EIGHTEENTH – CENTURY
—— *English Poetry* ——
THE ANNOTATED ANTHOLOGY

edited by
NALINI JAIN
and
JOHN RICHARDSON

HARVESTER WHEATSHEAF

New York London Toronto Sydney Tokyo Singapore

First published 1994 by
Harvester Wheatsheaf
Campus 400, Maylands Avenue
Hemel Hempstead
Hertfordshire, HP2 7EZ

A division of
Simon & Schuster International Group

Typeset in 10/12pt Palacio
by Mathematical Composition Setters, Salisbury

Printed and bound in Great Britain by
Biddles Ltd, Guildford and King's Lynn

British Library Cataloguing in Publication Data

A catalogue record for this book is available from
the British Library

ISBN 0-7450-1607-3 (pbk)

---

1 2 3 4 5 98 97 96 95 94

CONTENTS

◇

CONTENTS

CONTENTS

CONTENTS

PREFACE

◇

The readership of traditional English poetry has changed markedly over the last two or three decades in two important ways. First, there has been a spread outwards, so that what was once (more or less) the preserve of British and American educated elites is now being read by more kinds of people and in more countries. Secondly, even the members of those elites have usually a less substantial grounding in the Bible, in history and in classical literature than their forebears.

These changes mean that the knowledge which poets once took for granted can now no longer be assumed. An echo of the Bible will be recognised as such by only a small number of readers, an echo of a classical text by an even smaller.

But if there has been a change in readership, there has by and large been no corresponding change in the kind of editions available to these new readers. Poems are still usually presented without annotations, or are only sparsely annotated, or if copiously annotated, then with the kind of specialised notes that are intended chiefly for the scholar.

It is the aim of this edition to offer detailed annotations for students rather than scholars, that is, for 'A' level students and for undergraduates. Thus, we concentrate on words of which the meanings have changed, on primary allusions, and on relevant details of social and political history. We do not gloss every learned allusion to every recondite text.

With respect to the choice of poems, our principle has been to create a balanced, representative variety of good eighteenth-century (and five seventeenth-century) works. The selection is arranged according to the dates of poems rather than of poets. Although nothing is included just as an example of a genre or a type, many poems are (inevitably) excluded through considerations of space and coverage.

The texts of the poems have been modernised throughout. We have preserved archaic spellings only where a change would affect the metre. Where an extra syllable in modern spelling would be suppressed in spoken reading, we have taken the modern spelling (e.g. 'amorous causes' not 'am'rous causes').

We are greatly indebted to the scholars who have in this century laboured over the poems of the major poets of this selection. Though it is impossible here to list all our debts, the text bears ample witness to them.

INTRODUCTION

◇

Literary revolutions, like those in society and in science, have the irritating tendency to ignore the pattern of the centuries. Occasionally, 'epoch-making' works will land neatly and gratifyingly, like the *Lyrical Ballads* of 1798, close to the turn of the century. More often, however, they are wide of the mark and occur in such otherwise insignificant years as 1579 or 1667 or 1922. This presents a problem for the editors of anthologies. They can either choose works which fall within the confines of an (in terms of writing) arbitrary hundred years, or they can attempt to represent an 'age of literature'. The second alternative is fraught with difficulties since the limits and the characters of literary ages are the subjects of intense critical squabbles. Nevertheless, the present editors have chosen that alternative in preference to the arbitrariness of the first.

Although this anthology is entitled *Eighteenth-Century Poetry*, it begins well before the start of the eighteenth century and ends somewhat before the finish of it. Our earliest poet (though he did not write the earliest poem) is Dryden, because he exercised such a pervasive influence over the poets who came after him. On the subject of versification Pope wrote that Dryden 'had improved it much beyond any of our former poets, and would probably have brought it to its perfection, had he not been unhappily obliged to write so often in haste'. Needless to say, Milton was also influential but his influence is less marked and less central to the poetry of this period, and since a line must be drawn somewhere, it is with Dryden that we have chosen to draw it. At the other end of the anthology, we draw our line after Cowper and before Blake. However much Blake may belong to the eighteenth century, he succeeded (in Dostoyevsky's

I

phrase) in saying 'a new word'. We thought it appropriate to close before that word was spoken.

Thus, this is an anthology of the eighteenth and the later part of the seventeenth centuries, a period which today is neither popular nor fashionable. Like every other period it has its bands of industrious scholars working away at their books and articles, and fighting their corners in academic debate, but otherwise the poetry is largely unread. Today's 'common reader' (a phrase coined by one of our writers) is perhaps the graduate of English literature. But since many English degrees offer a selective coverage of literary history, even that graduate may have only the slightest acquaintance with the work of Dryden, Pope and Johnson. Certainly, he or she will know a good deal more of Donne from the previous century and of Keats from the next.

The modern indifference has recently been strikingly displayed in the *New Oxford Anthology of Seventeenth-Century Verse*, whose editor devotes much less than half his space to the poetry of the latter half of the century. Dryden, one of the major poets of the whole century and the single most important figure in the last quarter of it, is given less space than Donne, Jonson, Herbert, Herrick, Milton and Marvell, and only slightly more than Chapman, Drayton and Cowley. Even William Drummond of Hawthornden, a poet of the early century and a minor poet by any estimation, is judged to merit a coverage only one page shorter than that of the writer of *Absalom and Achitophel*.

The history of taste can furnish many earlier examples of such a general neglect by one age of another. Readers in the early eighteenth century had no time for medieval writing, while many in the early twentieth rejected Romantic and Victorian poetry. Usually such reactions have their source in differences of value: eighteenth-century readers disliked medieval poetry because of the formlessness, obscurity and religious fanaticism which they detected in it. And usually, with hindsight, these reactions appear to be narrow and limiting. The same may be true of the current neglect of the poetry represented in this volume. The poems betray different attitudes of mind from ours, and offend many of our unspoken canons of taste. But rather than ignoring them for those reasons, we might be better advised to read and to learn: to understand how and why the poets thought differently from us, to discover what they knew that we have forgotten.

One of the most crucial elements in any 'attitude of mind' is the definition of virtue. Towards the end of *Epistle to Dr Arbuthnot* (1735), Pope includes a passage in praise of his dead father:

> Stranger to civil and religious rage,
> The good man walked innoxious through his age,
> No courts he saw, no suits would ever try,
> Nor dared an oath, nor hazarded a lie. (lines 394–7)

The word 'innoxious', a synonym for 'innocuous', is the most interesting here. While Pope uses it positively to figure forth a life of humdrum virtue, it is hard to imagine anyone in our day being flattered by the adjective. Like the word 'unexceptional', it has changed its sense, as people have grown to value the extraordinary and the bizarre, at the cost of the simple and the everyday. Similar traces of former values are evident throughout Pope's lines. His father was unambitious (anathema to us!), and a 'stranger to civil rage', that is, uninvolved in affairs and not 'active' in politics – a deplorable abdication of responsibility according to twentieth-century standards. Moreover, he never 'dared an oath', unlike some of the heroes of our fictions, who curse their way through their futile lives.

Pope's description of his father is in some ways typical of representations of the good life in the period of this anthology, especially in the central part of it. By and large, the writers of that time rejected the extreme or the extravagant. Swift scoffed at heroism in all forms, especially the military, Pope (a Roman Catholic) took care to distance himself from the asceticism of the monks and hermits of the Middle Ages, and Johnson warned against the 'dangerous prevalency of the imagination'. Instead, these men preferred the unheroic, social virtues of good sense and good humour, and (at least in Johnson's case) the religious value of a resigned, unambitious will. Again, it is worth emphasising how different these values are from those which prevail in our century, and again it is perhaps true that the difference is not entirely to our credit.

The kind of values I have been sketching are connected with another feature of the period, its confidence in human reason.

The bulk of the eighteenth century, together with the last part of the seventeenth, is sometimes known as the Age of Reason, and though the title has been much and rightly questioned in recent years, there is some truth in it. Two influences are crucial. The first is that of Isaac Newton (1642–1727), his discoveries in physics and the progress which was being made in the natural sciences generally. In the eighteenth century, people were aware, with varying degrees of dimness, of this progress, and many were made excited, enthusiastic and optimistic because of it, for knowledge, perhaps absolute knowledge, seemed attainable. The second influence was that of John Locke (1632–1704), who wrote in the last decade of the seventeenth century on the human mind, on government, on tolerance and on Christianity. Locke propounds a number of views, including (limited) religious toleration, a rational Christianity that anticipates deism, and the belief that at birth human beings possess no 'innate ideas' (described by Swift as a 'dangerous tenet'). But it was as much his reasoned, empirical method that was important as the positions he argued, for his writings exemplify how reason may be put to work.

The rationalism of eighteenth-century attitudes affected its religion. Generally distrustful of anything that smacked of fanaticism ('enthusiasm' was the eighteenth-century word), many Christians sought a religion that was restrained and sensible. At its worst, this led to a set of beliefs so diluted that hell could not be mentioned to 'ears polite' nor heaven contemplated with any degree of excitement. At its best, it led to humanity, openness and tolerance. However, if eighteenth-century Christianity is often a rather milk-and-water affair, this is also the period of a remarkable 'fundamentalist' revival, that of Methodism. John Wesley (1703–91) through his exceptional energy and powers of organisation formed a movement which spread rapidly among the poorer sections of the population and which remains today the largest non-established church. The influence of Methodism is evident in this volume in the poetry of Cowper and in the hymns of John's brother, Charles.

The attitude towards reason among the writers represented here is not always simple. After a struggle, Dryden finally put faith before reason by accepting miracles, and Johnson shows the limitations of philosophy in *The Vanity of Human Wishes*

(1749) and in *Rasselas* (1759). Perhaps most memorable of all is Swift's attack on human claims to reason in the fourth book of *Gulliver's Travels* (1726). Yet even Swift, while deploring the absence of reason, elevates it as an unquestionable good – if only we possessed it. Certainly, for him the imagination was no alternative to reason for, in the earlier work *A Tale of a Tub* (1704), he represents that as an unruly horse which needs to be beaten into submission. Others were more sanguine than Swift. In the second epistle of his *Essay on Man* (1732–4), for example, Pope sees reason as the ruling moral faculty of a well-ordered individual, the faculty which restrains self-love and regulates the passions.

The confidence in reason sprang in part from ideas about 'nature', a word which occurs frequently in writings of the period, and which was used to mean many different things. Essentially, however, it connotes qualities which are universal and fixed, and which by diligent enquiry might be discovered beneath the variety and flux of life. Thus, when Pope in *An Essay on Criticism* (1711) urges the critic to 'follow nature', he is recommending attention to those elements of human nature which are not merely local. Something similar is at work in the contention of Imlac, the poet/adviser of Johnson's *Rasselas*, that the poet should examine 'not the individual but the species'. The poet's concern, like that of any rational person, should not be with details and particulars which change and dazzle, but with nature and the general which remain and reassure. Once again, we might underscore the difference in this from our own age. Increasingly suspicious of claims to authority and truth, many contemporary readers deny universality, and actively seek out individuality and variety.

The association of nature with absolutes led to two distinctive and related features of the period: the admiration of the ancients and the emphasis upon correctness and the rules. Many writers looked back to the classical age with veneration, and indeed, the term Augustan, which is sometimes applied to the period (strictly to the first four decades of the eighteenth century but more loosely to the whole age), refers to the way in which writers like Pope modelled their writing on that produced by poets, especially Virgil (70–19 BC) and Horace (65–8 BC), in the reign of Augustus. The explanation for this reverence is fairly simple. Since nature does not change and since the ancients had the best opportunity of representing it, later and less fortunate people can learn of nature by reading their works.

A similar explanation can be given for the stress which was laid on correctness. The belief was that certain kinds of literature, certain genres, were by virtue of their distinctive language, their kinds of plot, their characteristic subjects, particularly well adapted to representing certain features of nature. Thus, pastoral poetry could show love and innocence, the epistle could deal with the 'middle kind' of subject, and the epic could represent the noble and heroic. Since the ancients had already discovered these genres, modern writers wishing to write truthfully should observe the rules implicit in ancient writings and follow these. In this way, the adherence to rules was based upon the desire to be truthful rather than simply the desire to be obedient. It should also be added that every major writer of the period saw the need for departing from the rules in order to achieve a greater flourish or a more magnificent beauty. Moreover, the respect for rules and the traditional hierarchies of genres was eroding quite rapidly in the final third of the period of this anthology.

All the elements mentioned thus far combined to make the poets of the day write in ways which are unfamiliar in the twentieth century. Our preferred genre is the lyric, and most students, when asked, will confirm that to them the word 'poem' means something of twenty or thirty lines. The period of this anthology, however, is principally a period of the long poem, and particularly of the long meditative poem and the long satiric poem, in which virtues are praised and vices excoriated. But even the lyrics of the period, at least those belonging to its largest body of lyrics, are not such as would immediately appeal to modern readers. The Christian hymns of the eighteenth century are probably as strange to many of us as its strange genres.

Choices of genre reflect taste and the more general ideas and values which lie behind taste. In other words, the poets of this anthology wrote differently from their twentieth-century successors because, as I have been very briefly showing, they thought differently. This view, or at least its emphasis, has sometimes been challenged in recent years. Critics have (as I have said) rejected old phrases such as 'the age of reason' and the 'peace of the Augustans', concentrating instead upon the eighteenth century's fascination with madness, the oddness of its poets and the deformity of their productions. Rather than a rational age, so goes the argument, this was (at its most interesting) an age of the irrational, the violent, the eccentric and the idiosyncratic.

No doubt, there is a good deal of truth in this. Certainly, it is remarkable that, with the exception of *Paradise Lost* (1667 and 1674), which belongs in a sense to an earlier age, there is no epic from the period. The hierarchies of genres put the epic firmly at the top, as the production that the true poet should aspire to. And aspire they did. The doctor/poet Sir Richard Blackmore (1654–1729) wrote, between his sickbed visits, no fewer than four epics, all of them scorned in his lifetime and forgotten soon after it. A serious poet like Pope shared the same ambitions, and planned throughout his life to write a *Brutiad* which would account for the origins of the British in the way that the *Aeneid* accounts for the origins of the Romans. However, Pope never wrote his own epic, producing instead his translations of Homer, his poetical essays, and most notably of all, his satires – many of them the kind of ill-shaped, passionate and local works which seem to deny his own rules of taste.

So, to some extent, it is true that this was an age that failed to achieve its ideals, that was not as rational as might at first appear, nor as regulated, nor as peaceful. But this is both a limited and a limiting truth, for to represent the 'age of reason' as an age of unreason is to remake it in our own image. And we need no more versions of our own image. Far better, as was suggested earlier in this introduction, to recognise the difference between the poets of this anthology and ourselves, to accept it, to learn from it and ultimately to learn from them.

Some historical knowledge is useful, even essential, in reaching an understanding of the writing of any period. Such knowledge, however, should always be applied carefully. Historical circumstances influence writers, as is clear from the way that there are sudden flowerings of poetry or drama or fiction, and from the way that writings contemporary with each other tend to share family features. Yet, as critics have sometimes pointed out, literary revolutions do not follow social or economic revolutions in any very obvious manner, and, we might add, individual writers respond to the currents of their ages in different ways. Thus, in talking of the effect of history upon literature, we should be careful not to look for correspondences that are too close or laws of development that are too strictly defined. Perhaps the best rule is to keep the word 'influence' in mind. Writers and their writings, like other people and other kinds of behaviour, are influenced by their ages, not formed and determined by them.

One element of history consists of great events, and we will turn to those in a moment. But great events should also be seen in the context of the way that people lived when they happened. Most people during the period covered by this anthology lived in the country in small villages. Great changes were taking place there (as I discuss below) but at the beginning of the period, rural life retained much of the character it had possessed for the last 150 years. Social distinctions were quite clearly marked, with the village divided into gentry, yeomen, tradesmen (blacksmiths, wheelwrights, coopers) and labourers. The labourers were those who possessed little land and worked mostly for wages. Their work was extremely arduous and provided little return, so that up to half the rural population could be defined as paupers who at some time or other were forced to depend upon parish charity. The yeomen were middling landowners. It was they who formed the backbone of the village by assuming the responsibilities of constable and church warden, and who are celebrated by Goldsmith in *The Deserted Village* (1770) as 'a country's pride'. In most villages, the gentry consisted only of the families of the parson and the squire, and of all the inhabitants of the country, it was the male members of these families (with a few 'gentle' women) who would have read the poetry in this anthology.

At the end of the seventeenth century, the poetry of the countryside looked back to the classical models of the pastoral or the Georgic. Of these, the former deals with the lives of idealised shepherds, and the latter exploits the form of a treatise on husbandry in order to offer implicit moral advice, to comment on political events and to write of the origins of things. The publication in 1709 of two rival sets of pastorals, one by Pope and one by Ambrose Philips (1664–1749), really marks the end in English poetry of that genre. The Georgic exerted a greater influence in the eighteenth century. Although most poets of the country did not write formal Georgics in the way that sixteenth- and seventeenth-century poets had written formal pastorals, the seriousness of the mode is evident in much of the rural poetry of the eighteenth century. It is present in the political commentary of Pope's *Windsor-Forest* (1713), in the philosophical reflections of Thomson's *Seasons* (1726–30) and in the gravity of Goldsmith's *The Deserted Village*.

If most people lived in the country, publishing and literary activity was concentrated in the city, that is, in London. London was growing throughout the period, its population doubling during the course of the eighteenth century to stand at about one million at the end of it. Often this growth was greeted with excitement, as in Defoe's comment in his *Tour Through the Whole Island of Great Britain* (1724–6): 'New squares and new streets rising up every day to such a prodigy of buildings that nothing in the world does, or ever did, equal it, except old Rome in Trajan's times.' Much of the spread of the city was westward, where large houses were being built to accommodate the wealthy. The reason for the choice of the west as the site for expansion was simple: the prevailing easterly winds kept the stink of the city to the east away from the area.

That smell was caused by the practice of burning 'sea-coal' from Newcastle and by the general unsanitariness of eighteenth-century London. The central and eastern parts of the city were a dark warren in which disease and crime prospered. The sewage from urban households was deposited in cesspits in gardens or cellars until it was removed by the night-soil man, to be taken by him to the Thames or to the market gardeners who used it as a fertiliser. Other waste was dumped in the streets, in Fleet Ditch or in the river. The river was also, of course, the city's reservoir, its already dirty water being pushed by the force of the rapids under London Bridge along rotten wooden pipes, through filth-impregnated soil, to the public pumps in streets and squares.

Not surprisingly, many Londoners were driven by their circumstances to crime and to drink. Some parts of the city, at least in the first half of the eighteenth century, were (in a grotesque distortion of the medieval sanctuaries they had once been) havens for criminals and 'no-go areas' for the inadequate forces of the law. But all over the city, there were dangers, especially at night in the unlit or ill-lit streets, from pickpockets and footpads. For the adult poor, the danger was less from criminals and more from lethal gin, advertised by the no-nonsense slogan of 'drunk for a penny, dead drunk for twopence'. Because of the low duty on the drink (a government measure to encourage a native industry), it was cheap and easy to set up a gin shop, so that by 1736 there were 6000 to 7000 in London – one for every hundred inhabitants. Eventually in 1751, a popular outcry moved Parliament to pass effective measures for the curbing of this evil. But perhaps no fact or figure can illustrate the harshness of London life so vividly as the infant mortality rates. Parish registers show that in the better parishes of the 'inner' city, only one in four babies survived longer than a year. In the worst parishes, the infant mortality rate was 100 per cent.

Although some of the poetry of the period deals with the city, little of it (in the present writer's opinion) conveys any sense of the toughness of urban life. Gay's *Trivia* (1716), though full of concrete local details, is so engrossed with its own wit and allusiveness that the ultimate effect is one of trivialisation. This is perhaps most evident in the myth he invents in the second canto to describe the origins of the shoe-shine boy, where he wittily adapts classical myths in order to provide the boy with brush and polish. A modern equivalent might be the poet who used a colourful ancient mythology to describe the lives of the street children of South America. Even Johnson, who knew at close hand the poverty of the city, failed to find adequate means of conveying it in his poem *London* (1738), where the xeno-phobic accounts of the Spanish and the French and the sensational descriptions of crime have the effect of reducing the impact. Perhaps it was simply that the poetry of the period (the poetry of any period) was the wrong form for describing city life. And if we want an idea of what life was like in the city we must turn to the novel, in particular to Defoe's novels, *Moll Flanders* (1722), *Colonel Jack* (1722), or even the historical *Journal of the Plague Year* (1722).

One other element of the social life of the period should be mentioned before moving on to great events – the life of women. Throughout the seventeenth century the responsibilities of well-to-do women were gradually eroded. In the sixteenth century, a 'housewife' was the chief of a household, in effect a small workplace, and she had a large number of duties, including managing staff, overseeing cookery, cleaning, herb and medical gardening, and the manufacture of all manner of household goods from clothes to candles. Before the Protestant Reformation at the beginning of that century, she also had a key position in the religious life with her responsibility for the regulation of diet. In the seventeenth century, however, many of these duties disappeared, and by the end of it, the role of a wealthy woman was to drink coffee and gossip. It is this kind of life which is exposed in Pope's *The Rape of the Lock* (1712–14), and Montagu's *Saturday: The Small-Pox* (1716). Mary Leapor's *Man the Monarch* (1745–6) shows a different kind of female experience, that of the domestic worker.

Among events, probably the most significant in the period covered by this anthology is a series just before it: the Civil Wars (1642–51) and the commonwealth that followed them (1649–60). The enormous and traumatic upheaval of these two decades was important in two principal ways. First, it provided an example for many years afterwards of the suffering which could be caused by tyranny, rebellion and faction. The physical scars remain on our landscape today in the form of partly ruined castles and despoiled cathedrals. In the century following the Restoration of King Charles II (1660), not only were scars such as these far more evident than they are now, but the more painful wounds of families destroyed and lives disrupted were still relatively fresh in the memory. It was at least in part that memory that led to Dryden's adoption of an apparently reasonable tone in *Absalom and Achitophel* (1681), and to Pope's praise of the qualities of good humour, good sense and moderation. Pope, like many of his contemporaries, feared fanaticism because he knew from recent history the straits to which it could lead.

The second important effect of the period of Civil Wars and commonwealth was the shift it caused, or helped to cause, in the balance of power between king and Parliament. The issues at stake in the Civil Wars were partly religious and partly political, with the political question turning upon the king's authority. To some extent, the curbing of that authority – represented in Parliament's military victory of 1648, the execution of Charles I in 1649, and the crushing defeat of Charles II at the Battle of Worcester in 1651 – seems to have been short-lived. The return of Charles II in 1660 and the popularity of his Restoration appear to spell a revival of the king's power, and to some extent that is true. Though challenged by such events as the Exclusion Crisis (1678–81) during his reign, Charles held firmly to his kingly authority, and when he died (1685) he bequeathed, as one historian has put it, 'to his brother the strongest prerogative in modern English history'.

Yet despite the reign of Charles II and his tenacious grip on power, English history was moving towards a system of government in which the monarch would play a less commanding role. Three years into his reign, James II, a Roman Catholic and feared for that reason, was deposed by the arrival in England of the Dutch Protestant, William of Orange (1688). William's claim to the English throne was based partly upon the fact that he was married to James's daughter Mary, but chiefly upon the invitation sent to him by a group of English notables, and (later but most significantly) upon Parliament's confirmation of his kingship (1689). This so-called Revolution Settlement did not quite mark the end of the royal attempts to assert a wide range of hereditary powers, but it marked a decisive phase in them.

Thereafter, the 'true kings' of England, James and his Stuart heirs, established a little court in exile in France, at which they continued to claim the privileges of monarchs and from which they planned to wrest back their rightful crown. The most important attempts at this were 'the fifteen' and 'the forty-five', the risings of 1715 and 1745. During the first the Jacobites, the adherents of the 'true king' (James III according to them), rose in Scotland and penetrated as far south as Preston. The second was the romantic, or perhaps more accurately romanticised, expedition of Bonnie Prince Charlie, James II's grandson, which is colourfully retold by Walter Scott in *Waverley* (1814). The Jacobites, again rising in Scotland, enjoyed a successful start to their campaign, and had reached as far south as Derby before beginning their retreat back to the north. That retreat ended in the decisive defeat of Culloden (April 1746), and in the pursuit of the highlanders which followed it. The English commander, the Duke of Cumberland, nick-named the 'Butcher Cumberland', spent three months hunting down the rebels, killing them and destroying their homes.

Thus ended both the hopes of the Jacobites and the ancient way of life of the highlanders. Thirty years later Johnson wrote in *A Journey to the Western Isles of Scotland* (1775) of his visit to the highlands:

> We came thither too late to see what we expected, a people of peculiar appearance, and a system of antiquated life. The clans retain little now of their original character, their ferocity of temper is softened, their military ardour is extinguished, their dignity of independence is depressed, their contempt of government subdued, and their reverence for their chiefs abated. Of what they had before the late conquest of their country, there remain only their language and their poverty.

The highlanders had become objects of pity and regret, no longer a potential threat with their Stuart allegiances to the political status quo in England.

The claims of the Stuarts were received differently by the poets of this anthology. Dryden, a recently converted Catholic at the time of the Revolution and an old servant of the Stuarts, naturally resented the deposition of James II. Later, Prior was probably an active Jacobite (he was investigated in 1715), while Pope seems to have nourished an affection for the old royal family. Such an affection was essentially conservative, a nostalgic yearning for an old way of life, or for what appeared to be an old way of life. But conservative impulses could also affect writers in different ways. Swift, for example, remained loyal throughout his life to the Revolution Settlement, even though he was associated with Jacobites and his church career was effectively halted because of the association. His knowledge of the Civil Wars and his conservative belief that most changes are changes for the worse made him dread disruption more than he disliked the status quo.

The claims of kings, then, were kept alive in the Jacobitism of 1688–1746, but still the Revolution Settlement represented a decisive victory in favour of Parliament. By passing an act ruling that James II's departure from England in the face of William's army was an abdication, Parliament in effect took upon itself the responsibility of deciding who was king. It exercised the same responsibility in the Act of Settlement in 1701. This limited the succession of William to his descendants (should he have had any), to Princess Anne (like Mary, a Protestant daughter of James II) and her descendants, and to the Electors of Hanover. In the event, Anne took the throne in 1702, and died in 1714, to be succeeded by the German George I. His claim was weaker than the Stuart Pretender's in every respect except that he was Protestant and that he had the support of an Act of Parliament.

The new power of Parliament represented an important political change, but one that must be considered in its context. Eighteenth-century monarchs retained considerable power, and the democratic process was very different from that we know today. Only a small percentage of men (no women) were entitled to vote, the numbers of those eligible varied greatly in different constituencies, and ballots were not secret. The consequences in some boroughs were the bribery and violence depicted in William Hogarth's four 'Election' pictures of 1753–4. Nevertheless, Parliament acquired a new power, prestige and earnestness under its Hanoverian kings, so that it was, in the words of one historian, 'generally accepted at its own valuation as the principal organ of the nation's will'. This fact is quite strikingly conveyed by the way that histories of the eighteenth century tend to be organised around ministries, not (as with histories of earlier centuries) around reigns.

One man who should be mentioned in connection with the new prestige of Parliament is Robert Walpole (1676–1745). During his ministry (1721–42), the House of Commons was transformed from an arena for complaint into a genuine chamber of government. What is more, Walpole himself, through his authority and effective control of all aspects of government, became known as the 'chief minister' and is recognised by historians today as the first prime minister. The extent of his power, the way that it was consolidated through the appointment of his followers to office, the widespread nepotism and corruption of his ministry, were all matters of concern for some of his contemporaries. Of the poets of this anthology, Swift, Gay and (especially) Pope spent their last years as fierce critics of the government. Their criticisms were conservative, in that they wished to see a return to what they regarded as an older kind of honour, honesty and responsibility. And this is one of the interesting features of the period – that some of the most virulent critics of government were also some of the most conservative of men. Satire was written not with any wish to promote revolutionary change, but rather with the wish to inhibit what the satirists saw as the undesirable changes that were already taking place.

The new power of Parliament went hand in hand with economic and social changes. Political debate in the first part of the eighteenth century was sometimes couched in terms of a struggle between the 'Land Interest' and the 'Money Interest'. In this struggle, the land, the traditional source of wealth and power, was destined to lose to money, to the entrepreneurs and merchants of the city; in short, to trade. Trade had been increasing rapidly since the 1670s, and with the foundation of the Bank of England in 1694, London became an important financial centre. Perhaps the most immediately obvious effect of the growth was the availability of a wide range of luxury goods from abroad: the coffee, cocoa, ivory and chinoiserie referred to in *The Rape of the Lock* and *Saturday: The Small-Pox*. Less obvious and more fundamental effects were the gradual changes that were taking place in the nation's class structure, and in the relations between master and man. Nor should we forget that one important branch of trade and the source of much wealth in the eighteenth century was slavery: this is the period of the notorious 'middle passage' between Africa and the Americas.

The end of our period saw two other great changes: the agricultural and industrial revolutions. A number of factors contributed towards the first of these, including innovations in crop rotation, soil treatment and animal husbandry. Most important of all was the wave of enclosures that took place between 1750 and 1800. Enclosure had been occurring in the country for over two centuries and was identified as a problem in Thomas More's *Utopia* (1516), but the rate and extent of it in these fifty years effectively destroyed the old way of life. At the beginning of the century, the English countryside (if we can generalise about such a varied phenomenon) still looked much as it had since the Middle Ages. Agriculture was carried out in huge fields, divided into unevenly shaped 'strips', each belonging to a different villager. Cows and sheep grazed on common lands, while pigs foraged on the field (one of the village's three) which that year was lying fallow. All this meant that a 'farm' consisted of a number of scattered strips, varying according to the wealth of the farmer, and of grazing rights on the common. The farmer had to rely upon his neighbours for the drainage of his strips, since theirs bordered his, and for the health of his animals, since theirs lived with his. Enclosure changed all that. Farms became self-enclosed units like those we know today, with the farmer taking responsibility on himself for the upkeep of his fields and the health of his animals.

The effects were in part an astonishing improvement in the efficiency of farming: the size of oxen and sheep, for example, doubled in the course of the century. But enclosure also led to an increase in rural poverty. The cost of changing to the new enclosed system was so considerable that not only the village poor, but also the middling men, the yeomen, were ruined by it. This is the destruction of the peasantry that Goldsmith laments in *The Deserted Village*, and which was responsible for the bitter rural poverty that Crabbe exposes in *The Village* (1783).

The industrial revolution represented a change more important even than the agricultural. Insofar as it can be precisely dated, it occurred between 1760 and 1790, and the revolutionary effects of the changes were not at first apparent. Thus, it is not commented upon by any of our poets. Nevertheless, the harnessing of power, the concentration of workers in factories, the simplification and specialisation of tasks, the growth of towns and cities, the establishment of pure cash relations between master and man – all these various facets of the industrial revolution altered the way people lived. Historians who take a broad sweep identify two crucial changes in the history of humanity. The first is the development of agriculture and the settlement of wandering communities of hunters and gatherers into stable villages. The second is the industrial revolution.

In terms of literary history, or at least poetic history, the period can be divided fairly neatly into three sections of more or less equal length: the Age of Dryden (to 1700), the Age of Pope (to 1744) and the Age of Johnson (to 1784). In a nutshell, the first of these sees the establishment of classical principles, along with the heroic couplet as the predominant form; the second, the Augustan Age, sees the consolidation and culmination of that tendency; the third sees its gradual disintegration. Nutshells, however, are of very limited use in literary history, and such a generalisation contains as much distorting half-truth as it does real truth. The reader is best advised to turn directly to the poetry.

Two developments in literary history, which do not involve too much generalisation, can also be mentioned. These are the increasing independence of the writer, and the rise of the novel. For most of the seventeenth century, the writer had to depend upon patronage, upon politics or upon the stage to make a living. This changed at the end of it when Dryden, deprived of royal patronage by the departure of James II and the arrival of William of Orange, learnt how to make substantial amounts of money by publishing poetry. He contracted himself to translate Virgil, for which translation people paid in advance by subscription. In return for their payment they eventually gained not only the book, but also the pleasure of seeing their names in the list of subscribers at the beginning of it. In the following century, Pope adopted the same method of publication for his translation of Homer, and was able to live independently by his writing, something he boasts of in *Epistle to Dr Arbuthnot*. Indeed, subscription publication later became so common that it was attacked by satirists as a kind of charity for worthless authors – a sort of eighteenth-century equivalent of the Arts Council at its worst. The point, however, is that a new kind of independence was becoming possible for writers.

Between the years 1720 and 1750 the novel emerged as an important genre. Of course, the novel is the subject of much critical debate: what it is, when it started, if it rose. Nevertheless, it seems sensible to say that with the publication by Defoe of *Robinson Crusoe* (1719) and *Moll Flanders* (1722), by Samuel Richardson of *Pamela* (1740–1) and *Clarissa Harlowe* (1747–8) and by Henry Fielding of *Joseph Andrews* (1742) and

Tom Jones (1749), we see a new kind of prose fiction and one which is recognisable as the novel we know today. Although these novels are not now as widely read as their nineteenth-century successors, they established that form of writing which was to become the dominant literary genre for nearly two centuries. Even today, it tends to be novels which people read if they read anything.

It is an irony of literary history that the poetry of the age which gave us the novel should have become so generally neglected. Yet it is also an irony that can be understood. The interest in individual experience which (in part) fostered and informed the development of the novel led eventually to new kinds of poetry and to new conceptions about the nature of poetry. These ideas in time grew so pervasive that they filled the intellectual atmosphere, just as the noise of traffic fills the air outside our windows. And like the traffic noise, the pervasiveness of these ideas tends to block out other sounds and other voices, among them those of our poets. It is the task of the reader to put aside twentieth-century conceptions about the nature of poetry, and to find a quiet place away from their noise. Once that is achieved, the poets of this anthology can speak to us on their own terms and in their own way – directly, seriously, sanely and engagingly.

Further Reading

Chalker, John. *The English Georgic* (Baltimore: Johns Hopkins University Press, 1969).

Fussell, Paul. *The Rhetorical World of Augustan Humanism: Ethics and Imagery from Swift to Burke* (Oxford: Clarendon Press, 1965).

Jack, Ian. *Augustan Satire* (Oxford: Oxford University Press, 1952).

Ogg, David. *England in the Reign of Charles II* (1934; New York: Oxford University Press, 1984).

Plumb, J.H. *England in the Eighteenth Century* (1959; Harmonds-worth: Penguin, 1963).

Rogers, Pat. *The Eighteenth Century* (London: Methuen, 1978).

Rothstein, Eric. *Restoration and Eighteenth-Century Poetry 1660–1780* (London: Routledge and Kegan Paul, 1981).

Sutherland, James. *A Preface to Eighteenth Century Poetry* (Oxford: Clarendon Press, 1948).

Tillotson, Geoffrey. *Augustan Poetic Diction* (London: Athlone Press, 1964).

Tillotson, Geoffrey. *Augustan Studies* (London: Athlone Press, 1961).

Trickett, Rachel. *The Honest Muse* (Oxford: Clarendon Press, 1967).

Weinbrot, Howard D. *The Formal Strain: Studies in Augustan Imitation and Satire* (Chicago: University of Chicago Press, 1969).

Williams, Basil. *The Whig Supremacy, 1714–1760* (Oxford: Clarendon Press, 1939).

JOHN WILMOT, EARL OF ROCHESTER

(1647–80)

◇

The story of Rochester's life is one of debauchery, repentance and early death. Having joined the court of Charles II at the age of seventeen, he became known as a libertine, famous for intrigues, drinking, wild escapades, atheism and scandalous verses. In the last four years of his life, he became increasingly misanthropic as well as increasingly weak and ill. Finally, he was converted to Christianity a few months before his death.

Further Reading

For a long time Rochester's poetry was available only in expurgated editions. Now, though, there are two complete editions: David M. Vieth's *The Complete Poems of John Wilmot, Earl of Rochester* (New Haven and London: Yale University Press, 1968) and Keith Walker's *The Poems of John Wilmot, Earl of Rochester* (Oxford: Basil Blackwell, 1984). Rochester's was a colourful life and the standard biography remains Vivian de Sola Pinto, *Enthusiast in Wit: A Portrait of John Wilmot, Earl of Rochester, 1647–1680* (London: Routledge and Kegan Paul, 1962). There are not many full length books devoted to his poetry, but one that offers a general consideration is Dustin H. Griffin, *Satires Against Man: The Poems of Rochester* (Berkeley: University of California Press, 1973). More limited approaches are provided by Alan Roper in *Rochester and Court Poetry* (Los Angeles: University of California Press, 1988), and by Felicity Nussbaum in the relevant section of *The Brink of All We Hate: English Satires on Women, 1660–1750* (Lexington: University Press of Kentucky, 1984). Finally, two useful collections of essays are David M. Vieth (ed.), *John Wilmot, Earl of Rochester: Critical Essays* (New York:

Garland, 1988) and Jeremy Treglown (ed.), *Spirit of Wit: Reconsiderations of Rochester* (Oxford: Basil Blackwell, 1982).

————◇————

1/   **'Absent from thee'**

Absent from thee, I languish still;
   Then ask me not, when I return.
The straying fool 'twill plainly kill
   To wish all day, all night to mourn.

Dear! from thine arms then let me fly,   5
   That my fantastic mind may prove
The torments it deserves to try
   That tears my fixed heart from my love.

When, wearied with a world of woe,
   To thy sage bosom I retire   10
Where love and peace and truth does flow,
   May I contented there expire,

Lest, once more wandering from that heaven,
   I fall on some base heart unblessed,
Faithless to thee, false, unforgiven,   15
   And lose my everlasting rest.

The Restoration produced a good number of courtly love lyrics, as the reign of Charles I had before it. Many of these are purely conventional praises of (sometimes imaginary) mistresses, appeals for mercy, or complaints of amorous sufferings. This poem, by contrast, and in spite of the libertinism of its argument, conveys a genuine tenderness. Moreover, the attitude of the speaker is complex and mixed: he loves the mistress he addresses, wishes to leave her, expects only torments from his adventures with others, desires them nevertheless, and longs in the end to die with his beloved as a way of avoiding further temptation.

   The occasion for the lyric (supposing it to have had one) is unknown. Nevertheless, given Rochester's reputation as a rake, it is tempting to think of the verses as addressed to his wife, Elizabeth Malet. That he was fond of her, for all his affairs and his infidelity, is proved by his letters.

   The poem is written in alternately rhymed lines of iambic tetrameters (i.e. four iambic feet per line – dedum dedum dedum dedum). Part of the success of the lyric arises from the way in which Rochester introduces variations into this basic pattern. Each verse, for example, begins with a stressed syllable which works against the dominant rhythm.

[1] **Absent**
Later lines make it clear that the word is used to mean 'when I am absent' not 'absent as I am now'; *thee* a mistress, possibly a wife (see above); *languish* become feeble, lose health, pine with love.
[3] **straying fool**
himself, the speaker. There is an interesting and deliberate contradiction that runs throughout the poem: the speaker wishes to seek other mistresses, and yet recognises the folly of such behaviour. In this respect, the poem is close in subject, if not in tone, to some of Rochester's more sexually graphic satires, in particular *A Ramble in St James' Park*. This represents the speaker as himself a libertine, and one who professes to believe 'there's something generous in mere lust' (line 98). However, the poem's marked tone of disgust belies the profession; *'twill* it will; *kill* the anticipated effect of a prohibition of absence. If the speaker is kept at home he will pine away and die.
[4] **wish . . . mourn**
the homebound activities that will 'kill' the speaker.
[5] **let me**
The assumption that the addressed woman has authority to forbid reinforces the supposition that she is Rochester's wife. In another poem, 'Upon leaving his Mistress', the speaker asks no permission for infidelity, but urges the mistress to take a similar liberty. On the other hand, the epigram, 'To his more than Meritorious Wife', concedes the wife's authority, as Rochester gives her the right 'to wear the trousers', or (as he puts it) yields 'to your fair bum the breeches' (line 8).
[6] **fantastic**
perverse, extravagant, fanciful; *prove* test, try, experience.
[7] **torments**
another hint of the speaker's com-

plexity of attitude. The sexual adventures he wishes to embark upon are described as potential torments, and yet he wants them still.
[8] **fixed heart**
a paradox: that the speaker should proclaim his fixity in a poem about sexual infidelity.
[10] **sage**
wise; *bosom* The idea of retirement to a wise bosom not only continues the sexual theme of the poem, but anticipates the idea of death. To 'rest in Abraham's bosom' is to die, a phrase which, though used only once in the Bible (Luke 16: 22), is reasonably familiar.
[12] **expire**
die. 'Dying' is used frequently in sixteenth- and seventeenth-century poetry as a metaphor for sexual orgasm. There may be something of that sense here, especially as the speaker is figuratively 'on the bosom' of the woman he is addressing. But Rochester is also using the word in the literal sense as the following lines make clear.
[13] **Lest**
unless; *that heaven* i.e. of her bosom. The last verse makes use of a number of religious ideas: 'base', 'unblessed', 'everlasting rest'. The combination of the amorous and the religious in this way is somewhat reminiscent of John Donne's poetry from earlier in the century.
[15] **unforgiven**
The idea is that a second fall after conversion will not be forgiven. Rochester may have been thinking of the Epistle to the Hebrews: 'it is impossible for those who were once enlightened . . . if they shall fall away, to renew themselves again to repentance' (Hebrews 6: 4–6).
[16] **everlasting rest**
The phrase is curiously double-edged: it refers both to the benefits that the mistress can confer, and also to the expectation of everlasting life.

2 /   *Satyr*

Were I (who to my cost already am
One of those strange prodigious creatures, man)
A spirit free to choose for my own share,
What case of flesh and blood I pleased to wear,
I'd be a dog, a monkey, or a bear,   5
Or any thing but that vain animal,
Who is so proud of being rational.
　The senses are too gross, and he'll contrive
A sixth to contradict the other five;
And before certain instinct, will prefer   10
Reason which twenty times to one does err.
Reason, an ignis fatuus in the mind,
Which leaving light of nature, sense behind,
Pathless and dangerous wandering ways it takes,
Through Error's fenny bogs and thorny brakes   15
Whilst the misguided follower climbs with pain
Mountains of whimseys, heaped in his own brain,
Stumbling from thought to thought, falls head-long down,
Into Doubt's boundless sea, where like to drown
Books bear him up awhile, and make him try,   20
To swim with bladders of Philosophy,
In hopes still to o'ertake the escaping light.
The vapour dances in his dazzled sight,
Till spent, it leaves him to eternal night.
Then Old Age, and Experience, hand in hand,   25
Lead him to death, and make him understand,
After a search so painful and so long,
That all his life he has been in the wrong.
Huddled in dirt, the reasoning engine lies,
Who was so proud, so witty and so wise.   30
　Pride drew him in, as cheats their bubbles catch
And made him venture, to be made a wretch.
His wisdom did his happiness destroy,
Aiming to know that world he should enjoy.
And wit was his vain frivolous pretence,   35
Of pleasing others at his own expence.
For wits are treated just like common whores,
First they're enjoyed and then kicked out of doors.
The pleasure past, a threatening doubt remains,
That frights the enjoyer with succeeding pains.   40

Women and men of wit are dangerous tools,
And ever fatal to admiring fools.
Pleasure allures, and when the fops escape,
'Tis not that they're beloved but fortunate.
And therefore what they fear, at heart they hate.   45
    But now methinks some formal band and beard,
Takes me to task. 'Come on, Sir, I'm prepared.'
    'Then, by your favour, any thing that's writ
Against this gibing jingling knack called wit,
Likes me abundantly, but you take care,   50
Upon this point, not to be too severe.
Perhaps my muse were fitter for this part,
For I profess I can be very smart
On wit, which I abhor with all my heart.
I long to lash it in some sharp essay,   55
But your grand indiscretion bids me stay,
And turns my tide of ink another way.
What rage ferments in your degenerate mind,
To make you rail at reason and mankind?
Blessed glorious man! to whom alone kind heaven,   60
An everlasting soul has freely given,
Whom his great maker took such care to make
That from himself he did the image take,
And this fair frame in shining reason dressed,
To dignify his nature above beast.   65
Reason, by whose aspiring influence,
We take a flight beyond material sense,
Dive into mysteries, then soaring pierce
The flaming limits of the universe.
Search heaven and hell, find out what's acted there,   70
And give the world true grounds of hope and fear.'
    'Hold, mighty man,' I cry, 'all this we know,
From the pathetic pen of Ingello,
From Patrick's *Pilgrim*, Stillingfleet's replies,
And 'tis this very reason I despise,   75
This supernatural gift, that makes a mite,
Think he's the image of the infinite,
Comparing his short life, void of all rest,
To the eternal, and the ever blessed.
This busy, puzzling, stirrer up of doubt,   80
That frames deep mysteries, then finds 'em out,

24

Filling with frantic crowds of thinking fools,
Those reverend bedlams, colleges and schools,
Borne on whose wings, each heavy sot can pierce,
The limits of the boundless universe.   85
So charming ointments make an old witch fly,
And bear a crippled carcass through the sky.
'Tis this exalted power, whose business lies
In nonsense and impossibilities.
This made a whimsical philosopher   90
Before the spacious world his tub prefer,
And we have modern cloistered coxcombs, who
Retire to think 'cause they have naught to do.
   'But thoughts are given for action's government,
Where action ceases, thought's impertinent.   95
Our sphere of action is life's happiness,
And he who thinks beyond, thinks like an ass.
   'Thus, whilst 'gainst false reasoning I inveigh,
I own right reason which I would obey:
That reason that distinguishes by sense,   100
And gives us rules of good and ill from thence,
That bounds desires with a reforming will,
To keep 'em more in vigour, not to kill.
Your reason hinders, mine helps to enjoy,
Renewing appetites, yours would destroy.   105
My reason is my friend, yours is a cheat.
Hunger calls out, my reason bids me eat;
Perversely yours, your appetite does mock:
This asks for food, that answers what's a clock?
This plain distinction, Sir, your doubt secures,   110
'Tis not true reason I despise but yours.
   'Thus, I think reason righted. But for man,
I'll ne'er recant. Defend him if you can.
For all his pride, and his philosophy,
'Tis evident, beasts are in their degree,   115
As wise at least, and better far than he.
Those creatures, are the wisest who attain,
By surest means, the ends at which they aim.
If, therefore, Jowler finds and kills his hares
Better than Meres supplies committee chairs   120
(Though one's a statesman, the other but a hound)
Jowler, in justice, would be wiser found.

'You see how far man's wisdom here extends.
Look next, if human nature makes amends,
Whose principles most generous are and just,   125
And to whose morals you would sooner trust.
Be judge yourself, I'll bring it to the test,
Which is the basest creature, man or beast?
Birds feed on birds, beasts on each other prey,
But savage man alone does man betray.   130
Pressed by necessity, they kill for food,
Man undoes man to do himself no good.
With teeth and claws by nature armed, they hunt
Nature's allowance to supply their want.
But man with smiles, embraces, friendships, praise,   135
Inhumanly his fellow's life betrays,
With voluntary pains, works his distress,
Not through necessity, but wantonness.
    'For hunger or for love, they fight or tear,
Whilst wretched man is still in arms for fear.   140
For fear he arms, and is of arms afraid,
By fear to fear successively betrayed.
Base fear, the source whence his best passions came,
His boasted honour, and his dear bought fame.
That lust of power, to which he's such a slave,   145
And for the which alone he dares be brave:
To which his various projects are designed,
Which makes him generous, affable, and kind.
For which he takes such pains to be thought wise,
And screws his actions in a forced disguise,   150
Leading a tedious life in misery,
Under laborious, mean hypocrisy.
Look to the bottom of his vast design,
Wherein man's wisdom, power and glory join,
The good he acts, the ill he does endure,   155
'Tis all for fear, to make himself secure.
Merely for safety after fame we thirst,
For all men would be cowards if they durst.
    'And honesty's against all common sense,
Men must be knaves, 'tis in their own defence.   160
Mankind's dishonest, if you think it fair,
Amongst known cheats, to play upon the square,
You'll be undone . . .

Nor can weak truth your reputation save:
The knaves will all agree to call you knave.   165
Wronged shall he live, insulted o'er, oppressed,
Who dares be less a villain than the rest.
Thus, Sir, you see what human nature craves,
Most men are cowards, all men should be knaves.
The difference lies, as far as I can see,   170
Not in the thing itself, but the degree.
And all the subject matter of debate
Is only, who's a knave of the first rate?'

All this with indignation have I hurled,
At the pretending part of the proud world,   175
Who swollen with selfish vanity devise,
False freedoms, holy cheats and formal lies
Over their fellow slaves to tyrannise.
But if in court, so just a man there be,
(In court, a just man yet unknown to me.)   180
Who does his needful flattery direct,
Not to oppress and ruin, but protect
(Since flattery, which way so ever laid,
Is still a tax on that unhappy trade)
If so upright a statesman you can find,   185
Whose passions bend to his unbiased mind,
Who does his arts and policies apply,
To raise his country, not his family,
Nor, while his pride owned avarice withstands,
Receives close bribes from friends' corrupted hands.   190
Is there a churchman who on God relies?
Whose life his faith and doctrine justifies?
Not one blown up with vain prelatic pride,
Who for reproof of sins does man deride;
Whose envious heart with his obstreperous saucy eloquence 195
Dares chide at kings and rail at men of sense;
Who from his pulpit vents more peevish lies,
More bitter railings, scandals, calumnies,
Than at a gossipping are thrown about,
When the goodwives get drunk and then fall out.   200
None of that sensual tribe, whose talents lie
In avarice, pride, sloth, and gluttony.
Who hunt good livings, but abhor good lives,

Whose lust exalted to that height arrives,
They act adultery with their own wives.   205
And ere a score of years completed be,
Can from the lofty pulpit proudly see,
Half a large parish their own progeny.
Nor doting bishop who would be adored,
For domineering at the council board,   210
A greater fop in business at fourscore,
Fonder of serious toys, affected more,
Than the gay glittering fool at twenty proves,
With all his noise, his tawdry clothes and loves.
But a meek humble man of modest sense,   215
Who preaching peace does practice continence,
Whose pious life's a proof he does believe,
Mysterious truths which no man can conceive.
If upon earth there dwell such Godlike men,
I'll here recant my paradox to them,   220
Adore those shrines of virtue, homage pay,
And with the rabble world their laws obey.
If such there are, yet grant me this at least,
Man differs more from man, than man from beast.

Satyr imitates, in a fairly free manner, Nicolas Boileau's (1636–1711) eighth satire, in which man is compared (to his disadvantage) to beasts. It is perhaps more profoundly influenced by Thomas Hobbes' (1588–1679) political treatise *Leviathan* (1651). Hobbes' view of man, which is materialistic, goes back to the Roman poet Lucretius (*c*.100–*c*.55 BC). Lucretius's poem, *On the Nature of the Universe*, expounds the teachings of Epicurus, that wisdom and happiness have a physical (not a spiritual) basis.

First published in 1679, *Satyr* was probably circulated in manuscript in 1674, since the sermon attacking it was preached in early 1675 (see note to line 74). Its libertine philosophy belongs to the licence in thought and behaviour in the court of Charles II.

Although *Satyr* is (as the title suggests) a satire, it is a satire of a different kind from the others in this collection (*Absalom and Achitophel, Epistle to Dr Arbuthnot,* etc.). Rather than being an attack on individuals or general follies, it is a philosophical poem which attempts to define the fundamental nature of human beings. What makes the poem satiric is the tone, the anger and indignation, which are directed not only at those who disagree with Rochester but also at the human condition generally.

Satyr is written in rhymed couplets of iambic pentameters. The couplets are less 'closed' than those of Pope (in that they end less often in a period), and the verse moves more freely.

The argument proceeds rather swiftly and there are some internal inconsistencies. Nevertheless, the principal structure is as follows:

1. *Introduction*: the delusion of reason, and the life of the wit (lines 1–45),
2. The *opposing position*, in the mouth of a caricature clergyman, that reason is divine and human nature noble (lines 46–71).
3. *Rochester's reply* (lines 72–173):
   (a) no supernatural reason (lines 72–97);
   (b) right reason is sensual reason (lines 98–111);
   (c) human nature worse than animal nature (lines 112–40);
   (d) fear as the basic human motivation (lines 141–58);
   (e) the necessity of knavery (lines 159–73).
4. *Addendum* – reply to Stillingfleet, no man virtuous, therefore no man really believes in virtue.

Title

Satyr The contemporary spelling of 'satire' preserves the mistaken (and by Rochester's time known to be mistaken) derivation of the word from 'satyr', a mythological creature, half-man and half-beast, with a bent for lechery, drunkenness and violence. The Elizabethan satirists, trying consciously to reproduce the voice of a satyr in their poems, established a tradition in English poetry of biting, angry satire.

[1] **to my cost**
to my detriment.

[2] **prodigious**
unnatural, abnormal.

[3] **share**
quality allotted by Providence.

[5] **I'd be ... bear**
Rochester introduces the paradox at the heart of his argument, that animals are both better and better off than people. The idea is borrowed partly from Boileau: 'Of all the animals which fly through the air, walk upon the earth, or swim in the sea . . . man is, in my opinion, the most foolish' (*Satire*, 8, 1–4).

[6] **vain**
both proud and worthless or insignificant.

[7] **proud ... rational**
A standard definition of man, used in university logic courses, was 'rational animal'.

[8] **gross**
dull, stupid, rude; *contrive* implying

that the reason which Rochester attacks is the invention of man.

[9] **sixth**
i.e. the sixth sense, a means of perception (like the five senses) but only conjectured to exist. Reason is denigrated by being regarded as the sixth sense; *contradict* compare lines 104–9, in which Rochester argues that the false reason followed by man works against the wisdom of appetite and the senses.

[10–11] **And before ... reason**
i.e. He ('man' from line 8) prefers the dictates of reason over instinct; *certain instinct* implies the materialistic basis of the argument by elevating physical instinct above spiritual reason. Rochester follows Lucretius who argues that the origin of truth is the senses (*On the Nature of the Universe*).

[11] **ignis fatuus**
foolish fire, will o' the wisp. The flames produced by marsh gas over swampy areas were a danger to travellers tempted to follow them (in the hope of finding shelter) into danger. There are two sources for the long passage in which Rochester develops this idea (lines 11–30): (1) Francis Quarles' *Divine Fancies*, 2, 17, in which lust is represented as an ignis fatuus leading men astray, and (2) the Christian allegorical tradition in which the life of a man is represented as a pilgrimage towards enlightenment, through a countryside in which every mountain, river, lake and road has a

symbolic meaning. Here, the tradition is echoed in the creation of a symbolic landscape ('Error's . . . bogs', line 15), but subverted in terms of meaning.

[13] **light of nature, sense**
'Nature' and 'sense' are used to mean man's physical nature and the senses. The 'true' light of the physical is neglected in preference to the false light of speculative reason. The central argument later on is that 'right reason' is that which 'distinguishes by sense' (line 100).

[14] **Pathless . . . takes**
The course of the ignis fatuus.

[15] **fenny**
swampy; *brakes* clumps of bushes.

[16] **follower**
i.e. of the ignis fatuus of reason.

[17] **whimseys**
fantastic ideas.

[19] **boundless**
unlimited; *like* likely.

[20] **bear him up**
The books serve as floats in the sea.

[21] **bladders**
The treated bladders of animals were used as floats, balls and the sacks of bagpipes.

[22] **o'ertake**
catch up with; *escaping light* of the ignis fatuus.

[23] **vapour**
both gas (which causes the ignis fatuus) and a fantastic idea; *dazzled* confused by brightness.

[24] **spent**
exhausted, finished.

[29] **Huddled**
confused, jumbled; *Huddled in dirt* suggestive of the fate of the follower of the ignis fatuus and also of old age generally; *engine* The mechanical metaphor is influenced by Hobbes: 'what is the heart but a spring, and the nerves but so many strings, and the joints but so many wheels' (*Leviathan*, introduction).

[30] **witty**
wise, clever, as well as possessing wit.

[31] **drew him in**
cozened, ensnared; *bubbles* dupes, victims (of the cheats).

[32] **venture**
go forth, continuing the journey image; *made a wretch* the end of his venturing.

[34] **know . . . enjoy**
The heart of the argument – life should be experienced and enjoyed, not understood (see lines 94–5).

[35] **wit**
The word had several meanings. Rochester seems here to be using it in the sense of the court wit, the man who used his intellect to produce sparkling verbal sallies, which usually exposed and ridiculed the weaknesses of others. The following lines (lines 35–45) digress from the main argument, as Rochester turns from his attack on reason to a consideration of the difficulties of the life of the wit; *pretence* claim, not necessarily false.

[36] **pleasing others**
The wit's intellectual and verbal skills are practised for the pleasure of others.

[37] **common whores**
streetwalking prostitutes rather than kept mistresses, who were also frequently referred to as 'whores'.

[38] **kicked out of doors**
This may be an autobiographical reference, since Rochester was banished from the court a number of times. On one occasion, the cause of banishment was that, intending to show the king an obscene poem concerning prominent court ladies, he offered instead (and by mistake) a libel on kings, including Charles himself.

[39] **threatening doubt**
the fear of (1) infection (with venereal disease) by the prostitute and (2) ridicule by the wit.

[40] **enjoyer**
i.e. the person who has enjoyed the wit or whore; *succeeding* following; *pains* the pains of (1) being diseased and (2) being ridiculed.

[41] **men of wit**
see note to line 35.

[42] **fatal**
again referring to the dangerous consequences of consorting with wits or whores.

[43] **fops**
fools, dandies, here especially those who have enjoyed the wit's company; *escape* i.e. with reputation or body unharmed.

[44] **beloved**
i.e. the fop who escapes ridicule does so by chance.

[45] **therefore...hate**
The fops who fear the wit's attack (or the prostitute's disease) hate him for it.

[46] **But now**
back to the main argument; *formal* excessively concerned with forms, prim; *band* Geneva band, a collar made of a strip of cloth, of which the two ends hang down. This was the dress of the clergyman, the seventeenth-century equivalent of the modern dog collar; *beard* sometimes associated with gravity or (as here) affected gravity.

[47] **Come on...prepared**
supposed to be Rochester's words of challenge to the 'formal band'. The rest of the poem consists of the clergyman's argument (lines 48–71), followed by Rochester's rebuttal.

[48] **by your favour**
a set phrase for opening a speech, roughly equivalent to 'with your permission'.

[49] **gibing**
refers to the malicious element believed to be part of wit (see note to line 35); *jingling* playing with words; *knack* then as now carrying a negative sense.

[50] **likes me**
I like (anything written against wit – line 48); *you take care* a warning to Rochester, the wit, in particular.

[51] **this point**
i.e. attacking wit.

[52] **muse**
goddess of poetry (see *Rape of the Lock*, i, 3 and note), used here to mean simply my genius, my talent; *were* would be.

[53] **smart**
clever, witty, biting. Rochester's pompous clergyman vainly affects the quality of a wit in this respect.

[54] **abhor...heart**
The clergyman distinguishes between wit and reason (line 59).

[55] **lash**
attack – conventional verb for any strong verbal attack; *essay* the clergyman chooses an appropriately dull genre.

[56] **grand indiscretion**
great lack of judgement, referring to Rochester's attack on reason; *bids me stay* tells me to stop, wait – to postpone his attack on wit.

[57] **turns my...way**
His pen will be used to defend reason rather than attack wit.

[58] **ferments**
(figuratively) agitates, stirs up.

[59] **rail at**
attack with abusive language; *reason and mankind* The phrase exposes the poem's uncertainty of subject. Rochester claims to be attacking only those who pretend to reason (lines 174–5), but sections such as the extended journey metaphor (lines 12–30) seem to have the more general subject of all human life.

[61] **everlasting soul**
The clergyman echoes the conventional idea that reason is a faculty of the soul. In the late sixteenth century, for example, Sir John Davies called wit 'pupil of the soul's clear eye'.

[63] **from himself...take**
'So God created man in his own image, in the image of God created he him' (Genesis 1: 27). The clergyman interprets the text to mean that man is like God in being rational.

[64] **this fair...dressed**
Milton describes Adam and Eve before the fall: 'in their looks divine/ The image of their glorious maker shone,/ Truth, wisdom, sanctitude severe and pure' (*Paradise Lost*, iv, 291–3).

[65] **nature above beast**
'God said...let them have dominion over the fish of the sea, and over the fowl of the air, and over the cattle...' (Genesis 1: 26). The relative value of men and animals is a central idea of the poem.

[66] **aspiring**
mounting up.

[67] **material sense**
The clergyman opposes the materialistic doctrine that all we can know is what is conveyed to us by the physical senses.

[68] **mysteries**
implying religious ideas.

[69] **flaming... universe**
echoing a line of Lucretius, 'the flaming ramparts of the world'.

[70] **acted**
done; *find out... there* possibly a reference to Milton's descriptions of the deeds of angels and devils in *Paradise Lost*.

[71] **hope and fear**
the hope of heaven, fear of hell.

[72] **mighty man**
ironic address to the clergyman.

[73] **pathetic**
moving, affecting, not necessarily with a negative sense; *Ingello* puritan divine and author of a religious allegory, *Bentivolio and Urania*.

[74] **Patrick's *Pilgrim***
The Parable of the Pilgrim, by Simon Patrick, another religious allegory; *Stillingfleet* Edward Stillingfleet, royal chaplain, who was to preach a sermon before the king attacking lines 1–173 of *Satyr*, and provoking Rochester to compose the final section.

[75] **this very reason**
Rochester identifies the divine reason described by the clergyman as the specific object of his scorn.

[76] **mite**
small thing, insect.

[77] **image of the infinite**
referring back to the clergyman's argument (lines 60–5).

[80] **This**
refers to the reason.

[81] **frames**
creates, articulates. The sacred mysteries of religion are reduced to the invented puzzles of the reason; *finds 'em out* solves them.

[82] **frantic**
lunatic, insane, as well as wild.

[83] **bedlams**
psychiatric hospitals; a contraction of Bethlehem Hospital, one of the first public madhouses in Europe and always the most infamous in England. When Rochester wrote, it had recently been relocated to a new site and handsome building. Its evil reputation, however, survived the move. (See *Epistle to Dr Arbuthnot*, line 4 and note.)

[84] **heavy**
heaviness was later to be associated with dullness by Pope. Rochester uses it in the sense both of dull and of physically heavy (thus, unable to fly); *sot* stupid person, fool.

[84–5] **pierce... universe**
refers back to the argument of the clergyman that reason gives man this capacity (lines 68–9).

[85] **boundless universe**
The idea of an infinite universe was novel and unorthodox.

[86] **charming**
(literally) casting a charm or a spell; *ointments... fly* The sophisticate, Rochester, is contemptuous of the popular superstition that believed witches capable of flight through the application of a magic potion. Religious beliefs concerning the divinity of reason are reduced by the comparison to the level of superstitions.

[87] **crippled carcass**
the witch's body.

[88] **power**
reason again.

[90] **whimsical**
capricious, humorous – compare line 17 and note; *philosopher* Diogenes the Cynic, a Greek philosopher of the fourth century BC.

[91] **his tub prefer**
Diogenes was reputed to have retired from the world in disgust to live in a tub.

[92] **cloistered coxcombs**
fools, enclosed or shut away from the world – academics.

[94] **for action's government**
to direct (rule) behaviour: an important part of the argument, that life is to be enjoyed not studied (line 34).

[95] **impertinent**
irrelevant, absurd, presumptuous.

[96] **life's happiness**
implying that pleasure in the here and now should be our goal rather than heaven after death.

[97] **like an ass**
Though Rochester devotes a considerable part of the poem to arguing against conventional ideas about man's superiority to beasts, he borrows here the stock notion that asses are stupid.

[98] **inveigh**
speak in violent denunciatory language.

[99] **own**
admit; *right reason* a common term in contemporary controversy for the reason which can arbitrate between different opinions, the reason closest to the divine. Rochester cleverly turns the idea on its head by making his right reason materialistic.

[100] **distinguishes by sense**
makes judgements based on the physical senses (see line 13).

[101] **rules of good and ill**
moral codes; *thence* from the senses – morality is to be sensual in basis.

[102] **bounds**
limits; *reforming will* the intention to renew or restore.

[103] **more in vigour**
Desires are denied by right reason only in order to preserve their strength; *not to kill* The aim of the religious reason Rochester rejects is to destroy desires.

[104] **Your reason**
the idea of reason advanced by the clergyman.

[105] **Renewing appetites**
'Right reason' regulates the satisfaction of appetites only to preserve them in vigour.

[107] **bids**
tells.

[108] **Perversely**
wrongly, obstinately in error; *does mock* denies, as well as scorns.

[109] **This**
the speaker's kind of reason; *that* the clergyman's kind of reason.

[110] **your doubt secures**
satisfies your objection (i.e. that

Rochester should not 'rail at reason and mankind') (line 59).

[112] **righted**
vindicated, justified, set right (recalling the phrase 'right reason' from line 99); *But for man* Rochester turns to the clergyman's second objection, that against an attack on humanity in general – see previous note.

[113] **Defend ... can**
Despite this invitation, the clergyman does not speak again in the poem.

[114] **For**
despite.

[115] **degree**
position in the scale of creation.

[116] **better**
Rochester begins to introduce terms based upon the kind of moral evaluation which he has rejected.

[117–18] **Those creatures ... aim**
A general statement (that wisdom lies in the achievement of goals) used to prove the superiority of animals.

[119] **Jowler**
a beagle. As with Belinda's Shock the word is used both as a description of a species and a name of an individual (*Rape of the Lock*, i, 115).

[120] **Meres**
Sir Thomas Meres, MP for Lincoln; *supplies* fills, occupies; *committee chairs* Meres acted as chairman of a number of parliamentary committees.

[121] **Though ... hound**
Like the earlier comparison to asses (line 96) the line relies upon the negative connotations of the animal.

[122] **in justice**
implying that Rochester has proved his point, which he has not since it depends upon our acceptance of his first premise (lines 117–18).

[124] **Look ... amends**
i.e. since we have seen that human reason is inferior to that of beasts, we should turn to nature; *makes amends* i.e. for the lack of reason.

[125] **Whose ... just**
i.e. whether animals or people have better principles.

[127] **Be judge yourself**
addressed to the clergyman. Rochester

affects an air of fairness here to rein-
force his argument; *bring...test* a
common phrase, meaning simply to
test.

[130] **But savage...betray**
Boileau argued that men were worse
than animals in that they (men) attack
each other. Rochester's emphasis is
slightly different. He allows that
animals attack each other, but isolates
betrayal as the peculiar quality of
men. The 'smiles' and 'embraces' of
line 129 suggest a faint allusion to
Judas's betrayal of Jesus 'with a kiss'
(Luke 22: 48).

[131] **they**
animals.

[132] **undoes**
ruins, destroys.

[134] **Nature's allowance**
the portion allotted them by nature,
also implying a degree of moral
approval for their action; *want* lack,
need.

[136] **Inhumanly**
the adverb is used ironically. Actions
which are inhuman in the sense of
eminently cruel are also peculiarly
human; *fellow* partner, companion.

[137] **voluntary pains**
freely chosen (and unnecessary)
labours; *his* i.e. the fellow's; *distress*
implying a physical and material
condition, as well as a psychological.

[138] **wantonness**
caprice, gratuitous cruelty.

[139] **they**
animals.

[140] **for fear**
The passage which follows (lines
140–58) repeats a fairly commonplace
notion about human motivation.

[142] **betrayed**
placed in the power of an enemy; *By
fear betrayed* Fear delivers him to
greater fear in a successive cycle.

[143] **best passions**
a paradox since the passions were
generally regarded as belonging to the
worst part of man.

[144] **honour**
elevated character, respect for what is
right; *dear bought* expensive, not in

the sense of money; *fame* public
reputation, especially reputation for
virtue – not necessarily 'widely
known' or 'famous' in the modern
sense.

[145] **lust of power**
Hobbes wrote, 'in the first place, I put
for a general inclination of all
mankind, a perpetual and restless
desire of power after power, that
ceases only in death' (*Leviathan*, I, 11).

[146] **the which**
which.

[147] **To which**
i.e. to the achieving of which (power).

[148] **Which makes...kind**
a cruel paradox that human benevolence can be traced back to the
desire for power.

[149] **For which...wise**
an answer to the clergyman – our
claims to wisdom are means of
acquiring power.

[150] **screws**
stretches, strains the meaning of
something.

[152] **laborious**
requiring effort, but the word also
carries the snobbish sense of belonging to an inferior, labouring class;
mean low, contemptible – not necessarily parsimonious.

[153] **design**
purpose.

[155] **acts**
enacts, does.

[157] **fame**
reputation of virtue; see above line
144.

[158] **durst**
dared; *For all...durst* another
paradox, i.e. (following from the
previous line) we're too afraid of
public appearance to be the cowards
we'd like to be.

[159] **Honesty**
in the general sense of virtuous
behaviour, rather than specifically
truth-telling.

[160] **knaves**
unprincipled men, crafty rogues.

[161] **dishonest**
without virtue, wicked.

[162] **known cheats**
i.e. men generally; *play* implying card games involving gambling; *upon the square* in an honest, open manner.
[163] **undone**
destroyed, ruined – see line 132.
[164] **weak truth**
Rochester undermines all our cherished absolutes.
[166] **wronged**
in the sense of spoken badly (and untruthfully) of.
[168] **Sir**
another direct address to the clergyman – compare line 110.
[169] **Most men**
Rochester seems to have moved away slightly from the earlier opinion that 'all men would be cowards if they durst' (line 158); *all men...knaves* The 'should' lifts dishonesty from an unfortunate fact to a moral imperative. Again, this represents a shift from the earlier 'mankind's dishonest' (line 161).
[170] **difference**
i.e. between different men.
[171] **thing...degree**
The subsequent couplet makes it clear that Rochester refers to dishonesty here. This makes the 'should be' of line 169 rather inconsistent with his argument, as he's assuming that everyone is a knave (whatever everyone should be).
[172–3] **And all...first rate**
This is the final couplet of the earlier, shorter version of the poem, with which Rochester rounds off his reply to the clergyman. The phrase 'first rate' (which has a positive weight) implies that eminence in knavery confers as valuable a distinction as eminence in morality or wisdom.
[174] **All this...hurled**
The first line of the section of the poem added after Stillingfleet's sermon attack (see note to line 74). The sermon was directed against those who try to 'defend their extravagant courses' by making 'satirical invectives against reason'. It includes such remarks as 'it is a pity such had not

their wish to be beasts rather than men...that they might have been less capable of doing mischief among mankind'.
[175] **pretending**
aspiring to, claiming; *part* Rochester identifies his object of scorn as the claim to reason (and those who make it) rather than reason itself.
[177] **False freedoms**
referring to the notion that reason can give man access to higher knowledge – see the clergyman's argument in lines 66–70 and Rochester's reply in lines 80–7; *holy cheats* religious ideas; *formal* in the sense that the lies follow the forms of the church – see line 46.
[178] **Over their...tyrannise**
The motive behind the invention of reason by the clergy is the wish for power; *fellow slaves* in that none really possesses the freedom promised by religious ideas of the reason.
[179] **court**
the king's establishment of advisers, followers and hangers-on; *But if...be* In the remainder of the poem, Rochester conducts a kind of search for a good man, reminiscent of the search of the angels sent to Sodom (Genesis 18: 20–19: 25).
[180] **unknown to me**
Rochester draws upon his own experience of the court to state that no courtier is virtuous.
[181–2] **Who does...protect**
i.e. if there is a courtier so just (line 179) that he uses his flattery for the protection of others rather than their ruin; *needful* necessary, unavoidable (in court).
[183–4] **Since flattery...trade**
The clause seems to be explaining the use of the word 'needful' (line 181). Flattery is demanded from every courtier.
[183] **which way...laid**
i.e. directed to whatever ends, either ruin or protection.
[184] **tax**
in the sense that all courtiers have to 'pay' the king with flattery; *unhappy*

unlucky, wretched; *trade* i.e. of the courtier.

[186] **bend**
submit; *Whose passions... mind* i.e. who is ruled by reason rather than passion.

[187] **arts**
skills; *policies* shrewd courses of action.

[188] **not his family**
Officers of state often gave appointments to lucrative positions to their family members.

[189] **pride**
Just as earlier Rochester identified fear as the source of our best actions (line 143), here he fixes on pride; *owned* acknowledged, admitted, open.

[190] **close**
secret; *friends'... hands* i.e. although he avoids open corruption, his corrupt friends pass on some of their earnings to him.

[192] **justifies**
vindicates, shows to be right (i.e. whose life vindicates his faith).

[193] **prelatic**
like a bishop (or other churchman of high rank).

[194] **reproof**
reproach; *Who... man deride* who derides mankind under the cover of an attack on sin. Rochester accuses the churchman of his own fault of attacking mankind.

[195] **obstreperous**
angrily vociferous; *saucy* impudent, impertinent; *eloquence* a reference to Stillingfleet's sermon – see notes to line 74 and line 174.

[196] *chide at kings*
Stillingfleet's sermon (see previous note) could be interpreted as an attack on the king before whom it was preached, since Charles was associated with libertine wits such as Rochester; *rail* attack with abusive language; *men of sense* a term for the court wits, referred to in lines 35–45.

[197] **pulpit**
Stillingfleet's sermon again – see previous notes.

[198] **scandals**
Restoration London, and particularly the court, delighted in malicious gossip; *calumnies* false accusations.

[199] **gossipping**
meeting of women to exchange scandal.

[200] **goodwife**
mistress of a house and the formal term of address for yeoman's wife – the latter associated with Puritanism.

[201] **sensual tribe**
i.e. the clergy. Rochester accuses others of the very qualities he has earlier praised – see lines 106–9.

[202] **avarice, pride, sloth, gluttony**
four of the seven deadly sins. The other three are envy, anger and lust. The corrupted clergyman (implicitly Stillingfleet) has already been accused of envy in line 195, and been shown to be full of anger in lines 197–8. Rochester turns his attention to lust in line 204ff.

[203] **good living**
wealthy benefices, well paid jobs (as clergymen).

[204] **lust exalted**
refined or intensified lust. 'Exalted' also has a religious connotation, present here ironically.

[205] **act**
enact; *adultery... wives* in that they imagine themselves with others when they sleep with their wives. Ben Jonson's second epigram on 'Voluptuous Beast' (1611) makes the same point: 'Than his chaste wife though Beast now know no more,/ He adulters still. His thoughts lie with his whore.'

[206] **score of years**
i.e. in a good living – see line 203.

[207] **lofty**
Pulpits were literally high up, but the word also has an ironic (here) moral sense.

[208] **progeny**
offspring; *Half a... progeny* The clergyman has apparently gone beyond being adulterous in his mind (line 205) to father half the children of his parish.

[209] **doting**
displaying the weak-mindedness of old age; *adored* i.e. admired in the way that belongs to God.

[210] **council board**
table used at meetings of the ecclesiastical council, the governing body of the church.
[211] **fop**
fool, dandy; *business* the business of the church, not trade.
[212] **Fond**
affectionate towards, but also foolish, weak witted; *toys* trifles (rather than children's playthings).
[213] **gay glittering fool**
the kind of affected young beau common in the comedy of the period; *proves* shows himself to be.
[214] **tawdry**
showy but of poor quality; *loves* The beau is expected to have mistresses.
[215] **But**
i.e. not the kind of clergyman he has described in the preceding passage; *meek humble man* Rochester imagines an ideal of the kind of virtue which he has denied to exist.
[216] **continence**
chastity, fidelity to a spouse.
[218] **mysterious truths**
The attitude here is different from that earlier when Rochester seemed to deny the existence of such truths – see

line 81; *no man ... conceive* Although Rochester reaffirms that such knowledge is unattainable, he does not deny its existence.
[220] **recant**
take back. The word is usually applied to the heretic who returns to the fold; *paradox* unorthodox opinion (i.e. that man has no reason in the accepted sense).
[222] **rabble world**
people in general (with a negative weight). The opinions expressed in most of the poem have been opposed to those of the world. Now Rochester says he will accept the world's opinions if a virtuous man can be found.
[223] **grant me**
addressed to the clergyman of earlier (lines 46–71) with whom the whole argument has been conducted.
[224] **Man differs ... beast**
i.e. there is a greater distance between this imaginary virtuous man and the general run of men than there is between man as a species and animals. The idea goes back to Montaigne (1533–92) and before him, the Greek historian and essayist Plutarch.

JOHN DRYDEN

(1631–1700)

Born in 1631, Dryden grew up amidst the Civil Wars and came of age during the Commonwealth period. His literary career, however, belongs to the Restoration, and in the forty years which spanned from the return of Charles II in 1660 to his own death in 1700, he was, if we except the ageing John Milton (1608–74), the major literary figure in England. He wrote drama, poetry, translations and critical prose. During the reigns of the Stuart kings, he was a loyal servant of them, for which he was rewarded with the posts of Poet Laureate (1668) and historiographer (1670). He converted to Catholicism (1686) during the reign of the Catholic James II, a move for which he was branded a time-server. However, he remained loyal to his faith when the crown was taken by the Protestant William in 1688 (see introduction to this volume), losing his state offices as a result and being forced to turn again in old age to writing for a living.

As indicated above, the range of his writings is immense. Significant among them are heroic plays such as *All for Love* (1678), odes such as *Alexander's Feast* (1697) printed below, didactic religious poems such as *The Hind and the Panther* (1687), and the verse translation of Virgil (1697). He is, however, perhaps most remembered for his prose, in which he developed a lucid, plain and vigorous style, and above all, for his satirical poetry. In satires such as *Absalom and Achitophel* (1681) he displayed an acute insight into human character, and he deployed the heroic couplet with such variety and force that his poetic language was to exert a major influence on his successors.

Further Reading

Volumes of the authoritative, annotated *Works of John Dryden* are still appearing from the University of California Press (Berkeley) under the editorship of Edward Niles Hooker *et al.* Until that project is complete, James Kinsley's four-volume *The Poems of John Dryden* (Oxford: Clarendon Press, 1968) remains useful, as it has been to the present editors. The same text is also available without annotations in a single volume, *The Poems and Fables of John Dryden* (London: Oxford University Press, 1962).

Possibly the best introduction to a study of Dryden is James Anderson Winn's excellent biography, *John Dryden and His World* (New Haven: Yale University Press, 1987). Louis Bredvold's *The Intellectual Milieu of John Dryden* (Ann Arbor: University of Michigan Press, 1977) is a useful background work, while more recently David Bywaters has offered *Dryden in Revolutionary England* (Berkeley: University of California Press, 1991). Two full-length studies of *Absalom and Achitophel* provide valuable help with that difficult poem: Bernard Schilling's *John Dryden and the Conservative Myth: A Reading of Absalom and Achitophel* (New Haven and London: Yale University Press, 1961) and Robert W. McHenry's *Absalom and Achitophel* (Hamden, Conn.: Archon, 1987). Though rather shorter, Raman Selden's *John Dryden: Absalom and Achitophel* (Harmondsworth: Penguin, 1986) might also be of some help to new readers. Among collections of essays H.T. Swedenberg's *Essential Articles for the Study of John Dryden* (Hamden, Conn.: Archon, 1966) remains useful despite its age. Both more recent and more tendentious is Harold Bloom's collection, *John Dryden: Modern Critical Views* (New York: Chelsea House, 1987). Those interested in the way that opinions about Dryden have changed over the centuries should consult James Kinsley and Helen Kinsley (eds), *John Dryden: The Critical Heritage* (London: Routledge and Kegan Paul, 1971).

———◇———

3 / *Absalom and Achitophel*
A Poem

In pious times, ere priest-craft did begin,
Before polygamy was made a sin,
When man on many multiplied his kind,
Ere one to one was, cursedly, confined,
When nature prompted, and no law denied   5
Promiscuous use of concubine and bride,
Then Israel's monarch, after heaven's own heart,
His vigorous warmth did variously impart
To wives and slaves, and, wide as his command,
Scattered his maker's image through the land.   10
Michal, of royal blood, the crown did wear,
A soil ungrateful to the tiller's care.
Not so the rest, for several mothers bore
To godlike David several sons before.
But since like slaves his bed they did ascend,   15
No true succession could their seed attend.
Of all this numerous progeny was none
So beautiful, so brave as Absalon,
Whether inspired by a diviner lust
His father got him with a greater gust,   20
Or that his conscious destiny made way
By manly beauty to imperial sway.
Early in foreign fields he won renown,
With kings and states allied to Israel's crown.
In peace the thoughts of war he could remove,   25
And seemed as he were only born for love.
What e'er he did was done with so much ease,
In him alone, 'twas natural to please.
His motions all accompanied with grace,
And Paradise was opened in his face.   30
With secret joy, indulgent David viewed
His youthful image in his son renewed:
To all his wishes nothing he denied,
And made the charming Annabel his bride.
What faults he had (for who from faults is free?)   35
His father could not, or he would not see.
Some warm excesses, which the law forbore,
Were construed youth that purged by boiling o'er,
And Amnon's murder, by a specious name,

Was called a just revenge for injured fame.   40
Thus praised, and loved, the noble youth remained,
While David, undisturbed, in Sion reigned.
    But life can never be sincerely blessed:
Heaven punishes the bad, and proves the best.
The Jews, a headstrong, moody, murmuring race,   45
As ever tried th'extent and reach of grace;
God's pampered people, whom, debauched with ease,
No king could govern, nor no god could please;
(Gods they had tried of every shape or size
That God-smiths could produce or priests devise;)   50
These Adam-wits, too fortunately free,
Began to dream they wanted liberty,
And when no rule, no precedent, was found
Of men by laws less circumscribed and bound,
They led their wild desires to woods and caves   55
And thought that all but savages were slaves.
They who, when Saul was dead, without a blow
Made foolish Ishbosheth the crown forego,
Who banished David did from Hebron bring
And with a general shout proclaimed him king;   60
Those very Jews, who at their very best
Their humour more than loyalty expressed,
Now wondered why so long they had obeyed
An idol monarch which their hands had made,
Thought they might ruin him they could create,   65
Or melt him to that golden calf, a state.
But these were random bolts. No formed design,
Nor interest made the factious crowd to join.
The sober part of Israel, free from stain,
Well knew the value of a peaceful reign: 70
And, looking backward with a wise afright,
Saw seams of wounds, dishonest to the sight;
In contemplation of whose ugly scars,
They cursed the memory of civil wars.
The moderate sort of men, thus qualified,   75
Inclined the balance to the better side,
And David's mildness managed it so well,
The bad found no occasion to rebel.
But, when to sin our biased nature leans,
The careful devil is still at hand with means;   80

And providently pimps for ill desires:
The Good Old Cause revived, a plot requires.
Plots, true or false, are necessary things,
To raise up common-wealths, and ruin kings.
 Th'inhabitants of old Jerusalem   85
Were Jebusites, the town so called from them;
And theirs the native right –
But when the chosen people grew more strong,
The rightful cause at length became the wrong:
And every loss the men of Jebus bore,   90
They still were thought God's enemies the more.
Thus, worn and weakened, well or ill content,
Submit they must to David's government.
Impoverished, and deprived of all command,
Their taxes doubled as they lost their land,   95
And, what was harder yet to flesh and blood,
Their gods disgraced, and burnt like common wood.
This set the heathen priesthood in a flame;
For priests of all religions are the same.
Of whatsoe'r descent their Godhead be,   100
Stock, stone, or other homely pedigree,
In his defence his servants are as bold
As if he had been born of beaten gold.
The Jewish rabbins, though their enemies,
In this conclude them honest men and wise,   105
For 'twas their duty, all the learned think,
T'espouse his cause by whom they eat and drink.
 From hence began that plot, the nation's curse,
Bad in itself, but represented worse.
Raised in extremes, and in extremes decried,   110
With oaths affirmed, with dying vows denied.
Not weighed, or winnowed by the multitude,
But swallowed in the mass, unchewed and crude.
Some truth there was, but dashed and brewed with lies,
To please the fools, and puzzle all the wise.   115
Succeeding times did equal folly call,
Believing nothing, or believing all.
Th' Egyptian rites the Jebusites embraced,
Where Gods were recommended by their taste.
Such savoury deities must needs be good,   120
As served at once for worship and for food.

By force they could not introduce these gods,
For ten to one, in former days was odds.
So fraud was used (the sacrificer's trade)
Fools are more hard to conquer than persuade.   125
Their busy teachers mingled with the Jews,
And raked, for converts, even the court and stews,
Which Hebrew priests the more unkindly took,
Because the fleece accompanies the flock.
Some thought they God's anointed meant to slay   130
By guns, invented since full many a day.
Our author swears it not, but who can know
How far the devil and Jebusites may go?
This plot, which failed for want of common sense,
Had yet a deep and dangerous consequence: 135
For, as when raging fevers boil the blood,
The standing lake soon floats into a flood,
And every hostile humour, which before
Slept quiet in its channels, bubbles o'er,
So, several factions from this first ferment,   140
Work up to foam, and threat the government.
Some by their friends, more by themselves thought wise,
Opposed the power, to which they could not rise.
Some had in courts been great, and thrown from thence,
Like fiends, were hardened in impenitence.   145
Some by their monarch's fatal mercy grown,
From pardoned rebels, kinsmen to the throne;
Were raised in power and public office high:
Strong bands, if bands ungrateful men could tie.
   Of these the false Achitophel was first,   150
A name to all succeeding ages cursed,
For close designs and crooked counsels fit,
Sagacious, bold, and turbulent of wit,
Restless, unfixed in principles and place,
In power unpleased, impatient of disgrace.   155
A fiery soul, which working out its way
Fretted the pigmy body to decay,
And o'erinformed the tenement of clay.
A daring pilot in extremity,
Pleased with the danger when the waves went high   160
He sought the storms, but for a calm unfit,
Would steer too nigh the sands, to boast his wit.

Great wits are sure to madness near allied,
And thin partitions do their bounds divide.
Else, why should he, with wealth and honour blessed,　165
Refuse his age the needful hours of rest?
Punish a body which he could not please,
Bankrupt of life, yet prodigal of ease?
And all to leave what with his toil he won
To that unfeathered, two-legged thing, a son,　170
Got while his soul did huddled notions try
And born a shapeless lump like anarchy.
In friendship false, implacable in hate,
Resolved to ruin or to rule the state.
To compass this the triple bond he broke,　175
The pillars of the public safety shook,
And fitted Israel for a foreign yoke.
Then, seized with fear, yet still affecting fame,
Usurped a patriot's all-atoning name.
So easy still it proves in factious times,　180
With public zeal to cancel private crimes.
How safe is treason, and how sacred ill,
Where none can sin against the people's will,
Where crowds can wink, and no offence be known,
Since in another's guilt they find their own.　185
Yet, fame deserved, no enemy can grudge:
The statesman we abhor, but praise the judge.
In Israel's courts ne'er sat an Abbethdin
With more discerning eyes, or hands more clean.
Unbribed, unsought, the wretched to redress,　190
Swift of dispatch, and easy of access.
Oh, had he been content to serve the crown,
With virtues only proper to the gown,
Or, had the rankness of the soil been freed
From cockle, that oppressed the noble seed,　195
David, for him his tuneful harp had strung,
And heaven had wanted one immortal song.
But wild ambition loves to slide, not stand,
And fortune's ice prefers to virtue's land.
Achitophel, grown weary to possess　200
A lawful fame, and lazy happiness,
Disdained the golden fruit to gather free,
And lent the crowd his arm to shake the tree.

Now, manifest of crimes, contrived long since,
He stood at bold defiance with his prince, 205
Help up the buckler of the people's cause,
Against the crown, and skulked behind the laws.
The wished occasion of the plot he takes,
Some circumstances finds, but more he makes.
By buzzing emissaries, fills the ears 210
Of listening crowds, with jealousies and fears
Of arbitrary counsels brought to light,
And proves the king himself a Jebusite.
Weak arguments! which yet he knew full well,
Were strong with people easy to rebel. 215
For, governed by the moon, the giddy Jews
Tread the same track when she the prime renews,
And once in twenty years, their scribes record,
By natural instinct they change their lord.
Achitophel still wants a chief, and none 220
Was found so fit as warlike Absalon.
Not, that he wished his greatness to create,
(For politicians neither love nor hate)
But, for he knew, his title not allowed,
Would keep him still depending on the crowd, 225
That kingly power, thus ebbing out, might be
Drawn to the dregs of a democracy.
Him he attempts, with studied arts to please,
And sheds his venom, in such words as these.
    'Auspicious prince, at whose nativity 230
Some royal planet ruled the southern sky,
Thy longing country's darling and desire,
Their cloudy pillar, and their guardian fire,
Their second Moses, whose extended wand
Divides the seas, and shows the promised land, 235
Whose dawning day, in every distant age,
Has exercised the sacred prophet's rage,
The people's prayer, the glad diviner's theme,
The young men's vision, and the old men's dream!
Thee, saviour, thee, the nation's vows confess, 240
And, never satisfied with seeing, bless.
Swift, unbespoken pomps, thy steps proclaim,
And stammering babes are taught to lisp thy name.
How long wilt thou the general joy detain,

Starve, and defraud the people of thy reign? 245
Content ingloriously to pass thy days
Like one of virtue's fools that feeds on praise,
Till thy fresh glories, which now shine so bright,
Grow stale and tarnish with our daily sight.
Believe me, royal youth, thy fruit must be, 250
Or gathered ripe, or rot upon the tree.
Heaven has to all allotted, soon or late,
Some lucky revolution of their fate,
Whose motions, if we watch and guide with skill,
(For human good depends on human will) 255
Our fortune rolls, as from a smooth descent,
And, from the first impression, takes the bent,
But, if unseized, she glides away like wind,
And leaves repenting folly far behind.
Now, now she meets you, with a glorious prize, 260
And spreads her locks before her as she flies.
Had thus old David, from whose loins you spring,
Not dared, when Fortune called him, to be king,
At Gath an exile he might still remain,
And heaven's anointing oil had been in vain. 265
Let his successful youth your hopes engage,
But shun th'example of declining age.
Behold him setting in his western skies,
The shadows lengthening as the vapours rise.
He is not now, as when on Jordan's sand 270
The joyful people thronged to see him land,
Cov'ring the beach, and black'ning all the strand;
But, like the prince of angels from his height,
Comes tumbling downward with diminished light,
Betrayed by one poor plot to public scorn, 275
(Our only blessing since his cursed return)
Those heaps of people which one sheaf did bind,
Blown off and scattered by a puff of wind.
What strength can he to your designs oppose,
Naked of friends, and round beset with foes? 280
If Pharaoh's doubtful succour he should use,
A foreign aid would more incense the Jews.
Proud Egypt would dissembled friendship bring,
Foment the war, but not support the king.
Nor would the royal party e'er unite 285

46

With Pharaoh's arms t'assist the Jebusite;
Or if they should, their interest soon would break,
And with such odious aid make David weak.
All sorts of men by my successful arts,
Abhorring kings, estrange their altered hearts   290
From David's rule: And 'tis the general cry,
Religion, commonwealth, and liberty.
If you as champion of the public good,
Add to their arms a chief of royal blood,
What may not Israel hope? And what applause   295
Might such a general gain by such a cause?
Not barren praise alone, that gaudy flower,
Fair only to the sight, but solid power.
And nobler is a limited command,
Given by the love of all your native land,   300
Than a successive title, long and dark,
Drawn from the mouldy rolls of Noah's ark.'

  What cannot praise effect in mighty minds,
When flattery sooths, and when ambition blinds!
Desire of power, on earth a vicious weed,   305
Yet, sprung from high, is of celestial seed.
In God 'tis glory. And when men aspire,
'Tis but a spark too much of heavenly fire.
Th' ambitious youth, too covetous of fame,
Too full of angel's metal in his frame   310
Unwarily was led from virtue's ways.
Made drunk with honour, and debauched with praise.
Half loath, and half consenting to the ill,
(For loyal blood within him struggled still)
He thus replied, 'And what pretence have I   315
To take up arms for public liberty?
My father governs with unquestioned right,
The faith's defender, and mankind's delight,
Good, gracious, just, observant of the laws;
And heaven by wonders has espoused his cause.   320
Whom has he wronged in all his peaceful reign?
Who sues for justice to his throne in vain?
What millions has he pardoned of his foes,
Whom just revenge did to his wrath expose?
Mild, easy, humble, studious of our good;   325

47

Inclined to mercy, and averse from blood.
If mildness ill with stubborn Israel suit,
His crime is God's beloved attribute.
What could he gain, his people to betray,
Or change his right, for arbitrary sway?   330
Let haughty Pharaoh curse with such a reign,
His fruitful Nile, and yoke a servile train.
If David's rule Jerusalem displease,
The dog-star heats their brains to this disease.
Why then should I, encouraging the bad,   335
Turn rebel, and run popularly mad?
Were he a tyrant who, by lawless might,
Oppressed the Jews, and raised the Jebusite,
Well might I mourn, but nature's holy bands
Would curb my spirits, and restrain my hands.   340
The people might assert their liberty,
But what was right in them, were crime in me.
His favour leaves me nothing to require,
Prevents my wishes, and outruns desire.
What more can I expect while David lives?   345
All but his kingly diadem he gives,
And that . . . ' (But there he paused. Then sighing said,)
'Is justly destined for a worthier head.
For when my father from his toils shall rest,
And late augment the number of the blessed,   350
His lawful issue shall the throne ascend,
Or the collateral line where that shall end.
His brother, though oppressed with vulgar spite,
Yet dauntless and secure of native right,
Of every royal virtue stands possessed,   355
Still dear to all the bravest, and the best.
His courage foes, his friends his truth proclaim,
His loyalty the king, the world his fame.
His mercy even th' offending crowd will find,
For sure he comes of a forgiving kind.   360
Why should I then repine at heaven's decree,
Which gives me no pretence to royalty?
Yet, Oh, that fate propitiously inclined
Had raised my birth, or had debased my mind,
To my large soul, not all her treasure lent,   365
And then betrayed it to a mean descent.

48

I find, I find my mounting spirits bold,
And David's part disdains my mother's mould.
Why am I scanted by a niggard birth?
My soul disclaims the kindred of her earth, 370
And made for empire, whispers me within,
Desire of greatness is a Godlike sin.'
   Him staggering so when hell's dire agent found,
While fainting virtue scarce maintained her ground,
He pours fresh forces in, and thus replies, 375
   'Th'eternal God supremely good and wise,
Imparts not these prodigious gifts in vain;
What wonders are reserved to bless your reign?
Against your will your arguments have shown,
Such virtue's only given to guide a throne. 380
Not that your father's mildness I contemn,
But manly force becomes the diadem.
'Tis true, he grants the people all they crave,
And more perhaps than subjects ought to have,
For lavish grants suppose a monarch tame, 385
And more his goodness than his wit proclaim.
But when should people strive their bonds to break,
If not when kings are negligent or weak?
Let him give on till he can give no more,
The thrifty Sanhedrin shall keep him poor, 390
And every shekel which he can receive,
Shall cost a limb of his prerogative.
To ply him with new plots, shall be my care,
Or plunge him deep in some expensive war,
Which when his treasure can no more supply, 395
He must, with the remains of kingship, buy.
His faithful friends, our jealousies and fears
Call Jebusites and Pharaoh's pensioners;
Whom, when our fury from his aid has torn,
He shall be naked left to public scorn. 400
The next successor, whom I fear and hate,
My arts have made obnoxious to the state,
Turned all his virtues to his overthrow,
And gained our elders to pronounce a foe.
His right, for sums of necessary gold, 405
Shall first be pawned, and afterwards be sold,
Till time shall ever-wanting David draw,

To pass your doubtful title into law.
If not, the people have a right supreme
To make their kings, for kings are made for them. 410
All empire is no more than power in trust,
Which when resumed, can be no longer just.
Succession, for the general good designed,
In its own wrong a nation cannot bind.
If altering that the people can relieve, 415
Better one suffer, than a nation grieve.
The Jews well know their power. E'er Saul they chose,
God was their king, and God they durst depose.
Urge now your piety, your filial name,
A father's right, and fear of future fame. 420
The public good, that universal call,
To which even heaven submitted, answers all.
Nor let his love enchant your generous mind,
'Tis nature's trick to propagate her kind.
Our fond begetters, who would never die, 425
Love but themselves in their posterity.
Or let his kindness by th' effects be tried,
Or let him lay his vain pretence aside.
God said he loved your father. Could he bring
A better proof, than to anoint him king? 430
It surely shewed he loved the shepherd well,
Who gave so fair a flock as Israel.
Would David have you thought his darling son?
What means he then, to alienate the crown?
The name of godly he may blush to bear. 435
'Tis after God's own heart to cheat his heir.
He to his brother gives supreme command,
To you a legacy of barren land,
Perhaps th' old harp, on which he thrums his lays,
Or some dull Hebrew ballad in your praise. 440
Then, the next heir, a prince severe and wise
Already looks on you with jealous eyes,
Sees through the thin disguises of your arts,
And marks your progress in the people's hearts.
Though now his mighty soul its grief contains, 445
He meditates revenge who least complains,
And like a lion, slumbering in the way,
Or sleep-dissembling while he waits his prey,

His fearless foes within his distance draws,
Constrains his roaring, and contracts his paws,   450
Till at the last, his time for fury found,
He shoots with sudden vengeance from the ground,
The prostrate vulgar, passes o'er, and spares,
But with a lordly rage, his hunters tears.
Your case no tame expedients will afford.   455
Resolve on death, or conquest by the sword,
Which for no less a stake than life you draw,
And self-defence is nature's eldest law.
Leave the warm people no considering time,
For then rebellion may be thought a crime.   460
Prevail yourself of what occasion gives,
But try your title while your father lives,
And that your arms may have a fair pretence,
Proclaim you take them in the king's defence,
Whose sacred life each minute would expose,   465
To plots from seeming friends and secret foes.
And who can sound the depth of David's soul?
Perhaps his fear, his kindness may control.
He fears his brother, though he loves his son,
For plighted vows too late to be undone.   470
If so, by force he wishes to be gained,
Like women's lechery to seem constrained.
Doubt not, but when he most affects the frown
Commit a pleasing rape upon the crown.
Secure his person to secure your cause.   475
They who possess the prince, possess the laws.'
    He said, and this advice above the rest,
With Absalom's mild nature suited best.
Unblamed of life (ambition set aside)
Not stained with cruelty, nor puffed with pride,   480
How happy had he been, if destiny
Had higher placed his birth, or not so high!
His kingly virtues might have claimed a throne,
And blessed all other countries but his own.
But charming greatness, since so few refuse,   485
'Tis juster to lament him, than accuse.
Strong were his hopes a rival to remove,
With blandishments to gain the public love,
To head the faction while their zeal was hot,

And popularly prosecute the plot.   490
    To further this, Achitophel unites
The malcontents of all the Israelites,
Whose differing parties he could wisely join,
For several ends, to serve the same design.
The best, and of the princes some were such,   495
Who thought the power of monarchy too much,
Mistaken men, and patriots in their hearts,
Not wicked, but seduced by impious arts.
By these the springs of property were bent,
And wound so high, they cracked the government.   500
The next for interest sought t' embroil the state,
To sell their duty at a dearer rate,
And make their Jewish markets of the throne,
Pretending public good, to serve their own.
Others thought kings a useless heavy load,   505
Who cost too much, and did too little good.
These were for laying honest David by,
On principles of pure good husbandry.
With them joined all th' haranguers of the throng,
That thought to get preferment by the tongue.   510
Who follow next, a double danger bring,
Not only hating David, but the king,
The Solymean rout, well versed of old,
In godly faction, and in treason bold,
Cowering and quaking at a conqueror's sword,   515
But lofty to a lawful prince restored,
Saw with disdain an ethnic plot begun,
And scorned by Jebusites to be outdone.
Hot Levites headed these, who pulled before
From th'ark which in the judges' days they bore,   520
Resumed their cant, and with a zealous cry,
Pursued their old beloved theocracy.
Where Sanhedrin and priest enslaved the nation,
And justified their spoils by inspiration,
For who so fit for reign as Aaron's race,   525
If once dominion they could found in grace?
These led the pack, though not of surest scent,
Yet deepest mouthed against the government.
A numerous host of dreaming saints succeed,
Of the true old enthusiastic breed.   530

'Gainst form and order they their power employ,
Nothing to build and all things to destroy.
But far more numerous was the herd of such,
Who think too little, and who talk too much.
These, out of mere instinct, they knew not why,   535
Adored their fathers' God, and property,
And, by the same blind benefit of fate,
The devil and the Jebusite did hate,
Born to be saved, even in their own despite,
Because they could not help believing right.   540
Such were the tools, but a whole hydra more
Remains, of sprouting heads too long, to score.
    Some of their chiefs were princes of the land;
In the first rank of these did Zimri stand,
A man so various that he seemed to be,   545
Not one, but all mankind's epitome.
Stiff in opinions, always in the wrong,
Was everything by starts and nothing long;
But, in the course of one revolving moon,
Was chymist, fiddler, statesman and buffoon;   550
Then all for women, painting, rhyming, drinking,
Besides ten thousand freaks that died in thinking.
Blessed madman who could every hour employ
With something new to wish, or to enjoy.
Railing and praising were his usual themes,   555
And both (to show his judgement) in extremes;
So over violent or over civil
That every man with him was god or devil.
In squand'ring wealth was his peculiar art,
Nothing went unrewarded but desert.   560
Beggared by fools whom still he found too late,
He had his jests, and they had his estate.
He laughed himself from court, then sought relief
By forming parties, but could ne'er be chief,
For spite of him the weight of business fell   565
On Absalom and wise Achitophel.
Thus, wicked but in will, of means bereft,
He left not faction, but of that was left.
    Titles and names 'twere tedious to rehearse
Of lords, below the dignity of verse.   570
Wits, warriors, commonwealthsmen were the best.

Kind husbands and mere nobles all the rest.
And, therefore, in the name of dullness, be
The well hung Balaam and cold Caleb free.
And canting Nadab let oblivion damn, 575
Who made new porridge for the paschal lamb.
Let friendship's holy band some names assure,
Some their own worth, and some let scorn secure.
Nor shall the rascal rabble here have place,
Whom kings no titles gave, and God no grace, 580
Not bull-faced Jonas, who could statutes draw
To mean rebellion, and make treason law.
But he, though bad, is followed by a worse,
The wretch who heaven's anointed dared to curse.
Shimei, whose youth did early promise bring 585
Of zeal to God, and hatred to his king,
Did wisely from expensive sins refrain
And never broke the Sabbath, but for gain,
Nor ever was he known an oath to vent,
Or curse unless against the government. 590
Thus, heaping wealth by the most ready way
Among the Jews, which was to cheat and pray,
The city, to reward his pious hate
Against his master, chose him magistrate.
His hand a vare of justice did uphold, 595
His neck was loaded with a chain of gold.
During his office, treason was no crime,
The sons of Belial had a glorious time,
For Shimei, though not prodigal of pelf,
Yet loved his wicked neighbour as himself. 600
When two or three were gathered to declaim
Against the monarch of Jerusalem,
Shimei was always in the midst of them.
And, if they cursed the king when he was by,
Would rather curse, than break good company. 605
If any durst his factious friends accuse,
He packed a jury of dissenting Jews,
Whose fellow-feeling, in the godly cause,
Would free the suffering saint from human laws.
For laws are only made to punish those 610
Who serve the king and to protect his foes.
If any leisure time he had from power,

(Because 'tis sin to misemploy an hour)
His business was by writing to persuade,
That kings were useless, and a clog to trade,   615
And, that his noble style he might refine,
No Rechabite more shunned the fumes of wine.
Chaste were his cellars, and his shrieval board
The grossness of a City feast abhorred.
His cooks, with long disuse, their trade forgot,   620
Cool was his kitchen, though his brains were hot.
Such frugal virtue malice may accuse,
But sure 'twas necessary to the Jews.
For towns once burnt such magistrates require
As dare not tempt God's providence by fire.   625
With spiritual food he fed his servants well,
But free from flesh that made the Jews rebel,
And Moses' laws he held in more account,
For forty days of fasting in the Mount.
    To speak the rest, who better are forgot,   630
Would tire a well-breathed witness of the plot.
Yet, Corah, thou shalt from oblivion pass;
Erect thyself, thou monumental brass,
High as the serpent of thy metal made,
While nations stand secure beneath thy shade.   635
What though his birth were base, yet comets rise,
From earthly vapours ere they rise in skies.
Prodigious actions may as well be done
By weaver's issue, as by prince's son.
This arch-attestor for the public good   640
By that one deed ennobles all his blood.
Whoever asked the witnesses' high race
Whose oath with martyrdom did Stephen grace?
Ours was a Levite, and as times went then,
His tribe was godalmighty's gentlemen.   645
Sunk were his eyes, his voice was harsh and loud,
Sure signs he neither choleric was, nor proud;
His long chin proved his wit, his saintlike grace
A church vermilion and a Moses face.
His memory, miraculously great,   650
Could plots, exceeding man's belief, repeat,
Which, therefore, cannot be accounted lies
For human wit could never such devise.

Some future truths are mingled in his book,
But, where the witness failed, the prophet spoke. 655
Some things like visionary flights appear,
The spirit caught him up, the Lord knows where,
And gave him his rabbinical degree
Unknown to foreign university.
His judgement yet his memory did excel, 660
Which pieced his wondrous evidence so well,
And suited to the temper of the times,
Then groaning under Jebusitic crimes.
Let Israel's foes suspect his heavenly call,
And rashly judge his writ apocryphal. 665
Our laws for such affronts have forfeits made:
He takes his life, who takes away his trade.
Were I myself in witness Corah's place,
The wretch who did me such a dire disgrace,
Should whet my memory, though once forgot, 670
To make him an appendix of my plot.
His zeal to heaven, made him his prince despise,
And load his person with indignities,
But zeal peculiar privilege affords,
Indulging latitude to deeds and words, 675
And Corah might for Agag's murder call,
In terms as coarse as Samuel used to Saul.
What others in his evidence did join,
(The best that could be had for love or coin,)
In Corah's own predicament will fall, 680
For witness is a common name to all.

Surrounded thus with friends of every sort,
Deluded Absalom forsakes the court,
Impatient of high hopes, urged with renown,
And fired with near possession of a crown. 685
Th' admiring crowd are dazzled with surprise,
And on his goodly person feed their eyes.
His joy concealed, he sets himself to show,
On each side bowing popularly low.
His looks, his gestures, and his words he frames, 690
And with familiar ease repeats their names.
Thus, formed by nature, furnished out with arts,
He glides unfelt into their secret hearts.

Then with a kind compassionating look,
And sighs, bespeaking pity ere he spoke,   695
Few words he said, but easy those and fit,
More slow than Hybla drops, and far more sweet.
   'I mourn, my countrymen, your lost estate,
Though far unable to prevent your fate.
Behold a banished man, for your dear cause   700
Exposed a prey to arbitrary laws!
Yet oh! that I alone could be undone,
Cut off from empire, and no more a son!
Now all your liberties a spoil are made,
Egypt and Tyrus intercept your trade,   705
And Jebusites your sacred rites invade.
My father, whom with reverence yet I name,
Charmed into ease, is careless of his fame,
And, bribed with petty sums of foreign gold,
Is grown in Bathsheba's embraces old,   710
Exalts his enemies, his friends destroys,
And all his power against himself employs.
He gives (and let him give) my right away,
But why should he his own, and yours betray?
He, only he, can make the nation bleed,   715
And he alone from my revenge is freed.
Take then my tears (with that he wiped his eyes)
'Tis all the aid my present power supplies.
No court informer can these arms accuse,
These arms may sons against their fathers use,   720
And, 'tis my wish, the next successor's reign
May make no other Israelite complain.'
   Youth, beauty, graceful action, seldom fail,
But common interest always will prevail,
And pity never ceases to be shown   725
To him, who makes the people's wrongs his own.
The crowd (that still believe their kings oppress)
With lifted hands their young messiah bless,
Who now begins his progress to ordain,
With chariots, horsemen, and a numerous train.   730
From east to west his glories he displays,
And, like the sun, the promised land surveys.
Fame runs before him, as the morning star,
And shouts of joy salute him from afar.

Each house receives him as a guardian God; 735
And consecrates the place of his abode,
But hospitable treats did most commend
Wise Issachar, his wealthy western friend.
This moving court, that caught the people's eyes,
And seemed but pomp, did other ends disguise. 740
Achitophel had formed it, with intent
To sound the depths, and fathom where it went,
The people's hearts, distinguish friends from foes,
And try their strength, before they came to blows.
Yet all was coloured with a smooth pretence 745
Of specious love, and duty to their prince.
Religion, and redress of grievances
(Two names that always cheat and always please)
Are often urged, and good King David's life
Endangered by a brother and a wife. 750

    Thus, in a pageant show, a plot is made,
And peace itself is war in masquerade.
Oh foolish Israel! never warned by ill,
Still the same bait, and circumvented still!
Did ever men forsake their present ease, 755
In midst of health imagine a disease?
Take pains contingent mischiefs to foresee,
Make heirs for monarchs, and for God decree?
What shall we think! Can people give away
Both for themselves and sons their native sway? 760
Then they are left defenceless to the sword
Of each unbounded arbitrary lord;
And laws are vain, by which we right enjoy,
If kings unquestioned can those laws destroy.
Yet, if the crowd be judge of fit and just 765
And kings are only officers in trust,
Then this resuming cov'nant was declared
When kings were made, or is for ever barred;
If those who gave the scepter could not tie
By their own deed their own posterity, 770
How then could Adam bind his future race?
How could his forfeit on mankind take place?
Or how could heavenly justice damn us all
Who ne'er consented to our father's fall?

Then kings are slaves to those whom they command, 775
And tenants to their people's pleasure stand.
Add, that the power for property allowed
Is mischievously seated in the crowd;
For who can be secure of private right
If sovereign sway may be dissolved by might? 780
Nor is the people's judgement always true;
The most may err as grossly as the few,
And faultless kings run down by common cry
For vice, oppression and for tyranny.
What standard is there in a fickle rout, 785
Which flowing to the mark runs faster out?
Nor only crowds, but Sanhedrins may be
Infected by this public lunacy,
And share the madness of rebellious times
To murder monarchs for imagined crimes. 790
If they may give and take whene'er they please
Not kings alone (the godhead's images)
But government itself at length must fall
To nature's state, where all have right to all.
Yet, grant our lords the people kings can make, 795
What prudent men a settled throne would shake?
For whatsoe'er their sufferings were before
The change they covet makes them suffer more.
All other errors but disturb a state,
But innovation is the blow of fate. 800
If ancient fabrics nod and threat to fall,
To patch the flaws and buttress up the wall,
This far 'tis duty; but here fix the mark,
For all beyond it is to touch our ark.
To change foundations, cast the frame anew, 805
Is work for rebels who base ends pursue,
At once divine and human laws control
And mend the parts by ruin of the whole.
The tampering world is subject to this curse,
To physic their disease into a worse. 810
  Now what relief can righteous David bring?
How fatal 'tis to be too good a king!
Friends he has few, so high the madness grows,
Who dare be such, must be the people's foes.
Yet some there were, even in the worst of days; 815

Some let me name, and naming is to praise.
   In this short file Barzillai first appears,
Barzillai crowned with honour and with years.
Long since, the rising rebels he withstood
In regions waste, beyond the Jordan's flood, 820
Unfortunately brave to buoy the state,
But sinking underneath his master's fate.
In exile with his godlike prince he mourned,
For him he suffered, and with him returned.
The court he practised, not the courtier's art, 825
Large was his wealth, but larger was his heart,
Which, well the noblest objects knew to choose,
The fighting warrior, and recording muse.
His bed could once a fruitful issue boast,
Now more than half a father's name is lost. 830
His eldest hope, with every grace adorned,
By me (so heaven will have it) always mourned,
And always honoured, snatched in manhood's prime
By th'unequal fates, and providence's crime.
Yet not before the goal of honour won, 835
All parts fulfilled of subject and of son.
Swift was the race, but short the time to run.
Oh narrow circle, but of power divine,
Scanted in space, but perfect in thy line!
By sea, by land, thy matchless worth was known, 840
Arms thy delight, and war was all thy own.
Thy force, infused, the fainting Tyrians propped
And haughty Pharaoh found his fortune stopped.
Oh ancient honour, Oh unconquered hand,
Whom foes unpunished never could withstand! 845
But Israel was unworthy of thy name,
Short is the date of all immoderate fame.
It looks as heaven our ruin had designed,
And durst not trust thy fortune and thy mind.
Now, free from earth, thy disencumbred soul 850
Mounts up, and leaves behind the clouds and starry pole:
From thence thy kindred legions mayst thou bring
To aid the guardian angel of thy king.
Here stop, my muse, here cease thy painful flight,
No pinions can pursue immortal height. 855
Tell good Barzillai thou canst sing no more,

60

And tell thy soul she should have fled before.
Or fled she with his life, and left this verse
To hang on her departed patron's hearse?
    Now take thy steepy flight from heaven, and see   860
If thou canst find on earth another he.
Another he would be too hard to find,
See then whom thou canst see not far behind.
Zadoc the priest, whom shunning power and place,
His lowly mind advanced to David's grace,   865
With him the Sagan of Jerusalem,
Of hospitable soul and noble stem.
Him of the western dome, whose weighty sense
Flows in fit words and heavenly eloquence.
The prophets' sons by such example led,   870
To learning and to loyalty were bred.
For colleges on bounteous kings depend,
And never rebel was to arts a friend.
To these succeed the pillars of the laws,
Who best could plead and best can judge a cause.   875
Next them a train of loyal peers ascend,
Sharp judging Adriel the muse's friend,
Himself a muse – In Sanhedrin's debate
True to his prince, but not a slave of state.
Whom David's love with honours did adorn,   880
That from his disobedient son were torn.
Jotham of piercing wit and pregnant thought,
Indewed by nature, and by learning taught
To move assemblies, who but only tried
The worse awhile, then chose the better side,   885
Nor chose alone, but turned the balance too,
So much the weight of one brave man can do.
Hushai the friend of David in distress,
In public storms of manly steadfastness.
By foreign treaties he informed his youth,   890
And joined experience to his native truth.
His frugal care supplied the wanting throne,
Frugal for that, but bounteous of his own.
'Tis easy conduct when exchequers flow,
But hard the task to manage well the low,   895
For sovereign power is too depressed or high,
When kings are forced to sell, or crowds to buy.

Indulge one labour more my weary muse,
For Amiel, who can Amiel's praise refuse?
Of ancient race by birth, but nobler yet   900
In his own worth, and without title great.
The Sanhedrin long time as chief he ruled,
Their reason guided and their passion cooled.
So dexterous was he in the crown's defence,
So formed to speak a loyal nation's sense,   905
That as their band was Israel's tribes in small,
So fit was he to represent them all.
Now rather charioteers the seat ascend,
Whose loose careers his steady skill commend.
They like th'unequal ruler of the day,   910
Misguide the seasons and mistake the way,
While he withdrawn at their mad labour smiles,
And safe enjoys the Sabbath of his toils.

These were the chief, a small but faithful band
Of worthies, in the breach who dared to stand,   915
And tempt th'united fury of the land.
With grief they viewed such powerful engines bent,
To batter down the lawful government,
A numerous faction with pretended frights,
In Sanhedrins to plume the regal rights,   920
The true successor from the court removed,
The plot, by hireling witnesses improved.
These ills they saw, and as their duty bound,
They showed the king the danger of the wound,
That no concessions from the throne would please,   925
But lenitives fomented the disease,
That Absalom, ambitious of the crown,
Was made the lure to draw the people down,
That false Achitophel's pernicious hate,
Had turned the plot to ruin church and state,   930
The council violent, the rabble worse
That Shimei taught Jerusalem to curse.

With all these loads of injuries oppressed,
And long revolving, in his careful breast,
Th'event of things. At last his patience tired,   935
Thus from his royal throne by heaven inspired,

The God-like David spoke. With awful fear
His train their maker in their master hear.
   'Thus long have I, by native mercy swayed,
My wrongs dissembled, my revenge delayed. 940
So willing to forgive th'offending age,
So much the father did the king assuage.
But now so far my clemency they slight,
Th'offenders question my forgiving right.
That one was made for many, they contend, 945
But 'tis to rule, for that's a monarch's end.
They call my tenderness of blood, my fear:
Though manly tempers can the longest bear.
Yet, since they will divert my native course,
'Tis time to show I am not good by force. 950
Those heaped affronts that haughty subjects bring,
Are burthens for a camel, not a king:
Kings are the public pillars of the state,
Born to sustain and prop the nation's weight.
If my young Samson will pretend a call 955
To shake the column, let him share the fall.
But Oh, that yet he would repent and live!
How easy 'tis for parents to forgive!
With how few tears a pardon might be won
From nature, pleading for a darling son! 960
Poor pitied youth, by my paternal care,
Raised up to all the height his frame could bear.
Had God ordained his fate for empire born,
He would have given his soul another turn.
Gulled with a patriot's name, whose modern sense 965
Is one that would by law supplant his prince.
The people's brave, the politicians' tool,
Never was patriot yet, but was a fool.
Whence comes it that religion and the laws
Should more be Absalom's than David's cause? 970
His old instructor, ere he lost his place,
Was never thought endued with so much grace.
Good heavens, how faction can a patriot paint!
My rebel ever proves my people's saint.
Would they impose an heir upon the throne? 975
Let Sanhedrins be taught to give their own.
A king's at least a part of government,

And mine as requisite as their consent.
Without my leave a future king to choose,
Infers a right the present to depose. 980
True, they petition me t'approve their choice,
But Esau's hands suit ill with Jacob's voice.
My pious subjects for my safety pray,
Which to secure they take my power away.
From plots and treasons heaven preserve my years, 985
But save me most from my petitioners.
Unsatiate as the barren womb or grave,
God cannot grant so much as they can crave.
What then is left but with a jealous eye
To guard the small remains of royalty? 990
The law shall still direct my peaceful sway,
And the same law teach rebels to obey.
Votes shall no more established power control,
Such votes as make a part exceed the whole.
No groundless clamours shall my friends remove, 995
Nor crowds have power to punish e'er they prove.
For Gods, and godlike Kings their care express,
Still to defend their servants in distress.
Oh that my power to saving were confined;
Why am I forced, like heaven, against my mind 1000
To make examples of another kind?
Must I at length the sword of justice draw?
Oh cursed effects of necessary law!
How ill my fear they by my mercy scan,
Beware the fury of a patient man. 1005
Law they require, let law then show her face;
They could not be content to look on grace,
Her hinder parts, but with a daring eye
To tempt the terror of her front, and die.
By their own arts 'tis righteously decreed 1010
Those dire artificers of death shall bleed.
Against themselves their witnesses will swear
Till viper-like their mother plot they tear,
And suck for nutriment that bloody gore
Which was their principle of life before. 1015
Their Belial with their Beelzebub will fight;
Thus, on my foes my foes will do me right.
Nor doubt th'event, for factious crowds engage

In their first onset all their brutal rage.
Then, let them take an unresisted course,   1020
Retire and traverse and delude their force;
But when they stand all breathless, urge the fight,
And rise upon them with redoubled might,
For lawful power is still superior found,
When long driven back, at length it stands the ground.'   1025

He said. Th'Almighty nodding gave consent,
And peals of thunder shook the firmament.
Henceforth, a series of new time began,
The mighty years in long procession ran.
Once more the godlike David was restored   1030
And willing nations knew their lawful lord.

Absalom and Achitophel is a political poem which responds to and comments upon the so-called 'Exclusion Crisis' of 1678–81. The word 'exclusion' refers to the attempts of Parliament to exclude King Charles II's brother, James, from the throne to which he was heir presumptive. Two issues were principally involved. First, there was the issue of the king's prerogative and the extent of his power relative to that of Parliament. It was Parliament which sought to exclude James, and by doing so, to establish that kings were chosen by the people. The second issue was religious. James was a Roman Catholic, and the Protestant Parliamentarians wanted to ensure that no Catholic became king.

The crisis began with the revelations (most of them spurious) of a 'Popish [Catholic] Plot' to kill Charles and establish a Catholic government with James as king. Opposition leaders (such as Shaftesbury) used the anti-Catholic sentiment created by news of the 'plot' to push for the recognition of Charles's illegitimate son, the Duke of Monmouth, as his successor, and for the exclusion of James. By the time *Absalom and Achitophel* was published (early November 1681) the excluders had lost their momentum and their leader, the Earl of Shaftesbury, was in the Tower awaiting trial on a charge of treason.

Further details of the political background to the poem are given in the notes. More are to be found in James Kinsley's edition, to which we are indebted.

Absalom and Achitophel is a heroic satire which addresses its subject by use of allegory. Heroic satire is satire using some heroic forms and diction, and treating an elevated subject in an elevated manner. The seriousness of the subject distinguishes it from 'mock-heroic' satire such as *The Rape of the Lock*. It should be noted that Dryden occasionally uses mock-heroic methods, and that he mixes panegyric (formal praise in verse) of those he supports and political discussion in with his satire.

An allegory is a narrative in verse or prose in which all the characters, events and settings have a hidden meaning in addition to their surface meaning. Dryden uses the biblical story of the revolt of Absalom against his father, King David (2 Samuel 13–18), as a parallel to the 'revolt' of Monmouth against his father, King Charles. Further details of the allegory are given in the notes.

The poem is written in heroic couplets, in rhymed pairs of regular iambic pentameters, usually with a period or a pause at the end of the second line. Dryden exploits the form in a freer way than Pope. Fewer of his couplets end with a period, and he uses less antithesis. The general effect of the couplet here is one of elevation.

The structure is as follows:

1. Lines 1–149: Introduction; first, to the king and Absalom, and then to the situation in general.
2. Lines 150–490: Achitophel and his tempting of Absalom to rebel against his father.
3. Lines 491–681: portraits of Achitophel's fellow conspirators – Zimri, Shimei, Corah and others.
4. Lines 682–752: Absalom's siding with Achitophel and his tour in search of popular support.
5. Lines 753–810: exposition of political ideas.
6. Lines 811–932: portraits of the king's supporters.
7. Lines 933–1031: the king's intervention, his speech and the conclusion.

Absalom's Conspiracy

The story of Absalom's attempted usurpation of his father's throne occurs in the second book of Samuel. It is particularly suited to Dryden's aim of reconciliation (declared in 'To the Reader') since it tells not only of Absalom's revolt but also of David's love for his son. Nevertheless, Dryden still had to adapt his source to fit contemporary events, and sometimes he departs from it. An outline of the biblical narrative follows.

After this Absalom got himself a chariot and horses, and fifty men to run before him. He used to rise early and stand beside the way at the gate, and when any man had a suit to come before the king for judgement, Absalom would call to him, 'From what city are you?' And when the man answered, he would say to him, 'Your claims are good and right; but there is no man deputed by the king to hear you' – adding – 'Oh that I were judge in the land! Then every man with a suit or cause might come to me, and I would give him justice.'

And whenever a man came near to bow to him, he would put out his hand, and take hold of him, and kiss him. He did this to all the Israelites who came to the king for judgement, and in that way he stole their hearts.

At the end of forty years, Absalom said to the king, 'Pray let me go and fulfil the vow I made to the Lord by going to Hebron. For I made a vow while I dwelt at Geshur in Aram, that if the Lord brought me back to Jerusalem, I would worship Him.'

The king said to him, 'Go in peace.'

So Absalom went to Hebron, and with him two hundred invited men from Jerusalem, who went innocently knowing nothing of the plot. And he sent secret messengers throughout all the tribes of Israel with the message: 'As soon as you hear the sound of the trumpet, then announce that Absalom is king at Hebron!'

While Absalom was offering sacrifices, he sent for Ahithopel the Gilonite, David's counsellor, from his city Giloh. So the conspiracy grew strong, and the people with Absalom kept increasing.

A messenger came to David with the news that Absalom had won the hearts of the Israelites. Then David said to all the servants with him at Jerusalem: 'Let us flee, or there will be no escape for us from Absalom. Go quickly in case he overtakes us, and brings down evil upon us, and puts the city to the sword . . . (2 Samuel 15: 1–14).

When King David came to Bahurim, a man of the family of the house of Saul came out, whose name was Shimei, the son of Gera. As he came he cursed continually. And he threw stones at David, and at all the servants of David; and all the people and all the mighty men were on his right hand and on his left. And Shimei said as he cursed, 'Begone, begone, you man of blood, you worthless fellow! The Lord has avenged upon you all the blood of the house of Saul, in whose place you have reigned; and the Lord has given the kingdom to your son Absalom. See, your ruin is on you, for you are a man of blood . . .' (2 Samuel 16: 5–8).

So the army went out into the field against Israel, and the battle was fought in the forest of Ephraim. The men of Israel were defeated there by the servants of David, and there was great slaughter, of twenty thousand men. The battle spread over the face of all the country; and the forest devoured more people that day than the sword . . . (2 Samuel 18: 6–8).

And [after the battle] the Cushite came, and said, 'Good tidings for my lord the king! For the Lord has delivered you this day from the power of all who rose up against you.'

The king said to the Cushite, 'Is it well with the young man Absalom?'

And the Cushite answered, 'May the enemies of my lord the king, and all who rise up against you for evil, be like that young man.'

And the king was deeply moved, and went up to the chamber over the gate, and wept; and as he went, he said, 'O my son Absalom, my son, my son Absalom! Would I had died instead of you, O Absalom, my son, my son!' (2 Samuel 18: 31–3).

To the Reader

[Dryden's preface to his poem. Sparse editorial notes are given in square brackets in the text.]

> si propius stes/ te capiet magis
> (the closer you stand, the truer it looks)
>
> Horace, *Art of Poetry*, 361–2

It is not my intention to make an apology for my poem. Some will think it needs no excuse, and others will receive none. The design, I am sure, is honest, but he who draws his pen for one party, must expect to make enemies of the other. For, wit and fool, are consequents of Whig and Tory [political groupings during the crisis]; and every man is a knave or an ass to the contrary side. There's a treasury of merits in the fanatic church [Protestant fundamentalists], as well as in the papist [Roman Catholic]; and a pennyworth to be had of saintship, honesty, and poetry, for the lewd, the factious, and the blockheads. But the longest chapter in Deuteronomy, has not curses enough for an anti-Bromingham [an anti-Whig, a Tory, a supporter of the king]. My comfort is, their manifest prejudice to my cause, will render their judgement of less authority against me.

Yet if a poem have a genius, it will force its own reception in the world. For there's a sweetness in good verse, which tickles even while it hurts. And no man can be heartily angry with him, who pleases him against his will. The commendation of adversaries, is the greatest triumph of a writer, because it never comes unless extorted. But I can be satisfied on more easy terms. If I happen to please the more moderate sort, I shall be sure of an honest party, and in all probability of the best judges, for the least concerned are commonly the least corrupt. And I confess I have laid in for those by rebating [softening] the satire (where justice would allow it) from carrying too sharp an edge.

They who can criticise so weakly as to imagine I have done my worst may be convinced, at their own cost, that I can write severely with more ease than I can gently. I have but laughed at some men's follies when I could have declaimed against their vices. And other men's virtues I have commended as freely as I have taxed their crimes. And now if you are a malicious reader I expect you should return upon me that I affect to be thought more impartial than I am. But if men are not to be judged by their professions God forgive you common-wealthsmen for professing so plausibly for the government. You cannot be so unconscionable as to charge me for not subscribing of my name, for that would reflect too grossly upon your own party who never dare though they have the advantage of a jury to secure them [it was common practice to publish anonymously]. If you like not my poem the fault may possibly be in my writing (though it is hard for an author to judge against himself) but more probably it is in your morals, which cannot bear the truth of it.

The violent on both sides will condemn the character of Absalom [i.e. Monmouth] as either too favourably or too hardly drawn. But they are not the violent whom I desire to please. The fault on the right hand is to extenuate, palliate and indulge, and to confess freely I have endeavoured to commit it. Besides the respect which I owe his birth I have a greater for his heroic virtues, and David [Charles] himself could not be more tender of the young man's life than I would be of his reputation. But since the most excellent natures are always the most easy, and (as being such) are the soonest perverted by ill counsels (especially when baited with fame and glory), it is no more a wonder that he withstood not the temptations of Achitophel [Shaftesbury] than it was for Adam not to have resisted the two devils: the serpent and the woman. The conclusion of the story I purposely forbore to prosecute, because I could not obtain from myself to show Absalom unfortunate. The frame of it was cut out but for a picture to the waist, and if the draft be so far true it is as much as I designed.

Were I the inventor who am only the historian I should certainly conclude the piece with the reconcilement of Absalom to David. And who knows but this may come to pass? Things were not brought to an extremity where I left the story. There seems yet to be room left for a composure. Hereafter there may only be for pity. I have not so much as an uncharitable wish against Achitophel, but am content to be accused of a good natured error, and to hope with Origen that the devil himself may at last be saved [Origen was an influential theologian of the third century who believed in universal salvation]. For which reason in this poem he is neither brought to set his house in order nor to dispose of his person afterwards as he in wisdom shall think fit. God is infinitely merciful, and his viceregent [the king] is only not so because he is not infinite.

The true end of satire is the amendment of vices by correction. And he who writes honestly is no more an enemy to the offender than the physician to the patient when he prescribes harsh remedies to an inveterate disease, for those are only in order to prevent the surgeon's work, which I wish not to my very enemies. To conclude all: if the body politic have any analogy to the natural in my weak judgement an Act of Oblivion were as necessary in a hot distempered state as an opiate would be in a raging fever. [After his restoration, Charles chose not to pursue his former enemies, preferring to show mercy with an Act of Indemnity which consigned the acts of all but thirty-two to oblivion. Dryden suggests that a second such Act would have the beneficial effects of a medicine.]

Title
By adding the sub-title 'a poem', Dryden claims a certain dignity and stature for his work. This is not an ephemeral lampoon or a piece of opportunistic politicking.

[1] pious times
The reign of David. David himself is represented in the Bible as being chosen by God (1 Samuel 16: 12), and his reign which represents the high point of Hebrew history is here ironically defined by its tolerance of polygamy; *ere* before; *priest-craft ... begin* priests were established among the Hebrews as keepers of the ark and the altar long before the reign of David (Exodus 28: 1). However, Dryden means by 'priest-craft' (his coinage) not the real business of priests but their policy and cunning, attributes which (he suggests) developed after the time of David.

[2] Before ... made a sin
implies that it is priests who have attached a sinful character to polygamy, indeed, to any kind of promiscuity. Here, Dryden faces the problem of anyone trying to write in support of Charles II, namely the king's notorious womanising. He jocularly turns the weakness into an advantage by comparing Charles with the Old Testament kings who had several wives and many concubines.

[4] cursedly
The speaker jokingly signals his own attitude.

[6] concubine
a 'secondary' wife with a lower status in law than the primary wife. The word is used to refer both to David's concubines and to Charles's mistresses.

[7] Israel
England; *monarch* at the biblical level, David; at the level of contemporary history, Charles II. Each was 30 when he began his reign (2 Samuel 5: 4); *after heaven's own heart* Samuel the prophet says of David, 'the LORD

hath sought him a man after his own heart' (1 Samuel 13: 14). Dryden implies that Charles is a king with a divine sanction, and thus takes a distinctive position in contemporary debates about kingship.

[8] warmth
vital spirits; again the king's promiscuity is cast in a positive light.

[9] To wives and slaves
Charles's conquests spanned the social scale.

[10] scattered
the image is that of the farmer sowing seed; *his maker's image* 'God created man in his own image, in the image of God created he him' (Genesis 1: 27).

[11] Michal
In the contemporary context, this is Catherine of Braganza, Charles's legal wife, who had failed to produce any children. The biblical Michal is one of David's wives who is rendered barren after he curses her for mocking the way that he has danced in public upon the arrival of the ark of the covenant in Jerusalem (2 Samuel 6: 20–3).

[12] tiller
a cultivator of crops, or more specifically, one who tills or ploughs, picking up the metaphor of 'scattered' (line 10); *A soil ... tiller's care* a reference to Charles's wife's infertility. The ploughing image carries a bawdy innuendo. Cf. 'She made great Caesar lay his sword to bed;/ He ploughed her, and she cropped' (*Antony and Cleopatra*, II, ii, 227–8).

[13] Not so the rest
both Charles and David had numerous offspring.

[14] godlike David
refers primarily to classical rather than Christian or Jewish myth. There are numerous stories of gods producing children, both with goddesses and mortal women.

[16] No true ... attend
The succession to David's throne was decided by the king himself, while the

succession to Charles's fell automatically to his oldest legitimate son (if he had had any). Dryden implies a kind of Old Testament equivalent to modern illegitimacy in the manner of David's wives' lovemaking ('like slaves').

[17] **progeny**
issue, offspring.

[18] **So beautiful ... Absalon**
The biblical Absalom is David's beloved son who rebels against his father, and in the poem he represents James Scott, Duke of Monmouth. Monmouth was Charles II's illegitimate son and a favourite among his children. Many of the Protestants who wished to prevent the succession to the throne of the Catholic James (Charles's brother and eventually James II) pinned their hopes on Monmouth, claiming either that Charles had been married to Lucy Walter (Monmouth's mother), or simply that Monmouth would be a good king. Dryden describes his Absalom as 'beautiful' and 'brave', and Monmouth shared these qualities with the character from the Bible. Just as 'in all Israel there was none so much praised for his beauty as Absalom' (2 Samuel 14: 25), so Monmouth was noted for his physical attractiveness. Moreover, both had some success as soldiers. It should be added that Dryden is careful, while praising Monmouth, not to give him any of the outstanding intellectual or moral qualities which might fit him for the crown.

[19] **diviner lust**
referring again to classical myths of sexually active gods.

[20] **gust**
a sudden rush of wind, here the sexual act; also, taste, savour.

[21–2] **Or that ... imperial sway**
i.e. or whether his fate made a concession to the overpowering influence of the king in the form of manly beauty. The idea is that fate did not have much in store for this illegitimate son but gave him beauty because of the king.

[23] **foreign fields**
Monmouth had fought in Holland in 1672–3 and Scotland in 1679.

[24] **allied**
In Holland he had fought for the French.

[25] **remove**
i.e. put away from himself.

[26] **only born for love**
Possessing personal charm and beauty, Monmouth was a great favourite among the women at court.

[27] **ease**
social grace, a quality much commended in the period; compare Pope's *Rape of the Lock*, ii, 15 and *Epistle to Dr Arbuthnot*, line 196.

[31] **indulgent David**
The biblical David is rebuked by his general Joab for caring more about his traitorous son than about his loyal allies (2 Samuel 19: 4–7), and here Dryden implies that Charles may have been too fond of Monmouth. It is characteristic of his political poetry that, while he remains loyal to the Stuarts, he exploits his position as the loyal poet to offer advice.

[34] **Annabel**
Anne, Countess of Buccleugh, a rich heiress.

[37] **warm excesses**
Among Monmouth's 'excesses' was the murder of a beadle; *forbore* pardoned.

[38] **construed**
interpreted, taken to be; *purged* purified; *boiling o'er* While the boiling of liquids to distil (purify) them is controlled, Dryden's phrase suggests an uncontrolled boiling.

[39] **Amnon's murder**
probably the attack on Sir John Coventry by Monmouth's troops in retaliation for a derogatory remark about the king. The biblical Amnon was killed by Absalom's servants for sleeping with his sister Tamar (2 Samuel 13: 1–29); *specious* showy but false.

[40] **fame**
reputation; referring to the motive for the attack on Coventry.

[41] **remained**
despite the serious faults just mentioned.

[43] **sincerely**
purely, completely.

[44] **punishes**
a veiled warning; *proves* tests.

[45] **Jews**
English Protestants; *headstrong... murmuring* The verb to 'murmur' is that used of the complaining of the Jews in the wilderness: 'the... congregation... murmured against Moses and Aaron in the wilderness' (Exodus 16: 2). The English Protestants had also shown these qualities in rebelling against, and executing, Charles II's father (Charles I).

[46] **tried**
tested; *grace* favour of God.

[47] **God's pampered people**
The Jews are traditionally 'God's chosen people'. Dryden glances at the numerous Protestants of the period who believed that the return of Christ was at hand and that they had been chosen to share His thousand-year kingdom.

[49–50] **Gods they had... priest devise**
In the wilderness, Aaron (the priest) makes a golden calf for the Israelites to worship (Exodus 32: 1–6), and later, Moses prophesies that the Israelites 'shall serve gods, the work of men's hands, wood and stone' (Deuteronomy 4: 28). Dryden is referring in part to the many different Christian opinions and sects which had sprung up in the 150 years since the Reformation. However, Jewish idolatry, a kind of religious disloyalty, is also a recurring metaphor in the poem for English political disloyalty.

[51] **Adam-wits**
like Adam in being both free and dissatisfied with his one constraint, i.e. the injunction not to eat the fruit of 'the tree of the knowledge of good and evil' (Genesis 2: 16–17); *too... free* a reference to English political liberty (compared to French servitude), and suggesting, with the word 'too',

the poem's conservative idea of the danger of freedom; also, implicitly, the English Protestants by seeking greater freedom are repeating the sin of Adam.

[52] **wanted**
lacked.

[53–6] **And when... slaves**
i.e. lacking historical examples of organised societies with greater freedom than theirs, they began to wish to live in the complete freedom of unorganised societies. Dryden refers to Thomas Hobbes' (1588–1679) idea that in the 'state of nature' (before organisation) human life is 'solitary, poor, nasty, brutish and short' (*Leviathan*, I, xiii), and implies his opponents prefer anarchy to order.

[57] **Saul**
David's predecessor; also, Oliver Cromwell, the 'Lord Protector' of England during the Commonwealth period; thus, the leader (not the king) who preceded Charles.

[57–8] **Ishbosheth**
David's rival for the throne upon Saul's death; also, Cromwell's son, Richard, Charles's potential rival; *without a blow* While David only became king of all the Hebrews after the murder of Ishbosheth (2 Samuel 4: 7), Charles ascended peacefully to his throne.

[59] **banished**
Charles was effectively banished during the period in which Cromwell was in power, just as David had fled the country during the reign of Saul (1 Samuel 21: 10 & 1 Samuel 27: 1); *Hebron* David's city of residence when he was king only of Judah, i.e. not of Judah and Israel (2 Samuel 5: 1–5); in the contemporary context, Scotland where Charles was crowned king of the Scots four months before being crowned king of England as well.

[60] **a general shout**
Charles's return in 1660 was popularly acclaimed.

[62] **humour**
character, disposition, whim.

[64] **idol**
The Protestants think Charles an 'idol monarch' because he has ascended the throne at the invitation of Parliament. Thus, he has been made, in the same way as idols, of metal and wood. The irony is that the Protestants want to replace him with a state, described here as itself an idol, the Golden Calf (line 66 & Exodus 32: 7–8).

[66] **golden calf**
see previous note and the note to lines 49–50; *state* i.e. a republic.

[67] **bolts**
arrows; *design* plan.

[68] **interest**
share, stake, self-interest.

[69] **sober**
moderate, temperate; *stain* sin, blame.

[71] **afright**
fear. The terror of a return to the Civil Wars of the 1640s played a prominent part in political discussion for many years to come.

[73] **scars**
The physical scars of the Civil Wars were still evident in England in gaping castle walls and partially ruined cathedrals.

[75] **qualified**
modified, made temperate (i.e. by the memory of the past).

[78] **found**
suggests an active seeking of occasion; *occasion* opportunity.

[79] **sin**
the Christian doctrine that all people are born to sin; *biased . . . leans* a metaphor from bowls. The bias (a weight in the side) causes the bowl to lean and to follow a curve.

[80] **careful**
conscientious, painstaking.

[81] **providently**
prudently, thriftily; *pimps* procures (literally procures customers for prostitutes).

[82] **Good Old Cause**
supporters of Parliament and the Puritans in the Civil Wars; republicans; Whigs. Dryden implies that the discontents are republicans; *plot* the first mention of the Popish Plot, used

by Shaftesbury and his followers to foment discord – see introduction.

[84] **To raise . . . kings**
A source of discontent in the early 1640s, and one cause of the Civil Wars, was the plotting of the royalists exposed in the First and Second Army Plots. Dryden suggests the Parliamentarians exploited the exposure of these plots for their own ends.

[86] **Jebusites**
a tribe of Canaanites from whom David seized Jerusalem (2 Samuel 5: 6–9); also, a derogatory term for the Jesuits, and used here to mean Roman Catholics in general; *town . . . them* not the real origin of the name.

[87] **native right**
(an incomplete line, the only one in the poem). The Catholics (like the Jebusites) could claim a certain precedence by virtue of the fact that England had once been a Catholic country.

[88] **chosen people**
Protestants – see note to line 47.

[89] **The rightful . . . wrong**
refers to the Reformation at the beginning of the sixteenth century. Dryden was later (1686) to convert to Catholicism.

[91] **God's enemies**
refers to two strains in Protestant thinking: (1) that the Catholic Church was anti-Christ and (2) that since God's favour shows itself in material prosperity the dispossession of the Catholics must signal disfavour.

[92] **worn and weakened**
English Catholics had suffered restrictions, fines, imprisonment and sometimes death for over a century.

[93] **Submit**
The implication is that the Catholics are naturally opposed to Charles's Anglican government, but must submit to it.

[94] **deprived . . . command**
They were barred from positions of trust in the state.

[95] **taxes doubled**
anti-Catholic legislation; *lost their land* the effect of decades of fines.

[97] **Their gods...wood**
Although the widescale destruction of sacred objects which took place at the Reformation had ceased, the authorities still seized and destroyed Catholic crucifixes, statues and pictures. Dryden's Protestantism is evident in the phrase 'their gods', for the Catholic position was that these were objects of veneration not worship.

[98] **heathen**
i.e. the Jebusites or Catholics.

[99] **For priests...same**
echoing the anti-clericism of the opening couplet.

[101] **Stock**
log of wood. Dryden plays very ingeniously with his biblical and modern contexts here. The non-Jewish tribes are frequently represented in the Old Testament as idolaters (worshippers of stock and stone), just as contemporary Protestant propaganda accused the Catholics of worshipping their holy images – see notes to lines 49–50, 64 & 97.

[103] **gold**
i.e. like the calf; ironic since the calf, though gold, remains an idol (see line 66).

[104] **rabbins**
rabbis, experts in Jewish law, usually priests; the Protestant clergy.

[105] **In this...wise**
Even the Protestant clergy admire Catholic obstinacy.

[107] **his cause**
their God's cause and that of James, the Catholic heir presumptive, whose accession to the throne was expected to ease the position of other Catholics.

[108] **plot**
the 'Popish Plot' – see introductory notes.

[109] **Bad in...worse**
Dryden's consistent position, that the real villains are not the misguided plotters but those who used the Plot to whip up a crisis.

[110] **extremes**
The appeal to the middle road (present here) had long been a favourite ploy in English political rhetoric.

[111] **oaths**
of the perjured witnesses; *dying vows* refers to those condemned to death for their part in the Plot, particularly to five Jesuits who affirmed their innocence on the scaffold.

[112] **winnow**
to separate grain from chaff by wind; *multitude* Typically Dryden lays a good deal of blame for the unrest on the people, represented here as without judgement.

[113] **swallowed...mass**
swallowed whole; *crude* undigested.

[114] **Some truth**
Historians are still unsure exactly how much; *dashed* mixed with some (inferior) substance.

[116] **Succeeding times**
i.e. the times after the reign of David, and after the Plot. Dryden's use of an ancient parallel allows him to claim a historical hindsight he did not possess.

[118] **Th'Egyptian rites**
Egyptian religion, known for its grotesque beliefs and ceremonies, is used here to mean Catholic France and Catholicism in general. At this point Dryden turns his attention to Catholic beliefs and behaviour in order to weigh the Plot allegations. He is careful to distance himself from Catholicism in order to preempt attempts to portray this as a Catholic poem.

[119] **by their taste**
a mocking reference to the Catholic belief (which Dryden eventually accepted) in transubstantiation; i.e. that the bread and wine of the mass become the real body and blood of Christ.

[121] **worship...food**
referring both to transubstantiation (see previous note) and to Catholic adoration of the Host.

[123] **ten to one**
an estimate of the proportion of Protestants to Catholics; *odds* superior position, advantage.

[124] **fraud**
According to popular belief, the Catholic missionaries in England (in particular the Jesuits) were deceitful and untrustworthy; *sacrificer's* The Catholic belief in the mass as a sacrifice (of Christ's body) was rejected by Protestants.

[125] **Fools ... persuade**
contempt for the multitude again – see note to line 112.

[126] **busy teachers**
Catholic priests had moved around England in disguise in order to succour the faithful and (secondarily) to seek converts since the Elizabethan period.

[127] **court**
The most famous court convert to Catholicism was James, the heir presumptive; *stews* brothels.

[129] **Because ... flock**
Since 'fleece' refers to the priests' tithe money and 'flock' to their congregation, Dryden is charging them with greed. See Ezekiel 34: 2–3: 'Son of man, prophesy against the shepherds of Israel ... woe be to the shepherds of Israel that do feed themselves! should not the shepherds feed the flocks? Ye eat the fat, and ye clothe you with the wool ... '

[130] **God's anointed**
David was anointed king by the prophet Samuel (1 Samuel 16: 1–13), and Charles was also, in the opinion of conservative royalists like Dryden, divinely appointed.

[131] **By guns**
Two of the plotters were found guilty of having planned to shoot Charles; *invented ... day* not, of course, true of David's time.

[132] **Our author ... not**
Dryden's consistent position: that he does not know how much truth there is in the allegations, though he thinks not much.

[134] **want**
lack.

[136] **as when**
The phrase introduces a heroic simile, a lengthy, detailed and elevated comparison, like those to be found in

heroic poetry; *raging fevers* in the body politic, an idea which Dryden refers to in his prefatory 'Letter to the Reader', and which had been developed by Thomas Hobbes in the introduction to *Leviathan*: 'a commonwealth ... is but an artificial man ... sovereignty an artificial soul ... magistrates and other officers of the judicature artificial joints; reward and punishment are the nerves ... etc.' The image probably goes back to St Paul's account of the Church as a body (1 Corinthians 12: 12–27).

[137] **flood**
The image of deluge, which is interwoven with that of fever, goes back to the Bible, where (leaving Noah aside) the threat of flood is quite a common part of the prophet's rhetorical armoury. Thus, Isaiah warns of the threat from Assyria (Isaiah 8: 7–8): 'behold, the Lord bringeth upon them the waters of the river, strong and many, even the king of Assyria ... he shall come up over all his channels, and go over all his banks ... '

[138] **humour**
one of the four principal fluids which combine in a person and determine his character; also, whim.

[140] **factions**
parties, with a strong negative weight; *ferment* the action of yeast on dough and some liquids; here, agitation.

[141] **foam**
the result of fermentation; the sea; the foam on the lips of the madman.

[144] **thrown from hence**
applies to Zimri/Buckingham – see lines 544ff.

[145] **hardened ... impenitence**
the condition of a fiend, just as Milton's Satan rejects repentance (*Paradise Lost*, iv, 79–86).

[146] **fatal**
dangerous.

[147] **pardoned rebels**
Charles's policy at the Restoration had been to extend mercy to most of the former rebels. Lines 147–9 apply to Shaftesbury – see introduction and below.

[150] **these**
the discontents (lines 140–9); *Achitophel* Absalom's chief adviser in rebellion, representing, in the contemporary context, Antony Ashley Cooper, first Earl of Shaftesbury (1621–83). Although at one time Charles's chancellor, he had been dismissed in 1673, and had moved into opposition, becoming one of the leading opposition figures. His political position was against Roman Catholicism, and in favour of toleration of non-Anglican Protestants and limitation on the power of the king. By 1681, when *Absalom and Achitophel* was published, Shaftesbury was on trial for high treason.

His treasonable actions had come in the wake of the 'Popish Plot' and the events which followed it. The so-called plot was exposed in a series of dramatic trials, and was supposed to have included a number of plans to kill the king. As the trials progressed, publicity spread, and political unrest resulting from the 'revelations' increased, further accusations were added to the original list. Anti-Catholics, like Shaftesbury, used the unrest caused by the trials to whip up feeling against the Catholic James, and to press for the succession of Monmouth. During a sitting of Parliament at Oxford in March 1681, Shaftesbury made a public appeal that Charles should legitimise Monmouth. However, the tide of opinion had begun to turn against the opponents of the succession of James, and by July 1681 Shaftesbury was in the Tower.

On 24 November, shortly after the publication of *Absalom and Achitophel*, he stood trial for intending to levy war against the king, a charge of which he was acquitted. Dryden may have hoped to prejudice the jury against Shaftesbury with his poem, and if he did, his hope was unfulfilled. The portrait of Achitophel, like those later in the poem, reproduces some real features of the original model but is also strongly coloured by the poet's political opinions.

[151] **A name . . . cursed**
implies a connection between Shaftesbury and Satan. Satan is, of course, the arch-rebel.

[152] **close designs**
secret plans; *crooked counsels* dishonest advice. Shaftesbury is made the instigator of the crisis (thus taking away some of the blame from Monmouth); in the Bible, on the other hand, Absalom sends for Achitophel (2 Samuel 15: 12).

[153] **wit**
the mental faculty generally.

[154] **unfixed**
i.e. a turncoat; he sided with both Parliamentarians and Royalists in the 1640s and 1650s and he once served Charles; *place* position; glances at Shaftesbury's loss of the chancellorship in 1673 and seat on the privy council in 1680.

[156] **fiery soul**
suggestive of dangerous energy; *working . . . way* bringing about its aim.

[157] **fretted**
ravaged, tortured.

[158] **o'erinformed**
To inform is to pervade, to animate. 'Overinformed' suggests the fiery soul is too large a presence for the body; *tenement of clay* body.

[159] **daring plot**
refers to the idea of the 'ship of state'.

[162] **Would . . . wit**
There is some ambiguity in the line: (1) he would steer too near the sands in order to be able to boast of his cleverness; (2) he got too close to the sands to be able to boast of his cleverness (i.e. his reckless steering made any boast of cleverness empty).

[163] **Great wits . . . allied**
'There is no great genius without some admixture of madness' (Seneca). Dryden here exposes his period's distrust of excess.

[166] **needful**
necessary.

[168] **life**
both energy and, figuratively, blessedness – 'your life is hid with Christ in
God' (Colossians 3: 3); *prodigal* recklessly wasteful; *ease* comfort. The line
suggests the perversity of one who,
lacking vitality and blessedness, still
throws away every possibility of
comfort.

[169] **what... won**
i.e. that which he won with his toil.

[170] **unfeathered... thing**
a definition of man attributed to Plato,
and a mocking reference to Shaftesbury's reputedly foolish son, Antony.
There is a contrast between this
description of Shaftesbury's son and
the earlier one of Monmouth, Charles's
son (lines 17ff.).

[171] **got**
conceived; *huddled* confused. Shaftesbury's son was born in 1652, i.e.
during the Commonwealth period,
regarded by Dryden as one of confusion and disorder.

[172] **shapeless lump**
refers to the popular belief that a bear
is born formless and only takes on its
bear's shape after being licked by its
mother; *anarchy* the chaos existing
before God created earth, and referring to the disorder of the Civil War
and the commonwealth periods.

[175] **triple bond**
usually taken as referring to Shaftesbury's part in breaking the Triple
Alliance between England, Holland
and Sweden (1670). The breaking of
this treaty led to war with Holland.
Dryden may, however, have been
thinking of the 'three estates' of the
body politic (commons, lords and
bishops), whose balanced interdepen-
dence was thought to ensure stability.
By claiming extra powers for Parliament and trying to reduce the extent
of the king's sway, Shaftesbury is
threatening the balance.

[176] **The pillars... shook**
i.e. like Samson. Weakened by
Delilah's cutting of his hair and
blinded by his Philistine enemies,
Samson is placed between two pillars

in a Philistine hall during a religious
festival. By pushing the pillars he
makes the building collapse, 'so the
dead which he slew at his death were
more than those which he slew in his
life' (Judges 16: 21–30).

[177] **a foreign yoke**
domination by a foreign power. The
breaking of the Triple Alliance led to a
treaty with France. Dryden may also
be implying that Shaftesbury's
advocacy of Monmouth tended to
weaken the country and to create the
possibility of foreign domination.

[178] **Then**
i.e. after his dismissal from office and
his move into opposition (1773);
affecting aspiring for; *fame* good
reputation.

[179] **Usurped... name**
i.e. declared his motive for opposition
to be patriotism. Then (as now) the
claim of patriotism was the politician's
stock in trade.

[180] **factious**
divided (see line 140 and note).

[181] **With... crimes**
i.e. to cover up wrong-doing by claims
of patriotism.

[182–3] **How safe... people's will**
When the only wrong-doing is that
which the people regard as wrong-
doing, treason is safe and mis-
behaviour sacred. The idea is that in
'factious times' (line 180), the people
become sovereign and sense and
judgement are lost; part of Dryden's
overall attack on the people – see line
112 & line 125.

[184] **wink**
in the sense of ignore misdemeanours,
wink at crimes.

[185] **Since... own**
As Shaftesbury and the people share
the same faults of faction and rebellion, they ignore his in order to remain
blind to their own.

[186] **Yet fame... grudge**
rhetorically signalling the writer's
fairness, a quality mentioned in the
prefatory letter. Dryden must allow
Shaftesbury, the former servant of the
king, some virtue.

[187] **statesman**
one involved in affairs of state (lacking the positive weighting of modern usage); *praise the judge* Shaftesbury was Lord Chancellor from 1672 to 1673, an office in which he acquitted himself well.

[188] **Abbethdin**
presiding judge in the Jewish civil court; referring to the chancellorship.

[189] **hands ... clean**
i.e. unstained by partiality or bribes.

[190] **redress**
compensate, restore to prosperity.

[193] **gown**
the chancellor's robe of office.

[194] **rankness**
grossly fertile, tending to produce luxuriant growth.

[195] **cockle**
a weed that grows in corn; here seen as choking the good seed of Shaftesbury's virtue. There may be a subdued reference to the Parable of the Sower (Matthew 13: 3–8).

[196–7] **David for him ... song**
If Achitophel had stayed on the right path (lines 192–5), David would have composed songs in praise of him instead of psalms in praise of God. David is the preeminent poet of the Old Testament.

[198] **slide**
fitting with the ice imagery of the following line; also suggestive of a moral decline. The sense here and in the following lines of Achitophel as a restless, reckless lover of danger fits with the earlier part of the portrait (lines 156–63).

[199] **And fortune's ... land**
back to the pilot imagery – see lines 159–63.

[200] **weary to possess**
weary of possessing.

[202] **gold fruit**
In Greek myth three nymphs (the Hesperides) and a dragon guard a tree of golden apples, the fruit of immortality.

[203] **crowd**
another derogatory reference to the people (see lines 112, 125 & 182–3);

shake the tree i.e. to make the fruit fall; recalling the comparison to Samson (line 176).

[204] **manifest of crimes**
his crimes apparent, obviously guilty.

[205] **prince**
leader; here the king.

[206] **buckler**
shield; *people's cause* associating Shaftesbury with democratic aspirations – see line 227.

[208] **occasion**
opportunity; *takes* Shaftesbury, the chief parliamentary investigator of the Plot, encouraged Oates in his 'revelations'.

[209] **makes**
So eager was Shaftesbury to collect 'evidence' that he recorded statements from 15-year-old boys concerning what was said by a 6-year-old.

[210] **emissaries**
people sent out to do some (underhand) task; Shaftesbury's agitators.

[211] **crowds**
distrust of popular opinion again – see line 203 and note.

[212] **arbitrary**
(in contemporary usage) authoritarian to the point of tyranny. Among the evidence collected were the letters of Edward Coleman, the Roman Catholic secretary to the Duchess of York (wife of James whom the plotters were supposed to be trying to put on the throne). On the back of one was recorded the 'arbitrary' sentiment, 'king's power to command his subjects' service against all acts of parliament'; *counsels* pieces of advice.

[213] **king ... Jebusite**
Rumours of Charles's Catholicism, presented by Dryden as wild allegations, were later proved true when he was reconciled with the church at death.

[215] **easy to rebel**
the character of the Jews (or English) given earlier – see line 48.

[216] **governed**
in the astrological sense of having the moon as a ruling planet; *moon* a symbol of inconstancy.

[217] **she**
the moon; *prime* the beginning of a lunar cycle.

[218] **twenty years**
The struggle for power leading to the downfall of Charles I and the rule of Cromwell began in 1640; the restoration of Charles II took place in 1660; and the crisis following the Plot revelations occurred 1680–1. Thus, an interval of twenty years separates each change or attempted change; *scribe* Jewish interpreter of the Law; writer – here historian.

[219] **instinct**
The stress falls on the second syllable.

[220] **wants**
lacks.

[222] **greatness . . . create**
Shaftesbury does not want to invest real power in Monmouth.

[223] **politician**
cunning, deceitful intriguer.

[224] **for**
because; *title not allowed* As an illegitimate son, Monmouth had no real claim to the throne.

[225] **depending**
dependent; *crowd* Lacking a proper claim, Monmouth could only be crowned by popular assent and by Act of Parliament.

[227] **Drawn**
made to flow out; *democracy* in line with the earlier references to crowds and the people.

[228] **arts**
types of conduct, tricks.

[229] **sheds his venom**
In *Paradise Lost* Satan is represented as attempting to 'inspire' venom into the blood of Eve (iv, 804). Like Satan with Eve, Achitophel persuades to evil by means of flattery and deceit; *words as these* The poem, general and discursive to this point, suddenly becomes particular and dramatic, and invites comparison with Satan's temptation of Eve.

[230] **Auspicious**
promising well for the future; *nativity* Shaftesbury and Monmouth were both interested in astrology.

[231] **southern**
Monmouth was born in Rotterdam and brought up in Paris.

[233] **cloudy pillar**
A pillar of cloud and fire protected the Hebrews as, led by Moses, they fled from their Egyptian captors (Exodus 13: 21 & 14: 24–5).

[234] **Moses**
who led the Hebrews out of bondage. The Messiah hoped for by the Old Testament prophets is to be a second David (Isaiah 11: 1–2). Achitophel prefers the model of the liberator, Moses, to that of the anointed king, David; *wand* Moses divides the Red Sea by stretching his rod, given to him as a sign from God (Exodus 4: 2–5), over its waters (Exodus 14: 16).

[235] **seas**
the Red Sea whose waters parted in front of the fleeing Hebrews and allowed them to escape; *shows . . . land* Although the Hebrews did not see the land to which they were travelling and which they had been promised as they crossed the Red Sea, the passage was the decisive event in their journey there.

[237] **rage**
prophetic inspiration. According to Christian belief, Christ's coming was predicted by the prophets; Shaftesbury impiously compares Monmouth to Christ.

[238] **diviner**
foreteller of the future, prophet.

[239] **The young . . . dream!**
The prophecy of Joel that 'your old men shall dream dreams, your young men shall see visions' (Joel 2: 28) was repeated by St Peter after the coming of the Holy Spirit at Pentecost (Acts 2: 17). Again Achitophel's reference is distinctly impious.

[240] **saviour**
a title of Christ; *confess* a word with strong religious connotations.

[241] **bless**
used in the sense of to adore as holy.

[242] **unbespoken**
not arranged, spontaneous; *pomps* processions, demonstrations of loyalty and affection.

[244] **general joy**
joy of all.

[248] **fresh glories**
Monmouth returned from a successful military campaign in Scotland at the end of 1679. The argument at this point is both flattering and opportunistic, for while referring glowingly to Monmouth's victories, Shaftesbury also reminds him that the memory of them will not last forever.

[249] **tarnish**
(of metals) to become discoloured; picking up the image of brightness in the previous line.

[250] **royal**
a flattering half-truth, since Monmouth was illegitimate.

[251] **Or...or**
either...or.

[253] **revolution**
turn or twist.

[256] **from...descent**
as down a smooth hill.

[257] **impression**
indentation, hollow (in the hill); also impact; *bent* direction. The image is of a rolling fortune whose path is determined by the lie of the ground.

[258] **glides away**
down the hill.

[260] **she**
the goddess Fortune, sometimes represented as seated on the rolling stone implied in the previous lines.

[261] **And spreads...flies**
Though Fortune has hair streaming in front of her, she is bald at the back; thus, she must be seized as she comes towards you, for there's only one chance.

[262] **from whose loins**
another half-truth since it suppresses mention of Monmouth's illegitimacy.

[263] **Not dared...king**
Shaftesbury compares the position of Monmouth with that of Charles when invited back to be king – a strained comparison since Charles's return was based not on opportunism but on a legitimate and universally recognised claim.

[264] **Gath**
David took refuge from Saul at Gath (1 Samuel 27: 1–3); also Breda in the Netherlands, where Charles spent part of his exile and whence he returned to England.

[265] **anointing oil**
see note to line 130. Shaftesbury shows scant respect for the divine election of the king; *had* would have.

[268] **setting...skies**
like the sun.

[269] **vapours**
Evening mists were associated with disease. The word also implies those bodily 'vapours' which were thought (according to the medical theory of the day) to cause madness.

[270] **Jordan's sand**
Although David would not have crossed the river Jordan when he moved from Hebron to Jerusalem to rule the combined tribes (2 Samuel 5: 5–6), he does later when he returns after the death of Absalom (2 Samuel 19: 9–15). In the contemporary context the reference is to Dover beach where Charles landed at his restoration.

[271] **The joyful...land**
Compare Dryden's *Astræa Redux* (lines 27o–9): 'Methinks I see those crowds on Dover's strand/ Who in their haste to welcome you to land/ Choked up the beach with their still growing store.'

[272] **strand**
beach.

[273] **prince of angels**
Satan. Ironically, Shaftesbury himself is represented as a tempter by Dryden.

[274] **tumbling downward**
like the rebel angels driven down from heaven; *diminished light* In *Paradise Lost* Satan addresses his companion Beelzebub (i, 84–7): 'how changed/ From him who in the happy Realms of Light/ Clothed with transcendent brightness didst outshine/ Myriads though bright.'

[275] **poor plot**
Shaftesbury's real opinion of the allegations.

[276] **Our only ... return**
Shaftesbury's argument is not self-consistent; while he seems sometimes to praise the young Charles, asides like this reveal different feelings.

[277] **sheaf did bind**
were bound together in one bundle.

[279] **your designs**
your plans. Shaftesbury cleverly attributes his own plans to Monmouth.

[280] **round beset**
beset round.

[281] **Pharaoh**
the ruler of Egypt; here Louis XIV of France – see note to line 117. The autocratic French government was a stock example of foreign tyranny (as opposed to English liberty – line 51). Charles had conducted secret negotiations with France by which he was to receive French money and French military support in a campaign to reconvert England to Catholicism; *doubtful succour* dubious help.

[283] **dissembled**
false, pretended.

[284] **foment**
encourage.

[285] **royal party**
Dryden assigns the guilt for any rumoured dealings with France to Charles's advisers rather than Charles himself – see line 281 and note.

[286] **arms**
used to mean military strength.

[287] **interest**
cause.

[289] **arts**
stratagems, wiles.

[290] **altered hearts**
in that they have formerly professed loyalty to Charles.

[291] **general cry**
everyone's cry, demand.

[292] **Religion**
i.e. the religion of the Low Church Nonconformists as opposed to the Anglicanism of Charles or the Catholicism of his brother James and the plotters; *commonwealth* republic; *liberty* from the tyranny of kings.

[298] **solid power**
Shaftesbury's deceit is clear at this point since his real interest in Monmouth has been given earlier as the desire to create a figurehead dependent upon him – see lines 222–5.

[299] **limited command**
that which Shaftesbury will give; compare the 'solid power' offered in the previous line.

[300] **Given ... land**
implying that Monmouth will be an elected king.

[301] **successive title**
a genuine claim. Dryden makes Shaftesbury admit that Monmouth's claim does not rest upon inheritance.

[302] **rolls**
parchments, documents. The idea is that a real king's real title could be traced back to the flood.

[303] **What cannot ... minds**
Compare the sentiment expressed by Milton in *Lycidas* (lines 70–1): 'Fame is the spur that the clear spirit doth rise/ (That last infirmity of noble mind).'

[305] **vicious**
given to vice (not necessarily cruelty); *weed* recalling the imagery of lines 194–5, and the Parable of the Sower.

[306] **celestial**
heavenly. Dryden gives a noble colouring even to Monmouth's ambition.

[307] **In ... glory**
i.e. the desire for power.

[309] **covetous**
desirous.

[310] **angel's**
both the angel of heaven and the gold coin called an angel; *metal* both the gold of the coin and 'mettle' (disposition, especially vigour); *frame* body, constitution.

[315] **pretence**
claim. Monmouth begins his speech by recognising that he ought not rebel.

[318] **faith's defender**
The title 'Defender of the Faith' was conferred on Henry VIII before his break with Rome for writing a book against Luther. The faith Monmouth refers to is Anglicanism. Charles's

supporters (like Dryden) were keen to stress the king's loyalty to the Church of England, though he was in fact a 'closet' Catholic.

[320] **wonders**
In *Annus Mirabilis* (the 'Year of Wonders') Dryden writes of the English successes against the Dutch and of the Fire of London. If these might be taken as God's endorsement of Charles by his supporters, the Great Plague of 1665 could be interpreted as a sign of disapproval for the moral laxity of the court by his critics; *espoused* taken on.

[323] **What millions**
a reference to Charles's merciful attitude at the Restoration – see note to line 146.

[324] **Whom just ... expose**
Charles's return was so popular that he could (if he had wished) have pursued his former enemies with far more severity than he did.

[325] **easy**
Social ease was an admired acquirement throughout the period – see line 27 and note.

[326] **Inclined ... blood**
the virtue upon which Dryden lays the greatest stress.

[327] **If mildness ... suit**
i.e. if mildness does not fit well ...

[328] **crime**
used ironically for mercy; *God's ... attribute* mildness and mercy again. According to St John, 'God is love' (1 John 4: 8).

[330] **arbitrary**
tyrannical. Charles himself rejected arbitrary government; *sway* domination.

[331–2] **Pharaoh**
an example of a tyrant because of his treatment of the captive Jews (Exodus 5: 6–7); Louis XIV again – see note to line 281; *curse ... Nile* Pharaoh's ill treatment of the Jews is answered by Moses turning the Nile to blood (Exodus 7: 19–21): 'and the fish that was in the river died; and the river stank; and the Egyptians could not drink of the water of the river'; *yoke*

put a yoke upon, make subject; *train* of followers.

[333] **If ... displease**
i.e. if David's rule displeases Jerusalem.

[334] **dog-star**
Sirius, associated with summer heat and with madness – compare *Arbuthnot*, lines 3–4. As Monmouth made his challenging progress through Somerset and Devon in the late summer of 1680 (lines 729–52), this dialogue is probably supposed to take place in the summer months before that; *heats their brains* i.e. the rebellious Jews are mad.

[336] **popularly**
like the people; another gibe at democracy.

[337] **Were he**
if he were.

[338] **raised**
aided, encouraged.

[339] **bands**
ties, constraints. Monmouth's argument is that even if Charles were a wicked king, his filial duty would forbid rebellion.

[340] **curb**
restrain.

[341] **The people might**
allowing the possibility of legitimate rebellion, a point half granted later in the political heart of the poem – see line 795.

[342] **were**
would be; *crime in me* i.e. even if the people could rightfully turn against the king, a son could not do so against his father.

[344] **Prevents**
forestalls. Charles sees what his son wants and gives it before he can ask; *outruns* runs faster than. The sense is that Monmouth is given more than he wants.

[346] **kingly diadem**
his crown.

[347] **But there**
To this point, Monmouth has been staunchly loyal, but the pause signals his doubt and the change in direction of his argument.

[348] **worthier head**
i.e. the Duke of York, later James II.
[350] **late**
i.e. let it be late; *augment* increase;
blessed those in heaven.
[351] **issue**
offspring. As a bastard Monmouth is
not lawful issue.
[352] **collateral line**
the line of Charles's brother James. In
the event of the king's death without
legitimate offspring, the inheritance
passes first to his brother, then his
brother's children; *where that shall
end* if there is no lawful issue ('that').
[352] **vulgar**
(literally) of the people; *spite* Numerous attacks on James followed in the
wake of the Plot. The House of
Commons declared that, though
James was not directly implicated,
his Catholicism had given great
encouragement to the plotters, and
they voted repeatedly to have him
excluded from the throne on account
of his religion.
[356] **Still dear**
James was, of course, not dear to
those MPs who had voted to have him
excluded from the throne (previous
note).
[357] **courage**
James had been a successful Admiral
of the Fleet; *truth* faithfulness, loyalty.
[358] **His ... king**
i.e the king proclaims his loyalty.
[360] **forgiving kind**
As Charles's brother he shares his
merciful temper – see line 323.
[361] **repine**
feel discontent, dissatisfaction.
[362] **pretence**
claim, but also (as now) with the sense
of a false claim. Dryden has Monmouth
confess that he possesses no real right
to the throne.
[363] **that fate**
if only fate ... ;*propitiously* fortunately.
[364] **debased my mind**
Monmouth begins clearly to lament
his position, giving himself credit for
the 'spark too much of heavenly fire'
mentioned earlier (line 308).

[365] **her**
fate; *To my ... lent* going back to line
363; if only fate had not lent all her
treasure to my large soul.
[366] **betrayed**
a definite repining at heaven's decree
(line 361); *mean descent* base birth, his
bastardy.
[367] **David's part**
that part of Monmouth inherited from
Charles; *mother's mould* Lucy Walter.
The word 'mould' suggests both the
mould which gives a shape and the
mould of the dirty earth.
[369] **scanted**
stinted, provided with inadequate
means; *niggard* parsimonious, miserly,
mean.
[370] **her earth**
i.e. his mother's substance.
[371] **empire**
rule, power; *whispers me* whispers to
me.
[372] **Desire ... Godlike sin**
recalling lines 305–10. In Monmouth's
mouth the claim to be transgressing in
a divine manner is impious.
[373] **Him staggering**
describing the perilous condition of
Monmouth as he becomes increasingly
resentful; *hell's dire agent* Shaftesbury is again compared to a devil –
compare line 151 and line 229.
[374] **fainting**
growing weak (rather than swooning);
maintained her ground a metaphor
from battle.
[375] **fresh forces**
another battle metaphor.
[376] **Th'eternal God ...**
Shaftesbury's argument is clothed in
virtue and religion, recalling the
proverbial belief that 'the devil can
cite scripture for his purpose' (*The
Merchant of Venice*, I, iii, 93).
[377] **prodigious**
marvellous. Shaftesbury pounces upon
the weakness exposed in Monmouth's
speech, namely the sense that his talents
are going to waste – see lines 363–6.
[378] **What wonders**
recalling Monmouth's words about
his father's reign – see line 320.

[379] **Against your will**
Shaftesbury flatters Monmouth that he has no real wish to rebel.

[380] **Such virtue's...throne**
referring to Monmouth's argument that he feels like a king – see lines 368–71. 'Virtue' connotes strength.

[381] **father's mildness**
another reference to Charles's merciful disposition – see lines 323, 326, etc.; *contemn* have contempt for.

[382] **manly force**
a reference to Monmouth's military successes (see line 23 & line 248) and a contrast to Charles's 'unmanly' mercy; *diadem* the crown.

[383] **grants...crave**
perhaps alluding to the way that Charles let the law take its course during the Popish Plot, though he did not believe in the guilt of all the plotters.

[384] **And more...have**
This sentiment is at odds with Shaftesbury's championing of democracy, and reveals the falsity of his claims to be working for the public good.

[385] **suppose**
argue, suggest that he is.

[386] **wit**
wisdom.

[388] **negligent or weak**
The difference, which Shaftesbury ignores, between the qualities of negligence and weakness exposes the dishonesty of his argument. There is the same kind of blurring of distinctions in the way that the 'mildness' of line 381 becomes 'tameness' by line 385 and 'weakness' here.

[390] **thrifty**
frugal, economical, mean; *Sanhedrin* the supreme legislative body of the Jews; also, Parliament which had the right to vote or to refuse money to the king.

[391] **shekel**
Jewish currency (later than the time of David); money.

[392] **prerogative**
rights and privileges. In late 1680, for example, the Commons tried to bargain that Charles agree to the exclusion of his brother (see note to line 353) in exchange for a vote of supplies. Matters of succession lay within the king's prerogative, though (in English law) even the king cannot simply decide to appoint a successor, because the laws of succession are already fixed. This is something that Dryden makes much of in the political discussion at the heart of the poem (lines 759–810).

[394] **war**
In the middle of the previous decade the Commons had urged Charles to join the Dutch in war against France.

[396] **He must...buy**
he must pay for with the remains of his royal prerogative. If Charles became embroiled in a war, he would, dependent upon Parliament for money, be in a very weak bargaining position.

[397–8] **His faithful friends... Jebusites**
we accuse them (his faithful friends) of Catholicism (Jebutism) and disloyalty (servitude to the Pharaoh) out of fear and jealousy; *Pharaoh's pensioners* i.e. Louis XIV's hirelings.

[399] **Whom...torn**
and when our fury has torn them (whom) from his protection.

[400] **naked**
unprotected without his friends.

[401] **next successor**
James.

[402] **arts**
plots, wiles; *obnoxious* unpleasing, causing aversion.

[404] **elders**
Parliament; the word is associated with Low Church dissent; *pronounce a foe* referring to the Exclusion Bills – see note to line 353.

[405] **necessary**
needed (since Charles will need money from Parliament).

[406] **pawned**
given as collateral in return for a loan of money; *first be...sold* Shaftesbury proposes that they proceed step by step.

[407] **ever-wanting**
always in need.

[409] **If not...**
The true politician, Shaftesbury, can discard plans and change the direction of his argument as circumstances demand. The idea he espouses here was declared by the Commons towards the end of the Civil Wars: 'the people are, under God, the original of all just power.'

[410] **To make...them**
compare line 795.

[411] **empire**
power, rule.

[412] **resumed**
taken back; here, by the people who have given Charles power in trust until they decide to take back the gift. By this point, Shaftesbury is denying the existence of any hereditary right to kingship.

[413] **Succession...designed**
Laws of hereditary are no longer divinely given and binding, but rather an expedient instituted for the good of the state.

[414] **In...wrong**
to the general detriment.

[415] **If altering...relieve**
if a change in succession can relieve the people.

[416] **Better one suffer**
The words have an ominous ring when it is remembered that Charles's father was executed 'for the nation'.

[417–18] **E'er Saul...depose**
Between the death of Charles I (1649) and the elevation of Cromwell (here Saul) to Lord Protector (1653) England was a republic and supposedly a theocracy (government in which God is the supreme ruler). In Jewish history, Saul was the first king, replacing the rule of divinely inspired judges, but the notion of 'deposing' God also returns us to the imagery of idolatry – see lines 49–50 and note; *durst* dared.

[419] **Urge**
put forward strongly in argument; *piety* The religious appeal of the rebellion was rather to factionalism and anti-Catholicism than to real piety.

[420] **father's right**
that fatherhood (legitimate or not) confers an absolute right; a spurious argument since Monmouth is about to rebel against his father; *fear...fame* i.e. that the judgement of history will be against him if he fails to take his chance.

[422] **even heaven submitted**
When Samuel, the last of the great judges (see note to lines 417–18), was old he appointed his sons in his place, but the Jews, dissatisfied with the sons, asked for a king instead: 'And Samuel prayed unto the Lord. And the Lord said unto Samuel, hearken unto the voice of the people in all they say unto thee, for they have not rejected thee, but they have rejected me that I should not reign over them' (1 Samuel 8: 1–7); *answers all* is sufficient argument in itself.

[424] **'Tis nature's...kind**
i.e. nature plants in people the love of their offspring in order to encourage procreation (propagation). The phrase 'nature's trick' is reductive of the bond between parent and child.

[425] **fond**
both affectionate and foolish; *begetters* parents.

[426] **posterity**
offspring. The argument is that hinted at in line 424.

[427] **Or**
either; *tried* tested; *Or...tried* either let his affection be proved by what it produces...

[428] **vain**
both empty and proud.

[429] **God...father**
David is a king 'after heaven's own heart' (1 Samuel 13: 14) – see line 7.

[430] **anoint him king**
i.e. as God showed his love for David by making him king, so David should show love for Absalom in the same way.

[431] **shepherd**
David's task in his family when he is anointed king (1 Samuel 16: 11).

[432] **so fair a flock**
ironic given the description of the Jews earlier.

[434] **alienate**
distance, transfer (from Monmouth); another false argument since the active nature of the verb implies that Charles has stolen from Monmouth something rightfully his (which kingship was not).

[436] **God's own heart**
see note to line 429; *cheat his heir* Upon the death of Saul, David has a rival for king in Ishbosheth, Saul's son (2 Samuel 2: 8–10). God might be (impiously) said to have cheated Saul's heir by choosing David (1 Samuel 16: 12).

[437] **supreme command**
James had been Admiral of the Fleet.

[438] **barren land**
possibly a reference to lands owned by Monmouth's wife.

[439] **th'old harp**
Charles brought a guitar to England at the Restoration, just as David possessed a harp; *thrum* to pluck mechanically and unskilfully; *lays* songs.

[440] **dull ... ballad**
a reference more to the pedestrian nature of Charles's versifying than to the Hebrew psalms traditionally ascribed to David.

[441] **next heir**
James – see line 352 and note; *wise* referring here to the politician's wisdom of recognising a rival.

[443] **arts**
cunning behaviour. Dryden makes Shaftesbury imply that Monmouth is a dissembler.

[444] **marks**
remarks, notices.

[445] **mighty soul**
a compliment to James; *grief contains* James spent most of the period of the crisis abroad.

[447] **like a lion**
the beginning of another heroic simile – see line 136 and note; *lion* Dryden has Shaftesbury concede James's claim to the throne by using the comparison of the lion, the king of beasts.

[448] **sleep-dissembling**
pretending to be asleep; *waits* awaits.

[449] **distance**
his area, his reach; *draws* The subject of the verb is 'he' of line 446.

[450] **contracts**
draws in.

[453] **prostrate**
lying face down; *vulgar* the ordinary people. It was believed that the lion's noble nature caused him to ignore vulnerable prey. Even so, the extended simile (begun on line 447) goes slightly awry at this point, since there is no reason for lion hunters – see next line – to be preceded by 'prostrate vulgar'.

[454] **his hunters tears**
i.e. James's vengeance will concentrate on leaders. Shaftesbury deploys many different kinds of argument, this one being akin to threat.

[455] **expedients**
courses of action; *afford* allow.

[457] **Which ... draw**
continuing the argument that James is a threat to Monmouth.

[458] **Self-defence**
In *Leviathan* Thomas Hobbes argues that the preservation of one's own life is a 'right of nature' (I, xiv).

[459] **warm people**
i.e. warm with indignation from the Plot revelations.

[460] **rebellion ... crime**
Dryden makes Shaftesbury half admit both that their actions are rebellious and that rebellion is wrong.

[461] **Prevail**
avail; *occasion* opportunity. See lines 258–62.

[462] **But**
only.

[463] **arms**
taking up arms; *fair pretence* pleasing appearance.

[464] **king's defence**
Because the Plot was supposed to be against the king and in favour of James, the exclusionists could argue that their sole motive was to protect the king. In the second Exclusion Parliament (1680) Monmouth claimed to be acting from filial duty.

[465] **sacred life**
Shaftesbury has sneered at the idea of

a divinely given kingship – see line 265 & line 411; *each minute* the subject of the verb 'would expose'.

[467] **sound the depth**
(literally) of sailors, to use a line and weight to ascertain depth.

[468] **his fear**
strengthening the suggestion of earlier that Charles is weak – see lines 381–8.

[470] **For**
on account of; *plighted* promised; *vows* In March 1679 Charles signed a declaration that he had never married anyone except his consort, thus establishing both Monmouth's illegitimacy and James's claim to the throne beyond all doubt.

[471] **If so... gained**
i.e. Charles is so weak that he longs to be ruled by Monmouth.

[472] **Like women's... constrained**
Charles secretly wishes to be forced (constrained) to make Monmouth heir just as women secretly wish to be forced to make love. This view of female psychology (saying 'no' while meaning 'yes') was widespread. It is, of course, highly comic to picture the promiscuous Charles as a coy woman.

[473] **affects the frown**
pretends to be stern.

[474] **pleasing rape**
looking back to line 472.

[475] **Secure**
seize and confine; *person* body. By now Shaftesbury has advanced from hints and innuendos to open treason; *secure* make safe.

[476] **They who... laws**
proposing a kind of rule by kidnap which is at odds with the noble ideals professed earlier.

[478] **mild nature**
somewhat ironic since the advice is to imprison his father.

[479] **Unblamed of life**
of blameless life.

[480] **Not stained... pride**
Monmouth's life had not been as virtuous as this suggests – see lines 35–40 and notes; *puffed* stock description of the effect of pride. See

'charity vaunteth not itself, is not puffed up' (1 Corinthians 13: 4); and *Arbuthnot*, 232.

[481–2] **How happy... high!**
echoing Monmouth's own arguments about his unlucky fate – see lines 363–6.

[484] **And blessed... own**
i.e in other countries he might have been able to ascend the throne on the strength of royal virtue alone.

[485] **refuse**
deny (that Monmouth possesses 'charming greatness').

[486] **'Tis juster... accuse**
Charles strikes a similarly merciful attitude in his speech at the end of the poem – see lines 957–60.

[487] **rival**
his uncle, James.

[488] **blandishments**
flatteries.

[489] **faction**
like 'party', a negative word; *zeal* a word associated with Nonconformist Christianity. Ben Jonson's hypocritical Puritan in *Bartholomew Fair* (1614), for example, is called Zeal-of-the-Land Busy.

[490] **popularly**
with the support of the people (compare line 336); *prosecute the plot* both to lead the reaction against the Popish Plotters, and to pursue (put into action) the plan of action (plot) of Achitophel.

[492] **malcontent**
a discontented person, especially in the political sense of one inclined to rebellion. Earlier in the century, the word meant someone pathologically melancholy, a sense which is preserved here.

[494] **ends**
motives, purposes; *design* overall plan.

[495] **princes**
leaders, in Parliament.

[498] **impious**
irreligious, wicked; *arts* cunning wiles.

[499] **these**
i.e. these 'impious arts'; *property*

·wealth. The Whig Parliamentarians
(see line 495) wanted to see more
power and influence vested in City
financiers, rather than in courtiers and
country squires. Dryden identifies
self-interest as the motive for
rebellion.

[500] **wound**
continuing the image of the tightened
spring from the previous line; *cracked
the government* Between 1679 and
1681 Charles summoned three Parliaments, only to dissolve each of them
because of opposition.

[501] **next**
i.e. of the differing parties joined by
Achitophel (line 493); *interest* both
self-interest, and the interest earned
from loans to the state; *embroil*
entangle.

[503] **Jewish markets**
referring to City merchants; the Jews
had long been famous as bankers.

[505] **others**
the next group, those who try to
assess monarchy in terms of cost and
profit.

[508] **husbandry**
economy, thrift. The word was
associated with small farmers, and
was thus ironically inappropriate to
kings and matters of state.

[509] **haranguers**
makers of loud, stirring speeches;
mob orators, demagogues; *throng*
crowd, mob.

[510] **preferment**
material (or job) advancement. Like
the merchants (of lines 501–5) these
demagogues are motivated by profit.

[511] **who follow next**
i.e. the next of the 'differing parties'
(line 593).

[512] **not only ... king**
i.e. the true republicans who are
ideologically opposed to all idea of
kingship.

[513] **Solymean rout**
the London mob. Solyma is the
Latin name for Jerusalem; *versed*
experienced.

[514] **godly faction**
There were numerous dissenting

Protestant sects; *treason bold* referring to the part played by Londoners
in the Civil Wars and in the execution
of Charles I.

[515] **conqueror's sword**
refers to Cromwell's power during the
Commonwealth period.

[516] **lofty**
haughty, proud; *prince* king.

[517] **ethnic**
gentile. Since the Jebusites were not
Jews (gentiles) Dryden refers to the
Catholics in the same way.

[519] **Levites**
Jewish priests, and here Presbyterian
ministers; *pulled before* taken away
from at an earlier date.

[520] **th'ark ... bore**
It was the special duty of the Levites
to look after the Ark of the Covenant
and to carry it when it moved, a duty
which continued in the reign of David
(1 Chronicles 15: 2), though later they
were to lose some of their status
(2 Chronicles 11: 14–15). The contemporary reference is to the Presbyterian
ministers who were deprived of their
livings by the Act of Uniformity in
1662.

[521] **cant**
a special dialect, usually of the underworld; here, the language of false
piety; also perhaps the whining
manner of speaking associated (by
their opponents) with the dissenters;
zealous a word associated with dissent
– see line 489.

[522] **theocracy**
rule in which God is the supreme
sovereign, His laws are the laws of the
land – see lines 417–18 and note.

[523] **Sanhedrin**
Parliament – see line 390; *enslaved*
Since the complaint against Charles is
that he is arbitrary or tyrannical, it is a
clever gambit to make the same charge
against the democrats.

[524] **spoils**
plunder; *inspiration* Some radical
Protestants (most notably the Quakers)
sought authority for their beliefs in
neither the Bible nor the church but in
inspiration, adopting such 'inspired'

practices as speaking in tongues, having fits and 'going naked for a sign'.

[525] **Aaron's race**
Moses's brother, Aaron, and his sons were the Levites (Exodus 28: 41). Aaron was also the maker of the golden calf – see line 66 and note.

[526] **dominion**
power; *found* establish; *grace* both the special favour of God and the divine influence at work in men. The word was associated with dissenting Protestants.

[527] **These**
i.e. the different groups just listed; *scent* referring back to the image of the pack (of hounds).

[528] **deepest mouthed**
loudest.

[529] **saints**
a word used of themselves by some radical Protestants (as now by the Mormons, the 'latterday saints').

[530] **enthusiastic**
religiously fanatical, extremist; *old . . . breed* a reference to the pre-Restoration days.

[533] **far more numerous**
the final group of rebels.

[534] **Who think . . . much**
i.e. those who get involved for the sake of involvement.

[535] **mere**
pure.

[536] **property**
wealth.

[537] **benefit**
used ironically.

[539] **Born . . . saved**
two references: (1) to the Jews as the 'chosen people' (see line 47 and note); (2) to the Calvinist idea of predestination, that God chose those to be saved at the beginning of time; *even . . . despite* against their own wishes.

[541] **tools**
i.e. simply Shaftesbury's dupes; *hydra* in Greek myth a many-headed monster killed by Heracles. Dryden has portrayed the rebels as divided into many groups.

[543] **princes**
men with power.

[544] **Zimri**
There is no Zimri in the biblical account of Absalom's rebellion, although two Zimris appear elsewhere in the Old Testament. The first is killed for an illicit sexual relationship with a Midianite woman, that is, a woman from an enemy tribe (Numbers 25: 6–18). The second is a high-ranking servant of Elah who conspires against and kills his master (1Kings 6: 8–10). In the contemporary context, Zimri is George Villiers, second Duke of Buckingham (1628–87), who, though previously one of Charles's ministers, had joined in the opposition to James. A wit and a lover of pleasure, he was marked by the inconstancy of his character. Thus, he was like the first of the biblical Zimris in his dissolution, and like the second in his treachery. Dryden plays upon the inconstancy of Buckingham to create a portrait which is less individual than that of Shaftesbury and more typical of any inconstant man. He had a personal reason for attacking Buckingham in addition to the political motive, for the duke had ridiculed him in his play *The Rehearsal* (1671). Indeed, the prominence given to Zimri in the poem seems to owe more to the desire for revenge than to political expediency. However, Dryden was astute enough to know that a tone of detached mockery is more effective in satire than one of outraged indignation, and he kept his personal resentment out of the portrait.

In a famous passage of 'A Discourse Concerning the Original and Progress of Satire' (1693) Dryden praises his portrait:

there is still a vast difference between the slovenly butchering of a man, and the fineness of stroke that separates the head from the body, and leaves it standing in its place The character of Zimri in my *Absalom* is in my opinion

[546] **epitome**
a summary, a representation of a larger whole in miniature.

[548] **starts**
sudden fits of passion.

[549] **revolving**
refers to the phases of the moon; *moon* traditionally associated with changeableness.

[550] **chymist**
chemist, but still carrying a strong connotation of alchemy rather than scientific chemistry; *fiddler* a trifler, one who acts idly and frivolously; *buffoon* Although Zimri resembles Achitophel in some respects, Dryden makes him clownish and absurd rather than demonic and threatening. The sandwiching of Zimri's role as a 'statesman' between those of 'fiddler' and 'buffoon' is satirically very telling.

[551] **rhyming**
Dryden betrays something of his professional contempt for the amateur poet.

[552] **freaks**
capricious whims, the products of an undisciplined mind.

[553] **Blessed madman**
cf. line 163 and note; *every hour employ* i.e. who could employ every hour with . . .

[555] **railing**
abusing, reviling. Dryden may have Buckingham's 'railing' against him in *The Rehearsal* in mind here.

[557] **civil**
polite.

[559] **art**
skill.

[560] **desert**
that which has deserved reward. Zimri gives money to everyone except those who deserve it.

[561] **still**
constantly; *found* discovered, found out.

[564] **parties**
factions. Political parties in the modern sense did not yet exist. In the seventeenth century, the word 'party' was usually employed in a negative sense. Parties and factions accused their opponents of 'forming parties', but denied their own factionalism; *ne'er be chief* In keeping with the rest of the portrait, Dryden emphasises Zimri's folly and lack of political stature.

[566] **wise Achitophel**
'Wise' is used in the sense of 'cunning' here. Even so, the contrast reflects badly on Zimri, for Achitophel possesses greater 'wisdom', greater cunning; he is superior in evil.

[567] **wicked but in will**
i.e. he wanted to be wicked but lacked the ability to be; *means* instruments; *bereft* deprived of.

[569] **rehearse**
repeat. The list of heroes is an epic device – see *Rape of the Lock*, iii, 37ff.

[570] **dignity of verse**
Poetry was thought nobler than prose – see *Arbuthnot*, line 188.

[571] **commonwealthsmen**
supporters of the commonwealth, republicans.

[572] **Kind husbands . . . rest**
These figures contrast with the heroic dignity suggested in the preceding three lines.

[574] **well hung**
both fluent and sexually potent; *Balaam* Theophilus Hastings, Earl of Huntingdon, a leader of the agitation against James, later reconciled with Charles. The name derives from a Hebrew who is reconciled with God after attempting to join the Moabites (Numbers 22 : 21–34); *Caleb* probably Arthur Capel, Earl of Essex; *free* from being attacked here.

[575] **canting**
using affectedly pious language (cf. line 521); *Nadab* Lord Howard of Esrick, formerly a dissenting preacher;

in the Old Testament, a Levite who
'offered strange fire before the Lord'
(Leviticus 10: 1), another image of
idolatry; *oblivion damn* hurt by being
forgotten rather than by being
described.

[576] **paschal lamb**
the sacrifice made by the Jews to
commemorate the Passover; for
Christians, the body of Christ in the
bread of Holy Communion; *who
made... lamb* Howard was said to
have mocked Holy Communion in the
Tower by performing the Prayer Book
(Church of England) service using
beer and roast apples instead of bread
and wine.

[577] **holy band**
i.e. friends of Dryden will not be
named; *assure* protect, make safe.

[578] **scorn secure**
those who are already the butt of
public scorn will not be left out.

[581] **Jonas**
Sir William Jones, Attorney General,
and initially the chief prosecutor
against the plotters; *statutes draw*
draft laws.

[582] **To mean... law**
Jones played a part in drafting bills to
exclude James from the throne and to
limit the king's power – see line 353
and note.

[584] **heaven's anointed**
See note to line 130; *dared to curse*
Shimei was a member of the tribe of
Benjamin who cursed David during
Absalom's rebellion (2 Samuel 16:
5–8). Although David spared Shimei
(2 Samuel 16: 11), on his deathbed
he requested his son and successor,
Solomon, to put him to death, a
request which Solomon carried out
(1 Kings 2: 8–9 & 36–46).

[585] **Shimei**
In the contemporary context, this is
Slingsby Bethel, one of the two
sheriffs of London, and for the poet a
representative City merchant. He was
a republican, a tradesman and a
dissenter, all of which qualities made
him a natural ally for Shaftesbury. As
sheriff, Bethel played a part in the

selection of juries, and for trials of
political consequence he could pack
juries with his own men. Shaftesbury's acquittal shortly after the publication of *Absalom and Achitophel* owed
much to this kind of manoeuvring.

[586] **zeal to God**
ironic. 'Zeal' was a word associated
with sectarian claims to extraordinary
piety – line 489 and note; *hatred to the
king* Bethel fought against the king in
the Civil Wars.

[587] **from expensive sins refrain**
i.e. hypocritical and mean. Dryden
echoes popular prejudices by giving
his City merchant these qualities.

[588] **And never... for gain**
implicitly giving Shimei the character
of the Pharisee and the Puritan.
Dryden may be recollecting the incident in which the Pharisees try to trick
Jesus with the question of whether or
not it is legal to heal on the sabbath.
Jesus replies by asking whether any of
them would fail to rescue a sheep
fallen into a pit on that day, and thus
implies that the Pharisees are ready
enough to break the sabbath in their
own interest (Matthew 12: 10–13).
The Puritans, too, preserved a great
respect for Sundays – see, for instance,
John Bunyan's *Grace Abounding* (1666),
where the author recollects his sinful
life as one who would play games on
the day of rest.

[589–90] **oath & curse**
Prohibitions against cursing and
swearing oaths, like the exaggerated
respect for the sabbath, belong with
the legalistic religion characteristic of
Puritan and Pharisee. Shimei's
hypocrisy is again evident in the way
that he is ready to break these
prohibitions.

[591] **heaping wealth**
Dryden betrays the seventeenth-
century conservative's distrust of the
London merchant's money-making.

[593] **The city**
i.e. the City of London, associated
with merchants and trade.

[594] **his master**
i.e. Charles; *magistrate* his position as

sheriff. 'Magistrate' was often used at the time to mean any administrator of the law, not simply a 'justice of the peace'.

[595] **vare**
a rod or staff; one of the sheriff's badges of office.

[596] **chain of gold**
another badge of office.

[598] **sons of Belial**
Shimei accuses David of being a 'man of belial' (2 Samuel 16: 7). In the Old Testament, belial is not a proper name, but a description of worthlessness, the 'children of belial' being associated particularly with rebellion (2 Samuel 20: 1–2). In *Paradise Lost*, Belial is the last of the fallen angels (i, 490–92), a figure of drunkenness and lust (i, 501–5).

[599] **prodigal**
recklessly wasteful; *pelf* money.

[600] **loved . . . as himself**
Jesus gives the second great commandment (after the love of God) as 'thou shalt love thy neighbour as thyself' (Mark 12: 31). Shimei perverts it.

[601–3] **When . . . midst of them**
Jesus says, 'where two or three are gathered together in my name, there am I in the midst of them' (Matthew 18: 20). While the allusion suggests someone with pious words on his lips, the inversion of its meaning shows the falseness of this piety.

[605] **break good company**
spoil a pleasant social gathering.

[606] **durst**
dared; *factious* given to faction – see line 514.

[607] **packed**
selected the members to ensure the desired verdict.

[608] **godly**
used ironically and with a hint of the 'good old cause' – see line 82.

[609] **saint**
used (ironically) to mean a Protestant fanatic – see line 529 and note; *human laws* contrasting with 'saint'; Bethel abuses his legal position to help like-minded people.

[613] **sin . . . hour**
recalling the proverb, 'the devil finds work for idle hands'.

[615] **clog**
impediment; *trade* emphasising his greed.

[616] **noble style**
Avoiding elevated and ornamented writing as vanity, some of the Puritans adopted a plain, unadorned style. Dryden uses the adjective 'noble' ironically.

[617] **Rechabite**
member of teetotal family in the Old Testament (Jeremiah 35: 2–8).

[618] **Chaste . . . cellars**
i.e. he kept no wine; *shrieval* of the sheriff; *board* table.

[619] **grossness**
both lacking in delicacy and overweight; *City feast* Bethel avoids the sheriff's duty of giving banquets, implicitly out of meanness.

[621] **Cool**
with fires unlit; *hot* used to connote fanaticism – compare line 489 & line 519.

[622] **frugal**
prudent, abstemious, penny-pinching.

[624] **towns once burnt**
referring to the fire of London of 1666, which started in a baker's in Pudding Lane.

[625] **providence**
God's government; *by fire* glancing ironically at the unused fires in Bethel's kitchen; also, according to Christian belief, the end of the world will come by fire.

[626] **spiritual food**
i.e. nothing more substantial.

[627] **Jews rebel**
In the wilderness the Jews complained to Moses that he had taken them from the 'flesh pots' of Egypt to a barren land (Exodus 16: 2–3).

[629] **forty days . . . Mount**
Moses fasted forty days on Mount Sinai before the covenant with God was renewed (Exodus 34: 28): Bethel's respect for fasting is motivated by greed.

[631] **well-breathed**
sound of wind, not out of breath. The

word refers derisively to the ability of witnesses to keep on talking and, implicitly, inventing; *plot* the 'Popish Plot' to kill the king and reestablish Catholicism in England. It was largely the invention of the witnesses who appeared in the trials of those supposed to have been involved in it. David Ogg sums up the substance of the wild, anti-Catholic allegations:

Pope Innocent XI had deputed to the Jesuits supreme control of the Roman Catholic interest in England for the purpose of overthrowing king and government; money was to be provided by the Spanish Jesuits and by the French king's confessor, père la Chaise; two Jesuits had been paid to shoot the king, four Irish ruffians to stab him, and Sir George Wakeman, the queen's physician, to poison him. In addition to all this, there was to be a massacre of Protestants and a French invasion of Ireland; the Duke of York [Charles's Catholic brother, James] was to become king, and rule under the direction of the Jesuits. (*England in the Reign of Charles II*, ii, 563–4)

[632] **Corah**
Like Zimri, Dryden found the name not in the story of Absalom but elsewhere in the Old Testament. Korah is the leader of a rebellion against Aaron and Moses (Numbers 16: 1–3). His reward for rebellion is to be swallowed up by the earth (Numbers 16: 31–3), and Dryden may have hoped that the contemporary Corah would come to a similarly violent end. In the contemporary context, Corah is Titus Oates (1649–1705), the chief witness of the Popish Plot trials. A Church of England minister, he spent some time as a naval chaplain before discovering his true vocation as an informer, spy and fantasiser. In 1677, he joined the Jesuits and spent several months abroad with them, apparently training to become a priest but in reality monitoring their activities. On his return in 1678, he and his associate,

Ezerel Tonge, put together the Popish Plot, partly from the information he had gathered and partly from their own imaginations. The popular mood of anti-Catholicism which the trials gave rise to was, as mentioned above, manipulated by Shaftesbury and others in an attempt to have James excluded from the throne, and they and their chief witnesses were important elements in the whole 'Exclusion Crisis'.

[633] **Erect thyself . . . brass**
A 'monumental brass' is an engraved brass plaque placed over a tomb and representing the deceased as a supine figure – it cannot stand up, that is, 'erect itself'. 'Brass' also implies impudence, as in the expression 'bold as brass'.

[634] **the serpent**
In the wilderness, Moses made a bronze serpent in order to protect his people from a plague of serpents (Numbers 21: 6–9). However, Dryden is probably referring to a later reference to the bronze serpent. King Hezekiah (the twelfth king of Judah after the division of the kingdom which followed Solomon's reign) set about a campaign of religious reform which included breaking 'the brazen serpent that Moses had made; for unto those days the children of Israel did burn incense to it' (2 Kings 18: 4). By then the serpent had ceased to be a symbol of faith as it was regarded to have been in Moses' day (see Wisdom 16: 5–7), and had become instead an object of idolatry. In similar fashion, Oates with his tales and perjuries was a kind of idol of the credulous English, another use of the imagery of idolatry.

[635] **nations . . . beneath thy shade**
In a warning to the Pharaoh, Ezekiel represents Assyria as having been a great cedar: 'All the fowls of heaven made their nests in his boughs, and under his branches did all the beasts of the field bring forth their young, and under his shadow dwelt all great nations' (Ezekiel 31: 6). But God is angry with the the country 'because

he hath shot his top among the thick boughs, and his heart is lifted up in his height', and He decrees its destruction (Ezekiel 31: 10–12). Dryden's 'secure' is heavily ironic; otherwise, he deploys the reference to suggest a deserved and severe punishment.

[636–7] **birth were base**
Oates was the son of a Norfolk weaver; *yet comets . . . in skies* Comets were believed to be formed out of vapours drawn up from the earth by the sun. They were also believed to be portents of disaster.

[638] **prodigious**
marvellous, magnificent; also, ominous, portentous.

[639] **weaver's issue**
See note to lines 636–7; *prince's son* a reference to Monmouth.

[641] **ennobles**
At the height of his reputation Oates tried to concoct for himself a nobler lineage than his real one.

[642–3] **Whoever asked . . . Stephen grace**
Stephen was the first Christian martyr, stoned to death in Jerusalem (Acts 7: 58). The people were 'stirred' against him by men 'suborned' for the task, and he was testified against before the council by 'false witnesses' (Acts 6: 11–14). Dryden likens Oates to these perjurers.

[644] **Levite**
a disparaging term for a clergyman – see line 519. Korah is a leader of the Levite tribe (Numbers 16: 8–10), just as Oates had taken orders in the Church of England.

[645] **godalmighty's gentlemen**
those who hope to derive gentility (in the sense of belonging to the gentry) from sanctity rather than rank. Dryden glances towards the radical dissenters who looked forward to the establishment of a classless, Christian republic. What is more, 'God-a-mighty' was sometimes used in the seventeenth century as a derisive term for someone who posed as powerful or omnipotent.

[646] **Sunk were . . . harsh and loud**
Oates's real features.

[647] **choleric**
having an excess of choler. In the old physiology, choler was one of the four bodily humours which determined an individual's temperament. It was associated with strong memory, keen mind, vindictiveness and bad temper. The physical features described in the previous line are, of course, those of a choleric person.

[649] **vermilion**
scarlet. 'Church vermilion' recalls one of the colours of Roman Catholic vestments, and alludes to Oates's period as a priest; *Moses face* When Moses descended from Mount Sinai with the 'tables of testimony' his face shone from his contact with God (Exodus 34: 29–30). A derisive way of referring to Oates's red face.

[650] **His memory . . . great**
As the trials proceeded, the accusations became so involved and complicated that it was impossible to unravel the various strands of the plots which the witnesses invented.

[653] **wit**
intelligence.

[654] **future truths**
repeating the idea (of line 114) that the plot allegations had some substance.

[655] **prophet**
used ironically; when Oates had nothing to expose, he invented something.

[656] **visionary**
continuing the ironic prophet reference.

[657] **The spirit . . . up**
a phrase affected by 'inspired' dissenters. The biblical source is the incident in which Philip baptises an Ethiopian eunuch, 'and when they were come out of the water, the Spirit of the Lord caught away Philip' (Acts 8: 39); *the Lord . . . where* expressive of disbelief, then as now.

[658] **rabbinical**
priestly; *degree* Oates claimed to have been awarded the degree of Doctor of Divinity at Salamanca (Spain).

[659] **Unknown**
Salamanca denied his claim (see note to previous line).

[660] **yet**
even.

[661] **pieced**
united. Oates's evidence was so disparate and self-contradictory that it needed an exceptional mind to hold it all together.

[662] **suited**
refers to his judgement (of line 660); *temper* disposition, inclination.

[665] **writ**
anything written, sacred writings, orders from a court of law; *apocryphal* spurious, unreliable; used especially of those books of the Old Testament excluded from the Bible by the Protestants.

[666] **affronts**
insults; i.e. the suggestion that Oates's testimony is untrue.

[667] **life**
used partly in the sense of livelihood; *trade* implying that Oates makes his living by making allegations.

[669] **did me ... disgrace**
i.e. as to cast doubt on his authenticity.

[670] **whet my memory**
sharpen it, refresh it. The suggestion here that Oates often made allegations out of personal malice appears to have been true. His servant, John Lane, for example, having unsuccessfully accused Oates of sodomy, was himself charged under the Plot trials.

[672] **zeal**
a word associated (negatively) with Puritanism. See line 586 & line 489.

[673] **And load ... indignities**
Although Oates stopped short of insulting the king, he used his privilege as a witness to go as close as he could, accusing the queen, for example, of treason.

[674] **affords**
allows.

[675] **latitude**
freedom.

[676] **Agag's murder**
Probably referring to the execution of

Lord Stafford on Oates's evidence. The biblical Agag is a king of the Amalekites, captured by Saul and killed by Samuel (1 Samuel 15: 8–33).

[677] **terms as coarse**
When Saul (the king) returns with the captured (but still alive) Agag, Samuel (the judge) accuses him of rebellion and stubbornness (1 Samuel 15: 23).

[678] **others ... join**
Oates's fellow witnesses.

[680] **Corah's own predicament**
By the time Dryden wrote, the tide had turned against Oates, he had had to move lodgings and was no longer attended to with such respect as formerly.

[681] **witness**
used as a derogatory term.

[682] **friends**
highly ironic after the preceding descriptions.

[683] **forsakes the court**
The biblical Absalom sets himself up as a kind of rival king to David (2 Samuel 15: 1–6). Similarly, Monmouth left his father's circle of family, friends and advisers, moved into opposition and conducted the pseudo-royal progress of lines 729ff.

[684] **urged with renown**
motivated by (the desire for) fame.

[686] **Th' admiring ... surprise**
It is in keeping with Dryden's representation of the people that they should be so impressed by novelty.

[687] **goodly person**
referring to his physical appearance – see line 187 & lines 29–30.

[688] **sets ... show**
presents himself as a spectacle.

[689] **popularly**
the third use of the adverb – see line 336 & line 490; *low* implying a self-abasement before the crowd.

[690] **his looks ... frames**
suggesting self-conscious artifice.

[691] **familiar**
i.e. with unkingly closeness; *ease* social grace again – see line 27 and note.

[692] **furnished**
supplied, provided (softening the

criticism of Monmouth by suggesting his arts are from others); *arts* wiles, cunning ways.

[693] **secret hearts**
just as the biblical Absalom 'stole the hearts of the men of Israel' (2 Samuel 15: 6).

[694] **compassionating**
understanding. Absalom claimed to understand the grievances of those who came to Jerusalem for justice (2 Samuel 15: 3–4).

[695] **bespeaking**
expressing.

[697] **Hybla drops**
honey; the town of Hybla is famous for it.

[698] **my countrymen**
Absalom is represented as speaking to his fellow Englishmen and tempting them to rebellion. In this respect, the speech echoes Achitophel's temptation speech of earlier (lines 230–302); *estate* condition, worldly prosperity, status. The word is (deliberately) vague, just as the grievances of Monmouth and his supporters are somewhat unreal.

[699] **far unable**
far from able.

[700] **banished man**
Charles exiled Monmouth to Holland in September 1679, to defuse some of the tension of the situation, but he returned without permission in November; *your dear cause* the politician's perennial claim that he is acting for the good of others.

[701] **arbitrary**
tyrannical – see lines 212, 330 & 762.

[702] **undone**
in the sense of materially ruined.

[703] **empire**
power. The dishonesty of Monmouth's argument is particularly clear here since he cannot be cut off from a right to rule which he (as a bastard) does not possess; *no...son!* ironic since it is Monmouth's unfilial behaviour which is denying the relationship.

[704] **liberties**
reflecting English pride in the country's relative freedom – see line 51 and note; *spoil* plunder.

[705] **Egypt and Tyrus**
France and Holland; *intercept your trade* by piracy.

[706] **invade**
encroach on; Monmouth plays on popular anti-Catholicism, by referring to disputes concerning Church of England liturgy and music, and the extent to which those might reflect Catholic models.

[707] **ease**
(here) idleness; *fame* reputation.

[708] **foreign gold**
money received from France – see line 285 and note.

[710] **Bathsheba**
Louise Renée de Kéroualle, Duchess of Portsmouth and Charles's principal mistress. One of the most famous incidents in the biblical David's life is his illicit liaison with Bathsheba, wife of Uriah the Hittite (2 Samuel 11: 2–4); *old* Monmouth repeats Shaftesbury's sneering reference to Charles's 'declining age' – line 267.

[711] **enemies**
a perverse description of the loyal ministers praised by Dryden later (lines 817ff.); *friends destroys* possibly referring to Shaftesbury's removal from office and Monmouth's exile.

[712] **power against himself**
highly ironic in view of Monmouth's position.

[713] **He gives...away**
referring to Charles's declaration of Monmouth's illegitimacy – see line 470 and note. The argument of this poem, of course, is that Monmouth possesses no real right; *let him give* the pretence of altruism again – cf. line 700.

[714] **his own...betray**
The argument seems to be that by allowing the accession of a Catholic king, Charles will destroy the rights of Anglicans.

[715] **He only...bleed**
laying the blame for the anticipated Civil War with Charles.

[716] **he alone...freed**
Monmouth's promised revenge on all his opponents except his father stands

in contrast with Charles's much emphasised mercy – see lines 146 & 939.

[717] **wiped his eyes**
a deliberate theatrical gesture – cf. line 690.

[719] **court informer**
Monmouth's apparent distaste for informers creates another intense irony since his rebellion has been made possible by the revelations of informers like Oates; *arms* weapons.

[720] **These . . . use**
a flat contradiction of the fifth commandment, 'honour thy father and thy mother' (Exodus 20: 12).

[721] **next successor**
Monmouth is deliberately vague about the identity of this person.

[722] **May . . . complain**
like Absalom in the Bible (2 Samuel 15: 4) and like politicians ever since, Monmouth promises to please everybody once he is in power.

[724] **common interest**
i.e. the rebels are acting not out of patriotism or love of Monmouth but simply out of hope for gain.

[726] **people's wrongs . . . own**
The drift of Monmouth's speech is that he is acting for the good of others (not himself).

[728] **messiah**
echoing Shaftesbury's preposterous flattery – see line 240.

[729] **progress**
a royal journey, with a numerous retinue, to a part of the kingdom, to be met there and entertained by the principal people. In July 1680, Monmouth made a pseudo-royal progress through Somerset, Devon and Exeter; *ordain* prepare.

[730] **chariots**
carriages; also military vehicles of ancient times; *horsemen . . . train* The details of the retinue betray the treasonable nature of the progress. The biblical Absalom, too, 'prepared him chariots and horses, and fifty men to run before him' (2 Samuel 15: 1).

[731] **east to west**
the direction of Monmouth's progress and of the sun's path.

[732] **sun**
See previous note; also by a pun a further reference to Jesus, the Son of God; *promised land surveys* just as Moses sees Canaan before he dies (Deuteronomy 34: 1–4) – for an earlier reference to Moses see lines 234–5.

[733] **morning star**
the planet Venus; continuing the imagery of the sun's diurnal progress as Venus appears before it. Also, a name for Jesus, as the harbinger of a new way of life (Revelation 22: 16).

[734] **salute**
greet.

[735] **guardian god**
In Roman religion, each family had its 'household god' – another idol image.

[736] **consecrates**
makes holy.

[737] **commend**
recommend.

[738] **Wise**
(here) implicitly, cunning; *Issachar* Thomas Thynne of Wiltshire, an ally of Monmouth.

[739] **court**
the servants and advisers of a sovereign. Monmouth's creation of a rival court is, like his progress, a usurpation of royal privilege.

[740] **but pomp**
only show.

[742] **sound the depths**
of sailors, to use weight and line to ascertain depth – see line 467; *fathom . . . went* discover the direction of tides and currents; continuing the sea imagery.

[743] **The people's hearts**
A clumsy construction, this phrase seems to be a second object of the verb 'to sound' in the previous line.

[744] **try**
test; *blows* The earlier hints of approaching civil war become explicit here – see lines 715 & 730.

[746] **specious**
of pleasing appearance but false; *duty . . . prince* referring to Monmouth's argument that he was acting from filial love – see line 464 and note.

[749] **urged**
used in argument; *king . . . life* a third argument urged by the rebels.

[750] **Endangered . . . wife**
Both James, the king's brother, and the queen were eventually implicated in the Plot allegations.

[751] **Thus**
a break in the poem. Dryden moves from description of Monmouth's allies and activities to comment on and analysis of the crisis; *pageant show* Monmouth's progress, a deliberately reductive description; *plot* turning the word which Monmouth and his allies had used to whip up feeling against James back on them. They are the plotters now.

[752] **masquerade**
costumes worn at a masked ball; a pretence. The sense of the line is that underlying the peaceful nature of Monmouth's progress is a conflict equivalent to war. The word also repeats the sense of 'pageant show' in the previous line.

[754] **same bait**
i.e. the arguments of religion, liberty and public good are the same as those used in the Civil Wars; *circumvented* overcome by deceit and cunning.

[755] **ease**
(here) comfort and security.

[757] **contingent mischiefs**
evils dependent upon some possible future event; referring to the fears aroused by the possibility of James (a Catholic) becoming king.

[758] **heirs for monarchs**
a key phrase for the ensuing argument. Dryden contends that any attempt to change the succession is (1) illegal and (2) dangerous; *God . . . decree* in that it is God's decree which creates the king.

[760] **sons**
successors; *native sway* innate power of command; conceding that power is ultimately invested in the people rather than the king. Although elsewhere in the poem Dryden refers to the divine sanction of kings he does not emphasise it here (but see line 792

and note). His argument is that the popular destruction of a king also destroys the law and with that the rights of the people.

[761] **defenceless**
the consequence of destroying the law.

[762] **unbounded**
unrestrained; *arbitrary* absolute, tyrannical – see line 701 and note.

[763–4] **right**
justice; *And laws . . . destroy* If the king alters the method of succession, he is breaking the law, and thus destroying the rule of law which provides justice for all.

[765] **fit**
proper, right. The clause means 'if the crowd is judge of what is right and just'. Dryden has shifted from the 'people', a neutral term, to the 'crowd', a negative one.

[766] **officers in trust**
alludes to the idea of an agreement between king and people; recalling Shaftesbury's argument – see lines 409–14.

[767] **resuming**
beginning again for each new generation, with reference here to the succession; *cov'nant* i.e. covenant, a mutual agreement, binding on both those who made it and their successors. The word 'resume' echoes its use earlier – see line 412. 'Covenant' recalls the relationship between God and the Jews in the Old Testament, itself a continuing agreement.

[768] **barred**
made null. Dryden gives his readers a rather bleak choice by arguing that either an eternally binding agreement was made between king and people when monarchy was first established or there can be no monarchy (which to his contemporaries meant anarchy).

[769] **scepter**
ornamental rod, the traditional badge (along with the crown) of kingly office; *tie* i.e. bind to a hereditary king.

[770] **posterity**
collective descendants.

[771] **How then... future race**
According to Christianity, the fall of Adam has caused every human being to be born tainted by original sin. Dryden suggests a parallel between the inheritance of sin and the inheritance of a binding contract between king and people, a contract which includes unbreakable laws of succession.

[772] **forfeit**
i.e. his loss of innocence, eternal life and bliss in Paradise; *take place* take effect, be accomplished, be realised.

[773–4] **How could... father's fall?**
The punishment of Adam's successors is used as an example of divine justice, equivalent to the continuing subjection of people to king and the 'resuming covenant' of inherited succession.

[775] **Then**
A new stage of the argument begins. 'Then' does not mark a direct consequence of the earlier ideas of a 'resuming' bond, but a general recapitulation and moving on; *slaves ... command* note the paradox. From here on, Dryden emphasises the vulnerability of kings and the dangers of democracy.

[775–6] **Then... pleasure stand**
back to the idea that kings hold their authority by the will of the people.

[776] **tenants**
i.e. he holds his office by the agreement of the people.

[777–8] **Add**
The argument moves to a further example of the power invested in the people; *mischievously* unfortunately; also suggesting the people's inclination for evil; *the pow'r... the crowd* i.e. laws of ownership are created by Parliament, the people.

[779–80] **private right**
justifiable claim to personal possessions; *For who... by might?* implies that the power of Parliament threatens the livelihood of every citizen; now Parliament (rather than the king) is a threat to individual liberties.

[783] **faultless kings**
referring to the execution of Charles I; the conservatives' stock proof of the danger of popular power; *run down* be overthrown, be hunted down.

[785] **standard**
definite, fixed quality; *fickle* changeable, without standard; *rout* crowd, mob.

[786] **Which flowing... faster out?**
The image is that of the tide, approaching the high tide mark only to ebb away.

[787] **Sanhedrins**
Parliament.

[788] **lunacy**
referring back to the tide imagery; caused (like madness) by the moon.

[790] **murder monarchs**
another reference to the death of Charles I. The tone becomes more vigorous as Dryden moves from theoretical discussion to denunciation. He has saved his direct reference to the execution of Charles I to this point.

[791] **give and take**
repeating the premise of line 777.

[792] **the godhead's images**
because their position reflects that of God, and because they are divinely appointed.

[793] **government... must fall**
echoing the argument of lines 779–80, that the fall of a king must have further consequences of damage to all.

[794] **nature's state**
suggesting anarchy – see the note to lines 53–6; *all... all* describing the disappearance of property rights in a lawless state.

[795] **Yet**
announcing a shift in the argument; *grant... make* i.e. grant that the people, who are our lords, create kings.

[796] **What prudent... shake**
the main point of the concluding section, that change is dangerous.

[798] **makes**
i.e. will make.

[800] **fate**
used here less in its usual sense of destiny, than in its occasional poetic sense of an instrument of destruction.

[801–2] **fabrics**
buildings; *buttress* strengthen with a buttress, i.e. a structure of wood or stone built against a wall; *If ancient ... the wall* This imagery of shattered buildings must have been particularly evocative at a time when the fire of London was still well within living memory and its effects were still evident in the city.

[803] **fix the mark**
set the limit.

[804] **touch our ark**
The Ark of the Covenant was the container made by the Hebrews in the wilderness to contain the tables of law which Moses brought down from Sinai. It was so sacred that to touch it meant death (1 Chronicles 13: 9–10).

[805] **frame**
structure, building.

[807] **control**
dominate, command; *At once... control* These are the 'base ends' of the rebels, to alter human and divine law.

[810] **physic**
treat, in the medical sense. The last couplet sums up the conservative's belief that any change is likely to be a change for the worse.

[811] **relief**
remedy, deliverance from hardship.

[812] **fatal**
dangerous; recalling the phrase 'fatal mercy' (of line 146).

[816] **Some let me name**
Dryden announces that the next section will be a list of the king's loyal supporters.

[817] **short file**
The small number of those loyal to Charles contrasts with the hydra-headed crowd of those against him (line 541); *Barzillai* James Butler, Duke of Ormonde (1610–88), an old and unfailingly loyal servant of both Charles and his father. The biblical Barzillai was like Ormonde both in his age and in taking David's part during Absalom's rebellion (2 Samuel 19: 31–2).

[818] **with years**
Ormonde was born in 1610.

[820] **regions waste**
Ireland. Ormonde had been Lord Lieutenant four times; *beyond... flood* over the Irish Sea; also the biblical Barzillai lived 'over the Jordan'.

[821] **buoy**
keep from sinking; adopting the 'ship of state' imagery used earlier – see line 159.

[822] **sinking... fate**
Ormonde went into exile during the Commonwealth period.

[823] **godlike prince**
Charles before his restoration.

[825] **practised**
frequented; *courtier's art* the false behaviour of kings' followers. Ormonde was laughed at by some of the wits of Charles's court.

[826] **larger... heart**
Ormonde was something of a patron.

[827] **noblest objects**
Dryden was among those Ormonde patronised.

[828] **recording muse**
referring to Dryden.

[829] **fruitful issue**
He fathered ten children.

[830] **now more... lost**
Six of the children had died.

[831] **eldest hope**
Thomas, Earl of Ossory, who died in 1680. The reference to the outstanding qualities of this eldest son recalls the references to Charles's son and Shaftesbury's – see line 70 and note. His behaviour contrasts with that of Monmouth.

[833] **honoured**
Dryden had included a passing reference to the Earl's bravery in a prologue he wrote for *Oedipus; manhood's prime* at the age of 46.

[834] **th'unequal fates**
The three fates of classical mythology allot differing portions to different people; *providence* God's divine plan; therefore, incapable of crime.

[835] **Yet not... won**
Ossory distinguished himself as a soldier before his death.

[836] **All parts ... son**
Ossory's loyalty to father and king stands in contrast with Monmouth.
[839] **perfect in thy line**
The circle was regarded as a perfect shape, which reflected divine perfection.
[840] **By sea, by land**
Ossory fought against the Dutch at sea and the French on land.
[842] **infused**
poured in; *fainting* growing weak; *Tyrians* Dutch (see note to line 705). Ossory had been part of a contingent of English troops assisting the Dutch against the French.
[843] **Pharaoh**
Louis XIV of France – see note to previous line.
[844] **ancient honour**
It is characteristic of many ages to imagine that honour and virtue were more alive in earlier times than in their own.
[847] **immoderate**
exceptional, eminent.
[848] **as**
as if; *designed* planned.
[849] **durst**
dared; if Ossory had been left alive the plan of heaven for the ruin of England (mentioned in the previous line) would have been spoilt; *fortune* used in the sense of wealth. Again there is a contrast with a Monmouth who uses his wealth for treason.
[850] **free from earth**
The body is a 'tenement of clay' (line 158), and a prison for the immaterial soul; *disencumbred* unburdened.
[851] **Mounts up ... pole**
an alexandrine, a line of twelve syllables, or here, six iambic feet; *starry pole* the starry sky (poetic).
[852] **kindred legions**
i.e. squads of angels.
[853] **to aid ... king**
emphasising Ossory's loyalty as against Monmouth's treachery.
[854] **muse**
goddess of poetry – see *Rape of the Lock*, i, 3 and note; *painful* difficult; *flight* a common idea for the action of

poetic imagination (muse) – cf. 'Oh for muse of fire that would ascend/ The brightest heaven of invention' (prologue, *Henry V*).
[855] **pinions**
wings; *immortal height* in that he is attempting to follow Ossory into heaven.
[856] **thou**
the muse.
[857] **fled before**
i.e. if she wanted to follow Ossory.
[858] **Or fled ... life**
suggesting that the death of Ossory might have meant the death of Dryden's muse; an elegant compliment.
[859] **hearse**
a structure built over a bier (the cart which bore coffin and corpse), decorated with banners and epitaphs. The idea is that this verse, the section dealing with Ossory, is an epitaph dedicated to him; *patron* Ossory's father rather than Ossory himself – see note to line 827.
[860] **take ... from**
descend; *steepy* steep (an archaism).
[861] **he**
Ossory.
[862] **Another he**
rather clumsy repetition.
[864] **Zadoc the priest**
William Sancroft, Archbishop of Canterbury. The biblical Zadok was high priest during Absalom's rebellion (2 Samuel 15: 24–9).
[865] **lowly**
humble, meek; *David's* The appointment of the Archbishop of Canterbury was the privilege of the monarch.
[866] **Sagan**
the deputy of the Jewish high priest; here, Henry Compton, Bishop of London (as hinted by the reference to Jerusalem – see line 513 and note).
[867] **noble stem**
He was the youngest son of the Earl of Northampton.
[868] **Him of the western dome**
John Dolben, Dean of Westminster ('the western dome'), until he was made Archbishop of York.

[869] **fit words ... eloquence**
referring to Dolben's pulpit oratory.

[870] **The prophets' ... led**
referring to Westminster school which, in the middle of London, had its share of sons of dissenting fathers (the 'prophets' sons'). The word 'prophet' glances ironically at the claims of contemporary fanatics to prophetic gifts – compare line 529. References to the 'sons' or the 'children' of prophets in the Bible provide little illumination.

[871] **To learning ... bred**
i.e. even with such (for Dryden) unpromising material as Nonconformist boys Dolben was a successful teacher of duty.

[872] **colleges**
a further reference to Westminster school; *bounteous* generous.

[873] **never ... friend**
rebels are never patrons of arts and learning. The ideal of patronage was that a wealthy lover of learning provided for a protégé – Dryden himself earned some of his money in this way. For an account of the debasement of patronage, see Pope's portrait of Bufo (*Arbuthnot*, 231ff.).

[875] **plead**
make a formal plea in a court of law.

[876] **Next them**
after them; *train* group.

[877] **Adriel**
John Sheffield, Earl of Mulgrave; *the muse's friend* Mulgrave was a patron of poets, among them Dryden.

[878] **Himself a muse**
Author of a number of poems, he was attacked by Rochester as 'My Lord All-Pride'.

[880] **Whom David's ... adorn**
In 1679 he was made Lord Lieutenant of the East Riding of Yorkshire and Governor of Hull, offices previously held by Monmouth.

[881] **That from ... torn**
See previous note.

[882] **Jotham**
George Savile, Earl of Halifax. He argued with great eloquence against the Exclusion Bill (see line 353 and note) in the House of Lords in 1680.

The biblical Jotham (no part of the Absalom story) is also an eloquent man who pleads against rebels (Judges 9: 1–21).

[883] **Indewed**
endowed.

[884] **To move assemblies**
referring to his success in the Lords.

[885] **The worse ... side**
Halifax was no party man but tried to judge each situation as well as he could. He worked with Shaftesbury from 1674 to 1679, before deciding against exclusion.

[886] **Nor chose alone**
in the sense of 'and didn't only choose but ... '

[888] **Hushai**
Laurence Hyde, First Lord of the Treasury. The biblical Hushai is a loyal servant of David who deceives the rebels (2 Samuel 16: 16–19).

[890] **By foreign treaties**
He had negotiated the Anglo–Dutch alliance of 1679.

[891] **native truth**
inherent loyalty and honour.

[892] **frugal**
careful with money; *supplied* i.e. in his role as First Lord of the Treasury; *wanting* needy.

[894] **exchequers**
(here) the money gathered by the Treasury.

[895] **low**
referring to Charles's money difficulties which Shaftesbury had hoped to exploit – see line 390.

[897] **When kings ... buy**
cf. line 392.

[898] **Indulge**
allow.

[899] **Amiel**
Edward Seymour, Speaker of the House of Commons. The biblical Amiel is not an important figure and no part of the Absalom story; he is someone mentioned in passing as deputed to guard the House of Asuppim (1 Chronicles 26: 4–15).

[900] **ancient race**
belonging to the old Seymour family.

[902] **The Sanhedrin ... ruled**
referring to his position as Speaker of the House.

[903] **passion cooled**
Acting as a kind of chairman, the Speaker must try to keep debate as calm as possible.

[906] **as their ... small**
just as Parliament (their band – the Sanhedrin) was a little version of the whole nation.

[908] **charioteers**
a lowly occupation in ancient times; also beginning the image of the following lines; *seat* the Speaker's seat.

[909] **loose**
uncontrolled (in the charioteer image, of the reins); *careers* gallops (of the chariots); *commend* recommend (i.e. their lack of skill serves as recommendation for his possession of it).

[910] **th'unequal ... day**
According to classical myth Phaethon, a son of Helios, the sun god, persuaded his father to lend him his chariot (the sun).

[911] **Misguide ... way**
Phaethon's unskilful driving of the chariot has serious results, almost causing a universal conflagration.

[912] **withdrawn**
Seymour's period as Speaker ended in 1679. The gods' response to Phaethon's ride is less carefree – he was struck by a thunderbolt to prevent further harm.

[913] **Sabbath**
day of rest; used here to mean the period of retirement after a lifetime's work.

[915] **breach**
a gap in a fortification.

[916] **th'united fury**
continuing the military image of the previous line.

[917] **engines**
machines, especially military machines, cannon; *bent* aimed, determined.

[918] **batter**
an image of peculiar force in the second half of the seventeenth century, since the Civil Wars had seen the widespread use of cannon to destroy what had once been impregnable fortified buildings.

[919] **frights**
fears; referring to the supposed fear of a Catholic revival should James become king – see line 757.

[920] **In Sanhedrins**
i.e. through Parliaments; *plume* pluck, reduce.

[921] **removed**
James spent most of the crisis away from England.

[922] **hireling witnesses**
cf. line 679.

[923] **they**
i.e. the faithful band.

[926] **lenitives**
medicines which tend to allay or soften; continuing the suggestion that Charles may have been too mild – see line 146; *foment* make worse, aggravate.

[928] **lure**
meat used to bring the falcon back to the falconer; *draw ... down* referring both to the the downward flight of the hawk attracted to the lure and to the moral fall of the people in rebelling against their king.

[929] **pernicious**
harmful, destructive.

[930] **turned**
formed.

[931] **council**
group of advisers, especially the Privy Council, to which Shaftesbury had once belonged.

[932] **Shimei ... curse**
cf. line 584.

[934] **careful**
(literally) full of care, laden with anxiety.

[935] **event**
outcome.

[937] **spoke**
Dryden's version of Charles's speech, the last major section of the poem, is compiled in part from real speeches and pamphlets; *awful* (literally) full of awe.

[938] **their maker ... hear**
As 'God's anointed' (line 130) Charles can be said to speak for God.

[939] **native mercy**
perhaps the characteristic of Charles which Dryden emphasises most – see line 326; *swayed* ruled.

[940] **dissembled**
made to appear different from their real nature.

[942] **assuage**
soften, mitigate, appease; *So much...assuage* so much did the inclinations of the father for mercy soften those of the king for justice.

[943] **clemency**
mercy; *slight* make little of.

[944] **question...right**
The king's prerogative to pardon condemned criminals was attacked by the Commons on at least two occasions.

[945] **That one...contend**
the notion of the king as servant of the people – see lines 409–14 & line 766.

[947] **tenderness of blood**
unwillingness to shed blood, merciful disposition; *They call...fear* the misconstruction of Charles's mercy which Shaftesbury makes in his second speech, see lines 381–2.

[948] **tempers**
dispositions, characters; *the longest bear* i.e. his long-suffering is evidence of manliness not cowardice.

[949] **native**
natural.

[950] **good by force**
i.e. merciful out of fear of their power.

[955] **Samson**
returning to the image of line 176 (see note). The image is more sustained here, beginning with the idea of the king as pillar of the state, and developing into that of Monmouth who shakes the pillars and threatens to bring the whole building down; *call impulse*; a cant term among the Puritans.

[956] **share the fall**
Samson was killed by the collapsing building (see note to line 176). There is a thinly veiled threat here that Monmouth could face execution for his treasonable activities.

[957] **But Oh...live!**
While the line sustains the overall sense of the poem that Monmouth's virtues are deserving of mercy, it also reinforces the threat of the previous line – if Monmouth does not repent he may not live.

[960] **nature**
the natural wish of fathers to forgive children; *darling son* a phrase earlier used by Shaftesbury – see line 433.

[962] **frame**
constitution. In contrast to Monmouth's claims, Charles argues that his son is unfit for the throne both by birth and by character – see line 371.

[963] **Had God...born**
if he had been designed by God to rule...

[964] **another turn**
a different complexion. Dryden has earlier reminded us that, despite Monmouth's physical beauty and military dash, he is not without serious faults – see lines 35–40.

[965–6] **Gulled**
cheated, tricked; *patriot's name...prince* for an earlier note to the rebel use of 'patriot' see line 179; *prince* ruler, (here) king.

[967] **brave**
bully, hired thug.

[969] **Whence comes it**
from where does it come, for what reason is it (surviving in the colloquial expression, 'how come?'); *religion and the laws* the rebels claim to be protecting these – see lines 292 & 747.

[971] **instructor**
Achitophel/Shaftesbury; *lost...place* referring to his removal from office – see line 154 and note.

[972] **endued**
invested, endowed; *grace* referring to religious grace, and implying that Shaftesbury's championship of dissenting Christianity is a politician's expedient – see line 526 and note.

[973] **patriot paint**
i.e. disguise someone to look like a patriot.

[975] **Would they...throne**
cf. line 758.

[976] **give their own**
offer what is their own.

[978] **mine**
i.e. my consent.
[979] **Without my . . . choose**
to choose a future king without my leave . . .
[980] **Infers**
(here) implies.
[981] **petition**
request through a written petition; referring to Shaftesbury's faction's frequent use of this device.
[982] **Esau's hands . . . voice**
Jacob usurps his brother Esau's birthright by disguising his hands with goatskin, so that they felt to the touch of their blind father Isaac like Esau's hairy hands rather than Jacob's smooth ones. However, Isaac notes that 'the voice is Jacob's voice, but the hands are the hands of Esau' (Genesis 27: 15–22). The sense is that the petitioners pretend to be loyal subjects (like Jacob pretending to be Esau) while they are really intent upon usurping power.
[983–4] **My pious subjects . . . away**
exposing the contradiction in Shaftesbury's argument that they should rebel for the sake of the king – see lines 471–4.
[986] **petitioners**
a term for the opponents of the king (Whigs) who presented him with petitions.
[987] **womb or grave**
According to Proverbs there are four insatiable things, 'the grave; the barren womb; the earth that is not filled with water; and the fire that saith not, It is enough' (Proverbs 30: 15–16).
[989] **left**
i.e for Charles.
[991] **sway**
rule.
[992] **teach . . . obey**
another threat that severe punishment might be dealt on the rebels.
[993] **established power**
referring to the power of the king.
[994] **part . . . whole**
A group in the Commons (a part) can vote in such a way as to give the

House (and themselves as the controlling group in the House) greater power.
[995] **groundless**
unfounded; *clamours* outcries, especially popular outcries; *my friends* Shaftesbury's group sought to direct Charles in his choice of advisers.
[996] **punish . . . prove**
Charles Osborne, Earl of Danby and Lord Treasurer, was impeached by the Commons in 1678 and resigned from the treasurership in 1679.
[997] **care express**
show their wish.
[998] **defend their servants**
Charles pardoned Danby.
[999] **Oh that . . . confined**
Dryden emphasises the king's desire to show clemency. The references to 'power' and 'healing' allude to Charles's reintroduction of 'touching' as a cure for the king's evil, or scrofula.
[1000] **like heaven**
i.e. like God; *against my mind* against my inclination.
[1001] **examples of another kind**
i.e. examples of a kind different from those of the people cured by Charles's touch. The phrase refers to the possibility of punishment.
[1004] **How ill . . . scan**
i.e. how inaccurately they perceive me to be fearful because I am merciful. Achitophel has earlier suggested that Charles must be weak because he is benevolent (lines 381–7).
[1006] **let law . . . her face**
Dryden seems to be writing with the forthcoming trial of Shaftesbury in mind.
[1007–9] **grace**
mercy; *They could . . . and die* The lines refer to the incident in which God allows Moses to see His 'back parts' only, since, as He explains, 'thou canst not see my face; for there shall no man see me and live' (Exodus 33: 20–3). So far, Charles has shown only the 'hinder parts' of the law, her mercy, but he may be forced to display her punitive front.

[1012] **Against themselves ... swear**
Some of the informers who had worked for Shaftesbury were to act as witnesses against him.

[1013] **viper-like**
It was believed that the young of the viper fed on their mother. In *Paradise Lost*, sin is represented as half woman, half snake (ii, 650–3). The hell-hounds produced by her incestuous union with Death return 'hourly' to her womb and 'gnaw/ My bowels, their repast' (ii, 796–800).

[1015] **principle**
source.

[1016] **Belial**
a devil, see line 598 and note; *Beelzebub* a Philistine god, here used (as in *Paradise Lost*) as the name of one of the chief devils.

[1017] **on my foes ... me right**
i.e. some of my enemies will exact justice for me from other of my enemies.

[1018] **Nor doubt**
The king begins to address a third party; *event* outcome, result.

[1021] **delude**
befuddle, frustrate; *traverse* pass through. The image is that of the movement of armies.

[1023] **rise upon**
take arms against.

[1025] **stands the ground**
another military image.

[1026] **Th'Almighty ... consent**
In *Aeneid*, Jove is represented as ratifying his own judgement in a similar way: 'He said, and shook the skies with his imperial nod' (Dryden's translation, bk ix).

[1027] **peals of thunder**
Thunder is associated with Jove (the Thunderer) and also sometimes with the God of the Old Testament (Exodus 19: 16).

[1028] **a series of new time**
a new age. Dryden announced the beginning of a new age in two earlier poems: 'And now time's whiter series is begun' (*Astraea Redux*, 292). 'And now a round of greater years begun' (*Annus Mirabilis*, 71). The idea goes back to two sources. First, there is Virgil's famous fourth *Eclogue*: 'The last great age, foretold by sacred rhymes,/ Renews its finished course; Saturnian times/ Roll round again, and mighty years, begun/ From their first orb, in radiant circles run' (Dryden's translation, 5–8). Secondly, there is an older and possibly more important source in the messianic strain of Old Testament prophecy, in the prediction of a future saviour for the Jews, a kind of second, and superior, David:

For unto us a child is born, unto us a son is given: and the government shall be upon his shoulder; and his name shall be called Wonderful, Counsellor, The Mighty God, The Everlasting Father, The Prince of Peace. Of the increase of his government and peace there shall be no end, upon the throne of David, and upon his kingdom, to order it and to establish it with judgment from henceforth even for ever. (Isaiah 9: 6–7)

[1030] **Once ... restored**
Dryden imagines the new age as a second Restoration.

4 / *To the Memory of Mr Oldham*

Farewell, too little and too lately known,
Whom I began to think and call my own.
For sure our souls were near allied, and thine
Cast in the same poetic mould with mine.
One common note on either lyre did strike,   5
And knaves and fools we both abhorred alike.
To the same goal did both our studies drive,
The last set out the soonest did arrive.
Thus Nisus fell upon the slippery place,
While his young friend performed and won the race.   10
O early ripe – to thy abundant store
What could advancing age have added more?
It might (what nature never gives the young)
Have taught the numbers of thy native tongue.
But satire needs not those, and wit will shine   15
Through the harsh cadence of a rugged line.
A noble error and but seldom made,
When poets are by too much force betrayed.
Thy generous fruits, though gathered ere their prime
Still showed a quickness, and maturing time   20
But mellows what we write to the dull sweets of rhyme.
Once more, hail and farewell; farewell thou young
But, ah, too short Marcellus of our tongue,
Thy brows with ivy and with laurel bound,
But fate and gloomy night encompass thee around.   25

In this poem of 1684 Dryden laments the early death from smallpox of John Oldham (1653–83), who was regarded by a number of contemporaries as a poet of great promise. The poem is a stately elegy written in rhyming couplets of iambic pentameters.

[1] **Farewell**
The valedictory opening is a fairly common device in elegiac poems. Compare Ben Jonson's epigram on the death of his son, 'Farewell, thou child of my right hand...'; *too little and too lately known* The dead Oldham is addressed not by name but by epithets. This contributes to the formality and dignity of the poem. The nature of the epithets is explained

by the fact that Dryden probably knew Oldham only for the last two years of his short life.
[3] **near allied**
similar in nature. Dryden uses the same phrase in *Absalom*, line 163.
[4] **Cast ... mould**
The metaphor, taken from metalwork, probably still retained some of its power in 1684, not having quite yet degenerated into a dead, clichéd

metaphor. Certainly, it is used forcefully in Andrew Marvell's famous lines of 1650 concerning the actions of Oliver Cromwell, 'And cast the kingdoms old/ Into another mould' ('A Horatian Ode Upon Cromwell's Return from Ireland', lines 35–6).

[5] **either**
each; *lyre* a stringed instrument, like a small harp – the traditional instrument of the Greek poet/singer, and thus, a conventional description of poetic aptitude. Compare *Alexander's Feast*, line 22.

[6] **knaves**
villains, unscrupulous men; *knaves and fools* It was common to divide the 'unblessed' part of humanity into these two categories; *abhorred alike* in that both Oldham and Dryden were satirists, whose literary job was to attack knaves and fools. *Mr Oldham* was written after Dryden's greatest satirical poems, *Macflecknoe* (publ. 1682) and *Absalom* (1681).

[7] **To**
i.e. towards.

[8] **last ... arrive**
Oldham was the last to set out in that he was over twenty years younger than Dryden, and thus began to write later. However, he 'arrived sooner' than Dryden in that his *Satyrs upon the Jesuits* achieved renown in 1679, two years before *Absalom*.

[9] **Nisus**
In the fifth book of Virgil's *Aeneid*, Nisus is the athlete who outstrips his opponents at the beginning of a race, only to lose his lead when he slips in a pool of blood from an earlier sacrifice. Here, Dryden is Nisus, the early starter but eventual loser (to Oldham). The comparison elevates the metaphorical race between the two writers to the level of a race between epic heroes; *slippery place* the pool of blood.

[10] **young friend**
Oldham. The comparison with the race in the *Aeneid* is not exact, for there the race is won by Nisus's friend, Euryalus, only after he (Nisus)

has tripped the other main contender, Salius.

[11] **early ripe**
another address by epithet – see note to line 1. Oldham was 'early ripe' because he had achieved some fame in his twenties.

[13] **It ... nature**
i.e. it (age) might have taught that which nature never gives the young.

[14] **numbers**
metres, correct versification – suggesting that Oldham, though gifted, lacked polish.

[15] **satire needs not**
Dryden draws upon the idea, common since the late sixteenth century, that satire is a rude, violent genre, for which correctness and polish are not suited; *those* i.e. numbers, smoothness.

[16] **harsh ... line**
Though an apt description of one conception of satire, this does not fit Dryden's own in *Absalom*.

[17] **noble error**
i.e the ruggedness referred to in the last line and the force in the next.

[18] **When**
used in the sense of 'that'. The line describes the nature of the 'noble error' of the previous line – i.e. it is in some way noble to be led astray ('betrayed') by an excess of poetic power ('too much force').

[19] **ere**
before; *fruits* continuing the metaphor of line 11; *prime* best.

[20] **quickness**
life, vigour, briskness.

[21] **But**
only; *mellows* of fruit (as here) ripens, produces softness and sweetness; *dull sweets ... rhyme* still exploiting the metaphor of ripening fruit. The word 'dull' implies that more polished poetry from a more mature Oldham would not have been as exciting as his crude but lively, youthful work.

[22] **hail**
greetings. The coupling of this word with 'farewell' reemphasises the brevity of the acquaintance between Dryden and Oldham.

[23] **Marcellus**
nephew of Augustus (Virgil's emperor) and a young man of great promise who, like Oldham, died before that promise could be fulfilled. A famous passage celebrating him in the sixth book of the *Aeneid* is supposed, when recited, to have moved his mother so much that she fainted.

[24] **ivy...laurel**
Ivy and laurel, sacred to Bacchus and Apollo respectively, made, when woven together, the crown of the poet. Compare the opening of Milton's *Lycidas*, in which he announces his return to poetry: 'Yet once more, O ye laurels, and once more/ Ye myrtles brown, with ivy never sere.'

―――――◇―――――

5 /   *Alexander's Feast: or The Power of Music*
An Ode in Honour of St Cecilia's Day

I

'Twas at the royal feast, for Persia won
    By Philip's warlike son:
   Aloft in awful state
   The god-like hero sat
    On his imperial throne.   5
His valiant peers were placed around,
Their brows with roses and with myrtles bound
  (So should desert in arms be crowned).
The lovely Thais by his side,
Sat like a blooming Eastern bride   10
In flower of youth and beauty's pride.
    Happy, happy, happy pair!
   None but the brave
   None but the brave
   None but the brave deserves the fair.   15

CHORUS

Happy, happy, happy pair!
None but the brave
None but the brave
None but the brave deserves the fair.

II

Timotheus placed on high   20
  Amid the tuneful choir,
  With flying fingers touched the lyre.
The trembling notes ascend the sky,
    And heavenly joys inspire.
The song began from Jove,   25
Who left his blissful seat above,
(Such is the power of mighty love)
A dragon's fiery form belied the god.
Sublime on radiant spires he rode,
  When he to fair Olympia pressed,   30
  And while he sought her snowy breast.
Then, round her slender waist he curled,
And stamped an image of himself, a sovereign of the world.
The listening crowd admire the lofty sound,
'A present deity,' they shout around.   35
'A present deity,' the vaulted roofs rebound.
    With ravished ears
    The monarch hears,
    Assumes the god,
    Affects to nod,   40
  And seems to shake the spheres.

CHORUS

    With ravished ears
    The monarch hears,
    Assumes the god,
    Affects to nod,   45
  And seems to shake the spheres.

III

The praise of Bacchus then the sweet musician sung,
  Of Bacchus ever fair and ever young.
    The jolly god in triumph comes!
    Sound the trumpets, beat the drums!   50
      Flushed with a purple grace
      He shows his honest face,
Now give the hautboys breath; he comes, he comes!

Bacchus, ever fair and young,
   Drinking joys did first ordain, 55
Bacchus' blessings are a treasure,
Drinking is the soldier's pleasure.
     Rich the treasure,
     Sweet the pleasure;
   Sweet is pleasure after pain. 60

CHORUS

Bacchus' blessings are a treasure,
Drinking is the soldier's pleasure.
     Rich the treasure,
     Sweet the pleasure;
   Sweet is pleasure after pain. 65

IV

Soothed with the sound the King grew vain,
   Fought all his battles o'er again;
And thrice he routed all his foes, and thrice he slew the slain.
     The master saw the madness rise,
     His glowing cheeks, his ardent eyes; 70
     And while he heaven and earth defied,
     Changed his hand, and checked his pride.
       He chose a mournful muse
       Soft pity to infuse.
     He sang Darius great and good, 75
       By too severe a fate,
   Fallen, fallen, fallen, fallen,
     Fallen from his high estate
       And weltering in his blood;
   Deserted at his utmost need 80
By those his former bounty fed.
On the bare earth exposed he lies,
With not a friend to close his eyes.

With downcast looks the joyless victor sat,
   Revolving in his altered soul 85
     The various turns of chance below,
And, now and then, a sigh he stole,
     And tears began to flow.

CHORUS

Revolving in his altered soul
  The various turns of chance below,   90
And, now and then, a sigh he stole,
  And tears began to flow.

V

The mighty master smiled to see
That love was in the next degree.
'Twas but a kindred sound to move,   95
For pity melts the mind to love.
  Softly sweet, in Lydian measures
  Soon he soothed his soul to pleasures.
  'War', he sung, 'is toil and trouble,
  Honour but an empty bubble.   100
    Never ending, still beginning,
  Fighting still, and still destroying.
    If the world be worth the winning,
  Think, O think, it worth enjoying.
    Lovely Thais sits beside thee,   105
    Take the good the gods provide thee.'

The many rend the skies with loud applause.
So Love was crowned, but Music won the cause.
  The prince, unable to conceal his pain,
      Gazed on the fair   110
      Who caused his care,
  And sighed and looked, sighed and looked,
  Sighed and looked, and sighed again.
At length, with love and wine at once oppressed,
The vanquished victor sunk upon her breast.   115

CHORUS

The prince, unable to conceal his pain,
      Gazed on the fair
      Who caused his care,
  And sighed and looked, sighed and looked,
Sighed and looked, and sighed again.   120
At length, with love and wine at once oppressed,
The vanquished victor sunk upon her breast.

VI

Now strike the golden lyre again,
A louder yet, and yet a louder strain.
Break his bands of sleep asunder, 125
And rouse him, like a rattling peal of thunder.
   Hark, hark, the horrid sound
    Has raised up his head,
    As awaked from the dead,
   And amazed he stares around. 130
'Revenge, revenge!' Timotheus cries,
  'See the Furies arise!
  See the snakes that they rear,
  How they hiss in their hair,
 And the sparkles that flash from their eyes! 135
  Behold a ghastly band,
  Each a torch in his hand!
Those are Grecian ghosts that in battle were slain,
     And unburied remain
     Inglorious on the plain. 140
   Give the vengeance due
   To the valiant crew.
Behold how they toss their torches on high,
   How they point to the Persian abodes,
And glittering temples of their hostile gods!' 145
The princes applaud with a furious joy,
And the king seized a flambeau, with zeal to destroy.
   Thais led the way
   To light him to his prey,
And, like another Helen, fired another Troy. 150

CHORUS

And the king seized a flambeau, with zeal to destroy.
   Thais led the way
   To light him to his prey,
And, like another Helen, fired another Troy.

VII

 Thus, long ago, 155
Ere heaving bellows learned to blow,
 While organs yet were mute;

Timotheus, to his breathing flute
    And sounding lyre,
Could swell the soul to rage, or kindle soft desire.   160
    At last divine Cecilia came,
    Inventress of the vocal frame,
The sweet enthusiast, from her sacred store,
    Enlarged the former narrow bounds,
    And added length to solemn sounds,   165
With nature's mother wit, and arts unknown before.
    Let old Timotheus yield the prize,
    Or both divide the crown.
    He raised a mortal to the skies,
    She drew an angel down.   170

GRAND CHORUS

At last divine Cecilia came,
Inventress of the vocal frame,
The sweet enthusiast, from her sacred store,
    Enlarged the former narrow bounds,
    And added length to solemn sounds,   175
With nature's mother wit, and arts unknown before.
    Let old Timotheus yield the prize,
    Or both divide the crown.
    He raised a mortal to the skies,
    She drew an angel down.

Alexander's Feast was commissioned in 1697 for a musical entertainment held by a society of musicians on St Cecilia's Day (22 November). She is the patron saint of music and musicians. The concert series had begun in 1683 and Dryden had contributed *A Song for St Cecilia's Day* in 1687.

The poem, set to music by Jeremiah Clarke, won great public acclaim, and Dryden himself admitted he thought it 'the best of all my poetry'. Though Clarke's music is lost, *Alexander's Feast* is still performed today to the later setting by Handel.

Alexander's Feast is an ode, that is, a serious poem, written in an elevated style and using complex stanzas. The classical, Pindaric, ode arranges its stanzas in groups of three, with the same form being repeated for the first, second and third of the stanzas in each group throughout the poem. *Alexander's Feast*, however, is an irregular ode, a form introduced by Abraham Cowley (1618–67), in which each stanza is formed to fit its particular subject.

The complex stanzas allow Dryden to vary line lengths and metres' and to display considerable virtuosity in matching the style to the subject. Thus, although the dominant metre is iambic (-/ -/ or dedum dedum), he introduces other rhythms to capture other moods. For example, the approach of Bacchus is announced with the line (line 50): 'Sound the trumpets, beat the drums' (/ -/- / -/ or dum dedumde – dum dedum). And a song of revenge is heralded with (line 127): 'Hark, hark, the horrid sound' (/ / -/- / or dum dum dedumde dum). More generally, one of the strengths of the poem is the way in which sound is made to be the echo of sense. A final example might be the gentle lines which introduce a song of love (lines 97–8): 'Softly sweet, in Lydian measures,/ Soon he soothed his soul to pleasures.'

Dryden announces the subject in the second title, the power of music. He imagines a victory feast at which the musician Timotheus moulds the moods of his hearers by varying the kinds of music he sings. The climax of the poem comes when the music drives the victorious army to fire the defeated city of Persepolis (lines 131–50).

Title

Alexander's Feast Alexander III of Macedonia, known as Alexander the Great. The feast is a victory celebration; *Ode* see the introductory notes; *St Cecilia's Day* see the introductory notes.

[1] **'Twas at**
it was at, i.e. that which is going to be described took place at; *for Persia won* the occasion of the feast was the capture of the Persian capital, Persepolis. However, the poem is not precise in its historical references, for Darius, whose death Timotheus sings (lines 75–82), survived the fall of the city. More importantly, it was the courtesan, Thais (see line 9), and not the power of music which drove Alexander to ignite the city.

[2] **Philip's warlike son**
Alexander was son of Philip II and Olympias of Epirus.

[3] **Aloft**
i.e. sitting on a raised throne; *awful* inspiring awe.

[4] **god-like**
Rumours of Alexander's divine nature existed during his lifetime and were apparently encouraged by him. Arrian, among others, records the occasion on which he visited the oracle of Zeus in Libya specifically in order to ask whether that god was his father (*Life of Alexander*, bk 4). On receiving a positive answer he thereafter 'not only allowed himself to be called the son of Jupiter [Zeus] but commanded it' (Quintus Curtius, *History of Alexander*, bk 4). A slightly different view of Alexander is given by Plutarch in his *Life*: he argues that although he may have exploited rumours of divinity, he was never foolish enough to believe them himself; *sat* pronounced 'sate' and a true rhyme with 'state'.

[5] **imperial**
because he has conquered the Persian empire.

[6] **peers**
men of high rank (rather than equals). Alexander did not admit other men to be his equals; in a letter to Darius he commands, 'do not write to me as an equal' (*Arrian*, bk 2).

[7] **roses . . . myrtles**
plants sacred to Venus (in Greek, Aphrodite), the goddess of love. According to classical sources, women were present at Alexander's feasts: 'he took part in long banquets there were women . . . for whores lived licentiously with soldiers' (Quintus Curtius, *History*, bk 5).

[8] **desert in arms**
military excellence.

[9] **Thais**
a courtesan from Athens who had followed Alexander's army in its victorious journey from Greece across Asia. She is described by Quintus Curtius as a 'drunken strumpet' (bk 5), and by Plutarch as 'mistress of Ptolemy'.

[10] **Eastern bride**
After the sack of the city, Thais is dressed in the stolen clothes of the vanquished Persians. Since ancient Persian dress was famed for its

sumptuousness, the image of the orientally attired Thais adds to the splendour of the feast.

[11] **flower**
picking up the metaphorical 'blooming' of the previous line.

[15] **None but ... fair**
This epigrammatic statement, though it seems proverbial, is not.

[16] **chorus**
Since Timotheus, the minstrel at the feast (line 20), bears the fame of having invented choral music, it is appropriate that this ode should have a chorus.

[20] **Timotheus**
poet of Macedonia (Alexander's homeland), reputed inventor of choral music, and imagined here as the conqueror's master of music.

[22] **lyre**
a stringed instrument, like a small harp – the traditional instrument of the Greek poet/singer.

[23] **ascend the sky**
rise into the sky.

[24] **inspire**
excite, animate (i.e. in the hearers).

[25] **began**
used here to mean that the song concerned Jove; *Jove* Zeus or Jupiter, the chief god in the Greek and Roman pantheon.

[26] **seat**
throne; *above* the classical gods were thought to reside on Olympus, a name which referred originally to a Greek mountain but which gradually took on the more general meaning of a heavenly dwelling place.

[27] **love**
i.e. the love felt by Jove/Zeus for Olympias.

[28] **dragon's fiery form**
Plutarch records that a serpent found lying by Alexander's mother Olympias as she slept was interpreted as a sign she had slept with a god. Dryden transforms the serpent into a dragon; *belied* disguised.

[29] **Sublime**
aloft, proud; *radiant spires* The phrase describes the beams of light

surrounding the flying god, and evokes the pictures of the crowded, light-filled heavens of the decorative art of the period. The most famous example in England of this kind of large-scale baroque production was (and is) the ceiling of the Banqueting House, Whitehall, painted by Peter Paul Rubens (1577–1640). From the early 1670s onwards, a number of country houses were also being fitted with painted rooms and ceilings.

[30] **Olympia**
Olympias, mother of Alexander; *pressed* suggesting sexual union.

[31] **snowy**
conventional epithet for a beautiful breast.

[32] **curled**
recalling the serpent-form of Zeus (see note to line 28).

[33] **stamped an image of himself**
The metaphor is from coining. Zeus stamps his image when he presses against Olympias, just as the coiner stamps an image in a coin; *a sovereign of the world* Alexander is like his father Zeus in that both are kings.

[34] **listening crowd**
the scene shifts back to the feast.

[35] **present deity**
i.e. Alexander.

[36] **rebound**
The echoing shout of the adoring crowd is a motif of heroic poetry, which Dryden uses mockingly in *Macflecknoe*. The dunce poet Fleckno imagines the triumphant coronation of his dunce son Shadwell: 'Echoes from Pissing-Alley, "Shadwell" call,/ And "Shadwell" they resound from Aston Hall' (line 47–8).

[37] **ravished**
entranced, enraptured.

[39] **assumes**
takes upon himself (the character of) the god. This is another instance of Dryden's freedom with his historical sources since Alexander 'assumed' godhead at his visit to the Libyan shrine (note to line 4), before the feast at Persepolis.

[40] **affects**
performs the action pretentiously.

[41] **seems**
The word is carefully included to remind us that Alexander, in fact, did not possess divine power; *spheres* the huge crystal globes which, according to the old astronomy (already obsolete in Dryden's time), rotated round the world carrying on them the sun and the stars (compare *Rape of the Lock*, i, 107); *shake the spheres* The image continues the comparison of Alexander with Zeus, since as the god of the heavens, Zeus was responsible for all celestial manifestations of this kind.

[47] **praise of Bacchus**
the first of the changes in musical mood which evidences the power of music; *Bacchus* (in Greek, Dionysius) god of wine and mystic ecstasy.

[48] **ever fair ... young**
Bacchus is conventionally represented in pictures as a young god.

[49] **jolly**
convivial, festive; *in triumph* Bacchus's victorious campaign in India led to the founding of the triumphal procession which usually accompanies him in legend and picture. The god himself rides a chariot drawn by panthers, and he is surrounded by satyrs and worshippers. As with the image of the flying Jove (line 29 and note), Dryden's description here owes much to contemporary painting.

[50] **trumpets ... drums**
played by the revellers in the triumphant procession.

[51] **purple**
used in the Latinate sense of 'bright'; *grace* attractiveness, charm. The word, applied as it is here to a drunken flush, is probably ironic.

[52] **honest**
honourable, respectable, virtuous (ironic).

[53] **hautboys**
oboes; *give ... breath* blow.

[55] **first ordain**
According to the legend, Bacchus became the god of wine, because he discovered it.

[67] **Fought ... o'er again**
i.e. the song led him to relive his battles in memory.

[68] **thrice**
The description of an action as performed three times is characteristic of heroic poetry (compare *Rape of the Lock*, i, 17).

[69] **master**
Timotheus. He is a master both of song and, as the poem demonstrates, of this situation through the power of song.

[70] **His**
i.e. Alexander's; *ardent* literally, red-hot, burning; *glowing cheeks ... ardent eyes* features characteristic of one excited either by battle or by drink.

[71] **he**
still Alexander.

[72] **Changes his hand**
the subject is Timotheus. The sense is that he changes the way that he plays; *his pride* Alexander's.

[73] **muse**
literally one of the nine sister goddesses of the arts (see *Rape of the Lock*, i, 3 and note), used here to denote the style of song Timotheus elects to play.

[75] **Darius**
Darius III, King of Persia, Alexander's defeated enemy; *great and good* Dryden confers these characteristics upon Darius in order to heighten the poem. Arrian writes of a weak and incompetent soldier, though someone decent enough in other ways (*Life of Alexander*, bk 3).

[77] **Fallen**
In fact he fell after the sack of Persepolis – see note to line 1.

[78] **estate**
position, status.

[79] **weltering**
rolling, twisting, writhing.

[80] **Deserted**
He ended his life by being stabbed and abandoned by his own followers.

[82] **exposed**
in the sense of shown up, his true nature laid bare.

[84] **downcast looks**
Alexander has suffered a swift change
of mood from line 70. Plutarch
describes Alexander displaying
sorrow at the sight of the body of his
former rival.

[85] **Revolving**
turning over in the mind.

[86] **turns of chance**
the uncertainty of fortune is a standard theme of poetry; *below* on earth.

[87] **stole**
breathed.

[93] **mighty**
The word is used as more than a filler
epithet, since it refers to Timotheus's
power, the subject of the whole poem;
master Timotheus again.

[94] **degree**
position in a scale of rank, or here a
scale of feeling.

[95] **but**
only; *kindred* i.e. the sound of love is
close to that of mourning which
Timotheus has just uttered.

[97] **Lydian**
a type of ancient Greek music, soft in
character; *measures* rhythms, tunes.

[99] **toil and trouble**
part of the opening incantation of the
witches at the beginning of *Macbeth*,
'Hubble, bubble, toil and trouble'.

[100] **Honour**
referring particularly to the soldier's
honour; *bubble* commonly used
figuratively to denote something
insubstantial and worthless.

[105] **Thais**
see note to line 9.

[107] **The many**
i.e. the assembled crowd.

[108] **crowned**
The applause is figuratively the same
as the giving of a victor's crown in that
it recognises the supremacy of love;
Music...cause Though love is recognised by the applause, it is really
music which won the recognition.

[109] **prince**
used generally for someone of power
and authority – here, of course,
Alexander; *pain* The pleasurable pain
of love is a commonplace of poetry.

[110] **fair**
the beautiful woman, i.e. Thais.

[111] **care**
mental suffering, the pain referred to
in line 109.

[114] **oppressed**
with the sense of being beaten in
battle.

[115] **vanquished victor**
A neat paradox, which conveys
Alexander's position not only now but
throughout the feast as he is overcome
by music.

[123] **strike**
The verb is put in the imperative
mood as befits the new mood of poem
and music.

[125] **bands**
restraints, chains, shackles, fetters;
sleep Alexander nodded off at the end
of the last section.

[130] **amazed**
astounded, greatly astonished, with a
stronger weight than in current usage.

[132] **Furies**
The Roman Furies are identified with
the Greek Erinyes, violent goddesses
with snakes in their hair and whips in
their hands who pursued victims in
order to send them mad. Their special
function was to avenge crime; hence
their association with revenge here.
There is also a hint at the role of Thais
in suggesting the burning – see note
to line 1.

[133] **snakes**
those that live in the Furies' hair – see
previous note; *rear* breed, raise.

[136] **ghastly band**
In Timotheus's imagination the furies
are accompanied by a crowd of
unburied ghosts.

[139] **Unburied**
According to Greek belief, the burial
rites opened the gates of Hades (the
underworld) for the dead, and made
possible their departure from this
world.

[140] **Inglorious**
in that they have been denied the
proper honours of burial rites.

[142] **valiant crew**
i.e. the dead Greek heroes.

[144] **Persian abodes**
the houses of Persepolis – see note to line 1.
[145] **their**
the Persian; *hostile gods* The gods of Persia, envisaged as in enmity to the gods of Greece.
[146] **princes**
the assembled chiefs.
[147] **flambeau**
torch.
[148] **Thais led**
as in the historical record – see note to line 1.
[150] **Helen**
Helen, the wife of the Greek king Menelaus, was abducted by the Trojan, Paris, a theft which led to the siege of Troy. Her legend is that of the beautiful but dangerous woman; *fired another Troy* The firing of Troy by the victorious Greeks may be regarded as Helen's responsibility, since she was the ultimate cause of the war.
[156] **heaving bellows**
i.e. those which provide the wind for organs.
[157] **organs**
see line 161 and note.
[158] **breathing**
speaking, uttering, as well as exhaling.
[159] **sounding**
conveying ideas and impressions, as well as making noise.
[161] **divine Cecilia**
a Roman virgin martyr of the third century. It was very late (in the sixteenth century) that she was

associated with the invention of the organ and became the patron saint of music.
[162] **vocal frame**
the organ.
[163] **enthusiast**
one possessed by a god; one who receives divine communications; negatively (not implied here) a religious fanatic.
[165] **added length**
in that the organ notes can be sustained by the working of the bellows.
[166] **mother wit**
common sense, inborn practical intelligence; *arts* skills, techniques.
[167] **yield the prize**
i.e. give up the claim to be the greatest musician.
[168] **crown**
the laurel crown of the victor, the prize referred to in the previous line.
[169] **raised a mortal to the skies**
The line refers to music's power to make Alexander appear like a god – see lines 25–36.
[170] **drew an angel down**
In *A Song for St Cecilia's Day* (1687), Dryden includes a reference to the appearance of an angel at Cecilia's invention of the organ – hearing the music, the angel had mistaken earth for heaven (lines 52–4). This may be a distortion of an older part of her legend; married against her will to a pagan, Valerian (later converted), she was protected on her wedding night by an angel.

MATTHEW PRIOR

(1664–1721)

Prior's life included a distinguished career as a diplomat, the crowning achievement of which was the negotiation of the Treaty of Utrecht (1713). Upon the death of Queen Anne (1714), however, he was suspected of Jacobitism (see general introduction), placed under house arrest and investigated. Although he was eventually released, it was to a life without position or influence. He attempted to mend his situation by publishing his *Poems on Several Occasions* (1718), from the subscription sale of which (see general introduction) he earned the princely sum of 4,000 guineas.

Further Reading

The standard edition of Prior's works is the two-volume H. Bunker Wright and Monroe K. Spears (eds), *The Literary Works of Matthew Prior* (Oxford: Clarendon Press, 1959).

Charles Kenneth Eves' *Matthew Prior, Poet and Diplomatist* (New York: Columbia University Press, 1939) is a reasonable biography. Like many other minor poets of the eighteenth century, Prior has been comparatively neglected by critics. One general introductory book is of use: Frances Mayhew Rippy, *Matthew Prior* (Boston, Mass.: Twayne, 1986).

6/ ## To a Child of Quality, Five Years Old, The Author Forty

Lords, knights, and squires, the numerous band
   That wear the fair Miss Mary's fetters,
Were summoned by her high command,
   To show their passions by their letters.

My pen amongst the rest I took,   5
   Lest those bright eyes that cannot read
Should dart their kindling fires, and look
   The power they have to be obeyed.

Nor quality nor reputation
   Forbid me yet my flame to tell.   10
Dear five years old befriends my passion,
   And I may write till she can spell.

For while she makes her silkworms beds
   With all the tender things I swear,
Whilst all the house my passion reads   15
   In papers round her baby's hair,

She may receive and own my flame,
   For though the strictest prudes should know it,
She'll pass for a most virtuous dame,
   And I for an unhappy poet.   20

Then too, alas, when she shall tear
   The lines some younger rival sends,
She'll give me leave to write, I fear,
   And we shall still continue friends;

For, as our different ages move,   25
   'Tis so ordained (would fate but mend it!)
That I shall be past making love
   When she begins to comprehend it.

To a Child of Quality (1704) belongs in no strictly defined genre. There are examples of seventeenth-century poems about children, of which perhaps the most famous is Andrew Marvell's *A Picture of Little T.C. in a Prospect of Flowers.*

But *A Child of Quality* is probably best considered simply as occasional verse. It is a poem written in the first place for the amusement of its intended recipient and her family circle. Among the poets of this anthology, it is Swift (along with Prior) who wrote most often in this way.

The poem is written in iambic tetrameters, lines of four iambic feet (dedumdedumdedumdedum). It is arranged in stanzas of four lines with alternate lines rhyming. This is a common form for a song.

Title
child Lady Mary Villiers, daughter of the first Earl of Jersey; *quality* refers to the child's rank rather than to intrinsic worth.

[1] **Lords, knights and squires**
Her admirers are properly grouped in descending order of rank. The listing of these important men is a heightening device, which is ironically inappropriate for the little girl. The exploitation of such devices links the poem to the mock-heroic – it might be called 'mock-amorous'. Its general tenor, however, is more affectionate than most mock-heroic poems.

[2] **fetters**
bonds, shackles. The word is a conventional metaphor for the bondage of men in love with a woman – part of the mock-amorous structure.

[3] **summoned ... high command**
more ironic heightening of tone.

[4] **letters**
writing, literature; also, in the context of childhood, the alphabet that must be learnt.

[6] **bright eyes**
a conventional attribute of beauty; compare Montagu's *Saturday: The Small-Pox*, line 12; *cannot read* a humorous deflation of the earlier praise of her eyes.

[7] **dart ... fires**
conventional again – compare the lightnings of Belinda's eyes, *Rape of the Lock*, i, 144.

[9] **Nor ... nor**
neither ... nor; *quality* rank; *reputation* i.e. the kind of reputation for purity of life that might, with an adult woman, prevent a male poet from proclaiming his love for her.

[10] **flame**
love; a conventional poetic metaphor.

[12] **may write ... spell**
The sense is that once Mary is sufficiently adult to be able to spell, propriety will demand that Prior stop writing love verses to her. There may also be a hint at the stock joke about female spelling: see Swift's *Verses Wrote in a Lady's Ivory Table-Book* where the lady is represented as spelling 'for an ell breadth' as 'far an el breth' (line 10).

[13–15] **For while ... Whilst**
Two subordinate clauses, with the second repeating the structure of the first, represent another heightening device.

[13] **silkworms beds**
Mary uses the paper of Prior's poems as litter for the beds of her pet silkworms.

[14] **all ... swear**
i.e. his poetic professions of love; by transference, the paper on which they are written.

[16] **papers**
used for curling hair. It was a stock satirical joke that the works of bad poets ended up as curlers, pie-cases or toilet paper. Here, Prior turns the joke against himself; *baby's* doll's.

[17] **own**
admit.

[18] **prudes**
regarded in society as the bearers of gossip, but in this case, the relationship is such that no gossip can harm it.

[19] **virtuous dame**
ironically inappropriate phrase for a 5-year-old.

[20] **unhappy**
a conventional state for the lovelorn poet.

[21] **when ... tear**
looking ahead to the time when Mary,

as a young woman, will respond with appropriate understanding and scorn to proposals of love.

[22] **younger rival**
The rival of the future, a young man, when Prior will be approaching old age.

[23] **leave...I fear**
The permission to write is (according to the decorum of the age) a sign that Prior can at his advanced age have no pretence to be a lover.

[24] **continue friends**
i.e. friends and not lovers.

[28] **comprehend it**
as shown by her tearing of the letter of the 'younger rival' (line 22).

---

7 | *A Better Answer – To Chloe Jealous*

Dear Chloe, how blubbered is that pretty face!
　Thy cheek all on fire, and thy hair all uncurled!
Prithee quit this caprice, and (as old Falstaff says)
　Let us e'en talk a little like folks of this world.

How canst thou presume thou hast leave to destroy　　5
　The beauties which Venus but lent to thy keeping?
Those looks were designed to inspire love and joy.
　More ordinary eyes may serve people for weeping.

To be vexed at a trifle or two that I writ,
　Your judgement at once and my passion you wrong.　10
You take that for fact which will scarce be found wit –
　Od's life! Must one swear to the truth of a song?

What I speak, my fair Chloe, and what I write, shows
　The difference there is betwixt nature and art;
I court others in verse, but I love thee in prose;　　15
　And they have my whimsies, but thou hast my heart.

The god of us verse-men (you know, child) the sun,
　How after his journeys he sets up his rest;
If at morning o'er earth 'tis his fancy to run,
　At night he reclines on his Thetis's breast.　　20

So when I am wearied with wandering all day,
    To thee, my delight, in the evening I come;
No matter what beauties I saw in my way –
    They were but my visits, but thou art my home.

Then finish, dear Chloe, this pastoral war;   25
    And let us like Horace and Lydia agree:
For thou art a girl as much brighter than her,
    As he was a poet sublimer than me.

A Better Answer (publ. 1718) is a love lyric aimed at the reconciliation of a jealous
mistress. The poem closest to it in subject in this volume is Rochester's 'Absent
from thee'.
    The poem is unusual in that it does not follow any strict syllable/stress metre.
Its metrical principle is, like that of much medieval poetry, based upon the
number of stresses in each line. Here there are (again as in much medieval
poetry) four stresses in each line, and a pause somewhere in the middle:
    Prithee quit this caprice // and (as old Falstaff says)
    (--/-/- ---/-/) or (dededumdedumde dedededumdedum)
    Let us e'en talk a little // like folks of the world.
    (---/-/- -/-/) or (dedededumdedumde dedumdededum)
Prior's handling, however, does not admit as much variation in line length as
this form allows. Underlying the poem (though by no means consistent
throughout) is an anapestic rhythm, that is, two unstressed syllables followed
by a stressed syllable (dededum):
    To be vexed at a trifle or two that I writ
    (--/ --/ --/ --/) or (dededum dededum dededum dededum)

Title
Chloe a conventional, poetic name for
a mistress. Here, it is especially
appropriate as that is the name of the
rival in the debate between the poet
and his mistress, Lydia, in Horace's
Ode, III, ix, which is alluded to in the
final stanza. It is impossible to tell
from the poem whether or not Prior
was addressing a real woman.
[1] blubbered
swollen; disfigured by weeping.
[2] uncurled
The gravity of such a condition for an
eighteenth-century woman is evident
in the consequences which follow upon
the loss of a curl in *The Rape of the Lock*.
[3] caprice
whim, sudden change of mind or
mood; *old Falstaff* Sir John Falstaff

is the fat, dissolute knight who is companion to Prince Hal in Shakespeare's
two Henry IV plays. 'Old' is used
both to denote his age and as an
adjective of affection.
[4] e'en
even; *like folks of this world* in *Henry
IV, Part Two*, Falstaff bids Pistol deliver
his news (that Prince Hal is now
become Henry V) 'like a man of this
world' (V,iii,96). The allusion is rather
an odd one in the context of a poem of
reconciliation. When he hears of his
friend's coronation, Falstaff promises
himself great things. However, his
only rewards for having formerly been
friend (and bad influence) to the new
king are to be banished his presence
upon pain of death and committed to
prison.

[6] **Venus**
the goddess of love; *but lent* only lent.
The idea of physical beauty as a loan
from Venus is a witty distortion of the
Christian idea that innate capacities
are loans from God to be put to proper
use. The idea goes back to the parable
of the talents, in which the servant
who receives one coin from his master
and promptly buries it is rebuked for
making no better use of the loan
(Matthew 25: 14–30). The modern use
of the word 'talent' to mean 'skill'
derives from the parable.

[10] **at once**
simultaneously.

[11] **scarce . . . wit**
a modest disclaimer of his own poetic
talent.

[12] **Od's life**
God's life; an oath; *swear . . . song*
The rhetorical question may have the
force of undermining rather than
strengthening his argument. If songs
are not to be accounted for, why
should this one be believed?

[16] **whimsies**
i.e. his poems.

[17] **god . . . sun**
Phoebus Apollo, the god of poetry
and music, is sometimes also regarded
as the god of the sun.

[18] **journeys**
the daily chariot ride of the sun across
the heavens from east to west.

[19] **o'er earth**
Apollo's heavenly journey above the
earth. There is also a reference to the
speaker indulging his fancy by court-
ing earthly beauties with his poems.

[20] **Thetis**
a sea-nymph, one of the daughters of
the Old Man of the Sea. Apollo rests
on her breast at night because the sun
sinks into the western sea.

[21] **So**
Prior begins to apply the Apollo
comparison.

[25] **pastoral war**
One form of pastoral poetry (see
introductory notes to *Saturday: The
Smallpox*) was the debate between
rival shepherd lovers. Prior here compares the debate between estranged
lover and mistress in Horace's *Ode*
(see subsequent note) with the
debates of pastoral poetry.

[26] **Horace and Lydia**
Horace is Quintus Horatius Flaccus,
the contemporary of Virgil, and famed
writer of satires, epistles and odes.
The ninth poem of his third book of
odes is an argument between the
speaker and Lydia, in which both
speak jealously of the new loves of the
other, before reaching a reconciliation
in the last two stanzas.

[27] **brighter . . . her**
i.e. brighter than Lydia. The compliment is rather conventional as Horace
does not remark upon Lydia's outstanding qualities in his poem. She is,
in fact, 'less stable than the stars'.

[28] **sublimer**
'Sublimity', the expression of lofty
ideas in elevated language, is a quality
more normally associated with Homer
than with Horace. Prior appears to be
using the word loosely.

ISAAC WATTS

(1674–1748)

◇

Isaac Watts, after being educated at the Dissenting Academy in Stoke Newington, became minister of Mark Lane Independent Chapel in 1702. An intended short visit in 1712 to Sir Thomas Abney of Hertfordshire for reasons of health was prolonged for the rest of his life. Watts is remembered today chiefly for his hymns, and is regarded of as the father of the English hymn. In *The Day of Judgement*, however, we see him attempting to follow (to adapt the title of another poem) his adventurous muse.

Further Reading

Although there is no modern edition of Watts' poems, there is a six-volume reprint of the eighteenth-century *The Works of the Reverend and Learned Isaac Watts* (New York: AMS Press, 1971). Interested readers without access to a good academic library might find it easier to look in anthologies. Perhaps the most readily available is Roger Lonsdale's *The New Oxford Book of Eighteenth-Century Verse* (Oxford: Oxford University Press, 1987), which reproduces ten poems by Watts.

A biography is available in Arthur Paul Davis, *Isaac Watts, His Life and Works* (New York: Dryden Press, 1943). Two recent books which contain critical material are: Madeleine Marshall Forell and Janet Todd, *English Congregational Hymns in the Eighteenth Century* (Lexington: University of Kentucky Press, 1982) and Donald Davie, *Dissentient Voice: Enlightenment and Christian Dissent* (Notre Dame: University Press of Notre Dame, 1982).

———◇———

8 / The Day of Judgement
An Ode

Attempted in English Sapphic

When the fierce north wind with his airy forces
Rears up the Baltic to a foaming fury,
And the red lightning with a storm of hail comes
    Rushing amain down,

How the poor sailors stand amazed and tremble!   5
While the hoarse thunder like a bloody trumpet
Roars a loud onset to the gaping waters
    Quick to devour them.

Such shall the noise be, and the wild disorder,
(If things eternal may be like these earthly)   10
Such the dire terror when the great archangel
    Shakes the creation,

Tears the strong pillars of the vault of heaven,
Breaks up old marble, the repose of princes.
See the graves open, and the bones arising,   15
    Flames all around 'em.

Hark the shrill outcries of the guilty wretches!
Lively bright horror and amazing anguish
Stare through their eyelids, while the living worm lies
    Gnawing within them.   20

Thoughts like old vultures prey upon their heartstrings,
And the smart twinges, when their eye beholds the
Lofty Judge frowning, and the flood of vengeance
    Rolling afore him.

Hopeless immortals! how they scream and shiver   25
While devils push them to the pit wide yawning
Hideous and gloomy, to receive them headlong
    Down to the centre.

Stop here, my fancy. (All away, ye horrid
Doleful ideas). Come, arise to Jesus, 30
How he sits god-like! And the saints around him
    Throned, yet adoring!

O may I sit there when he comes triumphant
Dooming the nations. Then ascend to glory,
While our hosannas all along the passage 35
    Shout the Redeemer.

Like *Alexander's Feast, The Day of Judgement* (1706) is an irregular ode in that it avoids any strict pattern of strophe, antistrophe and epode. Watts, however, does not like Dryden adapt the form of each stanza to its subject but uses throughout the same pattern – the sapphic (see below).

The poem is, as the title suggests, a 'last days' poem, that is, one which envisages the end of the world expected by all Christians. As such it has a long line of ancestors, including seventeenth-century religious lyrics by John Donne and George Herbert. The theme was to be given a new treatment later in the eighteenth century in Swift's hands. He imagines a Jove who when he sees humanity waiting for judgement dismisses them as beneath his notice.

The 'sapphic' is a stanza form written in a complex quantitative metre and adapted from the poetry of the Greek poetess, Sappho. Quantitative metres are based upon the length of syllables rather than upon stressed and unstressed syllables as most English metres are. Indeed, English is so strongly accentual a language that classical quantitative metres can only be adapted, not reproduced, in the language.

Sapphic stanzas consist of three lines of eleven syllables, followed by a line of five syllables. The eleven-syllable lines contain a trochee (long/short), a spondee (long/long), a dactyl (long/short/short), a trochee and a spondee. There is a pause (caesura) after the fifth syllable. The short line at the end of the stanza is an Adonic, that is, a dactyl (long/short/short) and a spondee (long/long).

Thus each verse runs (it is an idea to read out loud):
Lahlilahlahlah [pause] lililahlilahlah
Lahlilahlahlah [pause] lililahlilahlah
Lahlilahlahlah [pause] lililahlilahlah
    Lahlililahlah

English sapphics were attempted before Watts by some of the Elizabethan poets, among them Sir Philip Sidney:
If the spheres senseless do yet hold a music,
If the swan's sweet voice be not heard but at death,
If the mute timber when it hath the life lost
    Yieldeth a lute's tune.

Later, a number of Victorian poets made the same attempt, and below is part of Algernon Charles Swinburne's:
Faded all their crowns, but about her forehead,
Round her woven tresses and ashen temples
White as dead snow, paler than grass in summer,
Ravaged with kisses.

Title
Day of Judgement the end of the world as described by Jesus in the first three gospels (Matthew 24 & 25, Mark 13, Luke 21), by the writer of Revelation and by some of the prophets of the Old Testament. Watts assumes for himself some freedom in assembling details from different parts of the Bible in order to create an impressionistic picture of the confusion and terror that accompany the end; *Attempted* The word perhaps indicates the difficulty of the task of writing in sapphics.

[1] **north wind . . . airy forces**
The north wind is personified as a military god in charge of an army. The classical god of the north wind is Boreas. However, Watts is drawing more upon Christian and Judaic ideas of natural tumults at the end of the world and of the north as the place from which destruction comes. Jeremiah, the prophet of the fall of Jerusalem, exclaims: 'evil looms out of the north, and great destruction' (Jeremiah 6: 1). More specifically, the devil is traditionally associated with the north. In the passage of Isaiah from which he gets his name of Lucifer, the devil says in his heart: 'I will set my throne on high; I will sit on the mount of assembly in the far north' (Isaiah 14: 12–13). And in *Paradise Lost,* Satan retires to his possessions in the north in order to organise his rebellion (v, 755); *airy* 'Prince of air' is a title given to Satan in *Paradise Lost* (xii, 454). Milton derived the title from St Paul's phrase, the 'prince of the power of the air' (Ephesians 2: 2).

[2] **Baltic**
Although there is, of course, no mention of the Baltic Sea in biblical

accounts of the last days, the notion of a stormy northern sea fits with references to natural disasters. Jesus mentions 'the roaring of the sea and the waves' (Luke 21: 25) and predicts more generally: 'the sun will be darkened, and the moon will not give its light, and the stars will fall from heaven' (Matthew 24: 29). In the Old Testament, Zephaniah (among others) warns: 'the great day of the Lord is near . . . a day of wrath is that day . . . a day of darkness and gloom, a day of clouds and thick darkness' (Zephaniah 1: 14–15).

[3] **red lightning . . . hail**
In Revelation, one series of convulsions in nature begins with one of seven angels blowing a trumpet: 'and there followed hail and fire, mixed with blood, which fell on the earth' (Revelation 8: 7).

[4] **amain**
violently, at full speed.

[5] **poor sailors**
'Shipmasters and seafaring men' are described in Revelation as standing far off and crying as they witness the destruction of Babylon (Revelation 18: 17). Watts, however, is also referring more generally to biblical accounts of the terror aroused by the last days, of 'men fainting with fear and with foreboding of what is coming to the world' (Luke 21: 26), of the way that 'everyone, slave and free, hid in the caves and among the rocks of the mountains' (Revelation 6: 15).

[6] **hoarse thunder . . . bloody trumpet**
The sounds of both thunder and trumpets are described in Revelation as accompanying the various convulsions of the end. The adjective 'bloody' is applied to trumpets because seven trumpets are blown by seven angels, and the first six of these

bring plagues and death (Revelation 8: 7–19).

[7] **onset**
attack, assault; here, used to mean the trumpets' signal to attack; *gaping* broken apart by the winds.

[8] **Quick...them**
It is the thunder which is ready to devour the waters. At the blowing of the trumpet of the second angel, 'something like a great mountain, burning with fire, was thrown into the sea, and a third of the sea became blood' (Revelation 8: 8–9).

[10] **If things...earthly**
The problem of describing the spiritual in physical terms is raised by Milton's Raphael when he embarks upon his relation to Adam of the war in heaven: 'how shall I relate/ To human sense th'invisible exploits/ Of warring spirits...yet for thy good/ This is dispensed, and what surmounts the reach/ Of human sense, I shall delineate so/ By likening spiritual to corporal forms/ As may express them best' (*Paradise Lost*, v, 564–74).

[11] **great archangel**
Michael. The prophet Daniel speaks of Michael's role during the last days: 'at that time shall arise Michael, the great prince who has charge of your people...and many of those who sleep in the dust of the earth shall awake' (Daniel 12: 1–2). The archangel is also named in Revelation: 'Now war arose in heaven, Michael and his angels fighting against the dragon' (Revelation 12: 7).

[12] **Shakes...creation**
The opening of the sixth seal in Revelation shows 'a great earthquake' (Revelation 6: 12) and Jesus foretells that the 'powers of heaven will be shaken' (Matthew 24: 29, Mark 13: 25 & Luke 21: 26).

[13] **Tears...pillars**
The metaphor refers to Samson, who, blinded and shackled by his enemies the Philistines, is brought into their feast to be mocked. Placed between the supporting pillars of the building, Samson grasps them, and wreaks

vengeance on his captors by bringing the building down on top of them (Judges 16: 23–31). Like the roof of the Philistines' hall, the stars of the sky are destined to fall at the end of the world (Matthew 24: 29 & Revelation 6: 13); *vault* arched roof.

[14] **Breaks...marble**
Both the destruction of the Philistines' hall and the general destruction of buildings during the last days; *repose* Sleep is a common biblical metaphor for death. Before raising the dead Lazarus, Jesus says: 'our friend Lazarus is fallen asleep, but I go to awake him out of sleep' (John 11: 11); *princes* men of authority. In Revelation, the 'kings of the earth and the great men and the generals' go into hiding (Revelation 6: 15).

[15] **graves open**
'For the trumpet will sound and the dead will be raised imperishable' (1 Corinthians 15: 52); *bones* This detail goes back to the Old Testament, to Ezekiel's vision of a valley of dry bones which are first brought together, then clothed with flesh, then given life (Ezekiel 37: 1–10).

[16] **flames**
Watts gets a little ahead of himself here. According to biblical accounts, it is only the guilty dead who will be consigned to 'eternal fire' (Matthew 25: 41), to 'the lake of fire' (Revelation 20: 14–15). Watts seems to imagine all the dead as surrounded by flames.

[17] **outcries...wretches**
The day of judgement is the day of condemnation for the guilty – see previous note.

[18] **amazing**
frenzied, stupefied.

[19] **Stare...eyelids**
rather a grotesque image; *living worm* The gnawing of the living worm is one of the pains of hell. The last words of Isaiah describe the fate of rebels: 'their worm shall not die, their fire shall not be quenched, and they shall be an abhorrence to all flesh' (Isaiah 66: 24). This is extended in Mark into a description of hell 'where their worm

does not die and the fire is not quenched' (Mark 9: 48).

[21] **old vultures ... heartstrings** a (for this poem) rare classical reference. The giant Tityus, having tried to attack Leto, was punished in the underworld by having his liver gnawed by vultures or eagles. Virgil refers to this when Aeneas visits the underworld: 'There Tityus was to see, who took his birth/ From heaven, his nursing from the foodful earth./ Here his gigantic limbs, with large embrace,/ Enfold nine acres of infernal space./ A rav'nous vulture, in his opened side,/ Her crooked beak and cruel talons tried,/ Still for the growing liver digged his breast;/ The growing liver still supplied the feast' (*Aeneid*, bk vi – Dryden's translation). The age of the vultures and their preference for heartstrings over liver are Watts' inventions; *their* i.e. the guilty's.

[23] **Lofty judge** i.e. Jesus, who will preside over the judging of humanity at the Last Judgement. He is lofty (in part) because of His elevation on a 'great white throne' (Revelation 20: 11 & Matthew 25: 31); *flood of vengeance* The image goes back to Old Testament prophecy. Jeremiah warns: 'Behold! Waters rise up out of the north and shall be an overflowing flood' (Jeremiah 47: 2). Similarly, Nahum describes Jehovah's vengeance as 'an overflowing flood' (Nahum 1: 8), and Amos calls on judgement to 'run down as waters, and righteousness as a mighty stream' (Amos 5: 24). The prophets, of course, are drawing upon the idea of Noah's flood.

[25] **immortals** i.e. all human beings, because all are eternal.

[26] **devils push** The image of devils herding the damned into hell with pitchforks is more traditional than biblical. It is, in particular, part of the painting (known as the 'doom') which filled the top of the arch leading into the eastern end

of a medieval church. By Watts's time most such paintings had disappeared, destroyed in the vandalism of the sixteenth-century Reformation. Nevertheless, their images remained in people's minds; *pit wide yawning* The 'bottomless pit' is hell (Revelation 9: 2).

[27] **headlong** with head down. The word recalls the fall of Satan as described by Milton: 'Him the Almighty Power/ Hurled headlong flaming from th'etherial sky/ With hideous ruin and combustion down/ To bottomless perdition' (*Paradise Lost*, i, 44–7).

[28] **centre** i.e. the centre of the world, hell. The word was sometimes used simply as a noun for hell, as in Fulke Greville's poem: 'Down in the depth of mine iniquity,/ That ugly centre of infernal spirits' (lines 1–2).

[29] **fancy** imagination.

[30] **Doleful** sad, gloomy.

[31] **sits god-like** 'When the Son of Man comes in his glory, and all the angels with him, then he will sit on his glorious throne' (Matthew 25: 31). This position is 'god-like' because God the Father is also envisaged as seated upon a throne (Revelation 4: 2).

[32] **Throned** Jesus promises his followers that they will be enthroned in the new world (Matthew 19: 28). The idea is repeated in the vision of a reign of throned martyrs in Revelation (Revelation 20: 4); *yet adoring* The saints continue to worship God, despite their elevation.

[34] **dooming** judging. See note to line 26; *the nations* 'Before him [Jesus] will be gathered all the nations' (Matthew 25: 2).

[35] **hosannas** shouts of praise to God. On Christ's entry into Jerusalem, the crowd shouted 'Hosanna to the son of

David! Blessed is he who comes in the name of the Lord! Hosanna in the highest!' (Matthew 21: 9). Milton imagines the song of heavenly choirs: 'Heaven rung/ With jubilee, and loud hosannas filled/ Th'eternal regions' (*Paradise Lost*, iii, 347–9); *passage* way, route.

[36] **Shout** shout in greeting; ***Redeemer*** Jesus Christ. According to Christian teaching, the death and resurrection of Jesus redeem (save) humanity from its enslavement to death and sin.

———◇———

9 | *'Our God, our help'*

Our God, our help in ages past,
    Our hope for years to come,
Our shelter from the stormy blast,
    And our eternal home:

Under the shadow of thy throne   5
    Thy saints have dwelt secure.
Sufficient is thine arm alone,
    And our defense is sure.

Before the hills in order stood
    Or earth received her frame,   10
From everlasting thou art God,
    To endless years the same.

Thy word commands our flesh to dust,
    'Return, ye sons of men';
All nations rose from earth at first,   15
    And turn to earth again.

A thousand ages in thy sight
    Are like an evening gone;
Short as the watch that ends the night
    Before the rising sun.   20

The busy tribes of flesh and blood,
    With all their lives and cares,
Are carried downwards by thy flood,
    And lost in following years.

Time, like an ever-rolling stream,   25
   Bears all its sons away.
They fly forgotten, as a dream
   Dies at the opening day.

Like flowery fields the nations stand,
   Pleased with the morning light;   30
The flowers beneath the mower's hand
   Lie withering ere 'tis night.

Our God, our help in ages past,
   Our hope for years to come,
Be thou our guard while troubles last,   35
   And our eternal home.

'Our God, our help' (1719) is Watts's most famous hymn, and one that is still sung in churches today. As a metrical rendition of one of the Psalms of David (no. 90), it has a lineage which reaches back to the biblical translations of sixteenth-century Protestants. Most prominent among these are the metrical psalms of Thomas Sternhold and John Hopkins. Watts, however, does not attempt to translate the whole psalm, but rather selects certain parts of it, and even makes some additions of his own. Thus, it is rather more of an adaptation than a translation.

Although this poem is a rendition of a psalm, it should also be seen alongside Watts's hymns, such as 'When I behold the wondrous cross'. Congregational hymn-singing is an integral art of Protestant worship which goes back to Luther's German hymns. In England, however, the peculiar religious situation meant that hymns (as opposed to translations of the psalms) were not written until the eighteenth century. On the one hand, the Church of England stuck to the liturgical music which it had inherited from Catholicism. On the other, the independent, dissenting churches followed the view of Calvin that only psalms should be sung. In the eighteenth century, this belief was finally abandoned, with the result that there was a flowering of hymns, represented in this volume by Wesley and Cowper.

The poem is written in the popular ballad measure of alternate lines of four and three iambic feet. Each four-line stanza is alternately rhymed.

This is a form which can easily degenerate into an over-regular and uninteresting, dog-trot rhythm. Watts, however, introduces sufficient variation to prevent this. There is, for example, often a stress, or half a stress, on the first syllable of a line, which disrupts the iambic metre.

[1] **our help ... ages past**
Although there is no reference to God's former help in Psalm 90, the idea is present in many other psalms. They often refer in particular to the flight of the Hebrews out of Egypt and

to God's destruction of the Egyptian pursuers:

Marvellous things did he in the sight of their fathers, in the land of Egypt, in the field of Zoan. He divided the sea and caused them to pass through; and he made the waters to stand as a heap. In the daytime also he led them with a cloud, and all the night with a light of fire. He clave the rocks of the wilderness, and gave them drink as out of great depths. (Psalms 78: 12–15).

Such references to an oppressed nation saved by God were particularly congenial to Nonconformists like Watts, who often saw themselves as persecuted.

[4] **eternal home**
Again Watts adapts his source. Although the psalm refers to God as 'a dwelling place' or a 'refuge' (Psalms 90: 1), the word 'eternal' is his addition. It is a crucial one, for the word gives a colouring of immortality and heaven to the expression of human transience in lines 13–28. In the psalm, by contrast, the sense is simply that human life passes 'like a dream, like grass' (Psalms 90: 5).

[5] **Under...throne**
an echo rather of Psalm 91 than Psalm 90: 'he that dwells in the secret place of the most High shall abide under the shadow of the Almighty' (Psalms 91: 1); *thy* 'Thou', 'thee', 'thy', and 'thine' are the familiar forms of 'you' and 'yours', and were at this time becoming less common in ordinary speech. They remained in use, however, as the proper form of address to God.

[6] **saints**
the chosen people of God. The title was adopted by many Nonconformist Protestants of the seventeenth century and became associated with them.

[7] **arm**
strength; a common metaphor of the Old Testament in general, the psalms in particular. See 'thou hast scattered thine enemies with thy strong arm' (Psalms 89: 10).

[9–12] **Before the hills...same**
a close rendition of the second verse of the psalm in which Watts borrows some of his phrasing from the

Authorised Version: 'before the mountains were brought forth, or ever thou hadst formed the earth and the world, even from everlasting to everlasting, thou art God.' The eternal and unchanging nature of God is a common theme of Old and New Testaments alike.

[10] **frame**
form, structure. Compare 'this goodly frame, the earth, seems to me a sterile promontory' (*Hamlet*, II, ii, 291–2). Also, 'These are thy glorious works, parent of good,/ Almighty, thine this universal frame' (*Paradise Lost*, v, 153–4).

[13–14] **Thy word...men**
'Thou turnest man to destruction; and sayest, return, ye children of men' (Psalms 90: 3); *dust* 'And the Lord God formed man of the dust of the ground' (Genesis 2: 7).

[17–20] **A thousand...sun**
'For a thousand years in thy sight are but as yesterday when it is past, and as a watch in the night' (Psalms 90: 4); *watch* The Israelites divided the night into three watches. Eighteenth-century Englishmen like Watts, of course, did not keep night watches.

[23] **Are carried...flood**
'Thou carriest them away as with a flood' (Psalms 90: 5).

[27] **fly...dream**
The psalmist talks of men's lives 'flying away' (Psalms 90: 10) and compares them to a 'sleep' (90: 5). Otherwise, this line and the others of the verse are Watts' own.

[29–32] **Like flowery...night**
'they are like grass which groweth up. In the morning it flourisheth, and groweth up; in the evening it is cut down and withereth' (Psalms 90: 5–6).

[32] **ere**
before; '*tis* it is.

[35] **Be thou...last**
Watts introduces a variation in the first stanza, repeated here as the last. 'Be thou' is a request cast as an imperative and corresponds to the supplications at the end of the psalm. Watts'

method of repeating the first verse is, however, a considerable simplification of his original:

So teach us to number our days, that we may apply our hearts unto wisdom. Return, O Lord, how long? And let it repent thee concerning thy servants. O satisfy us early with thy mercy, that we may rejoice and be glad all our days. Make us glad according to the days wherein thou hast afflicted us, and the years wherein we have seen evil. Let thy work appear unto thy servants, and thy glory unto their children. And let the beauty of the Lord our God be upon us, and establish thou the work of our hands upon us. Yea, the work of our hands establish thou it. (Psalms 90: 12–17)

JONATHAN SWIFT

(1667–1745)

◇

Swift is famous today both as a writer of prose satire, in particular *A Tale of a Tub* (1704) and *Gulliver's Travels* (1726), and as
a former 'Irish Patriot' Dean of St Patrick's in Dublin. As far as
the latter is concerned, the decisive event was the death of
Queen Anne in 1714. This led to the collapse of the Tory
ministry with which Swift had been associated for four years,
and to his return to Ireland, a return he regarded as a virtual
exile. In Ireland he agitated against English oppression, and
wrote *Gulliver's Travels*. His poetry, for many years neglected,
has recently received greater critical attention.

Further Reading

The standard edition of Swift's poems is Harold Williams (ed.),
The Poems of Jonathan Swift, 3 vols (Oxford: Clarendon Press,
1937). A good text without annotations is also available in
Herbert Davies (ed.), *Swift: Poetical Works* (London: Oxford
University Press, 1967), and in Pat Rogers (ed.), *Swift: The
Complete Poems* (London: Oxford University Press, 1985).

Swift has been well served by biographers. Irvin Ehrenpreis's
three-volume *Swift: The Man, his Works and the Age* (London:
Methuen, 1962–83) is one of the monuments of postwar
eighteenth-century scholarship. Among the shorter modern
biographies perhaps the best is David Nokes' *Jonathan Swift, a
Hypocrite Reversed: A Critical Biography* (Oxford: Oxford
University Press, 1989).

Academic critics have traditionally concentrated on Swift's
prose. In recent years, however, a number of studies devoted to
the poetry have appeared. Perhaps the most substantial is

Louise K. Barnett's *Swift's Poetic Worlds* (Newark: University of Delaware Press, 1981), while a feminist reading appears in Ellen Pollak's *The Poetics of Sexual Myth: Gender and Ideology in the Verse of Swift and Pope* (Chicago: University of Chicago Press, 1985). Useful collections of essays are David M. Vieth (ed.), *Essential Articles for the Study of Jonathan Swift's Poetry* (Hamden, Conn.: Archon, 1984), and John Irwin Fischer, Donald C. Mell and David M. Vieth (eds), *Contemporary Studies of Swift's Poetry* (Newark: University of Delaware Press, 1981). Different opinions of Swift over history can be found in Kathleen Williams (ed.), *The Critical Heritage* (London: Routledge and Kegan Paul, 1970).

———◇———

10 /   *A Description of the Morning*

Now, hardly here and there a hackney-coach
Appearing, showed the ruddy morn's approach.
Now Betty from her master's bed had flown,
And softly stole to discompose her own.
The slipshod prentice from his master's door   5
Had pared the dirt, and sprinkled round the floor.
Now Moll had whirled her mop with dext'rous airs,
Prepared to scrub the entry and the stairs.
The youth with broomy stumps began to trace
The kennel edge where wheels had worn the place.   10
The smallcoal man was heard with cadence deep
'Till drowned in shriller notes of chimney sweep.
Duns at his lordship's gate began to meet
And brickdust Moll had scoured through half the street.
The turnkey now his flock returning sees,   15
Duly let out a-nights to steal for fees.
The watchful bailiffs take their silent stands,
And schoolboys lag with satchels in their hands.

A Description of the Morning was published in *The Tatler* on 30 April 1709, during Swift's residence in London as the emissary of the Church of Ireland. The poem refers to and rejects conventional, idealised descriptions of morning, offering instead a series of gritty, unromantic details. There are two more specific sources. The first is Milton's *L'Allegro*, which includes a long passage describing morning in the country. The second is classical rural poetry (pastoral and georgic), the conventions of which are wittily applied to a description of the city, a hint that Gay was to follow in *Trivia*. Swift's poem coincides with a renewed interest in these forms, as evidenced in the poetry of Gay and Ambrose Philips (1674–1749) and the early poetry of Pope.

The eighteen lines of the poem are in rhyming couplets of iambic pentameters. More usual in Swift's poetry is the rhymed tetrameter (see *Verses on the Death of Dr Swift*).

[1–2] **Now . . . approach**
i.e the approaching morning became evident now, with hardly a hackney-coach in sight; **hackney-coach** a horse-drawn carriage let out for hire. This is the poem's first realistic detail of city life; **ruddy morn's approach** Swift parodies pastoral and romantic descriptions of the morning. See, for example, Milton's *L'Allegro*: 'Right against the eastern gate/ Where the great sun begins his state/ Robed in flames and amber light/ The clouds in thousand liveries dight' (lines 59–62).

[3] **Betty**
a stock name for a maid. In listing the various occupations of the morning, Swift follows (and alters) Milton: 'While the ploughman near at hand/ Whistles o'er the furrowed land,/ And the milkmaid singeth blithe,/ And the mower whets his scythe' (*L'Allegro*, lines 63–6).

[4] **discompose**
the maid ruffles the sheets on her own bed to make it appear to others that she has slept there.

[5] **slipshod prentice**
untidy apprentice. 'Slipshod' probably does not imply carelessness in his work.

[6] **sprinkled**
the apprentice throws water on the stone floor to keep the dust down.

[9–10] **broomy stumps**
remains of a worn broom.

[10] **kennel**
the large, open drain in the middle of the road. The youth is sweeping the road in front of his master's house.

[11–12] **smallcoal man**
seller of household coal. The crude domestic coal brought to London from Newcastle and used for cooking and heating was the cause of the smog that hung over the city even in the eighteenth century; **cadence deep . . . shriller notes** London streets in the eighteenth century were crowded with street vendors of various kinds, most of whom advertised their wares or their services by shouting, often in rhyme. Swift wrote some humorous rhymes of this kind, one of which is intended for a seller of asparagus: 'Ripe 'sparagus,/ Fit for lad and lass/ To make their waters pass./ O 'tis pretty picking/ With a tender chicken.'

[13] **Duns**
tradesmen gathering to ask the lord to pay his debts to them.

[14] **brickdust Moll**
Brickdust was used for cleaning knives and pans. Brickdust Moll, like the coalman and the chimney sweep, is shouting her wares.

[15] **turnkey**
gaoler; **flock** The word, then as now, was associated with those under a clergyman's, not a gaoler's, care; **sees** At this point the poem shifts from the past to the present tense.

[16] **steal for fees**
In the eighteenth century prisoners paid for certain privileges. Swift jokingly suggests that these prisoners have been allowed out by the gaoler so that they can steal the money which they need to pay him.

[17] **bailiffs**
officers of a court waiting to serve a warrant on someone, presumably for debt. They are doing the same job as the 'duns' of line 13.

11 /   *A Description of a City Shower*

Careful observers may foretell the hour
(By sure prognostics) when to dread a shower.
While rain depends, the pensive cat gives o'er
Her frolics, and pursues her tail no more.
Returning home at night, you'll find the sink   5
Strike your offended sense with double stink.
If you be wise, then go not far to dine –
You'll spend in coach-hire more than save in wine.
A coming shower your shooting corns presage,
Old aches throb, your hollow tooth will rage.   10
Sauntering in coffee-house is Dulman seen.
He damns the climate, and complains of spleen.

Meanwhile the south rising with dabbled wings,
A sable cloud athwart the welkin flings,
That swilled more liquor than it could contain,   15
And like a drunkard gives it up again.
Brisk Susan whips her linen from the rope,
While the first drizzling shower is borne aslope.
Such is that sprinkling which some careless queen
Flirts on you from her mop, but not so clean.   20
You fly, invoke the gods, then turning, stop
To rail. She singing, still whirls on her mop.
Not yet, the dust had shunned th'unequal strife,
But aided by the wind, fought still for life,
And wafted with its foe by violent gust,   25
'Twas doubtful which was rain, and which was dust.
Ah! where must needy poet seek for aid,
When dust and rain at once his coat invade,
His only coat, where dust confused with rain
Roughen the nap, and leave a mingled stain   30

Now in contiguous drops the flood comes down,
Threatening with deluge this devoted town.
To shops in crowds the daggled females fly,
Pretend to cheapen goods, but nothing buy.
The templar spruce while every spout's abroach   35
Stays till 'tis fair, yet seems to call a coach.
The tucked-up seamstress walks with hasty strides,
While streams run down her oiled umbrella's sides.

Here various kinds by various fortunes led,
Commence acquaintance underneath a shed.   40
Triumphant Tories, and desponding Whigs,
Forget their feuds, and join to save their wigs.
Boxed in a chair the beau impatient sits,
While spouts run clatt'ring o'er the roof by fits.
And ever and anon with frightful din   45
The leather sounds, he trembles from within.
So when Troy chair-men bore the wooden steed,
Pregnant with Greeks, impatient to be freed,
(Those bully Greeks, who, as the moderns do,
Instead of paying chair-men, run them through.)   50
Laocoon struck the outside with his spear,
And each imprisoned hero quaked for fear.

Now from all parts the swelling kennels flow,
And bear their trophies with them as they go.
Filth of all hues and odours seem to tell   55
What street they sailed from, by their sight and smell.
They, as each torrent drives, with rapid force
From Smithfield, or St. Pultre's shape their course,
And in huge confluent join at Snow Hill ridge,
Fall from the conduit prone to Holborn Bridge.   60
Sweepings from butchers stalls, dung, guts, and blood,
Drowned puppies, stinking sprats, all drenched in mud,
Dead cats and turnip-tops come tumbling down the flood.

A Description of a City Shower was published in *The Tatler* in October 1710. Like
the companion poem, *A Description of the Morning*, it invokes idealised pastoral
descriptions of rain in order to contrast them with realistic details of city life.
Also like that poem, it is written in rhymed couplets of iambic pentameters.
Swift himself preferred this poem of the two.

[2] **sure prognostics**
reliable omens, certain signs. The passage which follows (lines 3–12) is a list
of the different omens which betray
the approach of the shower. It is based
upon a description of the signs of the
rain in Virgil's *Georgics* together with
Swift's own observations. Dryden
translates the appropriate passage in
Georgics (bk 1) thus: 'Wet weather
seldom hurts the most unwise,/ So

plain the signs, such prophets are the
skies:/ The wary crane foresees it first,
and sails/ Above the storm and leaves
the lowly vales:/ The cow looks up
and from afar can find/ The change of
heaven and snuffs it in the wind./ The
swallow skims the river's watery
face,/ The frogs renew the croaks of
their loquacious race . . . '
[5] **sink**
pit made to receive dirty water and/or

sewage, cesspool. These were located in gardens and cellars. In general, the sanitary arrangements of eighteenth-century London were inadequate for the size of the growing city.

[6] **offended sense**
i.e. of smell; *double stink* The sultry, still atmosphere that precedes a summer shower would increase the smell from a cesspool.

[8] **You'll spend ... wine**
i.e. the return coach fare will be more than the savings made by dining at someone else's expense. Swift's care with money is well documented. It was perhaps particularly acute at this period of life when (though by no means poor) he was the acquaintance of great men without the wealth of a great man.

[9] **presage**
tell of, warn of; *shooting* giving pain; *A coming ... presage* i.e. the pain in your corns foretells a shower.

[10] **aches**
pronounced as two syllables; *aches ... hollow tooth* other physical signs of the coming storm. Popular superstition concerning human barometers persists in the stories of the forecasting powers of war wounds.

[11] **Sauntering**
the behaviour of one in dissatisfied mood because of the close weather; *coffee-house* The coffee-houses of early eighteenth-century London were popular places of meeting and resort.

[12] **spleen**
discontent, bad temper – see the Cave of Spleen in *Rape of the Lock*, canto iv.

[13–14] **Meanwhile ... flings**
Swift elevates the tone by personifying the south wind and using archaisms such as 'welkin', thus achieving a mock-heroic, more exactly a mock-Georgic, effect.

[13] **the south**
i.e. the south wind; *dabbled* bespattered, besprinkled, wet.

[14] **sable**
black; *athwart* across; *welkin* sky, firmament. The word is poetic and its use draws the reader's attention to

idealised descriptions of the sky with which this contrasts.

[15] **swilled**
the colloquial verb punctures the heightened tone created by the previous couplet (as does the comparison of the following line); *liquor* liquid (not alcohol).

[16] **drunkard ... again**
Presumably a drunkard is picked for this comparison because of the copiousness of his urine. There may be a faint echo of Virgil's description of a downpour: 'And oft whole sheets descend of sluicy rain,/ Sucked by the spongy clouds from off the main' (*Georgics*, bk 1 – Dryden's translation).

[17] **rope**
(here) washing line.

[18] **borne**
carried; *aslope* crosswise, athwart.

[19] **queen**
usually, harlot; here, simply a generally abusive term for a woman, especially a slatternly woman.

[20] **flirts**
flicks, throws with a sudden jerk; *not so clean* referring to the spray from the mop.

[21] **invoke the gods**
Two senses: (1) call upon the gods in the manner of the pastoral or heroic poet; (2) utter an oath involving the name of God or one of the classical gods.

[22] **rail**
use angry and abusive language (towards the woman); *on* suggesting the continuance of the whirling.

[23] **Not yet ... shunned**
i.e. the dust had not yet shunned. The inversion of 'not yet' is mock-heroic heightening; *th'unequal strife* between dust and rain. Again, the representation of a conflict between dust and rain is mock-heroic.

[25] **its foe**
the dust's foe, the rain (both being driven by the wind).

[27] **needy poet**
References, usually contemptuous, to the poverty of poets are common in the period.

[29] **confused**
mingled, mixed.

[30] **Roughen the nap**
The nap is the smooth surface, the pile, given to cloth by small fibres on the surface. It is 'roughened' by the rain raising the fibres; *mingled stain* of moisture and dust.

[31] **contiguous**
close, here continuous; *flood* downpour, but also containing a reference to Noah's flood in preparation for the next line.

[32] **Threatening...town**
referring to Noah's flood. The word 'devoted' is lightly ironic: (1) because London is not pious; (2) because the biblical flood was sent to punish impiety not devotion.

[33] **daggled**
wet with mud, bedraggled.

[34] **cheapen**
bargain over, haggle over. The women use this as an excuse to take shelter in the shops.

[35] **templar**
a law student, resident at one of the two Inns of Court known as Temples; *spruce* templars had the reputation of being minor town dandies – see *Epistle to Dr Arbuthnot*, line 211; *abroach* literally, about to be pierced; here, full.

[36] **Stays**
remains (in shelter); *seems...coach* The templar affects to be waiting for the kind of transport he cannot afford.

[37] **tucked-up**
i.e. her skirts raised to keep them out of the mud.

[38] **oiled**
Umbrellas were covered with oiled cotton or silk; *umbrella* Although umbrellas existed in England as early as the seventeenth century, they were uncommon until the late eighteenth.

[39] **various kinds**
of people.

[40] **Commence acquaintance**
get to know each other; *shed* open shelter.

[41] **Triumphant Tories...Whigs**
Names of the two political groupings

(not yet quite parties in the modern sense) and used here to denote their supporters. In October 1710, when the poem was published, the Tories had just won a landslide election victory, which accounts for the differing moods of Whigs and Tories.

[42] **Forget their feuds**
by taking shelter together; *save their wigs* A soaking would ruin their expensive wigs.

[43] **chair**
sedan chair – compare *Rape of the Lock*, i, 46; *beau* fashionable young man.

[44] **spouts**
The word for the short pipes which discharged the rain from the roofs is used for the streams of water coming from them; *clatt'ring* i.e. the noise of the water on the sedan chair roof; *o'er* over; *by fits* The streams strike the roof of the chair intermittently, presumably because of the way that the water comes out of the spout in trickles and spurts (line 47).

[45] **ever and anon**
every now and then; *frightful din* of the water on the roof; mock-heroic heightening.

[46] **leather**
of the sedan chair roof; *trembles* from fear. The notion of the terrified beau inside the chair prepares for the mock-heroic comparison of the following lines (lines 47–52).

[47] **So when**
in the same way as when; introducing a comparison; *Troy* used as an adjective, Trojan. The Greek army gained access to the city of Troy by pretending to lift its siege, and leaving behind a large wooden horse, inside which a number of Greek warriors were hidden. The Trojans bore the horse into their city, and in the middle of the night the concealed Greeks emerged to open the city gates for their comrades who had returned under cover of darkness. Swift humorously compares the situation of the beau in his chair with that of the Greek heroes hidden in the horse; *chair-men* the

bearers of sedan chairs. The word is
ludicrously inappropriate for the
Trojan warriors who carried the horse
into the city.

[49–50] Those bully...through
The Greek warriors who left the horse
to slaughter their Trojan enemies are
compared to the modern thug who
attacks the chair-man with his sword
('runs him through') instead of paying
him for the ride.

[51] Laocoon...spear
Laocoon was the Trojan who suspected trickery when he saw the wooden
horse, and endeavoured to prove his
suspicions by throwing a spear at it
(*Aeneid*, ii). The noise of the spear on
the side of the horse is likened to the
rain on the roof of the chair.

[52] each...fear
The point of the long comparison is
finally made explicit.

[53] kennels
the open drains which ran down the
middle of the street; used here to
mean the water flowing down them.

[54] trophies
spoils of war exhibited in triumph; an
inappropriately elevated word for the
filth described in the succeeding lines.

[55] Hues
colours.

[56] What...smell
i.e. the origin of the water in the
drains is betrayed by the kinds of filth
in it.

[57] They
the different streams caused by the
downpour; *each torrent* Swift goes on
to imagine the sources and routes of a
number of streams.

[58] Smithfield
famous for its meat markets and
responsible for much of the filth in line
61; *St. Pultre's* St Sepulchre's church,
another London landmark.

[59] confluent
flowing together; *join* i.e. They (line
57) (the streams from Smithfield and
St Sepulchre's)...join; *Snow Hill* the
site of the conduit referred to in the
next line.

[60] conduit
canal, large kennel; *prone* straight
down; *Holborn Bridge* the point at
which the conduit joined Fleet Ditch,
the large stream, famous for its filth,
which led into the Thames.

[61–3] Sweepings...flood
The poem ends with a triplet (three
rhymed lines) rather than a couplet, in
which Swift lists the various types
of waste carried by the swollen
kennels.

---

12 / From *Verses on the Death of Dr Swift*

The time is not remote when I
Must by the course of nature die.
When I foresee my special friends
Will try to find their private ends,
Though it is hardly understood   5
Which way the death can do them good.
Yet, thus, methinks, I hear them speak,
'See how the Dean begins to break.
Poor gentleman, he droops apace,

You plainly find it in his face: 10
That old vertigo in his head,
Will never leave him, till he's dead.
Besides, his memory decays,
He recollects not what he says;
He cannot call his friends to mind;   15
Forgets the place where last he dined:
Plies you with stories o'er and o'er,
He told them fifty times before.
How does he fancy we can sit,
To hear his out-of-fashion wit?   20
But he takes up with younger folks,
Who for his wine will bear his jokes:
Faith, he must make his stories shorter,
Or change his comrades once a quarter.
In half the time, he talks them round;   25
There must another set be found.'

.   .   .   .

    My female friends, whose tender hearts
Have better learned to act their parts,
Receive the news in doleful dumps,
'The Dean is dead, (and what is trumps?)   30
Then Lord have mercy on his soul.
(Ladies I'll venture for the vole.)
Six Deans they say must bear the pall.
(I wish I knew what king to call.)
Madam, your husband will attend   35
The funeral of so good a friend.'
'No, madam, 'tis a shocking sight,
And he's engaged to-morrow night!
My Lady Club would take it ill,
If he should fail her at quadrille.   40
He loved the Dean (I lead a heart)
But dearest friends, they say, must part.
His time was come, he ran his race;
We hope he's in a better place.'

.   .   .   .

'The Dean, if we believe report,   45
Was never ill received at court.
As for his works in verse and prose,
I own myself no judge of those,
Nor can I tell what critics thought 'em,
But this I know – all people bought 'em.   50
As with a moral view designed
To cure the vices of mankind,
His vein, ironically grave,
Exposed the fool, and lashed the knave.
To steal a hint was never known,   55
But what he writ was all his own.

   . . . .

'Perhaps I may allow, the Dean
Had too much satire in his vein,
And seemed determined not to starve it,
Because no age could more deserve it.   60
Yet, malice never was his aim,
He lashed the vice but spared the name.
No individual could resent,
Where thousands equally were meant.
His satire points at no defect,   65
But what all mortals may correct,
For he abhorred that senseless tribe,
Who call it humour when they jibe.
He spared a hump or crooked nose,
Whose owners set not up for beaux.   70
True genuine dullness moved his pity,
Unless it offered to be witty.
Those, who their ignorance confessed,
He ne'er offended with a jest,
But laughed to hear an idiot quote,   75
A verse from Horace, learned by rote.

   . . . .

He gave the little wealth he had
To build a house for fools and mad,
And showed by one satiric touch,

No nation wanted it so much: 80
That kingdom he hath left his debtor,
I wish it soon may have a better.'

In *Verses on the Death of Dr Swift* (written 1731), Swift both imagines his own death and gives a humorous account of his career. *Verses* takes as its epigraph a maxim from La Rochefoucauld's *Réflexions* (1665), to the effect that we find a source of pleasure even in the gravest misfortunes of our best friends. This is Swift's starting point: his death will inconvenience no one greatly.

The poem is written in rhymed couplets of iambic tetrameters, a verse form more characteristic of Swift's poetry than the pentameters of the two 'descriptions' also included in this anthology. In this poem, as in others, Swift uses the tetrameters to create a light and humorous effect.

[2] **course of nature**
natural progression.

[4] **private ends**
personal benefit in the death, referring to the maxim of the French writer, Rochefoucauld, with which the poem begins (see above). The imagined reactions of Swift's friends to his death are testimony to its truth.

[7] **speak**
In Ireland, where Swift had lived for seventeen years when he wrote the poem (and many more before that), speak is pronounced 'spake', and thus makes a true rhyme with 'break'.

[8] **Dean**
Swift had been Dean of St Patrick's (the Anglican Cathedral), Dublin, since 1713; *break* sink towards death.

[9] **apace**
swiftly.

[10] **You plainly ... face**
The friends' complacent observations are contrasted with the death.

[11] **vertigo**
(pronounced here with the stress on the middle syllable: ver-TEE-go) dizziness. Swift suffered from Ménière's Syndrome, a disease of the ear, which causes deafness and dizziness to the victim.

[13–14] **Besides his memory ... says**
The couplet begins a list of common complaints (then as now) against the elderly (lines 13–23).

[17] **Plies you with**
demands your attention.

[20] **out-of-fashion**
Swift was 64 when he wrote *Verses*,

and his period of greatest influence and public prominence, the period of the Tory ministry of 1710–14, was an age away from 1731, in the midst of the long Whig supremacy.

[23] **Faith**
a contraction of the mild oath 'in faith'.

[24] **quarter**
three months.

[25] **them**
his stories; *talks them round* recounts his full set of stories.

[26] **set**
of friends. The idea is that the aged Swift needs to acquire a new group of friends for each retelling of his worn stories.

[28] **better**
In the immediately preceding section Swift has been imagining the insouciant reactions of his male friends; *act their parts* The phrase makes it clear that their sorrow is in appearance only.

[29] **doleful dumps**
sorrowful mood. The expression belongs to an affected feminine vocabulary.

[30] **trumps**
the most powerful suit of cards in certain card games. Swift imagines that the news of his death will not disturb the ladies' cards.

[31–2] **Then Lord ... vole**
The couplet's contrast between the pious prayer for his soul and the worldly interest in cards typifies the comedy of the whole scene.

[32] **vole**
a term for the acquisition of all the

tricks in the card games ombre and quadrille. For ombre, see note to *The Rape of the Lock*, ii, 27.

[33] **Six Deans**
The number of church dignitaries attending at the funeral is a measure of his eminence; *bear the pall* The coffin was covered with a cloth (the pall), the edges of which were held up by pall-bearers.

[34] **king to call**
a reference to the card game.

[38] **engaged**
is busy, has an appointment.

[39] **Lady Club**
satirical name for a lady who hosts card parties.

[42] **But dearest ... part**
a proverb, apparently repeated without real feeling for the loss.

[43–4] **His time ... place**
Having cited a proverb, the speaker rattles off quickly three trite platitudes, her use of cliché exposing her lack of sorrow.

[45–82]
Swift finishes his poem by imagining how an impartial witness might represent his character and life history.

[45] **report**
rumour.

[46] **never ... court**
never snubbed by the monarch's servants and advisers.

[48] **I**
i.e. the imaginary impartial adviser; *own myself no* do not claim to be any.

[49] **critics thought 'em**
a contemptuous opinion of critics' judgements is implied.

[51] **view**
aim, intention.

[52] **To cure ... mankind**
the satirist's standard claim concerning his intention.

[53] **vein**
characteristic style.

[54] **exposed**
exposure to public ridicule is the main weapon in the satirist's armoury; *lashed* standard metaphor for the action of satire.

[55] **steal ... known**
Though proud of his own originality, Swift sometimes offered fruitful suggestions to his friends, among them that of a 'Newgate Pastoral' to John Gay, which became *The Beggar's Opera*.

[56] **writ**
wrote.

[57] **Dean**
pronounced 'dane' in Ireland and making a true rhyme with 'vein'. In Dublin Swift was known simply as 'the Dane'.

[58] **vein**
see line 53 above.

[59] **not to starve it**
i.e. he gave his tendency for satire full rein.

[60] **deserve it**
Again (see notes to lines 7 and 57) the Irish pronunciation ('desarve') creates a true rhyme; *no age ... deserve it* It has been the common defence of satirists since Juvenal (*c.* AD 55–140), and probably before, that they write only because the wickedness of the age forces them to.

[61] **malice**
in the sense of the wish to injure individuals.

[62] **He lashed ... name**
another standard defence (untrue in Swift's case), that the satire stops short of naming names.

[66] **But**
except; *But what ... correct* i.e. he only aimed (and this was another golden rule for satirists) at minor and corrigible faults.

[68] **jibe**
mock maliciously.

[70] **beaux**
fashionable, and implicitly handsome, young men; *Whose owners ... beaux* i.e. he would mock physical ugliness only if the ugly people pretended to be handsome.

[72] **Unless ... witty**
Again Swift claims that he reserved his mockery for the affectation of intelligence, sparing those who were unaffectedly stupid.

[74] **ne'er**
never.

[76] **Horace**
Quintus Horatius Flaccus, the Roman poet of the first century, whose style and ideals were a great influence on Pope; *by rote* i.e. the idiot has no real knowledge of Horace, only a few scraps which he has learnt so as to be able to shine.

[78] **house . . . mad**
The bulk of Swift's estate was, in fact, left for the founding of a lunatic hospital in Dublin.

[79] **satiric touch**
It is characteristic of Swift that he should represent his act of charity as a joke.

[80] **wanted**
needed.

[81] **That kingdom . . . debt**
i.e. he has left the kingdom (of Ireland) in debt to him.

[82] **a better**
a better benefactor than Swift.

ANNE FINCH, COUNTESS OF WINCHILSEA

(1661–1720)

◇

After a brief spell at court in the 1680s, Anne Finch spent much of her life in retirement in the country. There, she wrote and was the friend of leading literary figures, such as Pope and the playwright, Nicholas Rowe (1674–1718).

Further Reading

There is no complete, modern edition of Finch's poetry, but a selection exists in Denys Thomson (ed.), *Selected Poems: Anne Finch, Countess of Winchilsea* (Manchester: Fyfield, 1987).

The most famous critical comments are those made by Wordsworth in the prefatory matter to his *Poetical Works* of 1815. More recently, articles have begun to appear in scholarly journals and collections of essays. A full length book is Jean M. Ellis D'Allesandro's *When in the Shade: Imaginal Equivalents in Anne, the Countess of Winchilsea's Poetry* (Udine, Italy: Del Bianco, 1989), while Jean Mallinson offers a substantial chapter in Anne Messenger (ed.), *Gender at Work: Four Women Writers of the Eighteenth Century* (Detroit: Wayne State University Press, 1990).

13 / # A Nocturnal Reverie

In such a night, when every louder wind,
Is to its distant cavern safe confined,
And only gentle Zephyr fans his wings,
And lonely Philomel, still waking, sings,
Or from some tree, famed for the owl's delight   5
She, hollowing clear, directs the wanderer right;
In such a night, when passing clouds give place,
Or thinly veil the heaven's mysterious face,
When in some river overhung with green,
The waving moon and trembling leaves are seen;   10
When freshened grass now bears itself upright,
And makes cool banks to pleasing rest invite,
Whence springs the woodbine and the bramble rose,
And where the sleepy cowslip sheltered grows,
Whilst now a paler hue the foxglove takes,   15
Yet chequers still with red the dusky brakes;
When scattered glowworms, but in twilight fine,
Show trivial beauties, watch their hour to shine,
Whilst Salisbury stands the test of every light,
In perfect charms and perfect virtue bright;   20
When odours which declined repelling day,
Through temperate air uninterrupted stray;
When darkened groves their softest shadows wear,
And falling waters we distinctly hear;
When through the gloom more venerable shows   25
Some ancient fabric, awful in repose,
While sunburnt hills their swarthy looks conceal,
And swelling haycocks thicken up the vale;
When the loosed horse now, as his pasture leads,
Comes slowly grazing through th'adjoining meads,   30
Whose stealing pace and lengthened shade we fear,
Till torn-up forage in his teeth we hear;
When nibbling sheep at large pursue their food,
And unmolested kine rechew the cud;
When curlews cry beneath the village walls   35
And to her straggling brood the partridge calls,
Their short-lived jubilee the creatures keep,
Which but endures whilst tyrant man does sleep;
When a sedate content the spirit feels,
And no fierce light disturbs whilst it reveals,   40

But silent musings urge the mind to seek
Something too high for syllables to speak,
Till the free soul to a composedness charmed,
Finding the elements of rage disarmed,
O'er all below a solemn quiet grown,   45
Joys in th'inferior world and thinks it like her own:
In such a night let me abroad remain,
Till morning breaks, and all's confused again,
Our cares, our toils, our clamours are renewed
Or pleasures, seldom reached, again pursued.   50

A Nocturnal Reverie (publ. 1713) is, as the title suggests, a night poem, that is,
one which exploits the setting and the mood of falling evening or deep night in
order to convey an emotion and to pursue philosophical or religious reflections.
Its forebears include the night sonnets of the Elizabethans (among them
Shakespeare and Sidney), the religious poetry of Henry Vaughan, and parts of
Milton's *Il Penseroso*. Variations of the genre were to become particularly popular in the eighteenth century with poems like Edward Young's *Night Thoughts*
(1742–45), and Gray's *Elegy*. It reached perhaps its highest expression among
the Romantics with Coleridge's *Frost at Midnight* (1798).

The poem is written in heroic couplets. Its most remarkable stylistic feature is
that its fifty lines comprise one sentence. The first forty-six lines contain a series
of subordinate clauses ('in such...', 'while...'), and the main clause comes
only in line 47 ('let me abroad remain'). The effect of this is to allow the poet
to accumulate descriptions of different aspects of the falling night; these details,
without the progression of successive sentences, seem fixed in one moment.

Title

nocturnal used in the modern way as
an adjective meaning 'of night', but
also retaining some of its original
sense. A 'nocturn' was part of the
office of matins which medieval
monks sang at midnight, an appropriate ancestor for a contemplative poem
of the night. John Donne draws upon
this when he uses 'nocturnal' (as a
noun) in the title of one of his poems
(*A Nocturnal Upon St Lucy's Night*);
reverie fit of abstracted musing.

[1] In such a night

The repetition of this phrase (lines 7 &
47) harks back to *The Merchant of
Venice* (V, i, 1–14):

Lorenzo: The moon shines bright.
          In such a night as this,

When the sweet wind did gently
                    kiss the trees,
And they did make no noise; in
                    such a night
Troilus methinks mounted the
                    Trojan walls,
And sighed his soul towards the
                    Grecian tents
Where Cressid lay that night.
Jessica: In such a night
Did Thisbe fearfully o'ertrip the dew,
And saw the Lion's shadow ere
                    himself,
And ran dismayed away.
Lorenzo: In such a night
Stood Dido with a willow in her
                    hand
Upon the wild sea banks, and
                    waft her love
To come again to Carthage.

Jessica: In such a night
  Medea gathered the enchanted
                                 herbs
  That did renew old Aeson. (etc.)

louder
Finch mentions the softer winds in
line 3.

[2] **distant cavern**
In the first book of the *Aeneid*, Virgil
writes of the dispensation that has
prevented unruly winds from causing
chaos in the earth: 'In fear of this, the
Father of the Gods/ Confined their
[the winds'] fury to those dark
abodes,/ And locked 'em safe within,
oppressed with mountain loads'
(Dryden's translation). In their cavern
prisons ('dark abodes') they are ruled
by the god Aeolus.

[3] **Zephyr**
the god of the west wind; by transference, a wind or (since the west is supposed to be gentle) a soft breeze. This
reference implies that the night being
described is a summer night, something later confirmed by the references
to flowers and to the 'sunburnt hills'
(line 27). The echo of *A Midsummer
Night's Dream* (lines 12–14) suggests
an even more specific date – some
time close to 21 June, the summer
solstice; *fans his wings* i.e. in order to
produce the breeze. This notion of the
source of wind is classical.

[4] **Philomel**
the nightingale. In legend, Philomel
and her sister, Procne, sought revenge
on the latter's husband (Tereus), for
his abduction, rape and imprisonment
of the former. To this end, they
slaughtered, cooked and served to
him his own son (Itys). When Tereus
learnt the nature of his horrid meal, he
turned on the sisters, but they were
promptly turned into the lark (Procne)
and the nightingale (Philomel), while
Tereus himself later became the
hoopoe. The song of the nightingale
was generally celebrated for its
beauty. In *A Midsummer Night's
Dream*, Philomel is invoked as the
singer of sweet lullabies that will help

the fairy queen to her sleep (II, ii,
13–19). Milton associated the song
with solitude, melancholy and
wisdom: 'In her sweetest, saddest
plight/ Smoothing the rugged brow of
night . . . Sweet bird that shunn'st the
noise of folly,/ Most musical, most
melancholy!' (*Il Penseroso*, lines
57–62).

[5] **famed . . . delight**
rather a ponderous construction.

[6] **hollowing**
halloaing; the call made by huntsmen
to their hounds, and used here
metaphorically for the cry of the owl;
directs . . . right The image of the wanderer seeking signs is commonplace,
and occurs in *Il Penseroso* in reference
to the moon shortly after the lines on
Philomel: 'Like one that had been led
astray/ Through the Heavens' wide,
pathless way' (69–70). What is
unusual is that the owl, usually a bird
of ill luck, should be represented as
guiding the traveller correctly.

[7] **give place**
give way to, get out of the way. It is a
rather awkwardly courtly expression
for the context.

[8] **mysterious**
because veiled by thin cloud.

[10] **waving . . . trembling**
the effects of the moving water of the
river on the reflections of moon and
leaves.

[12–13] **banks . . . rose**
These idyllic banks of evening seem,
with their flowers and their invitations
to rest, to owe something to Oberon's
description of the sleeping place of
Titania, queen of the fairies: 'I know a
bank where the wild thyme blows,/
Where oxlips and the nodding violet
grows,/ Quite overcanopied with
luscious woodbine,/ With sweet musk
roses and with eglantine./ There
sleeps Titania sometime of the night'
(*Midsummer Night's Dream*, II, i,
249–53).

[14] **cowslip**
The cowslip's bowed head might give
the appearance of sleepiness; the
flower is also related to the oxlip from

Oberon's description (see previous note).

[15] **paler hue**
the foxglove's colour is muted in the dusk light.

[16] **chequers**
diversifies with a different colour; *still* i.e. the red of the foxgloves is still visible despite the weakening light. Milton uses the phrase 'chequered shade' in *L'Allegro* (line 96); *brakes* clumps of bushes, thickets.

[17] **but**
only. The glowworms appear bright ('fine') only at this time of day.

[18] **trivial beauties**
the small, weak lights of the glow-worms.

[19] **Salisbury**
Anne Tufton, Countess of Salisbury, and sister to Finch's closest friend; *stands ... light* The idea is that a strong beauty does not, like the beauty of glowworms, need a weak light to shine in.

[20] **charms ... virtue**
The linking of physical and moral beauty is conventional.

[21] **declined ... day**
Certain smells turn away from the day, which repels them with its busi-ness and brightness.

[24] **falling waters**
the kind of muted sound that is normally drowned in the noise of the day.

[25] **venerable**
revered, august.

[26] **fabric**
building; *awful* impressive, inspiring awe; *in repose* presumably referring to the occupants' being at rest.

[27] **swarthy**
dark, blackish, dusky. The grass of the hills has been dried up by the mid-summer heat.

[28] **swelling**
The hayricks have just been enlarged by the second harvest of hay; *thicken* darken, become more obscure.

[29] **loosed**
i.e. after his day's labour; *pasture* feeding, grazing.

[30] **meads**
meadows. The word originally meant not just grass fields, but fields reserved for the production of hay.

[32] **forage**
food for cattle; *we hear* The noisy chewing of the horse would compete easily with such other nocturnal sounds as that of falling waters (line 24).

[33] **at large**
freely, without hindrance; over a wide area.

[34] **kine**
cows; *rechew the cud* cows, like other ruminants, bring their food back out of their stomachs to chew it at leisure.

[35] **curlews**
Finch appears to be thinking of the stone curlew, or thickknee, a slightly smaller bird than the true curlew and one more common inland. A summer visitor, it feeds mostly at night, when it seeks moister and more fertile places than its usual dry heathland habitat – hence, the closeness to the village. It is also known for the croaking cry it makes at dusk.

[36] **brood**
chicks, family; *partridge* grey par-tridge. The bird prefers to live on farmland, where in summer family groups forage for their food of seeds and insects.

[37] **jubilee**
a season of rejoicing; also a release from slavery.

[38] **but**
only; *tyrant man* Man is a tyrant in that he hunts and kills animals.

[42] **Something too high**
The vagueness of the formulation is characteristic of one strand of religious feeling in the eighteenth century, that of deism and the kind of non-doctrinaire Christianity that tends towards deism. The deist believes in God insofar as His existence is re-vealed by reason, but rejects faith based upon revelation, and in effect, rejects those specifics of different religions which have their source in revelation. A useful comparison in

this respect might be Henry Vaughan's mid-seventeenth-century poem *The Night*. Its many biblical references make that poem specifically Christian in a way Finch's is not.

[45] **below**
i.e. beneath, below the heavens, on earth; refers also to the inferior elements of the soul; *solemn quiet* perhaps a source for Gray's phrase 'solemn stillness' (*Elegy*, line 6).

[46] **Joys...own**
The subject of the verb ('joys' = enjoys) is the 'free soul' (line 43), who takes pleasure in the material ('inferior') world, which in its evening stillness seems now to resemble her ('the soul's') superior and spiritual world.

[47] **In such...remain**
the main clause of the single sentence of which the poem consists. The verb is cast as an imperative ('let me...remain') which emphasises the

strength of the wish; *abroad* outside, outdoors.

[48] **confused**
emotionally bewildered; chaotic.

[49] **clamours**
outcries, importunate demands; like the other nouns of the lines, an attribute of the day. The characterisation of day is somewhat reminiscent of Vaughan's description of his 'loud, evil days': 'But living where the sun/ Does all things wake, and where all mix and tire/ Themselves and others, I consent and run/ To every mire,/ And by this world's ill-guiding light/ Err more than I can do by night' (*The Night*, lines 43–8).

[50] **Or pleasures...pursued**
Although there is a shift in this line with the word 'pleasures' from the cares of the previous two, the sense remains gloomy. Those pleasures we seek in the day are usually unobtainable.

―――――◇―――――

14 /　　　　　*To the Nightingale*

Exert thy voice, sweet harbinger of spring!
　　This moment is thy time to sing.
　　This moment I attend to praise
And set my numbers to thy lays.
　　Free as thine shall be my song,　　　　　　　　　　5
　　As thy music, short or long.
Poets wild as thou were born,
　　Pleasing best when unconfined,
　　When to please is least designed,
Soothing but their cares to rest.　　　　　　　　　　10
　　Cares do still their thoughts molest.
　　And still th'unhappy poet's breast,
Like thine, when best he sings, is placed against a thorn.

She begins. Let all be still!
　　Muse, thy promise now fulfil!　　　　　　　　　　15

Sweet, oh sweet, still sweeter yet!
Can thy words such accents fit,
Canst thou syllables refine
Melt a sense that shall retain,
Still some spirit of thy brain,   20
Till with sounds like these it join?
    'Twill not be! Then change thy note –
Let division shake thy throat
Hark! Division now she tries,
Yet as far the muse outflies.   25
    Cease, then, prithee, cease thy tune.
    Trifler, wilt thou sing till June?
Till thy business all lies waste,
And the time of building's past!
    Thus, we poets that have speech,   30
Unlike what thy forests teach,
    If a fluent vein be shown
    That's transcendent to our own,
Criticise, reform, or preach,
Or censure that we cannot reach.   35

Although Finch does not announce the poem's genre in the title, it is a short, irregular ode (published 1713). The poet considers a serious subject in a fairly elevated style, in this case by addressing the nightingale. The subject is the relation of poetry to music, and the inferiority of the former.

The poem's lines are adapted to fit the different thoughts and moods of its different parts. The way that changes in style reflect changes in the nightingale's music invites comparison with the method of *Alexander's Feast*.

Finch adapts her lines in terms both of their length and their rhythm to the mood at hand. There is, however, one kind of line which recurs throughout the poem, and which by doing so creates a rhythmic pattern. This is a seven-syllable line, with four trochaic feet (stress/unstress), the last foot dropping its second (unstressed) syllable.

Trifler, wilt thou sing till June?
(Dumde dumde dumde dum)

Nevertheless, it should be emphasised that despite this repeated line the poem remains fairly irregular, or to use Finch's own word, 'free'.

Title
The poem shares its title with an early sonnet by Milton. There is also the similarity that both poems associate the nightingale with the poet.

[1] **harbinger**
forerunner, announcer. The nightingale arrives in Britain in mid-April, and the first hearing of its song is (as with the cuckoo) a sign of the arrival

of spring. Finch begins by drawing upon the happiest associations of the nightingale's song. In this, she may be thinking back to the first lines of Milton's sonnet: 'O Nightingale, that on yon bloomy spray/ Warblest at eve, when all the woods are still,/ Thou with fresh hope the lover's heart dost fill/ While jolly hours lead on propitious May.'

[3] attend
Finch places herself in an inferior position to the bird. The inferiority is important throughout the poem.

[4] set my...lays
'Numbers' are poems and 'lays' songs. The sense is that Finch intends to follow, to copy, in verse the nightingale's music. The argument of the poem shows this to be a vain ambition, since music is superior to poetry.

[5] Free
The word announces Finch's poetic approach.

[6] short or long
referring to the way in which styles and moods in music and poetry are determined by the length of syllable, note or line.

[7] Poets wild
In the early and mid-eighteenth century, discussions of the poet tended to lay less emphasis on unruly genius than do modern discussions. Nevertheless, notions of poetic madness were not unknown; **born** Finch refers to a Latin proverb, repeated by Sir Philip Sidney in the *Apology for Poetry* (1595): 'orators are made but poets are born.' The idea was so current in the early seventeenth century that Ben Jonson could play upon it in his poem *To the Memory of My Beloved... William Shakespeare*: 'For a good poet's made as well as born' (line 64).

[9] designed
planned, meant, intended.

[10] Soothing...rest
This is the notion of poetry as therapy, memorably expressed over a century earlier in Donne's *The Triple Fool*: 'Grief brought to numbers cannot be

so fierce,/ For he tames it that fetters it in verse' (lines 10–11); **but** only (the adverb belongs with 'soothing' – only soothing); **cares** The emphasis shifts from the joyfulness of the nightingale's song to its melancholy.

[12–13] And still...thorn
The nightingale's music is traditionally associated with pain, as can be seen both in the myth of Philomel (see note to line 4 of *A Nocturnal Reverie*) and in the picturesque belief that the bird sings while transfixing itself on a thorn. After her rape, Shakespeare's Lucrece addresses the nightingale: 'And whiles against a thorn thou bearst thy part/ To keep sharp woes waking' (*Rape of Lucrece*, lines 1135–6). Here, the link between pain and beautiful birdsong is extended to human poetry.

[14] She...still
The two short sentences have the effect of slowing the verse down and changing the mood of the poem.

[15] Muse
goddess of poetry. In the following lines, Finch uses the word to mean her own inspiration, which she addresses as 'thou'.

[17] Can...fit
The question is whether poetry (and language generally) can reach the heights of the bird's music ('accents'). Finch has earlier promised to follow the bird's music (line 4); she now doubts whether that is possible. This is the heart of the poem's subject.

[18–21] Canst...join?
These four lines reiterate the question of line 17. Can words ('syllables') be refined so far as to reproduce music ('sounds like these') while still making sense (retaining 'some spirit of the brain')?

[22] change
announcing another shift of mood.

[23] division
a musical term for a rapid passage of melody (in contrast to the sweet stillness of lines 14–21).

[24] she
Finch follows the myth of Philomel

(see note to lines 12–13) and poetic tradition by making her nightingale female. In fact, only the male nightingale sings.

[25] **Yet ... outflies**
She (the nightingale) outdoes the muse of poetry as thoroughly ('as far') with fast music ('division') as she did with slow.

[26] **Cease**
The command is no longer addressed to the muse but to the 'trifler' of the following line. This is the nightingale herself as the final lines of the poem make clear (the poet says she has criticised what she cannot attain – i.e. the nightingale's singing); *prithee* a contraction of 'I pray thee'.

[28–9] **Till ... past**
Finch ironically represents herself (or her speaker) taking the high moral ground, and upbraiding the nightingale for wasting time.

[30] **Thus**
used to mean 'in this way' and to refer to the ironic moralising of lines 26–9.

[31] **Unlike ... teach**
The speech of poets is different from the music of birds.

[32] **vein**
characteristic style.

[34–5] **Criticise ... censure**
the activities represented in lines 26–9. Finch closes by representing the petty carping of verbal composers when faced with the superiority of musical composers; *reach* attain.

JOSEPH ADDISON

(1672–1719)

Joseph Addison was born on 1 May 1672, the son of the rector of Milston, in Wiltshire. He finished school at the Charterhouse from where he went up to Queen's College in Oxford. Shortly afterwards he was elected to a demyship at Magdalen College where he later became a fellow. A long wooded walk along the Isis near Magdalen is still referred to as 'Addison's walk'. He did a 'grand tour' of Europe from 1699 to 1703. In later life he held political positions and became Secretary of State for just under a year in 1718–19.

Addison's literary career began with his contributions to *The Tatler*, the popular periodical edited by his friend Richard Steele. Addison and Steele collaborated on *The Spectator*, which followed soon after the last *Tatler* was published in January 1711. *The Spectator* ran to an impressive 555 numbers and was extremely popular in its time. It bears the mark of Addison's personality and sense of purpose. In 1713 Addison published *Cato: A Tragedy*, which, though it elicited high praise from Johnson, is of only historical interest today.

Further Reading

Although editions of the *Tatler* and *Spectator* are readily available, Addison's poetry is not easy to find, and readers might be best advised to look in anthologies.

There is a well-documented biography in Peter Smithers, *The Life of Joseph Addison* (Oxford: Clarendon Press, 1954), and a collection of earlier reactions in Edward A. Bloom and Lillian D. Bloom (eds), *Addison and Steele: The Critical Heritage* (London: Routledge and Kegan Paul, 1980).

15 / *Ode*

The spacious firmament on high,
With all the blue ethereal sky,
And spangled heavens, a shining frame,
Their great original proclaim:
Th'unwearied sun, from day to day, 5
Does his creator's power display,
And publishes to every land
The work of an almighty hand.

Soon as the evening shades prevail,
The moon takes up the wondrous tale, 10
And nightly to the listening earth
Repeats the story of her birth:
Whilst all the stars that round her burn,
And all the planets, in their turn,
Confirm the tidings as they roll, 15
And spread the truth from pole to pole.

What though, in solemn silence, all
Move round the dark terrestrial ball?
What though nor real voice nor sound
Amid their radiant orbs be found? 20
In reason's ear they all rejoice,
And utter forth a glorious voice,
For ever singing, as they shine,
'The hand that made us is Divine.'

Addison's hymns occur in the context of his best known work, *The Spectator* (1711–12). In the *Spectator* essays Addison conversed politely with his readers on social issues, and aimed to instruct them in matters of religion, morality, philosophy and science. He was interested in disseminating the ideas of contemporary thinkers, in particular Newton and Locke.

Addison's poems reveal a nice blend of faith and 'philosophy'. Deriving inspiration from both the psalmist of the Old Testament and the scientific thinkers of the period, he achieves a tone that reconciles the two. Similarly, as in 'How are thy servants blest', he can redefine personal experience in terms of the traditional religious metaphor. In the process the poem arrives at a voice of both individual intensity and public fervour. Poised thus at a point of configuration of the public and private, the poems are ideally suited to be hymns.

Addison is experimental in his verse form, using for eulogistic purposes the octosyllabic couplet in the first hymn printed here. He adheres to the metre and rhyme scheme with strict regularity, however. In 'How are thy servants blest' the four-line stanza of alternate long and short lines serves both to express and formalise experience.

Addison first published the poem in *The Spectator*, No. 465 of 23 August 1712. This hymn and the next one appeared in Saturday *Spectators* as material suitable to be read on Sundays as well. Addison introduced it as follows:

Faith and devotion naturally grow in the mind of every reasonable man, who sees the impressions of divine power and wisdom in every object on which he casts his eye. The Supreme Being has made the best arguments for his own existence, in the formation of the heavens and the earth, ... Aristotle says, that should a man live under ground, and there converse with works of art and mechanism, and should afterwards be brought up into the open day, and see the several glories of heaven and earth, he would immediately pronounce them the works of such a being as we define God to be.

He turned next to Psalm 19: 1–4 to illustrate his position, and perhaps to protect himself against charges of 'deism':

The Psalmist has very beautiful strokes of poetry to this purpose, in that exalted strain, *The heavens declare the glory of God: And the firmament showeth his handy work. One day telleth another: and one night certifieth another. There is neither speech nor language: but their voices are heard among them. Their sound is gone into all lands: and their works into the ends of the world.*

[1] **spacious**
extensive; *firmament* heavens.
[2] **ethereal**
heavenly; as in 'Thrones, and imperial powers, offspring of heaven/ Ethereal virtues', *Paradise Lost*, ii, 310–11.

[3] **spangled**
besprinkled; *shining* in the sense of 'eminent' or 'conspicuous' as well as 'bright' or 'gleaming'; *frame* a structure or fabric of parts fitted harmoniously together; cf. 'Divine Cecilia came,/ Inventress of the vocal frame', Dryden, *Alexander's Feast*, line 162.
[4] **original**
primary source; Addison means God; *proclaim* manifest or make known; make a public declaration of.
[6] **creator's**
God's; *display* exhibit to the sight or mind.
[7] **publishes**
discovers to mankind, makes generally known.
[9] **prevail**
gain influence.
[10] **wondrous**
marvellous; creating a sense of wonder.
[13] **burn**
give light, shine.
[14] **planets**
stars that move, are not fixed; not necessarily confined to revolution round the sun as yet. The idea is continued in the 'roll' of the next line.
[16] **spread**
disseminate.
[18] **dark terrestrial ball**
referring to the earth; Addison refers to the view that the moon and stars move around the earth, which has no light. He could also be using 'dark' in the sense of ignorant or wanting knowledge.
[19] **nor real voice nor sound**
debunking the idea of the music of the spheres.
[20] **radiant orbs**
shining spheres, as opposed to the 'dark ... ball'.
[21] **reason**
conviction through argument and evidence; *rejoice* exult.

16 / *Divine Ode*

How are thy servants blest, O Lord!
How sure is their defence!
Eternal wisdom is their guide,
Their help omnipotence.

In foreign realms, and lands remote, 5
Supported by thy care,
Through burning climes I passed unhurt,
And breathed in tainted air.

Thy mercy sweetened every soil,
Made every region please; 10
The hoary Alpine hills it warmed,
And smoothed the Tyrrhene seas:

Think, O my soul, devoutly think,
How with affrighted eyes
Thou sawest the wide extended deep 15
In all its horrors rise!

Confusion dwelt in every face,
And fear in every heart;
When waves on waves, and gulfs in gulfs,
O'ercame the pilot's art. 20

Yet then from all my griefs, O Lord,
Thy mercy set me free,
Whilst in the confidence of prayer
My soul took hold on thee;

For though in dreadful whirls we hung 25
High on the broken wave,
I knew thou wert not slow to hear,
Nor impotent to save.

The storm was laid, the winds retired,
Obedient to thy will; 30
The sea, that roared at thy command,
At thy command was still.

In midst of dangers, fears, and death,
Thy goodness I'll adore,
And praise thee for thy mercies past;   35
And humbly hope for more.

My life, if thou preservest my life,
Thy sacrifice shall be;
And death, if death must be my doom,
Shall join my soul to thee.   40

This poem, which Addison called 'a divine ode made by a gentleman upon the conclusion of his travels', first appeared in his *Spectator* No. 489 of Saturday 20 September 1712. The essay reveals his deistic cast of mind: 'Such an object (the ocean) naturally raises in my thoughts the idea of an Almighty Being, and convinces me of his existence, as much as metaphysical demonstration.' In the poem, however, Addison talks of the tumultuous ocean not only as a physical reality, but with connotations of spiritual upheaval. Clearly Psalm 107, from which he quotes in the *Spectator* essay, was his inspiration:

They that go down to the sea in ships, that do business in great waters: these see the works of the Lord, and his wonders in the deep. For he commandeth and raiseth the stormy wind, which lifteth up the waters thereof. They mount up to the heaven, they go down again to the depths, their soul is melted because of trouble. They reel to and fro, and stagger like a drunken man, and are at their wits' end. Then they cry unto the Lord in their trouble, and he bringeth them out of their distresses. He maketh the storm a calm, so that the waves thereof are still. Then they are glad because they be quiet; so he bringeth them unto their desired haven.

The experience of a violent storm in the Gulf of Genoa during his 'grand tour' of Europe was the 'occasion' of the poem.

[2] **sure**
'certain, unfailing, infallible', Johnson, *Dictionary*; Johnson illustrates the sense from Psalm 19: 7: 'The testimony of the Lord is sure and giveth wisdom unto the simple'; *defence* protection.
[8]
referring to the risk of pestilence in Rome during the 'grand tour'.
[11] **hoary**
white with snow.
[12] **the Tyrrhene seas**
The Tyrrhene Sea between the west coast of Italy and the islands of Corsica, Sardinia and Sicily. Addison had sailed along the west coast after visiting Naples.
[15] **wide extended deep**
periphrasis for the ocean.
[20] **o'ercame**
The word is used in both its literal sense of 'flowed over' and the more usual metaphorical meaning of 'vanquished' or 'defeated'.
[28] **impotent**
without power.
[29] **laid**
quietened, made still.

JOHN GAY

(1685–1732)

Gay was born into a family of the gentleman class in Barnstaple, Devon, but his father's early death did not leave him financially independent. He started on a literary career in London in the full knowledge that it would also have to be a source of livelihood. He was lucky in contracting a friendship with Pope only a few years after he launched on his writings; this matured later into a relationship with Swift, Arbuthnot and Parnell. Under the patronage of the Earl of Oxford the five friends formed the Scriblerus Club.

Gay's first poem *Wine* appeared in 1708 and *Rural Sports* in 1712. In *The Shepherd's Week* (1714) he burlesqued the pastorals of Pope's rival Ambrose Philips. The poem is also a stimulating piece of social realism. *Trivia* (1716) was clearly the greatest poem on London life. Gay carefully revised his poems for later editions and collections. The farce, *Three Hours After Marriage*, in which Gay collaborated with Pope and Arbuthnot, was successful; even more successful was *The Beggar's Opera* (1728). Unfortunately Gay was not able to cope with the political realities of the time. *Polly* (1729), a sequal to *The Beggar's Opera*, in which he further satirised Walpole, was banned before it could be produced. Gay died fairly young, from ill-health, and was buried in Westminster Abbey. Pope's famous epitaph is inscribed on his grave:

Of manners gentle, of affections mild;
In wit, a man; simplicity, a child;
With native humour tempering virtuous rage,
Formed to delight at once and lash the age;
Above temptation, in a low estate,
And uncorrupted, ev'n among the great;

A safe companion, and an easy friend,
Unblamed through life, lamented in thy end.
These are thy honours! not that here thy bust
Is mixed with heroes, or with kings thy dust;
But that the worthy and the good shall say,
Striking their pensive bosoms – Here lies Gay.

Further Reading

The standard edition of Gay's poetry is to be found in Vinton A. Dearing (ed.) with Charles Beckwith, *John Gay: Poetry and Prose*, in two vols (Oxford: Clarendon Press, 1974), which the editors have found useful. A useful selection is Marcus Walsh (ed.), *Selected Poems: John Gay* (Manchester: Carcanet, 1979).

The standard biography is W.H. Irving's *John Gay: Favourite of the Wits* (Durham, NC: Duke University Press, 1940). Few books are devoted to his work, but among them S.M. Armens' *John Gay: Social Critic* (New York: King's Crown Press, 1954) remains a good full-length study, as does Patricia Meyer Spacks, *John Gay* (New York: Twayne, 1965). A useful collection of modern essays is Peter Lewis and Nigel Wood (eds), *John Gay and the Scriblerians* (London: Vision, 1988), while a very brief account of the works is offered by Oliver Warner in *John Gay* (London: Longmans, 1964). For a translation of Virgil's *Georgics* see L.P. Wilkinson, *Virgil, 'The Georgics'* (Harmondsworth: Penguin, 1982).

————◇————

17 | From *Trivia*
Or, The Art of Walking the Streets of London

From *Book II*

Thus far the muse has traced in useful lays,
The proper implements for wintry ways:
Has taught the walker, with judicious eyes,
To read the various warnings of the skies.
Now venture, muse, from home, to range the town,   5
And for the public safety risk thy own.

. . . .

If clothed in black you tread the busy town,   *What trades*
Or if distinguished by the reverend gown,   *prejudicial*
Three trades avoid; oft in the mingling press,   *to walkers*
The barber's apron soils the sable dress: 10
Shun the perfumer's touch with cautious eye,
Nor let the baker's step advance too nigh:
Ye walkers too that youthful colours wear,
Three sullying trades avoid with equal care;
The little chimney-sweeper skulks along,   15
And marks with sooty stains the heedless throng;
When smallcoal murmurs in the hoarser throat,
From smutty dangers guard thy threatened coat;
The dustman's cart offends thy clothes and eyes,
When through the street a cloud of ashes flies;   20
But whether black, or lighter dyes are worn,
The chandler's basket, on his shoulder borne,
With tallow spots thy coat; resign the way,
To shun the surly butcher's greasy tray,
Butchers, whose hands are dyed with blood's foul stain,   25
And always foremost in the hangman's train.

Let due civilities be strictly paid.   *To whom to*
The wall surrender to the hooded maid: *give the*
Nor let thy sturdy elbow's hasty rage   *wall*
Jostle the feeble steps of trembling age: 30
And when the porter bends beneath his load,
And pants for breath; clear thou the crowded road.
But, above all, the groping blind direct,

And from the pressing throng the lame protect.
You'll sometimes meet a fop, of nicest tread,   35
Whose mantling peruke veils his empty head,
At every step he dreads the wall to lose,
And risks, to save a coach, his red-heeled shoes;
Him, like the miller, pass with caution by,
Lest from his shoulder clouds of powder fly;   40
But when the bully, with assuming pace,   *To whom*
Cocks his broad hat, edged round with tarnished lace,   *to*
Yield not the way; defy his strutting pride,   *refuse*
And thrust him to the muddy kennel's side;   *the wall*
He never turns again, nor dares oppose,   45
But mutters coward curses as he goes.

.   .   .   .

Though expedition bids, yet never stray   *Of*
Where no ranged posts defend the rugged way;   *narrow*
Here laden carts with thundering wagons meet,   *streets*
Wheels clash with wheels, and bar the narrow street;   50
The lashing whip resounds, the horses strain,
And blood in anguish bursts the swelling vein.
O barbarous men, your cruel breasts assuage,
Why vent ye on the generous steed your rage?
Does not his service earn your daily bread?   55
Your wives, your children by his labours fed!
If, as the Samian taught, the soul revives,
And shifting seats, in other bodies lives;
Severe shall be the brutal coachman's change,
Doomed in a hackney horse, the town to range: 60
Carmen, transformed, the groaning lord shall draw,
Whom other tyrants, with the lash, shall awe.

.   .   .   .

Winter my theme confines; whose nitry wind   *Frosty*
Shall crust the slabby mire, and kennels bind.   *weather*
She bids the snow descend in flaky sheets,   65
And in her hoary mantle clothe the streets;
Let not the virgin tread these slippery roads,
The gathering fleece the hollow patten loads;

But if thy footsteps slide with clotted frost,
Strike off the breaking balls against the post;   70
On silent wheel the passing coaches roll,
Oft look behind and ward the threatening pole.
In hardened orbs the school-boy moulds the snow,
To mark the coachman with a dextrous throw.
Why do ye, boys, the kennel's surface spread,   75
To tempt with faithless pass the matron's tread?
How can ye laugh, to see the damsel spurn,
Sink in your frauds and her green stocking mourn?
At White's, the harnessed chairman idly stands,
And swings, around his waist, his tingling hands;   80
The sempstress speeds to 'Change with red-tipt nose;
The Belgian stove beneath her foot-stool glows,
In half-whipt muslin needles useless lye,
And shuttle-cocks across the counter fly.
These sports warm harmless; why then will ye prove,   85
Deluded maids, the dangerous flame of love?

    Where Covent-garden's famous temple stands,   The
That boasts the work of Jones' immortal hands: dangers
Columns, with plain magnificence, appear,   of football
And graceful porches lead along the square;   90
Here oft my course I bend, when lo! from far,
I spy the furies of the foot-ball war:
The 'prentice quits his shop, to join the crew,
Increasing crowds the flying game pursue.
Thus, as you roll the ball o'er the snowy ground,   95
The gathering globe augments with every round:
But whither shall I run? the throng draws nigh,
The ball now skims the street, now soars on high;
The dextrous glazier strong returns the bound,
And jingling sashes on the pent-house sound.   100

    O roving muse, recall that wondrous year,
When winter reigned in bleak Britannia's air:
When hoary Thames, with frosted osiers crowned,
Was three long moons in icy fetters bound.
The waterman, forlorn along the shore,   105
Pensive reclines upon his useless oar,
Sees harnessed steeds desert the stony town,

And wander roads unstable, not their own;
Wheels o'er the hardened waters smoothly glide,
And rase with whitened tracks the slippery tide.   110
Here the fat cook piles high the blazing fire,
And scarce the spit can turn the steer entire.
Booths sudden hide the Thames, long streets appear,
And numerous games proclaim the crowded fair.
So when a general bids the martial train   115
Spread their encampment o'er the spacious plain;
Thick-rising tents a canvas city build,
And the loud dice resound through all the field.
'Twas here the matron found a doleful fate:
Let elegiac lay the woe relate,   120
Soft, as the breath of distant flutes, at hours,
When silent evening closes up the flowers;
Lulling, as falling water's hollow noise;
Indulging grief, like Philomela's voice.

    Doll every day had walked these treacherous roads: 125
Her neck grew warped beneath autumnal loads
Of various fruit; she now a basket bore,
That head, alas! shall basket bear no more.
Each booth she frequent passed, in quest of gain,
And boys with pleasure heard her shrilling strain.   130
Ah Doll! all mortals must resign their breath,
And industry itself submit to death!
The cracking crystal yields, she sinks, she dies,
Her head, chopped off, from her lost shoulders flies:
'Pippins' she cried, but death her voice confounds,   135
And 'pip-pip-pip' along the ice resounds.
So when the Thracian Furies Orpheus tore,
And left his bleeding trunk deformed with gore,
His severed head floats down the silver tide,
His yet warm tongue for his lost consort cried;   140
'Eurydice', with quivering voice, he mourned,
And Heber's banks 'Eurydice' returned.

    But now the western gale the flood unbinds,   A
And blackening clouds move on with warmer winds;   thaw
The wooden town its frail foundation leaves,   145
And Thames' full urn rolls down his plenteous waves:

167

From every penthouse streams the fleeting snow,
And with dissolving frost the pavements flow.

.   .   .   .

O ye associate walkers, O my friends,   The
Upon your state what happiness attends!   happi-
What, though no coach to frequent visit rolls,   ness of
Nor for your shilling chairmen sling their poles: walkers
Yet still your nerves rheumatic pains defy,
Nor lazy jaundice dulls your saffron eye;
No wasting cough discharges sounds of death,   155
Nor wheezing asthma heaves in vain for breath;
Nor from your restless couch is heard the groan
Of burning gout, or sedentary stone.
Let others in the jolting coach confide,
Or in the leaky boat the Thames divide: 160
Or, boxed within the chair, contemn the street,
And trust their safety to another's feet,
Still let me walk; for oft the sudden gale
Ruffles the tide, and shifts the dangerous sail,
Then shall the passenger, too late, deplore   165
The whelming billow, and the faithless oar;
The drunken chairman in the kennel spurns,
The glasses shatters, and his charge o'erturns.
Who can recount the coach's various harms:
The legs disjointed, and the broken arms?   170

.   .   .   .

What walker shall his mean ambition fix,
On the false lustre of a coach and six?
Let the vain virgin, lured by glaring show,
Sigh for the liveries of th'embroidered beau.

See, yon bright chariot on its braces swing,   175
With Flanders mares, and on an arched spring,
That wretch, to gain an equipage and place,
Betrayed his sister to a lewd embrace:
This coach, that with the blazoned scutcheon glows,
Vain of his unknown race, the coxcomb shows.   180

Here the bribed lawyer, sunk in velvet, sleeps;
The starving orphan, as he passes, weeps;
There flames a fool begirt with tinselled slaves,
Who wastes the wealth of a whole race of knaves;
That other, with a clustering train behind,   185
Owes his new honours to a sordid mind.
This next in court fidelity excels,
The public rifles, and his country sells.
May the proud chariot never be my fate,
If purchased at so mean, so dear a rate;   190
Or rather give me sweet content on foot,
Wrapped in my virtue, and a good surtout.

There were a few poems before *Trivia* to which we can look for a background to Gay's poem. John Philips' *Cider* is perhaps the closest; it had already been the inspiration for his mock work *Wine*. Swift's two 'description' poems may also have been influential. But on the whole in *Trivia* Gay must be credited with originality, especially in his combination of the classical, the mock-epic and realistic modes.

The eighteenth century greatly admired Virgil's *Georgics*. Dryden in the Dedication to his translation of 1697 referred to *Georgics* as 'the best poem of the best poet' and declared that Virgil wrote it in the 'full strength and vigour of his age'. The poem described the lives of husbandsmen, the rearing of livestock, and the cultivation of land. Gay's *Trivia*, which is modelled on Virgil's poem, may be considered an urban georgic in which city sights and city life, with all their hazards and vitality, are described.

Trivia is written in the ten-syllabled rhymed couplet, the favourite verse form of the age. Gay's language is relatively simple and clear. Published in 1716, after *The Rape of the Lock* had run into several editions, Gay's poem, too, adopts the mock-heroic stance; in terms of the style Gay, like Pope, often applies an elevated style informed with classical allusions to trivial occurrences. His overall subject is, again like Pope's, an important and serious one, and the tone both ironic and celebratory. There are many passages in the poem, however, like the evocative descriptions of life in the streets of London, that may also be read straight.

Title
Trivia means streets. There was a Roman goddess called Trivia; she was not really the goddess of streets and highways, but another version of Hecate. In her form as Trivia she was to be found at night, in association with demons, at street junctions (the root meaning of *trivia*).
Epigraph
Quo te Moeri pedes? An, quo via ducit, in Urbem? (Whither afoot,

Moeris? Is it, as the path leads, to town?, Virgil, *Eclogues*, ix, i).
[2] **implements**
equipment. In the first book Gay had been talking about overcoats, shoes, umbrellas, etc.
[1–6] **Thus far...thy own**
Gay appears to have modelled his opening on: 'Thus far my song has been of tilth below/ And stars above; now, Bacchus, it shall be/ Of you, and with you of the woodland saplings/

And the rearing of the slow-maturing olive./ Come father of the winepress: yours are the gifts/ That here abound; for you the land burgeons/ Pregnant with vine-leafed autumn, and the vats/ Foam to the brim. Come, Father of the winepress,/ Swiftly pull off your buskins, and with me/ Dip your bare legs deep in the new must', Virgil, *Georgics*, ii, 1–8, trans. Wilkinson.

[9] **mingling press**
the crowd that presses.

[10–11] **The barber ... the perfumer's**
they would have powder on their clothes.

[12] **baker's step ... too nigh**
'allow the baker to come too close'. The baker would have flour on his clothes and hands.

[15] **little chimney-sweeper**
small boys sent inside the chimneys to clean them; *skulks* moves stealthily, so as to escape notice.

[16] **heedless throng**
periphrastic usage for people among the crowd who unknowingly get smeared.

[17] **smallcoal**
coal in small pieces or charcoal, i.e. household coal.

[15–17] **The little ... hoarser throat**
'The smallcoal man was heard with cadence deep,/ Till drowned in shriller notes of chimney-sweep', Swift, *Description of the Morning*, lines 11–12.

[19] **offends**
assails, injures.

[22] **chandler's**
candlemaker.

[23] **tallow**
grease or animal fat.

[28] **The wall surrender**
Walking the streets of London was a hazardous exercise. By far the safest and cleanest part of the road was that nearest the walls of buildings. To give up one's place along the wall was a choice to be made carefully. Boswell in his *Life* quotes Johnson as saying:

In the last age, when my mother lived in London, there were two sets of people, those who gave wall, and those who took it; the peaceable and the quarrelsome. When I returned to Lichfield, after having been in London, my mother asked me, whether I was one of those who gave the wall, or those who took it. Now it is fixed that every man keeps to the right; or, if one is taking the wall, the other yields it; and it is never a dispute.

[30] **trembling age**
old people unsure of their footing.

[35] **nicest tread**
in the sense of 'mincing steps'.

[36] **mantling**
spreading; *peruke* French form that was altered in English to 'periwig'; *mantling peruke* elaborate wig.

[38] **to save**
to avoid; *red-heeled shoes* These were fashionable in the reign of Queen Anne.

[41] **assuming**
arrogant, haughty; *pace* manner of walking.

[44] **kennel's**
'The watercourse of the street', Johnson, *Dictionary*. A drain of dirty water flowed down a rough channel in the middle of the roads in London in those days; see 'The kennel edge, where wheels had worn the place', *Description of the Morning*, line 10.

[46] **coward**
cowardly.

[48] **defend**
fence off; *ranged posts ... rugged way* a line of posts separated the broad flat-stoned pavements of 'High' streets from the rougher surface of the road.

[57] **Samian**
referring to Pythagoras who was born in the island of Samos.

[58] **seats**
abodes.

[57–8] **If as ... lives**
Pythagorean doctrine of the trans-migration of the soul.

[60] **hackney horse**
a horse kept for hire.

[61] **Carmen**
those who drew cars.
[62] **awe**
subdue.
[63] **my theme confines**
my theme is tied to; *nitry* nitre, which
was believed to cause frost or ice.
[64] **slabby**
'Wet; floody', Johnson, *Dictionary*.
[67] **slippery**
both literally, and also suggesting
'sliding virtue'.
[68] **patten**
'A shoe of wood with an iron ring,
worn under the common shoe by
women', Johnson, *Dictionary*. Such
shoes gave protection against the wet
by raising the wearer an inch or two
from the ground.
[72] **pole**
coach-pole.
[76] **faithless pass**
treacherous passage.
[77] **spurn**
stumble.
[79] **White's**
a famous chocolate house and gaming
house in St James's Street. It later
became a club; *harnessed* a harness
worn by chair-men to make it easier
for them to carry chairs.
[81] **'Change**
the New Exchange where items of
fashion such as dresses, hats, ribbons,
etc., were sold.
[82] **Belgian stove**
a footwarmer heated by burning charcoal, originally from Belgium.
[83] **half-whipt muslin**
In needlework 'whip' meant 'to trim
or ornament with embroidery', *OED*;
muslin fine cotton material; the muslin
is 'half-whipt' because the girls are
keeping themselves warm by playing
shuttlecock.
[85] **prove**
make a trial of.
[87] **temple**
St Paul's church in Covent Garden,
built by Inigo Jones in 1631. He also
designed rows of houses with arcades
that extended on two sides of the
square.

[90] **porches**
arcades with roofs supported by pillars.
[99] **glazier**
'one whose trade is to make glass
windows', Johnson, *Dictionary*. ·
[100] **sashes**
windows; *pent-house* 'A shed hanging
out aslope from the main wall',
Johnson, *Dictionary*.
[101] **that wondrous year**
the prolonged winter of 1709–10
when the Thames was frozen for three
months. The event was marked by
'frost-fairs', with bull and bear-
baiting, puppet shows and market-
stalls. The roasting of a whole ox on
the ice was a characteristic feature of
these fairs.
[103] **osiers**
'A tree of the willow kind, growing by
the water', Johnson, *Dictionary*.
[105] **waterman**
a ferryman, a boatman.
[107–9] **sees harnessed ... glide**
cf. 'In running rivers sudden sheets of
ice/ Congeal, until the water's back
can bear/ Iron bound wheels, and that
which recently/ Welcomed light craft
now welcomes lumbering wagons',
Virgil, *Georgics*, iii, 360–2, trans.
Wilkinson.
[110] **rase**
to scratch; *slippery tide* the frozen
Thames.
[112] **steer**
young ox.
[115–18]
in the mode of the mock-epic simile.
[121] **hours**
appointed times for prayers.
[124] **Philomela's**
In Greek mythology the sister-in-law
of the King of Thrace who outraged
her and then cut off her tongue so that
she could not tell of her ill-usage.
Philomela was changed into a nightingale. Gay makes a mocking comparison, but the story that follows is also
tragic.
[133] **cracking crystal**
the cracking ice.
[135] **Pippins**
one of the cries of London.

[137–42]

Cf. 'But Thracian women,/ Deemed themselves despised by such devotion,/ Amid their Bacchic orgies in the night/ Tore him apart, this youth, and strewed his limbs/ Over the countryside. And so it was/ That as the river of his fatherland/ The Hebrus, bore in the middle of its current/ His head, now severed from his marble neck,/ "Eurydice!" the voice and frozen tongue/ Still called aloud, "Ah, poor Eurydice!"/ As life was ebbing away, and the river banks/ Echoed across the flood, "Eurydice!"', Virgil, *Georgics*, iv, 520–7, trans. Wilkinson.

[146] **Thames' full urn**

rivers were personified as divinities holding urns from which the water flowed.

[149] **associate**

companion.

[154] **saffron**

of orange-red colour.

[158] **burning gout**

painful arthritic inflammation; *sedentary* unmoving; *stone* 'Calculous concretion in the kidneys or bladder', Johnson, *Dictionary*.

[159] **confide**

trust.

[149–70]

A parody of Virgil, *Georgics*, ii, 458–74.

[171–2]

Cf. 'The soul's calm sunshine, and the heartfelt joy,/ Is virtue's prize: A better would you fix?/ Then give humility a coach and six', Pope, *An Essay on Man*, iv, 168–70.

[175] **chariot**

a light four-wheeled carriage; *braces* 'Thick straps of leather on which it (the coach) hangs', Johnson, *Dictionary*.

[176] **Flanders mares**

Flemish mares that drew the coaches of the aristocracy.

[177] **equipage**

a carriage; *place* office or employment.

[179] **blazoned ... glows**

displays ostentatiously its coat of arms.

[180] **coxcomb**

'a superficial pretender', Johnson, *Dictionary*; *shows* reveals.

[183] **flames**

shines; *begirt ... slaves* surrounded by showily dressed servants.

[184] **the wealth ... of knaves**

the ill-gotten gains of several corrupt people.

[187] **court fidelity**

conforms to the mores at court.

[192] **wrapped ... virtue**

Cf. 'I clothe me in my virtue', Horace, *Odes*, III, xxix, 54–5; *surtout* an overcoat.

LADY MARY WORTLEY MONTAGU

(1689–1762)

◇

Born the daughter of a duke, Lady Mary Wortley Montagu lived a varied and colourful life which included elopement and marriage against her father's wishes, friendship with many of the leading writers of the day (most famously with Pope), life in Turkey as wife of the ambassador there, the pioneering in England of inoculation against smallpox, literary squabbles (especially with Pope after the ending of their friendship), flight in middle age with a much younger man to the continent, and years of life abroad. Her literary fame rests chiefly on the 'Embassy Letters' she wrote from Turkey (1716–18). Recently, her poetry has been more widely anthologised than heretofore, but there is still little criticism of it.

Further Reading

Lady Mary Wortley Montagu is unusual among female poets of the eighteenth century in that there are good modern editions of her works. Her poetry is to be found in Robert Halsband and Isobel Grundy (eds), *Essays and Poems and Simplicity: A Comedy* (Oxford: Clarendon Press, 1977). There is also an excellent biography by Halsband, *The Life of Lady Mary Wortley Montagu* (Oxford: Clarendon Press, 1956). Although her poetry has been increasingly anthologised in recent years, there is little critical comment on it. The bulk of critics who write about her at all concentrate on her letters, and in particular, on the 'Embassy Letters' from Turkey.

18 /   *Saturday: The Small-Pox*

Flavia

The wretched Flavia, on her couch reclined,
Thus breathed the anguish of a wounded mind.
A glass reversed in her right hand she bore,
For now she shunned the face she sought before.

'How am I changed! Alas, how am I grown   5
A frightful spectre, to myself unknown!
Where's my complexion? Where the radiant bloom,
That promised happiness for years to come?
Then, with what pleasure I this face surveyed!
To look once more, my visits oft delayed!   10
Charmed with the view, a fresher red would rise,
And a new life shot sparkling from my eyes!
Ah, faithless glass, my wonted bloom restore!
Alas, I rave, that bloom is now no more!

'The greatest good the gods on men bestow,   15
Ev'n youth itself, to me is useless now.
There was a time (oh, that I could forget!)
When opera tickets poured before my feet.
And at the Ring, where brightest beauties shine,
The earliest cherries of the spring were mine.   20
Witness, Oh Lilly, and thou, Motteux, tell,
How much japan these eyes have made you sell.
With what contempt ye saw me oft despise
The humble offer of the raffled prize.
For at each raffle still the prize I bore,   25
With scorn rejected, or with triumph wore.
Now beauty's fled, and presents are no more.

'For me the patriot has the House forsook,
And left debates to catch a passing look;
For me the soldier has soft verses writ;   30
For me the beau has aimed to be a wit;
For me the wit to nonsense was betrayed;
The gamester has for me his dun delayed,
And overseen the card he would have played;

The bold and haughty by success made vain,   35
Awed by my eyes, has trembled to complain;
The bashful squire, touched with a wish unknown,
Has dared to speak with spirit not his own;
Fired by one wish, all did alike adore
Now beauty's fled, and lovers are no more.   40

'As round the room I turn my weeping eyes,
New unaffected scenes of sorrow rise.
Far from my sight that killing picture bear,
The face disfigure, or the canvas tear!
That picture, which with pride I used to show −   45
The lost resemblance but upbraids me now.
And thou, my toilette, where I oft have sat,
While hours unheeded passed in deep debate,
How curls should fall, or where a patch to place,
If blue or scarlet best became my face,   50
Now on some happier nymph your aid bestow.
On fairer heads, you useless jewels, glow!
No borrowed lustre can my charms restore,
Beauty is fled, and dress is now no more.

'You meaner beauties, I permit you shine.   55
Go, triumph in the hearts that once were mine,
But, midst your triumphs with confusion know,
'Tis to my ruin all your charms you owe.
Would pitying heaven restore my wonted mien,
You still might move unthought of and unseen.   60
But oh, how vain, how wretched is the boast
Of beauty faded, and of empire lost!
What now is left but weeping to deplore
My beauty fled, and empire now no more?

'You cruel chymists, what withheld your aid?   65
Could no pomatums save a trembling maid?
How false and trifling is that art you boast;
No art can give me back my beauty lost!
In tears, surrounded by my friends I lay,
Masked o'er, and trembling at the light of day.   70
Mirmillio came my fortune to deplore

(A golden-headed cane well carved he bore):
Cordials, he cried, my spirits must restore!
Beauty is fled, and spirit is no more!
Galen the grave, officious Squirt was there,   75
With fruitless grief and unavailing care.
Machaon too, the great Machaon, known
By his red cloak and his superior frown.
"And why," he cried, "this grief and this despair?
You shall again be well, again be fair.   80
Believe my oath." (With that an oath he swore.)
False was his oath! My beauty is no more.

   'Cease, hapless maid, no more thy tale pursue.
Forsake mankind, and bid the world adieu.
Monarchs and beauties rule with equal sway,   85
All strive to serve, and glory to obey.
Alike unpitied when deposed they grow,
Men mock the idol of their former vow.

   'Adieu, ye parks – in some obscure recess,
Where gentle streams will weep at my distress,   90
Where no false friend will in my grief take part,
And mourn my ruin with a joyful heart.
There let me live in some deserted place,
There hide in shades this lost inglorious face.
Plays, operas, circles, I no more must view!   95
My toilette, patches, all the world, adieu!'

Saturday: The Small-Pox was written in 1716 soon after Montagu's recovery from
smallpox. It is one of six 'town eclogues', one for each of the days of the week
except Sunday. One of the six was written by Gay, and two of the earlier ones
involved collaboration with him and with Pope.
   A 'town eclogue' is a work of a similar kind to Swift's two description poems
and to Gay's *Trivia*. Just as they borrow from and parody Virgil's *Georgics* in
order to describe the city and city life, so this draws upon his *Pastorals* or
Eclogues (42–35 BC). A group of ten poems, the *Pastorals* are set in Arcadia,
representing the (sometimes idealised) life of shepherds. One type is the complaint, usually the lover's complaint, and Montagu adapts the language of
unlucky pastoral love in order to bewail the after-effects of smallpox. However,
the poem she seems to have had most in mind was not a lover's complaint but
the first pastoral. In this Meliboeus, bereft of his farm, must leave the happy
shepherd's life (in the same way that Flavia is forced to abandon the life of the

society beauty). He cries:

> Farewell my pastures, my paternal stock,
> My fruitful fields, and my more fruitful flock!
> No more, my goats, shall I behold you climb
> The steepy cliffs, or crop the flowery thyme! . . .
> No more my sheep shall sip the morning dew,
> No more my song shall please the rural crew –
> Adieu, my tuneful pipe! And all the world, adieu!
> (Dryden's translation)

The first three *Town Eclogues* (one of them by Gay) were circulated in manuscript, then later pirated by the notorious publisher, Edmund Curll (see *Epistle to Dr Arbuthnot*, 53 and note). In revenge, Pope (the friend of Gay and at that time of Montagu) met Curll for a drink, secretly added an emetic to his wine, and published a lively account of his sufferings. The three later poems (of 1716) were not published until 1747.

Like most of the poems in this volume, *Saturday: The Small-Pox* is written in heroic couplets. Montagu exploits the balance of the paired lines for witty and satiric effect, exposing the folly of Flavia and the triviality of her world. But she also seeks to represent the strong regret of one who has lost her beauty. The latter use of the couplet has its precedent in Dryden's translations of the *Eclogues* and in English pastoral elegy.

Title

Saturday Though not strictly the first English pastoral poet, Edmund Spenser introduced the formal pastoral into English poetry in 1579. He also introduced, in his cycle 'The Shepherd's Calendar', the device of fitting each poem to a month or a season of the year. Gay adapted the convention in his poem of 1714, 'The Shepherd's Week', by matching six poems to six of the days of the week. Montagu follows Gay, and follows him also in using the device simply as a way of giving some structure to a group of poems; there is no real Saturday quality in the poem at hand. In this respect, both Gay and Montagu depart from their Spenserian model, even though Gay claims him (wrongly) as a precedent; *Small-pox* a feared disease in the eighteenth century, and until it was declared eradicated in 1977. It was sometimes fatal, and left many of those who survived it badly scarred. Montagu emerged with pitted skin and no eyelashes; *Flavia* The name appears to have no special significance beyond being common among the Romans and suitable for a pastoral (compare *Epistle to a Lady*, line 87). Since the poem is partly autobiographical, Flavia represents (to some extent) Montagu herself.

[1] **reclined**
in eighteenth-century poetry, a stock posture for a suffering, possibly self-indulgent, women. Compare *Rape of the Lock*, iv, 23 & 35. Many of ways in which women are represented here echo that poem.

[2] **Thus breathed**
i.e. in this way spoke. The phrase introduces Flavia's monologue which, from line 5 onwards, makes up the poem. The structure of a short introduction followed by a monologue or dialogue is common in pastoral poetry.

[3] **glass**
mirror. The woman holding a mirror is an old image of pride. Spenser's Lucifera 'held a mirror bright,/ Wherein her face she often viewed fain,/ And in her self-loved semblance took delight;/ For she was wondrous fair as any living wight', *Faerie Queene*,

1.4. Flavia's mirror is reversed, turned away from her, so that she avoids seeing her own scarred reflection.

[4] sought before
The notion of a woman as obsessed with her own reflection is reminiscent of Belinda in *The Rape of the Lock*, i, 125–6.

[6] myself unknown
The phrase both conveys the situation of the survivor of smallpox, hardly able to discern her old self under the scars, and harks back to the ghost metaphor ('spectre') earlier in the line. Ghosts were thought to be difficult to recognise. When Aeneas enters the underworld, he meets his recently dead helmsman Palinurus: 'The Trojan fixed his view,/ And scarcely through the gloom the sullen shadow knew' (*Aeneid*, vi – Dryden's translation). Aeneas encounters the same problem later on when he meets the shade of his former lover, Dido.

[7] bloom
the reddish tint of the cheek, a mark of beauty; also, figuratively, beauty in general.

[8] years to come
deliberately ironic. The word 'bloom' in the previous lines introduces the idea of flowers, a stock image for transient beauty.

[10] visits
By the eighteenth century, wealthy women had lost their traditional role as 'housewives', a word which had once comprehended the host of duties, responsibilities and skills involved in managing a large household. Instead, they were reduced to the round of pointless social activities represented in *The Rape of the Lock*, and implied here in the word 'visits'.

[11] fresher red
i.e. she used to flush with pleasure at her own beauty. This is slightly different from Belinda raising 'a purer blush' with rouge – *Rape of the Lock*, i, 143.

[12] a new life . . . eyes
The brightness of the eyes was another conventional attribute of beauty.

Belinda quickens 'keener lightnings' in her eyes with cosmetics (*Rape of the Lock*, i, 144); Flavia's 'new life' comes from satisfied vanity. In the context of Montagu's recovery from smallpox, the poem's references to eyes are poignant since hers had become disfigured by the loss of lashes – see introductory notes.

[13] faithless
treacherous; in her distress, Flavia cannot believe that the scarred image the mirror now presents is true; *wonted* customary, former.

[14] rave
literally, think and speak like a mad person.

[15] the gods
As a pastoral, the poem refers to the classical gods, rather than to the Christian God. The avoidance of Christian reference is also more generally in keeping with Montagu's sceptical temper.

[16] Ev'n youth itself
the 'greatest good' of the previous line. There may be a faint echo of the myth of Tithonus here. He was granted immortality by Zeus, but his lover, Eos (the goddess of dawn), forgot to ask also for youth, and he had to live a life of aged misery. Thus, youth, not immortality, represents the 'greatest good' a human being could possess.

[18] opera tickets
gifts from lovers. Italian opera enjoyed great popularity in London in the early decades of the eighteenth century. Pope refers to some of its special effects in *The Rape of the Lock*, iv, 43–6; *poured . . . feet* conventional expression for the giving of gifts.

[19] Ring
a fashionable meeting-place in Hyde Park. Compare *Rape of the Lock*, i, 44.

[20] earliest cherries
another valued lovers' gift.

[21] Witness
in the imperative, commanding Lilly to bear witness, to admit; *Lilly . . . Motteux* Charles Lilly and Peter Motteux, both (among other occupations)

dealers in oriental luxuries. Motteux is now better known as a minor dramatist and the translator of *Don Quixote*, but in a *Spectator* of 1712, Richard Steele describes his 'spacious warehouses filled and adorned with tea, China and Indian wares'.

[22] **japan**
articles of lacquered wood from Japan – compare *Rape of the Lock*, iii, 107; *made you sell* i.e. in former times these merchants sold japan to Flavia's lovers who were buying gifts for her.

[24] **raffled prize**
Raffles and lotteries were fashionable pastimes – compare *Epistle to a Lady*, line 266.

[25] **For at ... bore**
The sense is that at every raffle the gentleman who won the prize would gallantly offer it to Flavia; *bore* The verb 'to bear' is used here in the sense (which it does not have) of 'to be offered'; Flavia did not 'bear' ('carry') every prize for, as the next line tells us, she chose to reject some. Presumably, this is an example of a word chosen for its virtue as a rhyme rather than for its meaning.

[27] **beauty's fled ... no more**
Variations of these phrases are used as a refrain at the end of each of the next five verse paragraphs.

[28] **For me**
The following lines catalogue the various sacrifices of Flavia's various lovers. Montagu may have had some of her own former suitors in mind. Before her marriage she was much courted, and she was later to claim that even during the weeks before her elopement in 1712, when the marriage planned for her by her father was imminent, she had had many offers. However, the characters are general types, and probably have little specific reference; *patriot* a title claimed by the adherents of both parties. One of Montagu's suitors, and her eventual husband, was the ambitious young Whig politician, Edward Wortley Montagu. Here, she may be looking back, at a time when their conjugal

bliss was already less than complete, to his earlier ardour; *House* i.e. the House of Commons.

[29] **left debates**
the supreme sacrifice (for a politician).

[30] **soft verses**
an unnatural occupation for a soldier, and therefore one which expresses the depth of his love.

[31] **beau**
fashionable young man about town, fop; *aimed ... wit* rather a less surprising ambition than that of the soldier to be a poet, since the beaux and fops of the stage usually attempt wit.

[33] **gamester**
gambler, especially with cards; *dun* a demand for the payment of a debt. Like the politician (line 29), the gambler gives up that which is dearest to him.

[34] **overseen**
failed to notice. Her beauty ruins his card-playing.

[36] **trembled**
been afraid to.

[37] **bashful squire**
the image of the rude country gentleman, the bumpkin, thrown into confusion by beauty; *unknown* The word may imply previously unknown, or unrecognised by himself. Or it may simply be included to provide the rhyme in the following line.

[38] **spirit not his own**
The eloquent, vigorous declaration of love is, it is implied, the prerogative of the educated metropolitan. The bumpkin only rises to such heights by virtue of Flavia's beauty.

[40] **no more**
If the poem is autobiographical, the prediction proved to be untrue. Whether or not there was ever any physical relationship between them, Pope's passionate *Eloisa to Abelard* was composed with Montagu in mind, and she later left England with a man much younger than herself.

[42] **New**
in that the articles she goes on to describe were not previously associated with sorrow; *unaffected* not

influenced by sorrow; or, possibly, without affectation of sorrow. The use of the word here is rather obscure.

[43] **killing picture**
a portrait which kills because it reminds of lost beauty. A painting of Montagu by Charles Jervas in 1710 shows a handsome young woman leaning pensively against a tree trunk and attended by a fittingly pretty lamb.

[46] **upbraids**
finds fault with.

[47] **thou**
Flavia addresses her toilet – a deliber- ately artificial poetic device for height- ening the tone; *toilette* toilet, dressing table; *sat* pronounced 'sate'.

[48] **unheeded**
unnoticed (in that she's so engrossed in her own beautification); *deep debate* (ironic) description of the discussion between maid and mistress about hair, dress and face.

[49] **patch**
small patch of black cloth worn by fashionable women on the face; one of the articles on Belinda's dressing table – *Rape of the Lock*, i, 138.

[50] **became**
suited.

[51] **nymph**
(figurative) a beautiful young woman – see *Epistle to a Lady*, line 5, and note; *your aid* Flavia is still addressing her toilet (line 47).

[53] **lustre**
gloss, bright light, splendour. It is bor- rowed because imparted by the jewels.

[55] **meaner**
lower, less splendid. The ensuing verse paragraph represents Flavia achieving a kind of triumph over her former rivals in the thought that they can win only because she is out of the reckoning.

[57] **midst**
in the middle of; *confusion* mental distress.

[59] **wonted**
customary, former; *mien* bearing, air. Montagu, though, seems to be using

the word in its occasional late seventeenth-century sense of 'facial expression'.

[60] **unthought ... unseen**
the condition of rival beauties when Flavia was still fair.

[61] **vain**
useless, futile.

[62] **empire**
power, dominion, sway. Flavia refers to her own former power over men.

[65] **chymists**
chemists, alchemists. The reference to alchemy is appropriate since the aim of that science to transform base metals into gold is similar to Flavia's wish to have her ugliness transformed into beauty. The word is applied in the ensuing verse paragraph to makers of cosmetics and to doctors.

[66] **pomatums**
pomades, scented ointments for the skin or hair; appropriate since it is the smallpox victim's skin that requires restoration; *trembling* i.e. in fear; but the adjective seems rather redundant here.

[67] **art**
skill.

[70] **trembling ... day**
Flavia dreads the light because it exposes her new ugliness.

[71] **Mirmillio**
the first of four doctors, this one iden- tified by Horace Walpole's marginal note as Sir Hans Sloane (1660–1753), who had advised Queen Anne. His hobby of collecting curiosities prompted Edward Young to describe him as 'the foremost toyman of his age'. The name 'Mirmillio' is an early reference to what we call 'the bedside manner'. The doctor 'murmurs' his diagnosis and advice in comfortingly subdued tones; *deplore* lament.

[72] **golden-headed**
a fashionable accessory (compare Sir Plume in *The Rape of the Lock*, iv, 124), and presumably one associated with Sloane.

[73] **Cordials**
medicines which stimulate heart and circulation.

[75] **Galen**
the second doctor. The name is that of a Roman court physician and writer of medical books of the second century BC; with Hippocrates, one of the two most famous doctors of the ancient world. Montagu's contemporary reference (if any) is not known; *officious* obliging, kind; but also pejoratively, over-obliging, meddlesome; *Squirt* the third doctor. The name is appropriate since an important part of the doctor's duty was the administration of enemas by means of squirting with a large syringe.

[77] **Machaon**
the fourth doctor, identified by Walpole as Sir Samuel Garth (1661–1719), famous as a wit and a poet as well as a doctor. His mock-heroic poem *The Dispensary* was a source to Pope for *The Rape of the Lock*. Like Sloane and Montagu, he was a firm Whig. The name 'Machaon' goes back to the second book of the *Iliad* in which that person is one of two sons of Asclepius described as doctors. Later in the epic, he heals Menelaus (bk iv).

[83] **hapless maid**
unfortunate maid. Flavia addresses herself.

[85] **Monarchs...sway**
The comparison may have been prompted by recent events, for the limited power ('sway') of monarchs had just been demonstrated in the unsuccessful Jacobite rising of 1715 (see the introduction to the volume). The claims of 'the Pretender' were unquestionable, but he still failed to win back his crown. The rising was led by Montagu's brother-in-law, the Earl of Mar, who had fled to France with his lord in February 1716.

[86] **All**
i.e. all men, not all monarchs; *glory* are proud to.

[87] **unpitied**
refers now to monarchs, not men. Montagu may be alluding to a cruel pun which circulated after her illness. The fullness of the pocks (spots) of smallpox was associated with the depth of the pits, the scars, it left behind. The joke went that though her pocks had been full, yet she was not pitted. (not pitied); *deposed...grow* a clumsy construction since the deposition of monarchs (or of beauties in this case) is not a gradual process as the verb 'grow' implies.

[88] **idol**
Kings are compared to idols in *Absalom and Achitophel* (line 64), as are beauties in *The Rape of the Lock* (v, 12).

[89] **Adieu**
The sad farewell to the pleasures of the town echoes the farewell of Virgil's shepherd, Meliboeus, to the pleasures of the country life. See introductory note. Here, the poem is perhaps somewhat more satirical than in the sections which deal directly with the effects of smallpox.

[90] **streams...weep**
The comparison of the noise of streams to the sounds of mourning is both old and conventional. Desdemona's 'song of willow' in the fourth act of *Othello* includes the line, 'The fresh streams ran by her, and murmured her moans' (IV, iii, 44).

[92] **mourn...heart**
This is the secret delight we all experience in another's distress which Swift later takes as his starting point for *Verses on the Death of Dr Swift*.

[95] **circles**
galleries of the theatre.

———◇———

19 / *A Receipt to Cure the Vapours*

Why will Delia thus retire,
   And idly languish life away?
While the sighing crowd admire
   'Tis too soon for hartshorn tea.

All these dismal looks and fretting   5
   Cannot Damon's life restore.
Long ago the worms have ate him,
   You can never see him more.

Once again consult your toilette,
   In the glass your face review;   10
So much weeping soon will spoil it,
   And no spring your charms renew.

I, like you, was born a woman;
   Well I know what vapours mean;
The disease – alas – is common;   15
   Single, we have all the spleen.

All the morals that they tell us
   Never cured the sorrow yet.
Choose among the pretty fellows,
   One of honour, youth and wit.   20

Prithee hear him every morning,
   At the least, an hour or two.
Once again at night returning –
   I believe the dose will do!

The poem was published in 1748, but probably written earlier. It is a witty, almost cynical, reflection on love, somewhat reminiscent of the cavalier poems of the previous century. Montagu may have known Sir John Suckling's (1609–42) poem, *Why so Pale and Wan*. In this, as in hers, the speaker addresses a lovelorn youth, and offers advice on how to overcome melancholy. Moreover, both poems end with similarly vigorous and dismissive lines: 'I believe the dose will do' and 'The Devil take her'. The difference is that Montagu is concerned with a bereaved young woman and Suckling with a scorned young man.

The poem is a lyric, written in alternately rhyming lines of trochaic (stress/unstress) tetrameters (four stresses to the line). The last syllable of the last foot is usually omitted.

Title

receipt recipe, prescription; *vapours* the fumes which were supposed to rise from the body and overspread the mind, at the expense of sanity. By transference, a morbid and hysterical condition, especially of women. Pope's 'Cave of Spleen' (in the fourth canto of *The Rape of the Lock*) is an allegorical representation of a vapourish condition.

[1] Delia

a stock poetic name – like Flavia in *Saturday*; *retire* withdraw from public life, specifically from the public life of a society beauty.

[3] sighing crowd

her male suitors, sighing with love.

[4] hartshorn tea

An infusion of horn scrapings creates an ammonia solution, which was once used medicinally. Various horns are still employed in this way in traditional Chinese medicine; *tea* pronounced 'tay'.

[6] Damon

another stock poetic name; *life* Delia's melancholy is caused by the death, rather than the desertion, of her lover.

[7] ate him

The rhyme with 'fretting' (line 5) causes 'ate him' to be pronounced 'et 'im', and conveys the idea of the worm's meal with great comic gusto.

[9] toilette

dressing table and cosmetics.

[14] Well I ... mean

Montagu accepts the opinion of her age that spleen and vapours were particularly feminine complaints.

[16] Single

i.e. if we are single; *spleen* a synonym for the vapours of the title.

[19] pretty fellow

fashionable young man; beau; fop.

[19–20] Choose ... wit

The speaker advises pleasure rather than morality to drive away sorrow. This is the cure for the vapours promised in the title.

[21] Prithee

a contraction of 'I pray thee'.

[21–3] every morning ... night

In specifying that the lover's addresses have to be 'taken' in morning and evening, Montagu mimics the style of a prescription.

ALEXANDER POPE

(1688–1744)

The literary career of Alexander Pope can be divided into three parts. Precocious in his youth, he established himself as probably the foremost poet of his generation well before he was 30, producing in this period such works as *An Essay on Criticism* (1711), *Windsor-Forest* (1713) and *The Rape of the Lock* (1712 & 1714). Having made his name as a poet, he turned to translating Homer, a task which occupied him for thirteen years (1713–26) during which he wrote very little original work. With Homer finally out of the way, he entered the third stage of his career with the publication of the first *Dunciad* in 1728 within days of his fortieth birthday. In his remaining years, he wrote most of his finest poetry, including the revised *Dunciad* (1742), the *Epistles to Several Persons* (1731–5), the *Imitations of Horace* (1733–8), to which series *Arbuthnot* belongs, and the philosophical *Essay on Man* (1732–4).

Although a highly successful poet and the friend of many of the most prominent men and women of his age, Pope remained always something of an outsider. Tuberculosis of the spine, contracted when he was a child, left him stunted, deformed, and the victim of precarious health throughout his life. His religion also tended to cut him off from his contemporaries for he was a Roman Catholic, which meant that he was excluded from public office, from university education and from residence in London. Finally, he spent his last years as a bitter opponent of Robert Walpole's administration and of what he saw as the general drift of society away from its traditional values.

Pope's reputation as a poet declined rather drastically with the rise of Romanticism at the end of his century, and although many readers in our century have found much to admire in his work, his standing is probably still less high than it was in his own day.

Further Reading

The standard edition of Pope's poetry is the eleven-volume *Twickenham Edition of the Poems of Alexander Pope* edited by John Butt and others (London: Methuen, 1939–69). Good single-volume editions are also available, among them a condensed version of the Twickenham edition. Herbert Davis's *Pope: Poetical Works* (Oxford: Oxford University Press, 1966) provides reliable texts, and early as well as late editions of *The Rape of the Lock* and *The Dunciad*. Rather less authoritative, but still usable and cheap, is Bonamy Dobrée's *Alexander Pope: Collected Poems* (London: J.M. Dent, 1924). The editors also wish to acknowledge use of the following: Francis Howes' translation of Horace, *Epistle VI*, in *The Complete Works*, ed. C.J. Kraemer (New York: Random House, 1936); H. Caplan's translation of Cicero, *Rhetorica ad Herrenium* (London: Heinemann, 1936); B. Radice's translation of Pliny, *Epistles* (London: Heinemann, 1942); H.E. Butler's translation of Quintilian, *Institutio Oratoria* (London: Heinemann, 1920); and Niall Rudd's translation, *The Satires of Horace and Persius* (Harmondsworth: Penguin, 1973).

The standard biography is Maynard Mack's *Alexander Pope: A Life* (New Haven: Yale University Press, 1985). Pope's poetry has been more thoroughly discussed by modern critics than that of any other writer in this volume. Geoffrey Tillotson's *On the Poetry of Pope* (Oxford: Clarendon Press, 1938) is still useful, and Reuben Brower's *Alexander Pope: The Poetry of Allusion* (London: Oxford University Press, 1959) remains an essential statement of the poet's method. A comprehensive account of the poetry is also attempted, though perhaps less successfully, by David B. Morris, *Alexander Pope: The Genius of Sense* (Cambridge, Mass.: Harvard University Press, 1984). Dustin H. Griffin's interesting book, *Alexander Pope: The Poet in the Poems* (Princeton: Princeton University Press, 1978), considers the self-expressive qualities of Pope's poetry, while Laura Brown's *Alexander Pope* (Oxford: Basil Blackwell, 1985) is one of a number of attempts to read it in the light of recent critical theory. A valuable introductory account of the late satires is provided by Peter Dixon, *The World of Pope's Satires: An Introduction to the 'Epistles' and 'Imitations of Horace'* (London: Methuen, 1968).

Articles on all aspects of Pope are legion. One of the most influential, which focuses upon the *Epistle to Dr Arbuthnot* in order to make a general point, is Maynard Mack's 'The Muse of Satire', *Yale Review* 41 (1950–1): 80–92. The new student is perhaps best advised to turn to collections of essays in order to gain a sense of different critical perspectives. John Dixon Hunt's *The Rape of the Lock: A Casebook* (London: Macmillan, 1968) is still useful, as are Maynard Mack (ed.), *Essential Articles for the Study of Alexander Pope* (Hamden, Conn.: Archon, 1964), and Maynard Mack and James A. Winn (eds), *Pope: Recent Essays by Several Hands* (Hamden, Conn.: Archon, 1980). A sense of how Pope has been differently regarded in different periods is provided by John Barnard (ed.), *Pope: The Critical Heritage* (London: Routledge and Kegan Paul, 1973). The editors are indebted to John Butt's *The Poems of Alexander Pope* (London: Methuen, 1963) and Raymond Southall's (ed.) *An Essay on Criticism* (Plymouth: Northcote House, 1973/1988).

———◇———

20 /   From *An Essay on Criticism*

'Tis hard to say, if greater want of skill
Appear in writing or in judging ill;
But, of the two, less dangerous is th'offence,
To tire our patience, than mis-lead our sense;
Some few in that, but numbers err in this,   5
Ten censure wrong for one who writes amiss;
A fool might once himself alone expose,
Now one in verse makes many more in prose.

'Tis with our judgements as our watches, none
Go just alike, yet each believes his own.   10
In poets as true genius is but rare,
True taste as seldom is the critic's share;
Both must alike from heaven derive their light,

These born to judge, as well as those to write:
Let such teach others who themselves excel,   15
And censure freely who have written well.
Authors are partial to their wit, 'tis true,
But are not critics to their judgement too?

.   .   .   .

First follow Nature, and your judgement frame
By her just standard, which is still the same;   20
Unerring Nature, still divinely bright,
One clear, unchanged, and universal light,
Life, force, and beauty, must to all impart,
At once the source, and end, and test of art.
Art from that fund each just supply provides,   25
Works without show, and without pomp presides;
In some fair body thus th'informing soul
With spirits feeds, with vigour fills the whole,
Each motion guides, and every nerve sustains,
Itself unseen, but in th'effects, remains.   30
Some, to whom heaven in wit has been profuse,
Want as much more, to turn it to its use;
For wit and judgement often are at strife,
Though meant each other's aid, like man and wife.
'Tis more to guide than spur the muse's steed,   35
Restrain his fury, than provoke his speed;
The winged courser, like a generous horse,
Shows most true mettle when you check his course.

Those rules of old discovered, not devised,
Are nature still, but nature methodised: 40
Nature, like liberty, is but restrained
By the same laws which first herself ordained.

.   .   .   .

You then whose judgement the right course would steer,
Know well each Ancient's proper character,
His fable, subject, scope in every page,   45
Religion, country, genius of his age:
Without all these at once before your eyes,

Cavil you may, but never criticise.
Be Homer's works your study, and delight,
Read them by day, and meditate by night: 50
Thence form your judgement, thence your maxims bring,
And trace the muses upward to their spring;
Still with itself compared, his text peruse,
And let your comment be the Mantuan muse.

When first young Maro in his boundless mind   55
A work t'outlast immortal Rome designed,
Perhaps he seemed above the critic's law,
And but from nature's fountains scorned to draw;
But when t'examine every part he came,
Nature and Homer were, he found, the same.   60
Convinced, amazed, he checks the bold design,
And rules as strict his laboured work confine,
As if the Stagyrite o'erlooked each line.
Learn hence for ancient rules a just esteem,
To copy nature is to copy them.   65

Some beauties yet, no precepts can declare,
For there's a happiness as well as care;
Music resembles poetry, in each
Are nameless graces which no methods teach,
And which a master-hand alone can reach.   70
If, where the rules not far enough extend,
(Since rules were made but to promote their end)
Some lucky licence answer to the full
Th'intent proposed, that licence is a rule;
Thus Pegasus, a nearer way to take,   75
May boldly deviate from the common track.
From vulgar bounds with brave disorder part,
And snatch a grace beyond the reach of art,
Which, without passing through the judgement, gains
The heart, and all its end at once attains.   80
In prospects thus, some objects please our eyes,
Which out of nature's common order rise,
The shapeless rock or hanging precipice.
Great wits sometimes may gloriously offend
And rise to faults true critics dare not mend;   85
But though the Ancients thus their rules invade,

(As kings dispense with laws themselves have made)
Moderns, beware! Or if you must offend
Against the precept, ne'er transgress its end,
Let it be seldom, and compelled by need,   90
And have, at least, their precedent to plead;
The critic else proceeds without remorse,
Seizes your fame, and puts his laws in force.

. . . .

   A little learning is a dangerous thing,
Drink deep, or taste not the Pierian spring;   95
There shallow draughts intoxicate the brain,
And drinking largely sobers us again.
Fired at first sight with what the muse imparts,
In fearless youth we tempt the heights of arts,
While from the bounded level of our mind,   100
Short views we take, nor see the lengths behind,
But more advanced, behold with strange surprise
New, distant scenes of endless science rise!
So pleased at first, the towering Alps we try,
Mount o'er the vales, and seem to tread the sky;   105
Th'eternal snows appear already past,
And the first clouds and mountains seem the last;
But those attained, we tremble to survey
The growing labours of the lengthened way,
Th'increasing prospect tires our wandering eyes,   110
Hills peep o'er hills, and Alps on Alps arise!

   A perfect judge will read each work of wit
With the same spirit that its author writ;
Survey the whole, nor seek slight faults to find,
Where nature moves, and rapture warms the mind;   115
Nor lose, for that malignant dull delight,
The generous pleasure to be charmed with wit.
But in such lays as neither ebb, nor flow,
Correctly cold, and regularly low,
That shunning faults, one quiet tenor keep,   120
We cannot blame indeed – but we may sleep.
In wit, as nature, what affects our hearts
Is not th'exactness of peculiar parts,

'Tis not a lip, or eye, we beauty call,
But the joint force and full result of all.　　　　　125
Thus when we view some well-proportioned dome,
(The world's just wonder, and ev'n thine O Rome!)
No single parts unequally surprise,
All comes united to th'admiring eyes;
No monstrous height, or breadth, or length appear,　　　　　130
The whole at once is bold, and regular.

.　.　.　.　.　.　.　.　.　.　.　.

Some to conceit alone their taste confine,
And glittering thoughts struck out at every line;
Pleased with a work where nothing's just or fit,
One glaring chaos and wild heap of wit;　　　　　135
Poets like painters, thus, unskilled to trace
The naked nature and the living grace,
With gold and jewels cover every part,
And hide with ornaments their want of art.
True wit is nature to advantage dressed,　　　　　140
What oft was thought, but ne'er so well expressed;
Something, whose truth convinced at sight we find,
That gives us back the image of our mind:
As shades more sweetly recommend the light,
So modest plainness sets off sprightly wit:　　　　　145
For works may have more wit than does 'em good,
As bodies perish through excess of blood.

Others for language all their care express,
And value books, as women men, for dress;
Their praise is still – The style is excellent:　　　　　150
The sense, they humbly take upon content.
Words are like leaves; and where they most abound,
Much fruit of sense beneath is rarely found.
False eloquence, like the prismatic glass,
Its gaudy colours spreads on every place;　　　　　155
The face of nature we no more survey,
All glares alike without distinction gay;
But true expression, like th'unchanging sun,
Clears, and improves whate'er it shines upon,
It gilds all objects, but it alters none.　　　　　160

Expression is the dress of thought, and still
Appears more decent as more suitable.

.   .   .   .

But most by numbers judge a poet's song,
And smooth or rough, with them, is right or wrong;
In the bright muse though thousand charms conspire,   165
Her voice is all these tuneful fools admire,
Who haunt Parnassus but to please their ear,
Not mend their minds; as some to church repair,
Not for the doctrine, but the music there:
These equal syllables alone require,   170
Though oft the ear the open vowels tire,
While expletives their feeble aid do join,
And ten low words oft creep in one dull line,
While they ring round the same unvaried chimes,
With sure returns of still expected rhymes.   175
Where-e'er you find the cooling western breeze,
In the next line, it whispers through the trees;
If crystal streams with pleasing murmurs creep,
The reader's threatened (not in vain) with sleep;
Then, at the last, and only couplet fraught   180
With some unmeaning thing they call a thought,
A needless Alexandrine ends the song,
That like a wounded snake, drags its slow length along.
Leave such to tune their own dull rhymes, and know
What's roundly smooth, or languishingly slow;   185
And praise the easy vigour of a line,
Where Denham's strength, and Waller's sweetness join.
True ease in writing comes from art, not chance,
As those move easiest who have learned to dance.
'Tis not enough no harshness gives offence,   190
The sound must seem an echo to the sense:
Soft is the strain when zephyr gently blows,
And the smooth stream in smoother numbers flows;
But when loud surges lash the sounding shore,
The hoarse, rough verse should like the torrent roar.   195

.   .   .   .

But where's the man, who counsel can bestow,
Still pleased to teach, and yet not proud to know?
Unbiased, or by favour or by spite,
Not dully prepossessed, nor blindly right;
Though learned, well-bred; and though well-bred, sincere,   200
Modestly bold, and humanly severe?
Who to a friend his faults can freely show,
And gladly praise the merit of a foe?
Blessed with a taste exact, yet unconfined,
A knowledge both of books and humankind;   205
Generous converse; a soul exempt from pride,
And love to praise, with reason on his side?

Such once were critics, such the happy few,
Athens and Rome in better ages knew.
The mighty Stagyrite first left the shore,   210
Spread all his sails, and durst the deeps explore;
He steered securely, and discovered far,
Led by the light of the Maeonian star.
Poets, a race long unconfined and free,
Still fond and proud of savage liberty,   215
Received his laws, and stood convinced 'twas fit
Who conquered nature, should preside o'er wit.

Horace still charms with graceful negligence,
And without method talks us into sense,
Will like a friend familiarly convey   220
The truest notions in the easiest way.
He, who supreme in judgement, as in wit,
Might boldly censure, as he boldly writ,
Yet judged with coolness though he sung with fire,
His precepts teach but what his works inspire.   225
Our critics take a contrary extreme,
They judge with fury, but they write with phlegm;
Not suffers Horace more in wrong translations
By wits, than critics in as wrong quotations.

See Dionysius Homer's thoughts refine,   230
And call new beauties forth from every line!

Fancy and art in gay Petronius please,
The scholar's learning, and the courtier's ease.

In grave Quintilian's copious work we find
The justest rules, and clearest method joined;   235
Thus useful arms in magazines we place,
All ranged in order, and disposed with grace,
But less to please the eye, than arm the hand,
Still fit for use, and ready at command.

Thee, bold Longinus! all the nine inspire,   240
And blessed their critic with a poet's fire;
An ardent judge, that zealous in his trust,
With warmth gives sentence, yet is always just;
Whose own example strengthens all his laws,
And is himself that great sublime he draws.   245

.   .   .   .

But soon by impious arms from Latium chased,
Their ancient bounds the banished muses passed;
Thence arts o'er all the northern world advance,
But critic learning flourished most in France.
The rules, a nation born to serve, obeys,   250
And Boileau still in right of Horace sways.
But we, brave Britons, foreign laws despised,
And kept unconquered, and uncivilised,
Fierce for the liberties of wit, and bold,
We still defied the Romans, as of old.   255
Yet some there were, among the sounder few
Of those who less presumed, and better knew,
Who durst assert the juster ancient cause,
And here restored wit's fundamental laws.
Such was the muse, whose rules and practice tell,   260
Nature's chief master-piece is writing well.
Such was Roscommon – not more learned than good,
With manners generous as his noble blood;
To him the wit of Greece and Rome was known,
And every author's merit, but his own.   265
Such late was Walsh, – the muse's judge and friend,
Who justly knew to blame or to commend;

To failings mild, but zealous for desert,
The clearest head, and the sincerest heart.
This humble praise, lamented shade! receive,   270
This praise at least a grateful muse may give!
The muse, whose early voice you taught to sing,
Prescribed her heights, and pruned her tender wing,
(Her guide now lost) no more attempts to rise,
But in low numbers short excursions tries;   275
Content, if hence th'unlearned their wants may view,
The learned reflect on what before they knew;
Careless of censure, nor too fond of fame,
Still pleased to praise, yet not afraid to blame,
Averse alike to flatter, or offend,   280
Not free from faults, nor yet too vain to mend.

Written in 1711, *An Essay on Criticism* is a verse essay, a genre seldom attempted today but one popular in the seventeenth and eighteenth centuries. Probably the most important ancient example to which Pope looks back is Horace's *Art of Poetry*.

Like nearly all Pope's poetry the *Essay* is written in heroic couplets. For a full note on these, see the introductory notes to *Rape of the Lock*.

Epigraph
'... Si quid novisti rectius istis,/ Candidus imperti; si non, his utere mecum.' (... and if my doctrine seem amiss,/ with candour set me right – If not, take this – last lines of Horace, *Epistles*, 1.vi. Trans. Howes).

[1] **want**
lack; *skill* 'Knowledge of any practice or art; readiness in any practice; knowledge; dexterity', Johnson, *Dictionary*.

[2] **judging**
'judge: One who has skill sufficient to decide upon the merit of anything', Johnson, *Dictionary*; *ill* 'Not well; not rightly in any respect', Johnson, *Dictionary*.

[3] **dangerous**
hazardous.

[4] **sense**
understanding.

[5] **numbers**
many.

[5]
Not as many make the mistake of writing badly as do of passing wrong judgements on other people's writing.

[6] **censure wrong**
reprimand wrongly; *amiss* faultily.

[7] **expose**
to lay open to censure or ridicule.

[8]
For every one person that writes poor poetry, there are many more that make erroneous critical assessments.

[9–10]
Pope points out how each individual is partial to his or her own judgement.

[12] **True taste**
Pope probably has in mind an ideal or faultless taste capable of full appreciation of a work of genius.

[11–12]
Just as real poetic genius is very rare, the capacity to properly discern and appreciate poetry is the privilege of very few critics.

[13] **heaven**
from a shared natural and superior source, as different from artificial and subjective measures.

[15]
'Thus the artistic writer will find it easy to discern what has been skilfully written by others', Cicero, *Ad Herrenium*, 4, 4. Pope's note (trans. Caplan); 'Judgement of painters, sculptors, creators of art, is not possible except by an artist', Pliny, *Epistles*, 1, 10. Pope's note (trans. Radice). This presents a slightly more extreme position than the one drawn from the *Ad Herrenium*.

[17] **wit**
imaginative powers; writings, products of genius. The word 'wit' is used in this poem in many different senses.

[19] **Nature**
the idea of creativity, order and harmony which reflects the divine mind of its Creator. Man, created in God's image, can realise a share in this idea even in his fallen condition. Man can do this through art; *frame* compose, regulate.

[20] **just**
proper; according to reason; *still the same* uniform, unchanged by time.

[21–2]
The lines incorporate the Platonic image of light as divine truth. The image had been used by Spenser and Milton, among others. See: 'Hail, holy light, off-spring of heaven first born,/ Or of the eternal co-eternal beam/ May I express thee unblamed? Since God is light,/ And never but in unapproached__ light/ Dwelt from eternity, dwelt then in thee,/ Bright effluence of bright essence increate', *Paradise Lost*, iii, 1–6.

[24]
Simultaneously the origin and the end of art, and also its standard of measurement.

[25] **just supply provides**
provides what is needed.

[26] **without show**
Horace had advised that art should conceal its presence.

[27] **informing**
endowing with form or essential qualities.

[28] **spirits**
powers of mind, moral or intellectual; *vigour* energy.

[29] **nerve**
sinew; *sustains* supports.

[31] **wit**
the word retains here the sense of the combined power of the imagination and intellect; in the next line Pope extends the meaning to include acumen. Judgement, he believes, is a proper constituent of wit, in the sense of 're-straint' or 'tact'. 'Wit' and 'judgement', though often conceived of as anti-thetical, are viewed as complementary.

[36] **provoke**
to incite.

[37] **generous**
spirited.

[38] **mettle**
'spirit, spritliness, courage', Johnson, *Dictionary*; *check* restrain in order to regulate; *check his course* control his race or speed.

[35–8]
In Greek myth Pegasus, the winged horse, caused the spring Hippocrene to well forth on Mount Helicon, the home of the muses. Hence Pegasus offers an image for poetry. In Plato the image of horse and bridle represents the proper and balanced relationship between reason and the passions; hence the unbridled horse came to signify the governance of the reason by the passions.

[39–40]
The ancient rules about the arts are inherent in the divine order of nature; man has not devised them, but only discovered them.

[41–2]
Man in society could protect his liberty only by formulating laws that governed his behaviour. Similarly nature ordains those laws that are both inherent and immanent in her and give her best expression.

[44] **Ancients**
'Those that lived in old times,

opposed to the moderns', Johnson, *Dictionary*. By 'old times' Johnson means in ancient Greece and Rome as opposed to the writers of the Renaissance and onwards. It appears from a note by Pope that he was also directly referring to the French writer Perrault's *Parallèle des Anciens et des Modernes* in which he had put the modern writers above the ancient writers and criticised Homer. Swift had taken a stand in favour of the Ancients in his *A Tale of a Tub*, and also in *The Battle of the Books*; **character** 'particular constitution of the mind', Johnson, *Dictionary*.

[45] fable
The main thread of the story of a work of literature; 'The series or contexture of events that constitute a poem', Johnson, *Dictionary*; **subject** chosen material; 'That on which any operation either mental or material is performed', Johnson, *Dictionary*; **scope** 'aim, intention', Johnson, *Dictionary*.

[46] genius of his age
inclination of the particular time.

[44–6]
The historical method in criticism, which encourages detailed knowledge of the age in which a particular author wrote, is recommended, but mainly as an aid to correct judgement. Pope is not advocating relativism of any kind.

[48] cavil
find fault unfairly; *criticise* judge well.

[50] meditate
revolve in the mind, muse upon.

[51] maxims
an axiom or general principle.

[52] spring
source.

[53]
The first thing is to study the text with an eye to its internal structure and organisation. In a more general sense the advice is to immerse yourself fully in Homer.

[54]
Virgil's epics provide the best commentary on Homer.

[54–5] Mantuan muse ... young Maro
Virgil (Virgilius Maro) was born near Mantua in northern Italy.

[55ff.]
'Virgil, Eclogue. 6. Whilst I sang of kings and battles, Apollo whispered to me – It is a tradition preserved by Servius, that Virgil began with writing a poem of the Alban and Roman affairs; which he found above his years, and descended first to imitate Theocritus on rural subjects, and afterwards to copy Homer in heroic poetry.' Pope's note translated.

[56]
a hyperbole, as something cannot 'outlast' that which is 'immortal'; *designed* planned; the word hints at another sense which Johnson defines and illustrates with reference to Addison: 'The idea which an artist endeavours to execute or express', *Dictionary*.

[58]
wished to 'imitate' only 'nature'.

[59–60]
Pope undoubtedly held Homer in very high estimation. The lines can be simply interpreted to mean that Virgil discerned that nature and Homer were identifiable. The lines also raise the question of the relationship between nature and the artist. The artist, as a man, is part of nature; he can also give form to the laws that are essential to nature, and thereby explicate them.

[61] convinced
overcome; *amazed* astonished; *checks* examines; *design* scheme.

[61–2]
Pope makes the point that Homer's work is governed by strict rules, which later artists can learn from him.

[63] Stagyrite
Aristotle, born in Stagira in 384 BC. Known for his treatise on tragedy, *The Poetics*, in which he extrapolated the chief characteristics of existing plays as essential to the form.

[64]
Pope appears to advise honouring the

'rules' of Aristotle. Actually it was the neo-classical critics of the late seventeenth and early eighteenth centuries who had crystallised Aristotle's ideas into rules. Soon after Pope makes clear that he is not advocating a servile adherence to any set of prescriptions.

[65] **copy**
in the sense of emulation, not slavish imitation.

[66] **precepts**
mandates; rules authoritatively given.

[67] **happiness**
artistic felicity for which there is no explanation; *care* attention.

[66–70]
Pope here subscribes to Longinus and the ideas of the School of Taste. He expresses the belief that the inspired genius may skirt the rules and achieve his end inexplicably.

[69] **nameless graces**
undefinable beauties; *methods* prescribed ways of doing something.

[71ff.]
Pope quotes from Quintilian, *Institutio Oratoria* at some length to elaborate his point:

For these rules have not the formal authority of laws or decrees of the plebs, but are, with all they contain, the children of expediency. I will not deny that it is generally expedient to conform to such rules ... but if our friend expediency suggests some other course to us, why, we should disregard the authority of the professors and follow her. (bk II, xiii, 6–7. Pope's note, trans. Butler.)

[72]
Rules are secondary to the goal or purpose for which they are contrived.

[73–4]
If the desired end is fully achieved, even if by some deviation from the established rule, then that deviation itself is as good as a rule.

[75] **Pegasus**
Pope draws once again upon the image of the mythical horse whose unconfined nature is associated with poetry.

[77] **vulgar bounds**
the limitations suitable for the ordinary.

[79] **judgement**
the faculty of the mind that compares and assesses. In the hierarchy of mental faculties it occupied an elevated position, second only to reason.

[80] **The heart**
the inmost part; used here in an all-inclusive sense as the seat of total satisfaction.

[83] **hanging**
overhanging, protruding.

[81–3]
The wild and irregular landscape which would create the Longinian emotion of the sublime; Pope may have in mind contemporary landscape paintings that depicted such wild mountainous scenery. Later Burke was to explore the idea in his *Enquiry into ... the Sublime and Beautiful.*

[84] **gloriously offend**
Pope uses the oxymoronic phrase to illustrate his point that apparently contradictory positions are not meaningless. It must be noted that the passage goes on to warn against the needless transgression of the rules.

[85] **rise to faults**
another oxymoron.

[86] **invade**
violate.

[91] **their precedent to plead**
the example of the ancients as support. There is a legalistic colour to the phrase.

[93] **seizes**
also probably used in the legal sense of 'to take possession of ... in pursuance of a judicial order'.

[95] **Pierian spring**
the spring of the muses, who were first worshipped in Pieria, a coastal region in ancient Macedonia.

[97] **largely**
abundantly.

[98] **Fired**
enthused; *imparts* communicates.

[99] **tempt**
attempt.
[100] **bounded level**
restricted plain.
[103] **science**
knowledge.
[110] **wandering**
journeying uncertainly.
[98–111]
Johnson considered this

comparison of a student's progress in the sciences with the journey of a traveller in the Alps . . . perhaps the best that English poetry can show. The simile of the Alps has no useless parts, yet affords a striking picture by itself; it makes the foregoing position better understood, and enables it to take faster hold on the attention; it assists the apprehension and elevates the fancy. (*Life of Pope*)

The strength and economy of the lines lie in the fact that the young student's responses in the first part are conceived in terms of landscape metaphors that are activated in the image of the Alps in the second part. The image is integrated with the movements of the student's mind, which it seeks to illustrate. The shift in tense from past to present endows a vibrant presence to the mountain image itself. All through, Pope's visual and verbal imagination work together.
[112] **perfect judge**
the phrase has a religious resonance, as too do 'spirit' and 'author' of the next line; *read* to understand properly or fully; *work of wit* product of the creative mind or genius.
[113] **spirit**
'likeness; essential qualities', Johnson, *Dictionary*.
[114] **Survey the whole**
attempt a view of the complete work; later, especially in *An Essay on Man*, Pope explores the idea that as man can see but in part, he cannot fully appreciate the justness and perfection of God's creation.

[115] **nature moves**
a proper presentation of human emotions stirs the heart of the reader; *rapture warms the mind* the mind is elevated to a state of ecstasy.
[116] **malignant dull delight**
the malicious pleasure of finding fault.
[117] **generous pleasure**
the pleasure of a magnanimous mind; *to be charmed with wit* to be responsive to intelligence.
[118] **lays**
songs; *as neither ebb, nor flow* that have no movement at all, static, dull.
[119] **Correctly cold**
exact but without feeling; *regularly low* governed by strict rules and hence subdued.
[120] **tenor**
constant mode, continuity.
[123] **exactness**
strict conformity; *peculiar* particular or single.
[125] **full result**
total effect.
[126] **dome**
building.
[128] **unequally surprise**
draw attention disproportionately.
[130] **monstrous**
enormous in an irregular way.
[131] **at once is bold, and regular**
simultaneously conforming to the rules and executed with spirit.
[132] **conceit**
'Sentiment, as distinguished from imagery', Johnson, *Dictionary*; Johnson illustrates this sense by this line from Pope.
[134] **just or fit**
proportionate or suitable.
[135] **glaring chaos**
continuing the idea of 'glittering' accompanied with the sense of disorder and confusion; *wild heap of wit* pile of irregular ideas.
[136] **Poets like painters**
a popular feature of eighteenth-century criticism was to draw a parallel between poetry and painting.
[137] **naked nature**
unconcealed form; *living grace* natural perfection or excellence.

[139] **want of art**
lack of skill.
[140] **True wit**
great literature.
[140–3]
Pope glossed this famous passage with a reference to Quintilian, *Institutio Oratoria*, viii, 3: 'Fix your eyes on nature and follow her. ... the mind is always readiest to accept what it recognises to be true to nature'. Pope's note (trans. Butler). Despite Pope's gloss Johnson confined his attention to the first couplet, 'True wit is nature to advantage dressed, / What oft was thought, but ne'er so well expressed', and criticised it as follows: 'Pope's account of wit is undoubtedly erroneous: he depresses it below its natural dignity, and reduces it from strength of thought to happiness of language', *Life of Cowley*. Johnson's criticism is particularly puzzling in the light of Pope's effort in *An Essay on Criticism* to direct the critic's attention away from particular parts to the larger sequences of thought in works of art.
[143] **image**
'An idea; a representation of anything to the mind', Johnson, *Dictionary*.
[142–3]
Pope suggests an intuitive recognition based on an existing idea in the mind. Johnson defines 'intuition' in his *Dictionary* as 'Sight of anything; immediate knowledge'.
[144] **recommend**
make more desirable.
[145] **modest**
in a low key, not impudent or arrogant; *plainness* unadorned, not showy; *sprightly* gay, lively; *wit* fancy; *modest plainness* the phrase carries a subdued personification, as too does *sprightly wit*.
[146] **wit**
quickness of fancy.
[147]
The metaphor of the human body was a common basis for comparison with all human creations and activities.

[151] **content**
'acquiescence; satisfaction in a thing unexamined', Johnson, *Dictionary*; this sense is illustrated by the same passage from Pope.
[153] **sense**
meaning, import.
[154] **False**
deceptive, treacherous; *eloquence* 'Elegant language uttered with fluency', Johnson, *Dictionary*, with an illustrating quotation from Pope; *prismatic glass* a particular geometrical formation in glass through which light is refracted into varied colours.
[155] **gaudy colours**
as above. The effects of verbal eloquence are once again described in the language of visual experience.
[157]
Everything is indiscriminately bright and decorated.
[158] **true expression**
as opposed to 'false eloquence' of line 156; *unchanging sun* the constant and self-generated light of the sun was a popular metaphor for truth, especially as opposed to the changing and borrowed light of the moon.
[159] **Clears**
brightens, makes more luminous; *improves* 'improve: To advance anything nearer to perfection', Johnson, *Dictionary*.
[160] **gilds**
brightens or illuminates.
[161] **Expression is the dress of thought**
Pope is not assigning an adventitious and secondary position to language in poetry. He is, rather, expressing the old belief that expression, like dress, was a materialisation of the inner self.
[162] **decent**
becoming; *suitable* appropriate, proper.
[163] **numbers**
versification, metre.
[163ff.]
'What you'd expect – that poems at least have a smooth-flowing rhythm; where the joint occurs, it sends the critical nail skidding across the

polished surface', Persius, *Satire*, i, 63–6. Pope's note (trans. Rudd).

[165] **conspire**
unite.

[167] **Parnassus**
the mountain in Greece associated with the worship of Apollo and the muses, especially the muse of poetry.

[166–7]
Though many things go into the making of a poem, these people admire only its sound or versification.

[167–8] **please their ear,/ Not mend their minds**
Pope points to the overbalance of sensuous pleasure that some people derive from poetry. In this connection it is interesting to note Johnson's comparison between Dryden and Pope: 'Pope is read with calm acquiescence, Dryden with turbulent delight; Pope hangs upon the ear, and Dryden finds the passes of the mind', *Life of Pope*.

[168] **repair**
to go; to betake oneself.

[169] **doctrine**
'The principles or position of any sect or master', Johnson, *Dictionary*.

[170] **equal syllables**
even versification.

[171] **open vowels**
produced with a wide opening of the oral cavity as opposed to 'close vowels'.

[172] **expletives**
'Something used only to take up room', Johnson, *Dictionary*.

[173]
the line illustrates what it criticises, the stringing together of ten monosyllabic words of little consequence; *low words* words lacking in resonance of meaning, confined in their application to mundane ideas; *oft creep* move slowly.

[174]
Repeat the same sound again and again.

[176–8]
Pope mocks the stock language of poetry.

[180] **fraught**
charged.

[182] **needless**
unnecessary; *Alexandrine* 'A kind of verse borrowed from the French, first used in a poem called *Alexander*. This verse consists of twelve syllables'. Johnson's definition in his *Dictionary* is illustrated by the same lines from Pope.

[183]
The line is an alexandrine in form, and the meaning elucidates what is, in Pope's view, the slow and ineffectual nature of the alexandrine.

[184] **dull**
lacking in meaning.

[185] **roundly smooth**
completely even; *languishingly* 'Weakly; feebly; with feeble softness', Johnson, *Dictionary*, illustrated with the same lines from Pope.

[186] **easy vigour**
concentration of meaning, forcefully expressed, but in a flowing manner.

[187] **Denham's strength ... Waller's sweetness**
See 'This sweetness of Mr. Waller's lyric poesy was afterwards followed in the epic by Sir John Denham, in his *Cooper's Hill*, a poem which your Lordship knows for the majesty of the style', Dryden, *Epistle Dedicatory of the Rival Ladies*. Johnson, in his *Life of Denham*, had defined the word 'strength' as 'lines and couplets, which convey much meaning in few words, and exhibit the sentiment with more weight than bulk'; Spence records in his *Anecdotes* Pope's statement: 'In versification there is a sensible difference between softness and sweetness that I could distinguish from a boy. Thus on the same points, Dryden will be found to be softer, and Waller sweeter.'

[188] **ease**
facility; *art* skill attained through practice.

[190] **harshness**
roughness to the ear.

[191]
Pope's famous sound and sense dictum. In his notes to his translation of the *Iliad* and *Odyssey* Pope often

claimed that his versification represented the meaning of his lines. In line 1005 of Book XIII of his *Iliad*: 'Wide-rolling, foaming high, and tumbling to the shore', for instance, he said he had endeavoured to imitate the confusion and the broken sound of the original, which he conceived as imaging the tumult and roaring of the waters. He discerned a particular beauty in *Iliad* XIII: 'every word has a melancholy cadence, and the poet has not only made the sands and the arms, but even his very verse, to lament with Achilles'. A critic like Johnson who disagreed with the basic premise of the 'sound and sense' dictum would have attributed the sense of sorrow as much to the diction as to the metre. He said in his *Life of Pope* that the 'notion of representative metre, and the desire of discovering frequent adaptations of the sound to the sense' had produced 'many wild conceits, and imaginary beauties'.

[192] **strain**
sound, note; *zephyr* the west wind.
[194]
the sound of the line, Pope suggests, reflects its meaning; this is further exemplified in the next line.
[198] **or by favour or by spite**
neither by undue partiality nor by rancour.
[199] **dully prepossessed**
uncritically prejudiced against something; *blindly right* in favour of without proper examination.
[200] **well-bred**
elegant of manners, polite; *sincere* honest, not hypocritical.
[200]
Pope lists qualities that do not normally go together.
[201] **Modestly bold**
confident without being arrogant; *humanly severe* strict in a good natured way.
[204] **taste exact, yet unconfined**
an intellect that perceives in an accurate, but not too restricted a manner.
[206] **Generous converse**
well-bred social intercourse.

[210] **Stagyrite**
Aristotle, who was born in Stagira.
[210–12]
Aristotle's work conceived in the terms of a seafaring explorer.
[213] **Maeonian star**
Homer. Maeonia was the name given to Lydia, where Homer was supposed to have been born.
[215] **savage liberty**
unconstrained freedom.
[216] **Received his laws**
accepted his rules.
[217] **conquered nature**
Aristotle investigated many aspects of the physical world; could refer also to his understanding of how nature was best represented in art; *preside o'er* have authority over; *wit* communication of knowledge or intelligence as in a piece of writing.
[218] **Horace**
Quintus Horatius Flaccus, a contemporary of Virgil; well known for his *Ars Poetica*, the basis for many seventeenth- and eighteenth-century treatises on poetry in France and England; *graceful negligence* beautiful and dignified but uncontrived.
[219] **without method**
without proceeding in due order; *talks us into sense* is persuasive of sound reason.
[220] **familiarly**
informally.
[221] **notions**
thoughts; *easiest way* in the most smooth and flowing style.
[222] **supreme ... wit**
he who is master of both critical assessment and the lively presentation of life and knowledge.
[223]
His criticism may be as forceful as his creative presentations.
[224]
Exercised his judgement in a cool frame of mind, even though his poetry is full of passion.
[225]
His prescriptions accord with the spirit of his writings.

[227] **judge with fury**
censure with ardour; *write with phlegm* write in a cold, sluggish manner.

[229] **than critics**
than by critics.

[230] **Dionysius**
Dionysius of Halicarnassus, a Greek writer who lived in Rome in the days of Augustus and was the author of several important treatises in criticism.

[232] **Petronius**
Petronius Arbiter, one of Nero's inner circle in which he was regarded as an arbiter of taste; *Fancy . . . please* probably because Petronius was the author of the *Satyricon* in which there is great vivacity in presentation as well as inventiveness and ribaldry.

[233] **courtier's ease**
the courtier's relaxed and well-bred social intercourse.

[235] **Quintilian**
Marcus Fabius Quintilianus who lived around the first century AD, best known for his *Institutio Oratoria*. Quintilian's work exemplifies the greatest propriety in rules and the clearest order in the organisation of his materials.

[236–40]
See *Institutio Oratoria*, II, i, 12 and VII, x, 14: 'These are weapons which we should always have stored in our armoury ready for immediate use as the occasion may command', and 'The gift of arrangement is to oratory what generalship is to war. The skilled commander will know how to distribute his forces for battle', Pope's note (trans. Butler). Pope applies to Quintilian one of that writer's own favourite comparisons.

[240] **Longinus**
Dionysius Longinus, supposed author of the *Treatise on the Sublime*. The concept of the sublime appealed to the eighteenth century. John Dennis elaborated on it in his criticism of Milton. Later Edmund Burke wrote his famous *Enquiry . . . the Sublime and Beautiful*. Of course, in this process

Longinus's ideas underwent considerable modification; *all the nine* all the nine muses.

[241]
Referring to the expansive and emotionally charged nature of the sublime as delineated by Longinus.

[242] **ardent**
passionate; *ardent judge* a deliberate oxymoronic usage suggesting a fruitful combination of different faculties; *zealous in his trust* passionately involved in what is in his charge.

[243]
His assessment is always charged with feeling, but nevertheless fair.

[244]
Pope suggests that the best critics exemplify the rules they advocate.

[245]
Longinus's writings may be identified with idea of the sublime that he delineates.

[246] **impious arms from Latium chased**
Rome was sacked in 1527 by the troops of the Emperor Charles V under the leadership of the Duke of Bourbon. Pope suggests that learning fled to other parts of Europe.

[247]
The muses, exiled from Rome, went beyond their traditional habitation.

[249–51]
Classical criticism flourished in France in its most rigid form. Pope comments on the servility of the French, a popular theme in the satires of this period. Johnson refers to it in *London*. Pope may also have in mind French subservience to the despotic government of Louis XIV, as opposed to the British rebellion against Charles I and the Glorious Revolution of 1688.

[251] **Boileau**
Nicolas Boileau-Despreaux (1636–1711), the influential French critic and poet who was a friend of Molière, La Fontaine and Racine. In Pope's context he is remembered for his *L'Art Poétique*, a treatise on poetry in the tradition of Horace's *Ars Poetica*.

Boileau was known as the *législateur du Parnasse*.

[252–3]
British freedom, Pope says, amounts to lack of culture.

[257] **less presumed**
had fewer baseless opinions; **better knew** had sounder knowledge.

[258] **juster ancient cause**
the better arguments of the writers of ancient Rome.

[259] **wit's fundamental laws**
the primary rules of writing well.

[260]
'*Essay on Poetry*, by the Duke of Buckingham. Our poet is not the only one of his time who complimented this *Essay*, and its notable author. Mr Dryden had done it very largely in his Dedication to his translation of the *Aeneid*; and Dr Garth in the first edition of the *Dispensary* says, "*The Tyber now no courtly Gallus sees,/ But smiling Thames enjoys his Normanbys.*" . . . This nobleman's (the Duke of Buckingham's) true character had been very well marked by Mr Dryden before, "*the muse's friend,/ Himself a muse. In Sanadrin's debate/ True to his prince, but not a slave of state*", *Absalom and Achitophel*, 877–9.' Pope's note abbreviated.

[262] **Roscommon**
Wentworth Dillon, fourth Earl of Roscommon (1630–85). He translated Horace's *Ars Poetica* (1680) and wrote *An Essay on Translated Verse* (1684). He was one of the first critics to praise Milton's *Paradise Lost*.

[263] **manners generous**
noble in his conduct.

[264] **wit of Greece and Rome**
the understanding the ancient civilisations had of creative writing.

[266] **Walsh**
William Walsh (1663–1708), a poet and critic whose views were appreciated by Dryden. He encouraged Pope in his early years. Walsh is best remembered for his poem *The Despairing Lover*.

[268] **zealous for desert**
passionate in the cause of true merit.

[271] **grateful muse**
Pope himself.

[272]
Pope expresses gratitude to Walsh for his early encouragement.

[273] **pruned**
to trim or dress the feathers with a beak. Used in the more general sense of to divest of superfluities.

[275] **low numbers**
in a low key.

[276] **unlearned their wants may view**
those ignorant in the art of verse may learn their deficiencies.

[278] **careless**
not worried about.

[279] **pleased to**
happy to; *blame* point out faults.

[280] **averse**
unwilling to.

———◇———

21 / *Windsor-Forest*
To the Right Honourable George Lord Lansdowne

Thy forests, Windsor! and thy green retreats,
At once the monarch's and the muse's seats,
Invite my lays. Be present, sylvan maids!
Unlock your springs, and open all your shades.
Granville commands: Your aid O muses bring!   5
What muse for Granville can refuse to sing?

The groves of Eden, vanished now so long,
Live in description, and look green in song;
These, were my breast inspired with equal flame,
Like them in beauty, should be like in fame.   10
Here hills and vales, the woodland and the plain,
Here earth and water seem to strive again,
Not chaos-like together crushed and bruised,
But as the world, harmoniously confused;
Where order in variety we see,   15
And where, though all things differ, all agree.
Here waving groves a checkered scene display,
And part admit and part exclude the day;
As some coy nymph her lover's warm address
Nor quite indulges, nor can quite repress.   20
There, interspersed in lawns and opening glades,
Thin trees arise that shun each other's shades.
Here in full light the russet plains extend;
There wrapped in clouds the blueish hills ascend;
Ev'n the wild heath displays her purple dyes,   25
And midst the desert fruitful fields arise,
That crowned with tufted trees and springing corn,
Like verdant isles the sable waste adorn.
Let India boast her plants, nor envy we
The weeping amber or the balmy tree,   30
While by our oaks the precious loads are borne,
And realms commanded which those trees adorn.
Not proud Olympus yields a nobler sight,
Though gods assembled grace his towering height,
Than what more humble mountains offer here,   35
Where, in their blessings, all those gods appear.
See Pan with flocks, with fruits Pomona crowned,
Here blushing Flora paints th'enamelled ground,

Here Ceres' gifts in waving prospect stand,
And nodding tempt the joyful reaper's hand,   40
Rich industry sits smiling on the plains,
And peace and plenty tell, a Stuart reigns.

    Not thus the land appeared in ages past,
A dreary desert and a gloomy waste,
To savage beasts and savage laws a prey,   45
And kings more furious and severe than they;
Who claimed the skies, dispeopled air and floods,
The lonely lords of empty wilds and woods.
Cities laid waste, they stormed the dens and caves,
(For wiser brutes were backward to be slaves).   50
What could be free, when lawless beasts obeyed,
And ev'n the elements a tyrant swayed?
In vain kind seasons swelled the teeming grain,
Soft showers distilled, and suns grew warm in vain:
The swain with tears his frustrate labour yields,   55
And famished dies amidst his ripened fields.
What wonder then, a beast or subject slain
Were equal crimes in a despotic reign;
Both doomed alike for sportive tyrants bled,
But while the subject starved, the beast was fed.   60
Proud Nimrod first the bloody chase began,
A mighty hunter, and his prey was man.
Our haughty Norman boasts that barbarous name,
And makes his trembling slaves the royal game.
The fields are ravished from th'industrious swains,   65
From men their cities, and from gods their fanes;
The levelled towns with weeds lie covered o'er,
The hollow winds through naked temples roar;
Round broken columns clasping ivy twined;
O'er heaps of ruin stalked the stately hind;   70
The fox obscene to gaping tombs retires,
And savage howlings fill the sacred quires.
Awed by his nobles, by his commons cursed,
Th' oppressor ruled tyrannic where he durst,
Stretched o'er the poor, and church, his iron rod,   75
And served alike his vassals and his God.
Whom ev'n the Saxon spared, and bloody Dane,
The wanton victims of his sport remain.

But see the man who spacious regions gave
A waste for beasts, himself denied a grave!   80
Stretched on the lawn his second hope survey,
At once the chaser and at once the prey.
Lo Rufus, tugging at the deadly dart,
Bleeds in the forest, like a wounded hart.
Succeeding monarchs heard the subjects' cries,   85
Nor saw displeased the peaceful cottage rise.
Then gathering flocks on unknown mountains fed,
O'er sandy wilds were yellow harvests spread,
The forests wondered at th'unusual grain,
And secret transport touched the conscious swain.   90
Fair liberty, Britannia's goddess, rears
Her cheerful head, and leads the golden years.

Ye vigorous swains! while youth ferments your blood,
And purer spirits swell the sprightly flood,
Now range the hills, the gameful woods beset,   95
Wind the shrill horn, or spread the waving net:
When milder autumn summer's heat succeeds,
And in the new-shorn field the partridge feeds,
Before his lord the ready spaniel bounds,
Panting with hope, he tries the furrowed grounds,   100
But when the tainted gales the game betray,
Couched close he lies, and meditates the prey:
Secure they trust th'unfaithful field, beset,
Till hovering o'er 'em sweeps the swelling net.
Thus (if small things we may with great compare)   105
When Albion sends her eager sons to war,
Some thoughtless town, with ease and plenty blest,
Near, and more near, the closing lines invest:
Sudden they seize th'amazed, defenceless prize,
And high in air Britannia's standard flies.   110

See! from the brake the whirring pheasant springs,
And mounts exulting on triumphant wings:
Short is his joy! he feels the fiery wound,
Flutters in blood, and panting beats the ground.
Ah! what avail his glossy, varying dyes,   115
His purple crest, and scarlet-circled eyes,
The vivid green his shining plumes unfold;
His painted wings, and breast that flames with gold?

Nor yet, when moist Arcturus clouds the sky,
The woods and fields their pleasing toils deny.   120
To plains with well-breathed beagles we repair,
And trace the mazes of the circling hare.
(Beasts, urged by us, their fellow beasts pursue,
And learn of man each other to undo.)
With slaughtering guns th'unwearied fowler roves,   125
When frosts have whitened all the naked groves:
Where doves in flocks the leafless trees o'ershade,
And lonely woodcocks haunt the watery glade.
He lifts the tube, and levels with his eye;
Straight a short thunder breaks the frozen sky.   130
Oft, as in airy rings they skim the heath,
The clamorous lapwings feel the leaden death;
Oft as the mounting larks their notes prepare,
They fall, and leave their little lives in air.

In genial spring, beneath the quivering shade   135
Where cooling vapours breathe along the mead,
The patient fisher takes his silent stand
Intent, his angle trembling in his hand:
With looks unmoved, he hopes the scaly breed,
And eyes the dancing cork and bending reed.   140
Our plenteous streams a various race supply:
The bright-eyed perch with fins of Tyrian dye,
The silver eel, in shining volumes rolled,
The yellow carp, in scales bedropped with gold,
Swift trouts, diversified with crimson stains,   145
And pikes, the tyrants of the watery plains.

Now Cancer glows with Phoebus' fiery car,
The youth rush eager to the sylvan war:
Swarm o'er the lawns, the forest walks surround,
Rouse the fleet hart, and cheer the opening hound.   150
Th'impatient courser pants in every vein,
And pawing, seems to beat the distant plain,
Hills, vales, and floods appear already crossed,
And ere he starts, a thousand steps are lost.
See! the bold youth strain up the threatening steep,   155
Rush through the thickets, down the valleys sweep,
Hang o'er their coursers heads with eager speed,

And earth rolls back beneath the flying steed.
Let old Arcadia boast her ample plain,
Th'immortal huntress, and her virgin train;   160
Nor envy Windsor! since thy shades have seen
As bright a Goddess, and as chaste a queen;
Whose care, like hers, protects the sylvan reign,
The earth's fair light, and empress of the main.

Here too, 'tis sung, of old Diana strayed,   165
And Cynthus' top forsook for Windsor shade:
Here was she seen o'er airy wastes to rove,
Seek the clear spring, or haunt the pathless grove:
Here armed with silver bows, in early dawn,
Her buskined virgins traced the dewy lawn.   170

Above the rest a rural nymph was famed,
Thy offspring, Thames! the fair Lodona named,
(Lodona's fate, in long oblivion cast,
The muse shall sing, and what she sings shall last)
Scarce could the goddess from her nymph be known,   175
But by the crescent and the golden zone,
She scorned the praise of beauty, and the care;
A belt her waist, a fillet binds her hair,
A painted quiver on her shoulder sounds,
And with her dart the flying deer she wounds.   180
It chanced, as eager of the chase the maid
Beyond the forest's verdant limits strayed,
Pan saw and loved, and burning with desire
Pursued her flight; her flight increased his fire.
Not half so swift the trembling doves can fly,   185
When the fierce eagle cleaves the liquid sky,
Not half so swiftly the fierce eagle moves,
When through the clouds he drives the trembling doves;
As from the god she flew with furious pace,
Or as the god, more furious, urged the chase.   190
Now fainting, sinking, pale, the nymph appears,
Now close behind his sounding steps she hears,
And now his shadow reached her as she run,
(His shadow lengthened by the setting sun)
And now his shorter breath with sultry air   195

Pants on her neck, and fans her parting hair.
In vain on Father Thames she calls for aid,
Nor could Diana help her injured maid.
Faint, breathless, thus she prayed, nor prayed in vain;
'Ah Cynthia! ah – though banished from thy train,   200
Let me, O let me, to the shades repair,
My native shades – there weep, and murmur there.'
She said, and melting as in tears she lay,
In a soft, silver stream dissolved away.
The silver stream her virgin coldness keeps,   205
For ever murmurs, and for ever weeps;
Still bears the name the hapless virgin bore,
And bathes the forest where she ranged before.
In her chaste current oft the goddess laves,
And with celestial tears augments the waves.   210
Oft in her glass the musing shepherd spies
The headlong mountains and the downward skies,
The watery landscape of the pendant woods,
And absent trees that tremble in the floods;
In the clear azure gleam the flocks are seen,   215
And floating forests paint the waves with green.
Through the fair scene roll slow the lingering streams,
Then foaming pour along, and rush into the Thames.

Thou too, great father of the British floods!
With joyful pride surveyest our lofty woods,   220
Where towering oaks their growing honours rear,
And future navies on thy shores appear.
Not Neptune's self from all his streams receives
A wealthier tribute, than to thine he gives.
No seas so rich, so gay no banks appear,   225
No lake so gentle, and no spring so clear.
Nor Po so swells the fabling poet's lays,
While led along the skies his current strays,
As thine, which visits Windsor's famed abodes,
To grace the mansion of our earthly gods.   230
Nor all his stars above a lustre show,
Like the bright beauties on thy banks below;
Where Jove, subdued by mortal passion still,
Might change Olympus for a nobler hill.

Happy the man whom this bright court approves,   235
His sovereign favours, and his country loves;
Happy next him who to these shades retires,
Whom nature charms, and whom the muse inspires,
Whom humbler joys of home-felt quiet please,
Successive study, exercise and ease.   240
He gathers health from herbs the forest yields,
And of their fragrant physic spoils the fields;
With chymic art exalts the mineral powers,
And draws the aromatic souls of flowers.
Now marks the course of rolling orbs on high;   245
O'er figured worlds now travels with his eye.
Of ancient writ unlocks the learned store,
Consults the dead, and lives past ages o'er.
Or wandering thoughtful in the silent wood,
Attends the duties of the wise and good,   250
T'observe a mean, be to himself a friend,
To follow nature, and regard his end.
Or looks on heaven with more than mortal eyes,
Bids his free soul expatiate in the skies,
Amid her kindred stars familiar roam,   255
Survey the region, and confess her home!
Such was the life great Scipio once admired,
Thus Atticus, and Trumbal thus retired.

Ye sacred nine! that all my soul possess,
Whose raptures fire me, and whose visions bless,   260
Bear me, oh bear me to sequestered scenes,
The bowery mazes and surrounding greens:
To Thames's banks which fragrant breezes fill,
Or where ye muses sport on Cooper's Hill.
(On Cooper's hill eternal wreaths shall grow,   265
While lasts the mountain, or while Thames shall flow)
I seem through consecrated walks to rove,
I hear soft music die along the grove;
Led by the sound I roam from shade to shade,
By God-like poets venerable made: 270
Here his first lays majestic Denham sung;
There the last numbers flowed from Cowley's tongue.
O early lost! what tears the river shed
When the sad pomp along his banks was led?

His drooping swans on every note expire,   275
And on his willows hung each muse's lyre.

Since fate relentless stopped their heavenly voice,
No more the forests ring, or groves rejoice;
Who now shall charm the shades where Cowley strung
His living harp, and lofty Denham sung?   280
But hark! the groves rejoice, the forest rings!
Are these revived? or is it Granville sings?

'Tis yours, my lord, to bless our soft retreats,
And call the muses to their ancient seats,
To paint anew the flowery sylvan scenes,   285
To crown the forests with immortal greens,
Make Windsor hills in lofty numbers rise,
And lift her turrets nearer to the skies:
To sing those honours you deserve to wear,
And add new lustre to her Silver Star.   290

Here noble Surrey felt the sacred rage,
Surrey, the Granville of a former age;
Matchless his pen, victorious was his lance;
Bold in the lists, and graceful in the dance:
In the same shades the Cupids tuned his lyre,   295
To the same notes, of love, and soft desire:
Fair Geraldine, bright object of his vow,
Then filled the groves, as heavenly Myra now.

Oh wouldst thou sing what heroes Windsor bore,
What kings first breathed upon her winding shore,   300
Or raise old warriors whose adored remains
In weeping vaults her hallowed earth contains!
With Edward's acts adorn the shining page,
Stretch his long triumphs down through every age,
Draw monarchs chained, and Cressy's glorious field,   305
The lillies blazing on the regal shield.
Then, from her roofs when Verrio's colours fall,
And leave inanimate the naked wall;
Still in thy song should vanquished France appear,
And bleed for ever under Britain's spear.   310

Let softer strains ill-fated Henry mourn,
And palms eternal flourish round his urn.
Here o'er the martyr-king the marble weeps,
And fast beside him, once-feared Edward sleeps;
Whom not th'extended Albion could contain,   315
From old Belerium to the Northern Main,
The grave unites; where ev'n the great find rest,
And blended lie th'oppressor and th'oppressed!

Make sacred Charles's tomb for ever known,
(Obscure the place, and uninscribed the stone)   320
Oh fact accurst! What tears has Albion shed,
Heavens! what new wounds, and how her old have bled;
She saw her sons with purple deaths expire,
Her sacred domes involved in rolling fire,
A dreadful series of intestine wars,   325
Inglorious triumphs, and dishonest scars.
At length great Anna said – Let discord cease!
She said, the world obeyed, and all was peace!

In that blessed moment, from his oozy bed
Old Father Thames advanced his reverend head.   330
His tresses dropped with dews, and o'er the stream
His shining horns diffused a golden gleam;
Graved on his urn appeared the moon, that guides
His swelling waters, and alternate tides;
The figured streams in waves of silver rolled,   335
And on their banks Augusta rose in gold.
Around his throne the sea-born brothers stood,
Who swell with tributary urns his flood.
First the famed authors of his ancient name,
The winding Isis, and the fruitful Tame: 340
The Kennet swift, for silver eels renowned;
The Loddon slow, with verdant alders crowned:
Cole, whose dark streams his flowery islands lave;
And chalky Wey, that rolls a milky wave:
The blue, transparent Vandalis appears;   345
The gulfy Lee his sedgy tresses rears:
And sullen Mole, that hides his diving flood;
And silent Darent, stained with Danish blood.

High in the midst, upon his urn reclined,
(His sea-green mantle waving with the wind)   350
The god appeared; he turned his azure eyes
Where Windsor-domes and pompous turrets rise,
Then bowed and spoke; the winds forget to roar,
And the hushed waves glide softly to the shore.

Hail sacred peace! hail long-expected days,   355
That Thames's glory to the stars shall raise!
Though Tiber's streams immortal Rome behold,
Though foaming Hermus swells with tides of gold,
From heaven itself though sevenfold Nilus flows,
And harvests on a hundred realms bestows: 360
These now no more shall be the muse's themes,
Lost in my fame, as in the sea their streams.
Let Volga's banks with iron squadrons shine,
And groves of lances glitter on the Rhine,
Let barbarous Ganges arm a servile train;   365
Be mine the blessings of a peaceful reign.
No more my sons shall dye with British blood
Red Iber's sands, or Ister's foaming flood:
Safe on my shore each unmolested swain
Shall tend the flocks, or reap the bearded grain;   370
The shady empire shall retain no trace
Of war or blood, but in the sylvan chase,
The trumpets sleep, while cheerful horns are blown,
And arms employed on birds and beasts alone.
Behold! th'ascending villas on my side   375
Project long shadows o'er the crystal tide.
Behold! Augusta's glittering spires increase,
And temples rise, the beauteous works of peace.
I see, I see where two fair cities bend
Their ample bow, a new White-Hall ascend!   380
There mighty nations shall inquire their doom,
The world's great oracle in times to come;
There kings shall sue, and suppliant states be seen
Once more to bend before a British queen.

Thy trees, fair Windsor! now shall leave their woods,   385
And half thy forests rush into my floods,
Bear Britain's thunder, and her cross display,

To the bright regions of the rising day,
Tempt icy seas, where scarce the waters roll,
Where clearer flames glow round the frozen pole;   390
Or under southern skies exalt their sails,
Led by new stars, and borne by spicy gales!
For me the balm shall bleed, and amber flow,
The coral redden, and the ruby glow,
The pearly shell its lucid globe infold,   395
And Phoebus warm the ripening ore to gold.
The time shall come, when free as the seas or wind
Unbounded Thames shall flow for all mankind,
Whole nations enter with each swelling tide,
And seas but join the regions they divide;   400
Earth's distant ends our glory shall behold,
And the new world launch forth to seek the old.
Then ships of uncouth form shall stem the tide,
And feathered people crowd my wealthy side,
And naked youths and painted chiefs admire   405
Our speech, our colour, and our strange attire!
Oh stretch thy reign, fair peace! from shore to shore,
Till conquest cease, and slavery be no more:
Till the freed Indians in their native groves
Reap their own fruits, and woo their sable loves,   410
Peru once more a race of kings behold,
And other Mexicos be roofed with gold.
Exiled by thee from earth to deepest hell,
In brazen bonds shall barbarous discord dwell:
Gigantic pride, pale terror, gloomy care,   415
And mad ambition, shall attend her there.
There purple vengeance bathed in gore retires,
Her weapons blunted, and extinct her fires;
There hateful envy her own snakes shall feel,
And persecution mourn her broken wheel: 420
There faction roar, rebellion bite her chain,
And gasping furies thirst for blood in vain.

    Here cease thy flight, nor with unhallowed lays
Touch the fair fame of Albion's golden days.
The thoughts of gods let Granville's verse recite,   425
And bring the scenes of opening fate to light.
My humble muse, in unambitious strains,

Paints the green forests and the flowery plains,
Where peace descending bids her olives spring,
And scatters blessings from her dove-like wing.   430
Ev'n I more sweetly pass my careless days,
Pleased in the silent shade with empty praise;
Enough for me, that to the listening swains
First in these fields I sung the sylvan strains.

'The design of *Windsor-Forest* is evidently derived from *Cooper's Hill*, with some attention to Waller's poem *The Park*.' Johnson considered Pope's poem part of the 'local poetry' tradition, 'of which the fundamental subject is some particular landscape, to be poetically described, with the addition of such embellishments as may be supplied by historical retrospection or incidental meditation'. He also drew attention to its descriptive nature in which the different scenes, though exhibited successively, 'are all subsisting at the same time' (*Life of Pope*).

'This poem was written at two different times: the first part of it which relates to the country, in the year 1704, at the same time with the Pastorals; the latter part was not added till the year 1713, in which it was published.' (Pope's note.) The 'first part' ended at line 290.

Pope's epigraph for *Windsor-Forest* is chosen from the sixth *Eclogue* of Virgil in which the poet apologises for taking shelter in pastoral poetry, instead of writing about his friend Varus. In fact Virgil takes the opportunity to write about all kinds of political and philosophical subjects, including the formation of the world from the four elements and the separation of land from water, in the course of his 'pastoral poetry'. Similarly, Pope finds in *Windsor-Forest* a suitable 'location' for both political commentary and philosophical musings. Windsor Forest was famous for the hunting activities of a generation of kings; at the same time it was believed to be the seat of the muses. It also lent itself to visual descriptions of great beauty that play such an important part in Pope's poems.

Epigraph
Non inussa cano: Te nostrae, Vare,
Myricae/ Te Nemus omne canet; nec
Phoebo gratior ulla est/ Quam sibi
quae Vari praescripsit Pagina nomen.
(I was moving from my pastoral into
epic poetry when Apollo, god of
poesy, turned me back. It will be a
rural poem, then, that I shall present
to you, Varus. But even a rural poem
can bestow a lasting fame – Virgil,
Eclogues, vi, 9–12).

[2] **the monarch's ... seats**
Windsor Forest had been the seat of
kings from Norman, but possibly even
earlier times. According to legend
Arthur founded his court of the
Round Table here. It was also considered home of the muses as Denham

and Cowley had lived close by. See
261ff.

[3] **sylvan maids**
nymphs – dryads and naiads.

[4] **Unlock your Springs**
Open up your sources of power; cf.
'Once more unlock for thee the sacred
spring', Dryden, *Georgics*, ii, 245; *open
all your shades* reveal all that is
hidden.

[6] **Granville**
George Granville (1667–1735), Baron
Lansdowne, poet and playwright.

[7–8]
Alluding to the 'Eden' in Genesis 2:
8–10: 'And God planted a garden
eastward in Eden; ... And a river went
out of Eden to water the garden'; cf. 'I
look for streams immortalised in

song, . . . / . . . / Yet run for ever by the muse's skill,/ And in the smooth description murmur still', Addison, *Letter from Italy*, lines 32, 35–6; *song* referring to Milton's *Paradise Lost*: The beauty of the biblical garden of Eden now survives in the poetic descriptions of Milton's *Paradise Lost*.

[9] **These**
the groves of Windsor Forest.

[9]
Cf. 'O, could the muse my ravished breast inspire/ With warmth like yours, and raise an equal fire', Addison, *Letter from Italy*, lines 51–2. Pope laments that he has not got the same inspiration as Milton.

[9–10]
Cf. 'Like him in birth, thou shoudst be like in fame,/ As thine his fate, if mine had been his flame', Waller, *Cooper's Hill*, lines 71–2.

[12] **strive**
to contend for mastery; *seem to strive again* alludes to Virgil's description of the warring elements and the formation of the world.

[13] **Not chaos-like**
Cf. 'In the beginning how heaven and earth/ Rose out of Chaos', Milton, *Paradise Lost*, i, 10; see also 'where eldest night/ And chaos, ancestors of nature, hold/ Eternal anarchy, amidst the noise/ of endless wars', ii, 894–7.

[14] **harmoniously confused**
oxymoronic usage suggesting the blending or reconciliation of contraries.

[17] **waving groves a checkered scene display**
Cf. 'Dancing in the chequered shade', Milton, *L'Allegro*, line 96.

[20] **repress**
check or restrain.

[21] **lawns**
open spaces between woods; glades.

[22]
Thin trees grow, in which the shade of one does not extend to that of the other.

[23] **russet**
of a reddish-brown colour; *russet plains* cf. 'Russet lawns, and fallows

grey', Milton, *L'Allegro*, line 71; *extend* stretch out.

[25] **purple dyes**
the colour of the heather on the heath. 'Purple' is often used by Pope in its Latinate sense to mean bright and vibrant colours.

[27] **tufted trees**
small groups of trees or bushes. Milton had the phrase: 'Towers and battlements it sees/ Bosomed high in tufted trees', *L'Allegro*, lines 77–8.

[28] **verdant**
green; *sable* black.

[30] **weeping amber**
so called because the tree dropped liquid gum; *balmy tree* a tree yielding balm or an aromatic substance. Cf. 'Groves whose rich trees wept odorous gums and balms', Milton, *Paradise Lost*, iv, 248. Ovid, in *Metamorphoses*, tells of Myrrha who, changed into a tree, weeps myrrh, and the sisters of Phaeton, transformed into poplars, shed tears which harden in the sun, and turn to amber.

[31] **oaks**
referring to the ships built of English oak which carried spices to England and enabled her to have political authority in distant lands; *precious loads* spices.

[33] **Olympus**
the mountain whose summit was regarded as the seat of the gods in Greek mythology.

[36]
The hills round Windsor are blessed with all the beauties and virtues that the Greek gods could have bestowed on Olympus.

[37] **Pan**
the Greek god of flocks and shepherds. He invented the musical pipe of seven reeds, which he named Syrinx, after the nymph whom he loved and who was changed into a reed in order that she might escape him; *Pomona* the Roman goddess of fruit.

[38] **Flora**
an old Italian deity of fertility and flowers; *enamelled ground* a technical

process by which the ground or main surface is prepared with a coating of metal paint for other colours. The word had been used in descriptions of nature since the seventeenth century. See 'O'er the smooth enamelled green', Milton, *Arcades*, line 84.

[39] **Ceres**
a deity representing the generative power of nature; cf. 'Bacchus and fostering Ceres, powers divine', Dryden, *Georgics*, i, 9; *waving prospect* the wind blowing over a field of ripened grain creates a sense of waves.

[40–1]
Note the gentle sense of personification created by the use of the present participles 'nodding' and 'smiling'. The suggestion here is that of nature co-operating with man.

[42] **tell**
bear evidence; *Stuart* Queen Anne (1702–14).

[44] **dreary**
'gloomy, dismal', Johnson, *Dictionary*.

[45] **savage laws**
'The Forest Laws.' Pope's note. These laws laid down severe punishments for hunting in the New Forest.

[46] **furious**
'raging, violent', Johnson, *Dictionary*; *severe* 'cruel, inexorable', Johnson, *Dictionary*.

[43–86]
Refers to the use of New Forest as a game preserve by Norman kings, especially by William I. Their indiscriminate hunting is used as a metaphor for the other tyrannies they were supposed to have committed. The fact that so many members of William the Conqueror's family had met their death in the New Forest led to the belief that these deaths were a form of divine vengeance against the creation of royal preserves. Pope's poem follows this tradition.

[47] **dispeopled**
the non-human inhabitants of earth, air, and water were often called 'people', e.g. 'feathered people'. Pope is, of course, exaggerating through indignation; *floods* the rivers.

[50] **backward**
slow.

[51] **lawless**
'not subject to law', Johnson, *Dictionary*.

[52]
And even the elements were swayed by a tyrant. A typical inversion in the tradition of Milton. Later poets like Thomson followed the practice.

[53] **teeming grain**
burgeoning crops; *swelled the teeming grain* cf. 'to swell the teeming grain', Dryden, *Georgics*, i, 156.

[54] **distilled**
'To drop; to fall by drops', Johnson, *Dictionary*; Johnson illustrates this sense by these same lines from Pope.

[55] **swain**
the peasant, farm-labourer; *frustrate labour yields* gives up his work defeated and disappointed.

[56]
A severely ironical picture of the young man dying of starvation amidst a field full of ripe grain. Cf. 'Starves in the midst of nature's bounty curst,/ And in the loaden vineyard dies for thirst', Addison, *Letter from Italy*, lines 117–18.

[57 & 60]
'*No wonder savages or subjects slain* – / *But subjects starved while savages were fed*. It was originally thus, but the word savages is not properly applied to beasts but to men; which occasioned the alteration.' Pope's note; here an example of his careful and precise use of language.

[58] **despotic**
absolute in power.

[59] **doomed**
doomed to death; *sportive* 'wanton, playful', Johnson, *Dictionary*. Johnson illustrates this sense by these same lines from *Windsor-Forest*.

[61–2] **Nimrod ... A mighty hunter**
'the mighty hunter before the lord', Genesis 10: 9; *prey was man* Nimrod was considered a tyrant.

[63] **haughty Norman**
William the Conqueror, who came from Normandy.

[65]
'Alluding to the destruction made in the New Forest, and the tyrannies exercised there by William I.' Pope's note.

[66] **fanes**
temples.

[67] **levelled**
destroyed.

[68] **hollow**
like sound reverberated from a cavity; *naked* defenceless.

[70] **heaps of ruin**
mounds of rubble; *stalked* walked with proud steps.

[71] **obscene**
abominable, disgusting; *gaping* exhumed, opened, suggesting the barbarous acts of William I.

[72] **quires**
ruins, perhaps those of churches or monasteries, hence 'sacred'. It is interesting to note that originally Pope had 'wolves with howling fill' instead of 'savage howlings'. He rejected the former because he felt that there were no wolves in England by the time of William the Conqueror. Despite his expansive and often exaggerated statements, therefore, Pope still has a concern for facts.

[73] **awed**
struck with fear.

[74] **where he durst**
only where he dared.

[75–6]
Pope's characteristic compression makes the lines difficult to understand. 'The King treated all with equal tyranny, his subjects and his God.' Pope is close to the irony of the zeugma, the rhetorical device that exposes the false equations established between things. In this instance the zeugma revolves round the verb 'served' with its double sense of 'doing one's duty towards' and 'meting out punishment', on the one hand, and the ironic equation between 'vassals' and 'God', on the other.

[77–8]
Those spared by the Saxons and the Danes were victimised by William I.

[80] **denied a grave**
at William I's funeral a knight claimed that the land belonged to him.

[81] **second hope**
'Richard, second son of William the Conqueror.' Pope's note; *survey* view.

[83–4]
William Rufus (William II) was killed while hunting in the New Forest. There is, of course, a pun on the word 'hart' in these lines.

[79–84]
William I and William III both died after falling from their horses while hunting. These accidents were seen as enactments of divine justice by the opponents of William III.

[87] **unknown**
because hitherto forbidden to them.

[90] **secret transport**
undisplayed ecstasy; *conscious* aware.

[94] **purer spirits**
animal spirits that were believed to move in the blood.

[95] **the gameful woods beset**
surround the woods full of game, with the intent of hunting.

[96] **Wind the shrill horn**
blow the loud hunting horn. cf. 'the grey-fly winds her sultry horn', Milton, *Lycidas*, line 28.

[97]
When milder autumn follows after the heat of summer. Note the characteristic inversion, and the placing of the verb at the end of the line. The next line follows the same pattern.

[98] **new-shorn**
freshly harvested.

[99] **ready**
nimble; *spaniel* dog used for hunting; *bounds* jumps, springs.

[100] **tries**
examines; *furrowed grounds* ploughed into long shallow trenches; cf. 'who ploughs across the furrowed grounds', Dryden, *Georgics*, i, 141.

[101] **tainted**
with the scent of animals; *betray* show or discover.

[102] **Couched close**
concealed; *meditates* observes intently.

[103] **they**
refers to the hunted animals, probably hares; *unfaithful field, beset* the treacherous field, because 'beset' or laid over with nets.

[105]
Cf. 'If little things with great we may compare', Dryden, *Georgics*, iv, 266.

[106] **Albion**
Britain; *eager* full of ardour.

[107] **thoughtless**
without a care.

[108] **closing lines**
advancing lines of soldiers; *invest* enclose or hem in; besiege.

[109] **th'amazed defenceless prize**
The besieged town is described by Pope in the terms usually applied to a hunted animal. In this connection it is worth noting the long epic simile in lines 93–104.

[105–10]
Perhaps inspired by the fall of Gibraltar in 1704.

[111] **brake**
thicket; *whirring* 'A word formed in imitation of the sound expressed by it', Johnson, *Dictionary*. Illustrated by the same lines from Pope.

[112] **triumphant wings**
a case of the transferred epithet. It is the pheasant who is triumphant, not its wings.

[113] **fiery wound**
of gunshot.

[114] **beats the ground**
strikes the ground.

[115] **glossy**
shining; *varying dyes* changing colours.

[117] **vivid**
striking; *unfold* display.

[115–18]
the description of the pheasant in the language of painting is typical of the period. External nature was frequently presented through the language of the arts, and Pope did so often. He was influenced by the *ut pictura poesis* dictum to which both Dryden and Addison subscribed. It has been suggested that at times he even referred to particular paintings.

Certainly in the year of the publication of *Windsor-Forest* Pope was living with his artist friend Jervas. The pheasant viewed as a dying hero harks back to the dying ox in the third book of Virgil's *Georgics*.

[119] **Arcturus**
The Great Bear, or one of its stars. It was believed that the weather was stormy through those days in September when Arcturus rose at the same time as the sun; cf. 'When cold Arcturus rises with the sun', Dryden, *Georgics*, i, 102.

[120] **deny**
give up; renounce.

[121] **well-breathed beagles**
beagles were the smallest of the type of English hunting hounds. It was believed that they had a particular physiological particularity by which they could, better than other dogs, catch the scent of animals; *well-breathed* could mean that the animals were well-exercised, in good shape for a hunt; it would also refer to their particularly sharp noses. Cf. 'Thus o're the Elean plains, thy well-breathed-horse/ Impels the flying car, and wins the course', Dryden, *Georgics*, iii, 315–16.

[126] **naked groves**
referring to the trees shedding their leaves during the winter. Even so the word 'naked' carries a hint of personification.

[127]
When, instead of leaves, the trees are crowded with flocks of doves which give shade.

[128] **woodcocks**
'a bird of passage with a long bill', Johnson, *Dictionary*; *watery* abounding with water; *glade* 'a lawn, or opening in a forest', Johnson, *Dictionary*.

[129] **tube**
the barrel of the gun; *levels* takes aim; cf. 'And bends his bow, and levels with his eyes', Dryden, *Georgics*, ii, 774.

[130] **straight**
immediately; *breaks* bursts upon;

rends; *frozen sky* referring here literally to the wintry cold, but also the freeze in terms of activity onto which the gunman's action bursts so rudely.
[131] **airy rings**
making circles in the air; *skim the heath* glide lightly over the heath.
[132] **clamorous lapwing**
'A clamorous bird with long wings', Johnson, *Dictionary*; 'clamorous' would refer to its noise; cf. 'The crow with clamorous cries the show'r demands', Dryden, *Georgics*, i, 533; *leaden death* death by the leaden bullet, a characteristic Popean compression.
[133] **mounting larks their notes prepare**
birds known for singing as they ascend into the air.
[134]
The bodies of the larks fall, but their music or spirits are left in the air. There is a mild pun here on the word 'air' in the sense of literal air, and musical airs; a further unstated meaning of air in the sense of spirit is also present; cf. 'From clouds they fall, and leave their souls above', Dryden, *Georgics*, iii, 815.
[135] **genial**
'that which contributes to propagation', Johnson, *Dictionary*; cf. 'The womb of earth the genial seed receives', Dryden, *Georgics*, ii, 439; *quivering* tremulous, because of the gentle breeze or 'cooling vapours breathe along the mead' of the next line.
[136] **cooling vapours**
gentle winds that cool; *breathe along the mead* blow in the meadow.
[138] **Intent**
concentrating.
[139] **looks unmoved**
absolutely still; *hopes* hopes to catch, an elision in the interest of compression; *scaly breed* fish; this is an example of the scientific formula of genus plus differentia used as periphrasis. See 'scaly flocks', Dryden, *Georgics*, iv, 568; 'venomed race', iii, 629.

[141] **plenteous streams**
streams full of fish; *various race* different kinds of fish.
[142] **Tyrian dye**
purple or crimson dye anciently made in Tyre, the Phoenician city on the Mediterranean.
[143] **volumes**
coils, folds, as of a serpent; cf. 'ended foul in many a scaly fold/ Voluminous and vast', Milton, *Paradise Lost*, ii, 651–2.
[144] **bedropped**
besprinkled.
[145] **diversified**
variegated; *stains* markings, colouring.
[147] **Cancer**
the zodiacal sign of the crab, into which the sun enters from around the summer solstice, i.e. 22 June; *Phoebus* the sun, which is in the constellation of the Twins, the zodiacal sign of Gemini, 21 May–22 June.
[150] **Rouse**
a hunting term; to rouse a hart is to raise him from his harbour, to drive a beast from his lair; *opening* giving tongue, beginning to cry in pursuit of a scent.
[151] **courser**
swift horse.
[152] **pawing**
to draw the forefoot along the ground; *seems to beat the distant plain* feels as though he is treading distant regions.
[154]
Before the horse actually starts on the hunt he has already spent much energy in his impatience.
[155] **strain up**
make strenuous efforts to climb; *threatening steep* dangerous ascent.
[158]
It appears as if the earth rolls backwards beneath the feet of the swiftly moving horse.
[159] **Arcadia**
a region in the very centre of the Peloponnese, associated with deities like Pan and Hermes. Its inhabitants claimed to be the oldest people in Greece, hence the adjective 'old';

ample plain though a mountainous area there were wide plains in the southern part of the region.

[160] **Th'immortal huntress**
the goddess Diana; *virgin train* Diana was also the goddess of chastity.

[162] **Queen**
Queen Anne.

[163]
A reference to Queen Anne's interest in hunting. She used to follow the hounds in a chaise which she drove herself.

[164] **The earth's fair light**
Diana, also associated with the moon; *empress of the main* Queen Anne could be compared to Diana on yet another point. Britannia ruled the seas, and Diana as goddess of the moon influenced the tides.

[166] **Cynthus**
a mountain in Delos sacred to Diana and Apollo. Diana was supposed to have been born on it.

[167] **airy wastes**
open lands.

[169]
Diana once again as the goddess of the hunt.

[170] **buskined**
wearing boots; *virgins* associated with the chaste Diana; *traced* traversed, trod.

[172] **Lodona**
a tributary of the Thames.

[172–204]
'The story of Lodona is told with sweetness; but a new metamorphosis is a ready and puerile expedient', Johnson, *Life of Pope*.

[173] **long oblivion cast**
forgotten for a long time.

[176] **crescent**
the crescent moon, emblem of Diana; *golden zone* girdle or belt.

[178] **fillet**
a band.

[179]
Cf. 'Diana's arms upon her shoulder sounds', Dryden, *Aeneid*, xi, 968; and 'A gilded quiver from his shoulder sounds', xi, 1140.

[180] **flying**
swift.

[182] **verdant limits**
green boundaries.

[183] **Pan**
the Greek god of flocks and shepherds, originally an Arcadian deity.

[183–4]
Cf. 'The lover gazed, and burning with desire,/ The more he looked the more he fed the fire', Dryden, *Aeneid*, xii, 108.

[186] **cleaves**
splits, divides; *liquid* in the Latinate sense of clear or transparent.

[189] **furious pace**
frenetic haste.

[190] **urged the chase**
pressed hard in pursuit.

[192] **sounding steps**
echoing steps.

[193] **as she run**
as she ran.

[195] **shorter breath**
panting breath; *sultry* hot.

[200] **Cynthia**
name given to Diana, derived from Cynthus, a mountain in their native Delos; see 'And Cynthus' top forsook', line 166.

[201] **to the shades repair**
to the underworld; a classical metaphor for dying.

[207] **Still bears the name**
'The River Loddon.' Pope's note. In using the Loddon Pope may have been inspired by the river in Arcadia called the Ladon where Syrinx met her fate. The story is told by Ovid in *Metamorphoses*, i, 702.

[209] **laves**
bathes.

[210]
'Her briny tears augment the briny flood', Dryden, *Art of Love*, i, 599.

[211] **her glass**
reflection in the river.

[212] **headlong**
head downwards, literally as reflected in the water. See 'And seeming stars fall headlong from the skies', Dryden, *Georgics*, i, 502; similarly *downward skies*.

[213] **watery landscape**
because reflected in the water; *pendant* hanging, suspended.
[214] **absent trees**
not fully there, because of the trembling image in the water.
[215] **clear azure gleam**
clear blue light.
[216]
The forests reflected in the water, and therefore 'floating', lend the waves a green colour.
[217]
Pope, who believed in a relationship between sound and sense, would have considered the slow movement of this line a reflection of the slower movement of the streams. See 'The sound must seem an echo to the sense', *An Essay on Criticism*, line 365.
[219] **great father**
the Thames.
[221] **growing honours rear**
exalt their high branches.
[222] **future navies**
the ships that will be made from the wood of the trees.
[223] **Neptune**
the Roman god of the sea.
[223–4]
Neptune, or the high seas attribute to you, Father Thames, greater honours through the navies you sent out, than the honours they receive from all their various tributaries.
[225–6]
Superlative praise bestowed on the Thames.
[227–8]
Because the constellation Eridanus was shaped like a winding river both Virgil and Ovid gave this name to the river Po in Italy. See 'that lord of floods,/ Eridanus', Virgil, *Georgics*, i, 484–5; and 'Eridanus/ Than whom none other through the laughing plains/ More furious pours into the purple sea', *Georgics*, iv, 371–3. Denham had compared the Thames to the Eridanus: 'Heaven her Eridanus no more shall boast,/ Whose fame in thine, like lesser currents lost', *Cooper's Hill*, lines 191–2.

[229] **Windsor's famed abodes**
Windsor Castle, the seat of the British monarchs.
[230] **the mansion of our earthly Gods**
the dwelling place of the kings and queens of England.
[231] **Nor all his stars above**
referring to the stars of the constellation Eridanus.
[233] **Jove**
Jupiter, the Roman god of the skies and light; came to be identified with the Greek Zeus. Particularly suitable in Pope's context because the oak is the special tree of Jupiter.
[234] **Olympus**
the mountain on whose summit the gods lived.
[235ff.]
Cf. 'Oh happy, if he knew his happy state!/ The swain, who free from business and debate,/ Receives his easy food from nature's hand,/ And just returns of cultivated land!', Virgil, *Georgics*, ii, 639–43; and 'But easy quiet, a secure retreat,/ A harmless life that knows not how to cheat,/ With homebred plenty the rich owner bless,/ And rural pleasures crown his happiness', ii, 655–8 (Dryden's translation).
[240] **successive**
following each other in due order.
[241] **the forest yields**
the forest produces.
[242]
Takes from the fields their sweet-smelling remedies.
[243] **chymic art**
the art of the chemist; *exalts* to intensify or render more powerful.
[244] **draws**
inhales; *aromatic* fragrant, strong-scented; *souls of flowers* the essence of flowers.
[245]
Cf. 'Give me the ways of wandering stars to know', Dryden, *Georgics*, ii, 677.
[246] **figured worlds**
to figure is to represent. The meaning could be over the Zodiac, or a globe of the world.

ALEXANDER POPE

[248]
The contemporary practice of talking
to the shades or ghosts of wisemen
from the past. Thomson, in *Winter*,
lines 431–4: 'There studious let me
sit,/ And hold high converse with the
mighty dead –/ Sages of ancient time,
as gods revered,/ As gods beneficent,
who blessed mankind', proceeds to
invoke the spirits of Socrates, Solon,
etc. This practice is probably a variation on the classical journey to the
underworld. Swift offers a satirical version of it in *Gulliver's Travels*, III, viii.
[250] **attends**
attends to.
[251] **T'observe a mean**
to follow the middle path.
[252] **regard his end**
to keep in mind why he was created.
[254] **expatiate**
to range at large.
[255] **her kindred stars**
of her own nature.
[256] **confess**
'to prove; to attest', Johnson,
Dictionary.
[257] **Scipio**
Scipio Africanus (c. 236–c. 183 BC),
the Roman general who defeated
Hannibal in 202 BC. After a period of
involvement in public affairs he lived a
retired life.
[258] **Atticus**
Titus Pomponius (109–32 BC),
Cicero's friend, who refused to be in
the public eye, and retired instead
from Rome to Athens. He is called
Atticus because of his long residence
in Athens; *Trumbal* 'Sir W. Trumbal
[1639–1716] was born in Windsor-
Forest, to which he retreated after he
had resigned the post of Secretary of
State to King William III.' Pope's note
on *Spring*, line 12.
[259] **Ye sacred nine**
the nine muses; *that all my soul
possess* who govern my whole being.
[259–60]
'Ye sacred muses, with whose beauty
fired,/ My soul is ravished, and my
brain inspired', Dryden, *Georgics*, ii,
673.

[261] **sequestered scenes**
private scenes, removed from public
life.
[262] **bowery mazes**
sheltering bowers, confused with the
branches of trees.
[265] **eternal ... grow**
because of Denham's poem *Cooper's
Hill*. Cooper's Hill is about eighteen
miles from London and from its top
one sees Windsor Castle to the left
and London, especially St Paul's, to
the right.
[266] **mountain**
often applied at this time to elevations
of moderate altitude.
[267] **consecrated walks**
sacred groves.
[268] **die**
fade.
[269–70] **shade to shade,/ By god-
like poets venerable made**
many poets have sung of the beauties
of the forest shades.
[271] **first lays**
referring to Denham's early works,
The Destruction of Troy, *The Sophy*, and
the first draft of *Cooper's Hill*, all of
which were written before the Civil
War began in 1642. Denham's house
near Windsor was taken by the republican forces in 1643; *majestic Denham*
Dryden considered *Cooper's Hill* to be
'a poem which ... for the majesty of
style is, and ever will be, the exact
standard of good writing', *Epistle
Dedicatory of the Rival Ladies*.
[272]
'Mr. Cowley died at Chertsey, on the
borders of the forest, and was from
thence conveyed to Westminster.'
Pope's note.
[273] **O early lost!**
Cowley died in 1667, at the age of 49.
His body was floated down the river to
London. Cf. 'O early ripe', Dryden,
To the Memory of Mr Oldham, line 11.
[276] **each muse's lyre**
Cowley experimented in many different genres. His epitaph in Westminster Abbey records his versatility in
calling him *Anglorum Pindarus,
Flaccus, Maro*.

[277] **relentless**
unpitying, unmoved by kindness.
[282] **these**
referring to Cowley and Denham;
revived returned to life; *Granville* see
note to line 6.
[284] **ancient seats**
old dwellings.
[285] **To paint anew**
to revive. Pope is fond of the language
of painting.
[286]
To adorn the forest with the unfading
colours of poetry.
[287]
Re-create the sublimity of Windsor's
hills in the elevated language of verse.
[288]
Add height to Windsor's towers
through the power of your poetry.
[290] **Silver Star**
'The Star of the Order of the Garter,
instituted at Windsor Castle by
Edward III. Edward reconstructed
Windsor Castle to provide a meeting-
place for the Order' (see John Butt,
1963). See 'Then didst thou found that
Order', *Cooper's Hill*, line 83. The 1704
version of the poem concluded with
the following lines that came after line
290: 'My humble muse in unambitious
strains/ Paints the green forests and
the flowery plains,/ Where I obscurely
pass my careless days,/ Pleased in the
silent shade with empty praise;/
Enough for me that to the listening
swains/ First in these fields I sung the
sylvan strains.'
[291] **Surrey**
'Henry Howard, Earl of Surrey, one of
the first refiners of the English poetry;
who flourished in the time of Henry
the VIIIth.' Pope's note.
[292] **Surrey, the Granville of a
former age**
Pope reverses the usual mode of comparison in which a later writer is
hailed with the name of an earlier one
as an encomium.
[294] **lists**
'Enclosed ground in which tilts are
run, and combats fought', Johnson,
Dictionary.

[295] **Cupids**
from Cupid, the boy-god of love,
Venus's son.
[297] **Fair Geraldine**
'Lady Elizabeth Fitzgerald (1528?–9),
youngest daughter of the Earl of Kil-
dare. Surrey's love poems were long
supposed to have been addressed to
her' (see John Butt, 1963).
[298] **Myra**
'The name Granville bestowed in his
songs, first to Mary of Modena, and
then upon Frances Brudenal, Countess of Newburgh, when the latter
became his mistress' (John Butt,
1963). Johnson said that Granville
'wrote verses to her before she was
three-and-twenty, and may be forgiven if he regarded the face more
than the mind. Poets are sometimes in
too much haste to praise', *Life of
Granville*.
[300] **winding shore**
Cf. 'The ports and creeks of every
winding shore', Dryden, *Aeneis*, i,
809.
[303]
'Edward III, born here.' Pope's note.
[299–303]
'Edward III (1312) and Henry VI (1421)
were born at Windsor, Edward IV,
Henry III and Charles I were buried
there' (see John Butt, 1963).
[303–10]
'Antonio Verrio (1639–1707) had
represented in St George's Hall at
Windsor the triumphal procession in
which King John of France was led
captive by the Black Prince' (see John
Butt, 1963). See also 'On painted ceilings you devoutly stare,/ Where
sprawl the saints of Verrio or
Laguerre', *Epistle to Burlington*, lines
145–6.
[304] **Stretch**
'display', Johnson, *Dictionary*.
[305] **monarchs chained**
'An allusion to David II, King of Scotland, taken prisoner at the battle of
Neville's Cross in 1346 and released in
1357; and to Jean le Bon, King of
France, whom the Black Prince
defeated and captured at Poitiers in

1356' (John Butt, 1963); *Cressy's glorious field* the village in France where Edward III defeated the French in 1346.

[306] **lillies**
the emblem of France; cf. 'But thee great Edward and thy greater son,/ The lillies which his father wore he won', Denham, *Cooper's Hill*, lines 77–8.

[306]
'In 1340 Edward III assumed the title of the King of France and quartered the lillies of France with the leopards of England' (John Butt, 1963).

[307]
Verrio's paintings on the ceilings had begun to deteriorate (see John Butt, 1963).

[308] **inanimate**
without life-like depictions; *naked* uncovered, in this instance with paintings or colour.

[309] **Still**
always, ever.

[311] **Henry**
'Henry VI.' Pope's note; *ill-fated Henry* Henry VI was taken prisoner in 1465, and after a short interlude on the throne in 1470 was murdered in 1471. He was buried in St George's chapel, in Windsor (see John Butt, 1963).

[312] **palms eternal**
symbols of martyrdom.

[314] **fast beside him**
close to, or next to him; *Edward* 'Edward IV.' Pope's note. Edward IV, who was at least partially victorious in his struggle for the throne with Henry VI, was also buried in St George's chapel in 1483 (see John Butt, 1963).

[316] **old Belerium**
the Latin name for Land's End; *Northern Main* the northern seas, may be the North Sea. The 'whom' of the previous line seems to refer to both Henry VI and Edward IV. Henry VI, it might be recalled, was a fugitive in the north before he was taken prisoner.

[315–16]
Cf. 'Whom Afric was not able to contain,/ Whose length runs level with th'Atlantic main', Dryden, *Tenth Satire of Juvenal*, lines 236–7.

[317] **The grave unites**
because, though enemies during their lives, they were buried close to each other.

[318] **blended**
mingled together.

[319] **Charles's tomb**
'The body of Charles I was buried in St George's Chapel in the same tomb as Henry VIII, and without any service', (John Butt, 1963).

[321] **fact**
evil deed; *accursed* 'execrable, detestable', Johnson, *Dictionary*.

[323] **purple deaths**
deaths from the Great Plague (1665).

[324] **domes**
stately building, mansion; *involved* enwrapped; *rolling fire* the Great Fire (1666).

[325] **intestine**
'domestic, not foreign', Johnson, *Dictionary*. Referring to the Civil Wars during the reign of Charles I.

[326] **Inglorious triumphs**
the Revolution of 1688; *dishonest* shameful, ignoble.

[327] **Anna**
Queen Anne.

[329] **oozy bed**
the slimy, muddy river-bed.

[330] **advanced**
lifted up.

[329–30]
Cf. 'Old Father Thames raised up his reverend head', Dryden, *Annus Mirabilis*, line 925; 'While starting from his oozy bed,/ Th'asserted ocean rears his reverend head', *Threnodia Augustalis*, lines 513–14; 'Addison had in his *Campaign* derided the "rivers" that "rise from their oozy beds" to tell stories of heroes, it is therefore strange that Pope should adopt a fiction not only unnatural but lately censured', Johnson, *Life of Pope*.

[331] **dropped**
dripping.

[332] **shining horns**
the river gods were often given the head or horns of a bull suggestive of

225

their strength and their usefulness in agriculture; *diffused* spread; *a golden gleam* a golden light.

[333] **Graved on his urn**
engraved on his urn; the Thames is personified as carrying an urn.

[334] **swelling waters**
rising in bulk; *alternate tides* in turns ebbing and flowing.

[335] **figured**
represented as figures on the urn; *waves of silver* in the image the urn is, perhaps, engraved in silver; referring also to the silvery colour of streams.

[336] **Augusta**
a name given to London by the Romans; *rose in gold* the new architecture after the Great Fire of 1666 was of brick and gilded decorations. Dryden described the city rebuilt after the fire: 'Me-thinks already, from this chymick flame,/ I see a city of more precious mould:/ Rich as the town which gives the Indies name,/ With silver paved, and all divine with gold', *Annus Mirabilis*, lines 1169–72. In the last section of *Windsor-Forest* Pope is indebted to the ending of *Annus Mirabilis*.

[337] **sea-born brothers**
It was believed that all rivers were born of Oceanus and Tethys.

[338] **tributary urns**
contributing urns; the image here is of water from different urns pouring into the Thames.

[339] **authors**
'he that effects or produces anything', Johnson, *Dictionary*; *famed authors* 'The Thames was thought to be the offspring of the Thame and the Isis' (see John Butt, 1963).

[342] **verdant alders**
green alders.

[343] **lave**
bathe.

[345] **Vandalis**
the Wandle.

[346] **gulfy**
full of gulfs or whirlpools; *sedgy tresses* rush-like growth that appears like hair; a muted personification.

[347] **sullen Mole**
'Or sullen Mole, that runneth under-

neath', Milton, *At a Vacation Exercise*, line 95; see also *A Tour Thro' the whole Island of Great Britain*, in which Defoe talks about a river 'called the Mole, from its remarkable sinking into the earth, at the foot of Box-Hill, near a village called Mickleham, and working its way under ground like a mole, rising again at or near this town of Leatherhead'; *diving flood* sinking waters.

[348] **stained with Danish blood**
the Danes were defeated in a bloody battle on the banks of the Darent in 1016.

[339–48]
Pope's catalogue of rivers is in the tradition of Milton and Spenser. See Milton, *At a Vacation Exercise*, lines 91ff. 'Rivers arise; whether thou be the son,/ Of utmost Tweed, or Ouse, or gulfy Dun,/ Or Trent...'. See also *Faerie Queene*, 4.11.

[351] **The god appeared**
Father Thames.

[352] **pompous turrets**
magnificent towers.

[354] **hushed**
quiet.

[353–4]
Cf. 'The winds their breath restrain,/ And the hushed waves lie flatted on the main', Dryden, *Aeneis*, x, 156.

[355] **Hail...days**
the speech of Father Thames; 'the preliminaries to the Peace Treaty of Utrecht were signed in London in 1711' (see John Butt, 1963).

[358] **Hermus**
An Italian river that Virgil has written about.

[359] **sevenfold**
alluding to its delta.

[363] **Volga's banks**
reference to the war Charles XII of Sweden lost against Russia.

[365] **Ganges**
an allusion to the Moghul emperor Aurangzeb's wars against the Marathas. Aurangzeb died in 1707.

[366]
Pope was hostile to Marlborough and his much glorified victories in battle.

[367] **dye**
an obvious pun on the word.
[368] **Iber's sands**
The river Ebro in Spain. The reference
is to the Allies' campaign in Spain in
1710, and the victory gained at
Saragossa; *Ister's foaming flood* The
Danube; a reference to Marlborough's
victory at Blenheim in 1704 (see John
Butt, 1963).
[369] **unmolested**
untroubled.
[371] **shady empire**
the forests.
[373] **trumpets**
blown during warfare; *horns* sounded
during hunts.
[375] **ascending villas**
rising country seats.
[376] **Project long shadows**
referring to the height and grandeur
of the country houses; *crystal tide* the
clear waters.
[377] **Augusta's glittering spires**
the shining spires of London.
[378] **temples rise**
'The fifty new churches.' Pope's note.
[379] **two fair cities**
London and Westminster, which at
that time were separate towns.
[379–80] **bend/ Their ample bow**
metaphorically for unite in the shape
of a curve; *White-Hall* White-Hall
Palace, burnt down in 1691 and 1697;
only Inigo Jones's banqueting hall survived. It was at different times the residence of British monarchs; *new White-
Hall ascend* the projected rebuilding
of the whole palace at Whitehall.
[381–422]
the influence of Isaiah 60 can be
discerned.
[383] **sue**
petition.
[384] **Once more**
the sovereignty of the United Provinces was offered to Queen Elizabeth
in 1575 and 1585 and her assistance
was sought in the struggles of the
Dutch against Philip of Spain (see
John Butt, 1963).
[386–7]
The trees of the forest will be made

into ships and carry British military
might and commerce all over the
world.
[387] **her cross**
the red cross of St George on the
Union Jack.
[388] **the bright regions of the rising
day**
literally the eastern part of the world.
[389] **tempt**
attempt, to risk the dangers of.
[392] **spicy gales**
winds fragrant with the scent of
spices.
[393] **balm shall bleed**
the juice was extracted from the bark
of the tree by a cut being made
on it.
[395] **lucid globe** ·
pearl, often considered a symbol of
the world; *infold* enclose.
[396] **ripening ore**
an allusion to the belief that the sun
ripened gold and precious stones into
maturity. Pope expressed a similar
idea later: 'The gen'rous God, who
wit and gold refines,/ And ripens
spirits as he ripens mines', *Of the
Characters of Women*, lines 289–90.
[398] **unbounded Thames**
'A wish that London may be made a
free port.' Pope's note. Cf. Sir
Andrew Freeport, the name that
Addison gave to the representative of
moneyed interests in his *Spectator*
papers.
[402]
There shall be movement in both
directions, from the old world to the
new, and from the new world to the
old.
[403] **uncouth form**
strange and unusual shapes; *stem the
tide* cross the current.
[404] **feathered people**
referring to the Red-Indians.
[405] **naked youths and painted
chiefs**
further images of Red Indians from
America; *admire* regard with wonder
and surprise; Milton used it in this
sense in 'Let none admire/ That riches
grow in hell', *Paradise Lost*, i, 690.

[409] **freed Indians** from the tyranny of Spain.

[413–14] Jupiter threw out Discord from heaven.

[414] **brazen** made of brass; strong, unyielding.

[417] **purple vengeance** vengeance coloured red because she is 'bathed in gore'.

[420] **broken wheel** Persons tortured at the wheel had their arms and legs broken during the process by being hit with a bar. Pope suggests a matching conclusion for the wheel itself.

[431ff.] Pope followed Virgil's *Georgics* in his conclusion: 'Thus have I sung of fields, and flocks, and trees,/ And of the waxen work of labouring bees;/ While mighty Caesar thund'ring from afar,/ Seeks on Euphrates' banks the spoils of war:/ With conquering arms asserts his country's cause,/ With arts of peace the willing people draws:/ On the glad earth the golden age renews,/ And his great father's path to heav'n pursues./ While I at Naples pass my peaceful days,/ Affecting studies of less noisy praise;/ And bold, through youth, beneath the beechen shade,/ The lays of shepherds, and their loves have played.' (Dryden's translation) Pope's final couplet echoes the opening of his Pastoral poem *Spring*: 'First in these fields I try the sylvan strains,/ Nor blush to sport on Windsor's blissful plains', just as Virgil closed his *Georgics* with the first line of his *Eclogues*.

––––––––◇––––––––

22 / *The Rape of the Lock*

Canto One

What dire offence from amorous causes springs,
What mighty contests rise from trivial things,
I sing – This verse to Caryll, Muse! is due;
This, even Belinda may vouchsafe to view:
Slight is the subject, but not so the praise,   5
If she inspire, and he approve my lays.
    Say what strange motive, goddess! could compel
A well-bred lord to assault a gentle belle!
Oh say what stranger cause, yet unexplored,
Could make a gentle belle reject a lord?   10
In tasks so bold, can little men engage,
And in soft bosoms dwells such mighty rage?
    Sol through white curtains shot a timorous ray,
And oped those eyes that must eclipse the day;
Now lapdogs give themselves the rousing shake,   15
And sleepless lovers, just at twelve, awake.

Thrice rung the bell, the slipper knocked the ground,
And the pressed watch returned a silver sound.
Belinda still her downy pillow pressed,
Her guardian sylph prolonged the balmy rest.   20
'Twas he had summoned to her silent bed
The morning-dream that hovered o'er her head.
A youth more glittering than a birth-night beau,
(That e'en in slumber caused her cheek to glow)
Seemed to her ear his winning lips to lay,   25
And thus in whispers said, or seemed to say:
   'Fairest of mortals, thou distinguished care
Of thousand bright inhabitants of air!
If e'er one vision touched thy infant thought,
Of all the nurse and all the priest have taught,   30
Of airy elves by moonlight shadows seen,
The silver token, and the circled green,
Or virgins visited by angel-powers,
With golden crowns and wreaths of heavenly flowers,
Hear and believe! thy own importance know,   35
Nor bound thy narrow views to things below.
Some secret truths, from learned pride concealed,
To maids alone and children are revealed.
What though no credit doubting wits may give?
The fair and innocent shall still believe.   40
Know then, unnumbered spirits round thee fly,
The light militia of the lower sky.
These, though unseen, are ever on the wing,
Hang o'er the box, and hover round the Ring.
Think what an equipage thou hast in air,   45
And view with scorn two pages and a chair.
As now your own, our beings were of old,
And once enclosed in woman's beauteous mould.
Thence, by a soft transition, we repair
From earthly vehicles to these of Air.   50
Think not, when woman's transient breath is fled,
That all her vanities at once are dead;
Succeeding vanities she still regards,
And though she plays no more, o'erlooks the cards.
Her joy in gilded chariots, when alive,   55
And love of ombre, after death survive.

For when the fair in all their pride expire,
To their first elements their souls retire:
The sprites of fiery termagants in flame
Mount up, and take a salamander's name.   60
Soft yielding minds to water glide away,
And sip with nymphs their elemental tea.
The graver prude sinks downward to a gnome,
In search of mischief still on earth to roam.
The light coquettes in sylphs aloft repair,   65
And sport and flutter in the fields of air.
　'Know farther yet; whoever fair and chaste
Rejects mankind, is by some sylph embraced.
For spirits, freed from mortal laws, with ease
Assume what sexes and what shapes they please.   70
What guards the purity of melting maids,
In courtly balls and midnight masquerades,
Safe from the treacherous friend, the daring spark,
The glance by day, the whisper in the dark,
When kind occasion prompts their warm desires,   75
When music softens, and when dancing fires?
'Tis but their sylph, the wise celestials know,
Though honour is the word with men below.
　'Some nymphs there are, too conscious of their face,
For life predestined to the gnomes' embrace.   80
These swell their prospects and exalt their pride,
When offers are disdained and love denied.
Then gay ideas crowd the vacant brain;
While peers and dukes and all their sweeping train,
And garters, stars, and coronets appear,   85
And in soft sounds, "Your Grace," salutes their ear.
'Tis these that early taint the female Soul,
Instruct the eyes of young coquettes to roll,
Teach infant-cheeks a bidden blush to know,
And little hearts to flutter at a beau.   90
　'Oft when the world imagine women stray,
The sylphs through mystic mazes guide their way,
Through all the giddy circle they pursue,
And old impertinence expel by new.
What tender maid but must a victim fall   95
To one man's treat, but for another's ball?
When Florio speaks, what virgin could withstand,

If gentle Damon did not squeeze her hand?
With varying vanities, from every part,
They shift the moving toyshop of their heart,   100
Where wigs with wigs, with sword-knots sword-knots strive,
Beaus banish beaus, and coaches coaches drive.
This erring mortals levity may call.
Oh blind to truth! the sylphs contrive it all.
   'Of these am I, who thy protection claim,   105
A watchful sprite, and Ariel is my name.
Late, as I ranged the crystal wilds of air,
In the clear mirror of thy ruling star
I saw, alas! some dread event impend,
Ere to the main this morning sun descend.   110
But Heaven reveals not what, or how, or where.
Warned by thy sylph, oh pious maid beware!
This to disclose is all thy guardian can.
Beware of all, but most beware of man!'
   He said; when Shock, who thought she slept too long,   115
Leapt up and waked his mistress with his tongue.
'Twas then, Belinda, if report say true,
Thy eyes first opened on a billet-doux.
Wounds, charms, and ardours, were no sooner read,
But all the vision vanished from thy head.   120
And now, unveiled, the toilet stands displayed,
Each silver vase in mystic order laid.
First, robed in white, the nymph intent adores
With head uncovered, the cosmetic powers.
A heavenly image in the glass appears,   125
To that she bends, to that her eyes she rears.
The inferior priestess, at her altar's side,
Trembling, begins the sacred rites of pride.
Unnumbered treasures ope at once, and here
The various offerings of the world appear.   130
From each she nicely culls with curious toil,
And decks the goddess with the glittering spoil.
This casket India's glowing gems unlocks,
And all Arabia breathes from yonder box.
The tortoise here and elephant unite,   135
Transformed to combs, the speckled and the white.
Here files of pins extend their shining rows,
Puffs, powders, patches, bibles, billet-doux.

Now awful Beauty puts on all its arms.
The fair each moment rises in her charms,   140
Repairs her smiles, awakens every grace,
And calls forth all the wonders of her face,
Sees by degrees a purer blush arise,
And keener lightnings quicken in her eyes.
The busy sylphs surround their darling care;   145
These set the head, and those divide the hair,
Some fold the sleeve, whilst others plait the gown,
And Betty's praised for labours not her own.

Canto Two

Not with more glories, in th'etherial plane,
The sun first rises o'er the purpled main,
Than issuing forth the rival of his beams
Launched on the bosom of the silver Thames.
Fair nymphs and well dressed youths around her shone,   5
But every eye was fixed on her alone.
On her white breast a sparkling cross she wore,
Which Jews might kiss and infidels adore.
Her lively looks a sprightly mind disclose,
Quick as her eyes, and as unfixed as those.   10
Favours to none, to all she smile extends,
Oft she rejects, but never once offends.
Bright as the sun, her eyes the gazers strike,
And like the sun, they shine on all alike.
Yet graceful ease and sweetness void of pride   15
Might hide her faults, if belles had faults to hide.
If to her share some female errors fall,
Look on her face and you'll forget them all.
    This nymph, to the destruction of mankind,
Nourished two locks which graceful hung behind   20
In equal curls, and well conspired to deck
With shining ringlets her smooth ivory neck.
Love in these labyrinths his slaves detains,
And mighty hearts are held in slender chains.
With hairy springes we the birds betray,   25
Slight lines of hair surprise the finny prey,
Fair tresses man's imperial race ensnare,
And beauty draws us with a single hair.

Th'adventurous Baron the bright locks admired.
He saw, he wished and to the prize aspired.   30
Resolved to win he meditates the way,
By force to ravish or by fraud betray.
For when success a lover's toils attends,
Few ask if fraud or force attained the ends.
  For this, ere Phoebus rose, he had implored   35
Propitious heaven, and every power adored,
But chiefly Love – to Love an altar built
Of twelve vast French romances, neatly gilt.
There lay three garters, half a pair of gloves,
And all the trophies of his former loves.   40
With tender billet-doux he lights the pyre,
And breathes three amorous sighs to raise the fire.
Then prostrate falls, and begs with ardent eyes
Soon to obtain and long possess the prize.
The powers gave ear, and granted half his prayer,   45
The rest, the winds dispersed in empty air.
  But now secure the painted vessel glides,
The sun beams trembling on the floating tides,
While melting music steals upon the sky,
And softened sounds along the water die.   50
Smooth flow the waves, the zephyrs gently play,
Belinda smiled, and all the world was gay.
All but the sylph – with careful thoughts oppressed,
Th'impending woe sat heavy on his breast.
He summons straight his denizens of air;   55
The lucid squadrons round the sails repair.
Soft o'er the shrouds aerial whispers breathe,
That seemed but zephyrs to the train beneath.
Some to the sun their insect wings unfold,
Waft on the breeze, or sink in clouds of gold,   60
Transparent forms, too fine for mortal sight,
Their fluid bodies half dissolved in light.
Loose to the wind their airy garments flew,
Thin glittering textures of the filmy dew,
Dipped in the richest tinctures of the skies,   65
Where light disports in ever mingling dyes,
While every beam new transient colours flings,
Colours that change whene'er they wave their wings.
Amid the circle, on the gilded mast,

Superior by the head, was Ariel placed. 70
His purple pinions opening to the sun,
He raised his azure wand, and thus begun.
    'Ye sylphs and sylphids, to your chief give ear,
Fays, fairies, genii, elves and daemons hear!
Ye know the spheres and various tasks assigned 75
By laws eternal to the aerial kind.
Some in the fields of purest ether play,
And bask and whiten in the blaze of day.
Some guide the course of wandering orbs on high,
Or roll the planets through the boundless sky. 80
Some less refined, beneath the moon's pale light
Pursue the stars that shoot athwart the night
Or suck the mists in grosser air below,
Or dip their pinions in the painted bow,
Or brew fierce tempests in the wintery main, 85
Or o'er the glebe distil the kindly rain.
Others on earth o'er human race preside,
Watch all their ways, and all their actions guide.
Of these the chief the care of nations own,
And guard with arms divine the British throne. 90
    'Our humbler province is to tend the fair,
Not a less pleasing, though less glorious care.
To save the powder from too rude a gale,
Nor let th'imprisoned essences exhale.
To draw fresh colours from the vernal flowers, 95
To steal from rainbows ere they drop in showers
A brighter wash, to curl their waving hairs,
Assist their blushes, and inspire their airs.
Nay oft, in dreams, invention we bestow
To change a flounce, or add a furbelow, 100
    'This day, black omens threat the brightest fair
That e'er deserved a watchful spirit's care.
Some dire disaster, or by force or slight,
But what or where the fates have wrapped in night.
Whether the nymph shall break Diana's law, 105
Or some frail China jar receive a flaw,
Or stain her honour, or her new brocade,
Forget her prayers, or miss a masquerade,
Or lose her heart, or necklace, at a ball,
Or whether heaven has doomed that Shock must fall. 110

Haste then, ye spirits! to your charge repair:
The fluttering fan be Zephyretta's care,
The drops to thee, Brillante, we consign,
And, Momentilla, let the watch be thine,
Do thou, Crispissa, tend her favourite lock,   115
Ariel himself shall be the guard of Shock.
   'To fifty chosen sylphs of special note,
We trust th'important charge, the petticoat.
Oft we have known that seven-fold fence to fail,
Though stiff with hoops, and armed with ribs of whale.   120
Form a strong line about the silver bound,
And guard the wide circumference around.
   'Whatever spirit, careless of his charge,
His post neglects, or leaves the fair at large,
Shall feel sharp vengeance soon o'ertake his sins,   125
Be stopped in vials, or transfixed with pins,
Or plunged in lakes of bitter washes lie,
Or wedged whole ages in a bodkin's eye.
Gums and pomatums shall his flight restrain,
While clogged he beats his silken wings in vain,   130
Or alum styptics with contracting power
Shrink his thin essence like a rivelled flower,
Or, as Ixion fixed, the wretch shall feel
The giddy motion of a whirling mill,
In fumes of burning chocolate shall glow,   135
And tremble at the sea that froths below!'
   He spoke. The spirits from the sails descend.
Some, orb in orb, around the nymph extend,
Some thrid the mazy ringlets of her hair,
Some hang upon the pendents of her ear.   140
With beating hearts the dire event they wait,
Anxious and trembling for the birth of fate.

Canto Three

Close by those meads, for ever crowned with flowers,
Where Thames with pride surveys his rising towers,
There stands a structure of majestic frame,
Which from the neighbouring Hampton takes its name.
Here Britain's statesmen oft the fall foredoom   5
Of foreign tyrants, and of nymphs at home.

Here thou, great Anna, whom three realms obey,
Dost sometimes counsel take – and sometimes tea.
   Hither the heroes and the nymphs resort
To taste awhile the pleasures of the court. 10
In various talk th'instructive hours they passed,
Who gave the ball, or paid the visit last.
One speaks the glory of the British queen,
And one describes a charming Indian screen,
A third interprets motions, looks and eyes – 15
At every word a reputation dies.
Snuff or the fan supply each pause of chat,
With singing, laughing, ogling and all that.
   Meanwhile, declining from the noon of day,
The sun obliquely shoots his burning ray. 20
The hungry judges soon the sentence sign,
And wretches hang that jurymen may dine.
The merchant from th'exchange returns in peace,
And the long labours of the toilet cease.
Belinda now, whom thirst of fame invites, 25
Burns to encounter two adventurous knights,
At ombre singly to decide their doom,
And swells her breast with conquests yet to come.
Straight the three bands prepare in arms to join,
Each band the number of the sacred nine. 30
Soon as she spreads her hand, the aerial guard
Descend and sit on each important card.
First Ariel perched upon a matador,
Then each, according to the rank they bore,
For sylphs, yet mindful of their ancient race, 35
Are, as when women, wondrous fond of place.
   Behold, four kings in majesty revered
With hoary whiskers and a forky beard,
And four fair queens whose hands sustain a flower,
Th'expressive emblem of their softer power, 40
Four knaves in garbs succinct, a trusty band,
Caps on their heads and halberds in their hand,
And parti-coloured troops, a shining train,
Draw forth to combat on the velvet plain.
   The skilful nymph reviews her force with care, 45
'Let spades be trumps!' she said, and trumps they were.
   Now move to war her sable matadors,

In show like leaders of the swarthy moors.
Spadillio first, unconquerable lord!
Led off two captive trumps and swept the board.   50
As many more Manillio forced to yield,
And marched the victor from the verdant field,
Him Basto followed, but his fate more hard
Gained but one trump and one plebeian card.
With his broad sabre next, a chief in years,   55
The hoary Majesty of spades appears,
Puts forth one manly leg, to sight revealed,
The rest, his many coloured robe concealed.
The rebel knave, who dares his prince engage,
Proves the just victim of his royal rage.   60
Ev'n mighty Pam, that kings and queens o'erthrew
And mowed down armies in the fights of Lu,
Sad chance of war! now destitute of aid,
Falls undistinguished by the victor spade!
   Thus far both armies to Belinda yield.   65
Now to the Baron fate inclines the field.
His warlike Amazon her host invades,
Th'imperial consort of the crown of spades.
The club's black tyrant first her victim died,
Spite of his haughty mien and barbarous pride.   70
What boots the regal circle on his head,
His giant limbs in state unwieldy spread,
That long behind he trails his pompous robe,
And, of all monarchs, only grasps the globe?
   The Baron now his diamonds pours apace,   75
Th'embroidered king who shows but half his face,
And his refulgent queen, with powers combined,
Of broken troops an easy conquest find.
Clubs, diamonds, hearts, in wild disorder seen,
With throngs promiscuous strow the level green.   80
Thus when dispersed a routed army runs,
Of Asia's troops and Afric's sable sons,
With like confusion different nations fly,
Of various habit and of various dye,
The pierced battalions disunited fall   85
In heaps on heaps; one fate o'erwhelms them all.
   The knave of diamonds tries his wily arts,
And wins (oh shameful chance!) the queen of hearts.

At this, the blood the virgin's cheek forsook,
A livid paleness spreads o'er all her look.   90
She sees and trembles at th'approaching ill,
Just in the jaws of ruin, and codille.
And now (as oft in some distempered state)
On one nice trick depends the general fate.
An ace of hearts steps forth. The king unseen   95
Lurked in her hand and mourned his captive queen.
He springs to vengeance with an eager pace
And falls like thunder on the prostrate ace.
The nymph exulting fills with shouts the sky,
The walls, the woods, the long canals reply.   100
     O thoughtless mortals! ever blind to fate,
Too soon dejected and too soon elate.
Sudden these honours shall be snatched away,
And cursed for ever this victorious day.
     For lo! the board with cups and spoons is crowned,   105
The berries crackle and the mill turns round.
On shining altars of Japan they raise
The silver lamp. The fiery spirits blaze.
From silver spouts the grateful liquors glide
While China's earth receives the smoking tide.   110
At once they gratify the scent and taste,
And frequent cups prolong the rich repast.
Straight hover round the fair her airy band.
Some, as she sipped, the fuming liquor fanned,
Some o'er her lap their careful plumes displayed,   115
Trembling, and conscious of the rich brocade.
Coffee, (which makes the politician wise,
And see through all things with his half-shut eyes)
Sent up in vapours to the Baron's brain
New stratagems the radiant lock to gain.   120
Ah cease, rash youth! desist ere 'tis too late,
Fear the just gods, and think of Scylla's fate!
Changed to a bird, and sent to flit in air,
She dearly pays for Nisus' injured hair!
     But when to mischief mortals bend their will,   125
How soon they find fit instruments of ill.
Just then, Clarissa drew with tempting grace
A two-edged weapon from her shining case,
So ladies in romance assist their knight,

Present the spear, and arm him for the fight.   130
He takes the gift with reverence, and extends
The little engine on his finger's ends.
This just behind Belinda's neck he spread,
As o'er the fragrant steams she bends her head.
Swift to the lock a thousand sprites repair,   135
A thousand wings, by turns, blow back the hair.
And thrice they twitched the diamond in her ear,
Thrice she looked back, and thrice the foe drew near.
Just in that instant, anxious Ariel sought,
The close recesses of the virgin's thought.   140
As on the nosegay in her breast reclined,
He watched th'ideas rising in her mind,
Sudden he viewed, in spite of all her art,
An earthly lover lurking in her heart.
Amazed, confused, he found his power expired,   145
Resigned to fate, and with a sigh retired.
    The peer now spreads the glittering forfex wide
T'inclose the lock, now joins it to divide.
Even then, before the fatal engine closed,
A wretched sylph too fondly interposed.   150
Fate urged the shears, and cut the sylph in twain
(But airy substance soon unites again),
The meeting points the sacred hair dissever
From the fair head for ever and for ever!
    Then flashed the living lightning from her eyes,   155
And screams of horror rend th'affrighted skies.
Not louder shrieks to pitying heaven are cast,
When husbands, or when lapdogs breathe their last,
Or when rich china vessels, fall'n from high,
In glittering dust and painted fragments lie!   160
    'Let wreaths of triumph now my temples twine,'
The victor cried, 'the glorious prize is mine!
While fish in streams, or birds delight in air,
Or in a coach and six the British fair,
As long as *Atalantis* shall be read,   165
Or the small pillow grace a lady's bed,
While visits shall be paid on solemn days,
When numerous waxlights in bright order blaze,
While nymphs take treats, or assignations give,
So long my honour, name and praise shall live!   170

What time would spare from steel receives its date,
And monuments, like men, submit to fate!
Steel could the labour of the gods destroy
And strike to dust th'imperial towers of Troy;
Steel could the works of mortal pride confound,   175
And hew triumphal arches to the ground.
What wonder then, fair nymph! thy hairs should feel
The conquering force of unresisted steel?'

Canto Four

But anxious cares the pensive nymph oppressed,
And secret passions laboured in her breast.
Not youthful kings in battle seized alive,
Not scornful virgins who their charms survive,
Not ardent lovers robbed of all their bliss,   5
Not ancient ladies when refused a kiss,
Not tyrants fierce that unrepenting die,
Not Cynthia when her manteau's pinned awry,
E'er felt such rage, resentment and despair,
As thou, sad virgin! for thy ravished hair.   10
    For, that sad moment, when the sylphs withdrew,
And Ariel, weeping, from Belinda flew,
Umbriel, a dusky, melancholy sprite,
As ever sullied the fair face of light,
Down to the central earth, his proper scene,   15
Repaired to search the gloomy Cave of Spleen.
    Swift on his sooty pinions flits the gnome,
And in a vapour reached the dismal dome.
No cheerful breeze this sullen region knows,
The dreaded east is all the wind that blows.   20
Here in a grotto, sheltered close from air,
And screened in shades from day's detested glare,
She sighs for ever on her pensive bed,
Pain at her side, and megrim at her head.
    Two handmaids wait the throne, alike in place,   25
But differing far in figure and in face.
Here stood Ill-Nature like an ancient maid,
Her wrinkled form in black and white arrayed.
With store of prayers for mornings, nights and noons,
Her hand is filled, her bosom with lampoons.   30

There Affectation, with a sickly mien,
Shows in her cheeks the roses of eighteen,
Practised to lisp and hang the head aside,
Faints into airs, and languishes with pride,
On the rich quilt sinks with becoming woe,   35
Wrapped in a gown, for sickness and for show.
The fair-ones feel such maladies as these,
When each new night-dress gives a new disease.
    A constant vapour o'er the palace flies,
Strange phantoms rising as the mists arise,   40
Dreadful as hermit's dreams in haunted shades,
Or bright, as visions of expiring maids.
Now glaring fiends, and snakes on rolling spires,
Pale spectres, gaping tombs, and purple fires,
Now lakes of liquid gold, Elysian scenes,   45
And crystal domes, and angels in machines.
    Unnumbered throngs on every side are seen,
Of bodies changed to various forms by Spleen.
Here living teapots stand, one arm held out,
One bent – the handle this, and that the spout;   50
A pipkin there like Homer's tripod walks;
Here sighs a jar, and there a goose-pie talks;
Men prove with child, as powerful fancy works,
And maids turned bottles, call aloud for corks.
    Safe passed the gnome through this fantastic band,   55
A branch of healing spleenwort in his hand.
Then thus addressed the power, 'Hail, wayward queen!
Who rule the sex from fifty to fifteen,
Parent of vapours and of female wit,
Who give th'hysteric, or poetic, fit,   60
On various tempers act by various ways,
Make some take physic, others scribble plays,
Who cause the proud their visits to delay,
And send the godly in a pet to pray.
A nymph there is that all thy power disdains,   65
And thousands more in equal mirth maintains.
But O! if e'er thy gnome could spoil a grace,
Or raise a pimple on a beauteous face,
Like citron waters matrons' cheeks inflame,
Or change complexions at a losing game,   70
If e'er with airy horns I planted heads,

Or rumpled petticoats, or tumbled beds,
Or caused suspicion where no soul was rude,
Or discomposed the headdress of a prude,
Or e'er to costive lap-dogs gave disease, 75
Which not the tears of brightest eyes could ease,
Hear me, and touch Belinda with chagrin.
That single act gives half the world the spleen.'
　The goddess with a discontented air
Seems to reject him, though she grants his prayer. 80
A wondrous bag with both her hands she binds,
Like that where once Ulysses held the winds.
There she collects the force of female lungs,
Sighs, sobs and passions, and the war of tongues.
A vial next she fills with fainting fears, 85
Soft sorrows, melting griefs and flowing tears.
The gnome rejoicing bears her gifts away,
Spreads his black wings and slowly mounts to day.
　Sunk in Thalestris' arms the nymph he found,
Her eyes dejected and her hair unbound. 90
Full o'er her head the swelling bag he rent,
And all the furies issued at the vent.
Belinda burns with more than mortal ire,
And fierce Thalestris fans the rising fire,
'O wretched maid!' she spread her hands and cried 95
(While Hampton's echoes, 'Wretched maid!' replied),
'Was it for this you took such constant care
The bodkin, comb and essence to prepare?
For this your locks in paper durance bound,
For this the tort'ring irons wreathed around? 100
For this with fillets strained your tender head,
And bravely bore the double loads of lead?
Gods! shall the ravisher display your hair,
While the fops envy, and the ladies stare?
Honour forbid! at whose unrivalled shrine 105
Ease, pleasure, virtue, all, our sex resign.
Methinks already I your tears survey,
Already hear the horrid things they say,
Already see you a degraded toast,
And all your honour in a whisper lost! 110
How, then, shall I your helpless fame defend?
'Twill then be infamy to seem your friend!

And shall this prize, th'inestimable prize,
Exposed through crystal to the gazing eyes,
And heightened by the diamond's circling rays,   115
On that rapacious hand for ever blaze?
Sooner shall grass in Hyde Park Circus grow,
And wits take lodgings in the sound of Bow,
Sooner let earth, air, sea, to Chaos fall,
Men, monkeys, lap-dogs, parrots, perish all!'   120
     She said. Then raging to Sir Plume repairs,
And bids her beau demand the precious hairs
(Sir Plume of amber snuff-box justly vain,
And the nice conduct of a clouded cane).
With earnest eyes, and round unthinking face,   125
He first the snuff-box opened, then the case,
And thus broke out, 'My lord, why, what the devil!
Zounds! Damn the lock! 'fore Gad, you must be civil!
Plague on't! 'tis past a jest – nay, prithee, pox!
Give her the hair,' he spoke, and rapped his box.   130
     'It grieves me much,' replied the peer again,
'Who speaks so well should ever speak in vain.
But by this lock, this sacred lock, I swear
(Which never more shall join its parted hair,
Which never more its honours shall renew,   135
Clipped from the lovely head where late it grew),
That while my nostrils draw the vital air,
This hand, which won it, shall for ever wear.'
He spoke, and speaking, in proud triumph spread
The long-contended honours of her head.   140
     But Umbriel, hateful gnome, forbears not so.
He breaks the vial whence the sorrows flow.
Then see! the nymph in beauteous grief appears,
Her eyes half-languishing, half-drowned in tears.
On her heaved bosom hung her drooping head   145
Which, with a sigh, she raised, and thus she said,
     'For ever cursed be this detested day
Which snatched my best, my favourite curl away!
Happy! ah ten times happy had I been,
If Hampton Court these eyes had never seen!   150
Yet am not I the first mistaken maid,
By love of courts to numerous ills betrayed.
O had I rather unadmired remained

243

In some lone isle, or distant northern land,
Where the gilt chariot never marks the way,   155
Where none learn ombre, none e'er taste Bohea!
There kept my charms concealed from mortal eye,
Like roses that in deserts bloom and die.
What moved my mind with youthful lords to roam?
O had I stayed, and said my prayers at home!   160
'Twas this the morning omens seemed to tell:
Thrice from my trembling hand the patch-box fell,
The tottering china shook without a wind,
Nay Poll sat mute and Shock was most unkind!
A sylph too warned me of the threats of Fate,   165
In mystic visions now believed too late!
See the poor remnants of these slighted hairs!
My hand shall rend what ev'n thy rapine spares.
These in two sable ringlets taught to break
Once gave new beauties to the snowy neck.   170
The sister lock now sits uncouth, alone,
And in its fellow's fate foresees its own.
Uncurled it hangs, the fatal shears demands,
And tempts once more thy sacrilegious hands.
O hadst thou, cruel, been content to seize   175
Hairs less in sight, or any hairs but these!'

Canto Five

She said. The pitying audience melt in tears.
But Fate and Jove had stopped the Baron's ears.
In vain Thalestris with reproach assails,
For who can move where fair Belinda fails?
Not half so fixed the Trojan could remain,   5
While Anna begged and Dido raged in vain.
The grave Clarissa graceful waved her fan.
Silence ensued, and thus the nymph began,
    'Say why are beauties praised and honoured most,
The wise man's passion, and the vain man's toast?   10
Why decked with all that land and sea afford,
Why angels called, and angel-like adored?
Why round our coaches crowd the white-gloved beaus,
Why bows the side-box from its inmost rows?
How vain are all these glories, all our pains,   15

Unless good sense preserve what beauty gains.
That men may say, when we the front-box grace,
"Behold the first in virtue as in face!"
O! if to dance all night, and dress all day,
Charmed the smallpox, or chased old age away,   20
Who would not scorn what huswife's cares produce,
Or who would learn one earthly thing of use.
To patch, nay ogle, may become a saint,
Nor could it sure be such a sin to paint.
But since, alas, frail beauty must decay,   25
Curled or uncurled, since locks will turn to grey,
Since painted, or not painted, all shall fade,
And she who scorns a man, must die a maid,
What then remains but well our power to use,
And keep good humour still whate'er we lose?   30
And trust me, dear, good humour can prevail,
When airs, and flights, and screams, and scoldings fail.
Beauties in vain their pretty eyes may roll,
Charms strike the sight but merit wins the soul.'
     So spoke the dame, but no applause ensued.   35
Belinda frowned, Thalestris called her prude.
'To arms! To arms!' the fierce virago cries,
And swift as lightning to the combat flies.
All side in parties and begin th'attack,
Fans clap, silks rustle and tough whalebones crack.   40
Heroes' and heroines' shouts confused'ly rise,
And base and treble voices strike the skies.
No common weapons in their hands are found,
Like gods they fight, nor dread a mortal wound.
     So when bold Homer makes the gods engage,   45
And heavenly breasts with human passions rage;
'Gainst Pallas, Mars; Latona, Hermes arms;
And all Olympus rings with loud alarms.
Jove's thunder roars, heaven trembles all around,
Blue Neptune storms, the bellowing deeps resound.   50
Earth shakes her nodding towers, the ground gives way,
And the pale ghosts start at the flash of day!
     Triumphant Umbriel on a sconce's height
Clapped his glad wings, and sat to see the fight.
Propped on their bodkin spears the sprites survey   55
The growing combat or assist the fray.

While through the press enraged Thalestris flies,
And scatters deaths around from both her eyes,
A beau and witling perished in the throng,
One died in metaphor and one in song.   60
'O cruel nymph, a living death I bear,'
Cried Dapperwit, and sunk beside his chair.
A mournful glance Sir Fopling upwards cast,
'Those eyes are made so killing,' was his last.
Thus on Meander's flowery margin lies   65
Th'expiring swan, and as he sings he dies.
   When bold Sir Plume had drawn Clarissa down,
Chloe stepped in and killed him with a frown.
She smiled to see the doughty hero slain,
But at her smile the beau revived again.   70
   Now Jove suspends his golden scales in air,
Weighs the men's wits against the lady's hair;
The doubtful beam long nods from side to side,
At length the wits mount up, the hairs subside.
   See fierce Belinda on the Baron flies,   75
With more than usual lightning in her eyes.
Nor feared the chief th'unequal fight to try,
Who sought no more than on his foe to die.
But this bold lord with manly strength endued,
She with one finger and a thumb subdued.   80
Just where the breath of life his nostrils drew
A charge of snuff the wily virgin threw.
The gnomes direct, to every atom just,
The pungent grains of titillating dust.
Sudden, with starting tears, each eye o'erflows,   85
And the high dome re-echoes to his nose.
   'Now meet thy fate,' incensed Belinda cried
And drew a deadly bodkin from her side,
(The same, his ancient personage to deck,
Her great great grandsire wore about his neck   90
In three seal-rings, which after, melted down,
Formed a vast buckle for his widow's gown.
Her infant grandame's whistle next it grew –
The bells she jingled and the whistle blew.
Then in a bodkin graced her mother's hairs,   95
Which long she wore and now Belinda wears.)
   'Boast not my fall,' he cried, 'insulting foe!

Thou by some other shalt be laid as low.
Nor think, to die dejects my lofty mind –
All that I dread is leaving you behind!   100
Rather than so, ah let me still survive,
And burn in Cupid's flames – but burn alive.'
    'Restore the lock!' she cries. And all around
'Restore the lock!' the vaulted roofs rebound.
Not fierce Othello in so loud a strain   105
Roared for the handkerchief that caused him pain.
But see how oft ambitious aims are crossed,
And chiefs contend 'till all the prize is lost!
The lock, obtained with guilt, and kept with pain,
In every place is sought but sought in vain.   110
With such a prize no mortal must be blessed,
So Heaven decrees! With Heaven who can contest?
    Some thought it mounted to the lunar sphere,
Since all things lost on earth are treasured there.
There heroes' wits are kept in ponderous vases,   115
And beaus' in snuff-boxes and tweezer-cases.
There broken vows and death-bed alms are found,
And lovers' hearts with ends of ribbons bound,
The courtier's promises and sick man's prayers,
The smiles of harlots, and the tears of heirs,   120
Cages for gnats and chains to yoke a flea,
Dried butterflies, and tomes of casuistry.
    But trust the Muse. She saw it upward rise,
Though marked by none but quick, poetic eyes
(So Rome's great founder to the heavens withdrew,   125
To Proculus alone confessed in view).
A sudden star it shot through liquid air,
And drew behind a radiant trail of hair.
Not Berenice's locks first rose so bright,
The heavens bespangling with dishevelled light.   130
The sylphs behold it kindling as it flies,
And pleased pursue its progress through the skies.
    This the beau-monde shall from the Mall survey,
And hail with music its propitious ray.
This the blessed lover shall for Venus take,   135
And send up vows from Rosamunda's lake.
This Partridge soon shall view in cloudless skies,
When next he looks through Galileo's eyes,

And hence th'egregious wizard shall foredoom
The fate of Louis and the fall of Rome.   140
   Then cease, bright nymph, to mourn thy ravished hair,
Which adds new glory to the shining sphere!
Not all the tresses that fair head can boast
Shall draw such envy as the lock you lost.
For, after all the murders of your eye,   145
Even after millions slain yourself shall die,
When those fair suns shall set as set they must,
And all those tresses shall be laid in dust,
This lock, the Muse shall consecrate to fame
And 'midst the stars inscribe Belinda's name.   150

The first version of *The Rape of the Lock* was written by Pope in 1711, at the
request of his friend John Caryll, in an attempt to heal the quarrel which had
arisen between two Catholic families. The cause of the quarrel was the cutting
of a lock of Arabella Fermor's hair by Robert, Lord Petre.

   The original poem was in two cantos. In 1714, Pope published an enlarged version in five cantos, with references to the supernatural world of sylphs and
gnomes included for the first time, and in 1717, he added Clarissa's speech in
Canto V. By its final version the poem had grown from 234 lines to 794 lines.

   The Rape of the Lock is a mock-epic or, alternatively, a mock-heroic poem. An
epic is a long narrative poem which deals with great characters and great
actions, following certain conventions and employing an elevated style. The
mock-epic applies the conventions and the style of the epic to trivial characters
and trivial actions. This allows the poet to place the pettiness of his society in
ludicrous contrast with the heroism of a former age.

   The epics most referred to in *The Rape of the Lock* are Homer's *Iliad*, which is
about the consequences of Achilles' wrath, and Virgil's *Aeneid*, about Aeneas'
adventures between leaving Troy and establishing the city of Rome. Pope
includes a great number of allusions to specific lines and phrases from these
poems in famous English translations, as well as references to larger scenes,
descriptions and incidents. The policy of the present editors has been to note
only some of the more important of the local allusions. Greater detail is provided
by Geoffrey Tillotson in the second volume of the Twickenham edition, to which
we must record our debt.

   The poem is written in heroic couplets, that is, in rhymed pairs of regular
iambic pentameters. Each line has a caesura (a pause), and Pope relieves
the potential monotony of the heroic couplet by deftly varying the position
of the caesura. See, for example, Canto I, 125–32, with the caesuras marked here
by //:

> A heavenly image // in the glass appears,
> To that she bends, // to that her eyes she rears;
> The inferior priestess, // at her altar's side,
> Trembling // begins the sacred rites of pride.

Unnumbered treasures ope at once, // and here
The various offerings // of the world appear.
From each // she nicely culls (/) with curious toil,
And decks the goddess // with the glittering spoil.

The structure is as follows:

Canto One: proposition and invocation; Belinda's dream; the supernatural world of salamanders, nymphs, sylphs and gnomes; the warning of coming danger; Belinda waking and making up.

Canto Two: Belinda on the Thames; her two locks; the Baron and his plans to cut one of them; the defence plans and preparations of Belinda's guardian sylphs.

Canto Three: Hampton Court and its activities; the first battle – the game of ombre between Belinda and the Baron; coffee drinking; Clarissa's scissors and the cutting of the lock; the Baron's speech of triumph.

Canto Four: Umbriel and the Cave of Spleen; Umbriel's request to the goddess of Spleen; her gifts of a bag of bad temper and vial of sorrow; Umbriel's spilling of the bag over Belinda and Thalestris; the consequences; Sir Plume as Belinda's champion; Umbriel's breaking of the vial over Belinda; her speech of grief.

Canto Five: Clarissa's intervention; her counsel of good humour; its failure; the final battle; the loss of the lock; its transformation into a star; closing advice and praise for Belinda.

Dedication to Mrs Arabella Fermor

[Added by Pope to the edition of 1714]
MADAM, – It will be in vain to deny that I have some regard for this piece, since I dedicate it to you. Yet you may bear me witness, it was intended only to divert a few young ladies, who have good sense and good humour enough to laugh not only at their sex's little unguarded follies, but at their own. But as it was communicated with the air of a secret, it soon found its way into the world. An imperfect copy having been offered to a bookseller, you had the good-nature for my sake to consent to the publication of one more correct. This I was forced to before I had executed half my design, for the machinery was entirely wanting to complete it.

The machinery, Madam, is a term invented by the critics to signify that part which the deities, angels, or demons are made to act in a poem: for the ancient poets are in one respect like many modern ladies – let an action be never so trivial in itself, they always make it appear of the utmost importance. These machines I determined to raise on a very new and odd foundation, the Rosicru-cian [see note to i, 60] doctrine of spirits.

I know how disagreeable it is to make use of hard words before a lady, but it is so much the concern of a poet to have his works understood, and particularly by your sex, that you must give me leave to explain two or three difficult terms.

The Rosicrucians are a people I must bring you acquainted with. The best account I know of them is in a French book called *Le Comte de Gabalis*, which, both in its title and size, is so like a novel that many of the fair sex have read it for one by mistake. According to these gentlemen, the four elements are inhabited by spirits which they call sylphs, gnomes, nymphs and salamanders. The gnomes, or demons of earth, delight in mischief, but the sylphs, whose habitation is in the air, are the best-conditioned creatures imaginable. For they say any mortals may enjoy the most intimate familiarities with these gentle spirits, upon a condition very easy to all true adepts, an inviolate preservation of chastity.

As to the following cantos, all the passages of them are as fabulous as the vision at the beginning, or the transformation at the end (except the loss of your hair, which I always mention with reverence). The human persons are as fictitious as the airy ones, and the character of Belinda, as it is now managed, resembles you in nothing but in beauty.

If this poem had as many graces as there are in your person, or in your mind, yet I could never hope it should pass through the world half so uncensured as you have done. But let its fortune be what it will, mine is happy enough, to have given me this occasion of assuring you that I am, with the truest esteem, Madam, your most obedient, humble servant,
A. POPE.

Canto One

[i, 1–3] **What dire offence ... I sing**
i.e. I sing of the dire offences which spring from amorous causes and of the mighty contests which rise from trivial things. Pope begins his poem with the conventional epic 'proposition', or statement of subject. Dryden's translation of the *Aeneid* begins in similar fashion, 'Arms, and the man I sing'. The delay of 'I sing' until the third line and the unnatural word order of object-subject-verb are heightening devices. Compare Milton, *Paradise Lost*, lines 1–6.

[i, 3] **Caryll**
John Caryll, Pope's friend, who urged him to write the poem. The verse, the poem, is due to him in the sense that he initiated it; *Muse* a goddess of poetry. In Greek mythology, the nine muses were sister goddesses, each responsible for one area of learning or the arts: epic, history, mime, music, dance, choral poetry, tragedy, comedy and astronomy. Pope's 'muse' is a kind of composite goddess. In addressing her, he is imitating the epic convention of invoking the muse.

[i, 5–6] **Slight is the subject ... lays**
anticipating and answering objections that his poem is too trivial to be considered seriously; *lays* verses; *Slight is the subject* Pope alludes to book four

of Virgil's *Georgics* (Dryden's translation): 'Slight is the subject, but the praise not small/ If Heaven assist and Phoebus hear my call.'

[i, 7] **goddess**
i.e. his muse; *Say what ... compel* The poet asks the muse to reveal the answer to his question. There is the epic implication that the muse has access to the truth, whilst a mere poet without the muse's aid does not.

[i, 8] **A well-bred lord ... belle**
i.e. explain why Lord Petre should have assaulted (cut the lock of) Arabella Fermor.

[i, 11] **tasks so bold**
mock-heroic heightening. Neither Lord Petre's 'rape' of the lock nor Pope's versifying of it is a bold task; *little men* Both Pope and Lord Petre were short.

[i, 13] **Sol**
the sun.

[i, 14] **those eyes ... eclipse the day**
Belinda's eyes are extravagantly praised as superior to the sun.

[i, 15] **lapdogs**
a fashionable possession.

[i, 16] **And sleepless lovers ... awake**
anticlimax. The lovers' boast of being kept awake by their passion is exposed as false by the fact that they have slept until midday.

[i, 17] **Thrice ... ground**
The bell and slipper are means of

calling a servant. The triple repetition is an epic convention. See *Aeneid*, bk 4 (Dryden's translation): 'Thrice Dido tried to raise her drooping head,/ And fainting thrice, fell grovelling on the bed.'

[i, 18] **the pressed watch**
The repeater watch, fashionable in the early eighteenth century, chimed the hour and the quarter when a pin was pressed.

[i, 19] **Belinda still ... pressed**
She has fallen back to sleep.

[i, 20] **Her guardian sylph**
Ariel (see i, 106). This introduces the supernatural world, an essential element in the epic, sometimes referred to by the word 'machinery' (see Pope's dedication). The supernatural in *The Rape of the Lock* corresponds to the natural world of the poem in being light and trivial, just as the natural world of war and heroism in the genuine epic is matched by martial and heroic gods and goddesses.

[i, 21–2] **'Twas he ... head**
Ariel has called up a dream so that he can warn Belinda of the impending attack on her lock.

[i, 23] **birth-night beau**
Courtiers dressed in their best clothes for the king's birthday.

[i, 27] **care**
object of care, charge.

[i, 29] **infant thought**
Ariel goes on to catalogue some of the beliefs which Belinda might have held in childhood, and he uses these beliefs to persuade her to accept the kind of supernatural realm he represents. See i, 35, 'Hear and believe'.

[i, 30] **nurse ... priest**
i.e. those responsible for passing on superstitions to children.

[i, 32] **silver token**
A number of country superstitions mention the silver coins which fairies are supposed to leave behind them (surviving today in the 'tooth fairy' which leaves a coin for a milk tooth); *circled green* rings of bright green grass. According to folklore, these rings (actually caused by the spores of fungi) mark the circles in which the fairies have danced.

[i, 33–4] **Or virgins ... heav'nly flowers**
the visions ascribed to virgin saints by popular Roman Catholic mythology. Arabella Fermor, the model for Belinda, was a Catholic, and Pope gives Belinda a distinctively Catholic imagination. He makes joking reference to this in his mock *Key to the Lock* where he argues the poem has 'a tendency to Popery, which is secretly insinuated throughout the whole'.

[i, 36] **bound**
limit.

[i, 38] **To maids ... revealed**
'Thou hast hid these things from the wise and the prudent, and hast delivered them unto babes' (Matthew 11: 25). As well as of this passage Pope seems to be thinking of the popular Catholic mythology which gave special status to virgins.

[i, 39] **doubting wits**
Scepticism about some of the tenets of Christianity became increasingly common among intellectuals, 'wits', in the late seventeenth and early eighteenth centuries. The line can be paraphrased 'what does it matter if sceptics do not believe?' See Rochester's *Satyr*.

[i, 37–40] **Some secret truths ... believe**
Pope plays upon the commonplace that the innocent may possess an insight into divine matters which is denied to the wise. The 'revelation' here comes ironically through Belinda's knowledge of coquetry.

[i, 42] **light militia**
Ariel represents the spirits as congregating in military formation; *lower sky* The sylphs occupy a relatively unimportant area of the heavens.

[i, 44] **box**
box at the theatre; *Ring* a fashionable meeting-place in Hyde Park.

[i, 45] **equipage**
carriage, horses and attendant footmen.

[i, 46] **chair**
sedan chair: an enclosed seat carried on two parallel poles by two bearers, one at the front and one at the back.

[i, 47–8] **As now . . . beauteous mould**
Ariel explains the origins of the sylphs, i.e. that mortal beauties like Belinda turn into these spirits after death.

[i, 49] **Thence**
from there; *repair* go.

[i, 50] **vehicles**
a fad word among certain thinkers (Platonists) for the material embodiment of something or the material habitation of a spirit. Pope puns on 'vehicle' meaning the female form as the 'home' of a potential sylph's spirit, and 'vehicle' meaning equipage.

[i, 52] **vanities**
both the unprofitable pastimes of society women like Belinda and their high opinion of their own beauty.

[i, 54] **And though . . . cards**
i.e. although a woman can no longer play at cards after death, she watches in spirit form the hands of living players.

[i, 55] **chariots**
carriages; also, formerly and in epic, military vehicles.

[i, 56] **ombre**
a popular card game, played by Belinda against the baron in Canto III.

[i, 58] **first elements**
Traditionally the four elements were earth, air, fire and water. Each element provided the essential substance of particular classes of being, and each class of being found its most natural surroundings in the element which formed it. (Hence the saying, 'to be in one's element'.) Thus, Pope's 'fiery termagants' return after death to fire, his 'yielding minds' to water, his heavy 'prudes' to earth, and his 'light coquettes' to air.

[i, 59] **sprites**
souls, spirits; *termagants* bad-tempered women.

[i, 60] **salamander**
lizardlike animal supposed to live in fire. Pope's four classes of supernatural being are salamanders, nymphs (i, 62), gnomes (i, 63) and sylphs (i, 65). He borrowed these terms from the Rosicrucian philosophy, a system of belief which, followed as it was by only a small number of people and those few widely regarded as eccentrics, was marginal and disreputable.

[i, 63] **gnome**
A prudish gnome descends to the Cave of Spleen in search of trouble in Canto IV.

[i, 65] **coquette**
a woman who uses beauty and artful behaviour to attract men, with no intention of returning or satisfying any feeling she may arouse. A coquette herself, Belinda is guarded by sylphs, the spirits into which coquettes change after death.

[i, 66] **fields of air**
a phrase from Dryden's translation of the *Aeneid*.

[i, 67–8] **Know farther . . . embraced**
Rosicrucianism included the notion of physical relationships between spirits and mortals (hinted at in the dedication). In the phrase 'fair and chaste', Pope is referring back to the earlier idea that pious virgins are given special visions. Belinda's coquetry is ironically called chastity and the reward for chastity is embraces.

[i, 70] **Assume what sexes**
the traditional idea that spirits can take on the form of either sex. Here, Ariel, the spirit of some dead female coquette, is appearing to Belinda as a man.

[i, 71] **melting**
being softened by compassion or love, or sweating excessively.

[i, 72] **masquerades**
fancy-dress balls at which the participants wore masks. Masquerades were often associated with uninhibited behaviour.

[i, 73] **safe**
i.e. 'What guards . . . safe' (i, 71–3); *the treacherous friend* here, the friend

who spreads gossip; *spark* a contemptuous term for a showy man about town.

[i, 74] **The glance ... dark**
The glance is the licentious glance of the spark, the whisper the malicious tale of the gossip.

[i, 75] **occasion**
opportunity.

[i, 76] **fires**
used as a verb. The dance has fired the blood of the melting maids.

[i, 77–8] **'Tis but ... men below**
Epic writers often draw the distinction between the names conferred by men and those conferred by gods. The idea is that supernatural beings ('the wise celestials') recognise that coquettes are protected by their sylphs, while ordinary mortals believe wrongly that it is honour which protects them.

[i, 79] **nymphs**
Demi-goddesses whose homes were in rivers and lakes; figuratively, young and beautiful women; *too conscious of their face* too aware of their own beauty.

[i, 80] **gnomes' embrace**
Those women who set so much store by their beauty that they refuse all suitors will eventually become ill-tempered and prudish old maids.

[i, 81] **these**
i.e. the gnomes; *prospects* imagined possibilities, ambitions.

[i, 82] **offers**
marriage proposals.

[i, 83] **gay ideas**
showy images, the nymphs' ambitious dreams.

[i, 84] **sweeping train**
trailing robes.

[i, 85] **garters ... coronets**
insignia of noble rank.

[i, 86] **Your Grace**
form of address for a duke or a duchess. The thought of being addressed as a duchess is one of the 'gay ideas' which crowd the mind of the young woman who sets too much store by her own beauty.

[i, 87] **early**
early in life.

[i, 89] **infant-cheeks**
Women learn the art of coquetry very early; *bidden blush* The blush is 'bidden' in the sense that it is made to come, i.e. by rouge.

[i, 92] **mystic**
esoteric, occult. The sylphs are supernatural.

[i, 93] **they pursue**
i.e. either the sylphs follow the nymphs or the nymphs follow circles.

[i, 94] **impertinence**
trifle. The idea is that the sylphs protect women by introducing them to a new temptation just as they are about to fall for an existing one. The entire passage (i, 91–104) is concerned with the changeableness of women.

[i, 96] **treat**
entertainment with food; *ball* The couplet might be paraphrased: what tender maid could avoid being seduced by the treat of one man if it were not for the ball of another?

[i, 97–9] **Florio & Damon**
conventional names for idealised pastoral lovers.

[i, 99] **vanities**
see note to i, 52.

[i, 100] **moving**
unstable; *toyshop* a shop selling fans, laces and other trinkets.

[i, 101] **sword-knots**
ribbons tied to the hilt of the sword for decoration. Pope assumes that young women will be attracted by these.

[i, 102] **coaches coaches drive**
i.e. coaches drive out coaches. A fresh interest in a new coach will drive out the existing interest in an old one from a woman's changeable heart.

[i, 103–4] **This erring mortals ... it all**
again the epic contrast between the perspectives of gods and of men. See i, 77–8 and note.

[i, 105] **thy protection claim**
claim the right to protect you.

[i, 106] **sprite**
spirit.

[i, 107] **crystal wilds**
Pope refers to the notion, already exploded in his day, that the sun, the

moon and the stars are fixed to enormous crystal spheres which rotate around a stationary earth. Ariel has been spending his time among the crystal spheres.

[i, 108] **clear mirror...star**
Pope added a note to the effect that the phrase 'clear mirror' was 'the language of the Platonists'. The mirror is clear because it is celestial; earthly mirrors and images are cloudy and obscure. The sense is simply that the 'clear mirror' of Belinda's 'ruling star' (i.e. the star which guides her fate) shows precisely and truly what will happen to her.

[i, 109] **impend**
to be imminent, about to happen; *I saw...impend* i.e. I saw a dreadful imminent event.

[i, 110] **main**
ocean.

[i, 112] **Warned...beware**
This kind of warning is another epic device; *pious* ironic.

[i, 115] **Shock**
both the name of Belinda's dog and that of its breed. The shock, or shough, was a fashionable lapdog.

[i, 117–18] **billet-doux**
a love letter, usually written in extravagant language; *'Twas then... a billet-doux* There is some ambiguity in the couplet. It could mean either (1) 'it was only at that point that your eyes opened and fell upon a love letter', or (2) 'it was at that point that your eyes opened and saw, for the first time ever, a love letter'. The second reading appears the more sensible because of the clause 'if report say true'. Gossip (report) would hardly be likely to consider the moment of waking, although it might well be concerned with the receipt of a first love letter. However, if that reading is correct, gossip must be mistaken; Belinda has other love letters on her dressing table (i, 138).

[i, 119] **wounds, charms, and ardours**
reproducing the extravagant contents of the letter.

[i, 120] **the vision**
i.e. of Ariel. The joke is that the earthly love letter distracts Belinda from her heavenly vision of the sylph.

[i, 121] **toilet**
dressing table.

[i, 122] **silver vase**
the containers of Belinda's cosmetics, and implicitly the sacred vessels of the mass (see below); *mystic order* an order which pertains to the religious mysteries. Pope goes on to describe the whole process of applying Belinda's make-up in mock religious terms. The description recalls the sacrifices and religious ceremonies of epic poems, and also the Catholic mass. The device makes a satirical point about Pope's society's worship of female beauty.

[i, 123] **First, robed...adores**
Belinda, dressed in a white dressing gown, is the priestess adoring the deity which appears in the mirror, that is, her own reflection. White vestments are worn in the Catholic Church on the feasts of confessors and virgins.

[i, 124] **head uncovered**
Pope's ironic *Key to the Lock* refers us to the bare-headedness of the Catholic priest.

[i, 125] **A heavenly image**
her reflection, the object of worship.

[i, 126] **To that...rears**
reminiscent of the Catholic priest adoring the host.

[i, 127] **The inferior priestess**
Belinda's maid. Actually helping Belinda with her make-up, she becomes in Pope's description an assistant priestess, helping with the rites.

[i, 130] **The various...appear**
The various items on Belinda's dressing table have been imported from all over the world. The international trade in superfluous luxury items which Pope hints at here was a relatively new phenomenon, and one much attacked by moralists (see v, 11).

[i, 131] **culls**
gathers; *curious* careful and skilful.

[i, 132] **decks the goddess**
the maid is presented as dressing the image in the mirror.

[i, 134] **Arabia**
famous for its perfumes.

[i, 135] **The tortoise ... unite**
Belinda's comb has a tortoise-shell spine and ivory teeth. The description of an everyday object, the comb, is mockingly heightened.

[i, 137] **files**
rows, suggestive of military order. The pins are for arranging clothing.

[i, 138] **patches**
small pieces of black cloth worn by fashionable women on the face; *bibles* Bibles printed in small format were fashionable accessories. Bibles, or at least mass books, belong on the Catholic altar, but their presence on the dressing table alongside the other items listed is incongruous and indicative of Belinda's confused system of values.

[i, 139] **awful**
inspiring awe; *beauty ... arms* Pope shifts from imitating one element of the epic, the religious rite, to imitating another, the arming of the hero. Belinda's face-painting, hair-setting and dressing are imagined in terms of a warrior being clothed in armour for the battle.

[i, 143] **a purer blush**
a blush created by cosmetics. 'Purer' is ironic.

[i, 144] **keener lightnings**
The eyes of a beautiful woman were conventionally praised as 'flashing lightning'. The lightnings in Belinda's eyes become 'keener' because she has applied eye make-up; *quicken* become animated, vigorous.

[i, 145] **The busy ... care**
Pope supplied a note directing the reader to the ancient traditions which record fallen angels becoming 'amorous of women'.

[i, 146] **set the head**
build the high tower, or head, into which fashionable women piled their hair.

[i, 147] **plait**
arrange in folds.

[i, 148] **Betty**
a stock name for a maid; *not her own* The effects which seem to be the results of the maid's work are really the results of the sylphs'.

Canto Two

[ii, 1] **th'etherial plane**
In traditional astronomy the space above the moon was thought to be filled by ether. 'Plane' is here used to mean an open space. Thus, 'the plane of ether', the realm of the sun.

[ii, 2] **purpled**
bright, made bright (by the rising sun) – a Latinate usage; *main* ocean, sea.

[ii, 3] **issuing forth**
coming out, setting off; *his beams* the sun's beams: compare i, 14.

[ii, 4] **Launched**
The Thames was a busy thoroughfare; *bosom* poetical term for the surface of a river or lake.

[ii, 1–4] **Not with ... Thames**
The sun does not rise in the heavens to light the sea with any more glory than his rival (Belinda) launched herself onto the Thames.

[ii, 5] **Fair**
beautiful; *nymphs* young women (see note to i, 75).

[ii, 7] **sparkling cross**
The decorated cross which Belinda wears again reminds readers of her Catholicism.

[ii, 8] **infidels**
non-believers, specifically Muslims; *Which Jews ... adore* Belinda's beauty overcomes the scruples of non-believers towards the cross. The word 'adore' again suggests Catholicism, since the meditation upon, and veneration of, holy images belong in the Catholic tradition.

[ii, 10] **quick**
animated, moving; *unfixed* Her mind, like her eyes, passes rapidly from object to object.

[ii, 11] **favours**
indulgences, possibly with the connotation of sexual indulgences.

[ii, 12] **Oft she . . . offends**
Her behaviour is that of the perfect society coquette.

[ii, 13] **Bright as the sun**
another comparison of Belinda's eyes with the sun.

[ii, 14] **shine on all alike**
Compare Matthew 5: 45: 'He maketh His sun to shine on the evil and on the good, and sendeth rain on the just and on the unjust.'

[ii, 15] **ease**
Social ease was a quality highly regarded by Pope (see *Arbuthnot*, 196); *void of* without.

[ii, 16] **her faults**
for example, her unfixed mind and the obvious vanity; *if belles* ironically mimicking the social convention which forbade criticism of women.

[ii, 18] **Look on . . . them all**
Flattering lines such as this ensured that Arabella Fermor, the model for Belinda, was at first quite proud of her place in the *Rape*.

[ii, 19] **destruction of mankind**
conventional overstatement.

[ii, 20] **Nourished**
The word had the specific meaning of 'to allow hair to grow'; *two locks* Her hair was tied up, with two thick ringlets allowed to hang down from the mass.

[ii, 21] **conspired**
in the sense of contrived; *deck* to cover, to clothe.

[ii, 23] **labyrinths**
The notion of female physical attributes as forming traps and chains for men was a common one. Compare Richard Lovelace's *To Althea, From Prison* (lines 5–6): 'When I lie tangled in her hair,/ And fettered to her eye.'

[ii, 25] **springes**
snares or traps for catching small animals and birds. Horse hair was used in the construction of them; *betray* used here in the sense of trap.

[ii, 26] **finny prey**
fish – sometimes caught with line only one hair thick.

[ii, 27] **tresses**
long locks of hair; *imperial* here,

domineering and powerful. The sense is that man, even though the stronger sex, can be subdued by female coiffure.

[ii, 29] **Th'adventurous Baron**
mock-heroic heightening. The Baron is Lord Petre – see introduction.

[ii, 30] **prize**
The word still carried a heavy military association – something won in battle.

[ii, 31] **meditates**
plans.

[ii, 32] **ravish**
to take by violence; *force . . . fraud* a common epic opposition.

[ii, 35] **this**
i.e. success; *Phoebus* Phoebus/Apollo, the god of the sun. The Baron, unlike Belinda (i, 16), has been up since before daybreak.

[ii, 36] **Propitious**
favourably inclined. The epithet implies that the Baron will have success; *power* divinity.

[ii, 37] **an altar built**
Like Belinda's toilet in the first canto, the Baron's altar recalls the religious ceremonies and sacrifices of the true epic (see note to i, 122).

[ii, 38] **vast French romances**
long and incredible fictions concerning love and battle. The Baron's altar is comically constructed from the possessions of the fashionable, modern lover; *gilt* gilded, covered with a thin layer of gold; a fashionable way of decorating the edges of the pages. The neatness of the gilding contrasts with the vastness of the books.

[ii, 40] **trophies**
prizes captured in war and kept as a memorial of victory.

[ii, 41] **billet-doux**
love letters (see note to i, 117–18); *pyre* the pile to be burnt.

[ii, 44] **prize**
i.e. Belinda's lock.

[ii, 45] **powers**
gods and goddesses; *gave ear* listened; *half his prayer* i.e. they granted him the quick seizure but not the long possession of the lock. The gods' granting of half a prayer is

another epic convention, and one which Pope echoes again at the end of *Epistle to a Lady* (lines 286–7).

[ii, 46] **The rest ... empty air**
another echo of the epic, as Pope's note indicates. In the *Aeneid* Arruns prays to Apollo as he throws his javelin at Camilla, with the result that in Dryden's translation (bk 2): 'Apollo heard, and granting half his prayer/ Shuffled in winds the rest and tossed in empty air.'

[ii, 47] **painted vessel**
The expression can refer both to the boat and to Belinda, since 'vessel' is sometimes used, especially in a religious context, to mean person or body.

[ii, 48] **tides**
When the *Rape* was written the Thames was tidal above London.

[ii, 49] **steals upon**
moves stealthily up to; *music* Presumably a small ensemble accompanies the party on the boat.

[ii, 50] **die**
fade away. Pope may also refer to the cadence of the music, as in Orsino's description of a 'strain' which had 'a dying fall' (*Twelfth Night*, I, i, 4).

[ii, 51] **zephyrs**
Greek gods of the winds; hence, any gentle breeze.

[ii, 52] **Belinda ... gay**
another elegant compliment to Arabella Fermor – see note to ii, 18.

[ii, 53] **the sylph**
i.e. Ariel; *careful* full of care, anxious.

[ii, 54] **Th'impending woe**
Ariel announces his vision of 'some dread event' in Belinda's ruling star in the first canto (i, 108–9).

[ii, 55] **straight**
immediately; *denizens* naturalised aliens, settlers. The sylphs are 'denizens of air' in that they have become inhabitants of the atmosphere after having been coquettes on earth (i, 65).

[ii, 56] **lucid**
having the quality of light; *repair* move to.

[ii, 57] **shrouds**
large ropes suitable for a sea-going ship rather than this river vessel – mock-heroic heightening.

[ii, 58] **that seemed but**
which seemed only; i.e. the whispers for the sylphs are taken to be breezes by the river party.

[ii, 60] **waft**
float; *clouds of gold* The idea of gilded clouds at the height of a mast owes more to contemporary painting (which sometimes used cherub-filled clouds for decorative effect) than to real life.

[ii, 61] **fine**
clear, pure, refined.

[ii, 63] **airy garments flew**
Again the image of translucent garments flying in the air owes a good deal to contemporary painting.

[ii, 64] **Thin, glittering ... dew**
Refers to the fine cobwebs, known as gossamers, which can be seen in the grass or floating in the air in spring and summer. These were thought to be formed through the action of the sun on dew.

[ii, 65] **tinctures**
colours, dyes.

[ii, 66] **disports**
plays freely, frolics.

[ii, 68] **Colours that change**
The changing colours caused by the sylphs reflect the unfixedness of Belinda's mind (ii, 10).

[ii, 69] **the circle**
i.e. of the sylphs gathered round him.

[ii, 70] **Superior by the head**
a head taller. The epic hero generally has the advantage of height.

[ii, 71] **purple**
a royal colour; *pinions* wings.

[ii, 72] **azure**
bright blue; *wand* Ariel's wand corresponds to an earthly king's sceptre as a badge of authority.

[ii, 73] **sylphids**
female sylphs.

[ii, 74] **Fays**
fairies; *genii* spirits belonging with a particular person or place; *daemons* inferior divinities or spirits, not necessarily evil.

[ii, 75] **spheres**
both the spheres of the old astronomy (see note to i, 107), and more generally areas of activity. The long list of the various tasks of Ariel's helpers is another epic device.

[ii, 77] **ether**
the gas filling the space above the moon – see note to ii, 1.

[ii, 78] **blaze of day**
living in ether they are exposed to the sun.

[ii, 79] **orbs**
globes; here, stars.

[ii, 81] **less refined**
They are less refined in that they occupy a less pure section of the heavens.

[ii, 82] **the starts that shoot**
comets; *athwart* across.

[ii, 83] **grosser**
less pure.

[ii, 84] **painted bow**
the rainbow.

[ii, 85] **main**
ocean, sea.

[ii, 86] **glebe**
field; *distil* let fall in drops, sprinkle.

[ii, 89] **Of these . . . own**
The chief of these (spirits who guard the welfare of people – ii, 87–8) take on, or own, the care of nations as their duty. The line alludes to the idea that each nation was assigned a guardian angel.

[ii, 91] **province**
sphere of activity; *fair* (used as a noun) women.

[ii, 92] **Not a . . . care**
The sylphs' job of looking after the likes of Belinda is just as pleasant as the more strenuous activities listed in the previous verse paragraph – another elegant compliment.

[ii, 93] **powder**
face powder; *rude* rough.

[ii, 94] **imprisoned essences**
the essences of flowers captured in liquids and in jars; i.e. perfumes; *exhale* evaporate.

[ii, 95] **vernal**
spring; *To draw . . . flowers* refers to the manufacture of paint for the face.

[ii, 97] **wash**
a liquid preparation for hair or skin, here specifically a curling lotion.

[ii, 98] **Assist their blushes**
with rouge – compare i, 89 & 143; *airs* behaviour, manners, affectations.

[ii, 99] **invention**
inventiveness, new ideas.

[ii, 100] **flounce**
a strip sewed by its upper edge to a dress; *furbelow* the border of a dress.

[ii, 101] **threat**
used as a verb, threaten; *fair* fair one, woman (see ii, 91).

[ii, 103] **or . . . or**
either . . . or; *force or slight* echoes the Baron's wish to gain the lock, whether by force or fraud (see ii, 32).

[ii, 104] **But what . . . night**
Ariel's vision has told him only of some dreadful doom, disclosing neither the nature nor the scene of it (see i, 111).

[ii, 105] **Diana's law**
Diana, the hunting goddess, was herself a virgin and was accompanied by female virgin attendants. Thus, 'Diana's law' refers to chastity.

[ii, 106] **Or some . . . flaw**
Implicitly, Belinda and her fellows are so morally confused that they recognise no difference between the loss of virginity and the cracking of a costly ornament.

[ii, 107] **brocade**
material richly decorated with raised patterns. Since brocade and honour are both objects of 'stain' the sentence gives them equal value, again implying moral confusion. The rhetorical figure by which one word in a sentence (here 'stain') is made to refer to two others ('honour' and 'brocade') is called zeugma, and Pope uses it to great effect in the *Rape* (see also iii, 65–8).

[ii, 110] **Shock**
Belinda's lapdog – see i, 115 and note; *fall* die, commit a misdemeanour.

[ii, 111] **charge**
particular duty; *repair* go, move.

[ii, 112] **Zephyretta's**
a female form of zephyr, breeze; an appropriate name for the guardian of a fan.

[ii, 113] **drops**
diamonds in the ear; *Brillante* 'Brilliants' was another word for diamonds; again an appropriately named guardian.

[ii, 115] **Crispissa**
'To crisp' is to crimp, or to curl into tight rings.

[ii, 116] **Ariel himself . . . Shock**
another comic reference to the death of a lapdog as a serious loss – see ii, 110 above, also iii, 158 & iv, 75.

[ii, 117–18] **To fifty . . . the petticoat**
The couplet carries a sexual innuendo – if Belinda's petticoat is lost, so too will be her honour.

[ii, 119–20] **seven-fold fence**
Pope describes Belinda's petticoat in terms similar to those used for the epic hero's shield. In the *Iliad* Vulcan arms Achilles (Pope's translation made after the *Rape*): 'Its utmost verge a threefold circle bound;/ . . . Five ample plates the broad expanse compose.'

[ii, 120] **hoops**
to hold out the skirts; *whale* whalebone, used for reinforcing dresses.

[ii, 121] **line**
in the military sense of a line of defence; *silver bound* Belinda's skirts are finished off with a silver border, just as Achilles' shield is rimmed with silver.

[ii, 123–36] **Whatever spirit . . . below**
These lines list, in comic fashion, the punishments awaiting negligent sylphs.

[ii, 124] **fair**
the fair one, Belinda; *at large* at liberty, undefended.

[ii, 126] **Be stopped . . . vials**
be shut up in cosmetic bottles (an amusingly fitting punishment for a sylph); *pins* used for arranging clothes, and present on Belinda's dressing table (i, 134).

[ii, 127] **Or plunged . . . lie**
As Satan is plunged in a lake of burn-

ing sulphur, transgressing sylphs will be plunged in bitter cosmetics.

[ii, 128] **bodkin**
a large needle used for drawing tapes through hems; another article of the lady's toilet.

[ii, 129] **gums**
resins; here, those used for perfumes; *pomatums* pomades, scented ointments used for the skin and hair.

[ii, 131] **alum**
a mineral salt; *styptics* astringent liquids used to close the pores.

[ii, 132] **rivelled**
shrivelled, wrinkled.

[ii, 133] **Ixion**
In Greek mythology Ixion was fastened by Zeus to a burning and continuously turning wheel in punishment for his vicious life.

[ii, 134] **whirling mill**
A stick (known as a molionet or mill) was introduced into the top of a pot of drinking chocolate and used to stir the liquid.

[ii, 135] **burning chocolate**
Pope imagines the erring sylph as tied to the top of the stirring stick (mill) and whirled around above the hot drinking chocolate, scalded by the steam. The punishment echoes the idea of hell as a place where the damned are burnt.

[ii, 136] **the sea that froths**
the drinking chocolate made to froth by the action of the mill.

[ii, 138] **orb in orb**
The spirits arranging themselves in circles recalls Milton's description of the heavenly host before God (*Paradise Lost*, v, 594–6): 'Thus when in orbs/ Of circuit inexpressible they stood,/ Orb within orb . . .'

[ii, 139] **thrid**
threaded; *mazy* maze-like; here, curly.

[ii, 140] **pendents of her ear**
ear-rings.

[ii, 142] **birth of fate**
can suggest both the birth of Belinda's peculiar destiny (fate), and the giving birth to the future by a personified Fate.

Canto Three

[iii, 1] **meads**
meadows; here the fields around London; *for ever ... flowers* Defoe described the gardens as extending 'almost to the river, yet are never overflowed' (*Tour*).

[iii, 2] **Where Thames ... towers**
refers to the fine houses and churches which had been built in London, especially since the fire (1666). 'I shall speak of the river as ... it really is made glorious by the splendour of its shores, gilded with noble palaces, strong fortifications, large hospitals and public buildings' (Defoe, *Tour*). Also, compare *Windsor-Forest*, lines 375–9.

[iii, 3] **structure of majestic frame**
Hampton Court Palace. Built by Cardinal Wolsey in the early years of the sixteenth century, and extended on a number of occasions since, the palace was frequently used in the reign of Queen Anne for the kind of private entertainment described here.

[iii, 5] **foredoom**
destiny (as a verb), decree.

[iii, 6] **nymphs at home**
zeugma used characteristically to create a comic anticlimax and to imply a confusion of values, since the statesmen's efforts are apparently equally divided between deciding foreign policy and planning seductions (see note to ii, 107).

[iii, 7] **great Anna**
Queen Anne, the reigning monarch; *three realms* Britain (England, Wales and Scotland had been one realm since union in 1707), Ireland and France (still claimed by the English monarch).

[iii, 8] **tea**
at that time pronounced tay; *sometimes ... tea* zeugma again (see note to ii, 107).

[iii, 10] **pleasures of the court**
Their business at Hampton is simply pleasure.

[iii, 11] **th'instructive**
heavily ironic; *In various ... passed* Compare Dryden's *Aeneid* (bk 6):

'While thus, in talk, the flying hours they pass.'

[iii, 12] **visit**
Fashionable ladies paid evening calls on one another.

[iii, 14] **charming**
mimicking the language of fashionable affectation (compare *Epistle to a Lady*, line 108); *Indian screen* Oriental accessories were the height of fashion (compare *Epistle to a Lady*, line 168).

[iii, 15] **interprets**
This person observes closely the behaviour of others to discover who is in love with whom (compare i, 73–4).

[iii, 17] **snuff**
a fairly recent fashion; *supply* help, fill in (the awkward silences).

[iii, 18] **ogling**
the casting of amorous looks.

[iii, 20] **obliquely**
slanting, sideways (since the sun is now no longer at the zenith). Ariel's vision has informed him that the catastrophe will happen before the sun sets – i, 110.

[iii, 21–2] **The hungry ... dine**
i.e. judges and jurymen pass sentence hastily in order to get away for an early dinner. The sudden insertion of this savage couplet suggests the extent and the seriousness of the moral confusion of the world of the *Rape*.

[iii, 23] **th'exchange**
The Royal Exchange in London, described by Defoe as 'the greatest and finest of the kind in the world' (*Tour*), was the place where merchants met to conduct business.

[iii, 25] **fame**
Just as epic heroes seek fame in battle, Belinda seeks it at cards. The passage which follows, in which the card game is treated as an epic battle, is the most elaborate piece of mock-heroic in the poem. The details of the game itself are accurate.

[iii, 26] **two adventurous knights**
Ombre was played with three participants, but only Belinda and the Baron really figure in Pope's account of this game.

[iii, 27] **ombre**
a kind of whist, played for money, in which each player attempts to win tricks (groups of cards, in this case groups of three) by beating the card played by an opponent or opponents with a higher card. At the beginning of the game one suit (diamonds, spades, hearts, clubs) is pronounced 'trumps', which gives the cards in that suit a higher value than the cards in the other suits. What distinguishes ombre from other forms of whist is that one player (called the 'ombre' in the cant of the game) takes on the other two. The identity of the ombre is decided by a system of bidding which Pope ignores; *singly* Belinda, as the ombre, opposes the two knights single-handedly.

[iii, 29] **bands**
The cards have been dealt, and in keeping with the military imagery, Pope refers to each hand as a band of soldiers.

[iii, 30] **sacred nine**
Each hand has nine cards in it. 'Sacred nine' is a conventional title for the nine muses (see note to i, 3), but it is more likely that Pope is thinking of the nine orders of angels (Seraphim, Cherubim, Thrones, Dominations, Virtues, Powers, Principalities, Archangels and Angels). At the end of the previous canto, the sylphs have been described in a way reminiscent of Milton's angels (note to ii, 138), and in the lines following this one they are first dubbed an 'aerial guard' (line 31), then imagined as organising themselves according to rank.

[iii, 31] **th'aerial guard**
the sylphs nominated to attend Belinda.

[iii, 33] **a matador**
The three matadors in ombre are the two black aces, plus either the seven of trumps (with black trumps) or the two of trumps (with red trumps). They are the highest cards in the game.

[iii, 34] **according . . . rank**
The gods in the *Aeneid* also place

themselves according to rank, as do the angels in *Paradise Lost* (v, 588–91).

[iii, 35] **yet mindful . . . race**
i.e. still remembering their previous existence (as women).

[iii, 36] **place**
rank, station.

[iii, 37] **Behold, four kings**
Pope accounts for the cards dealt to the three hands in imitation of the epic poet's detailing of the forces lined up for battle.

[iii, 38] **hoary . . . beard**
The kings are pictured with grey moustaches and forked beards.

[iii, 39] **sustain**
hold.

[iii, 40] **softer power**
The queens are weaker cards than the kings.

[iii, 41] **knaves**
or jacks; *succinct* gathered at the waist. The jacks are pictured in short, gathered tunics.

[iii, 42] **halberd**
weapon consisting of a metal head with a point and an axe-shaped blade, mounted on a long shaft.

[iii, 43] **parti-coloured**
of several colours. Pope refers to the number cards; *train* used in the sense of a body of (military) attendants.

[iii, 44] **velvet plain**
the green velvet cover of the card table, and the field of battle.

[iii, 46] **'Let . . . trumps'**
As ombre, Belinda chooses trumps.

[iii, 47] **sable matadors**
see note to iii, 33. With both the black aces and the two of trumps (spades), Belinda has the three highest cards in the pack and must win three tricks. She leads with her strongest cards.

[iii, 49] **Spadillio**
spadille, ace of spades, the highest matador.

[iii, 50] **two captive trumps**
Belinda wins two trump cards (spades) from the two other players who must put down the suit she has led.

[iii, 51] **Manillio**
manille, the two of spades, the second highest matador.

[iii, 52] **verdant**
green, the colour both of the table covering and the field of battle.

[iii, 53] **Basto**
the ace of clubs; *more hard* more difficult to bear, unpleasant.

[iii, 54] **one plebeian card**
one lower card, i.e. not a trump.

[iii, 55] **broad sabre**
pictured on the card; *chief in years* the greyness of the kings' whiskers is mentioned in the succeeding line and in iii, 38.

[iii, 56] **Majesty of spades**
Since spades are trumps the king is the highest card after the matadors.

[iii, 57–8] **Puts forth . . . concealed**
details of the picture on the card.

[iii, 59] **rebel knave**
the jack of spades, called rebel because he has engaged (fought against) his king; *prince* chief. The king of spades is the jack's prince because he is the highest card in that suit.

[iii, 61] **might Pam**
The jack of clubs is called Pam in the game of loo, where it is the highest card; *kings . . . o'erthrew* in that this jack is higher than kings and queens in loo.

[iii, 62] **Lu**
loo; see previous note. Pope comically elevates another card game to the status of an earlier battle or war.

[iii, 63] **destitute of aid**
in that this card has no special status in ombre.

[iii, 64] **victor spade**
the king of iii, 56.

[iii, 65] **Thus far . . . yield**
Belinda has led the four highest cards in the pack and won four of the total nine tricks.

[iii, 66] **the field**
of battle.

[iii, 67] **Amazon**
a Greek tribe of martial women; the Baron's queen of spades; *her host* i.e. Belinda's army, under attack by the Baron's Amazon.

[iii, 68] **Th'imperial . . . spades**
i.e. the wife (consort) of the king of spades, the queen. With the king and the three matadors gone, this is the highest card in the pack.

[iii, 69] **club's black tyrant**
the king of clubs. Having played her best cards, Belinda led this king, only to be beaten by the Baron, who was free to trump as he had no clubs left. If he had still had clubs he would have had to follow suit; *her victim died* died as her victim.

[iii, 70] **mien**
air, bearing.

[iii, 71] **What boots**
what does it profit, what does it matter; *regal circle* the pictured coronet.

[iii, 73] **pompous**
magnificent, splendid.

[iii, 74] **And, of . . . globe?**
Of the four kings in the pack only that of clubs is pictured with the royal orb.

[iii, 75] **The Baron . . . apace**
Having won the trick, the Baron now leads diamonds. There are no trumps left so he is assured of winning tricks with the high cards in this suit.

[iii, 76] **embroidered**
an epic epithet; *king* winning the Baron's second trick and the sixth of the game; *half his face* i.e. pictured in profile.

[iii, 77] **refulgent**
bright, radiant; another epic epithet; *queen* winning the Baron's third trick and the seventh of the whole game.

[iii, 78] **Of broken . . . find**
Most of the good cards in the pack are gone.

[iii, 79] **Clubs, diamonds, hearts**
Compare Dryden's translation of the *Aeneid* (bk 11): 'Arms, horses, men, on heaps together lie.'

[iii, 80] **promiscuous**
massed together without order; *level green* again both card table and battle field.

[iii, 82] **Asia's . . . Afric's**
comparable to the cards in that they provide a variety of types and colours.

[iii, 83] **like**
similar; *confusion* disorder.

[iii, 84] **habit**
dress; *dye* colour.

[iii, 85] **pierced**
in the military sense of breaking an enemy's line (see *Arbuthnot*, line 8).

[iii, 86] **heaps on heaps**
both the piles of the dead and the piles of tricks accumulating on the card table.

[iii, 87] **knave of diamonds**
winning the Baron's fourth trick and the eighth of the total nine. The Baron and Belinda now have four tricks apiece, so the trick after this one will decide who wins the game and the money gambled on it; *wily* in that he's a knave, a deceitful, untrustworthy person.

[iii, 88] **shameful chance**
since the queen falls to her inferior.

[iii, 89] **the blood . . . forsook**
Belinda is worried at losing such a valuable card and at the prospect of imminent defeat.

[iii, 90] **livid**
bluish.

[iii, 92] **codille**
the term for the outright defeat of the ombre (here Belinda) by one of the two players he or she is taking on. One more trick for the Baron will make codille.

[iii, 93] **distempered state**
troubled country.

[iii, 94] **nice**
critical, important; *trick* Pope plays upon trick as a group of cards and trick as an expedient; *general fate* the fate of all.

[iii, 95] **ace of hearts**
The Baron still has the lead and puts down the ace, which in ombre ranks below the jack.

[iii, 96] **mourned . . . queen**
taken by the jack of diamonds in iii, 87.

[iii, 97] **vengeance**
as a card superior to the ace; *eager pace* Belinda, the keen ombre player, apparently slaps her winning card down with some energy.

[iii, 98] **thunder**
the weapon of Jove, the chief of the Roman gods; *prostrate* the position both of the vanquished soldier and of the card.

[iii, 99–100] **The nymph . . . reply**
Another echo of Dryden's version of the *Aeneid* (bk 12): 'With groans the Latins rend the vaulted sky/ Woods, hills and valleys to the voice reply.'

[iii, 100] **woods . . . canals**
features of the grounds of Hampton Court.

[iii, 101–2] **Oh thoughtless . . . elate**
echoing the moralising interjection of the epic poet, and reminding us that some disaster is imminent.

[iii, 103] **Sudden**
swiftly.

[iii, 105] **board**
table. The passage which follows is a miniature version of the epic feast.

[iii, 106] **The berries . . . round**
refers to coffee making. The beans were first roasted, then ground in a mill.

[iii, 107] **altars of Japan**
another echo of the epic religious rite (see i, 120ff. & ii, 35ff.). These altars are tables japanned, or lacquered, in the fashion of the day.

[iii, 108] **silver lamp**
the heating device placed under the coffee pot.

[iii, 109] **grateful**
agreeable.

[iii, 110] **China's earth**
the clay of the coffee cups; *tide* China was known to suffer from flooding, and Pope plays upon the idea.

[iii, 112] **repast**
referring to the period of consumption rather than the food and drink consumed.

[iii, 113] **band**
of sylphs.

[iii, 115] **careful**
full of care, taking care; *plumes* feathers, suggestive of wings; *displayed* unfurled, spread out.

[iii, 116] **brocade**
referring back to the fear that the threatened disaster might be the staining of a brocade (ii, 107). The sylphs spread their wings over Belinda's lap in order to divert any coffee spills.

[iii, 117] **politician**
not in the modern sense of a professional statesman, but rather someone who discusses politics and gossip in the London coffee houses.

[iii, 118] **half-shut eyes**
The ancient seer, like Tiresias, is often represented as blind.

[iii, 119] **sent up in vapours**
In *A Tale of a Tub*, Swift describes the origin of new ideas in terms of ascending vapours: 'human understanding, seated in the brain, must be troubled and overspread by vapours, ascending from the lower faculties to water the invention and render it fruitful'.

[iii, 121] **rash youth**
the Baron. This kind of direct address to one of the participants in the action is sometimes used by epic poets at moments of great drama.

[iii, 122–4] **Scylla's fate . . . hair**
Nisus, king of Alcathous and father of Scylla, had a purple lock of hair on which the safety of his kingdom depended. When Alcathous was besieged by Minos, Scylla fell in love with the attacker and betrayed her father to him by cutting the purple lock. However, Minos shocked by the treachery rejected her, and she was eventually turned into a sea bird (by the 'just gods') and hunted by her father, himself now a sea eagle. Thus, Scylla provides a fitting classical parallel of someone punished for cutting a lock.

[iii, 125] **mischief**
harm or evil of a more serious kind than is generally implied in modern usage.

[iii, 126] **fit instruments**
suitable means.

[iii, 127] **Clarissa**
It is rather odd that Clarissa, who appears as the spokeswoman of good nature in the fifth canto (v, 9–34), should be the instigator of mischief here. The anomaly may be unintended. Clarissa's fifth canto speech was a late addition (see introduction and note to v, 7) and in early versions of the poem she is simply the provider of the scissors. Perhaps Pope chose her to make the speech simply because she was a named, but relatively uncharacterised, figure into whose mouth it could conveniently be put.

[iii, 128] **two-edged weapon**
scissors; *shining case* a newly fashionable 'tweezer case', containing a number of instruments for female beautification.

[iii, 129] **romance**
extravagant fiction centring upon love and battle; *knight* suggests that Clarissa has a special regard for the Baron, but see note to iii, 127 above.

[iii, 131] **extends**
holds out.

[iii, 132] **engine**
both any instrument (such as scissors) and a machine of warfare.

[iii, 134] **fragrant steams**
rising from the coffee.

[iii, 135] **thousand**
often used in epics to indicate large numbers; *sprites* spirits; here the sylphs.

[iii, 137] **thrice**
another common number in epics – see note to i, 17.

[iii, 140] **close**
hidden; *thought* used to mean thoughts, mind.

[iii, 141] **nosegay**
a small bunch of sweet-smelling flowers worn to keep away unpleasant odours; necessary at a time when drainage and the disposal of sewage were inadequate.

[iii, 143] **art**
used here to mean artifice, dissimulation.

[iii, 144] **earthly lover**
The identity of this lover (meaning only someone for whom she has a special regard, not someone with whom she has consummated physical love) is not revealed.

[iii, 145] **Amazed**
perplexed, astonished; *his power expired* The sylphs only protect those who 'reject mankind' (i, 68).

[iii, 146] **resigned**
in the sense of resigned himself.

[iii, 147] **forfex**
scissors (from the Latin).
[iii, 149] **fatal engine**
mock-heroic heightening; the phrase
is used for the wooden horse in
Dryden's *Aeneid*.
[iii, 150] **fondly**
foolishly.
[iii, 151] **in twain**
Pope's note draws attention to
Milton's description of Satan cut in
two by the Archangel Michael.
[iii, 152] **But airy...again**
as happens to Milton's Satan:
'...with swift wheel reverse, deep
entering sheared/ All his right side;
then Satan first knew pain,/ And
writhed him to and fro convolved; so
sore/ The grinding sword with discon-
tinuous wound/ Passed through him,
but th'etherial substance closed/ Not
long divisible...' (*Paradise Lost*, vi,
326–31).
[iii, 153] **dissever**
separate.
[iii, 155] **lightning**
previously an attribute of her beauty
(i, 144), now of her fierceness.
[iii, 157] **Not louder**
Such comparison is a common epic
device. Compare the *Iliad*, bk 14
(Pope's translation): 'Not half so loud
the bellowing deeps resound,/ When
stormy winds disclose the dark
profound.'
[iii, 158] **When husbands...last**
anticlimactic comparison.
[iii, 161] **wreaths of triumph**
In the ancient world laurel wreaths
were badges of victory.
[iii, 162] **prize**
in military sense, the spoils of
war.
[iii, 163] **While fish...**
Compare Dryden's rendering of
Virgil's *Eclogue V*: 'While savage boars
delight in shady woods,/ And finny
fish inhabit in the floods;/ While bees
on thyme and locusts feed on dew,/
Thy grateful swains these honours
shall renew.'
[iii, 164] **Or in...fair**
or while British women take delight in

a coach and six – a comic expression
of eternity.
[iii, 165] **Atalantis**
a notorious and popular *roman-à-clef*
dealing in the scandal of the day (see
Arbuthnot, line 302 and note).
[iii, 166] **small pillow**
an embroidered pillow case; a
fashionable accessory.
[iii, 167] **visits**
the formal visits mentioned in iii, 12;
solemn formal, appointed.
[iii, 168] **waxlights**
candles; wax was more expensive and
luxurious than tallow.
[iii, 169] **treat**
entertainment with food (see note to i,
95–6); *assignations* appointments to
meet (a lover).
[iii, 171] **What time...date**
The object which time would allow to
continue is ended by steel (i.e. the
steel of the scissors).
[iii, 172] **monuments**
built to preserve memory, therefore,
to last; the lock is here the monument.
[iii, 173] **labour of the gods**
Troy was thought to have been the
work of Apollo and Poseidon.
[iii, 176] **triumphal arches**
both the stone monuments built by
the ancients to commemorate victory,
and the curls of Belinda's hair.
[iii, 178] **unresisted**
irresistible.

Canto Four
[iv, 1–2] **But anxious...breast**
In Dryden's translation, the fourth
book of the *Aeneid* begins: 'But anxious cares already seized the queen;/
She fed within her veins a flame
unseen.'
[iv, 3] **Not youthful...**
Again Pope imitates epic heightening
through large comparison – see iii,
157 and note; *in battle...alive* a mark
of dishonour.
[iv, 4] **survive**
outlive; referring to those maids who
reject men for so long that they lose
their beauty and their suitors. Compare Clarissa's remark in v, 28.

[iv, 7] **Not tyrants . . . die**
Before his final battle and his death,
the tyrant Macbeth shouts, 'Blow
wind, come wrack!/ At least we'll die
with harness on our back' (*Macbeth*, V,
v, 61–2).
[iv, 8] **manteau**
mantua, a loose covering garment.
The juxtaposition of the rage of Cynthia with that of the dying tyrant is
comically anticlimactic.
[iv, 10] **ravished**
plundered, raped.
[iv, 13] **sprite**
spirit. Umbriel is a gnome (iv, 17), one
of the spirits associated in the first
canto with gravity, prudery, earth-
boundedness and mischief-making (i,
63–4).
[iv, 14] **sullied**
polluted, stained (since he is dusky).
[iv, 15] **central earth**
A visit to the underworld is part of the
epic poem (*Odyssey*, bk 11; *Aeneid*, bk
6), but Pope also draws upon the allegorical tradition of figuring forth
human attributes through the description of a symbolic place; *proper scene*
own place, the appropriate place for
him. The element of the gnomes is
earth just as that of the sylphs is air
(see note to i, 58).
[iv, 16] **repaired**
went; *gloomy* both dark and characterised by unhappiness; *spleen* a
malady (of the rich), characterised by
irritability and dejection of spirits, and
believed (among those like Pope)
to be caused by excessive idleness.
In *Gulliver's Travels*, Gulliver's
Houyhnhnm master relates that 'a
fancy would sometimes take a yahoo
to retire into a corner, to lie down
and howl, and spurn away all that
came near him, though he were
young and fat and wanted neither
food nor water.' Upon hearing
this Gulliver recognises 'the true
seeds of the spleen, which only
seizeth on the lazy, the luxurious and
the rich'.
[iv, 17] **pinions**
wings.

[iv, 18] **vapour**
both the mist which hangs in the cave
and the hysteric fit ('the vapours')
suffered by splenetic women.
[iv, 19] **sullen region**
the subject of the sentence.
[iv, 20] **east**
East winds were believed to cause
spleen.
[iv, 21] **grotto**
common in the gardens of the period
(see *Arbuthnot*, line 8 and note). The
spleen sufferer seeks the gloom
appropriate to her condition.
[iv, 22] **screened**
recalling the fashionable screens of the
period (see iii, 14).
[iv, 23] **she**
i.e. the goddess of Spleen; *pensive* the
adjective is applied to Belinda in iv, 1.
[iv, 24] **at her side**
The spleen after which the malady is
named is situated on the left side of
the body; *megrim* migraine.
[iv, 25] **Two handmaids**
These turn out to be Ill-Nature and
Affectation, one an old maid, the other
a hypochondriac girl; *wait* wait upon;
alike in place both enjoying the same
status.
[iv, 27] **Ill-Nature**
the first of the two handmaids, alle-
gorically representing an attitude of
mind; *ancient maid* an old maid.
[iv, 28] **form**
body; *black and white* both the
accepted dress of an old woman and
suggestive of a harsh, judgemental
disposition.
[iv, 29] **With store . . . noons**
The old woman affects religion.
[iv, 30] **lampoons**
scurrilous personal satires; *Her
hand . . . lampoons* While the prayers
are in her hand for everyone to see,
the lampoons are tucked away
secretly in the bosom of her dress.
[iv, 31] **Affectation**
the second of the two handmaids;
mien manner.
[iv, 32] **roses of eighteen**
Her colour betrays the real state of her
health – very good.

[iv, 33] **lisp ... hang the head**
fashionably affected behaviour.

[iv, 34] **Faints into airs**
sinks in affectation.

[iv, 35] **becoming**
Her concern is still primarily for her appearance; *rich quilt* Fashionable ladies would sometimes receive their visitors in bed.

[iv, 38] **new disease**
Pope comments on the changeableness of women in i, 91–104.

[iv, 39] **vapour**
see note to iv, 18.

[iv, 40] **Strange phantoms ... arise**
As with the image of ideas rising in the Baron's head (iii, 119 and note), Pope may have Swift's *Tale of a Tub* in mind. According to that, madness is the result of a 'redundancy [excess] of vapours' rising from the body into the brain. Swift himself was drawing upon seventeenth-century theories of the physiological origins of lunacy.

[iv, 41–2] **hermit's dreams ... maids**
Hermits, virgins and visions figured largely in popular Catholic legend. By associating them with the spleen, Pope distances himself from this kind of 'medieval' Catholicism. Compare *Arbuthnot*, line 398 and note.

[iv, 43–6] **Now glaring ... machines**
Pope moves from the visions of Catholic mystics to a list of the spectacular, crowd-pulling effects of contemporary opera, the measure (to his mind) of contemporary bad taste. 'Machines' is used in the theatrical sense of stage contrivances.

[iv, 47] **Unnumbered throngs**
the populousness of the underworld is commonly emphasised in epics.

[iv, 48] **changed ... by spleen**
The grotesque descriptions which follow represent the hallucinations of the splenetic.

[iv, 51] **pipkin**
small jar; *Homer's tripod* Pope's note directs the reader to the walking tripods made by Vulcan and described in the eighteenth book of the *Iliad*.

[iv, 52] **goose-pie talks**
Pope's note claims that this alludes to 'a real fact'.

[iv, 53] **Men ... with child**
alluding to the royal chaplain, Edward Pelling, who was said to have fancied himself pregnant.

[iv, 54] **And maids ... corks**
The line has a marked sexual meaning. In his comic *Sermon on Glass Bottles*, Pope writes of bottles, 'your neck most aptly represents what anatomists call the vagines uteri.'

[iv, 56] **A branch ... hand**
As Aeneas held the golden bough for safety in his passage through the underworld, Umbriel carries a fern supposed to be a cure for spleen.

[iv, 57] **the power**
the goddess.

[iv, 58] **the sex**
women.

[iv, 59] **female wit**
The spleen was associated with intellectual women, and more generally madness and genius were recognised as 'near allied' (see *Absalom*, line 163); *vapours* hysterics (see iv, 18 and note).

[iv, 60] **poetic**
referring not to the genuine poetic fit of the real poet, but rather to the fit of the lady poetaster.

[iv, 61] **tempers**
dispositions.

[iv, 62] **physic**
medicine.

[iv, 64] **pet**
peevish fit.

[iv, 65] **all thy power disdains**
another compliment to Arabella (see ii, 18 & 52) – she is not the usual splenetic woman.

[iv, 66] **mirth**
her power to create happiness has already been noted – ii, 53.

[iv, 67] **grace**
charm and refinement, the qualities possessed by Belinda. In the passage which follows Umbriel sets out his credentials as a destroyer of grace and a creator of spleen.

[iv, 68] **Or raise . . . face**
one of the means by which Umbriel will destroy Belinda's grace.

[iv, 69] **citron waters**
brandy and lemon, a popular drink among fashionable married women – see *To a Lady*, line 64. Umbriel boasts of his ability to raise ugly flushes similar to those caused by strong drink.

[iv, 70] **losing game**
A game of cards, like that of Canto Three, would cause a change in complexion.

[iv, 71] **airy horns**
Horns are the traditional sign of the cuckold, the cheated husband. Those planted by Umbriel are airy in that they exist only in a suspicious female imagination.

[iv, 72] **Or rumpled . . . beds**
clues of sexual misconduct. Again Umbriel is not exposing real sexual errors but rather leading splenetic women to suspect them.

[iv, 74] **a prude**
Prudes were more severe in both behaviour and dress than coquettes such as Belinda. Their headdress was a plain covering for the hair, but the line suggests that the prude's care for her plain clothing was as great as the coquette's for her more elaborate dress.

[iv, 75] **costive**
constipated.

[iv, 76] **ease**
refers to the disease. Even the belle's tears cannot cure the dog.

[iv, 77] **chagrin**
that which frets and worries; a true rhyme with spleen.

[iv, 78] **That single . . . spleen**
another compliment to Arabella (see ii, 18 & ii, 52). If she is made bad tempered half the world will be affected.

[iv, 80] **Seems to reject**
shows the perverse character of the goddess, who mixes her doing of a favour with unpleasantness.

[iv, 82] **Ulysses**
In the tenth book of the *Odyssey*, Odysseus is presented with a bag containing winds by Aeolus, the god of winds.

[iv, 83] **There**
i.e. in the bag.

[iv, 84] **Sighs . . . tongues**
appropriate gifts from the goddess of Spleen.

[iv, 85] **vial**
a small container. As the bag contains ill temper, the vial contains immoderate grief, another side of spleen.

[iv, 89] **Sunk . . . the nymph**
Belinda has already succumbed to spleen by fainting (or at least collapsing) into the arms of another woman; she is, thus, an easy victim for the grief and bad temper carried by Umbriel; *Thalestris* As Thalestris was a queen of the warlike Amazons, the name signifies female bellicosity. Pope may have been referring to Lady Browne, wife of Sir George Browne (Sir Plume – iv, 121ff.), and a relative of Arabella Fermor.

[iv, 90] **dejected**
both turned downwards (after her fit) and dispirited; *hair unbound* unbound hair was a conventional sign of female grief.

[iv, 91] **swelling bag**
i.e. the gift from the goddess of Spleen containing ill temper; *rent* tore.

[iv, 92] **furies**
avenging, appropriately female, deities of Roman mythology; *issued* came out; *vent* opening.

[iv, 93] **ire**
anger, fury.

[iv, 94] **fans**
the action to make a fire increase.

[iv, 95] **'O wretched maid'**
Thalestris's absurdly exaggerated reaction parodies the epic hero's speech of arousal and encouragement to his companions in battle.

[iv, 96] **Hampton's . . . replied**
The echo is used here as a heightening device – compare *Alexander's Feast*, line 36 and note.

[iv, 98] **bodkin**
large pin for holding the hair; *essence* here, a hair preparation.

[iv, 99] **durance**
constraint, forced confinement. Belinda's hair has been 'confined' in the strips of paper used to curl it.

[iv, 100] **tort'ring**
torturing; *iron* both the curling iron and (continuing the imagery of confinement and torture) the leg iron or shackle.

[iv, 101] **fillets**
headbands used in hairdressing.

[iv, 102] **loads of lead**
The curling papers were fastened with lead strips, just as lead might be employed to stretch or squash the victim of torture. The meaning of 'double' is obscure but it may be that lead was used for fastening the fillets as well as the curlers.

[iv, 103] **display**
in a ring or locket.

[iv, 104] **fops**
excessively concerned with his own appearance, the fop would be jealous of such an ornament as the lock.

[iv, 105] **Honour**
used to mean public reputation.

[iv, 106] **Ease...resign**
i.e. women give up everything to keep a good name, and even virtue is secondary to honour.

[iv, 107] **Methinks...survey**
Hecuba foreseeing the death of Hector uses similar words in Pope's *Iliad* (bk 12).

[iv, 108] **horrid**
a word which, while still retaining some of its original strength and meaning ('arousing horror'), was also a fashionably affected term for the disagreeable.

[iv, 109] **toast**
beautiful woman, in whose honour men frequently drink toasts.

[iv, 110] **whisper**
gossip – cf. i, 74 & *Arbuthnot*, line 356.

[iv, 111] **How then...defend?**
Thalestris reveals herself the slave of reputation.

[iv, 112] **infamy**
both vileness and of poor reputation.

[iv, 114–16] **Exposed through...blaze?**
Thalestris imagines the lock put in a hollow ring with a crystal face and a setting of diamonds ('circling' because of the shape of the ring's face), and worn and shown off by the Baron.

[iv, 117] **Hyde Park Circus**
the Ring, a fashionable meeting place so driven over by coaches that it was bare of grass (see i, 44 and note).

[iv, 118] **sound of Bow**
the bells of St Mary le Bow in Cheapside, an unfashionable district in the middle of London.

[iv, 119] **Chaos**
the confused mass of elements from which God created the world, described by Milton as 'a dark/ Illimitable ocean without bound/ Without dimension, where length, breadth and height/ And time and place are lost' (*Paradise Lost*, ii, 891–4).

[iv, 120] **Men...all**
Pope lists the exotic pets kept by fashionable ladies, comically including men in the list.

[iv, 121] **Sir Plume**
Sir George Browne (husband of Gertrude – see iv, 89), who was reputedly annoyed by the portrait. The name Plume suggests ornamental feathers, a dandy.

[iv, 123] **amber snuff-box**
identifies the owner as a follower of fashion.

[iv, 122] **her beau**
actually her husband.

[iv, 124] **nice**
precise; *conduct* handling, management. The fop would pride himself on the elegance with which he presented snuff and held his cane; *clouded* variegated in colour, veined; *cane* like the snuff box, a fashion accessory.

[iv, 126] **then the case**
i.e. he opened the case, he began speaking on the matter; zeugma again – see ii, 107.

[iv, 128] **Zounds**
an oath, a contraction of 'God's wounds'.

[iv, 129] **pox**
Sir Plume's sixth oath in two-and-a-half lines.
[iv, 131] **the peer**
i.e. the Baron.
[iv, 132] **who**
he who; it grieves me much . . . that he who . . .
[iv, 133–6] **By this . . . grew**
The oath is pure mock-heroic imitating, as Pope's note indicates, Achilles' oath in book 1 of the *Iliad* (Pope's translation): 'Now by this sacred sceptre hear me swear./ Which never more shall leaves of blossoms bear,/ Which severed from the trunk as I from thee/ On the bare mountains left its parent tree . . . '
[iv, 135] **honours**
an epic term for hair.
[iv, 137] **vital**
giving life.
[iv, 138] **This hand . . . wear**
referring to his plans to have the lock set in a ring mentioned by Thalestris (iv, 114–16 and note).
[iv, 140] **long-contended**
a common epic epithet.
[iv, 141] **forbears**
gives up, desists.
[iv, 142] **vial**
the second gift of the goddess of Spleen – see iv, 85–6 and note. Pope's note to this line indicates that the couplet was a late addition which assigns 'the cause of the different operations of the passions in the two ladies'. One purpose of the note seems to be to emphasise that while Thalestris has been shown in a fit of fury, Belinda is shown in a fit of grief, perhaps a less contemptible passion.
[iv, 143] **beauteous grief**
Pope continues to mix his satire of Belinda/Arabella with compliment.
[iv, 145] **heaved**
heaving.
[iv, 147] **'For ever cursed . . . '**
Belinda's lament for her snipped ringlet is modelled on Achilles' lament for his dead friend Patroclus (*Iliad*, bk 13).

[iv, 150] **If Hampton . . . seen**
i.e. if these eyes had never seen Hampton Court . . .
[iv, 152] **ills**
evils.
[iv, 154] **distant northern land**
For the Greeks or Romans the north was far off and barbaric. For Belinda, both Scotland with its strange customs and the north of England would have been provincial, dull and uncivilised.
[iv, 155] **gilt chariot**
ornate carriage of metropolitan fashion – cf. i, 55 and note; *marks the way* leaves the imprints of its wheels.
[iv, 156] **Bohea**
a type of strong tea, pronounced 'bohay'.
[iv, 159] **What moved . . . roam?**
Belinda has roamed not simply in that she has consorted with young lords but also in that she has nursed secret affections for one or more of them – see iii, 144.
[iv, 161] **omens**
The dire events of epics are usually preceded by omens.
[iv, 162] **Thrice**
a common epic number – cf. i, 17 & iii, 137–8; *patch-box* small patches of cloth were worn on the face for decoration – see i, 138 and note.
[iv, 163] **tottering china**
cf. ii, 106 & iii, 110.
[iv, 164] **Poll**
Belinda's pet parrot (see iv, 120 and note); *Shock* her lapdog (see i, 115 and note).
[iv, 165–6] **A sylph . . . too late!**
referring to the dream in which Ariel appears to Belinda in the first canto.
[iv, 167] **slighted**
both treated disrespectfully, and levelled to the ground, razed.
[iv, 168] **My hand**
Belinda threatens to cut off the remaining lock; *rapine* seizure by force, the same sense as the 'rape' of the title.
[iv, 169] **sable**
Although Arabella Fermor's hair was probably auburn, black was the most

fashionable colour; *taught to break* made to divide.

[iv, 171] **uncouth**
unseemly.

[iv, 172] **And in...own**
i.e. fears that the Baron will attack it as well.

[iv, 173] **Uncurled**
Presumably Belinda's weeping and hysterics have caused the ringlet to lose its curl; *fatal* deadly, destructive.

[iv, 174] **sacrilegious**
violating sanctity – the Baron calls the lock sacred when refusing to surrender it to Sir Plume (iv, 133).

[iv, 176] **Hairs less in sight**
Since it was pinned up some of Belinda's hair would have been less visible than the locks; *any hairs* carrying a strong sexual suggestion.

Canto Five

[v, 1] **The pitying audience**
Pope describes Belinda, in compliment to Arabella Fermor, by the effect she has on others – cf. ii, 52 & iv, 66.

[v, 2] **stopped**
blocked.

[v, 4] **For**
refers to the 'in vain' of the previous line. Thalestris's remonstrances must be in vain since the more powerful efforts of Belinda have failed already.

[v, 5] **the Trojan**
Aeneas, whose duty made him leave Carthage and Dido, the queen who loved him.

[v, 6] **Anna...Dido**
Anna was Dido's sister, and both women entreated him to stay in Carthage, though as the previous line makes clear he was not to be moved from his duty.

[v, 7] **Clarissa**
Pope's note states that this character was added only in later editions of the second version. In fact, it is Clarissa who supplies the Baron with his scissors, but it is questionable whether any significance should be placed upon this – see iii, 127 and note.

[v, 8] **began**
Clarissa's speech is modelled, as

Pope's note indicates, on the speech of Sarpendon in the twelfth book of the *Iliad* in which he characterises heroic conduct and urges Glaucus to join him in battle.

[v, 9] **most**
above others.

[v, 10] **vain man's toast**
The braggart might show off by drinking the health of women with whom he was unacquainted and who were oblivious of him.

[v, 11] **decked**
covered. Refers to the fine clothes and jewels worn by society beauties; *afford* provide; *sea* The fashionable articles from foreign countries brought in by trade and referred to earlier – see i, 133–4.

[v, 12] **angel-like adored**
Unlike Protestantism, Catholicism encourages the veneration (not the worship) of angels and saints; another reference to the Catholic milieu – see i, 33–4.

[v, 14] **Why bows...rows**
The boxes to the side of the stage were occupied by men while those facing it (the 'front boxes' of v, 17) were occupied by women. The sense of the line is that all the men in the crowded boxes bow towards beautiful women as they enter the theatre.

[v, 15] **vain**
futile, in vain; *pains* the pains required to cultivate beauty – compare Thalestris's description of Belinda's suffering in the cause of her ringlets (iv, 97–102).

[v, 16] **good sense**
the virtue, with good humour, most strongly urged by Clarissa; *what* that which, referring here to the admiration won by beauty but to be maintained by virtue.

[v, 17] **front-box**
see note to line 14 above; *grace* ornament.

[v, 20] **Charmed**
used to suggest both the charms of beauties and the charms used by witches to combat disease; *smallpox* widespread and virulent in the

eighteenth century, the disease caused disfigurement and, often enough, fatality – see *Saturday: The Small-Pox*, title note.

[v, 21] **Who ... scorn**
i.e. if you could be always young, why not be always frivolous; *what* that which; *huswife* housewife. The housewife of the sixteenth century and earlier had been the house manager, accountant, caterer, doctor and tailor. The word still implied something of this degree of responsibility when Pope wrote.

[v, 22] **use**
The practical cares of the housewife are contrasted with the pointless pastimes of Belinda and her fellows.

[v, 23] **To patch**
to apply beautifying patches – see i, 138 & iv, 163; *ogle* ogling, glancing lecherously, is given as one of the occupations of the young people in Canto Three (iii, 18); *may become* we are still in the sentence begun in line 19. The sense is, 'if we could always be young, it might be quite proper to use patches and face paint.'

[v, 25] **But since ...**
There is a sudden change of tone at this point.

[v, 28] **maid**
virgin.

[v, 29] **power**
the power over men described in the first part of the speech and seen throughout the poem in Belinda's effect on others – see note to v, 1.

[v, 30] **good humour**
essentially a social virtue, the antithesis of spleen, the poem's principal vice, which shuts the splenetic away in her moods and her darkened rooms – see iv, 19–24. The qualities prized by Pope in Martha Blount have a large proportion of good humour in them – see *Epistle to a Lady*, lines 257–68.

[v, 31] **prevail**
triumph.

[v, 32] **airs**
affectations, especially affected superiority; *flights* of passion.

[v, 36] **Belinda frowned**
still under the influence of Umbriel's vial (iv, 142); *prude* severe, censorious woman – see iv, 74 and note.

[v, 37] **virago**
female warrior, here Thalestris who has just shouted her battle cry.

[v, 39] **all side in parties**
i.e. all divide into groups.

[v, 40] **whalebones**
used to stiffen skirts – see ii, 120 and note; *fans ... crack* The whole line imitates the noise of epic battles.

[v, 41] **confused'ly**
suggestive of the disharmony which is opposite to Clarissa's good humour.

[v, 42] **base and treble**
the male and female voices.

[v, 44] **Like gods**
in that they do not use ordinary weapons and do not fear death; *nor ... mortal wound* They do not fear death since a squabble between fashionable young men and women involves no real danger. The line emphasises the distinctly unheroic nature of the people involved in the quarrel.

[v, 45] **Homer**
In the *Iliad* the gods involve themselves actively in battle, often by fighting each other – see line 47 below.

[v, 46] **heavenly breasts**
of both gods and belles.

[v, 47] **'Gainst ... arms**
The sense of the whole line is that Mars (the Roman god of war) fights ('arms') against Pallas (the Greek goddess of wisdom), and Hermes (the Greek messenger god) fights against Latona (a Roman goddess, mother of Apollo and Diana).

[v, 49] **Jove's thunder**
Thunder was the 'uncommon' weapon (line 43 above) of Jove or Zeus, the chief of the gods – see iii, 98 and note.

[v, 50] **Neptune**
the god of the sea and the creator of earthquakes, as in the following line.

[v, 52] **And the ... day!**
one of the poem's least melodious lines. The sense is that the quake of the previous line, tearing open the

earth, uncovers the underworld beneath and exposes the dead in it to a sudden unexpected flash of light.

[v, 53] **Triumphant**
Umbriel, the seeker of mischief and disunity, is the true victor of the battle; *sconce* a candle holder fixed to the wall.

[v, 54] **glad wings**
described earlier as 'sooty' (iv, 17) and 'black' (iv, 88).

[v, 55] **bodkin**
large needle for pinning hair (see iv, 98). The tininess of the sylphs' spears may be intended to recall Milton's famous description of Satan's huge one (*Paradise Lost*, i, 292–4): 'his spear, to equal which the tallest pine/ Hewn on Norwegian hills, to be the mast/ Of some great admiral, were but a wand...'

[v, 57] **press**
press of bodies, battle.

[v, 58] **death**
The language of wounding and death was a (by this time rather outmoded) convention of love poetry. 'Death' also carries the connotation of sexual fulfilment.

[v, 59] **witling**
a diminutive of wit, little wit.

[v, 60] **died in metaphor**
i.e. the beau used the metaphor of sexual fulfilment as death; also, implicitly, that the beau's conquests are simply imagined; *in song* the witling writes lyrics.

[v, 61] **cruel**
again the language of amorous compliment (see note to line 57 above).

[v, 62] **Dapperwit**
literally, neat, or well dressed wit – character in William Wycherley's *Love in a Wood*.

[v, 63] **Fopling**
little fop. Sir Fopling Flutter is a character in George Etherege's *Man of Mode*, and perhaps the most famous representation of the fop in Restoration comedy.

[v, 64] **'Those eyes...killing'**
Pope's note indicates that the words are taken from the contemporary opera *Camilla*. Opera, its strained conventions and the bad taste associated with it were to become principal objects of Pope's satire in *The Dunciad* (see iv, 43–6 and note).

[v, 65] **Meander**
a Greek river, mentioned by Ovid as the site of a dying swan; *margin* bank.

[v, 66] **Th'expiring...dies**
the idea of swans singing at death was common.

[v, 67] **When bold...down**
the battles of epic are often described in terms of individual combats; here also a sexual innuendo.

[v, 69] **doughty**
brave, noble; a comically archaic word.

[v, 70] **But at...again**
Sir Plume's involvement in the quarrel (his role as hero) is turned to elegant compliment (his role as beau) when Chloe smiles.

[v, 71] **Now Jove...air**
Jove's judging of the outcome of a battle by means of a pair of scales is a common epic device. Compare Dryden's translation of the *Aeneid* (bk 12): 'Jove sets the beam; in either scale he lays/ The champions' fate, and each exactly weighs.' Pope adapts the idea to make a telling attack on the stupidity of the affair and the world of belles and beaux.

[v, 72] **Weighs...hair**
'Wit' is used to mean intelligence and judgement, so the wisdom of the men involved in the squabble is found to be lighter than the lock of hair (line 74 below).

[v, 73] **doubtful**
of uncertain result; *beam* the bar of the scales.

[v, 74] **subside**
i.e. sink, proving themselves heavier than the men's wits.

[v, 76] **lightning**
cf. i, 144 & iii, 155.

[v, 77] **chief**
i.e. the Baron; *unequal* in the sense that she is stronger than him.

[v, 78] **Who sought...to die**
'To die' is used in the sexual sense,

the line being one of the sexually most graphic of the poem.

[v, 79] **endued**
endowed.

[v, 80] **finger ... thumb**
used to hold snuff (line 82 below) and matching the digits used by the Baron to hold the scissors.

[v, 81] **breath of life**
recalling the Baron's boast that he would retain the lock 'while my nostrils draw the vital air' (iv, 137).

[v, 82] **charge**
the measure of gunpowder rammed into a cannon or a gun.

[v, 83] **The gnomes**
Just as the sylphs involve themselves in the protection of Belinda in cantos two and three, the gnomes now involve themselves in causing mischief; *to every atom just* i.e. careful with each grain.

[v, 84] **pungent**
pricking, sharp; *titillating* tickling, stimulating.

[v, 85] **starting**
bursting out suddenly.

[v, 86] **dome**
of the chamber; *his nose* the sneeze is the explosion which follows the charge of line 82 above.

[v, 88] **bodkin**
a long pin, this one apparently fastened into the side of her dress (see v, 55).

[v, 89] **The same ...**
Pope's note indicates that the passage which follows parodies the 'progress of Agamemnon's sceptre in Homer'. The sceptre is described in the *Iliad* as having been owned successively by different gods (Pope's translation, bk 2): 'The golden sceptre of immortal fame,/ By Vulcan forged,/ from Jove to Hermes came:/ To Pelops he the immortal gift resigned,/ The immortal gift great Pelops left behind ...'

[v, 91] **seal-rings**
used for stamping wax seals.

[v, 93] **grandame**
grandmother. The great-great-grandfather's rings have been remodelled

first into a buckle for his widow (Belinda's great-great-grandmother), now into a whistle for their granddaughter (Belinda's grandmother).

[v, 94] **bells**
part of the child's whistle.

[v, 95] **her mother's**
Belinda's mother, the daughter of the whistling grandmother.

[v, 97] **my fall**
both his defeat in battle, and his sin in loving Belinda.

[v, 98] **laid as low**
another line of sexual suggestion (compare v, 78 and note).

[v, 99] **to die**
sexually suggestive.

[v, 101] **Rather than so**
i.e. rather than have to die and leave you behind

[v, 102] **Cupid's flames**
Cupid was the god of love, and his flames are those of passion.

[v, 103] **Restore**
return.

[v, 104] **'Restore ...' ... rebound**
another parody of echo writing (see iv, 96 and note).

[v, 105] **Not fierce Othello ... pain**
In Shakespeare's play, Othello is driven frantic with jealousy through the insinuations of his lieutenant (Iago) that his wife (Desdemona) has been unfaithful to him. Iago uses a handkerchief which had been a gift from Othello to Desdemona as part of his 'proof' of her infidelity.

[v, 113–14] **Some thought ... there**
Pope's note refers the reader to Ariosto's *Orlando Furioso*, in which Astolfo journeys to the moon and finds a mass of lost things, such as broken vows, useless deathbed alms, etc. The list of what is to be found on the moon which follows is made up of the useless and the vain.

[v, 115] **heroes'**
Pope may be referring to soldiers, whose leaden minds would match the vases; *ponderous* heavy; *vases* a true rhyme with cases.

[v, 116] **tweezer-cases**
decorated cases containing manicure instruments (see iii, 128).

[v, 117] **death-bed alms**
money given to the poor at the point of (the donor's) death in the fear of what is to follow, i.e. a false kind of charity.

[v, 118] **ends of ribbons**
i.e. not strongly fastened, suggesting inconstancy.

[v, 119] **courtier's promises**
insincere promises. Like the other things in the list, the promises are insubstantial; *sick man's prayers* prayers offered in extremity out of fear.

[v, 120] **smiles of harlots**
meaningless expressions offered to all; *tears of heirs* insincere because the heirs are glad to be inheriting the fortune of the deceased.

[v, 122] **Dried butterflies**
collected by the early natural scientists, a group frequently satirised by Pope and his circle; *tomes* large books; *casuistry* involved theological argument applying general ethical rules to particular cases, it was associated with Catholicism and particularly medieval Catholicism; again Pope distinguishes himself from part of the tradition of his Church – see iv, 41–2 and note.

[v, 123] **But trust**
addressing the reader.

[v, 124] **marked**
remarked, noticed; *quick* keen, sharp.

[v, 125] **Rome's . . . withdrew**
In legend Romulus, the founder of Rome, ascended into heaven in the chariot of his father, the god Mars.

[v, 126] **To Proculus . . . view**
Later he revealed ('confessed') himself to Julius Proculus.

[v, 127] **liquid**
clear.

[v, 128] **And drew . . . hair**
like a comet.

[v, 129] **Berenice**
offered a lock of her hair to the gods for the safe return of her husband from war. The lock was believed to have been changed into a constellation.

[v, 130] **bespangling**
to sprinkle with spangles (metal sequins); *dishevelled* negligently spread – referring both to the lock itself and to the light of the new star.

[v, 131] **kindling**
catching fire.

[v, 133] **beau-monde**
the world of the fashionable belles and beaux; *the Mall* an area in front of St James's Palace and a popular haunt of the fashionable.

[v, 134] **hail with music**
Musical entertainments were sometimes held in the Mall.

[v, 134] **propitious**
favourable.

[v, 135] **Venus**
both the planet which is a peculiarly bright star and the goddess of love. The planet appears in the morning and evening, perhaps the times when young men might most hope to be blessed in love.

[v, 136] **Rosamunda's lake**
in St James's Park; a popular place for lovers to meet.

[v, 137] **Partridge**
John Partridge, a well-known astrologer, became even more famous when Swift, under the name of Isaac Bickerstaff, published a series of rival predictions, the first of which concerned Partridge's imminent death.

[v, 138] **Galileo's eyes**
the telescope.

[v, 139] **egregious**
eminent or remarkable, usually for bad qualities; *wizard* i.e. Partridge; *foredoom* foretell the doom of.

[v, 140] **Louis**
Louis XIV of France. Partridge, a 'fundamentalist' Protestant, predicts the downfall of the Catholic monarch of France and of Catholicism generally (Rome).

[v, 141] **Then cease**
The poem's closing advice implicitly echoes Clarissa's counsel of good humour.

[v, 142] **shining sphere**
the heavens.

[v, 143–4] **Not all ... lost**
i.e. you will be more envied for the stolen lock than for those which remain.
[v, 145] **murders of your eye**
again the old fashioned convention that the eyes of beautiful women kill (see v, 58).
[v, 146] **millions slain**
Belinda's conquests.

[v, 147] **fair suns**
Belinda's eyes (see i, 14 & ii, 13–14).
[v, 149–50] **consecrate**
make sacred; *This lock ... name* Pope imitates the Elizabethan love poet's device of offering the loved one eternity in verse.

23 / *Epistle to Dr Arbuthnot*

'Shut, shut the door, good John,' fatigued I said,
'Tie up the knocker. Say I'm sick, I'm dead.'
The dog-star rages! Nay, 'tis past a doubt,
All Bedlam or Parnassus is let out:
Fire in each eye and paper in each hand, 5
They rave, recite and madden round the land.
    What walls can guard me, or what shades can hide?
They pierce my thickets, through my grot they glide,
By land, by water, they renew the charge,
They stop the chariot and they board the barge. 10
No place is sacred, not the church is free,
Ev'n Sunday shines no sabbath day for me.
Then, from the Mint walks forth the man of rhyme,
Happy to catch me just at dinner time.
    Is there a parson much bemused in beer, 15
A maudlin poetess, a rhyming peer,
A clerk foredoomed his father's soul to cross
Who pens a stanza when he should engross?
Is there, who locked from ink and paper scrawls
With desperate charcoal round his darkened walls? 20
All fly to Twit'nam, and in humble strain
Apply to me to keep them mad or vain.
Arthur whose giddy son neglects the laws,
Imputes to me and my damned works the cause.
Poor Cornus sees his frantic wife elope, 25
And curses wit and poetry and Pope.
    Friend to my life! (which did you not prolong
The world had wanted many an idle song)

What drop or nostrum can this plague remove?
Or, which must end me a fool's wrath, or love?   30
A dire dilemma! Either way I'm sped,
If foes they write, if friends they read me dead.
Seized and tied down to judge, how wretched I,
Who can't be silent and who will not lie.
To laugh were want of goodness and of grace,   35
And to be grave exceeds all power of face.
I sit with sad civility, I read
With honest anguish and an aching head,
And drop at last, but in unwilling ears,
This saving counsel, 'Keep your piece nine years.'   40
    'Nine years!' cries he, who high in Drury Lane
Lulled by soft Zephyrs through the broken pane
Rhymes ere he wakes, and prints before term ends,
Obliged by hunger and request of friends.
'The piece you think is incorrect? Why, take it.   45
I'm all submission. What you'd have it, make it.'
    Three things another's modest wishes bound,
My friendship, and a prologue, and ten pound.
    Pitholeon sends to me, 'You know his Grace.
I want a patron. Ask him for a place.'   50
Pitholeon libelled me – 'But here's a letter
Informs you, sir, 'twas when he knew no better.
Dare you refuse him? Curl invites to dine,
He'll write a journal, or he'll turn divine.'
    Bless me, a packet! – 'Tis a stranger sues,   55
A virgin tragedy, an orphan muse.
If I dislike it, 'Furies, death and rage!'
If I approve, 'Commend it to the stage.'
There (thank my stars) the whole commission ends,
The players and I are, luckily, no friends.   60
Fired that the house reject him, 'Sdeath I'll print it,
And shame the fools – Your interest, sir, with Lintot.'
'Lintot, dull rogue, will think your price too much.'
'Not, sir, if you revise it, and retouch.'
All my demurs but double his attacks.   65
At last he whispers, 'Do, and we go snacks.'
Glad of a quarrel, straight I clap the door,
'Sir, let me see your works and you no more.'
    'Tis sung when Midas' ears began to spring,

(Midas, a sacred person and a king)   70
His very minister who spied them first
(Some say his queen) was forced to speak or burst.
And is not mine, my friend, a sorer case
When every coxcomb perks them in my face?
    'Good friend, forbear. You deal in dangerous things.   75
I'd never name queens, ministers or kings.
Keep close to ears and let those asses prick,
'Tis nothing.' – Nothing? If they bite and kick?
Out with it, Dunciad, let the secret pass,
That secret to each fool that he's an ass.   80
The truth once told (and wherefore should we lie)
The queen of Midas slept, and so may I.
    You think this cruel? Take it for a rule,
No creature smarts so little as a fool.
Let peals of laughter, Codrus, round thee break,   85
Thou unconcerned canst hear the mighty crack.
Pit, box and gallery in convulsions hurled,
Thou stand'st unshook amidst a bursting world.
Who shames a scribbler? Break one cobweb through,
He spins the slight, self-pleasing thread anew.   90
Destroy his fib or sophistry – in vain,
The creature's at his dirty work again,
Throned in the centre of his thin designs,
Proud of a vast extent of flimsy lines!
Whom have I hurt? Has poet yet or peer   95
Lost the arched eyebrow, or Parnassian sneer?
And has not Colley still his lord and whore?
His butchers Henley, his freemasons Moore?
Does not one table Bavius still admit?
Still to one bishop Philips seem a wit?   100
Still Sappho – 'Hold! For God-sake, you'll offend,
No names – be calm – learn prudence of a friend.
I too could write and I am twice as tall,
But foes like these' – One flatterer's worse than all.
Of all mad creatures, if the learned are right,   105
It is the slaver kills and not the bite.
A fool quite angry is quite innocent.
Alas, 'tis ten times worse when they repent.
    One dedicates in high heroic prose,
And ridicules beyond a hundred foes;   110

One from all Grub Street will my fame defend,
And more abusive, calls himself my friend.
This prints my letters, that expects a bribe,
And others roar aloud, 'Subscribe, subscribe.'
There are, who to my person pay their court: 115
I cough like Horace, and though lean, am short.
Ammon's great son one shoulder had too high,
Such Ovid's nose and 'Sir, you have an eye...'
Go on, obliging creatures, make me see
All that disgraced my betters met in me.   120
Say for my comfort, languishing in bed,
'Just so immortal Maro held his head.'
And when I die, be sure to let me know
Great Homer died three thousand years ago.
Why did I write? What sin to me unknown   125
Dipped me in ink, my parents' or my own?
As yet a child, nor yet a fool to fame,
I lisped in numbers, for the numbers came.
I left no calling for this idle trade,
No duty broke, no father disobeyed.   130
The muse but served to ease some friend, not wife,
To help me through this long disease, my life,
To second, Arbuthnot, thy art and care,
And teach the being you preserved to bear.
But why then publish? Granville the polite   135
And knowing Walsh would tell me I could write.
Well natured Garth inflamed with early praise,
And Congreve loved, and Swift endured, my lays.
The courtly Talbot, Somers, Sheffield read,
Ev'n mitred Rochester would nod the head,   140
And St John's self (great Dryden's friends before)
With open arms received one poet more.
Happy my studies, when by these approved!
Happier their author, when by these beloved!
From these the world will judge of men and books,   145
Not from the Burnets, Oldmixons and Cooks.
Soft were my numbers. Who could take offence
While pure description held the place of sense?
Like gentle Fanny's was my flowery theme,
A painted mistress or a purling stream.   150
Yet then did Gildon draw his venal quill –

I wished the man a dinner and sat still.
Yet then did Dennis rave in furious fret –
I never answered, I was not in debt.
If want provoked or madness made them print,   155
I waged no war with Bedlam or the Mint.
   Did some more sober critic come abroad?
If wrong, I smiled – if right, I kissed the rod.
Pains, reading, study are their just pretence,
And all they want is spirit, taste and sense.   160
Commas and points they set exactly right,
And 'twere a sin to rob them of their mite.
Yet ne'er one sprig of laurel graced these ribbalds,
From slashing Bentley down to piddling Tibbalds.
Each wight who reads not, and but scans and spells, 165
Each word-catcher that lives on syllables,
Ev'n such small critics some regard may claim,
Preserved in Milton's or in Shakespeare's name.
Pretty! In amber to observe the forms
Of hairs, or straws, or dirt, or grubs, or worms!   170
The things, we know, are neither rich nor rare,
But wonder how the devil they got there?
   Were others angry? I excused them too.
Well might they rage. I gave them but their due.
A man's true merit 'tis not hard to find,   175
But each man's secret standard in his mind,
That casting-weight, pride adds to emptiness,
This who can gratify? For who can guess?
The bard whom pilfered pastorals renown,
Who turns a Persian tale for half a crown,   180
Just writes to make his barrenness appear,
And strains from hard-bound brains, eight lines a year;
He, who still wanting, though he lives on theft,
Steals much, spends little, yet has nothing left;
And he, who now to sense, now nonsense leaning,   185
Means not, but blunders round about a meaning;
And he, whose fustian's so sublimely bad,
It is not poetry but prose run mad;
All these my modest satire bad translate,
And own that nine such poets made a Tate.   190
How did they fume, and stamp, and roar, and chafe!
And swear not Addison himself was safe.

Peace to all such! But were there one whose fires
True genius kindles and fair fame inspires,
Blessed with each talent and each art to please,   195
And born to write, converse and live with ease.
Should such a man, too fond to rule alone,
Bear like the Turk, no brother near the throne,
View him with scornful, yet with jealous eyes,
And hate for arts that caused himself to rise,   200
Damn with faint praise, assent with civil leer,
And without sneering teach the rest to sneer,
Willing to wound and yet afraid to strike,
Just hint a fault and hesitate dislike,
Alike reserved to blame, or to commend,   205
A timorous foe, and a suspicious friend,
Dreading ev'n fools, by flatterers besieged,
And so obliging that he ne'er obliged,
Like Cato give his little senate laws
And sit attentive to his own applause,   210
While wits and templars every sentence raise,
And wonder with a foolish face of praise –
Who but must laugh if such a man there be?
Who would not weep if Atticus were he?
    What though my name stood rubric on the walls,   215
Or plastered posts, with claps, in capitals?
Or smoking forth, a hundred hawkers' load,
On wings of winds came flying all abroad?
I sought no homage from the race that write;
I kept, like Asian monarchs, from their sight: 220
Poems I heeded (now berhymed so long)
No more than thou, great George! a birthday song.
I ne'er with wits or witlings passed my days,
To spread about the itch of verse and praise;
Nor like a puppy, daggled through the town,   225
To fetch and carry sing-song up and down;
Nor at rehearsals sweat, and mouthed, and cried,
With handkerchief and orange at my side;
But sick of fops, and poetry, and prate,
To Bufo left the whole Castalian state.   230
    Proud as Apollo on his forked hill,
Sat full-blown Bufo, puffed by every quill;
Fed with soft dedication all day long,

Horace and he went hand in hand in song.
His library (where busts of poets dead   235
And a true Pindar stood without a head)
Received of wits an undistinguished race,
Who first his judgement asked, and then a place:
Much they extolled his pictures, much his seat,
And flattered every day, and some days eat: 240
Till grown more frugal in his riper days,
He paid some bards with port, and some with praise,
To some a dry rehearsal was assigned,
And others (harder still) he paid in kind.
Dryden alone (what wonder?) came not nigh,   245
Dryden alone escaped this judging eye,
But still the great have kindness in reserve,
He helped to bury whom he helped to starve.
    May some choice patron bless each grey goose quill!
May every Bavius have his Bufo still!   250
So when a statesman wants a day's defence,
Or envy holds a whole week's war with sense,
Or simple pride for flattery makes demands,
May dunce by dunce be whistled off my hands!
Blessed be the great! for those they take away,   255
And those they left me – for they left me Gay;
Left me to see neglected Genius bloom,
Neglected die, and tell it on his tomb:
Of all thy blameless life the sole return
My verse, and Queensberry weeping o'er thy urn!   260
    Oh let me live my own, and die so too!
(To live and die is all I have to do)
Maintain a poet's dignity and ease,
And see what friends, and read what books I please.
Above a patron, though I condescend   265
Sometimes to call a minister my friend.
I was not born for courts or great affairs:
I pay my debts, believe, and say my prayers;
Can sleep without a poem in my head,
Nor know if Dennis be alive or dead.   270
    Why am I asked what next shall see the light?
Heavens! was I born for nothing but to write?
Has life no joys for me? or (to be grave)
Have I no friend to serve, no soul to save?

'I found him close with Swift' – 'Indeed? No doubt,'   275
Cries prating Balbus, 'something will come out.'
'Tis all in vain, deny it as I will.
'No, such a genius never can lie still.'
And then for mine obligingly mistakes
The first lampoon Sir Will or Bufo makes.   280
Poor guiltless I! and can I choose but smile,
When every coxcomb knows me by my style?
    Cursed be the verse, how well soe'er it flow,
That tends to make one worthy man my foe,
Give virtue scandal, innocence a fear,   285
Or from the soft-eyed virgin steal a tear!
But he who hurts a harmless neighbour's peace,
Insults fallen worth, or beauty in distress,
Who loves a lie, lame slander helps about,
Who writes a libel, or who copies out;   290
That fop, whose pride affects a patron's name,
Yet absent, wounds an author's honest fame;
Who can your merit selfishly approve,
And show the sense of it without the love;
Who has the vanity to call you friend,   295
Yet wants the honour, injured, to defend;
Who tells whate'er you think, whate'er you say,
And if he lie not, must at least betray;
Who to the dean and silver bell can swear,
And sees at canons what was never there;   300
Who reads, but with a lust to misapply,
Makes satire a lampoon, and fiction lie;
A lash like mine no honest man shall dread,
But all such babbling blockheads in his stead.
    Let Sporus tremble – 'What? that thing of silk,   305
Sporus, that mere white curd of ass's milk?
Satire or sense, alas! can Sporus feel,
Who breaks a butterfly upon a wheel?'
    Yet let me flap this bug with gilded wings,
This painted child of dirt, that stinks and stings;   310
Whose buzz the witty and the fair annoys,
Yet wit ne'er tastes, and beauty ne'er enjoys:
So well-bred spaniels civilly delight
In mumbling of the game they dare not bite.
Eternal smiles his emptiness betray,   315

283

As shallow streams run dimpling all the way.
Whether in florid impotence he speaks,
And, as the prompter breathes, the puppet squeaks;
Or at the ear of Eve, familiar toad!
Half froth, half venom, spits himself abroad,   320
In puns, or politics, or tales, or lies,
Or spite, or smut, or rhymes, or blasphemies.
His wit all see-saw, between that and this,
Now high, now low, now master up, now miss,
And he himself one vile antithesis.   325
Amphibious thing! that acting either part,
The trifling head, or the corrupted heart;
Fop at the toilet, flatterer at the board,
Now trips a lady, and now struts a lord.
Eve's tempter thus the Rabbins have expressed,   330
A cherub's face, a reptile all the rest.
Beauty that shocks you, parts that none will trust,
Wit that can creep, and pride that licks the dust.
    Not fortune's worshipper, nor fashion's fool,
Not lucre's madman, nor ambition's tool,   335
Not proud, nor servile; be one poet's praise,
That, if he pleased, he pleased by manly ways:
That flattery, even to kings, he held a shame,
And thought a lie in verse or prose the same,
That not in Fancy's maze he wandered long,   340
But stooped to Truth, and moralised his song.
That not for Fame, but Virtue's better end,
He stood the furious foe, the timid friend,
The damning critic, half-approving wit,
The coxcomb hit, or fearing to be hit;   345
Laughed at the loss of friends he never had,
The dull, the proud, the wicked, and the mad,
The distant threats of vengeance on his head,
The blow unfelt, the tear he never shed,
The tale revived, the lie so oft o'erthrown,   350
The imputed trash and dullness not his own,
The morals blackened when the writings 'scape,
The libelled person, and the pictured shape;
Abuse on all he loved, or loved him, spread,
A friend in exile, or a father dead,   355
The whisper, that to greatness still too near,

Perhaps yet vibrates on his sovereign's ear.
Welcome for thee, fair Virtue, all the past.
For thee, fair Virtue, welcome even the last!
   'But why insult the poor, affront the great?'   360
A knave's a knave to me in every state.
Alike my scorn if he succeed or fail,
Sporus at court, or Japhet in a jail,
A hireling scribbler, or a hireling peer,
Knight of the post corrupt, or of the shire,   365
If on a pillory, or near a throne,
He gain his prince's ear, or lose his own.
   Yet soft by nature, more a dupe than wit,
Sappho can tell you how this man was bit.
This dreaded satirist Dennis will confess   370
Foe to his pride, but friend to his distress,
So humble, he has knocked at Tibbald's door,
Has drunk with Cibber, nay has rhymed for Moore.
Full ten years slandered, did he once reply?
Three thousand suns went down on Welsted's lie.   375
To please a mistress one aspersed his life
He lashed him not, but let her be his wife:
Let Budgell charge low Grub Street on his quill
And write whate'er he pleased, except his will;
Let the two Curlls of town and court abuse   380
His father, mother, body, soul, and muse.
Yet why? that father held it for a rule,
It was a sin to call our neighbour fool.
That harmless mother thought no wife a whore.
Hear this, and spare his family, James Moore!   385
Unspotted names, and memorable long,
If there be force in virtue, or in song.
   Of gentle blood (part shed in honour's cause,
While yet in Britain honour had applause)
Each parent sprung – What fortune, pray? – Their own,   390
And better got, than Bestia's, from the throne.
Born to no pride, inheriting no strife,
Nor marrying discord in a noble wife,
Stranger to civil and religious rage,
The good man walked innoxious through his age.   395
No courts he saw, no suits would ever try,
Nor dared an oath, nor hazarded a lie.

Unlearned, he knew no schoolman's subtle art,
No language, but the language of the heart.
By nature honest, by experience wise,   400
Healthy by temperance, and by exercise,
His life, though long, to sickness passed unknown,
His death was instant, and without a groan.
O grant me thus to live, and thus to die!
Who sprung from kings shall know less joy than I.   405
    O friend, may each domestic bliss be thine!
Be no unpleasing melancholy mine:
Me, let the tender office long engage
To rock the cradle of reposing age,
With lenient arts extend a mother breath,   410
Make languor smile, and smooth the bed of death.
Explore the thought, explain the asking eye,
And keep awhile one parent from the sky!
On cares like these if length of days attend,
May Heaven, to bless those days, preserve my friend,   415
Preserve him social, cheerful, and serene,
And just as rich as when he served a queen.
Whether that blessing be denied or given,
Thus far was right, the rest belongs to Heaven.

Epistle to Dr Arbuthnot was published in 1735, though parts of it had been written many years earlier. In his 'Advertisement' Pope claims the specific occasion to be the publication of two poems attacking him, and he suggests that he writes simply to put the record straight. In fact, the literary squabbles which inform the poem had a longer history and Pope was not always the innocent victim. John Butt's fourth volume of the Twickenham edition provides much information to which the present editors are indebted.

Pope calls the poem 'a sort of bill of complaint', and much of it turns upon his concern about the current state of literature. Indeed, the most famous parts are the portraits of the corrupt and corrupting literary figures – Sporus, Atticus and Bufo. Another important strand in the poem consists of self-portraiture and self-defence, as in the passage at the end where he describes his relationship with his dying mother.

The genre is announced in the title. The poem is a Horatian epistle, a letter containing morality, wit and satire. However, William Warburton, Pope's posthumous editor, added the letters P and A to parts of the poem, which make it read more like a dialogue. There is a good deal of sense in this reading. Lines 75–8, for instance, make better sense if we suppose them to be Arbuthnot's interjection. Consequently, the poem is treated in our notes as a dialogue, though we omit the Ps and As in the text.

It is possible to argue that the lines treated as interjections should be seen as

Pope's comments to himself, or his memory of earlier comments made to him by others. For example, the question 'why then publish?' in line 135 is clearly a question addressed by Pope to Pope. Other lines might be best read in the same way.

The structure of the poem is suggested by the phrase 'bill of complaint' in the 'Advertisement'. It is loosely structured, a poem that was (as Pope says) 'drawn up by snatches'.

Arbuthnot is written in heroic couplets (closed rhymed couplets of iambic pentameters), and one of its triumphs is the way in which Pope succeeds in this restricted form in capturing the flow and freedom of speech.

[Pope's] Advertisement

This paper is a sort of bill of complaint, begun many years since, and drawn up by snatches, as the several occasions offered. I had no thoughts of publishing it, till it pleased some persons of rank and fortune (the authors of *Verses to the Imitator of Horace*, and of an *Epistle to a Doctor of Divinity from a Nobleman at Hampton Court*) to attack, in a very extraordinary manner, not only my writings (of which, being public, the public is judge), but my person, morals, and family, whereof to those who know me not a truer information may be requisite. Being divided between the necessity to say something of myself and my own laziness to undertake so awkward a task, I thought it the shortest way to put the last hand to this Epistle. If it have anything pleasing, it will be that by which I am most desirous to please, the truth and the sentiment; and if anything offensive, it will be only to those I am least sorry to offend, the vicious or the ungenerous.

Many will know their own pictures in it, there being not a circumstance but what is true; but I have for the most part spared their names, and they may escape being laughed at if they please.

I would have some of them know it was owing to the request of the learned and candid friend to whom it is inscribed that I make not as free use of theirs as they have done of mine. However, I shall have this advantage and honour on my side, that whereas, by their proceeding, any abuse may be directed at any man, no injury can possibly be done by mine, since a nameless character can never be found out but by its truth and likeness.

Epigraph
Neque sermonibus vulgi dederis te, nec in praemiis humanis spem posueris rerum tuarum; suis te oportet illecebris ipsa virtus trahat ad verum decus. Quid de te alii loquantur, ipsi videant, sed loquentur tamen. Tully. (And do not yield yourself up to the speeches of the vulgar, nor in your affairs place hope in human rewards: virtue ought to draw you to true glory by its own allurements. Why should others speak of you? Let them study themselves – yet they will speak.)
Title
Dr Arbuthnot, Dr John Arbuthnot (1667–1735), physician to Queen Anne, friend of Pope, Gay and Swift,

and occasional writer; his works include the satirical *History of John Bull*. He was seriously ill in 1734, and died in February 1735, the month after the poem's publication.
[1] good John
John Serle, Pope's servant. The dramatic opening and the later interruptions make the poem read as much as a dialogue as a true epistle – but see introductory notes.
[2] Tie up the knocker
a tied-up doorknocker was a recognised sign of sickness or death.
[3] The dog-star
Sirius. Its reappearance in late summer was associated with heat and with the madness caused by heat.

Pope finished the *Epistle* in August 1734.

[4] **Bedlam**
Bethlehem hospital, London's famous asylum for the mad. The word can also be used for the inmate of a madhouse (see Rochester, *Satyr*, 82 and note); *Parnassus* a mountain in Greece sacred to Apollo and the muses; thus, figuratively, a place for poets.

[5] **fire...eye**
sign of madness.

[6] **madden**
both to become mad and to make others mad.

[8] **thickets**
hedges. Pope's garden in Twickenham was famous; *grot* His grounds were divided by a road, under which was built a tunnel, decorated as a kind of grotto.

[9] **charge**
one of a number of military images.

[10] **chariot**
a light carriage; here, Pope's vehicle, stopped by importunate poets; *barge* Pope's house stood on the Thames which was a busy thoroughfare.

[11] **not...free**
i.e. even the church is not free.

[12] **sabbath**
in the sense of day of rest – Sunday.

[13] **Then**
i.e. on Sunday; a debtor could leave his sanctuary on Sunday because it was a free day for bailiffs; *the Mint* an area in Southwark which, since bailiffs had no jurisdiction there, became a haven for insolvent debtors. The implication of the whole line is that the poetic visitor makes no money from his work.

[14] **Happy...dinner time**
The line is based on a real incident of an irritating interruption. The poet may be happy because his hour of arrival forces Pope to offer him a meal.

[15] **a parson**
probably Laurence Eusden, the Poet Laureate until his death in 1730; *bemused* confused, befuddled; also

(through a play on 'muse') made into a poet.

[16] **A·maudlin...peer**
In the final version, there are no particular references here. Much of Pope's satire is generalised, even where a particular reference lurks in the background.

[17] **his father's...cross**
i.e. to rebel against his father's will – the clerk wants to be a poet.

[18] **engross**
to write in large, legal hand, the proper occupation of the clerk. The word was a true rhyme with 'cross'.

[19] **Is there, who**
i.e. is there one who; *locked... scrawls* the inmate of Bedlam.

[21] **Twit'nam**
Pope's jocular name for his place of residence, Twickenham. To twit is to censure or to annoy. Thus, the name describes Pope's occupation as a satirist: twit'nam, twitten em, twitting them; *strain* passage of poetry.

[22] **Apply to me**
in that the visitors are asking for literary advice.

[23] **Arthur**
Arthur Moore, MP for Grimsby. His son, James Moore-Smythe, had been an aspiring writer, but was already dead by the time the *Epistle* was published. The line harks back to lines 17–18.

[24] **Imputes**
blames. Pope had once contributed some lines to a play of Smythe's.

[25] **Cornus**
In Latin 'cornu' means a horn, the traditional badge of the cheated husband.

[26] **wit**
wisdom, literary imagination, genius (see *An Essay on Criticism*).

[27] **Friend to my life**
i.e. Arbuthnot. He was friend to Pope's life in the special sense that, as Pope's doctor, he preserved it.

[28] **had wanted**
would have lacked.

[29] **drop or nostrum**
i.e. medicines, especially quack medicines; *plague* of bad poetry.

[31] **sped**
brought to end, killed.

[32] **write**
alluding to the written attacks of enemies; *read* in the sense that Pope will have to listen to their tedious writings.

[33] **Seized ... judge**
refers to his predicament when asked to listen to the writings of poetasters.

[35] **To ... want**
i.e. to laugh would be a lack of.

[36] **power of face**
refers to the power to avoid laughter in a humorous situation, to keep a straight face.

[37] **sad**
sober and serious as well as sorrowful; *I read* the poems brought to him.

[40] **saving**
both in that it will save Pope from further embarrassment and in that it will save the author from public exposure; *Keep ... nine years* Pope puns on piece and peace. The counsel echoes Horace's advice to a young poet in the *Ars Poetica*.

[41] **high**
As a general rule, the higher the room, the smaller, cheaper and dirtier it was; *Drury Lane* famous for its theatres and prostitutes – an undesirable location.

[42] **Zephyr**
the Greek god of the west wind; hence any mild breeze. The classical allusion is comically incongruous in the setting of the poet's slum dwelling; *broken panes* indicative of poverty.

[43] **Rhymes ... wakes**
contrasts with Pope's later claim to be able to sleep without thinking of poetry – line 269; *term* i.e. the legal term during which the courts were sitting. Books were published during the busy terms in order to catch more customers.

[44] **Oblige ... of friends**
Authors frequently asserted in prefaces that they published only because their friends pressed them to. Pope suggests hunger and the need for money as more plausible motives.

[45] **incorrect**
in the sense of not in accordance with the accepted 'rules' of poetry.

[47] **another's**
i.e. another visitor's.

[48] **prologue**
Plays were often provided with prologues by famous authors. The prologue might help sell tickets for the performance and copies of the printed version.

[49] **Pitholeon**
a foolish poet. Pope probably had a specific poet in mind when he composed the lines (Leonard Welsted), but they also have a general significance; *sends to me* i.e. sends a messenger to me; *his Grace* the term of address for a duke.

[50] **want**
desire, lack; *patron* Many authors still relied on the patronage of wealthy men for survival; *place* job, position. A patron could use his influence to acquire for the poet a sinecure.

[51] **Pitholeon libelled me**
Pope's reason for not wanting to do favours. 'Libel' is used in the sense of to write personal satire against; *'But here's ... '*: i.e. the messenger's answer.

[53] **Curl**
Edmund Curll (1675–1747), a notorious and unscrupulous publisher of scandal. The messenger replies to Pope's hesitation with the crude threat that Pitholeon is being courted by Curll, and might answer any refusal with a libel.

[54] **journal**
i.e. a short publication, often containing scandal; *divine* priest; probably an allusion to Welsted's religious writing.

[55] **packet**
the next incident, the arrival of a parcel.

[56] **A virgin ... orphan muse**
Virgins and orphans were stock materials in late seventeenth- and early eighteenth-century drama. Thus, the writing Pope has been sent is utterly derivative.

[57] **Furies**
three terrifying female deities of classical mythology associated with vengeance – used here as an oath.

[60] **players**
actors.

[61] **Fired**
made angry; *house* playhouse; *Sdeath* a contraction of the curse, 'God's death'.

[62] **the fools**
i.e. those who have rejected his play; *interest* personal influence. The writer asks Pope to use his influence to secure publication of the play; *Lintot* Bernard Lintot, a well-known publisher, formerly Pope's.

[63] **Lintot...too much**
Pope's reply to the proposal.

[66] **go snacks**
split the money two ways, go halves.

[67] **a quarrel**
The author's suggestion that Pope might be motivated solely by money is quite a serious breach of propriety, which can be exploited to make a quarrel; *clap* slam.

[69] **'Tis sung**
i.e. the story is. In ancient times most tales were sung; *Midas* a king in Greek myth. Pope alludes to the well-known story in which Midas is cursed with a pair of ass's ears by Apollo for interfering (in some versions for judging wrongly) in a singing competition between Apollo and Marsyas. Although Midas hides the ears under a headdress they are inevitably seen by his barber (in some versions by his wife). Unable to keep the secret, the barber digs a hole in the ground and tells it to the earth, whereupon it is picked up and repeated by reeds growing in the area, until it is a secret no longer.

[71] **minister**
Pope changes barber to minister in order to reflect contemporary politics. It was a constant complaint of the opposition that power was too much concentrated in the hands of Robert Walpole (1667–1745), the chief minister.

[72] **Some...queen**
see note to line 69.

[73] **sorer case**
more difficult position. Like the barber or the queen, Pope must speak out.

[74] **coxcomb**
the cap worn by a jester; hence, a fool; *perk* to thrust forward impudently.

[75] **'Good friend...'**
Treated by Warburton as Arbuthnot's interruption. See introductory notes.

[76] **I'd never...kings**
The line makes it clear that when Pope uses the Midas story he is thinking of Walpole, George II and Queen Caroline.

[77] **close**
reserved, uncommunicative. Thus, keep silent with respect to ears; *prick* to thrust, to irritate.

[78] **Nothing**
If the poem is a dialogue, Pope represents himself rudely interrupting Arbuthnot's counsel of moderation.

[79] **Dunciad**
Pope's long mock-heroic satire attacking what he saw as bad writing and bad writers. Here he addresses himself by the name of his poem.

[80] **ass**
continuing the allusion to Midas.

[81] **wherefore**
why.

[83] **this**
i.e. this exposure of folly.

[84] **smarts**
hurts. The sense is that fools are too thick-skinned to be wounded by satire.

[85–8] **Let peals...bursting world**
In these lines, Pope parodies Joseph Addison's version of part of Horace's *Ode* III, iii: 'Should the whole frame of nature round him break,/ In ruin and confusion hurled,/ He unconcerned would hear the mighty crack,/ And stand secure amidst a falling world.' Pope had previously used two of these lines in *Peri Bathous, or the Art of Sinking in Poetry. Peri Bathous* is a jocular treatise on bad poetry, consisting largely of

examples drawn from contemporary poets.

[85] **Codrus**
a poet ridiculed by Juvenal and Virgil. Pope imagines Codrus as an object of general and uncontrolled ridicule who is unaware of the fact.

[87] **Pit, box and gallery**
different parts of the theatre.

[89] **shames**
The power of satire was supposed to lie in its ability to shame people into amendment. Again, Pope adverts to the thick skins of his butts; *cobweb* The image of the hack writer as a spider is borrowed from Swift's *The Battle of the Books* (1704). It continues until line 94.

[91] **sophistry**
deceptive, false reasoning.

[92] **dirty work**
In *The Battle of the Books* Swift emphasises the dirtiness of the spider. His bee refers to it as a being 'which by a lazy contemplation of four inches round, by an overweening pride, feeding and engendering on itself, turns all into excrement and venom'.

[93] **thin designs**
the writer's inventions, the spider's web.

[94] **lines**
punning on spider's threads and lines of poetry.

[96] **Parnassian**
belonging to Parnassus, the place of poets.

[97] **Colley**
Colley Cibber (1671–1757), a comic actor, playwright and (since the death of Eusden in 1730) the Poet Laureate. He was later to become the principal figure in Pope's final revised version of *The Dunciad* (see note to line 79). Here, Pope suggests that satire has not cured Cibber of his vices of whoring and patron-hunting.

[98] **Henley**
John ('Orator') Henley, an eccentric preacher, one of whose sermons dealt with the theology of the butcher's vocation; *Moore* James Moore-Smythe

(see note to line 23) was believed to have been a freemason.

[99] **Bavius**
a poetaster enemy of Virgil and Horace, and a stock name for a bad poet; *one table . . . admit* i.e. Bavius is still treated to meals on the grounds that he is a poet.

[100] **Philips**
Ambrose Philips (1675?–1749), a writer of pastoral verses and an early rival of Pope's. In 1724 he had gone to Ireland as secretary to the Bishop of Armagh.

[101] **Sappho**
an ancient Greek poetess. Here, the name for a female poet, specifically for Lady Mary Wortley Montagu (1689–1762). A writer of some skill, she had been a friend of Pope's until a rupture some time in the late 1720s. One popular rumour had it that the two had fallen out after Pope had declared love to Lady Mary, only to be answered with a fit of immoderate laughter. Whatever the cause of the split, the ensuing quarrel was long-lived and bitter. In the 'Advertisement' to the *Epistle* Pope claimed that the immediate motive for writing was to reply to the attacks on him made by Lady Mary in two poems. For more details about her, see the introductory notes to *Saturday: The Small-Pox*; *Hold* Treated by Warburton as Arbuthnot's interruption of Pope – see introductory notes.

[103] **twice as tall**
Because of his physical deformity, Pope was very small.

[106] **slaver kills**
Rabies is transmitted through the animal's spittle.

[107] **innocent**
in the sense of unable to do harm.

[108] **repent**
i.e. repent of their former attacks on Pope, as in lines 51–2.

[109] **dedicates**
writes a dedication to Pope at the beginning of his book; *high heroic prose* The high heroic was associated with verse, and to write prose in a

high heroic manner was to offend against literary decorum.

[110] **ridicules ... foes**
His dedication makes Pope look more ridiculous than would a hundred attacks.

[111] **Grub Street**
a real street in London, but also a stock term for the area which housed hack writers, and for the hacks themselves.

[113] **prints my letters**
Edmund Curll (see note to line 53) had printed some of Pope's letters without permission in 1726. The attack here is directed chiefly at the supplier of the letters.

[114] **'Subscribe, subscribe.'**
Pope's translations of Homer had been published by subscription, that is, by wealthy people paying in advance for copies of the first deluxe edition. Here he complains that some of those who drummed up subscriptions for him made him ridiculous by their approach. Of course, he did not refuse any of the money raised in this way.

[115] **There are, who**
there are those who; *person* body, physical appearance.

[116] **I cough ...**
the first in a series of absurd flatteries.

[117] **Ammon's great son**
Alexander the Great was reputed to have been the son of Zeus (Ammon) – see *Alexander's Feast*, line 4, note; *one shoulder ... high* Pope had a deformed spine and a humped shoulder.

[119] **obliging creatures**
i.e. the flatterers.

[120] **Betters**
the exalted forebears with whom he is compared.

[122] **Maro**
Virgil.

[126] **Dipped me in ink**
alludes to the legend that Thetis, the mother of the Greek hero Achilles, dipped her son in the waters of the underworld river Styx in order to make his skin impenetrable. Pope had used the legend in 1728 in *The Dunciad*

when he imagined an underworld of hack writers: 'There in a dusky vale where Lethe rolls,/ Old Bavius sits to dip poetic souls,/ And blunt the sense and fit it for a skull/ Of solid proof, impenetrably dull' (iii, 23–6). His reworking of the allusion in the *Epistle* contains an ironic glance at himself.

[127] **fool to fame**
i.e. one who wishes foolishly for fame.

[128] **numbers**
verses.

[129] **calling**
vocation, especially religious vocation; *idle trade* Such ironically disparaging remarks about poetry are not uncommon in Pope's writing.

[130] **no father disobeyed**
referring back to James Moore-Smythe, line 23.

[131] **muse**
one of the nine sister goddesses of the arts; here, the goddess of poetry – see *Rape*, i, 7; *not wife* Pope remained unmarried.

[132] **this long disease, my life**
Pope was troubled by frailty and ill health throughout his life, and in the 1730s his afflictions were particularly severe.

[133] **To second**
to help. The sense of the line is that poetry has been a kind of second line of medicine (after that provided by Arbuthnot) for Pope.

[134] **And teach ... to bear**
i.e. While Arbuthnot has kept Pope (the being) alive, poetry has kept him in good spirits.

[135] **Granville**
George Granville, Baron Landsdowne (1667–1735). Pope knew, and was encouraged by, this statesman and minor poet at the beginning of his career, and he dedicated *Windsor-Forest* to him. In the passage which follows Pope tries to establish his poetic credentials by listing the luminaries who had approved his work early on.

[136] **Walsh**
William Walsh, poet and critic (thus, 'knowing').

[137] **Garth**
Sir Samuel Garth (1661–1719), doctor and poet, author of *The Dispensary*, a forerunner of *The Rape of the Lock*. As the epithet 'well natured' suggests, Pope had a high regard for Garth's character.

[138] **Congreve**
William Congreve, poet and playwright, author of *The Way of the World*; *Swift endured* Swift was a niggard with praise; *lays* poems.

[139] **Talbot**
Charles Talbot, Duke of Shrewsbury; *Somers* John, Baron Somers, statesman and patron of learning; *Sheffield* John Sheffield, Duke of Buckingham, statesman and minor author.

[140] **Rochester**
Francis Atterbury, Bishop of Rochester (thus 'mitred').

[141] **St John**
Henry St John, Viscount Bolingbroke (1678–1751), the leader of the opposition against Walpole's administration in the 1730s and a close associate of Pope's; *great Dryden's friends before* This applies to all the men on the list except Swift.

[144] **Happier . . . beloved!**
It is typical of Pope to celebrate friendship in this way.

[146] **Burnets, Oldmixons and Cooks**
Thomas Burnett, John Oldmixon and Thomas Cooke had all written attacks on Pope. The three obscure faultfinders are made contemptible by being placed next to Pope's noble, famous and intelligent encouragers.

[147] **Soft were**
Pope looks back to the beginnings of his poetic career as a writer of pastorals; *numbers* metre, verse; more generally poems.

[148] **While pure . . . sense**
i.e. while the poet described rather than moralised. Most of Pope's moral poetry belongs to the third phase of his career (1728 and after) when with his translations of Homer out of the way he settled down again to original composition.

[149] **gentle Fanny**
John Hervey, Baron of Ickworth (1696–1743). Hervey was Lady Mary's collaborator in the verse attacks on Pope which prompted the *Epistle* (see 'Advertisement' and note to line 101), and he appears later in the poem as Sporus (lines 305–33). Homosexuality is implied even in this early reference.

[150] **purling**
the sound or action of a small brook.

[151] **Gildon**
Charles Gildon, writer; *venal* hireling; *quill* pen.

[152] **dinner**
implying that Gildon wrote for food; *sat still* i.e. did not reply.

[153] **Dennis**
John Dennis. Critic, dramatist and old enemy of Pope, but already dead when the poem was published. He was known for his fiery temper, hence 'rave in furious fret'.

[155] **If want provoked**
i.e. if they were forced by need. As in the preceding lines Pope suggests that his enemies were motivated simply by money.

[156] **Bedlam**
madness – see note to line 4; *the Mint* see note to line 13. Pope's enemies are seen as belonging among debtors.

[157] **more sober**
i.e. than Gildon and Dennis.

[158] **kissed the rod**
accepted correction with submission.

[159] **their**
i.e. the critics'; *just pretence* true claim or profession.

[160] **want**
lack.

[161] **points**
punctuation marks, especially full stops.

[162] **'twere**
it would be; *mite* a small coin. The word is associated particularly with the poor woman whose small Temple offering is commended by Jesus as worth more than the larger offerings of the rich (Mark 12: 41–4).

[163] **ne'er**
never; *laurel* the traditional badge of

the true poet; *ribbalds* low fellows, users of base and offensive language.

[164] **slashing Bentley**
Richard Bentley, scholar and academic, dubbed 'slashing' because of passages omitted or marked as spurious in his editions of classic authors; *Tibbald* Pope's name for Lewis Theobald, a scholar who incurred his wrath by publishing an account of Pope's errors in his editing of Shakespeare. The adjective 'piddling' ('trifling') refers to his scholarly attention to detail. He became the first hero of *The Dunciad* (see note to line 79).

[165] **wight**
human being (archaic); *but* only.

[166] **syllables**
The last syllable must be unnaturally sounded to bring out the rhyme – a poetic joke.

[168] **Preserved . . . name**
Bentley had edited Milton and Theobald Shakespeare.

[169] **amber**
a waxy substance used in perfumes.

[170] **Of hairs . . . worms**
The critics preserved in the works of great writers are like these ugly, worthless things preserved in precious amber.

[171] **things**
the hairs, etc., in the amber – also critics.

[174] **I gave . . . due**
i.e. I judged them according to their deserts.

[176] **standard**
the authorised exemplar of a weight; here the measure by which people privately judge themselves.

[177] **casting-weight**
(continuing the imagery of weighing) the decisive added weight which tips the scales.

[179] **The bard**
Ambrose Philips again – see note to line 100; *renown* used as a verb, to make famous.

[180] **turns**
fashions, makes – the word is mildly pejorative; *Persian tale* Philips wrote

a book of *Persian Tales*; *half a crown* as an insult, this shows Pope having his cake and eating it. By mentioning money he implies that Philips writes only from motives of greed, and by mentioning the paltry amount he implies that Philips' poetry is insufficiently good to earn more.

[182] **hard-bound**
constipated. The whole line rests on the imagery of constipation.

[183] **wanting**
lacking, in need; *theft* i.e. plagiarism.

[184] **spends little**
i.e. gives away little of his own.

[186] **Means not**
in the sense of means nothing.

[187] **fustian**
thick cloth; figuratively, verbose language, bombast.

[189] **All these . . . translate**
i.e. all these (critics) interpret my modest satire badly.

[190] **own**
admit, concede; *such poets* i.e. such poets as Pope; *Tate* Nahum Tate, former Poet Laureate and bowdleriser of Shakespeare; an example of the weak poet.

[192] **Addison**
Joseph Addison, playwright, poet and journalist. Already fifteen years dead when the *Epistle* was published, Addison had been a prominent literary figure whom Pope had liked and admired. However, his encouragement of a rival translator of Homer had led to a breach and to Pope's satirical character sketch (Atticus), which was first drafted twenty years before the *Epistle*'s publication; *safe* from Pope's satire.

[193] **all such**
i.e. all such minor critics; *one* Atticus/Addison; *fires* sentiments, imaginations.

[196] **write, converse and live**
Typically, Pope considers the man as well as the writer; *ease* social grace as well as lacking in effort.

[197] **fond**
foolish.

[198] **Bear**
allow; *the Turk* a common exemplar of despotic behaviour.

[199] **him**
the rival brother.

[200] **arts**
skills; *hate...rise* The line refers to Pope's quarrel with Addison (see note to line 192). Addison turned against Pope, it suggests, out of envy at the possession of similar literary talents to his own.

[201] **Damn**
judge, condemn, express disapproval; *assent* presumably to praise given by others; *leer* a look of the eye expressive of malignity.

[202] **the rest**
i.e. his hangers on.

[205] **reserved**
unwilling.

[206] **timorous**
fearful, cowardly.

[208] **obliging**
courteous, civil, polite; *obliged* conferred favours, did services.

[209] **Like Cato**
Roman senator and patriot, and the hero of a play by Addison; *senate* the Roman parliament; used here ironically for the group of sycophants gathered round Addison.

[211] **wits**
used ironically for the followers of intellectual fashion; *templars* law students. Addison's admirers do not enjoy high social or intellectual status; *raise* add to reputation, lustre of.

[214] **Atticus**
Addison. The name 'Atticus' is appropriate in two ways: (1) it sounds like 'Addison'; (2) it recalls the Roman Atticus, correspondent of Cicero, whose determined neutrality betrayed a fear of taking sides and giving offence, one of the principal features of Addison as Pope portrays him.

[215] **What though...**
the phrase introduces a long passage of self-portraiture in which Pope implicitly contrasts himself with Atticus. He follows a similar procedure

after the portraits of Bufo and Sporus; *rubric* a heading in red on a printed page, popular with Lintot (see note to line 63) – referring to the contemporary practice of displaying title pages on boards and posts as a means of advertisement.

[216] **Or plastered ... capitals**
i.e. What if my name was stuck in capital letters on posts. Again, the reference is to the display of title pages; *claps* handbills.

[217] **smoking forth**
driving out at a rapid speed; *hawker* street-seller, used for the sale of books and pamphlets.

[219] **sought no homage**
in sharp contrast to Atticus with his tribe of sycophants.

[220] **like Asian monarchs**
His isolation is in this respect curiously similar to that of Atticus – see line 198.

[221] **berhymed**
written about, rhymed about; in the sense that Pope has been the subject of many derogatory verses.

[222] **George**
George II, well known for his dislike of poetry; *birthday song* large numbers of verses were produced to celebrate the king's birthday.

[224] **itch**
a common and extremely irritating skin disease. What follows is a list of the activities of the obscure writer, out to make a name for himself by making contacts. Pope claims never to have adopted such expedients.

[225] **puppy**
used sometimes as a contemptuous term for an upstart, a young pretender; *daggled* to drag or trail through mud.

[226] **fetch and carry**
the function of the dog; *sing-song* a diminutive.

[227] **sweat, and mouthed, and cried**
describing the author's behaviour during the rehearsal of his play.

[228] **handkerchief**
a scented handkerchief, the badge of a fop.

[229] **prate**
foolish talk.

[230] **Bufo**
suggestive of a toad. The character of a patron which follows, though based to some extent on real people (Bubb Dodington and the Earl of Halifax), is generalised; *Castalian state* Castalia is a spring on Mount Parnassus, sacred to the muses; thus, the realm of poetry.

[231] **Apollo**
the god of music and poetry, who (to give an example of pride) hung and flayed Marsyas for rivalling him in song (see note to line 68); *forked hill* Parnassus.

[232] **puffed**
blown up, made proud and boastful. The line employs the image of the toad blowing himself up to appear large; *quill* pen. Bufo is the patron willing to patronise those who will flatter his enormous pride.

[233] **dedication**
It was the custom to include flattering (sometimes fulsomely so) dedications to patrons at the beginning of books.

[234] **Horace ... in song**
He is compared to Horace in his hireling poets' writings.

[236] **And a ... head**
Pope is ridiculing those who collect, and place value upon, anything so long as it is antique; here, the absurd headless statue of a Greek poet.

[237] **Received ... race**
i.e. received (welcomed, gave hospitality to) an undistinguished race of wits.

[238] **place**
sinecure (see note to line 50).

[239] **extolled**
praised; *pictures* his collection of paintings; *seat* country seat, house and grounds.

[240] **some days eat**
the motive behind all the flattery, to get a good meal.

[241] **riper days**
old age.

[242] **port**
port wine, i.e. less than a meal now he has grown more frugal.

[243] **dry rehearsal**
a barren or futile rehearsal. The sense is that Bufo arranges a rehearsal for his protégé's play, but it leads nowhere.

[244] **paid in kind**
i.e. returned poem for poem. This is 'harder still' in that the poets hope for a more substantial payment.

[245] **Dryden alone**
Dryden possessed too much genius and integrity to seek patronage of that kind.

[247] **the great**
heavily ironic.

[248] **He helped ... to starve**
Having spent the closing years of his life in poverty, Dryden was buried with some magnificence, the funeral being paid for through a collection got up by the prominent and wealthy.

[249–50] **May some ... still!**
Let every poet still find a patron.

[249] **quill**
poet's pen.

[250] **Bavius & Bufo**
the undeserving poet and the undiscerning patron.

[251] **a statesman ... defence**
i.e. when he needs someone to write a quick defence of his actions.

[252] **Or envy ... sense**
referring to the public quarrels which flared up frequently in periodicals and other publications.

[253] **Or simple pride . : . demands**
i.e. when patrons demand written flattery in some form.

[254] **whistled off**
sent away, dismissed. The sense is that the close relationship between foolish poet and foolish patron ensures that neither troubles Pope.

[255] **great**
the powerful and wealthy; *take away* The 'great' keep bad poets out of Pope's hair by giving them patronage.

[256] **Gay**
John Gay, poet, dramatist and friend of Pope and Swift. He has been left to Pope because (like Dryden) he has not been courted by the Bufos of the world.

[257] **bloom**
Gay had a great success with *The Beggar's Opera* in 1728, though the sequel *Polly* was not allowed to be produced.

[258] **tell it on his tomb**
Pope wrote Gay's epitaph.

[260] **Queensberry**
Charles Douglas, Duke of Queensberry, and Gay's patron; *urn* vase used to hold the deceased's ashes or to decorate his tomb.

[261] **my own**
i.e. my own life, referring back to line 259.

[262] **To live...do**
This kind of moral statement is characteristic of the late Pope.

[263] **ease**
absence of constraint.

[265] **Above a patron**
i.e. above having a patron.

[267] **courts**
the monarch's residence, or (as here) his retinue of advisers, servants and flatterers.

[269] **Can sleep**
see line 43 and note.

[270] **Dennis**
John Dennis, playwright and critic (see note to line 153). He died in 1734.

[271] **what...light**
i.e. what he plans to publish next.

[275] **close with**
in the sense of talking confidentially with. The sentence is supposed to reproduce a piece of literary gossip from someone who, having seen Pope and Swift together, imagines they are planning a collaborative enterprise. Joint publishing projects were quite common.

[276] **prating**
foolishly talking; *Balbus* (from Latin) stammering, a stammerer; *come out* The sense is that something will be published as a result of the conversation.

[278] **No...lie still**
Balbus insists that Pope must be working on something.

[279] **obligingly**
used ironically.

[280] **lampoon**
a virulent satire on an individual; *Sir Will* Sir William Yonge, a proverbially corrupt and contemptible politician; *The first...makes* A lot of poems and tracts, particularly if they contained personal satire, were published anonymously, and guessing the authorship was a kind of game played by London readers. Balbus takes a scurrilous, doggerel lampoon to have been written by Pope.

[282] **coxcomb**
fool (see note to line 84); *by my style* Balbus and his like claim to recognise Pope as the author of a piece because of the style of it.

[285] **Give virtue scandal**
i.e. cursed be the verse that raises scandal and gossip concerning a virtuous person. This clause is part of a list of the possible effects of poetry (others' and his own) which Pope abhors.

[287] **But he**
i.e. on the other hand, verse should frighten, make a foe of, cause scandal about, this 'he'. The lines which follow (289–304) were first published as a paraphrase of part of one of Horace's satires.

[288] **fallen worth**
a virtuous person who has come down in the world.

[290] **copies out**
perhaps a hint at Hervey's role as Lady Mary's collaborator in the libels on Pope (see note to line 149).

[291–2] **That fop...honest fame**
the fop who claims to be patron in order to aggrandise himself, but who speaks ill of the patronised author behind his back.

[293] **Who can...approve**
refers to those who might praise distinction and virtue as a way of advertising their own.

[294] **sense**
perception, recognition (i.e. of 'your merit').

[296] **wants**
lacks; *Yet wants...defend* but lacks the courage to defend your reputation

when others speak against (injure) you.

[297] **tells**
makes public (even what is spoken in confidence).

[299] **dean**
Pope's note refers us to *Epistle to Burlington* (lines 141–50) and to the Dean who preached a sermon at Court in which he 'threatened sinners with punishment in "a place which he thought it not decent to name in so polite an assembly"'; *silver bell* used to summon worshippers to a private chapel service in which the participants' pride would be more prominent than their devotion (see *Epistle to Burlington*, lines 141–2). Both the dean and the bell suggest a very diluted religion.

[300] **canons**
the part of the mass in which the host is consecrated. Although it continues the religious imagery of the previous line, the meaning is obscure.

[301] **to misapply**
i.e. to find unintended hidden meanings.

[302] **Makes satire a lampoon**
One distinction drawn between satire and lampoon was that satire was general, lampoon personal. This person finds (unintended) personal references in general satire; *and fiction lie* A popular genre of the period was the *roman-à-clef*, in which the scandalous behaviour of the characters reflected that of prominent people. This person reads real fiction as if it were scandal.

[303] **lash**
a common term for the satirist's power to wound.

[305] **Sporus**
John Hervey (see note to line 149). The name refers to Suetonius's account of the boy Sporus whose testicles were cut off and who acted the woman; *'What...'* supposed (by Warburton – see introductory notes) to be Arbuthnot's interjection; *silk* anticipates both the grub imagery (silkworm – bug) and the portrait of Sporus as a bisexual courtier dressed effeminately.

[306] **curd**
the thick white substance which forms when milk separates; *ass's milk* frequently applied as a tonic, thus adverting to Sporus's frailty; also, asses imply stupidity.

[307] **can Sporus feel**
harks back to the argument of line 84 that fools are too dull to feel.

[308] **wheel**
a large wheel used as an instrument of torture or execution.

[309] **bug**
insect; here butterfly; also in slang usage, an inciter to homosexuality.

[310] **painted child**
Hervey used cosmetics to colour his face, and had no teeth.

[311] **the fair**
refers to court ladies.

[312] **tastes**
understands, appreciates; *enjoys* carries a sexual connotation and here suggests impotence.

[313] **spaniels**
were kept as lapdogs.

[314] **mumbling**
chewing, biting softly; another reference to Hervey's toothlessness; *game* animals or birds which are hunted for their flesh.

[316] **dimpling**
broken into ripples.

[317] **florid**
adorned, decorated language; also, of the complexion, bright and rosy – another reference to Hervey's use of face paint; *impotence* both since he is a puppet and since he is sexually ambiguous.

[318] **prompter**
Lady Mary; *squeaks* suggestive of sexual ambivalence.

[319] **ear of Eve**
In *Paradise Lost* Satan takes the form of a toad in order either to whisper dreams into the sleeping Eve or to breathe poison into her (iv, 799–809). Eve here is Queen Caroline, who lent a ready ear to Hervey's gossip; *familiar* both unduly intimate, and (in the context of the allusion to Satan) a familiar

spirit, a demon serving a witch in the form of an animal.

[320] **Half froth**
possibly a reference to the tendency of toothless people, like Hervey, to dribble.

[323–5] **His wit ... antithesis**
a (for Pope) rare triplet of rhymes.

[323] **His wit all see-saw**
contemporary decorum insisted that wit and language should be appropriate to their context, a rule Sporus flouts.

[324] **now ... miss**
implying bisexuality.

[325] **antithesis**
opposition, implicitly the opposition of goodness and naturalness.

[326] **Amphibious**
suggestive of sexual ambiguity; *acting ... part* continuing the puppet imagery.

[328] **toilet**
dressing table; *board* table, dinner.

[329] **Now ... lord**
The line in which Sporus's bisexuality is most explicitly alluded to.

[330] **Eve's tempter**
i.e. Satan disguised as the serpent in the Garden of Eden; *Rabbins* rabbis – who invented the image of Satan which follows.

[331] **cherub**
a kind of angel. The notion of Satan as a serpent with an angel's face existed among the Jews.

[332] **parts**
abilities, intellectual gifts (as in the expression 'man of parts').

[334] **Not fortune's ... fool**
the line begins a long passage in which Pope portrays himself as a direct contrast to Sporus; *fashion's fool* in the sense of a blind follower of fashion.

[335] **lucre**
gain, money; *ambition's tool* in the sense that he (Pope) would not allow himself to be exploited by the ambitious.

[337] **manly ways**
Pope contrasts himself with the sexually ambiguous Sporus and makes manliness something separate from size and physical robustness (qualities he did not possess).

[340] **That not ... long**
that he did not wander long in fancy's maze; *fancy* fantasy, pleasing (but trivial) imagination. Pope is thinking of his early works in terms similar to those of line 148.

[341] **stooped**
the image is from falconry, in which the hawk's dive on its prey is known as a stoop. Falconry was no longer a popular sport in Pope's day, but a number of hawking terms survived in the language, as they do now (e.g. to tower); *moralised his song* In his second phase of original writing (after the long period as a translator), Pope concentrated on satire, and broadly philosophical and moral works.

[343] **stood**
kept his ground, remained firm, withstood.

[344] **half-approving wit**
takes us back to Atticus damning with faint praise (line 201) and to the concessions of line 190.

[345] **coxcomb**
fool (see note to line 74); *hit* by Pope's satire.

[346] **friend he never had**
i.e. those claiming to have relinquished Pope's friendship who had never possessed it.

[349] **blow unfelt**
refers to a published account of a fictitious beating.

[350] **the tale ... the lie**
published attacks on Pope, concerning (for example) the circumstances of the composition of the portrait of Addison (Atticus) and Pope's financial dealings with publishers and collaborators.

[351] **imputed**
attributed. The line refers to scurrilous or profane works printed by unscrupulous publishers under Pope's name in order to help sales; *dullness* a selfish, dangerous kind of stupidity.

[352] **'scape**
escape.

[353] **person**
body. Published attacks on Pope sometimes included cruel references to his physical deformity; *pictured shape* caricature illustrations ridiculing his deformity.

[354] **all he loved**
Pope's note gives a list of friends who were publicly abused.

[355] **friend in exile**
Francis Atterbury was banished in 1723 for Jacobite plotting (see line 140 and note).

[356] **whisper**
the gossip of Hervey/Sporus; *greatness...near* refers to Hervey's closeness to the queen.

[357] **Perhaps...ear**
Hervey's gossip is still believed by the queen. The implication is that Pope remains out of favour with her because of this.

[358] **Welcome...the past**
i.e. Pope is happy to have suffered for the sake of virtue.

[359] **the last**
the last example, Pope's disfavour with the queen.

[360] **'But why...the great'**
Arbuthnot's interjection; *insult the poor* After the attack on hireling scribblers in *The Dunciad* Pope was accused of having used their poverty as a stick to beat them with. Material poverty is also seen as a sign of literary poverty in the *Epistle* (see lines 13, 42, 48, 50, 66, 154, 156, etc.).

[361] **knave**
a base, crafty, unprincipled man; *state* status, condition.

[362] **Alike my scorn**
I am equally scornful ...

[363] **Japhet**
Japhet Crook, the forger.

[365] **Knight of the post**
an informer, someone who lives by giving false evidence; *of the shire* i.e. knight of the shire, a Member of Parliament.

[366] **pillory**
a wooden frame in which an offender was exposed to the public. Occasionally the crowd's treatment of a pilloried offender was so rough that he or she died; *near a throne* Hervey again (see notes to lines 356 and 319).

[367] **lose his own**
The cropping of an ear, or ears, was a punishment for forgery.

[368] **soft by nature**
Pope; *dupe* one who is easily tricked.

[369] **Sappho**
Lady Mary (see line 101 and note); *bit* taken in, deceived.

[370] **This dreaded...confess**
i.e. Dennis (see note to line 153) will confess that this dreaded satirist (Pope) was ...

[371] **friend...distress**
Pope wrote a prologue for a benefit performance in aid of Dennis.

[372] **Tibbald**
Lewis Theobald (see note to line 164).

[373] **Cibber**
Colley Cibber (see note to line 97). Cibber and Pope were on friendly terms early in Pope's career; *Moore* James Moore-Smythe, to whose play Pope contributed some verses (see notes to lines 23 and 24).

[374] **Full ten...reply?**
Pope was not such an innocent victim as this suggests.

[375] **Welsted**
Leonard Welsted (see note to line 49). Pope's note refers to Welsted's false charge that he had caused a woman's death.

[376] **aspersed**
slandered, defamed. The reference is obscure.

[377] **let her be his wife**
i.e. Pope let the one who had aspersed him for the sake of a mistress marry her. The joke is that marriage to her was punishment enough.

[378] **Budgell**
Eustace Budgell; *charge...quill* i.e. falsely attribute bad writing to him.

[379] **except his will**
Budgell was (and is) believed to have forged Matthew Tindal's will in his own favour.

[380] **two Curlls**
Edmund Curll (see note to line 53) and Hervey. Hervey is the Curll of the

court in that he spreads gossip; *town* London.

[381] **father, mother**
Pope's note refers to a pamphlet of Curll's which described his father as a hatter, and to the poem by Hervey and Lady Mary which provoked the *Epistle* (see note to line 101) and which refers to his obscure birth; *body* see note to line 353.

[383] **sin . . . fool**
Pope's father's rustic good nature was not quite Pope's own, who made his living by calling others fools.

[385] **James Moore**
James Moore-Smythe again (see lines 28, 98 and 373).

[386] **Unspotted**
unspoilt by vice, honourable.

[387] **song**
poetry; the *Epistle* itself keeps alive the memory of Pope's parents.

[388] **Of gentle blood**
i.e. belonging to the gentry, the class composed of knights and esquires; *part shed . . . cause* Pope's long note to line 381 concerning his family mentions an uncle who 'died in the service of King Charles'. It was important for Pope as a Roman Catholic to be able to demonstrate his family's loyalty since Catholics were always regarded with suspicion by the Protestant majority.

[389] **While yet . . . applause**
It was the constant complaint of the opposition that the administration of Sir Robert Walpole had destroyed respect for honour and virtue by its emphasis on money. Gay's *The Beggar's Opera* (see note to line 257) provides a good example.

[390] **Each parent sprung**
i.e. each came (was sprung) from gentle blood; *Their own* A gentleman's wealth was inherited, not made by trade.

[391] **Bestia**
Roman senator who made a dishonourable peace – also suggestive of 'beast'. The line probably refers to the Duke of Marlborough, a general of the first and second decades of the

century, who received immense rewards for his campaigns.

[392] **inheriting no strife**
squabbles about wills and bequests were very common when wealth was still more often inherited than earned.

[393] **noble wife**
i.e. belonging to the aristocracy, the class above the gentry. Although there may be a specific reference intended, it is equally likely that Pope meant all those who marry for status, and whose marriages founder on argument and discontent ('discord').

[394] **Stranger to civil . . . rage**
i.e. keeping out of factiousness and political contention; *religious* The emphasis on religious moderation again reflects the insecurity of the Catholic.

[395] **good man**
i.e. Pope's father; *innoxious* without doing harm.

[396] **courts**
royal residences and places of royal business; *suits* law suits, litigation. Pope is stressing his father's peaceable character.

[398] **Unlearned**
not learned; *schoolman* medieval scholastic. 'Schoolmen' were known for their ingenious, tortuous argument ('subtle art') and for Pope they represented one of the worst aspects of the Middle Ages. They were Catholic theologians, and by distinguishing his father from them Pope represents his family's Catholicism as comparatively modern and rational.

[399] **No language**
i.e. no foreign language.

[402] **His life . . . unknown**
His life, though it was a long one, passed without sickness.

[405] **Who sprung . . . than I**
Even the offspring of kings will be less happy than I (if I live and die like my father). The irony is that the *Epistle* provides plentiful evidence that Pope's life and character have been, and are, very different from his father's.

[406] **friend**
Arbuthnot.
[408] **Me...engage**
i.e. Let the tender office long engage me; *office* task; here, the task of nursing his ailing mother.
[409] **cradle**
the metaphor transforms Pope into his parent's parent.
[410] **arts**
skills; *extend...breath* help a mother live longer.
[411] **languor**
faintness, tiredness of spirit caused by sorrow.
[413] **keep...sky**
In fact, Pope's mother died before publication of the poem, but these lines were composed during her lifetime.

[414–15] **On cares...my friend**
i.e. If I am given more time ('length of days') for such cares (looking after his mother), may heaven keep my friend alive to bless that time.
[416] **social**
Arbuthnot was known for his genial good nature, so much so that Swift once declared that if there had only been ten Arbuthnots he would not have needed to write his ferocious satire on humanity, *Gulliver's Travels*.
[417] **served a queen**
Arbuthnot had been Queen Anne's (d. 1714) doctor.
[418] **that blessing**
i.e. the blessing of Arbuthnot's continued existence.
[419] **Thus far was right**
presumably referring to Pope's wish.

---◇---

24 / *Epistle to a Lady*

Of the Characters of Women

Nothing so true as what you once let fall,
'Most women have no characters at all.'
Matter too soft a lasting mark to bear,
And best distinguished by black, brown or fair.
 How many pictures of one nymph we view,   5
All how unlike each other, all how true!
Arcadia's Countess, here, in ermined pride,
Is there, Pastora by a fountain side.
Here Fannia, leering on her own good man,
And there, a naked Leda with a swan.   10
Let then the fair one beautifully cry
In Magdalen's loose hair and lifted eye,
Or dress'd in smiles of sweet Cecilia shine,
With simpering angels, palms, and harps divine;
Whether the charmer sinner it, or saint it,   15
If folly grow romantic, I must paint it.

Come, then, the colours and the ground prepare!
Dip in the rainbow, trick her off in air;
Choose a firm cloud before it fall, and in it
Catch, ere she change, the Cynthia of this minute.   20
    Rufa, whose eye quick glancing o'er the park
Attracts each light gay meteor of a spark,
Agrees as ill with Rufa studying Locke,
As Sappho's diamonds with her dirty smock;
Or Sappho at her toilet's greasy task,   25
With Sappho fragrant at an evening mask:
So morning insects, that in muck begun,
Shine, buzz, and fly-blow in the setting sun.
    How soft is Silia, fearful to offend,
The frail one's advocate, the weak one's friend.   30
To her, Calista proved her conduct nice;
And good Simplicius asks of her advice.
Sudden, she storms! she raves! You tip the wink,
But spare your censure – Silia does not drink.
All eyes may see from what the change arose,   35
All eyes may see – a pimple on her nose.
    Papillia, wedded to her amorous spark,
Sighs for the shades – 'How charming is a park!'
A park is purchased, but the fair he sees
All bathed in tears – 'Oh odious, odious trees!'   40
    Ladies, like variegated tulips, show,
'Tis to their changes half their charms we owe.
Fine by defect, and delicately weak,
Their happy spots the nice admirer take.
'Twas thus Calypso once each heart alarmed,   45
Awed without virtue, without beauty charmed;
Her tongue bewitched as oddly as her eyes,
Less wit than mimic, more a wit than wise.
Strange graces still, and stranger flights she had,
Was just not ugly, and was just not mad.   50
Yet ne'er so sure our passion to create,
As when she touched the brink of all we hate.
    Narcissa's nature, tolerably mild,
To make a wash would hardly stew a child;
Has e'en been proved to grant a lover's prayer,   55
And paid a tradesman once, to make him stare;
Gave alms at Easter, in a Christian trim,

And made a widow happy for a whim.
Why then declare good-nature is her scorn,
When 'tis by that alone she can be borne? 60
Why pique all mortals, yet affect a name?
A fool to pleasure, yet a slave to fame:
Now deep in Taylor and the Book of Martyrs,
Now drinking citron with his Grace and Chartres.
Now conscience chills her, and now passion burns, 65
And atheism and religion take their turns,
A very heathen in the carnal part,
Yet still a sad, good Christian at her heart.
    See sin in state, majestically drunk;
Proud as a peeress, prouder as a punk, 70
Chaste to her husband, frank to all beside,
A teeming mistress, but a barren bride.
What then? let blood and body bear the fault,
Her head's untouched, that noble seat of thought.
Such this day's doctrine – in another fit 75
She sins with poets through pure love of wit.
What has not fired her bosom or her brain?
Caesar and Tall-boy, Charles and Charlemagne.
As Helluo, late dictator of the feast,
The nose of haut-gout and the tip of taste, 80
Critiqued your wine, and analysed your meat,
Yet on plain pudding deigned at home to eat:
So Philomede, lecturing all mankind
On the soft passion, and the taste refined,
The address, the delicacy – stoops at once, 85
And makes her hearty meal upon a dunce.
    Flavia's a wit, has too much sense to pray.
To toast our wants and wishes is her way,
Nor asks of God, but of her stars, to give
The mighty blessing, 'While we live, to live.' 90
Then all for death, that opiate of the soul!
Lucretia's dagger, Rosamonda's bowl.
Say, what can cause such impotence of mind?
A spark too fickle, or a spouse too kind.
Wise wretch! with pleasures too refined to please; 95
With too much spirit to be e'er at ease;
With too much quickness ever to be taught;
With too much thinking to have common thought;

Who purchase pain with all that joy can give,
And die of nothing but a rage to live. 100
    Turn then from wits; and look on Simo's mate,
No ass so meek, no ass so obstinate.
Or her that owns her faults, but never mends,
Because she's honest, and the best of friends.
Or her whose life the church and scandal share, 105
For ever in a passion or a prayer.
Or her who laughs at hell, but (like her grace)
Cries, 'Ah! how charming if there's no such place!'
Or who in sweet vicissitude appears
Of mirth and opium, ratafia and tears, 110
The daily anodyne, and nightly draught,
To kill those foes to fair ones, time and thought.
Woman and fool are two hard things to hit,
For true no-meaning puzzles more than wit.
    But what are these to great Atossa's mind? 115
Scarce once herself, by turns all womankind,
Who, with herself or others, from her birth
Finds all her life one warfare upon earth,
Shines in exposing knaves and painting fools,
Yet is whate'er she hates and ridicules. 120
No thought advances, but her eddy brain
Whisks it about, and down it goes again.
Full sixty years the world has been her trade,
The wisest fool much time has ever made.
From loveless youth to unrespected age, 125
No passion gratified, except her rage.
So much the fury still outran the wit,
The pleasure missed her, and the scandal hit.
Who breaks with her, provokes revenge from hell,
But he's a bolder man who dares be well. 130
Her every turn with violence pursued,
No more a storm her hate than gratitude.
To that each passion turns, or soon or late.
Love, if it makes her yield, must make her hate.
Superiors? Death! And equals? What a curse! 135
But an inferior not dependent? Worse!
Offend her, and she knows not to forgive.
Oblige her, and she'll hate you while you live:
But die, and she'll adore you – then the bust

And temple rise – then fall again to dust.   140
Last night, her lord was all that's good and great,
A knave this morning, and his will a cheat.
Strange! by the means defeated of the ends,
By spirit robbed of power, by warmth of friends,
By wealth of followers! Without one distress,   145
Sick of herself, through very selfishness!
Atossa, cursed with every granted prayer,
Childless with all her children, wants an heir.
To heirs unknown descends the unguarded store,
Or wanders, heaven-directed, to the poor.   150
    Pictures like these, dear Madam, to design,
Ask no firm hand, and no unerring line.
Some wandering touches, some reflected light,
Some flying stroke alone can hit them right:
For how should equal colours do the knack?   155
Chameleons who can paint in white and black?
    'Yet Chloe sure was formed without a spot.' –
Nature in her then erred not, but forgot.
'With every pleasing, every prudent part,
Say, what can Chloe want?' – She wants a heart.   160
She speaks, behaves, and acts, just as she ought,
But never, never reached one generous thought.
Virtue she finds too painful an endeavour,
Content to dwell in decencies for ever.
So very reasonable, so unmoved,   165
As never yet to love, or to be loved.
She, while her lover pants upon her breast,
Can mark the figures on an Indian chest;
And when she sees her friend in deep despair,
Observes how much a chintz exceeds mohair!   170
Forbid it, Heaven, a favour or a debt
She e'er should cancel – but she may forget.
Safe is your secret still in Chloe's ear,
But none of Chloe's shall you ever hear.
Of all her dears she never slandered one,   175
But cares not if a thousand are undone.
Would Chloe know if you're alive or dead?
She bids her footman put it in her head.
Chloe is prudent – would you too be wise?
Then never break your heart when Chloe dies.   180

One certain portrait may (I grant) be seen,
Which Heaven has varnished out, and made a queen,
The same for ever! And described by all
With truth and goodness, as with crown and ball.
Poets heap virtues, painters gems, at will, 185
And show their zeal, and hide their want of skill.
'Tis well – but, artists, who can paint or write,
To draw the naked is your true delight.
That robe of quality so struts and swells,
None see what parts of nature it conceals. 190
The exactest traits of body or of mind,
We owe to models of an humble kind.
If Queensberry to strip there's no compelling,
'Tis from a handmaid we must take a Helen.
From peer or bishop 'tis no easy thing 195
To draw the man who loves his God or king.
Alas! I copy (or my draught would fail)
From honest Mahomet, or plain Parson Hale.

But grant, in public, men sometimes are shown,
A woman's seen in private life alone. 200
Our bolder talents in full light displayed,
Your virtues open fairest in the shade.
Bred to disguise, in public 'tis you hide.
There, none distinguish 'twixt your shame or pride,
Weakness or delicacy, all so nice, 205
That each may seem a virtue or a vice.
In men we various ruling passions find.
In women, two almost divide the kind.
Those, only fixed, they first or last obey,
The love of pleasure, and the love of sway. 210
That, Nature gives, and where the lesson taught
Is but to please, can pleasure seem a fault?
Experience, this. By man's oppression cursed,
They seek the second not to lose the first.
Men, some to business, some to pleasure take, 215
But every woman is at heart a rake.
Men, some to quiet, some to public strife,
But every lady would be queen for life.
Yet mark the fate of a whole sex of queens!
Power all their end, but beauty all the means. 220
In youth they conquer with so wild a rage,

As leaves them scarce a subject in their age.
For foreign glory, foreign joy, they roam;
No thought of peace or happiness at home.
But wisdom's triumph is well-timed retreat,   225
As hard a science to the fair as great!
Beauties, like tyrants, old and friendless grown,
Yet hate repose, and dread to be alone.
Worn out in public, weary every eye,
Nor leave one sigh behind them when they die.   230
    Pleasures the sex, as children birds, pursue,
Still out of reach, yet never out of view;
Sure, if they catch, to spoil the toy at most,
To covet flying, and regret when lost.
At last, to follies youth could scarce defend,   235
It grows their age's prudence to pretend,
Ashamed to own they gave delight before,
Reduced to feign it, when they give no more:
As hags hold sabbaths, less for joy than spite,
So these their merry, miserable night.   240
Still round and round the ghosts of beauty glide,
And haunt the places where their honour died.
    See how the world its veterans rewards!
A youth of frolics, an old age of cards.
Fair to no purpose, artful to no end,   245
Young without lovers, old without a friend,
A fop their passion, but their prize a sot,
Alive, ridiculous, and dead, forgot!
    Ah, friend! to dazzle let the vain design.
To raise the thought and touch the heart be thine!   250
That charm shall grow, while what fatigues the Ring,
Flaunts and goes down, an unregarded thing,
So when the sun's broad beam has tired the sight,
All mild ascends the moon's more sober light,
Serene in virgin modesty she shines,   255
And unobserved the glaring orb declines.
    Oh! blessed with temper, whose unclouded ray
Can make to-morrow cheerful as to-day,
She who can love a sister's charms, or hear
Sighs for a daughter with unwounded ear;   260
She who ne'er answers till a husband cools,
Or, if she rules him, never shows she rules;

Charms by accepting, by submitting sways,
Yet has her humour most when she obeys,
Lets fops or fortune fly which way they will,   265
Disdains all loss of tickets, or codille,
Spleen, vapours, or smallpox, above them all,
And mistress of herself, though China fall.
   And yet, believe me, good as well as ill,
Woman's at best a contradiction still.   270
Heaven, when it strives to polish all it can
Its last best work, but forms a softer man;
Picks from each sex, to make the favourite blessed,
Your love of pleasure, our desire of rest;
Blends, in exception to all general rules;   275
Your taste of follies, with our scorn of fools:
Reserve with frankness, art with truth allied,
Courage with softness, modesty with pride,
Fixed principles, with fancy ever new;
Shakes all together, and produces – you!   280
   Be this a woman's fame. With this unblessed,
Toasts live a scorn, and queens may die a jest.
This Phoebus promised (I forget the year)
When those blue eyes first opened on the sphere.
Ascendant Phoebus watched that hour with care,   285
Averted half your parents' simple prayer,
And gave you beauty, but denied the pelf
That buys your sex a tyrant o'er itself.
The generous god, who wit and gold refines,
And ripens spirits as he ripens mines,   290
Kept dross for duchesses, the world shall know it,
To you gave sense, good humour and a poet.

First published in 1735, *Epistle to a Lady* appeared later as the second of the four
Epistles to Several Persons. In this format, the *Epistle* was intended to make part
of Pope's unfinished 'Opus Magnum', a large-scale philosophical work at the
centre of which was to have stood *An Essay on Man* (1733–4). The best annotated
version is F.W. Bateson's third volume of the Twickenham edition, and the
present editors are indebted to that.

   The poem is a Horatian epistle, that is, a poetic letter containing morality, wit
and satire. As such it is related to *Epistle to Dr Arbuthnot*, though it differs from
that poem in tone. Where in *Arbuthnot* Pope frequently adopts a voice of
exasperated rage, in *To a Lady* he is usually more detached and judicial.

   Like the other poems of Pope in this volume, *To a Lady* is written in heroic
couplets (see introductory notes to *The Rape of the Lock*). A comparative reading

of the different poems reveals the range of effects which Pope was able to achieve with this restricted form.

[Pope's] Argument

Of the characters of women (considered only as contradistinguished from the other sex). That these are yet more inconsistent and incomprehensible than those of men, of which instances are given even from such characters as are plainest and most strongly marked: as in the affected (line 7, etc.), the soft natured (line 29), the cunning (line 45), the whimsical (line 53), the wits and refiners (line 87), the stupid and silly (line 101) – how contrarieties run through them all.

But though the particular characters of this sex are more various than those of men, the general characteristic, as to the ruling passion, is more uniform and confined. In what that lies and whence it proceeds (line 207, etc.). Men are best known in public life, women in private (line 199). What are the aims and the fate of the sex both as to power and pleasure (lines 219, 231, etc.)? Advice for their true interest (line 249). The picture of an estimable woman, made up of the best kind of contrarieties (line 269, etc.).

[Pope's] Advertisement

The author being very sensible how particular a tenderness is due to the female sex, and at the same time how little they generally show to each other, declares upon his honour that no one character is drawn from the life in this epistle. It would otherwise be most improperly inscribed to a lady, who of all the women he knows is the last that would be entertained at the expense of another.

Title
to a Lady: Martha Blount (1690–1763), Pope's long-standing and intimate friend, possibly (but perhaps not probably) his mistress; *Of the* concerning the. Pope announces the subject of the epistle in the title.
[1] you
i.e. Martha. It is a clever ploy to begin a satire on women with a remark by a woman about women.
[2] no characters at all
Pope's note explains that Martha held that women's 'characters are not so strongly marked as those of men, seldom so fixed and still more inconsistent with themselves'.
[3] Matter
substance, the female substance.
[4] black, brown or fair
i.e. hair colours. John Donne distinguishes in the same way in the poem which begins, 'I can love both fair and brown'.

[5] nymph
a class of classical demi-goddesses who inhabit rivers etc., hence poetically, a woman especially a young and beautiful one.
[6] All how ... true
i.e. Wealthy women have themselves painted in a great variety of different poses and settings, yet all these portraits are in some way true of them. What follows is a list of the different kinds of portrait.
[7] Arcadia's Countess
A note, probably approved, if not written, by Pope, points out that in this satire on women there are no real names. However, the full title of Sir Philip Sidney's romance, *The Countess of Pembroke's Arcadia* (1593), suggests that a Pembroke may be intended; *ermined pride* ermine is worn by peers.
[8] Pastora
a name which derives from the word 'pastoral'. The portrait shows the

subject dressed as a shepherdess, a common pose – see note to line 43 of Montagu's *Saturday: The Small-Pox.*

[9] **leering**
the word did not necessarily carry a sexual connotation; *own good man* husband, i.e. in this portrait she is the besotted wife.

[10] **Leda**
In Greek mythology Leda was impregnated by Zeus disguised as a swan – a subject for semi-erotic painting.

[12] **Magdalen**
The weeping sinner who anointed Jesus' feet with tears and ointment (Luke 7: 37–8) is traditionally identified with Mary Magdalen (John 11: 2); *lifted eye* Painters frequently pictured saints and mystics with eyes raised heavenwards.

[13] **Cecilia**
The patron saint of music; see Dryden's *Alexander's Feast.*

[16] **romantic**
extravagant, showy; *I must* signalling a shift in focus from the portraitists to Pope.

[17] **the ground**
a technical term for the first coating of colour put on canvas by painters.

[18] **Dip**
immerse in colour; *rainbow* suggestive of the variety of women; *trick her off* sketch her; *in air* suggestive of the insubstantiality of women.

[20] **Cynthia**
the goddess of the moon, hence of change.

[21] **Rufa**
red haired. Red hair was associated with lechery. Pope probably has no individual woman in mind here.

[22] **Attracts**
The metaphor is from Newton's theory of attraction (gravity). Rufa's eye exerts a gravitational pull on the meteor-like fops; *spark* beau, fop.

[23] **Locke**
John Locke (1632–1704), late seventeenth-century philosopher and highly influential thinker throughout the eighteenth century.

[24] **Sappho**
Here there is a personal reference, for Pope had used the name of the Greek poetess (Sappho) in earlier poems to signify his enemy, Lady Mary Wortley Montagu. See *Epistle to Dr Arbuthnot,* line 101 and note; *smock* an undergarment.

[25] **toilet**
dressing table; *greasy* because of the application of face paint.

[26] **mask**
masked ball.

[27] **fly-blow**
lay eggs; figuratively, spread corruption.

[29] **Silia**
from the Latin 'silex', flint, hence connoting hardness.

[31] **Calista**
a guilty heroine; *nice* proper.

[32] **Simplicius**
The name suggests a simple man.

[33] **tip the wink**
give a private signal implying something (here drunkenness).

[37] **Papillia**
suggestive of a butterfly; *spark* fop, beau.

[38] **park**
refers here to the extensive grounds which might surround an estate in the country.

[39] **the fair**
The word was used to mean both women collectively and the individual woman.

[40] **odious, odious**
Both the word and the repetition suggest fashionable affectation.

[41] **variegated**
with petals of several colours.

[44] **happy**
fortunate; *spots* faults, defects; *nice* refined, fastidious.

[45] **Calypso**
the nymph with whom the shipwrecked Odysseus lived (against his will) for ten years. A specific reference to the Duchess of Hamilton may be intended here; *alarmed* called to arms, frightened.

[49] **flights**
of the imagination.

[51] **our passion**
Pope addresses the effect of women on men as well as women themselves.

[53] **Narcissa**
The Narcissus of myth fell in love with his own reflection in a stream. Narcissa is the female version of this kind of vanity.

[54] **wash**
liquid preparation for the skin, a cosmetic.

[55] **lover's prayer**
presumably to sleep with him.

[57] **alms**
money given to the poor; *trim* suit of clothes, dress. The line implies that the clothes were more important than the alms.

[58] **widow happy**
i.e. with the alms.

[59] **Why then declare**
It is presumably she who declares this.

[60] **can be borne**
i.e. it is only these occasional good-natured acts which make her bearable.

[61] **Why pique . . . name?**
Why does she deliberately offend ('pique') everybody, and yet still wish to be well thought of ('affect a name')?

[63] **Taylor**
Jeremy Taylor, a seventeenth-century writer of popular piety; *Book of Martyrs* Probably the most widely read book of the sixteenth century after the Bible and the Prayer Book, John Foxe's *Martyrs* is especially notable for its many accounts of Protestants who died under Catholic tyranny. By Pope's day the book was no longer so widely read.

[64] **citron**
brandy and lemon; *his Grace and Chartres* the Duke of Wharton and Francis Charteris, two men known for profanity and depraved living.

[68] **sad**
sober, serious.

[70] **punk**
whore.

[71] **frank**
here, free in a sexual sense.

[72] **teeming**
fecund, bearing many children.

[73] **blood**
supposed to be the seat of passion.

[75–6] **Such this . . . wit**
i.e. one day she claims that her sexual irregularities are purely physical, while the next she sleeps with a poet 'for his mind'.

[78] **Tall-boy**
a fool in a popular comedy; *Charles* The stock name for a footman, as Betty was the stock name for a maid; *Charlemagne* the eighth-century Holy Roman Emperor.

[79] **Helluo**
glutton.

[80] **haut-gout**
having a strong taste or smell; *tip* highest point.

[83] **So**
the woman is to be compared with Helluo who, while an epicure when invited out to eat, dines on plain fare at home; *Philomede* Pope finally provides the name of this character, 'lover (the Greek meaning of philo) of the Medes', implicitly of the strange.

[84] **the soft passion**
i.e. of love.

[85] **address**
refined courtship.

[87] **Flavia**
a common Roman name; *wit* used here to mean an intellectual; *too much sense to pray* ironic.

[88] **wants**
the things we lack.

[89] **but of her stars**
i.e. she indulges in astrology.

[90] **'While . . . live.'**
The wish typifies Flavia's irreligious cast of mind.

[91] **all for death**
Flavia's desire to live life for the moment is balanced by a morbid fascination with death; *opiate of the soul* i.e. she regards death in terms of deep sleep, not (as a Christian does) in terms of a definite hereafter.

[92] **Lucretia's dagger**
Lucretia was a legendary heroine of

ancient Rome who stabbed herself to
death after being raped; *Rosamonda's
bowl* In medieval legend Rosamund
was forced against her will to marry
King Alboin, who later made her
drink from her dead father's skull.
Having murdered Alboin, she went
on to marry a second husband, to plot
to murder him as well, to be discovered. She was then killed herself with
a poisoned cup by the intended
victim.

[94] **spark**
fop, here implicitly a lover; *fickle*
unreliable and false.

[97] **quickness**
in the sense of mental quickness.

[98] **common thought**
common sense. She's too much of an
intellectual to be sensible.

[99] **You . . . can give**
i.e. your pursuit of pleasure leads only
to pain.

[100] **rage**
intemperate desire, violent passion.

[101] **Turn then from wits**
The sentence reflects the ordered
character of the *Epistle*. To this
point Pope has systematically dealt
with types of women, illustrating
each type with an example. The
passage which follows sums up
the general point about female incon-
sistency with a rapid-fire list of
inconstant women; *Simo* suggests
snub-nosed.

[103] **owns**
admits; *mends* i.e. never improves.

[104] **she's honest**
her excuse for failing to overcome her
weaknesses.

[107] **Or her**
cf. Narcissa, lines 63–8; *her grace* the
title for a duchess. It is not clear
whether Pope had a specific duchess
in mind.

[108] **'how charming . . .'**
a fashionable, affected way of speaking; *no such place* Although this
woman claims to laugh at hell her
words expose a secret fear of it.

[109] **vicissitude**
change.

[110] **opium**
The soporific effects of opium are the
opposite of mirth; *ratafia* a kind of
cherry brandy, associated with social
merry-making.

[111] **anodyne**
painkiller; *draught* dose of liquid
medicine, implicitly a sleeping potion.

[112] **To kill . . . thought**
i.e. the medicines of the previous line
are taken to kill time and thought, the
enemies of women ('fair ones').

[113] **hit**
here, to represent, to hit off.

[114] **true no-meaning**
the central idea of the *Epistle*, that
women have no firm character.

[115] **what . . . mind?**
i.e. what are these compared with
Atossa's mind; *Atossa* The historical
Atossa was a daughter of Cyrus of
Persia and sister of his successor,
Cambyses. Although the character of
Atossa seems to be drawn from life,
scholars have disagreed as to the
identity of the original. In all probability Pope meant Katherine Darnley,
Duchess of Buckinghamshire
(1682?–1743). As natural daughter of
James II she was like Atossa in having
royal blood, and her half-brother was
James Edward (the Old Pretender)
who if he did not succeed his father
like Cambyses was at least a claimant
to the throne.

[116] **Scarce once . . . womankind**
Compare Dryden's portrait of Zimri
in *Absalom and Achitophel*, lines
544–50.

[117] **with herself**
i.e. she is at war with herself.

[118] **warfare upon earth**
Pope once declared the life of a wit to
be 'a warfare upon earth'. The wars of
the duchess took the form of civil litigation with her dead husband's
natural children over his will.

[119] **Shines**
excels; *knaves* deceitful, dishonest
men.

[121] **eddy brain**
Eddy (whirlpool) is used with the full
metaphorical sense as the following

line makes clear. The duchess became insane at the end of her life.

[123] **world**
high society, the polite world of politics and intrigue.

[124] **much time**
the long life referred to in the previous line. In fact, the duchess was still alive when Pope wrote. The couplet may have been carried over from another portrait.

[127] **wit**
used to mean reason, good sense. The line implies a connection between her bad temper and her eventual madness.

[128] **The pleasure . . . hit**
The sense is that she was so given to anger that she could not enjoy (implicitly) a liaison, though she still reaped the scandal of it. The duchess was supposed to have had an affair with her doctor.

[130] **be well**
be on good terms with.

[131] **turn**
action.

[132] **No more . . . gratitude**
i.e. her gratitude is as violent as her hate.

[133] **that**
i.e. hate; *or . . . or* either . . . or.

[138] **Oblige her**
do something for her.

[139] **But . . . you**
refers to the duchess's extravagant behaviour on the death of her husband; *bust* made in honour of the dead.

[140] **temple**
again erected in honour of the dead; *fall . . . dust* Inconstant even in extravagance, she soon loses interest.

[141] **her lord**
her husband.

[142] **his will a cheat**
see line 118 and note.

[144] **spirit**
vigour of mind, vivacity. The quality which would normally lead to power is so misdirected with Atossa that it deprives her of it; *warmth* affection, passion, anger. Warmth (affection)

usually wins friends but Atossa's warmth (ill temper) loses them.

[145] **wealth**
The wealth which usually attracts followers alienates them in Atossa's case, presumably because it is that which allows her to give her eccentricities full rein.

[147] **granted prayer**
in that she has got everything she wants.

[148] **Childless**
Her children died before her; *wants* lacks.

[149] **unguarded**
in that there are neither heirs nor a satisfactory will; *store* i.e. her wealth.

[151] **Pictures**
back to the imagery of painting – see lines 5–20; *dear Madam* Martha Blount – see the note to the title; *design* to sketch, to fashion the work of art.

[153] **touches**
of the pen or brush.

[154] **hit them**
in the sense of hit them (the pictures) off.

[155] **equal colours**
unmixed colours; *do the knack* do the trick, be adequate.

[156] **Chameleons**
i.e. who can paint chameleons in white and black? Chameleons are known for their ability to change into many colours.

[157] **'Yet . . .'**
Martha's interjection; *Chloe* a common name in pastorals. Some lines of the portrait which follows may describe Henrietta Howard, Countess of Suffolk (1681–1767); *without a spot* faultless.

[158] **Nature . . . forgot**
i.e. if nature gave Chloe no faults in making her, it left something out.

[159] **part**
attribute.

[160] **want**
lack. Martha is responding to Pope's imputation that nature forgot something with Chloe.

[164] **decencies**
i.e. minor social virtues. This sense of Chloe is already implied in Martha's defence of her in line 159. 'Prudent' and 'pleasing' are distinctly faint adjectives.

[168] **Indian chest**
Goods imported from the East were fashionable accessories. See *Rape of the Lock*, i, 133–6.

[170] **chintz**
painted calico imported from India; *mohair* fine cloth made from the hair of the angora goat.

[171–2] **Forbid it ... forget**
i.e. she will not blot out or deny the debts and favours she owes, but she might forget about them.

[175] **dears**
those close to her.

[176] **undone**
ruined in some way.

[181] **(I grant)**
he is conceding that this portrait is somewhat different from the others.

[182] **varnished out**
The painting has been finished and had varnish applied to it. The fact that Heaven has done the varnishing implies, with considerable irony, a perfect work; *a queen* Queen Caroline – see notes to *Epistle to Dr Arbuthnot*, lines 319 & 357.

[183] **described**
portrayed. It could be used to mean graphic as well as written portrayal.

[184] **ball**
the golden orb carried with the sceptre by the monarch; *With truth ... ball* i.e. portraitists of one kind or another conferred on her the virtues of truth and goodness as readily as they did her badges of rank.

[186] **zeal**
in the sense of loyalty. They show their zeal by picturing the queen with jewels and virtues; *want* lack.

[187] **To draw the naked**
Cf. *Essay on Criticism*, lines 293–5: 'Poets like painters, thus, unskilled to trace/ The naked nature and the living grace,/ With gold and jewels cover every part.'

[189] **robe**
Cf. *King Lear*, IV, vi, 163: 'Robes and furred gowns hide all'; *quality* in the sense of rank. The reference is clearly to the queen; *struts* here, bulges, protrudes.

[190] **None see ... conceals**
The implication is clear that the parts of nature concealed under the queen's robes are unpleasant.

[193] **Queensberry**
Catherine Hyde, Duchess of Queensberry, a notable beauty.

[194] **take**
copy, represent; *Helen* Helen of Troy. The sense of the couplet is: if we cannot induce Queensberry to take off her clothes we must paint the naked Helen with a maid for our model.

[195–6] **From peer ... or king**
Pope has claimed that it is never easy to paint the truth with those in high station because their rank hides their real nature (lines 189–90). The line reflects that idea, while also implying that peers and bishops tend to be disloyal atheists.

[197] **draught**
drawing, representation, portrait.

[198] **Mahomet**
Pope's note refers to the Turkish servant of the late king. The sense is that he may portray the servant not the king; *Hale* Dr Stephen Hales, a curate rather than a bishop.

[199] **But grant ... shown**
i.e. concede that you can sometimes discover the truth about a man from the way that he appears in public. Pope's note concedes that there is a lack of connection at this point, and certainly the transition is very abrupt.

[201] **Our**
belonging to us men; *bolder* used in the sense of striking and pronounced as well as of courageous.

[202] **open**
disclose themselves.

[204] **shame or pride**
i.e. whether it is modesty or hauteur which keeps the woman silent.

[205] **nice**
refined, shy, coy.

[207] **ruling passions**
Pope believed that every person had one dominant drive which was the key to his whole character and to all his actions. In *Epistle to Cobham* he writes (lines 174–8): 'Search then the ruling passion. There alone/ The wild are constant and the cunning known. ... This clue once found unravels all the rest.' The reference to 'ruling passions' introduces a philosophical note, and relates the poem to the others of the 'Opus Magnum' – see introductory notes.

[208] **the kind**
i.e. womankind. Pope's note maintains that, though each woman is more varied in herself than each man, the female sex as a whole is more uniform than the male.

[209] **only fixed**
the only fixed things where women are concerned.

[210] **sway**
dominance, control; *The love ... sway* the two ruling passions to which most women are subject. The *Epistle*, having offered a series of portraits of women in the earlier part, now considers the sex in general.

[211] **That**
i.e. the love of pleasure (is implanted by nature).

[212] **Is but to please**
is only to be happy, to give pleasure to others.

[213] **Experience, this**
experience gives this (the love of dominance).

[214] **They seek ... first**
i.e. they seek power in order to be able to pursue pleasure.

[215] **take**
as in betake, to give oneself to.

[216] **But**
The contrast is between the variety of men and the uniformity of women in this respect.

[218] **queen for life**
reflecting the female love of dominance.

[220] **Power ... means**
Though women all seek power, they can only obtain it through their beauty.

[221] **rage**
immoderate passion.

[222] **As leaves ... age**
i.e. they make conquests so promiscuously when they are young that few of their lovers remain loyal into old age.

[223] **foreign glory**
continuing the imagery of conquest.

[225] **But wisdom's ... retreat**
i.e. the victory won by wisdom depends upon the timely retreat. Still employing the imagery of war, Pope suggests that women need to know when to give up winning all hearts and (implicitly) to settle with one man.

[226] **science**
body of knowledge, intellectual discipline, not science in the modern sense of natural science.

[227] **like tyrants ... grown**
Pope may be thinking of Macbeth, a tyrant who recognises that in old age he cannot expect 'honour, love, obedience, troops of friends' (*Macbeth*, V, iii, 25).

[228] **hate repose ... alone**
Macbeth's sleep is disturbed by terrible dreams and he throws himself into frantic activity.

[229] **weary**
used as a verb, to make tired.

[230] **Nor leave one sigh**
i.e. no one sighs for them.

[231] **Pleasures ... pursue**
i.e. women ('the sex') pursue pleasures in the same way that children pursue birds.

[234] **covet flying**
i.e. to desire to catch the bird when flying.

[236] **to pretend**
to aspire to, to claim; also, the modern sense, to profess falsely. The sense of the couplet is that in old age women indulge in follies which even youth would shy from.

[237] **own**
admit; *before* i.e. in their youth (they would not admit sexual liaisons).

[238] **Reduced ... no more**
Unable to make conquests in old age, women pretend to them.

[239] **hags**
old women, witches; *sabbaths* sabbats, the witches' midnight meeting presided over by the devil.

[240] **night**
an evening set aside for receiving visitors.

[241] **round and round**
suggestive both of the witches' dance and of the aged socialites' trailing round London from one fashionable event to another.

[242] **haunt ... died**
The ghosts of murdered people are supposed to haunt the scene of the crime; likewise these women haunt the places where they surrendered themselves and lost their reputations.

[244] **cards**
Playing cards was commonly represented as the consuming activity of rich old women.

[245] **Fair**
beautiful; *artful* cunning, like the old women playing cards.

[246] **without lovers**
Young women, like Belinda in *The Rape of the Lock*, were deprived of lovers by their own coquetry.

[247] **sot**
a fool, specifically a drunken fool; *A fop ... sot* They loved a fop but they married a sot.

[249] **friend**
Martha again – see note to title; *design* plan, aspire.

[250] **raise**
to elevate, improve.

[251] **Ring**
a fashionable place of recreation in Hyde Park; *what fatigues the Ring* Rather a clumsy Latinate expression, it suggests someone who frequents the ring to a point of weariness and boredom.

[255] **virgin modesty**
Diana (or Artemis), the goddess of the moon, was a virgin.

[256] **glaring orb declines**
i.e. the sun goes down.

[257] **temper**
temperament, character, especially moderate equable character.

[259–60] **She who ... ear**
refers to common ideas about the jealousies subsisting even between women very close to each other.

[261] **cools**
i.e. calms down after anger.

[263] **sways**
dominates.

[264] **has her humour**
it suits her temperament best when.

[266] **tickets**
lottery tickets; *codille* a term in the card game, ombre. See *The Rape of the Lock* (iii, 25–100).

[267] **Spleen**
selfish and excessive dejection, peevishness. See the description of the Cave of Spleen in *The Rape of the Lock* (iv, 15–54); *smallpox* Martha had suffered from this.

[268] **though China fall**
refers to the excessive concern of women over expensive ornaments. Compare *The Rape of the Lock* (ii, 105–6): 'Whether the nymph shall break Diana's law/ Or some frail China jar receive a flaw'. See also Canto Three, 157–60, and Canto Four, 162–3.

[271] **polish**
finish, improve.

[272] **last best work**
Eve was, according to one biblical account, created after Adam (Genesis 2: 21–2). The word 'best', in part simply a compliment to women, also glances back to Milton's account of the creation of Eve (*Paradise Lost*, viii, 471–3): 'so lovely fair/ That what seemed fair in all the world, seemed now/ Mean or in her summed up'.

[273] **favourite**
i.e. the one chosen out to be polished.

[274] **rest**
in the sense of stillness or steadiness rather than repose.

[277] **art**
studied conduct, · self-conscious behaviour.

[282] **Toasts**
women to whom toasts are made, famous beauties. The sense is that without the qualities outlined above, even great beauties live to be scorned.

[283] **Phoebus**
Phoebus/Apollo, the god of poetry who is also associated with the sun; *the year* of Martha's birth.

[284] **those blue eyes**
i.e. Martha's; *the sphere* Phoebus's sphere, the sun.

[285] **Ascendant**
used in the astrological sense. Phoebus, the sun, appearing over the eastern horizon at Martha's birth, became the ascendant 'planet' in her life, the dominating force in her horoscope.

[286] **simple**
undesigning, straightforward.

[287] **pelf**
money, the second thing, with beauty, which Martha's parents asked for.

[288] **tyrant o'er itself**
Money, by allowing a woman to indulge every passion and fancy, reduces her to the subject of her own wayward desires. This is the case of Atossa.

[289] **wit and gold refines**
To refine is to separate the pure metal from the dross (the scum left behind in smelting). Phoebus can be said to refine wit as he is the god of poetry, and gold, since it was believed (by the uninformed) that gold was made by the sun's rays.

[290] **spirits**
i.e. of poets; *mines* i.e. gold mines.

[291] **dross**
impure elements left when metal is smelted – continuing the gold imagery; *the world shall know it* because Pope is telling the world in the *Epistle*.

[292] **good humour**
The value laid by Pope on this quality is clear from Clarissa's speech in *The Rape of the Lock* (v, 9–34).

JAMES THOMSON

(1700–48)

James Thomson was born in 1700 at Ednam in Roxburghshire. He was educated at Edinburgh College, now the University of Edinburgh, and then prepared to enter the Presbyterian ministry. In 1725, however, he left Scotland for good, and in London wrote *Winter*. He revised his poem and added a preface to it in the same year. In February 1727 he published *Summer*. Isaac Newton died on 20 March and Thomson's poem on his death, *A Poem sacred to the Memory of Sir Isaac Newton*, appeared in May. *Spring* followed in 1728, and in 1730 appeared the first collected edition of *The Seasons*, including *Autumn*. Alexander Pope was among the subscribers to *The Seasons*. Over the next few years Thomson travelled extensively in Europe as the tutor of Charles Talbot. By 1736 he had published the five parts of *Liberty*. *The Seasons* continued to occupy him, and in 1744 he published a greatly enlarged and much revised edition. A final edition of *The Seasons* appeared in 1746. In 1748 Thomson published *The Castle of Indolence*, a Spenserian imitation. *The Castle of Indolence* is markedly different from his other work, especially in its use of wit. Thomson died at Richmond in 1748.

Further Reading

The standard edition of Thomson's poetry is J.L. Robertson (ed.), *The Complete Poetical Works of James Thomson* (London: Oxford University Press, 1908). There are more modern editions of *The Seasons* edited by James Sambrook, of which the paperback, *The Seasons and the Castle of Indolence* (Oxford: Oxford University Press, 1972) has proved extremely useful to the present editors.

Two biographies might be consulted: Douglas Grant's, *James Thomson, Poet of the Seasons* (London: Cresset Press, 1961) contains no critical comment, while Johnson's *Life of Thomson* remains interesting. An account of the poetry in general is provided by Hilbert H. Campbell's *James Thomson* (Boston, Mass.: Twayne, 1979). Two books devoted specifically to *The Seasons* are Alan Dugald McKillop's *The Background of Thomson's Seasons* (Minneapolis: University of Minnesota Press, 1942), and Ralph Cohen's *The Unfolding of the Seasons* (London: Routledge and Kegan Paul, 1964).

The editors also wish to acknowledge L.P. Wilkinson's translation of Virgil, *The Georgics* (Harmondsworth: Penguin, 1984) and R.E. Latham's translation of Lucretius, *On the Nature of the Universe* (Harmondsworth: Penguin, 1951).

———————◇———————

25 /   From *Winter*

See! Winter comes, to rule the varied year,
Sullen, and sad; with all his rising train;
Vapours, and clouds, and storms. Be these my theme,
These, that exalt the soul to solemn thought,
And heavenly musing. Welcome, kindred glooms!   5
Cogenial horrors, hail! With frequent foot,
Pleased have I, in my cheerful morn of life,
When nursed by careless solitude I lived,
And sung of nature with unceasing joy,
Pleased have I wandered through your rough domain;   10
Trod the pure virgin-snows, myself as pure,
Heard the winds roar, and the big torrent burst:
Or seen the deep-fermenting tempest brewed
In the grim evening-sky. Thus passed the time,
Till, through the lucid chambers of the south   15
Looked out the joyous spring, looked out and smiled.

To thee, the patron of this first essay,
The muse, O Wilmington! renews her song.
Since she has rounded the revolving year:
Skimmed the gay Spring; on eagle-pinions borne,   20

Attempted through the summer-blaze to rise,
Then swept o'er Autumn with the shadowy gale.
And now among the Wintry clouds again,
Rolled in the doubling storm, she tries to soar,
To swell her note with all the rushing winds,   25
To suit her sounding cadence to the floods;
As is her theme, her numbers wildly great:
Thrice happy, could she fill thy judging ear
With bold description and with manly thought.
Nor art thou skilled in aweful schemes alone,   30
And how to make a mighty people thrive;
But equal goodness, sound integrity,
A firm, unshaken, uncorrupted soul
Amid a sliding age, and burning strong,
Not vainly blazing, for the country's weal,   35
A steady spirit, regularly free:
These, each exalting each, the statesman light
Into the patriot; these the public hope
And eye to thee converting, bid the muse
Record what envy dares not flattery call.   40

　　Now, when the cheerless empire of the sky
To Capricorn the Centaur-Archer yields,
And fierce Aquarius stains the inverted year;
Hung o'er the farthest verge of heaven, the sun
Scarce spreads o'er ether the dejected day.   45
Faint are his gleams, and ineffectual shoot
His struggling rays in horizontal lines
Through the thick air; as clothed in cloudy storm,
Weak, wan, and broad, he skirts the southern sky;
And, soon descending, to the long dark night,   50
Wide-shading all, the prostrate world resigns.
Nor is the night unwished; while vital heat,
Light, life, and joy, the dubious day forsake;
Meantime, in sable cincture, shadows vast,
Deep-tinged and damp, and congregated clouds,   55
And all the vapoury turbulence of heaven
Involve the face of things. Thus Winter falls,
A heavy gloom oppressive o'er the world,
Through nature shedding influence malign,
And rouses up the seeds of dark disease.   60

The soul of man dies in him, loathing life,
And black with more than melancholy views;
The cattle droop; and o'er the furrowed land,
Fresh from the plough, the dun discoloured flocks,
Untended spreading, crop the wholesome root.   65
Along the woods, along the moorish fens,
Sighs the sad genius of the coming storm,
And up among the loose disjointed cliffs
And fractured mountains wild, the brawling brook
And cave, presageful, send a hollow moan,   70
Resounding long in listening fancy's ear.

    Then comes the father of the tempest forth,
Wrapped in black glooms. First, joyless rains obscure
Drive through the mingling skies with vapour foul,
Dash on the mountain's brow, and shake the woods   75
That grumbling wave below. The unsightly plain
Lies a brown deluge; as the low-bent clouds
Pour flood on flood, yet unexhausted still
Combine, and deepening into night, shut up
The day's fair face. The wanderers of heaven,   80
Each to his home, retire; save those that love
To take their pastime in the troubled air,
Or skimming flutter round the dimply pool.
The cattle from the untasted fields return
And ask, with meaning low, their wonted stalls,   85
Or ruminate in the contiguous shade.
Thither the household feathery people crowd,
The crested cock, with all his female train,
Pensive and dripping; while the cottage-hind
Hangs o'er the enlivening blaze, and taleful there   90
Recounts his simple frolic: much he talks,
And much he laughs, nor recks the storm that blows
Without, and rattles on his humble roof.

    Wide o'er the brim, with many a torrent swelled,
And the mixed ruin of its banks o'erspread,   95
At last the roused-up river pours along;
Resistless, roaring, dreadful, down it comes,
From the rude mountain and the mossy wild,
Tumbling through rocks abrupt, and sounding far;

322

Then o'er the sanded valley floating spreads,   100
Calm, sluggish, silent; till again, constrained
Between two meeting hills, it bursts a way
Where rocks and woods o'erhang the turbid stream:
There, gathering triple force, rapid and deep,
It boils, and wheels, and foams, and thunders through.   105

   Nature! great parent! whose unceasing hand
Rolls round the seasons of the changeful year,
How mighty, how majestic, are thy works!
With what a pleasing dread they swell the soul,
That sees astonished, and astonished sings!   110
Ye too, ye winds! that now begin to blow
With boisterous sweep, I raise my voice to you;
Where are your stores, ye powerful beings! say,
Where your aerial magazines reserved
To swell the brooding terrors of the storm?   115
In what far-distant region of the sky,
Hushed in deep silence, sleep you when 'tis calm?

. . . .

   The keener tempests come: and, fuming dun
From all the livid east or piercing north,
Thick clouds ascend, in whose capacious womb   120
A vapoury deluge lies, to snow congealed.
Heavy they roll their fleecy world along,
And the sky saddens with the gathered storm.
Through the hushed air the whitening shower descends,
At first thin-wavering; till at last the flakes   125
Fall broad and wide and fast, dimming the day
With a continual flow. The cherished fields
Put on their winter-robe of purest white;
'Tis brightness all; save where the new snow melts
Along the mazy current. Low the woods   130
Bow their hoar head; and, ere the languid sun
Faint from the west emits his evening ray,
Earth's universal face, deep-hid and chill,
In one wild dazzling waste, that buries wide
The works of man. Drooping, the labourer-ox   135
Stands covered o'er with snow, and then demands

323

The fruit of all his toil. The fowls of heaven,
Tamed by the cruel season, crowd around
The winnowing store, and claim the little boon
Which Providence assigns them. One alone,   140
The redbreast, sacred to the household gods,
Wisely regardful of the embroiling sky,
In joyless fields and thorny thickets leaves
His shivering mates, and pays to trusted man
His annual visit. Half afraid, he first   145
Against the window beats; then brisk, alights
On the warm hearth; then, hopping o'er the floor,
Eyes all the smiling family askance,
And pecks, and starts, and wonders where he is:
Till, more familiar grown, the table-crumbs   150
Attract his slender feet. The foodless wilds
Pour forth their brown inhabitants. The hare,
Though timorous of heart, and hard beset
By death in various forms, dark snares, and dogs,
And more unpitying men, the garden seeks,   155
Urged on by fearless want. The bleating kind
Eye the bleak heaven, and next the glistening earth,
With looks of dumb despair; then, sad-dispersed,
Dig for the withered herb through heaps of snow.

Now, shepherds to your helpless charge be kind,   160
Baffle the raging year, and fill their pens
With food at will; lodge them below the storm,
And watch them strict: for, from the bellowing east,
In this dire season, oft the whirlwind's wing
Sweeps up the burden of whole wintry plains   165
In one wide waft, and o'er the hapless flocks,
Hid in the hollow of two neighbouring hills,
The billowy tempest whelms; till, upward urged,
The valley to a shining mountain swells
Tipped with a wreath high-curling in the sky.   170

As thus the snows arise, and foul, and fierce,
All Winter drives along the darkened air,
In his own loose-revolving fields, the swain
Disastered stands; sees other hills ascend,
Of unknown joyless brow; and other scenes,   175

Of horrid prospect, shag the trackless plain;
Nor finds the river nor the forest, hid
Beneath the formless wild; but wanders on
From hill to dale, still more and more astray;
Impatient flouncing through the drifted heaps,   180
Stung with the thoughts of home: the thoughts of home
Rush on his nerves and call their vigour forth
In many a vain attempt. How sinks his soul!
What black despair, what horror fills his heart,
When, for the dusky spot which fancy feigned   185
His tufted cottage rising through the snow,
He meets the roughness of the middle waste,
Far from the track and blessed abode of man,
While round him night resistless closes fast,
And every tempest, howling o'er his head,   190
Renders the savage wilderness more wild.
Then throng the busy shapes into his mind
Of covered pits, unfathomably deep,
A dire descent! beyond the power of frost:
Of faithless bogs; of precipices huge,   195
Smoothed up with snow; and what is land unknown,
What water, of the still unfrozen spring,
In the loose marsh or solitary lake,
Where the fresh fountain from the bottom boils;
These check his fearful steps, and down he sinks   200
Beneath the shelter of the shapeless drift,
Thinking o'er all the bitterness of death,
Mixed with the tender anguish nature shoots
Through the wrung bosom of the dying man,
His wife, his children, and his friends unseen.   205
In vain for him the officious wife prepares
The fire fair-blazing and the vestment warm,
In vain his little children, peeping out
Into the mingling storm, demand their sire
With tears of artless innocence. Alas!   210
Nor wife nor children more shall he behold,
Nor friends, nor sacred home. On every nerve
The deadly Winter seizes, shuts up sense,
And o'er his inmost vitals creeping cold,
Lays him along the snows a stiffened corpse,   215
Stretched out, and bleaching in the northern blast.

Ah! little think the gay licentious proud,
Whom pleasure, power and affluence surround,
They, who their thoughtless hours in giddy mirth,
And wanton, often cruel, riot waste;   220
Ah! little think they, while they dance along,
How many feel, this very moment, death
And all the sad variety of pain;
How many sink in the devouring flood,
Or more devouring flame; how many bleed,   225
By shameful variance betwixt man and man;
How many pine in want, and dungeon-glooms,
Shut from the common air and common use
Of their own limbs; how many drink the cup
Of baleful grief, or eat the bitter bread   230
Of misery; sore pierced by wintry winds,
How many shrink into the sordid hut
Of cheerless poverty; how many shake
With all the fiercer tortures of the mind,
Unbounded passion, madness, guilt, remorse,   235
Whence, tumbled headlong from the height of life,
They furnish matter for the tragic muse.
Even in the vale, where wisdom loves to dwell,
With friendship, peace, and contemplation joined,
How many, racked with honest passions, droop   240
In deep retired distress; how many stand
Around the death-bed of their dearest friends,
And point the parting anguish! Thought fond man
Of these, and all the thousand nameless ills
That one incessant struggle render life,   245
One scene of toil, of suffering, and of fate,
Vice in his high career would stand appalled,
And heedless rambling impulse learn to think.
The conscious heart of charity would warm,
And her wide wish benevolence dilate;   250
The social tear would rise, the social sigh;
And, into clear perfection, gradual bliss,
Refining still, the social passions work.

.   .   .   .

Thus in some deep retirement would I pass
The winter-glooms with friends of pliant soul,   255
Or blithe, or solemn, as the theme inspired:
With them would search if nature's boundless frame
Was called, late-rising, from the void of night,
Or sprung eternal from the Eternal Mind;
Its life, its laws, its progress, and its end.   260
Hence larger prospects of the beauteous whole
Would gradual open on our opening minds,
And each diffusive harmony unite
In full perfection to the astonished eye.
Then would we try to scan the moral world,   265
Which, though to us it seems embroiled, moves on
In higher order, fitted and impelled
By wisdom's finest hand, and issuing all
In general good. The sage historic muse
Should next conduct us through the deeps of time,   270
Show us how empire grew, declined, and fell
In scattered states; what makes the nations smile,
Improves their soil, and gives them double suns;
And why they pine beneath the brightest skies
In nature's richest lap. As thus we talked,   275
Our hearts would burn within us, would inhale
That portion of divinity, that ray
Of purest heaven, which lights the public soul
Of patriots and of heroes. But, if doomed
In powerless humble fortune to repress   280
These ardent risings of the kindling soul,
Then, even superior to ambition, we
Would learn the private virtues; how to glide
Through shades and plains along the smoothest stream
Of rural life: or, snatched away by hope   285
Through the dim spaces of futurity,
With earnest eye anticipate those scenes
Of happiness and wonder, where the mind,
In endless growth and infinite ascent,
Rises from state to state, and world to world.   290
But when with these the serious thought is foiled,
We, shifting for relief, would play the shapes
Of frolic fancy; and incessant form
Those rapid pictures, that assembled train

Of fleet ideas, never joined before,   295
Whence lively wit excites to gay surprise,
Or folly-painting humour, grave himself,
Calls laughter forth, deep-shaking every nerve.

.   .   .   .

   To thy loved haunt return, my happy muse:
For now, behold! the joyous Winter-days,   300
Frosty, succeed; and through the blue serene,
For sight too fine, the ethereal nitre flies,
Killing infectious damps, and the spent air
Storing afresh with elemental life.
Close crowds the shining atmosphere; and binds   305
Our strengthened bodies in its cold embrace,
Constringent; feeds, and animates our blood;
Refines our spirits, through the new-strung nerves
In swifter sallies darting to the brain,
Where sits the soul, intense, collected, cool,   310
Bright as the skies, and as the season keen.
All nature feels the renovating force
Of Winter, only to the thoughtless eye
In ruin seen. The frost-concocted glebe
Draws in abundant vegetable soul,   315
And gathers vigour for the coming year,
A stronger glow sits on the lively cheek
Of ruddy fire; and luculent along
The purer rivers flow, their sullen deeps,
Transparent, open to the shepherd's gaze,   320
And murmur hoarser at the fixing frost.

   What art thou frost? and whence are thy keen stores
Derived, thou secret all-invading power,
Whom even the illusive fluid cannot fly?
Is not thy potent energy, unseen,   325
Myriads of little salts, or hooked, or shaped
Like double wedges, and diffused immense
Through water, earth, and ether? Hence at eve,
Steamed eager from the red horizon round,
With the fierce rage of Winter deep suffused,   330
An icy gale, oft shifting, o'er the pool

328

Breathes a blue film, and in its mid-career
Arrests the bickering stream. The loosened ice,
Let down the flood, and half dissolved by day,
Rustles no more; but to the sedgy bank   335
Fast grows, or gathers round the pointed stone,
A crystal pavement, by the breath of heaven
Cemented firm; till, seized from shore to shore,
The whole imprisoned river growls below.
Loud rings the frozen earth, and hard reflects   340
A double noise; while, at his evening watch,
The village-dog deters the nightly thief;
The heifer lows; the distant waterfall
Swells in the breeze; and with the hasty tread
Of traveller the hollow-sounding plain   345
Shakes from afar. The full ethereal round,
Infinite worlds disclosing to the view,
Shines out intensely keen, and, all one cope
Of starry glitter, glows from pole to pole:
From pole to pole the rigid influence falls   350
Through the still night, incessant, heavy, strong,
And seizes nature fast. It freezes on;
Till morn, late-rising o'er the drooping world,
Lifts her pale eye unjoyous. Then appears
The various labour of the silent night: 355
Prone from the dripping eave, and dumb cascade,
Whose idle torrents only seem to roar,
The pendent icicle; the frost-work fair,
Where transient hues and fancied figures rise;
Wide-spouted o'er the hill the frozen brook,   360
A livid tract, cold-gleaming on the morn;
The forest bent beneath the plumy wave;
And by the frost refined the whiter snow
Incrusted hard, and sounding to the tread
Of early shepherd, as he pensive seeks   365
His pining flock, or from the mountain-top,
Pleased with the slippery surface, swift descends.

.   .   .   .

Still pressing on, beyond Tornea's lake,
And Hecla flaming through a waste of snow,

And farthest Greenland, to the pole itself,   370
Where failing gradual life at length goes out,
The muse expands her solitary flight;
And, hovering o'er the wild stupendous scene,
Beholds new seas beneath another sky.
Throned in his palace of cerulean ice,   375
Here Winter holds his unrejoicing court;
And through his airy hall the loud misrule
Of driving tempest is for ever heard:
Here the grim tyrant meditates his wrath;
Here arms his winds with all-subduing frost;   380
Moulds his fierce hail, and treasures up his snows,
With which he now oppresses half the globe.

  Thence winding eastward to the Tartar's coast,
She sweeps the howling margin of the main,
Where, undissolving from the first of time,   385
Snows swell on snows amazing to the sky,
And icy mountains high on mountains piled
Seem to the shivering sailor from afar,
Shapeless and white, an atmosphere of clouds.
Projected huge and horrid o'er the surge,   390
Alps frown on Alps; or, rushing hideous down,
As if old chaos was again returned,
Wide-rend the deep, and shake the solid pole.
Ocean itself no longer can resist
The binding fury; but, in all its rage   395
Of tempest taken by the boundless frost,
Is many a fathom to the bottom chained,
And bid to roar no more: a bleak expanse
Shagged o'er with wavy rocks, cheerless, and void
Of every life, that from the dreary months   400
Flies conscious southward. Miserable they!
Who, here entangled in the gathering ice,
Take their last look of the descending sun;
While, full of death and fierce with tenfold frost,
The long long night, incumbent o'er their heads,   405
Falls horrible! Such was the Briton's fate,
As with first prow (what have not Britons dared?)
He for the passage sought, attempted since
So much in vain, and seeming to be shut

By jealous nature with eternal bars.   410
In these fell regions, in Arzina caught,
And to the stony deep his idle ship
Immediate sealed, he with his hapless crew,
Each full exerted at his several task,
Froze into statues: to the cordage glued   415
The sailor, and the pilot to the helm.

    Hard by these shores, where scarce his freezing stream
Rolls the wild Oby, live the last of men;
And, half enlivened by the distant sun,
That rears and ripens men as well as plants,   420
Here human nature wears its rudest form.
Deep from the piercing season sunk in caves,
Here by dull fires and with unjoyous cheer
They waste the tedious gloom. Immersed in furs
Doze the gross race. Nor sprightly jest, nor song,   425
Nor tenderness they know; nor aught of life
Beyond the kindred bears that stalk without.
Till morn at length, her roses drooping all,
Sheds a long twilight brightening o'er their fields
And calls the quivered savage to the chase.   430

    What cannot active government perform,
New-moulding man? Wide-stretching from these shores,
A people savage from remotest time,
A huge neglected empire, one vast mind,
By heaven inspired, from Gothic darkness called.   435
Immortal Peter! first of monarchs! He
His stubborn country tamed, her rocks, her fens,
Her floods, her seas, her ill-submitting sons;
And, while the fierce barbarian he subdued,
To more exalted soul he raised the man: 440
Ye shades of ancient heroes, ye who toiled
Through long successive ages to build up
A labouring plan of state, behold at once
The wonder done! behold the matchless prince!
Who left his native throne, where reigned till then   445
A mighty shadow of unreal power;
Who greatly spurned the slothful pomp of courts;

And roaming every land, in every port
His sceptre laid aside, with glorious hand
Unwearied plying the mechanic tool,   450
Gathered the seeds of trade, of useful arts,
Of civil wisdom, and of martial skill.
Charged with the stores of Europe, home he goes!
Then cities rise amid the illumined waste;
O'er joyless deserts smiles the rural reign;   455
Far-distant flood to flood is social joined;
The astonished Euxine hears the Baltic roar,
Proud navies ride on seas that never foamed
With daring keel before; and armies stretch
Each way their dazzling files, repressing here   460
The frantic Alexander of the North,
And awing there stern Othman's shrinking sons.
Sloth flies the land, and ignorance and vice,
Of old dishonour proud: it glows around,
Taught by the royal hand that roused the whole,   465
One scene of arts, of arms, of rising trade:
For, what his wisdom planned and power enforced,
More potent still his great example showed.

.   .   .   .

'Tis done! Dread Winter spreads his latest glooms,
And reigns tremendous o'er the conquered year.   470
How dead the vegetable kingdom lies!
How dumb the tuneful! Horror wide extends
His desolate domain. Behold, fond man!
See here thy pictured life; pass some few years,
Thy flowering spring, thy summer's ardent strength,   475
Thy sober Autumn fading into age,
And pale concluding Winter comes at last
And shuts the scene. Ah! whither now are fled
Those dreams of greatness? those unsolid hopes
Of happiness? those longings after fame?   480
Those restless cares? those busy bustling days?
Those gay-spent festive nights? those veering thoughts,
Lost between good and ill, that shared thy life?
All now are vanished! Virtue sole survives,
Immortal, never-failing friend of man,   485

His guide to happiness on high. And see!
'Tis come, the glorious morn! the second birth
Of heaven and earth! awakening nature hears
The new-creating word, and starts to life
In every heightened form, from pain and death   490
For ever free. The great eternal scheme,
Involving all, and in a perfect whole
Uniting, as the prospect wider spreads,
To reason's eye refined clears up apace.
Ye vainly wise! ye blind presumptuous! now,   495
Confounded in the dust, adore that power
And wisdom oft arraigned: see now the cause
Why unassuming worth in secret lived,
And died neglected: why the good man's share
In life was gall and bitterness of soul: 500
Why the lone widow and her orphans pined
In starving solitude; while luxury
In palaces lay straining her low thought
To form unreal wants: why heaven-born Truth
And moderation fair wore the red marks   505
Of superstition's scourge; why licensed pain,
That cruel spoiler, that embosomed foe,
Embittered all our bliss. Ye good distressed!
Ye noble few! who here unbending stand
Beneath life's pressure, yet bear up awhile,   510
And what your bounded view, which only saw
A little part, deemed evil is no more;
The storms of wintry time will quickly pass,
And one unbounded Spring encircle all.

In his preface to the second edition of *Winter* Thomson wrote:

> I know no subject more elevating, more amusing, more ready to awake the
> poetical enthusiasm, the philosophical reflection, and the moral sentiment,
> than the works of Nature. Where can we meet with such variety, such
> beauty, such magnificence? All that enlarges and transports the soul!

The philosophical context of the poem is eighteenth-century deism, especially
as expounded by Shaftesbury and Francis Hutcheson. The deists believed that
man could arrive at an understanding of and faith in God, without the assistance
of revealed religion, if he worked backwards from the wondrous works of
Nature. Thomson's frequent revisions of his poem transformed it from a merely
descriptive to a reflective and philosophical work. The set-pieces of philo-

sophical reflection in Virgil's *Georgics* also provided him material. The poem has close literary links with *Paradise Lost* and the Book of Job.

Thomson was writing in the tradition of nature poetry of the eighteenth century. Inaugurated by Pope's *Pastorals* and *Windsor-Forest*, descriptive poetry in this period went hand in hand with a detailed interest in nature generated by the botanical sciences, and with gardening and landscaping through which landowners exhibited their cultivated tastes. Virgil's *Georgics* were ever present as both a model and a challenge for eighteenth-century poets. Thomson's descriptions of nature aim to paint detailed pictures. For this he seems to have been particularly well qualified. As Johnson said: 'he looks round on nature and on life, with the eye which nature bestows only on the poet; the eye that distinguishes, in everything presented to its view, whatever there is on which imagination can delight to be detained, and with a mind which at once comprehends the vast, and attends to the minute.' Accordingly, the scenes are organised in visual sequences and patterns; the reader may at times feel the lack of logical coherence, at which point it may be worth recalling Johnson's similar dissatisfaction with the lack of 'method' in *The Seasons*. But then he drew attention to the non-temporal sequence of the poem: 'of many appearances subsisting all at once, no rule can be given why one should be mentioned before another' (*Life of Thomson*).

The Seasons is written in blank verse which is quite deftly handled by Thomson. It suits the nature and scope of his subject matter. As Johnson explained: 'Thomson's wide expansion of general views, and his enumeration of circumstantial varieties would have been obstructed and embarrassed by the frequent intersections of the sense, which are the necessary effects of rhyme.' The influence of Milton is apparent in the versification, and a relationship with the early poems of Pope in the diction, and method of description.

Thomson is familiar with the eighteenth-century tradition of using abstract nouns, gently personified through the use of an animating verb. Throughout *The Seasons* periphrasis is used to evoke the system or order in which natural objects are located and also to particularise them. It is a device analogous to the terms of classification employed by seventeenth- and eighteenth-century scientists.

[2] **Sullen**
gloomy, dark; *train* retinue, followers.

[4–5]
The poet declares early that for him the experience of nature is inextricably linked with moral and philosophical reflections.

[6] **Cogenial**
congenial; 'partaking of the same genius; cognate', Johnson, *Dictionary*; *frequent foot* quick movement.

[15] **lucid**
transparent; *chambers of the south* the southern sky; cf. 'Which maketh Arcturus, Orion, and Pleiades, and the chambers of the south', Job 9: 9.

[17] **essay**
attempt.

[18] **Wilmington**
Sir Spencer Compton (1673–1743), Speaker of the House of Commons, was appointed Lord Privy Seal by Walpole and created Earl of Wilmington in 1730. Johnson, in his *Life of Thomson*, says that the poet's Dedication 'attracted no regard from him to the author; till Aaron Hill awakened his attention by some verses addressed to Thomson ... which censured the great for their neglect of ingenious men. Thomson then received a present of twenty guineas.'

[19] **rounded**
gone round; *the revolving year* moving in circular motion; cf. 'And the year rolls within itself again', Dryden, *Georgics*, ii, 557; *Winter* was

placed last in the collected edition, though it was written first.

[20] **skimmed**
glided lightly over.

[22] **gale**
a strong wind.

[24] **doubling**
fast increasing.

[19–24]
Thomson traces the course of his poetic writings, from the original *Winter* of 1726 through the other seasons, back to *Winter*.

[26] **suit**
to match; *sounding cadence* magnificent, resounding tone.

[27] **numbers**
verses; *wildly great* irregularly grand. The poet claims conformity of his versification with his subject matter.

[29] **manly**
firm, bold.

[30] **aweful**
inspiring awe.

[32] **equal**
'Like another in bulk, or any quality that admits comparison', Johnson, *Dictionary*.

[34] **sliding age**
declining imperceptibly from a virtuous existence; *burning strong* imbued with moral fervour and concern.

[35] **vainly blazing**
making ostentatious declarations; *weal* happiness, prosperity.

[36] **regularly free**
unrestrained, but committed to order.

[37] **each exalting each**
steadiness of spirit and a freedom, that yet conform to a certain method, help each other.

[37–8] **the statesman light/ Into the patriot**
the man versed in public affairs is imbued with a love for his country.

[39] **converting**
turning.

[42] **Capricorn**
the Goat, the tenth sign of the zodiac. The sun enters into Capricorn at the winter solstice (21 or 22 December); *Centaur-Archer* Sagittarius, the ninth

sign of the zodiac, into which the sun enters about 22 November.

[43] **fierce**
enraged; *Aquarius* the water-carrier, the eleventh sign of the zodiac, into which the sun enters on 21 January; cf. 'When chilly Aquarius, setting in February,/ Waters the skirts of the departing year', Virgil, *Georgics*, iii, 304–5; *stains* blots, makes its presence felt; *inverted year* see 'inverted year', Horace, *Satires*, I, i, 36.

[44] **verge**
the edge, the utmost border.

[45] **ether**
the matter of the highest regions; *dejected* low-spirited.

[49] **wan**
pale; *broad* spread out, extended, and hence diffused; cf. 'Low walks the sun, and broadens by degrees', *Summer*, line 1620; *southern sky* see 'Or under southern skies exalt their sails', Pope, *Windsor-Forest*, line 391.

[46–9]
These lines describe light refracted through layers of dense mist; see 'as when the sun new risen/ Looks through the horizontal misty air/ Shorn of his beams, or from behind the moon/ In dim eclipse disastrous twilight sheds/ On half the nations, and with fear of change / Perplexes monarchs', *Paradise Lost*, i, 594–9.

[50] **descending**
setting.

[51] **prostrate**
lying at the mercy of.

[52] **vital**
life-giving.

[53] **dubious**
uncertain.

[54] **sable**
black, dark; *cincture* garments.

[55] **Deep-tinged**
dark coloured; *congregated* gathered.

[57] **Involve**
envelop so as to obscure.

[57–60]
The lines hark back to Lucretius' description of the source of epidemics,

On the Nature of the Universe:

I will now explain the *nature of epidemics* and the source from which the accumulated power of pestilence is able to spring a sudden devastating plague upon the tribes of men and beasts. . . . This crop of pestilence and plague either comes through the sky from outside, like clouds and mists, or very often springs from the earth itself . . . (vi, 1091–4, 1098–101, trans. Latham)

[65] **Untended**
left out deliberately; *wholesome root* turnips.
[63–5]
Referring to the 'Norfolk system of husbandry' which was becoming popular in other parts of Britain. By this method the stubble was ploughed into the land after the harvest, and sheep were put out into the fields and fed with turnips through the winter so that their dung would restore the land's fertility (see Sambrook, 1972). Similarly Virgil in *Georgics* outlined a new and beneficial system of treating the land: 'Long practice has a sure improvement found,/ With kindled fires to burn the barren ground;/ When the slight stubble, to the flames resigned,/ Is driv'n along, and crackles in the wind', Dryden's translation, i, 122–5.
[67] **genius**
tutelary spirit.
[69] **fractured mountains wild**
mountains with broken rocks. This method of two adjectives, one on each side of the noun, is very Miltonic; *brawling* noisy, loud. As opposed to the usual 'purling' brook.
[70] **presageful**
foreboding.
[71] **listening fancy**
the imagination that perceives more than the simple sense of hearing.
[74] **mingling**
confused.
[76] **unsightly**
'Disagreeable to the sight', Johnson, *Dictionary*.

[79] **combine**
unite.
[80] **wanderers of heaven**
wild birds, not the 'household feathery people' of line 87. This is a typical periphrasis common in *The Seasons*, and other poems of the period. It follows the genus-cum-differentia formula of the eighteenth-century scientists, and indicates the place of the object described in the natural system or order. At the same time it focuses on a distinguishing characteristic.
[72–80]
Cf. 'And often too a mighty host of waters/ Invades the sky, and gathering from the deep/ Clouds roll and roll together an ugly storm/ Of murky rain. Down headlong falls the sky/ In sheets; the glad fruits of the oxen's labours/ Are washed away; dykes fill, low river-beds/ Swell to a roaring torrent, and the sea/ Foams with the seething of its estuaries./ The Father himself in the midmost night of cloud/ Wields thunderbolts amain. The mighty earth/ Quakes at that shock', Virgil, *Georgics*, i, 322–3, trans. Wilkinson. The 'Father' in Virgil is Jupiter, but Thomson seems to have the Old Testament Jehovah in mind; cf. 'All nature reels: till Nature's King, who oft/ Amid tempestuous darkness dwells alone,/ And on the wings of the careering wind/ Walks dreadfully serene, commands a calm;/ Then straight air, sea, and earth are hushed at once', *Winter*, lines 197–201.
[85] **meaning low**
meaningful cry; *wonted* usual.
[86] **ruminate**
chew over again; *contiguous* adjoining.
[89] **cottage-hind**
farm-labourer.
[90] **enlivening blaze**
cheerful fire; *taleful* telling of the events of the day.
[92] **recks**
heeds.
[95] **And . . . o'erspread**
covered with the debris of what the river has washed off its banks.

[96] **roused-up**
excited into action.

[97] **dreadful**
inspiring fear.

[98] **rude**
rugged.

[99] **rocks abrupt**
craggy; *sounding far* resounding.

[100] **floating**
covering over with water.

[101] **constrained**
confined.

[103] **turbid**
muddy, not clear.

[105] **boils**
agitated like boiling water; *wheels*
turns about.

[94-105]
A pictorial presentation of the wild
but grand course of the river that is
akin to paintings of the period. It
generates a sense of the sublime; the
idea of the sublime was to be analysed
later by Burke.

[106] **unceasing**
incessant, perpetual.

[109]
The sublime effect of Nature on the
human mind.

[110] **astonished**
amazed.

[106-10]
Apostrophe to Nature, part of Thomson's purpose in describing external
nature.

[112] **boisterous**
turbulent, tumultuous.

[113] **stores**
storehouse.

[114] **aerial magazines reserved**
stores kept in the regions of the sky.

[115] **brooding terrors**
emerging terrors.

[116] **region of the sky**
Cf. 'To the bright regions of the rising
day', Pope, *Windsor-Forest*, line 388.

[106-17]
Cf. 'The Father in his purpose hath
decreed,/ He in whose hand all time
and seasons roll', *Paradise Regained*,
iii, 186-7; the tone of Thomson's passage, however, is 'deistic', worshipping 'Nature' through which man

attains understanding of the 'first
mover' or God. See also: 'But looks
through nature, up to nature's God',
Pope, *An Essay on Man*, iv, 332. Curiously enough Dryden's lines: 'Happy
the man, who, studying Nature's
laws,/ Through known effects can
trace the secret cause', *Georgics*, ii,
698-9, suggest a similar attitude.
These ideas were forcefully expressed
by contemporary philosophers like
Shaftesbury. Notice the change in
pronoun from 'thy' to 'you' as
Thomson's subject shifts from
'Nature' to 'the winds'.

[118] **keener**
more severe, biting; *fuming* smoking;
dun dark, gloomy. 'Dun' was considered a 'low' word, unsuitable
for poetry, and Johnson had censured
its use in *Macbeth*; see *Rambler*,
No. 168.

[119] **livid**
discoloured.

[120] **in whose capacious womb**
the large womb of the clouds.

[121] **to snow congealed**
Cf. 'Of snow congealed', Dryden,
Georgics, iii, 568.

[123] **saddens**
becomes dark, gloomy, foreboding;
gathered thickened.

[127] **cherished**
well-nursed, looked-after.

[130] **mazy**
confused, not as yet flowing in a clear
direction.

[131] **languid**
weak, faint.

[132] **Faint**
faintly, weakly.

[133] **Earth's universal face**
the whole face of the earth.

[134] **wide**
widely.

[130-7]
Cf. 'Meantime perpetual sleet, and
driving snow,/ Obscure the skies, and
hang on herds below./ The starving
cattle perish in their stalls;/ Huge oxen
stand enclosed in wintry walls/ Of
snow congealed', Dryden, *Georgics*,
iii, 564-8.

[137] **fowls of heaven**
the birds.

[139] **winnowing store**
the barn in which the grain was winnowed, or the grain separated from
the chaff by throwing it up against the
wind. The birds often gathered round
the entrance to such barns to catch bits
of the flying grain. Cf. 'And winnowed
chaff, by western winds is blown',
Dryden, *Georgics*, iii, 217.

[142] **embroiling**
confusing in an agitated kind of way.

[144] **trusted**
in whom he places his trust.

[146] **brisk**
briskly.

[148] **askance**
sideways.

[151] **foodless wilds**
the uncultivated lands where, in
winter, there is nothing to eat.

[152] **brown inhabitants**
a periphrastic term for animals like the
hare and deer.

[153] **hard beset**
closely besieged.

[154] **dark snares**
hidden traps.

[156] **The bleating kind**
periphrasis for sheep.

[158] **sad-dispersed**
badly scattered.

[161] **Baffle**
confound, or perhaps in the stronger
sense of 'crush'. The latter would suit
better with 'raging'.

[162] **food at will**
food to be eaten when desired;
lodge ... storm shelter them in a place
that is too low for the storm.

[163] **strict**
carefully; *bellowing* roaring.

[164] **dire season**
dismal season.

[165] **burden ... plains**
all the snow of the plains.

[166] **wide waft**
broad sweep through the air; *hapless*
helpless.

[168] **billowy**
swelling; *whelms* covers; *urged* pushed
or impelled.

[170] **wreath**
a spiral of powdery snow blown by
the wind; something that curls. Suggests a sense of motion and continuity.

[173] **loose-revolving**
in which the snow swirls around.

[174] **Disastered**
stricken by calamity.

[175] **unknown joyless brow**
uncommunicative, sorrowful countenance.

[176] **horrid prospect**
rugged view; *shag* make rough;
shag ... plain cover, as if with rough
woolly hair, so that no tracks can be
seen on the plain.

[178] **formless wild**
large uninhabited areas covered with
snow so that no recognisable shapes
can be discerned in them.

[180] **Impatient flouncing**
moving impatiently, tumultuously.

[181] **Stung ... home**
stricken with the wish to get home.
Cf. 'Tis with this rage, the mother lion
stung/ Scours o'er the plains, regard-
less of her young', Dryden, *Georgics*,
iii, 381–2.

[185] **dusky**
dark, obscure; *fancy feigned* falsely
imagined.

[186] **tufted**
adorned with a tuft of protruding
straw, perhaps; see: 'That crowned
with tufted trees and springing corn',
Pope, *Windsor-Forest*, line 27.

[187] **roughness ... waste**
ruggedness of the faraway wilds.

[189] **closes**
gathers round; *fast* impregnable.

[191] **savage wilderness**
untamed, barbaric wastes.

[194] **dire descent**
horrible fall; *beyond ... frost* not
frozen, and therefore capable of
drowning him.

[195] **faithless bogs**
perfidious, treacherous swamps.

[196] **Smoothed ... snow**
covered with snow so as to appear
smooth.

[198] **loose marsh**
not firm, boggy and water-logged.

[199] **boils**
surges upwards.
[200] **check**
restrain; *fearful* full of fear.
[201] **Beneath the shelter**
underneath.
[202] **bitterness**
'implacability', Johnson, *Dictionary*.
[203] **tender . . . shoots**
delicate feelings of endearment which
are part of human nature; the image
here is of a young plant finding its way
through the surrounding dark soil.
[204] **wrung bosom**
tortured heart.
[206] **officious**
kind, obliging.
[207] **vestment**
garments.
[209] **mingling**
confusing.
[212] **sacred home**
his home blessed with family happiness; *nerve* organs of sensation.
[213] **shuts up sense**
blocks the capacity to feel.
[214] **inmost vitals**
the inner vital organs.
[216] **bleaching**
exposed to the elements.
[217] **licentious**
unrestrained.
[219] **thoughtless**
careless, negligent; often used in the
morally deprecatory sense of 'dull' or
'stupid' as: 'But lost in thoughtless
ease, and empty show', Johnson,
London, line 103.
[220] **riot**
dissipation.
[224] **devouring flood**
periphrasis for the ocean.
[225] **devouring flame**
periphrastic usage for a destructive
fire.
[226] **shameful . . . and man**
differences and quarrels between
people.
[229–30] **the cup/ Of baleful grief**
experience deep sorrow and misery.
See 'round he throws his baleful eyes/
That witnessed huge affliction and
dismay', *Paradise Lost*, i, 56–7.

[230–1] **the bitter bread/ Of misery**
suffer agony and unhappiness; *sore*
sorely, painfully.
[232–3] **sordid hut/ Of cheerless
poverty**
the mean abode of gloomy poverty;
the image is that of a small village
hut.
[235] **Unbounded passion**
unconfined, raging passion.
[236] **tumbled headlong**
falling precipitately. Cf. ' Some ask for
envy'ed pow'r; which public hate/
Pursues, and hurries headlong to their
fate', Dryden's Juvenal, *Satire X*,
85–6; see also: 'Oft in her glass the
musing shepherd spies/ The headlong
mountains and the downward skies',
Pope, *Windsor-Forest*, lines 211–12;
'Hurled headlong flaming from the
ethereal sky', Milton, *Paradise Lost*, i,
45; and: 'when his darling sons/
Hurled headlong to partake with us,
shall curse/ Their frail original', ii,
373–5.
[237] **furnish . . . muse**
Tragedy was generally supposed to
present the fall of a person from the
height of power and renown to
suffering and loss. This traditional
idea came under debate in the
eighteenth century. Johnson in his
Preface to Shakespeare points out the
limitation of viewing tragedy from the
perspective of a prescribed ending.
Accordingly, in his *Dictionary* he
defined 'tragedy' simply as ' a
dramatic representation of a serious
action'.
[240] **racked with honest passions**
tortured by justifiable passions.
[241] **retired distress**
private sorrow.
[243] **point**
regard or respect; *parting anguish* the
suffering of man at the time of death;
fond man foolish man.
[244] **and all . . . ills**
Cf. 'the thousand natural shocks',
Hamlet, III, i, 62.
[244–5]
A characteristic syntactical inversion.
The normal reading would be: And all

the thousand nameless ills that render life one incessant struggle.

[246] **fate**
doom.

[247] **Vice . . . career**
a personification of Vice as in the morality plays.

[248] **heedless rambling impulse**
negligent, directionless thoughts or ideas.

[249] **conscious heart**
knowing, not ignorant, mind.

[250] **benevolence**
kindness, disposition to do good; *dilate* extend; *her . . . dilate* an example of deliberate repetition for the sake of emphasis.

[251] **social**
relating to public interest, as opposed to 'private'.

[252] **clear perfection**
unmixed, pure perfection; *gradual bliss* bliss or happiness advancing step by step.

[253] **Refining still**
ever becoming more pure, more perfect. Social virtue is a theme that runs through much of Thomson's poetry and correspondence. See 'At last, extinct each social feeling, fell/ And joyless inhumanity pervades/ And petrifies the heart', *Spring*, lines 305–7; 'But to the generous, still improving mind/ That gives the hopeless heart to sing for joy,/ Diffusing kind beneficence around/ Boastless as now descends the silent dew –/ To him the long review of ordered life/ Is inward rapture only to be felt', *Summer*, 1641–6; see also *Autumn*, lines 1006–29. Thomson had written to Aaron Hill in 1726: 'Social love . . . is the very smile and consummation of virtue; 'tis the image of the fair perfection in the Supreme Being.'

[254] **deep retirement**
the theme of rural retirement is one that Thomson shares with poets like Pope and Goldsmith. See *Windsor-Forest*, lines 97–100, and *The Deserted Village*. Of course Virgil's *Georgics* is literally the original of all such passages in English poetry; see 'But easie quiet, a secure retreat,/ A harmless life that knows not how to cheat,/ With homebred plenty the rich owner bless,/ And rural pleasures crown his happiness', Dryden's translation, ii, 655–8.

[255] **pliant**
easily complying.

[256] **Or blithe, or solemn**
Either gay or serious.

[257] **search**
speculate; *frame* structure, applied to the heavens and the earth; see 'But of this frame the bearings, and the ties,/ The strong connections, nice dependencies,/ Gradations just, has thy pervading soul,/ Looked through?', Pope, *An Essay on Man*, i, 29–32; *nature's boundless frame* nature's enormous fabric or structure; see 'These are thy glorious works, parent of good,/ Almighty, thine this universal frame,/ Thus wondrous fair', *Paradise Lost*, v, 153–5; 'Lest fierce extremes/ Contiguous might distemper the whole frame', *Paradise Lost*, vii, 272–3; 'And all the world's fair frame', Spenser, *Faerie Queene*, 7.6. 5, 5.

[258] **void**
vacuum or empty space; *void of night* the darkness and emptiness of night. This refers to a traditional view that God created the world out of nothing. Cf. 'In the beginning God created the heaven and the earth. And the earth was without form, and void; and darkness was upon the face of the waters', Genesis 1: 1–2.

[259] **Or sprung . . . Eternal Mind**
The second explanation was that God created the material universe, not out of nothing, but out of his own being. In Platonic terms this meant that God formed the material world as a copy of an eternal pattern. See: 'My overshadowing spirit and might with thee/ I send along, ride forth, and bid the deep/ Within appointed bounds be heaven and earth,/ Boundless the deep, because I am who fill/ Infinitude, nor vacuous the space./ Though

I uncircumscribed myself retire,/ And put not forth my goodness, which is free/ To act or not, necessity and chance/ Approach not me, and what I will is fate', *Paradise Lost*, vii, 165–73 (see Sambrook, 1972).

[261–9]
Summary of the intention of *The Seasons*.

[262] **gradual**
by degrees; *opening* enlarging.

[263] **diffusive**
individual. The word could be read in the sense of 'scattered' or 'dispersed', in oxymoronic conjunction with 'harmony'.

[264] **astonished**
'amazed', Johnson, *Dictionary*.

[265] **scan**
to examine carefully.

[266] **embroiled**
confused and distracted.

[267] **fitted**
equipped; *impelled* urged onwards.

[268–9]
The thought of the period was dominated by the idea that a beneficent, omnipotent and omnipresent Universal Parent is working things towards a general good. The idea is expressed in Pope's *Essay on Man*: 'Safe in the hand of one disposing pow'r,/ Or in the natal, or the mortal hour./ All nature is but art, unknown to thee;/ All chance, direction, which thou canst not see;/ All discord, harmony, not understood;/ All partial evil, universal good', i, 287–92. Philosophers like Shaftesbury and Francis Hutcheson were exponents of this idea.

[269] **historic muse**
Clio, chief of the nine muses, who presided over history.

[272] **scattered**
dispersed.

[273] **gives them double suns**
Cf. 'each circling year,/ Returning suns and double seasons pass', *Summer*, lines 644–5; Thomson himself explained the line: 'In all places between the tropics the sun, as he passes and repasses in his annual motion, is twice a year perpendicular, which produces this effect.'

[272–5]
The influence of the climate on people's characters and developments in history was a favourite subject of the period. Johnson, in his *Life of Milton*, attributes to Milton the belief that he was born in too cold a climate to write an epic poem. Goldsmith in *The Traveller* also considers the influence of the climate on the growth of cultures.

[277] **portion of divinity**
consciousness of immortality; cf. 'the divinity that stirs within us', Addison, *Cato*, V, i, 7.

[278] **public soul**
the spirit that regards the general interest or the good of humanity.

[280] **repress**
'to crush', Johnson, *Dictionary*.

[281] **ardent**
hot, burning or fiery, moving metaphorically on to vehement, passionate; *kindling* burning, inflamed.

[282] **ambition**
'the desire or preferment of honour', Johnson, *Dictionary*.

[283] **private**
quiet, personal.

[283–5]
Cf. 'The country king his peaceful realm enjoys:/ Cool grots, and living lakes, the flow'ry pride/ Of meads, and streams that through the valley glide', Dryden, *Georgics*, ii, 660–2.

[285–6]
Transported by hope into the shadowy landscape of the future.

[287] **earnest**
eager; *anticipate* 'To foretaste, or take an impression of something, which is not as yet, as if it really was', Johnson, *Dictionary*.

[288–90]
The Renaissance idea of the chain of being was reinterpreted in the eighteenth century to incorporate the notion of progress. The future life then was seen as the infinite ascent of the mind from stage to stage. In this way the idea was subordinated to the deistic temper of the times. Samuel

Johnson criticised this view severely in his *Review* of Soame Jenyns' *A Free Inquiry into the Nature and Origin of Evil*. Jenyns had explored the idea of the chain of being, as too had Addison and Pope. See Addison, *Spectator*, No. 519; see also: 'Is the great chain, that draws all to agree,/ And drawn supports, upheld by God, or thee?', Pope, *Essay on Man*, i, 33–4; and *An Essay on Man*, i, 207–46. Arthur O. Lovejoy did an elaborate study of the idea in *The Great Chain of Being*: which he says was composed of

an immense, or ... infinite, number of links ranging in hierarchical order from the meagerest kind of existences, which barely escape non-existence, through 'every possible' grade up to the *ens perfectissimum* – or, ... to the highest possible kind of creature, between which and the Absolute Being the disparity was assumed to be infinite – every one of them differing from that immediately above and that immediately below it by the 'least possible' degree of difference.

[291] **foiled**
'defeated', Johnson, *Dictionary*.
[291]
When the mind is defeated by attempting these images of futurity.
[292] **play**
give play to.
[293] **frolic fancy**
imagination that is gay, or full of levity. The imagination, in the first half of the eighteenth century, was conceived of as a licentious faculty that could be dangerous if not kept under control by judgement. Johnson explores this idea in *Rasselas*, especially in chapter XLIV, 'The dangerous prevalence of imagination'.
[294] **rapid pictures**
succeeding quickly one after the other, ever-changing.
[295] **fleet**
fleeting, vanishing; *never joined before* in new combinations and arrangements. The idea of 'wit' as novel

assemblages of images otherwise unrelated to each other.
[292–6]
Cf. 'for wit lying most in the assemblage of ideas, and putting those together with quickness and variety, ... thereby to make up pleasant pictures and agreeable visions in the fancy', Locke, *Essay Concerning Human Understanding*, II, xi, 2.
[297–8]
Thomson's abstractions are gently personified.
[301] **succeed**
follow, one after the other; *blue serene* calm sky.
[302] **ethereal nitre**
The ether, it was believed, contained substances, the most important of which was an acid which formed saltpetre or nitre. Nitre supported vegetable life. 'The ancient philosophers supposed the ether to be igneous, and by its kind influence upon the air to be the cause of all vegetation', Pope, *Iliad*, i, 514, note (see Sambrook, 1972). See: 'Whate'er the wintry frost, Nitrous prepared, the various-blossomed spring/ Put in white promise forth', *Autumn*, lines 4–6; see also: 'With vigorous nitre', Dryden, *Georgics*, i, 281; 'Winter my theme confines; whose nitry wind', Gay, *Trivia*, line 319.
[303] **infectious**
causing mischief by contagion; *damps* 'a noxious vapour exhaled from the earth', Johnson, *Dictionary*; *spent* worn out.
[304] **elemental**
'arising from first principles', Johnson, *Dictionary*.
[304]
Providing once again elementary forms of life.
[305] **Close ... atmosphere**
In Winter the clear, gleaming air is filled thickly with emerging forms of life; *binds* enwraps; cf. 'While yet the spring is young, while earth unbinds/ Her frozen bosom to the western winds', Dryden, *Georgics*, i, 64–5.

[306] **strengthened**
made stronger by the life-giving power of nitre.

[307] **Constringent**
'Having the quality of binding or compressing', Johnson, *Dictionary*; *animates* quickens, makes alive; *animates our blood* imbues us with energy.

[308] **Refines**
makes more pure; *spirits* animal spirits; *new-strung nerves* nerves newly made taut or active. Cf. 'Ye vig'rous swains! while youth ferments your blood,/ And purer spirits swell the sprightly flood', Pope, *Windsor-Forest*, lines 93–4.

[309] **swifter sallies**
quick flights or rapid movements; *darting* flying like a dart.

[310] **intense**
attentive; *collected* self-possessed; *cool* not ruffled.

[311] **Bright as the skies**
as illuminated and shining as the heavens; *keen* sharp.

[312] **renovating force**
the power of renewal.

[313] **thoughtless eye**
dull, stupid viewer. Only the insensitive person perceives nothing but ruin in winter.

[313–14]
Thomson often suggests that the 'eyes' of fancy or reason can see far more of Nature's beauty and harmony than the ordinary physical eye. See: 'where the raptured eye/ Hurries from joy to joy, and, hid beneath/ The fair profusion, yellow Autumn spies', *Spring*, lines 111–13.

[314] **concocted**
solidified; 'heightened to perfection', Johnson, *Dictionary*; hence the sense also of 'ripened', cf. 'Whose high-concocted venom through the veins/ A rapid lightning darts', *Summer*, lines 909–10; 'and summer-suns/ Concocted strong, rush boundless now to view', *Autumn*, lines 6–7; suggesting therefore the productive part played by frost in the scheme of Nature; *glebe* soil.

[315]
Absorbs in plenty the power to regenerate vegetable life.

[316] **vigour**
life-force.

[317–18]
A gentle personification of 'fire' by the use of the word 'cheek'.

[318] **luculent**
full of light, clear.

[319] **The purer rivers flow**
purer because of the water given to them by melting snow; *sullen deeps* dark, intractable portions.

[320] **open**
clear, not hidden from.

[321] **fixing frost**
where the solidified portions of the water still make movement difficult. Hence the water there 'murmurs hoarser' or sounds louder.

[322] **keen stores**
sharp materials.

[324] **illusive fluid**
Ethyl alcohol, used in thermometers. Thermometers in a Lapland expedition were found to freeze, possibly because they contained some water as well; Thomson uses the idea to illustrate the power of frost (see Sambrook, 1972).

[327] **double wedges**
wedged or sharpened on two sides; *diffused immense* dispersed widely.

[322–8]
Cf.

Cold and freezing seem to proceed from some saline substance floating in the air; we see that all salts, but more eminently some, mixed with ice prodigiously increase the effects and force of cold. ... Microscopical observations inform us that the figures of some salts, before they shoot into masses, are thin double-wedged. ... The dimensions of freezed bodies are increased by the insinuations of these crystal wedges in their pores, and the particles of congealed water are kept at some distance from one another by the figure of these crystals which in freezing insinuate themselves in their pores. (George Cheyne, *Philosophical Principles of Religion: Natural and Revealed* (see Sambrook, 1972))

[329] **Steamed**
issuing vapours; *eager* keen, ardent.
[330] **deep suffused**
deeply informed.
[332] **Breathes a blue film**
covers as if with a blue mist.
[333] **Arrests**
stops from movement; *bickering stream* quivering; playing backwards and forwards; cf. 'And from him fierce effusion rolled/ Of smoke and bickering flame', Milton, *Paradise Lost*, vi, 765–6.
[335] **Rustles**
noise caused by movement, like of leaves or wind. In this instance the movement of the floating ice.
[336] **Fast grows**
attaches itself to; the half-dissolved ice gathers round the sedges, as its movement is arrested by them.
[337] **crystal pavement**
both in the scientific sense of congealed in the manner of crystal; and also bright and clear as perceived by the eye. Cf. 'And before the throne there was a sea of glass like unto crystal', Revelation 4: 6; *breath of heaven* the cold wind.
[338] **Cemented**
bonded firmly; *seized* arrested in movement.
[339]
The whole surface of the river is frozen, the water flowing beneath a cover of ice, and 'growling' or making an angry noise.
[340] **hard reflects**
both reflects loudly, and also reflects because of its own hardness in its frozen state.
[341] **double noise**
an echo.
[342] **deters**
discourages.
[343] **heifer lows**
the young cow bellows.
[344] **Swells in the breeze**
the spray of the water scattered by the breeze.

[345] **hollow-sounding**
echoing.
[338–45]
Thomson explores, by a process of association, the different sounds in the environment.
[346–8]
Elaborate descriptive periphrasis for the moon.
[348–9] **all one cope/ Of starry glitter**
canopy, referring to the starry sky.
[350] **rigid**
inflexible, unbending; *influence* 'power of the celestial aspects operating upon terrestrial bodies and affairs', Johnson, *Dictionary*. The phrase 'rigid influence' would signify the unremitting power of the celestial bodies. The idea is continued in the 'incessant' of the next line.
[352] **seizes nature fast**
grasps nature firmly, the cold having the effect of freezing all movement.
[354] **pale eye unjoyous**
the noun flanked by adjectives on either side; a Miltonic device; *appears* can be seen.
[356] **Prone**
hanging downward; *dripping eave* the edges of sloping roofs from which moisture drips; *dumb cascade* soundless waterfall, soundless because frozen.
[357] **idle torrents**
not really moving; *only seem to roar* do not in fact make any sound.
[358] **pendent**
hanging; see: 'Long icicles depend', Dryden, *Georgics*, ii; *frost-work fair* the beautiful designs of frost.
[359] **transient hues**
changing colours; *fancied figures* the many patterns that can be seen in frost.
[360] **Wide-spouted**
pouring in a broad collected body.
[361] **livid tract**
pale-coloured length; *cold-gleaming* shining cold.
[362] **plumy wave**
the snow in the trees giving the impression of hosts of bird-feathers.

[363] **refined**
made more pure, hence whiter.
[365] **pensive**
sad, melancholy.
[367] **Pleased with**
enjoying; *swift descends* slides down.
[368] **Tornea's lake**
A lake in northern Sweden near the border with Norway.
[369] **Hecla**
the volcano in Iceland.
[372] **expands**
spreads.
[374] **beneath another sky**
'The other hemisphere', Thomson's note.
[375] **cerulean**
blue, or sky-coloured.
[377] **airy hall**
the hall high up in the air; *misrule* tumult or confusion.
[378] **driving tempest**
the violent storm.
[379] **grim tyrant**
Winter; cf. 'Grim Death my son and foe', *Paradise Lost*, ii, 804.
[383] **Tartar's coast**
northern Siberia. Cf. 'Beyond this flood a frozen continent/ Lies dark and wild, beat with perpetual storms/ Of whirlwind and dire hail, which firm on land/ Thaws not, but gathers heap, and ruin seems/ Of ancient pile; all else deep snow and ice,/ A gulf profound', *Paradise Lost*, ii, 587–92. See also: 'Here walked the fiend at large in spacious field./ As when a vulture on Imaus bred,/ Whose snowy ridge the roving Tartar bounds', iii, 430–2. Carrying an association with *Tartarus*, in Greek mythology, part of the underworld, where the wicked suffer punishment for their misdeeds on earth. Ixion and Tantalus were both placed in Tartarus. See: 'and his throne itself/ Mixed with Tartarean sulphur, and strange fire,/ His own invented torments', Milton, *Paradise Lost*, ii, 68–70. Characteristically Miltonic adjectives like 'horrid' and 'hideous' that follow justify this association. In fact Thomson's

description of the wintry northern regions owes much to *Paradise Lost*.
[384] **She**
referring to the poet's muse; *howling margin of the main* the loud and horrible sound of the wind against the ocean's shore.
[386] **amazing**
a sight astonishing and perplexing to behold; cf. 'As we erewhile, astounded and amazed', *Paradise Lost*, i, 381; and: 'Under amazement of their hideous change', i, 13.
[389] **an atmosphere of clouds**
like the white clouds in the atmosphere.
[390] **projected**
protruding; *horrid* rough; *surge* the surge of the ocean.
[391] **hideous**
horribly; *rushing hideous down* cf. 'With hideous ruin and combustion down', *Paradise Lost*, i, 46; and: 'threatening hideous fall', ii, 177; 'Hell trembled at the hideous name', ii, 788.
[391–2]
The picture of an avalanche.
[392] **As if ... returned**
Cf. 'where eldest night/ And chaos, ancestors of nature, hold/ Eternal anarchy', *Paradise Lost*, ii, 894–6; and: 'Ye powers/ And spirits of this nethermost abyss,/ Chaos and ancient night', ii, 968–70.
[395] **binding fury**
the power of the descending snow to enchain or imprison.
[396–7]
A picture of the frozen ocean.
[399] **Shagged**
made rough; *wavy rocks* the waves of the ocean frozen into rocks.
[400–1] **dreary months ... southward**
referring to the migratory flight of the birds.
[402] **entangled ... ice**
caught in the accumulating ice.
[403] **descending sun**
the setting sun.
[405] **incumbent**
hanging over, threatening.

[406]
'Sir Hugh Willoughby, sent by Queen Elizabeth to discover the north-east passage', Thomson's note.
[406–15]

Willoughby and his crew entered an inlet, subsequently known as Arzina, near the present border between Norway and Russia, intending to pass the winter of 1553–54 there, but were ill-provisioned and all died. Their bodies were found some years afterwards, and Willoughby's journal was printed in Hakluyt's *Principal Navigations* and in many other collections. (see Sambrook, 1972)

[407] **prow**
ship.
[408–9] **since . . . in vain**
Later attempts on the north-east passage were made by Pete and Jackson in 1580, by Barents in 1594–97, and by expeditions sponsored by Peter the Great and commanded by Vitus Baring in 1725–8 and 1740–1 (see Sambrook, 1972).
[411] **fell regions**
cruel, inhuman parts.
[413] **Immediate sealed**
at once rendered fixed or immobile.
[414] **Each . . . task**
each fully engaged in his particular job.
[415] **cordage**
ropes.
[417] **Hard by**
close by.
[418] **Oby**
the river in Siberia; *the last of men*
oldest of men.
[419] **half enlivened**
only partly matured.
[421] **rudest**
most savage.
[424] **waste the tedious gloom**
pass the tedious and gloomy hours; cf. 'to drive the tedious hours away', Dryden, *Georgics*, iii, 583.
[428] **her roses drooping all**
the bright red hue, usually associated with morning, is faint.

[429] **twilight**
obscure, uncertain light.
[417–30]
Cf. 'The land lies shapeless under drifts of snow/ ·And piles of ice full seven cubits high./ Winter is endless there, and nor'west winds/ Whistle with endless cold; nor does the sun/ Ever disperse the pall of pallid fog/ Either in driving his chariot up the sky/ Or plunging it into the crimson ocean./ In running rivers sudden sheets of ice/ Congeal, until the water's back can bear/ Iron-bound wheels . . . ' Virgil, *Georgics*, iii, 355–64.
See also: 'clothing freezes/ On the body, an axe is used to serve the wine,/ Whole ponds are found turned into solid ice/ And uncombed beards bristle with icicles;/ Meanwhile the air is no less thick with snow,/ Beasts perish . . . ' Virgil, *Georgics*, iii, 364–9, trans. Wilkinson. Virgil's *Georgics* was the inspiration and source for many passages in *The Seasons*.
[435] **Gothic**
barbarous, savage.
[434–5]
One of powerful mind and extensive understanding retrieved from barbaric ignorance.
[436] **Immortal Peter**
Peter the Great of Russia (1672–1725).
[441] **Ye shades . . . heroes**
See *Winter*, lines 424–520, where Thomson calls up the shades of prominent classical figures like Socrates, Solon, Lycurgus, etc.
[448–53]
After becoming tsar he travelled through Western Europe to learn contemporary arts and sciences.
[450]
He worked as a carpenter. Cf. 'showed him how to raise/ His feeble force by the mechanic powers', *Autumn*, lines 76–7.
[454] **illumined waste**
the enlightened lands that were earlier wild and barbaric.
[454–62]
When Peter the Great returned to

Russia after his European travels he reorganised his country's armed forces, civil government and social life. Thomson admired material progress as is evident also from *Autumn*, lines 43–150.

[456] **is social joined**
connected in social harmony.

[457]
The Euxine (Black) Sea is connected with the Baltic by canals.

[460] **files**
'a line of soldiers ranged one behind another', Johnson, *Dictionary*.

[461] **Alexander of the North**
Charles XII of Sweden, defeated by the Russians at Poltava in 1709. Cf. Johnson, *The Vanity of Human Wishes*, lines 191–222.

[462] **Othman's ... sons**
The Turks, whom Peter did not succeed in defeating.

[464] **proud**
'impatient', Johnson, *Dictionary*; *it glows around* referring to 'the land' from which sloth, ignorance and other vices have fled.

[469] **'Tis done!**
it is all over!; *Dread Winter* frightening winter.

[470] **tremendous**
horrible.

[472] **How dumb the tuneful!**
How silent are the birds!; *Horror wide extends* Thomson often repeats for emphasis.

[473] **fond man**
foolish man.

[474] **See here ... life**
See here your life drawn out in a series of pictures.

[475] **ardent strength**
burning strength.

[477] **concluding ... at last**
another example of repetition.

[479] **unsolid**
without a foundation in reality, fanciful.

[482] **veering thoughts**
changing ideas.

[483] **Lost between good and ill**
uncertain of their moral position.

[484] **Virtue sole survives**
only virtue survives. Such apologues of 'virtue' were popular in the first half of the eighteenth century. See: 'Behold the first in virtue, as in face!', Pope, *Rape of the Lock*, v, 18; 'Know then this truth (enough for man to know)/ "Virtue alone is happiness below."/ The only point where human bliss stands still,/ And tastes the good without the fall to ill', *An Essay on Man*, iv, 309–12.

[486] **His guide ... on high**
his director to the happiness of another world.

[487] **the second birth**
the words thus ending the line suggest the second coming of Christ.

[487–8] **birth ... and earth**
the regeneration of the world after winter.

[489] **the new-creating word**
Cf. 'Light dies before thy uncreating word', Pope, *Dunciad*, iv, 654.

[491] **The great eternal scheme**
the whole plan of God, which is perfect and therefore everlasting.

[473–91]
Cf. Job 14: 1–15.

[492] **Involving**
comprising.

[494] **refined**
made more pure or clear; *reason's eye refined* Thomson suggests again that the eye of reason or fancy can see more in terms of nature's harmony and beauty than the ordinary physical eye.

[496] **Confounded in the dust**
utterly crushed.

[498–9]
Cf. 'Slow rises worth, by poverty depressed', Johnson, *London*, line 177.

[501] **lone widow**
an image of poverty and deprivation.

[502–4] **Luxury ... wants**
One of the many diatribes in the poetry of this period against 'luxury', or the artificial needs created by commerce, as opposed to requirements necessary for human life.

[506] **licensed**
with exorbitant liberty.

[507] **spoiler**
ravager; *embosomed foe* one who holds enmity with man in his deepest heart.
[511–12]
Cf. 'God sends not ill; if rightly understood,/ Or partial ill is universal good', Pope, *An Essay on Man*, iv,

113–14; see also: 'While from the bounded level of our mind,/ Short views we take, nor see the lengths behind', *An Essay on Criticism*, line 221.
[514] **unbounded ... encircle**
a nice play of images suggesting divine infinitude and human limitations.

SAMUEL JOHNSON

(1709–84)

Samuel Johnson was born in Lichfield near Birmingham in 1709. His father was a bookseller who sent him to Pembroke College, Oxford, for his education. Unfortunately Johnson did not survive at Oxford for financial reasons. He left the University without taking his degree. After a few experiments with school-teaching, in 1738 he went to London to try his luck in the literary capital. He had with him an unfinished draft of his tragedy *Irene*, and his friend David Garrick. Both men hoped to advance in a career in the London theatre. Garrick's success in the world of theatre is well known; Johnson moved into journalism with *The Gentleman's Magazine*, and published *London* in 1738. His interests in the next decade were to be lexicographical and editorial. In 1745 he first presented in his *Miscellaneous Observations on the Tragedy of Macbeth* a sample for what he hoped would be an edition of Shakespeare. When the edition did not seem immediately possible, he offered in 1747 his *Plan for a Dictionary*. In 1749 he published *The Vanity of Human Wishes*. The monumental *Dictionary* was published in 1755 and the *Edition of Shakespeare* in 1765. Of course, Johnson is also remembered for his *Rambler* essays and *The Lives of the Poets*. *On the Death of Dr Robert Levet* was published in 1783. Samuel Johnson died in 1784. To many people he is best known through his biography written by his friend James Boswell.

Further Reading

Johnson's poetry is available in David Nichol Smith and Edward L. McAdam (eds), *The Poems of Samuel Johnson* (1941; Oxford: Clarendon Press, 1974), and in the sixth volume of *The Yale*

Edition of the Works of Samuel Johnson, edited by E.L. McAdam and George Milne (New Haven, Conn.: Yale University Press, 1965). A reliable paperback edition is J.D. Fleeman (ed.), *Samuel Johnson: The Complete English Poems* (Harmondsworth: Penguin, 1971). The present editors have found the editions by Smith and McAdam and Fleeman extremely helpful. The editors also wish to acknowledge Peter Green's translation, *Juvenal: The Sixteen Satires* (Harmondsworth: Penguin, 1967).

We are lucky in having Johnson's life recorded in a biography which is itself a classic of English literature, James Boswell's *Life of Samuel Johnson, LL.D.* (many editions). There is also an excellent modern critical biography in Walter Jackson Bate's *Samuel Johnson* (London: Chatto and Windus, 1978). Probably still the best general introduction to Johnson's writing as a whole is Bate's *The Achievement of Samuel Johnson* (New York: Oxford University Press, 1955). Other valuable books of a general reach are John P. Hardy's *Samuel Johnson: A Critical Study* (London: Routledge and Kegan Paul, 1974), and Leopold Damrosch's *Samuel Johnson and the Tragic Sense* (Princeton, NJ: Princeton University Press, 1972). Although Johnson's writings have been extensively discussed by modern critics, his poetry has been relatively neglected. T.S. Eliot's article 'Johnson as Critic and Poet' in *On Poetry and Poets* (London: Faber and Faber, 1957) gives some insight, as does F.R. Leavis's 'Johnson as Poet' in *The Common Pursuit* (London: Chatto and Windus, 1952). An account of Johnson's theory of poetic language is provided by Nalini Jain in *The Mind's Extensive View: Samuel Johnson on Poetic Language* (Strathtay: Clunie Press, 1991).

————◇————

26 /   *London*

A Poem in Imitation of the Third Satire of Juvenal

Though grief and fondness in my breast rebel,
When injured Thales bids the town farewell,
Yet still my calmer thoughts his choice commend,
I praise the hermit, but regret the friend;
Resolved at length, from vice and London far,   5
To breathe in distant fields a purer air,
And fixed on Cambria's solitary shore,
Give to St. David one true Briton more.

  For who would leave, unbribed, Hibernia's land,
Or change the rocks of Scotland for the Strand?   10
There none are swept by sudden fate away,
But all whom hunger spares with age decay:
Here malice, rapine, accident, conspire,
And now a rabble rages, now a fire;
Their ambush here relentless ruffians lay,   15
And here the fell attorney prowls for prey;
Here falling houses thunder on your head,
And here a female atheist talks you dead.

  While Thales waits the wherry that contains
Of dissipated wealth the small remains,   20
On Thames's banks, in silent thought we stood,
Where Greenwich smiles upon the silver flood:
Struck with the seat that gave Eliza birth,
We kneel and kiss the consecrated earth;
In pleasing dreams the blissful age renew,   25
And call Britannia's glories back to view;
Behold her cross triumphant on the main,
The guard of commerce, and the dread of Spain,
Ere masquerades debauched, excise oppressed,
Or English honour grew a standing jest.   30

  A transient calm the happy scenes bestow,
And for a moment lull the sense of woe:
At length awaking, with contemptuous frown,
Indignant Thales eyes the neighbouring town.

Since worth, he cries, in these degenerate days,   35
Wants ev'n the cheap reward of empty praise;
In those cursed walls, devote to vice and gain,
Since unrewarded science toils in vain;
Since hope but soothes to double my distress,
And every moment leaves my little less;   40
While yet my steady steps no staff sustains,
And life still vigorous revels in my veins,
Grant me, kind heaven, to find some happier place,
Where honesty and sense are no disgrace:
Some pleasing bank where verdant osiers play,   45
Some peaceful vale with nature's paintings gay;
Where once the harassed Briton found repose,
And safe in poverty defied his foes;
Some secret cell, ye powers, indulgent give,
Let – live here, for – has learned to live.   50
Here let those reign, whom pensions can incite
To vote a patriot black, a courtier white;
Explain their country's dear-bought rights away,
And plead for pirates in the face of day;
With slavish tenets taint our poisoned youth,   55
And lend a lie the confidence of truth.

Let such raise palaces, and manors buy,
Collect a tax, or farm a lottery;
With warbling eunuchs fill a licensed stage,
And lull to servitude a thoughtless age.   60

Heroes, proceed! what bounds your pride shall hold?
What check restrain your thirst of power and gold?
Behold rebellious virtue quite o'erthrown,
Behold our fame, our wealth, our lives your own.

To such, a groaning nation's spoils are given,   65
When public crimes inflame the wrath of heaven:
But what, my friend, what hope remains for me,
Who start at theft, and blush at perjury?
Who scarce forbear, though Britain's court he sing,
To pluck a titled poet's borrowed wing: 70
A statesman's logic unconvinced can hear,
And dare to slumber o'er the Gazetteer;

Despise a fool in half his pension dressed,
And strive in vain to laugh at H—y's jest.

Others with softer smiles, and subtler art,   75
Can sap the principles, or taint the heart:
With more address a lover's note convey,
Or bribe a virgin's innocence away;
Well may they rise, while I, whose rustic tongue
Ne'er knew to puzzle right, or varnish wrong,   80
Spurned as a beggar, dreaded as a spy,
Live unregarded, unlamented die.

For what but social guilt the friend endears?
Who shares Orgilio's crimes, his fortune shares:
But thou, should tempting villainy present   85
All Marlborough hoarded, or all Villiers spent,
Turn from the glittering bribe thy scornful eye,
Nor sell for gold, what gold could never buy,
The peaceful slumber, self-approving day,
Unsullied fame, and conscience ever gay.   90

The cheated nation's happy favourites, see!
Mark whom the great caress, who frown on me!
London! the needy villain's general home,
The common shore of Paris and of Rome:
With eager thirst, by folly or by fate,   95
Sucks in the dregs of each corrupted state.
Forgive my transports on a theme like this,
I cannot bear a French metropolis.

Illustrious Edward! from the realms of day,
The land of heroes and of saints survey: 100
Nor hope the British lineaments to trace,
The rustic grandeur, or the surly grace,
But lost in thoughtless ease, and empty show,
Behold the warrior dwindled to a beau;
Sense, freedom, piety, refined away,   105
Of France the mimic, and of Spain the prey.

All that at home no more can beg or steal,
Or like a gibbet better than a wheel:

353

Hissed from the stage, or hooted from the court,
Their air, their dress, their politics import;   110
Obsequious, artful, voluble and gay,
On Britain's fond credulity they prey.
No gainful trade their industry can 'scape,
They sing, they dance, clean shoes, or cure a clap;
All sciences a fasting monsieur knows,   115
And bid him go to hell, to hell he goes.

Ah! what avails it, that, from slavery far,
I drew the breath of life in English air,
Was early taught a Briton's right to prize,
And lisp the tale of Henry's victories: 120
If the gulled conqueror receives the chain,
And flattery subdues when arms are vain?

Studious to please, and ready to submit,
The supple Gaul was born a parasite;
Still to his interest true, where'er he goes,   125
Wit, bravery, worth, his lavish tongue bestows:
In every face a thousand graces shine,
From every tongue flows harmony divine.
These arts in vain our rugged natives try,
Strain out with faltering diffidence a lie,   130
And get a kick for awkward flattery.

Besides, with justice, this discerning age
Admires their wondrous talents for the stage;
Well may they venture on the mimic's art,
Who play from morn to night a borrowed part: 135
Practised their master's notions to embrace,
Repeat his maxims, and reflect his face;
With every wild absurdity comply,
And view each object with another's eye;
To shake with laughter ere the jest they hear,   140
To pour at will the counterfeited tear,
And as their patron hints the cold or heat,
To shake in dog-days, in December sweat.

How, when competitors like these contend,
Can surly virtue hope to fix a friend?   145

Slaves that with serious impudence beguile,
And lie without a blush, without a smile;
Exalt each trifle, every vice adore,
Your taste in snuff, your judgement in a whore:
Can Balbo's eloquence applaud, and swear   150
He gropes his breeches with a monarch's air.

For arts like these preferred, admired, caressed,
They first invade your table, then your breast;
Explore your secrets with insidious art,
Watch the weak hour, and ransack all the heart: 155
Then soon your ill-placed confidence repay,
Commence your lords, and govern or betray.

By numbers here from shame or censure free,
All crimes are safe, but hated poverty:
This, only this, the rigid law pursues,   160
This, only this, provokes the snarling muse.
The sober trader at a tattered cloak,
Wakes from his dream, and labours for a joke;
With brisker air the silken courtiers gaze,
And turn the varied taunt a thousand ways.   165
Of all the griefs that harass the distressed,
Sure the most bitter is a scornful jest;
Fate never wounds more deep the generous heart,
Than when a blockhead's insult points the dart.

Has heaven reserved, in pity to the poor,   170
No pathless waste, or undiscovered shore?
No secret island in the boundless main?
No peaceful desert yet unclaimed by Spain?
Quick let us rise, the happy seats explore,
And bear oppression's insolence no more.   175
This mournful truth is every where confessed,
Slow rises worth, by poverty depressed:
But here more slow, where all are slaves to gold,
Where looks are merchandise, and smiles are sold;
Where won by bribes, by flatteries implored   180
The groom retails the favours of his lord.

But hark! th'affrighted crowd's tumultuous cries
Roll through the streets, and thunder to the skies;
Raised from some pleasing dream of wealth and power,
Some pompous palace, or some blissful bower,   185
Aghast you start, and scarce with aching sight
Sustain th'approaching fire's tremendous light;
Swift from pursuing horrors take your way,
And leave your little all to flames a prey:
Then through the world a wretched vagrant roam,   190
For where can starving merit find a home?
In vain your mournful narrative disclose,
While all neglect, and most insult your woes.

Should heaven's just bolts Orgilio's wealth confound,
And spread his flaming palace on the ground,   195
Swift o'er the land the dismal rumour flies,
And public mournings pacify the skies;
The laureate tribe in servile verse relate,
How virtue wars with persecuting fate:
With well-feigned gratitude the pensioned band   200
Refund the plunder of the beggared land.
See! while he builds, the gaudy vassals come,
And crowd with sudden wealth the rising dome;
The price of boroughs and of souls restore,
And raise his treasures higher than before.   205
Now blessed with all the baubles of the great,
The polished marble, and the shining plate,
Orgilio sees the golden pile aspire,
And hopes from angry heaven another fire.

Could'st thou resign the park and play content,   210
For the fair banks of Severn or of Trent:
There might'st thou find some elegant retreat,
Some hireling senator's deserted seat;
And stretch thy prospects o'er the smiling land,
For less than rent the dungeons of the Strand;   215
There prune thy walks, support thy drooping flowers,
Direct thy rivulets, and twine thy bowers;
And, while thy grounds a cheap repast afford,
Despise the dainties of a venal lord:
There every bush with nature's music rings,   220

There every breeze bears health upon its wings;
On all thy hours security shall smile,
And bless thine evening walk and morning toil.

Prepare for death, if here at night you roam,
And sign your will before you sup from home: 225
Some fiery fop, with new commission vain,
Who sleeps on brambles till he kills his man;
Some frolic drunkard, reeling from a feast,
Provokes a broil, and stabs you for a jest.
Yet ev'n these heroes, mischievously gay,   230
Lords of the street, and terrors of the way;
Flushed as they are with folly, youth and wine,
Their prudent insults to the poor confine;
Afar they mark the flambeau's bright approach,
And shun the shining train, and golden coach.   235

In vain, these dangers past, your doors you close,
And hope the balmy blessings of repose:
Cruel with guilt, and daring with despair,
The midnight murderer bursts the faithless bar;
Invades the sacred hour of silent rest,   240
And leaves, unseen, a dagger in your breast.

Scarce can our fields, such crowds at Tyburn die,
With hemp the gallows and the fleet supply:
Propose your schemes, ye Senatorian band,
Whose Ways and Means support the sinking land;   245
Lest ropes be wanting in the tempting spring,
To rig another convoy for the k—g.

A single jail, in Alfred's golden reign,
Could half the nation's criminals contain;
Fair justice then, without constraint adored,   250
Held high the steady scale, but dipped the sword;
No spies were paid, no special juries known,
Blesst age! but ah! how different from our own!

Much could I add, – but see the boat at hand,
The tide retiring, calls me from the land: 255
Farewell! – When youth, and health, and fortune spent,

357

Thou flyest for refuge to the wilds of Kent;
And tired like me with follies and with crimes,
In angry numbers warn'st succeeding times;
Then shall thy friend, nor thou refuse his aid,   260
Still foe to vice, forsake his Cambrian shade;
In virtue's cause once more exert his rage,
Thy satire point, and animate thy page.

London and *The Vanity of Human Wishes* were written during the first decade of Johnson's literary career. In *London* Johnson adopts the traditional posture of condemning the city, especially morally, and extolling the virtues of a civilised country retreat. This has puzzled some readers as in later life Johnson became very attached to London and is reported to have said, 'He who is tired of London, is tired of life'. On the other hand it is worth remembering that *London* was written when Johnson had just arrived in the metropolis, and his initial years there were fraught with disappointments. *London* is not the product, then, of insincerity, but rather of heartfelt experience for which Johnson found a suitable vehicle in Juvenal's poem on which his own is modelled. *The Vanity of Human Wishes*, of course, is so thoroughly Johnsonian that echoes of it can be found in almost all his other writings, including the Preface to the *Dictionary*.

Both *London* and *The Vanity of Human Wishes* are formal Imitations. Indeed, their subtitles, *A Poem in Imitation of the Third Satire of Juvenal*, and *The Tenth Satire of Juvenal Imitated*, declare as much. The formal Imitation was a new genre of which John Oldham is considered the founder. In the *Lives of the Poets* Johnson said of the genre:

> This mode of imitation, in which the ancients are familiarised by adapting their sentiments to modern topics, . . . was first practised in the reign of Charles the Second by Oldham and Rochester, . . . It is a kind of middle composition between translation and original design, which pleases when the thoughts are unexpectedly applicable and the parallels lucky.

In the seventeenth century Donne too had imitated various classical poets. The difference between his imitations and the formal Imitation was that poets like Pope and Johnson modelled their poems on a single classical poem, generally a satire, and drew attention to the relationship between the two poems. Indeed, for *London* Johnson published the parallel passages from Juvenal's *Satire III* at the foot of the page; for *The Vanity of Human Wishes* he cited the numbers of the verses of Juvenal's *Satire X*. Clearly he demanded from the reader a complex reading activity with the two poems reverberating in the reader's mind.

Johnson's two major poems, *London* and *The Vanity of Human Wishes*, are both written in the heroic couplet, a verse form that had reached its maturity in the hands of Pope. The form is particularly suited to the pointed wit of satiric writing. Brevity and compression are its chief characteristics. Johnson is also able to extend it into the larger unit of the verse paragraph, to express visions and analyses of greater scope. Characteristic of Johnson's use of the couplet is structural parallelism created by a careful division of the verse line into two parts. Within this parallelism Johnson often works through contrasts or repetitions. He skilfully varies the relationship between the different halves of the lines of the couplet to create intricate experience and commentary. Other rhetorical devices, especially the zeugma, abound in Johnson's writings, as they do in those of Pope; they have been pointed out in the notes. Johnson conforms to the Augustan use of abstractions, and the personification, if ever so slight, of abstract qualities. He does this without moving into the realm of allegory. A complexity in the weaving and interweaving of metaphors coupled with a tendency to rework the implications of certain key images during the course of the poem result in a complex and rich reading experience. It is an additional advantage to the modern reader if he has Latin; but despite Johnson's expectations we may dare to read his poems without it.

Epigraph
Quis ineptae/ Tam patiens urbis, tam ferreus ut teneat se? Juvenal (*Satire* I, 30–1) (For who could endure this monstrous city, however callous at heart, and swallow his wrath?). Trans. Peter Green.
[1] **grief and fondness**
Johnson's poem opens with typical Augustan abstractions personified through the use of the verb 'rebel' to which they both relate.
[2] **Thales**
There has been an extensive debate about the identity of Thales. Most often it has been assumed that the reference is to Johnson's friend Richard Savage who left London for Swansea in 1739. On the other hand Johnson himself is reputed to have said that by Thales he did not mean any particular person. The identity of Thales is less important than his function in the poem. Thales corresponds to Juvenal's Umbricius in the *Third Satire*. Like Umbricius who left Rome Thales leaves the city of London in disgust; *town* London.
[4] **hermit**
not literally an anchorite but one who lives a solitary life. The compressed antithesis in this line combines two ideas: 'I commend his decision to become a hermit' and 'I regret the loss of a friend'.
[5] **Resolved**
who is resolved; *from vice and London far* Johnson uses the rhetorical device of the zeugma in which the abstract and the concrete, the moral and the material, are pressed into an ironical relationship. The device, frequently used by Pope, is one of the sources of

compression and satire in eighteenth-century verse.
[7] **fixed**
settled; *Cambria* Wales.
[8] **St. David**
the patron saint of Wales; *true Briton* Thales' decision to leave London is a sign of his patriotism. It is parallel not only to Umbricius' departure from 'the Greek metropolis', but to the retreat into Wales of the original inhabitants of England, the Britons, who were harassed by the Anglo-Saxons.
[9] **Hibernia**
Ireland.
[10] **change**
exchange; *the rocks of Scotland* already there is an ambivalence in the speaker's attitude suggesting that the poem is not an undiluted statement in favour of the classical 'rural retreat'. It is well known that Johnson expressed a prejudice towards Scotland. When told that there were many fine prospects in Scotland, he is reported to have said, 'Sir, let me tell you, the noblest prospect that a Scotchman ever sees, is the high road that leads him to England', Boswell, *Life of Johnson*; *the Strand* a fashionable street in London.
[11] **There**
referring back to Scotland.
[12]
Again pointing to the economic hardships in Scotland or the countryside. The general thrust of the poem is towards an overall tragic vision of human life, not unlike that of *The Vanity of Human Wishes*.
[13] **Here**
referring to London; *conspire* plot.

359

[14]
Another interesting example of the zeugma in which a relationship is forged between 'rabble' and 'fire' through the verb 'rages'.

[15] **ambush**
'The post where soldiers and assassins are placed, in order to fall unexpectedly upon an enemy', Johnson, *Dictionary*; *relentless* 'unpitying; unmoved by kindness or tenderness', Johnson, *Dictionary*; *ruffians* 'A brutal, boisterous mischievous fellow; cutthroat; a robber; a murderer', Johnson, *Dictionary*.

[15]
Note the inverted syntax, the object preceding the subject, and the sentence ending with the verb. Here Johnson is working towards a certain emphasis; he is also concerned with the structure of the couplet. This inversion is not the habitual Miltonism of Collins and Thomson.

[16] **fell**
cruel and inhuman; *attorney* 'Such a person as by consent, commandment, or request, takes heed, fees, and takes upon him the charge of other men's business, in their absence', Johnson, *Dictionary*. Could also refer simply to an officer of the Common Law Court.

[18] **female atheist**
an example of unbearable loquacity; *talks you dead* bores you to death; cf. 'Nay, fly to Altars; there they'll talk you dead', Pope, *An Essay on Criticism*, line 624.

[19] **waits**
waits for; *wherry* a small boat; 'a light boat used on rivers', Johnson, *Dictionary*.

[22] **Greenwich**
a suburb of London on the banks of the river Thames; *silver flood* a periphrastic reference to the Thames.

[23] **Struck**
strongly impressed; *seat* place, situation; *Eliza* Queen Elizabeth I (1558–1603) who was born at Greenwich.

[24] **consecrated**
sacred, because Queen Elizabeth was born there.

[26] **call**
summon; *Britannia's glories* Britain's military, especially naval triumphs over the Spanish during the reign of Elizabeth I.

[27] **cross**
the cross of St George, the patron saint of England.

[28] **The guard of commerce**
the British navy guarded the country's trade routes to the Americas; *Spain* for much of Elizabeth's reign England was at war with Spain. The rivalry ended with success for the British and the defeat of the Spanish Armada in 1588.

[29] **masquerades**
'a diversion in which the company is masked', Johnson, *Dictionary*; *excise* a duty on the retailing of tea, coffee and a few other things. Robert Walpole, when he was prime minister, proposed an increase in the excise; defined in Johnson's *Dictionary* as: 'A hateful tax levied upon commodities, and adjudged not by the common judges of property, but wretches hired by those to whom excise is paid.'

[30]
Walpole's opponents wanted war with Spain, as an assertion of British rights in the American continent and the independence of British trading vessels.

[35]
The rest of the poem is a speech by Thales.

[37] **those cursed walls**
the city of London; *devote* devoted; *vice and gain* another example of a satiric equation established between the mental and the material through their dependence on the same verb. This method has been earlier referred to as the zeugma.

[38] **science**
intellectual work; 'any art or species of knowledge', Johnson, *Dictionary*; *unrewarded ... in vain* a deliberate pleonasm in order to create emphasis.

[39] **soothes**
assuages, mitigates.

[41] **steady . . . sustains**
note the alliteration and also the inversion.
[42] **revels**
is active, energetic.
[45] **verdant**
green; *osiers* 'a tree of the willow kind', Johnson, *Dictionary*.
[45–6] **pleasing . . . paintings**
Johnson's choice of language suggests a refined version of nature; he is certainly not thinking of a return to nature in any primitivist sense.
[47] **harassed Briton**
the reference is to the Anglo-Saxon invasions of the fifth and sixth centuries which caused the native inhabitants to retreat to Wales; see note to line 8.
[48] **defied**
challenged.
[49] **cell**
like the earlier 'hermit' of line 4 the word has religious connotations but does not imply religious retirement.
[50]
The blanks cannot be satisfactorily filled. It is possible that Johnson did not have any one person in mind.
[51] **pensions**
'In England it is generally understood to mean pay given to a state hireling for treason to his country', Johnson, *Dictionary*. State pensions were a common form of political bribery. Johnson himself was awarded a pension in 1762, but he did not change his *Dictionary* definition, though it was often turned against him.
[52] **patriot**
refers to the Tory opposition to Walpole, made up, by and large, of able writers who attacked the prime minister in political pamphlets and plays; the word was also applied to dissident Whigs; *courtier* the Whigs were called 'courtiers'.
[53] **Explain**
interpret in a way that justifies the surrender of British rights to Spain. Johnson said sarcastically of what he considered Walpole's policy of appeasement: 'The invasions of the

Spaniards were defended in the houses of Parliament'; cf. 'These leave the sense, their learning to display/ And those explain the meaning quite away', Pope, *Essay on Criticism*, lines 116–17; *dear-bought rights* commercial rights, especially in the slave-trade from Africa. Spain was anxious that Britain did not extend her rights in this area of trade.
[54] **pirates**
the Spanish seamen who carried out the then legal search of English vessels trafficking with her American possessions; *in the face of day* in broad daylight.
[55] **taint . . . poisoned**
taint so that it becomes poisoned.
[58] **farm a lottery**
lotteries in order to collect money for public projects were floated by the state, and patronised by all levels of society.
[59] **warbling eunuchs**
the *castrati*, or male sopranos of the Italian opera which was very popular at that time; *licensed stage* in 1737 Walpole passed the Licensing Act by which he hoped to control the attacks on him by contemporary dramatists like Fielding. Johnson satirised the Act's censorship of the stage in his *A Compleat Vindication of the Licensers of the Stage* (1739).
[60] **thoughtless**
unthinking. The word was often used in this sense, cf. 'Thoughtless as monarch oaks, that shade the plain', Dryden, *Macflecknoe*, line 27. Johnson used the word in a similar sense later in line 103.
[61] **Heroes**
satirical use of the word; *pride* complex use of the word such that it could be both subject and object to the verb: 'What can contain your pride?' or 'How boundless is your pride?', and 'How much can your pride hold?'.
[62] **thirst of power and gold**
Cf. 'Some through Ambition, or through thirst for gold', Dryden, *Georgics*, ii, 734.

[65] **a groaning nation's spoils**
spoils taken from a groaning nation;
but the suggestion that the nation is
groaning because it is being plundered is inescapable. Again a tightly
packed phrase which is characteristic
of the poem.

[66] **public crimes**
crimes against the people.

[68] **start**
'shrink', Johnson, *Dictionary*; *perjury*
false oaths.

[70]
To expose a titled poet as derivative.

[72] **Gazetteer**
The Daily Gazetteer, the official
newspaper of Walpole's ministry.
'The paper which at that time con-
tained apologies for the court',
Johnson's note.

[74] **H—y's**
i.e. Hervey's. John, Lord Hervey was
a supporter of Walpole. He was the
original of Pope's 'Sporus'.

[76] **sap**
undermine.

[77] **address**
'skill, dexterity', Johnson, *Dictionary*.

[79] **rustic tongue**
the simple and honest mode of
expression of the country as opposed
to the over-sophisticated and false language of the city. There is irony in the
speaker's view of his own expression
as simple and unsophisticated.

[80] **puzzle**
complicate, make obscure; *varnish*
gloss over.

[81–2]
Notice the patterns in the lines; the
first line offers parallelisms, the
second one presents the antithesis
between live/die with the adverbs
taking opposite positions in the two
phrases. The technique makes for
compression and variety.

[83]
Friendship is based on complicity in
crimes against society; *endears* there is
a slight pun on this word. The suggestion of making dear in the sense of
making valuable or expensive is a read

back in the context of the next line's
'fortune shares'.

[84] **Orgilio**
the name implies a proud, arrogant
person, cf. lines 194–209.

[86] **Marlborough**
John Churchill (1650–1722) was the
First Duke of Marlborough. He was a
famous general with victories at Blenheim (1704), Ramillies (1706) and Mal-
plaquet (1709) to his credit. Despite
handsome rewards for his military
successes he had a reputation for
avarice. 'That is no longer doubted, of
which the nation was then first
informed, that the war was unneces-
sarily protracted to fill the pockets of
Marlborough, and that it would have
been continued without end if he
could have continued his annual plunder', Johnson, *Life of Swift*; *Villiers*
George Villiers (1628–87) was the
second Duke of Buckingham. Dryden
portrayed him as 'Zimri' in *Absalom
and Achitophel*, and later Pope
described his unfortunate end in his
Epistle Of the Use of Riches, lines
299–314.

[89] **self-approving**
having a clear conscience. Cf. 'One
self-approving hour whole years out-
weighs', Pope, *An Essay on Man*, iv,
255.

[85–90]
These lines, it would seem, are
directly addressed by Thales to his
friend, though we still get them
within the framework of the friend's
reporting of Thales' speech.

[92]
The word 'who' refers back to 'the
great'.

[94] **common shore**
Oldham had translated Juvenal as follows: 'the Common-shore/ Where
France does all her filth and ordure
pour', lines 184–5. Johnson had in
mind 'sewer' which he substituted for
'shore' in later editions. In the *Dictionary* Johnson glossed 'sewer' as 'shore'
with the comment: 'the meaning is
the same: Shore: A drain; properly a
sewer.'

[97] **transports**
'to hurry by violence or passion', Johnson, *Dictionary*.

[98] **French metropolis**
the French provided both a military and cultural threat. France is a suitable counterpart to Juvenal's Greece. In attacking France Johnson also expressed opposition to Walpole's foreign policy of an alliance with France.

[99] **Edward**
Edward III (1312–77) most noted for his victory over the French at Crécy in 1346.

[99]
Extended metaphor of light. It is worth noting that Johnson mythologises earlier periods in British history as 'golden ages'.

[100] **heroes . . . saints**
in contrast to line 61 where heroism was coupled with 'virtue . . . o'erthrown'.

[101] **lineaments**
'feature; discriminating mark in the form', Johnson, *Dictionary*.

[102] **rustic**
as in line 79, simple and honest; *surly* rough.

[103] **lost**
there is a slight pun on the word as it relates to both 'thoughtless ease' and 'warrior'; *thoughtless* as in line 60, unthinking, almost in a stupor.

[105] **refined away**
used satirically; usually 'refined' carried a sense of upliftment.

[108] **gibbet**
gallows; *wheel* breaking on the wheel was a particularly painful method of execution used in France before the French Revolution when it was replaced by the guillotine.

[111] **voluble**
carries both senses of the word: 'changeable, inconstant', and 'having great fluency or readiness of speech'.

[112] **fond**
foolish, simple-minded.

[113] **industry**
diligence, assiduity.

[114] **clap**
venereal disease or gonorrhoea, 'the French disease'. Note the descending order in the kind of actions performed.

[116]
Cf. 'And bid him go to heav'n, to heav'n he goes', Dryden, *Third Satire of Juvenal*, line 141.

[117]
Cf. 'Ah! what avail his glossy, varying dyes', Pope, *Windsor-Forest*, line 115.

[120] **Henry's victories**
Henry V reigned from 1413 to 1422. He defeated the French in several battles, the best known of which is the battle of Agincourt (1415).

[121] **gulled**
tricked, defrauded.

[122] **vain**
there is a slight pun on this word owing to its connection with 'flattery' in the earlier part of the line. Hence it carries suggestions of 'false pride' as well as of 'what is useless' or 'ineffectual'.

[124] **supple**
flexible in assuming postures, especially of deference; 'flattering, fawning, bending', Johnson, *Dictionary*; *parasite* 'one that frequents rich tables, and earns his welcome by flattery', Johnson, *Dictionary*.

[126] **lavish tongue**
in contrast to Thales' 'rustic tongue', line 79.

[129–31]
A triplet, very rare in Johnson's mature verse.

[142] **patron**
Cf. 'Toil, envy, want, the patron, and the jail', *The Vanity*, line 160. Writers in Johnson's time were financially dependent on the patronage of the aristocracy.

[143] **dog-days**
the period when the dog-star Sirius rises and sets with the sun, from 3 July to 18 August, a season of intense heat and discomfort; Cf. ''Twas noon; the sultry dog-star from the sky/ Scorched Indian swains, the rivelled grass was dry', Dryden, *Georgics*, iv, 615.

[145] **surly**
rough, as in line 102; *fix a friend*
make a real friend. Cf. 'Who most
to shun or hate mankind pretend,/
Seek an admirer or would fix a
friend', Pope, *Essay on Man*, iv,
43–4.
[146] **Slaves**
stands in apposition to 'competitors',
line 144; *serious impudence* considered
unabashedness; *beguile* deceive,
delude.
[148–9]
The second line offers concrete examples for the 'trifle' and 'vice' of the first
line of the couplet. Cf. 'Then turns
repentant, and his God adores,/ With
the same spirit that he drinks and
whores', Pope, *Epistle to Cobham*, lines
188–9.
[150] **Balbo**
The name implies a stammerer, and
suits well with 'eloquence'.
[151] **gropes**
in the sense of to touch with the hand,
take hold of, grasp.
[153] **invade your table, then your
breast**
The verb functions in both its literal
and metaphorical senses to create a
satiric equation between 'table' and
'breast'. Johnson is referring to the
popularity of the French cuisine
among the rich in London. The
English considered it to be unwhole-
some, just as French influence in
general was believed to be morally
corrupting.
[154] **insidious**
cunning, wily.
[155] **weak hour**
moment of weakness.
[157] **Commence**
'to take a new character', Johnson,
Dictionary, hence 'to become' or 'turn
into'.
[158] **By numbers**
because of their large numbers.
[158–77]
Johnson here seems to be expressing
his own feelings.
[160] **rigid**
severe.

[161] **snarling muse**
the muse of satire.
[162] **sober**
serious, solemn.
[163] **dream**
of wealth, as in line 184; *labours for a
joke* tries hard to make a joke. It could
also mean that he works hard for very
little reward.
[164] **brisker air**
sharper, smarter manner; *silken
courtiers* in contrast to the 'tattered
cloak'.
[167] **scornful jest**
jests made at the expense of the poor;
the phrase glances back satirically at
'labours for a joke'.
[168] **generous**
'Noble of mind; magnanimous; open
of heart', Johnson, *Dictionary*.
[170] **pity to the poor**
Cf. 'with pity for the poor' , Dryden,
Georgics, ii, 714.
[172] **main**
'The ocean; the great sea, as distinguished from bays and rivers',
Johnson, *Dictionary*.
[173]
'The Spaniards at this time were said
to make claim to some of our
American provinces', Johnson's
note.
[174] **seats**
'situation; site', Johnson, *Dictionary*;
i.e. places to settle in; *explore* look
for.
[170–4]
Cf. 'Yet simple Nature to his hope has
giv'n,/ Behind the cloud-topt hill, an
humbler heav'n;/ Some safer world in
depth of woods embrac'd,/ Some happier island in the watery waste,' Pope,
Essay on Man, i, 102–6.
[177]
Johnson contrasts rises/depressed,
and worth/poverty; he draws satiric
attention to 'worth' as something cal-
culated in terms of wealth or poverty.
The idea is extended in the 'slaves to
gold' of the next line.
[179]
Where everything can be bought for
money.

[181] **retails**
retail: 'to sell at second hand',
Johnson, *Dictionary*.

[181]
Where the servants take money for
using the influence of their masters.

[182] **tumultuous**
violent, turbulent.

[185] **blissful bower**
Cf. Spenser's 'Bower of bliss'.

[186] **Aghast**
'Struck with horror, as at the sight of
a spectre', Johnson, *Dictionary*; **start**
rise suddenly.

[187] **Sustain**
endure, withstand; **tremendous**
Fleeman glosses it in its etymological
sense: to tremble, hence that which
causes to tremble.

[188]
Quickly remove yourself from the
terrible things that pursue you.

[192] **disclose**
'to reveal; to tell', Johnson, *Dictionary*.

[194] **heaven's just bolts**
divine punishment through lightning;
Orgilio the original draft had 'Sejano';
for the eighteenth-century reader
versed in the classics there was a line
of association linking Verres (the
wicked governor of Sicily), Sejanus
(the powerful favourite of Tiberius
whose fall is described in Juvenal,
Satire X), Wolsey (Henry VIII's
powerful Cardinal who fell out of
favour and had an ignominious death)
and Walpole; *confound* 'destroy',
Johnson, *Dictionary*.

[195] **spread**
extend or scatter through burning
down; *flaming palace* set on fire by
lightning.

[197] **pacify**
appease.

[194–7]
'This was by Hitch a Bookseller justly
remarked to be no picture of modern
manners, though it might be true of
Rome', Johnson's note. Charles Hitch
was one of the publishers of Johnson's
translation of Lobo's *Voyage to
Abyssinia* and of his *Plan of a
Dictionary*.

[198] **laureate tribe**
the poets who are in favour at the
court and therefore appointed as
court-poets or otherwise honoured;
servile verse slavish poetry.

[199]
a parody of the stock phrases used by
contemporary poets.

[200] **pensioned band**
see note to line 51.

[201]
Give Orgilio as much wealth as he had
lost in the fire, wealth originally
acquired by exploiting the poor.

[202] **gaudy**
'showy; splendid; pompous; ostentatiously fine', Johnson, *Dictionary*.

[203] **dome**
'a building, a house, a fabrick',
Johnson, *Dictionary*.

[204] **price of boroughs**
Certain small boroughs (pocket
boroughs) were controlled by wealthy
aristocrats who could, for an election,
give or sell the representation to men
in whom they were interested; *and of
souls* the ownership of a manor often
carried with it the right to appoint the
clergyman to the local church. The
criticism is of corrupt landlords who
used their influence over Parliament
and the Church.

[206] **baubles**
'a thing of more show than use',
Johnson, *Dictionary*.

[208] **aspire**
rise.

[210] **park**
London had several parks like St
James's Park and Hyde Park; *play* as
in the theatre. These were considered
the chief pleasures of London; *content*
contentedly.

[211] **Severn**
the river in the west of England
that forms its boundary with Wales;
Trent the river that forms the
traditional boundary between the
north and south of England. These
rivers were far enough away
from London to be considered virtuous, without actually being in wild
countryside.

[212] **elegant**
'pleasing with minor beauties', Johnson, *Dictionary*; carries a sense of the civilised and the cultured.
[213]
It was quite common for Members of Parliament from the rural areas to neglect their constituencies and live for long periods in London, where they functioned politically under the influence of their patrons.
[214] **prospects**
views.
[215] **dungeons**
basements or cellars.
[217] **Direct thy rivulets**
redirecting the courses of small rivers was part of the landscaping tradition of the century; *twine* to twist together and unite; *bowers* 'an arbour, a sheltered place covered with green trees, twined and bent', Johnson, *Dictionary*; *twine thy bowers* to create natural shelters by twisting together, as they grow, the branches of trees.
[216–17]
Johnson's description is in the Renaissance tradition of a tender and mutually beneficial relationship between man and nature; for example, Milton's description of Eve: 'oft stooping to support/ Each flower of slender stalk, whose head, though gay/ Carnation, purple, azure, or speck'd with gold,/ Hung drooping unsustain'd', *Paradise Lost*, ix, 427–30.
[218] **repast**
meal.
[219] **venal**
unprincipled, corrupt.
[222] **security**
freedom from anxieties and cares.
[223] **thine evening**
Johnson changed this to 'thy evening' in the 1755 text. In that same year he commented in his *Dictionary*: '*mine* and *thine* were formerly used before a vowel, as *mine amiable lady*; which though now disused in prose, might be still properly continued in poetry'.
[226] **Fop**
'a man of small understanding and much ostentation', Johnson,

Dictionary; *new commission* who has just become an officer.
[227] **brambles**
'Taken in popular language, for any rough, prickly plant', Johnson, *Dictionary*; nowadays 'thorns'. The phrase implied for extreme impatience.
[227]
Who is restless for military action.
[228] **frolic**
'gay, full of levity, full of pranks', Johnson, *Dictionary*.
[229] **broil**
'A tumult; a quarrel', Johnson, *Dictionary*.
[230] **heroes**
the word is used satirically; *mischievously* in a harmful, wicked way.
[232]
Cf. 'when the night/ Darkens the streets, then wander forth the sons/ Of Belial, swol'n with insolence and wine', *Paradise Lost*, i, 500–2.
[233]
prudently insult only the poor.
[216–33]
In the *Life of Savage* (1744) Johnson had written about the choice of making a retreat into the country:

As he was ready to entertain himself with future pleasures, he had planned out a scheme of life for the country, of which he had no knowledge but from pastorals and songs. He imagined that he should be transported to scenes of flowery felicity, like those which one poet has reflected to another, and had projected a perpetual round of innocent pleasures, of which he suspected no interruption from pride, or ignorance, or brutality. With these expectations he was so enchanted that when he was once gently reproached by a friend for submitting to live upon a subscription and advised rather by a resolute exertion of his abilities to support himself, he could not bear to debar himself from the happiness which was to be found in the calm of a cottage, or lose the opportunity of listening, without intermission, to the melody of the nightingale, which he believed was to be heard from every bramble, and which he did not fail to mention as a very important part of the happiness of a country life.

Despite the gentle satire in these lines of viewing the country as a pastoral idyll, it must be appreciated that for the young Johnson, just come from Lichfield to the metropolis, the initial experience of London must have been traumatic, and he was not altogether insincere in adopting the posture of Juvenal's Umbricius. The Johnson of 1738 is not the man who would have said that he who was tired of London was tired of life.

[234] **flambeau**
a lighted torch, usually made of thick wick dipped in wax; *bright approach* approaching light.

[235] **train**
retinue.

[237] **balmy**
soothing; *repose* sleep, rest.

[239] **bar**
the rod that secured the door by passing through two handles; *faithless* which gives way, unreliable.

[240] **Invades**
both literally enters the house through force, and also in the sense of violates the time designated for rest.

[242] **Tyburn**
the place in London where criminals were hanged till 1783. It was near Marble Arch.

[243] **hemp**
a fibrous plant used for making rope.

[242–3]
So much rope is needed to hang criminals at Tyburn that the farmers cannot produce enough hemp to meet the requirements of both the hangman and the British fleet.

[245] **Ways and Means**
Committee of Ways and Means, a committee of the House of Commons; 'Methods of procuring funds and supplies for the current expenditure of the state', *OED*; the dubious methods by which Parliament raised money.

[247] **rig**
there is a slight pun on the word in its sense from 'riggish' which Johnson defines in the *Dictionary* as 'an old name for a whore'.

[246–7]
The reference is to George II's frequent and prolonged trips to Hanover to be with his mistress.

[248] **Alfred**
(849–99) King of Wessex; warded off Danish invasions; an educator, chronicler, lawgiver.

[250–1]
Johnson presents the traditional emblem of Justice with the scales held up and the sword lowered and pointing downwards.

[252] **spies**
Walpole was believed to have an extensive network of spies to counteract the Jacobites; *special juries* 'a jury consisting of persons who (being on the Juror's book) are of a certain station in society, as esquires, bankers, or merchants, or occupy a house or other premises of a certain rateable value', *OED*. The *OED* gives the following illustration from Blackstone: 'Special juries were originally introduced in trials at bar when the causes were of too great nicety for the discussion of ordinary freeholders; or where the sheriff was suspected of partiality.'

[255] **retiring**
receding.

[257] **wilds**
Wealds (or wold) meaning woodland was often confused with 'wild' meaning untamed or savage. It appears that Johnson did not intend the fusion as he kept the words apart in his *Dictionary*.

[259] **angry numbers**
poetry expressing indignation.

[260] **aid**
Thales, unlike Juvenal's Umbricius, views himself as a co-author and not merely a listener to his friend's poem.

[262–3]
Thales makes specific how he will assist his friend, and what is his motivation in doing so; *rage* 'vehemence of

mind', Johnson, *Dictionary*; in this context carrying the sense of *furor poeticus*, poetic *inspiration*. [254–63]
The poem concludes with the older man predicting that his young friend will do later what he himself at present wishes to do. Thales also asserts his commitment to satirical verse to be more powerful than his

desire to live in the country. That he does so in a speech even before he has left for the country, or is rather outside the city, but not yet in the country, affirms that his consciousness is chiefly located in his poetry. And yet the situation is complicated by the fact that Thales' speech is framed in his friend's reporting voice.

———◇———

27 / *The Vanity of Human Wishes*

The Tenth Satire of Juvenal Imitated

Let observation with extensive view,
Survey mankind, from China to Peru;
Remark each anxious toil, each eager strife,
And watch the busy scenes of crowded life:
Then say how hope and fear, desire and hate   5
O'erspread with snares the clouded maze of fate,
Where wavering man, betrayed by venturous pride,
To tread the dreary paths without a guide,
As treacherous phantoms in the mist delude,
Shuns fancied ills, or chases airy good;   10
How rarely reason guides the stubborn choice,
Rules the bold hand, or prompts the suppliant voice;
How nations sink, by darling schemes oppressed,
When vengeance listens to the fool's request.
Fate wings with every wish th'afflictive dart,   15
Each gift of nature, and each grace of art,
With fatal heat impetuous courage glows,
With fatal sweetness elocution flows,
Impeachment stops the speaker's powerful breath,
And restless fire precipitates on death.   20

But scarce observed, the knowing and the bold
Fall in the general massacre of gold;
Wide-wasting pest! that rages unconfined,
And crowds with crimes the records of mankind:

For gold his sword the hireling ruffian draws,   25
For gold the hireling judge distorts the laws;
Wealth heaped on wealth, nor truth nor safety buys,
The dangers gather as the treasures rise.

   Let history tell where rival kings command,
And dubious title shakes the madded land,   30
When statutes glean the refuse of the sword,
How much more safe the vassal than the lord:
Low skulks the hind beneath the rage of power,
And leaves the wealthy traitor in the Tower,
Untouched his cottage, and his slumbers sound,   35
Though confiscation's vultures hover round.

   The needy traveller, serene and gay,
Walks the wild heath, and sings his toil away;
Does envy seize thee? crush th'upbraiding joy,
Increase his riches and his peace destroy: 40
Now fears in dire vicissitude invade,
The rustling brake alarms, and quivering shade;
Nor light nor darkness bring his pain relief,
One shows the plunder, and one hides the thief.

   Yet still one general cry the skies assails,   45
And gain and grandeur load the tainted gales:
Few know the toiling statesman's fear or care,
Th'insidious rival and the gaping heir.

   Once more, Democritus, arise on earth,
With cheerful wisdom and instructive mirth;   50
See motley life in modern trappings dressed,
And feed with varied fools th'eternal jest:
Thou who couldst laugh where want enchained caprice,
Toil crushed conceit, and man was of a piece;
Where wealth unloved without a mourner died,   55
And scarce a sycophant was fed by pride;
Where ne'er was known the form of mock debate,
Or seen a new-made mayor's unwieldy state;
Where change of favourites made no change of laws,
And senates heard before they judged a cause;   60
How wouldst thou shake at Britain's modish tribe,

Dart the quick taunt, and edge the piercing gibe?
Attentive truth and nature to descry,
And pierce each scene with philosophic eye.
To thee were solemn toys or empty show,   65
The robes of pleasure and the veils of woe:
All aid the farce, and all thy mirth maintain,
Whose joys are causeless, or whose griefs are vain.

   Such was the scorn that filled the sage's mind,
Renewed at every glance on humankind: 70
How just that scorn ere yet thy voice declare,
Search every state, and canvass every prayer.

   Unnumbered suppliants crowd preferment's gate,
Athirst for wealth, and burning to be great:
Delusive fortune hears th'incessant call,   75
They mount, they shine, evaporate, and fall.
On every stage the foes of peace attend,   ·
Hate dogs their flight, and insult mocks their end.
Love ends with hope, the sinking statesman's door
Pours in the morning worshipper no more;   80
For growing names the weekly scribbler lies,
To growing wealth the dedicator flies,
From every room descends the painted face,
That hung the bright Palladium of the place,
And smoked in kitchens, or in auctions sold,   85
To better features yields the frame of gold;
For now no more we trace in every line
Heroic worth, benevolence divine:
The form distorted justifies the fall,
And detestation rids th'indignant wall.   90

   But will not Britain hear the last appeal,
Sign her foe's doom, or guard her favourite's zeal?
Through freedom's sons no more remonstrance rings,
Degrading nobles and controlling kings;
Our supple tribes repress their patriot throats,   95
And ask no questions but the price of votes:
With weekly libels and septennial ale,
Their wish is full to riot and to rail.

In full-blown dignity, see Wolsey stand,
Law in his voice, and fortune in his hand: 100
To him the church, the realm, their powers consign,
Through him the rays of regal bounty shine,
Turned by his nod the stream of honour flows,
His smile alone security bestows:
Still to new heights his restless wishes tower,   105
Claim leads to claim, and power advances power;
Till conquest unresisted ceased to please,
And rights submitted, left him none to seize.
At length his sovereign frowns – the train of state
Mark the keen glance, and watch the sign to hate.   110
Where-e'er he turns he meets a stranger's eye,
His suppliants scorn him, and his followers fly;
At once is lost the pride of aweful state,
The golden canopy, the glittering plate,
The regal palace, the luxurious board,   115
The liveried army, and the menial lord.
With age, with cares, with maladies oppressed,
He seeks the refuge of monastic rest.
Grief aids disease, remembered folly stings,
And his last sighs reproach the faith of kings.   120

    Speak thou, whose thoughts at humble peace repine,
Shall Wolsey's wealth, with Wolsey's end be thine?
Or livest thou now, with safer pride content,
The wisest justice on the banks of Trent?
For why did Wolsey near the steeps of fate,   125
On weak foundations raise th'enormous weight?
Why but to sink beneath misfortune's blow,
With louder ruin to the gulfs below?

    What gave great Villiers to th'assassin's knife,
And fixed disease on Harley's closing life?   130
What murdered Wentworth, and what exiled Hyde,
By kings protected, and to kings allied?
What but their wish indulged in courts to shine,
And power too great to keep, or to resign?

    When first the college rolls receive his name,   135
The young enthusiast quits his ease for fame:

Through all his veins the fever of renown
Burns from the strong contagion of the gown;
O'er Bodley's dome his future labours spread,
And Bacon's mansion trembles o'er his head. 140
Are these thy views? proceed, illustrious youth,
And virtue guard thee to the throne of truth!
Yet should thy soul indulge the generous heat,
Till captive science yields her last retreat;
Should reason guide thee with her brightest ray, 145
And pour on misty doubt resistless day;
Should no false kindness lure to loose delight,
Nor praise relax, nor difficulty fright;
Should tempting novelty thy cell refrain,
And sloth effuse her opiate fumes in vain; 150
Should beauty blunt on fops her fatal dart,
Nor claim the triumph of a lettered heart;
Should no disease thy torpid veins invade,
Nor melancholy's phantoms haunt thy shade;
Yet hope not life from grief or danger free, 155
Nor think the doom of man reversed for thee:
Deign on the passing world to turn thine eyes,
And pause awhile from letters, to be wise;
There mark what ills the scholar's life assail,
Toil, envy, want, the patron, and the jail. 160
See nations slowly wise, and meanly just,
To buried merit raise the tardy bust.
If dreams yet flatter, once again attend,
Hear Lydiat's life, and Galileo's end.

Nor deem, when learning her last prize bestows, 165
The glittering eminence exempt from foes:
See when the vulgar 'scape, despised or awed,
Rebellion's vengeful talons seize on Laud.
From meaner minds, though smaller fines content,
The plundered palace or sequestered rent; 170
Marked out by dangerous parts he meets the shock,
And fatal learning leads him to the block:
Around his tomb let art and genius weep,
But hear his death, ye blockheads, hear and sleep.

The festal blazes, the triumphal show,   175
The ravished standard, and the captive foe,
The senate's thanks, the gazette's pompous tale,
With force resistless o'er the brave prevail:
Such bribes the rapid Greek o'er Asia whirled,
For such the steady Romans shook the world;   180
For such in distant lands the Britons shine,
And stain with blood the Danube or the Rhine;
This power has praise, that virtue scarce can warm,
Till fame supplies the universal charm.
Yet reason frowns on war's unequal game,   185
Where wasted nations raise a single name,
And mortgaged states their grandsire's wreaths regret,
From age to age in everlasting debt;
Wreaths which at last the dear-bought right convey
To rust on medals, or on stones decay.   190

On what foundation stands the warrior's pride,
How just his hopes let Swedish Charles decide:
A frame of adamant, a soul of fire,
No dangers fright him, and no labours tire;
O'er love, o'er fear, extends his wide domain,   195
Unconquered lord of pleasure and of pain;
No joys to him pacific scepters yield,
War sounds the trump, he rushes to the field;
Behold surrounding kings their power combine,
And one capitulate, and one resign;   200
Peace courts his hand, but spreads her charms in vain;
'Think nothing gained,' he cries, 'till nought remain,
On Moscow's walls till Gothic standards fly,
And all be mine beneath the polar sky.'
The march begins in military state,   205
And nations on his eye suspended wait;
Stern famine guards the solitary coast,
And winter barricades the realms of frost;
He comes, not want and cold his course delay;
Hide, blushing glory, hide Pultowa's day: 210
The vanquished hero leaves his broken bands,
And shows his miseries in distant lands;
Condemned a needy supplicant to wait,
While ladies interpose, and slaves debate.

But did not chance at length her error mend? 215
Did no subverted empire mark his end?
Did rival monarchs give the fatal wound?
Or hostile millions press him to the ground?
His fall was destined to a barren strand,
A petty fortress, and a dubious hand: 220
He left the name, at which the world grew pale,
To point a moral, or adorn a tale.

All times their scenes of pompous woes afford,
From Persia's tyrant to Bavaria's lord:
In gay hostility, and barbarous pride, 225
With half mankind embattled at his side,
Great Xerxes comes to seize the certain prey,
And starves exhausted regions in his way;
Attendant flattery counts his myriads o'er,
Till counted myriads soothe his pride no more; 230
Fresh praise is tried till madness fires his mind,
The waves he lashes, and enchains the wind;
New powers are claimed, new powers are still bestowed,
Till rude resistance lops the spreading god;
The daring Greeks deride the martial show, 235
And heap their valleys with the gaudy foe;
Th'insulted sea with humbler thoughts he gains,
A single skiff to speed his flight remains;
Th'incumbered oar scarce leaves the dreaded coast
Through purple billows and a floating host. 240

The bold Bavarian, in a luckless hour,
Tries the dread summits of Caesarean power;
With unexpected legions bursts away,
And sees defenceless realms receive his sway:
Short sway! fair Austria spreads her mournful charms, 245
The queen, the beauty, sets the world in arms;
From hill to hill the beacons' rousing blaze
Spreads wide the hope of plunder and of praise;
The fierce Croatian, and the wild Hussar,
And all the sons of ravage crowd the war; 250
The baffled prince in honour's flattering bloom
Of hasty greatness finds the fatal doom,

His foe's derision, and his subjects' blame,
And steals to death from anguish and from shame.

    Enlarge my life with multitude of days, 255
In health, in sickness, thus the suppliant prays:
Hides from himself his state, and shuns to know,
That life protracted is protracted woe.
Time hovers o'er, impatient to destroy,
And shuts up all the passages of joy: 260
In vain their gifts the bounteous seasons pour,
The fruit autumnal, and the vernal flower,
With listless eyes the dotard views the store,
He views, and wonders that they please no more;
Now pall the tasteless meats, and joyless wines, 265
And luxury with sighs her slave resigns.
Approach, ye minstrels, try the soothing strain,
Diffuse the tuneful lenitives of pain:
No sounds alas would touch th'impervious ear,
Though dancing mountains witnessed Orpheus near; 270
Nor lute nor lyre his feeble powers attend,
Nor sweeter music of a virtuous friend,
But everlasting dictates crowd his tongue,
Perversely grave, or positively wrong.
The still returning tale, and lingering jest, 275
Perplex the fawning niece and pampered guest,
While growing hopes scarce awe the gathering sneer,
And scarce a legacy can bribe to hear;
The watchful guests still hint the last offence,
The daughter's petulance, the son's expense, 280
Improve his heady rage with treacherous skill,
And mould his passions till they make his will.

    Unnumbered maladies his joints invade,
Lay siege to life and press the dire blockade;
But unextinguished avarice still remains, 285
And dreaded losses aggravate his pains:
He turns, with anxious heart and crippled hands,
His bonds of debt, and mortgages of lands;
Or views his coffers with suspicious eyes,
Unlocks his gold, and counts it till he dies. 290

But grant, the virtues of a temperate prime
Bless with an age exempt from scorn or crime:
An age that melts with unperceived decay,
And glides in modest innocence away;
Whose peaceful day benevolence endears,   295
Whose night congratulating conscience cheers;
The general favourite as the general friend:
Such age there is, and who shall wish its end?

Yet ev'n on this her load misfortune flings,
To press the weary minutes' flagging wings: 300
New sorrow rises as the day returns,
A sister sickens, or a daughter mourns.
Now kindred merit fills the sable bier,
Now lacerated friendship claims a tear.
Year chases year, decay pursues decay,   305
Still drops some joy from withering life away;
New forms arise, and different views engage,
Superfluous lags the veteran on the stage,
Till pitying nature signs the last release,
And bids afflicted worth retire to peace.   310

But few there are whom hours like these await,
Who set unclouded in the gulfs of fate:
From Lydia's monarch should the search descend,
By Solon cautioned to regard his end,
In life's last scene what prodigies surprise,   315
Fears of the brave, and follies of the wise?
From Marlborough's eyes the streams of dotage flow,
And Swift expires a driveler and a show.

The teeming mother, anxious for her race,
Begs for each birth the fortune of a face: 320
Yet Vane could tell what ills from beauty spring;
And Sedley cursed the form that pleased a king.
Ye nymphs of rosy lips and radiant eyes,
Whom pleasure keeps too busy to be wise,
Whom joys with soft varieties invite,   325
By day the frolic, and the dance by night,
Who frown with vanity, who smile with art,
And ask the latest fashion of the heart,

What care, what rules your heedless charms shall save,
Each nymph your rival, and each youth your slave? 330
Against your fame with fondness hate combines,
The rival batters, and the lover mines.
With distant voice neglected virtue calls,
Less heard and less, the faint remonstrance falls;
Tired with contempt, she quits the slippery reign, 335
And pride and prudence take her seat in vain.
In crowd at once, where none the pass defend,
The harmless freedom, and the private friend.
The guardians yield, by force superior plied;
By interest, prudence; and by flattery, pride. 340
Now beauty falls betrayed, despised, distressed,
And hissing infamy proclaims the rest.

   Where then shall Hope and Fear their objects find?
Must dull suspence corrupt the stagnant mind?
Must helpless man, in ignorance sedate, 345
Roll darkling down the torrent of his fate?
Must no dislike alarm, no wishes rise,
No cries attempt the mercies of the skies?
Enquirer, cease, petitions yet remain,
Which heaven may hear, nor deem religion vain. 350
Still raise for good the supplicating voice,
But leave to heaven the measure and the choice,
Safe in his power whose eyes discern afar
The secret ambush of a specious prayer.
Implore his aid, in his decisions rest, 355
Secure whate'er he gives, he gives the best.
Yet when the sense of sacred presence fires,
And strong devotion to the skies aspires,
Pour forth thy fervours for a healthful mind,
Obedient passions, and a will resigned; 360
For love, which scarce collective man can fill;
For patience sovereign o'er transmuted ill;
For faith, that panting for a happier seat,
Counts death kind nature's signal of retreat:
These goods for man the laws of heaven ordain, 365
These goods he grants, who grants the power to gain;
With these celestial wisdom calms the mind,
And makes the happiness she does not find.

[1–2]
The opening couplet has been the source of much controversy and commentary. The opinions of Wordsworth, Coleridge and Tennyson are contained in Coleridge's comment in his *Lectures on Shakespeare and Milton*: 'as much as to say "Let observation with extensive observation, observe mankind extensively"'. The lines are not in fact tautological, but an expression of the overview of the mind as it reflects on its own activity in the process of perception. Such an interpretation suits well with the structure of the poem in which large general truths are illustrated through concrete examples. Cf. 'Wand'ring from clime to clime, observant strayed,/ Their manners noted, and their states surveyed', Pope, *Odyssey*, lines 5–6.

[2] **China to Peru**
this very concretist phrase is nevertheless richly allusive. Cf. 'in all Nations from *China to Peru*', Sir William Temple, *Of Poetry*; 'From frozen Lapland to Peru', Soame Jenyns, *Epistle to Lord Lovelace*; 'All human Race, from China to Peru', Thomas Warton, *Of the Universal Love of Pleasure*. Johnson was using an accepted phrase for the idea of mankind in general.

[3] **anxious**
'disturbed about some uncertain event', Johnson, *Dictionary*; *eager* keen, sharp; *strife* striving.

[5] **Then say**
the subject is still 'Observation'.

[6] **snares ... clouded maze**
there is some overlap in these ideas for emphasis.

[7] **wavering**
to waver: 'to totter, to be in danger of falling', Johnson, *Dictionary*; *venturous* dangerous, rash.

[10] **airy**
insubstantial; 'wanting reality; having no steady foundation in truth or nature; trifling', Johnson, *Dictionary*.

[13] **darling**
cherished.

[15] **wings**
'throws' or possibly in the sense of

'trims with feathers as darts are trimmed'.

[16]
Cf. 'Thus with each gift of nature and art' , Pope, *Epistle to Cobham*, line 192.

[15–16]
The afflictive arrows of Fate are winged by every human wish, every gift of nature and each grace of art. In other words all aspects of existence contribute to human infelicity.

[17–18] **fatal**
destructive as well as 'what is doomed to be destroyed', Johnson, *Dictionary*.

[19] **Impeachment**
a parliamentary procedure by which the House of Commons could prosecute a person before the House of Lords; *stops the speaker's ... breath* in a literal sense with reference to the earlier 'elocution', and metaphorically related to 'death' of the next line.

[20] **fire**
refers back to the 'heat' and 'glow' of 'courage' in line 17; *precipitates* hurls.

[21] **the knowing and the bold**
the wise and the brave.

[22] **the ... massacre of gold**
the massacre caused by gold.

[23] **wide-wasting pest**
the first of many metaphors of disease.

[25] **hireling**
one who serves for wages; a mercenary.

[27] **Wealth heaped on wealth**
Cf. 'Get riches first, get wealth and treasure heap', *Paradise Regained*, ii, 427.

[28]
The risks and dangers in life increase in proportion with one's wealth.

[30] **dubious**
uncertain, contested; *madded* from 'to mad', meaning 'to be mad, to be furious', Johnson, *Dictionary*.

[31] **statutes**
Fiscal laws or taxation; cf. 'Refuse of swords, and gleanings of a fight', Addison, *The Campaign*, line 192. The idea is that those who have survived war are destroyed by tax laws.

[33] **skulks**
hides; *hind* 'a peasant; a boor; a mean rustic', Johnson, *Dictionary.*

[33]
The poor peasant's life is well below the level at which power-conflicts cause destruction.

[34]
The rich and powerful man almost inevitably faces charges of treachery and consequent imprisonment in the Tower of London. Johnson here generalises from the fate of the Earl of Cromartie, the Earl of Kilmarnock, Lord Balmerino, and Simon Fraser, Lord Lovat, all of whom were brought to the Tower of London for their part in the Jacobite rising of 1745, and the first three were executed on Tower Hill in 1746 (see Smith and McAdam, 1974).

[35] **his**
here referring back to 'vassal' of line 32.

[39] **upbraiding**
that which shows up faults through comparison; a source of reproach.

[40]
If you envy his happy lot, you can spoil his joy by giving him wealth.

[41] **dire vicissitude**
terrible succession; *invade* one of the many metaphors of warfare.

[42] **brake**
'a thicket of brambles, or of thorns', Johnson, *Dictionary*. The verb 'alarms' is understood after 'quivering shade'.

[45]
Cf. 'No cries attempt the mercies of the skies', line 348.

[46]
The winds are contaminated by a burden of prayers for gain and grandeur. In his *Dictionary* Johnson cites 'the spaniel struck stiff by the tainted gale', Thomson, *Autumn*, line 364.

[48] **insidious**
sly; *gaping* eagerly awaiting. Cf. 'I neither will, nor can prognosticate/ To the young, gaping heir', Dryden, *The Third Satire of Juvenal*, lines 81–2.

[49] **Democritus**
Democritus of Abdera (460–367 BC)

known later as 'the laughing philosopher' because of his treatise 'On Cheerfulness'. Was said to have found material for laughter in all human affairs.

[50] **cheerful wisdom and instructive mirth**
The pairs are a variation on the formula of 'instruction and delight' which was considered, since Horace, as the chief end of the art of poetry. By using one of the pair adjectivally in each case Johnson achieves compression and highlights the oxymoronic element.

[51] **motley**
many-coloured; associated with clownishness; *trappings* dress.

[52] **varied fools . . . eternal jest**
different clowns but the same, unending joke.

[53] **want enchained caprice**
'want' here is used in the sense of 'needs', in contrast to 'caprice', which relates to the idea of 'luxury' or whimsical desires unrelated to necessities.

[54] **conceit**
fanciful, exaggerated ideas, imagination; *man was of a piece* men were well-integrated. Johnson, like Pope, felt that the false needs created by a commercial society led to the disintegration of the self. Belinda's dressing table scene in *Rape of the Lock* reveals her complete lack of discrimination and awareness as 'Bibles' are strewn among 'powders', 'patches', etc. As a consequence Belinda never really sees her true self; only her reflection in the mirror of vanity.

[56] **sycophant**
a flattering parasite; *fed by pride* sycophants obtained free dinners from the proud men whom they flattered.

[57] **form**
'external appearance without the essential qualities; empty show', Johnson, *Dictionary.*

[58] **state**
'solemn pomp', Johnson, *Dictionary.*

[61] **shake**
with laughter; *modish* following the mode of the prevailing fashion.

[62] **Dart**
'to throw offensively' Johnson, *Dictionary*; *edge* as a verb, to sharpen or make more incisive; *gibe* jeer or taunt. Johnson creates emphasis here through repetition.

[63] **descry**
to investigate.

[63]
Careful to really find out what is true and according to human nature.

[64] **philosophic**
discerning, aiming to get at the truth.

[65–6]
To the seeker of truth the garments that betoken pleasure or woe are mere playthings, empty of real significance. Note the inverted syntax.

[67–8]
Another couplet relying on syntactical inversion and pointing to the insubstantial base on which human emotions often rest.

[72] **state**
condition of life; *canvass* 'to sift or examine', Johnson, *Dictionary*; or 'to scrutinise or examine carefully'; this sense is related to the 'search' of the first part of the line. The line looks forward to 'The secret ambush of a specious prayer', line 354.

[73] **preferment**
'advancement to a higher station', Johnson, *Dictionary*; *crowd preferment's gate* cf. 'crowd about Preferment's Gate', Swift, *To Doctor Delany*, line 93.

[76]
Image of fireworks referring back to 'burning to be great'. Cf. 'Like bubbles on the sea of matter born,/ They rise, they break, and to that sea return', Pope, *Essay on Man*, iii, 19–20.

[78] **dogs**
pursues, tracks.

[79] **Love ends with hope**
a slightly unusual construction implying that both 'love' and 'hope' end together.

[80] **morning worshipper**
men used to call on their patrons in the mornings.

[81] **the weekly scribbler**
writers in political weeklies.

[82] **dedicator**
'one who inscribes his work to a patron with compliment and servility', Johnson, *Dictionary*. This acerbic definition is the result of the insults and neglect Johnson suffered at the hands of Lord Chesterfield to whom he had dedicated *The Plan of a Dictionary* in 1745.

[83] **the painted face**
the portrait.

[84] **Palladium**
from the image of the goddess Pallas in the citadel of Troy which, it was believed, protected the city. Hence figuratively signifying anything on which the safety of a city or institution is thought to depend.

[85] **smoked**
exposed to smoke.

[86] **yields**
surrenders, gives up; *frame of gold* the more valuable and constant part of the picture is its frame, because it is made of gold.

[87] **line**
lineament, feature.

[89] **form distorted . . . fall**
Both the literal and the metaphorical senses are present, i.e. the man's features suddenly appear ugly, and the removal of the portrait seems justified by this ugliness; also the picture is no longer morally inspiring; rather it is morally 'fallen'.

[90] **indignant wall**
As so often in Johnson the adjective refers to a word other than the one to which it is immediately attached; in this case to 'detestation'.

[92] **zeal**
'passionate ardour for any person or cause', Johnson, *Dictionary*.

[93] **freedom's sons . . .**
remonstrance
alluding sarcastically to a people who have lost their best traditions of political justice and freedom; Johnson has in mind the Grand Remonstrance of 1641 in which the wrongs inflicted on the people by Charles I were

listed and proposals for reform put forward.

[95] supple
opposite of unbending, of unyielding rectitude; *tribes* the voting units of the Roman people, hence in concord with 'the price of votes' of the next line; *repress their patriot throats* keep in check patriotic utterances.

[96]
Their only concern is to be properly bribed for their votes.

[97] libels
Defamatory writing appearing in weeklies or pamphlets; *septennial ale* the length of a Parliament was seven years. Johnson writes sarcastically of the free beer provided in election campaigns as a bribe for votes.

[98] full
used as an intensive.

[97–8]
Protests are confined to drinking beer and bringing out weekly pamphlets of a controversial nature.

[99] full-blown
like a flower in full blossom, at the peak of his career; *Wolsey* Thomas Wolsey (1475–1530) was Lord Chancellor of England in the reign of Henry VIII. His was, in Johnson's terms, an exemplary case of a great man's downfall.

[99ff.]
See Shakespeare, *Henry VIII*, II, ii and III, ii.

[100] fortune in his hand
Cf. 'Not difficult, if thou hearken to me,/ Riches are mine, fortune is in my hand', *Paradise Regained*, ii, 428–9.

[101] the church, the realm
Wolsey was also cardinal of the Church of England. His power extended over both the religious and the secular spheres; *consign* yield, submit.

[102]
It is worth speculating on what image Johnson had in mind. A prism or a concave glass that disseminates the rays or 'bounty' comes to mind, rather than the more conventional image of stained glass. This bias towards

images drawn from the world of science is maintained in the next line.

[103]
The rather mundane image of sluice gates that control and direct the flow of water satirically counterpoints the more abstract 'stream of honour'.

[105–8]
Wolsey's political power here is conceived in the image of an advancing army.

[109] At length his sovereign frowns
Cf. 'What should this mean?/ What sudden anger's this? how have I reaped it?/ He parted frowning from me', *Henry VIII*, III, ii, 204–6; *train of state* retinue.

[113] the pride of aweful state
the ostentatious appurtenances to political power which are listed in the lines that follow.

[115] luxurious board
the well-supplied table.

[116] the menial lord
even the lords of the realm were subservient to Wolsey's uniquely powerful . position. The paradox also suggests the resentment that such power would create.

[117]
Images of warfare are often counterpointed by images of disease and the ravages of time.

[118] monastic rest
Wolsey retired to Cawood before he was arrested in 1530. He died in Leicester Abbey.

[120] faith of kings
an ironic reference to Henry VIII's title 'Defender of the Faith'.

[120]
Cf. 'Had I but served my God with half the zeal/ I served my King, he would not in mine age/ Have left me naked to mine enemies', *Henry VIII*, III, ii, 456–8.

[121] repine
'to be discontented', Johnson, *Dictionary*.

[125] steeps
precipices.

[128] ruin
in the sense of 'fall'.

[129] **Villiers**
George Villiers (1592–1628) was the first Duke of Buckingham. He was stabbed to death in 1628. The Villiers of line 86 of *London* was his son; *knife* Johnson had censured Shakespeare's use of the word in his comments on *Macbeth* in *Rambler*, No. 168; he viewed it as a 'low' word and would have considered it appropriate in the present satirical and reductive context.

[130] **Harley**
Robert Harley (1661–1724), Earl of Oxford, leader of the Tory party under Queen Anne, was later impeached. He was the owner of the great library which Johnson catalogued.

[131] **Wentworth**
Thomas Wentworth (1593–1641), Earl of Strafford, chief adviser to Charles I. He was impeached and executed in 1641; *Hyde* Edward Hyde (1609–74), Earl of Clarendon. He was Charles II's chancellor but was banished in 1667. He took refuge in France where he completed his famous *History of the Rebellion*.

[132] **to kings allied**
Hyde's daughter married the Duke of York, later James II.

[136] **enthusiast**
'one of elevated fancy, or exalted ideas', Johnson, *Dictionary*.

[137] **fever of renown**
continues the metaphor of disease which is taken up again in 'contagion' of the next line.

[138] **strong contagion of the gown**
the academic dress worn by the students at Oxford is conceived in terms of Nessus's shirt, which poisoned Hercules's body; cf. 'fierce contagion spreads', Gay, *Trivia*, iii, 337.

[139] **dome**
building, as in *London*, line 203.

[139]
His future writings spread throughout the Bodleian library. There is a subdued reference to the labours of Hercules. Bodleian is the name of the University Library at Oxford, so called after Sir Thomas Bodley who restored and endowed it in 1600.

[140] **Bacon's mansion**
The gatehouse of a bridge near Pembroke College, Oxford; *trembles* traditional lore had it that when a greater scholar than Roger Bacon passed under that bridge it would fall. Pembroke was Johnson's college in Oxford.

[143] **generous**
'noble of mind; magnanimous; open of heart', Johnson, *Dictionary*.

[144] **science**
means here knowledge, but there is some indication that Johnson is thinking of the contemporary scientists who investigated natural phenomena.

[144]
Cf. 'Counts death kind nature's signal of retreat', line 364. The line sustains the image of warfare and conquest.

[145–6]
Cf. 'If once right reason drives that cloud away,/ Truth breaks upon us with resistless day', Pope, *Essay on Criticism*, lines 211–12.

[147] **false kindness**
counterfeit love.

[149] **novelty**
spirit of innovation; *cell* cf. 'Some secret cell, ye powers indulgent give', *London*, line 49; *refrain* keep away from.

[150] **sloth**
one of the seven deadly sins. Johnson was always anxious about being slothful and in his diaries he recorded many resolutions against being idle and lazy; *effuse* pour out; *opiate* 'soporiferous; somniferous; narcotic', Johnson, *Dictionary*.

[151] **fops**
dandies.

[152] **lettered heart**
an educated person.

[153] **torpid veins**
so that they become torpid or sluggish.

[154] **melancholy**
much more than mere sadness; a condition of pathological depression with which Johnson himself was often afflicted; 'A gloomy, pensive, discontented temper', Johnson,

Dictionary; *phantoms* spectres; *shade* place of seclusion.

[156] **reversed**
turned to the contrary.

[158] **letters**
learning.

[160] **patron**
This famous alteration from the first edition, which had 'garret', was made in 1755. Johnson made the change in the wake of his disillusionment with Lord Chesterfield who, though he had not supported Johnson at all during his work over the *Dictionary*, claimed an interest in it when it came out in 1755. Johnson wrote a letter to him telling him how his concern came too late. The word 'patron' is defined in the *Dictionary* as 'commonly a wretch who supports with insolence, and is paid with flattery'.

[162] **the tardy bust**
The bust of Milton was placed in Westminster Abbey in 1737; the monument to Dryden was erected in 1720, and the monument to Shakespeare in 1741.

[163] **attend**
attend to.

[164] **Lydiat**
Thomas Lydiat (1572–1646), theologian, mathematician and astronomer. He was fellow of New College, Oxford. His contemporaries thought very highly of him as a scholar, but he lived and died in poverty; *Galileo* (1564–1642), who with the aid of the telescope established the validity of Copernicus's theory that in the planetary system the earth revolved round the sun; this view was unacceptable to the church authorities and Galileo was brought before the Inquisition in 1633. He passed the last eight years of his life under what we would call 'house arrest'.

[135–64]
The portrait of the scholar has many personal touches, and Johnson may be expressing his own difficulties here as he worked on his *Dictionary*. He was also harking back to his years of hardship at Oxford. Mrs Thrale records how affected he was when he read the poem to a circle of friends:

When Dr. Johnson read his own satire, in which the life of a scholar is painted, with the various obstructions thrown in his way to fortune and to fame, he burst into a passion of tears one day, the family and Mr. Scott only were present, who, in a jocose way, clapped him on the back, and said, What's all this, my dear Sir? Why you, and I, and Hercules, you know, were all troubled with melancholy . . . The Doctor was so delighted at this odd sally, that he suddenly embraced him, and the subject was immediately changed.

[166] **glittering eminence**
the prominent position.

[167] **awed**
feared rather than frightened.

[168] **Rebellion**
the Puritan rebels; *vengeful talons* note the compressed but powerful metaphor; *Laud* William Laud (1573–1645), authoritarian divine who supported the king in his conflict with the Commons; Chancellor of Oxford, 1629; Archbishop of Canterbury, 1633. Impeached for treason in 1640 and beheaded in 1645.

[169] **content**
content the persecutor.

[170] **sequestered**
sequestrated, diverted from its owner.

[171] **dangerous**
in the sense of 'powerful'; *parts* 'Qualities; powers, faculties, or accomplishments', Johnson, *Dictionary*.

[172] **fatal learning**
It was not strictly speaking Laud's learning that led to his death, but rather the part he played in the affairs of church and state.

[173] **art and genius**
Oxford University, of which Laud was benefactor.

[175] **festal**
of festivity and celebration; *blazes* Johnson could have in mind the sacrificial fires of the Roman altars; *triumphal show* victory parades.

[177] **gazette**
here, any newspaper; see note to *London*, line 72.
[179] **bribe**
'a reward given to pervert the judgement', Johnson, *Dictionary*; *rapid Greek* Alexander the Great (356–323 BC), King of Macedon. His empire stretched from the Danube eastwards to India and included Egypt. Some of his most spectacular victories such as that over the Indian King Porus resulted from his speed of movement.
[180] **steady**
F.R. Leavis comments: 'That "steady" turns the vague *cliché*, "shook the world" into the felt percussion of tramping legions', *Revaluation*.
[181] **shine**
win fame.
[182] **Danube**
The Duke of Marlborough's famous victory over the Bavarians in 1704 was at Blenheim on the river Danube; *Rhine* Marlborough laid siege to Bonn in 1703.
[183–4]
A difficult couplet of which the general sense is that praise has a kind of power which mere virtue does not have, to drive men; but fame has the final charm.
[185–6]
War is an iniquitous and irrational sport in which whole nations are devastated in order to raise to eminence a single person.
[187] **mortgaged states ... wreaths regret**
wreaths or laurels were signs of victories. These triumphs in battle were often, however, at a great expense to the nation.
[188] **debt**
The National Debt caused by military activities which had risen to over £77 million by 1749.
[189] **dear-bought right**
privilege purchased at a considerable cost.
[190]
Reduced to a mere decaying symbol.

[192] **Swedish Charles**
clearly introduced here as an exemplum of military glory. This has long been considered one of the finest passages in the poem. Charles XII of Sweden (1682–1718) came to power in 1697. He was faced with the hostile alliance between Denmark, Saxony and Russia. He managed to deal with the two former but the scorched earth policy of the Russians assisted by their terrible winter proved too much for him. Nevertheless Charles XII captured many a literary imagination of his age. Johnson had been interested in Charles XII for a long time, and had even thought of writing a play about him. Voltaire's *Histoire de Charles XII* had been published in 1732 and was well known in England, especially through a weekly translated serialisation. Charles was an ally of the Old Pretender and a favourite of the Tories. Cf. 'The frantic Alexander of the North', Thomson, *Winter*, line 980; also 'Heroes are much the same, the point's agreed,/ From Macedonia's madman, to the Swede', Pope, *An Essay on Man*, iv, 219–20.
[193] **adamant**
'a stone, imagined by writers, of impenetrable hardness', Johnson, *Dictionary*.
[197]
A peaceful reign gives him no pleasure.
[198] **trump**
the trumpet that is blown in warfare.
[200] **one capitulate**
Frederick IV of Denmark. He was defeated in the campaign which concluded in the Peace of Traventhal, 1700; *one resign* Augustus II of Poland. He was deposed in 1704, and succeeded by Stanislas I, who was Charles's choice (see Smith and McAdam, 1974).
[201] **spreads**
displays.
[202]
Consider that nothing has been achieved as long as something

remains to be conquered. The line is clearly proleptic and satirical in view of Charles's own defeat; *till nought remain*... applying to the complete demolition of Charles's power; cf. 'He reckons not the past, while aught remained/ Great to be done, or mighty to be gained', Lucan, *Pharsalia*, ii, 657 (trans. Rowe; see Smith and McAdam, 1974).

[203] **Gothic**
Swedish, though in Johnson's time it was commonly used in the sense of Teutonic.

[207] **Stern**
unrelenting.

[208] **winter barricades**
'General Winter', in popular humour the most effective commander of the Russian army.

[210] **Pultowa**
Charles was decisively defeated by Peter the Great at Pultowa or Poltova in 1709.

[211] **bands**
'a company of persons joined together', Johnson, *Dictionary*. In this context the battalions of his army; *broken bands* scattered battalions.

[211ff.]
After his defeat at Pultowa Charles fled to Bender in Turkish territory. He stayed there till 1714 but fell at the attack on Frederikshald in Norway in 1718 (see Smith and McAdam, 1974).

[214] **ladies interpose**
referring to the role of Catherine, the empress of Peter the Great, in July 1711, when the Russian army escaped from almost certain defeat near Pruth. At the treaty signed then it was agreed that Peter the Great should not oppose Charles's return to Sweden.

[216] **subverted**
overthrown.

[219] **barren strand**
unpopulated shore.

[220] **dubious hand**
Voltaire claims that Charles was killed by a stray cannon ball and not by one of his own army as popularly believed.

[221–2]
Charles of Sweden's name at one time struck terror into every heart, but survives now only as an exemplum of the tragic end of military glory.

[224] **Persia's tyrant**
Xerxes I, King of Persia (485–464 BC) who attacked Greece with both his navy and army. The Spartans offered resistance at the famous pass of Thermopylae. Xerxes was defeated decisively in the narrow strait between the island of Salamis and the mainland of Attica. He was assassinated in 465 BC; *Bavaria's lord* Charles Albert, Elector of Bavaria, was crowned as Charles VII in 1742. He was never a very effective emperor and died in 1745.

[225] **gay hostility**
showy, unconcealed enmity; *barbarous pride* unabashed, uncivilised pride.

[226] **embattled**
arrayed for war.

[228]
The reference is to the ruinous cost of feeding Xerxes' enormous army.

[229] **myriads**
in general, large numbers, but more specifically groups of 10,000.

[230] **soothe**
encourage, confirm.

[231]
Subjected to continuous flattery and praise, Xerxes' mind was inflamed with passion.

[232] **The waves he lashes**
When Xerxes' bridge over the Hellespont was destroyed by a storm he ordered the sea to be given 300 lashes. Dryden, *The Tenth Satire of Juvenal*: 'Who whipt the winds, and made the sea his slave', line 290.

[234] **rude**
unsophisticated, the rough and ready Greeks; *spreading god* the Hydra, the many-headed Greek god, who grew more heads if any were cut off.

[236]
The bodies of the dead fill the valleys.

[237] **Th'insulted sea**
see note to line 232.

[238] **skiff**
small, light boat.
[240] **host**
armed multitude of men.
[239–40]
According to Mrs Thrale Johnson had
said that this was his favourite couplet
in all his writings.
[241] **bold Bavarian**
Again, Charles Albert, Elector of
Bavaria. He asserted his claim to the
imperial throne in 1740 and was
crowned as Charles VII in 1742.
[242] **Tries**
attempts; *dread summits* the frightening heights.
[243] **unexpected legions**
large bodies of soldiers that have not
been provided against.
[244] **defenceless realms**
Upper Austria and Bohemia over
which Charles Albert had early
victories.
[245] **fair Austria**
Maria Theresa, Empress of Austria
(1717–80), who was supported by
England and Hanover in the War of
the Austrian Succession. Johnson
wrote an account of the Austrian succession and the part played by Maria
Theresa in his *Memoirs of Frederick III,
King of Prussia*, published in *The Literary Magazine*, 1756; *spreads* displays;
mournful charms Maria Theresa
appeared in mourning before the
Hungarian Diet in Pressburg in 1741
and made an emotional speech ending
in tears.
[247] **the beacons' rousing blaze**
the provocative light of the beacons as
they flashed messages from hilltop to
hilltop.
[248]
Opens the situation to all those who
aspire to gain or fame.
[249] **Croatian**
The Croatians and the Hungarians
formed part of the Hapsburg Empire.
'Croatian' implied savagery, as for
instance in 'And grin and whet like a
Croatian band', Dryden, *The Medal*,
line 240; *Hussar* a Hungarian light
cavalryman.

[250] **sons of ravage**
plunderers, looters.
[251] **flattering**
that which conceals the pitfalls and
precariousness of the situation.
[252] **hasty greatness**
greatness acquired too quickly; *fatal
doom* that which is destructive and
doomed itself to be destroyed. See
note to lines 17 and 18.
[255] **Enlarge**
prolong.
[256] **In health, in sickness**
Cf. 'In health and sickness, and in
turns of state', Dryden, *Georgics*, iv,
367.
[258]
Perhaps the most pessimistic line in
the poem.
[259] **Time hovers o'er**
'Time' conceived as a vulture; one of
Johnson's many images that depends
on the verb rather than the noun and
therefore does not address the sense
of sight.
[260] **passages of joy**
the senses.
[261–2]
Cf. 'Wherefore did Nature pour all her
bounties forth,/ With such a full and
unwithdrawing hand?', Milton,
Comus, lines 709–10.
[262] **The fruit autumnal, and the
vernal flower**
Johnson follows Milton in placing the
adjectives before and after the noun in
the two halves of the line.
[263] **store**
abundance.
[265] **pall**
become insipid or vapid.
[266] **luxury**
sensual pleasure, 'voluptuousness,
addictedness to pleasure', Johnson,
Dictionary. The word 'slave' later in
the line evokes a moral stance on
'luxury' as a kind of artificial and
insatiable appetite for exotic things
that was considered by the conservatives a serious social evil.
[266]
Death causes luxury to loosen her
hold over her victim.

[268] **Diffuse**
pour out; *tuneful* musical; *lenitives*
'Anything medicinally applied to ease
pain', Johnson, *Dictionary*.
[270] **Orpheus**
The Thracian god of music whose
power could draw trees, animals and
even rocks to listen. Pluto, the god of
the underworld, charmed by his
music, granted him back his Eurydice,
whom Orpheus lost, however, by
breaking the condition of not looking
back to see her.
[271] **attend**
listen to, regard.
[273] **everlasting dictates**
unending utterances of rules and
maxims; *crowd his tongue* pour out
one after another.
[274]
Grave when there was no need for
gravity, and dogmatic even when
wrong.
[275] **still returning tale**
oft repeated story; *lingering jest* the
long drawn out joke.
[276] **Perplex**
'vex' rather than 'puzzle'.
[277] **awe**
keep in check.
[279] **last**
latest, most recent.
[280] **petulance**
'immodesty' or 'wantonness' rather
than 'sulkiness'; *expense* extravagance.
[281] **Improve**
increase, augment; *heady* violent.
[282]
Note the pun on 'will'; cf. 'Obedient
passions and a will resigned', line 360.
[283–4]
The metaphor of warfare and attack is
sustained.
[286] **dreaded losses**
fear of anticipated losses.
[291] **prime**
'The spring of life; the height of
health, strength, or beauty', Johnson,
Dictionary.
[291–8]
Mrs Thrale reported that Johnson had
his own mother, Sarah Johnson, who

died at the age of 90, in mind in writing this passage.
[293–4]
Cf. 'Still quitting ground, by unperceived decay/ And steal from life and
melt away', Dryden, *The State of Innocence*, V, i, 349–50.
[300]
Puts a weight of sorrow on the already
weary old person.
[301] **as the day returns**
on each successive day.
[303] **kindred merit**
worthy relatives.
[304] **lacerated friendship**
friends sundered by death.
[305–6]
Cf. 'Years following years steal something every day,/ At last they steal us
from ourselves away;/ In one our
frolics, one amusements end,/ In one
a mistress drops, in one a friend',
Pope, *Imitations of Horace, Epistle 2*, ii,
72–5.
[309]
'Nature' is the subject here that
releases her 'prisoner'. Johnson sustains the image of warfare. Cf.
'Counts death kind Nature's signal of
retreat', line 364.
[310]
Death releases the worthy from the
afflictions of this life, and allows them
peace.
[312] **set unclouded**
a suppressed image of the sun setting;
unclouded not having any kind of
cloud over them; honourably; *gulfs*
depths.
[313] **Lydia's monarch**
Croesus ruled Lydia (560–546 BC)
with enormous wealth and power.
[314] **Solon**
a legal and economic reformer of
sixth-century Athens, known as one
of the seven sages of ancient Greece.
According to Herodotus he told Croesus that no man could be accounted
happy until he had ended his life
happily.
[315] **prodigies**
unexpected happenings; the word is
used satirically here.

[316] **Fears of the brave**
when the brave become fearful; *follies of the wise* when the wise become foolish.

[317] **Marlborough**
See note on *London*, line 86; *streams of dotage* Marlborough suffered two strokes before he died.

[318] **Swift**
Jonathan Swift (1667–1745), Dean of St Patrick's, Dublin; author of *A Tale of a Tub*, *Gulliver's Travels*, etc. Towards the end of his life he suffered from mental illness that rendered him a helpless invalid; *driveler* one who talks childishly or idiotically; *show* when Jonathan Swift died in his 78th year he had become extremely senile. It is said that his servants used to display him for tips.

[319] **teeming mother**
the expectant woman; *race* family.

[320] **fortune of a face**
beauty.

[321] **Vane**
Anne Vane (1705–36), mistress to Frederick, Prince of Wales. She lost her son when he was only 3 years old, and died herself a few weeks after this tragedy.

[322] **Sedley**
Catherine Sedley (1657–1717), mistress of James, Duke of York, for nearly ten years. Subsequently she was not entirely unhappy and is perhaps not the best example to illustrate Johnson's point.

[323] **nymphs**
'A lady. In poetry', Johnson, *Dictionary*.

[326]
Cf. 'Oh! if to dance all night, and dress all day', Pope, *Rape of the Lock*, v, 19. The tone of the passage is similar to that of Clarissa's speech in *The Rape*.

[329] **heedless**
inattentive, careless.

[331] **with fondness hate combines**
'fondness' refers back to 'youth' of the previous line; 'hate' looks back to 'nymph'; both combine to destroy her 'good name' or 'reputation'.

[332] **batters**
the gates of besieged cities were battered down with battering rams; *mines* walled cities were invaded by digging underneath the walls. Note the metaphor of attack is sustained even in this passage about love.

[334] **remonstrance**
protest against immorality.

[335] **she**
referring back to 'virtue'; *slippery* 'not chaste', Johnson, *Dictionary*.

[336] **pride and prudence**
not suitable substitutes for virtue.

[337] **the pass**
literally the low-lying region amongst mountains that grants access to outsiders. A suppressed sexual metaphor.

[338]. **harmless freedom ... private friend**
both phrases are ironical. The lady's free behaviour and her intimate friends will be the cause of her downfall.

[339] **The guardians**
the protectors of a woman's honour, prudence and dignity; *plied* 'bent, turned', Johnson, *Dictionary*.

[339]
Johnson continues the metaphor of warfare and attack.

[340] **interest**
share of pleasure; *and by flattery, pride* legitimate pride, in the sense of honour or dignity, is turned from its course by flattery.

[341–2]
The lines conjure, through the assonance in 'despised', 'distressed' and 'hissing', the image of the serpent and the fall of Eve.

[343] **objects**
'That about which any power or faculty is employed', Johnson, *Dictionary*.

[343]
Where will hope for happiness, and fear of not getting it (the primary constructs of the mind), find sustenance?

[344] **suspence**
not of judgement but of hope and fear and other human emotions; *corrupt the stagnant mind* the image is of unclean stagnant water.

[345] **sedate**
unruffled; calm.

[346] **darkling**
'Being in the dark; being without light: a word merely poetical', Johnson, *Dictionary*; *torrent of his fate* the phrase encapsulates the extended image of 'fate' in the opening lines of the poem. There is a shift here from the 'stagnant' of the earlier line, used in the sense of 'motionless', to the 'torrent' that carries one along helplessly.

[348] **attempt**
invoke.

[348]
Note the shift in vision from line 45 of the general cry that 'assails' the skies, to seeking the 'mercy' of heaven.

[350] **deem**
consider.

[354] **secret ambush**
hidden attack; *specious prayer* Cf. '"Give me good fame, ye powers, and make me just",/ Thus much the rogue to public ears will trust./ In private then,: "When wilt thou, mighty Jove,/ My wealthy uncle from this world remove?"', Dryden's *Persius*, 2, ii, 15–18.

[356] **secure**
calmly sure.

[361]
The scope of love is so wide that all of mankind cannot fill it.

[362]
Suffering ills patiently, without despairing, not only makes them endurable but transmutes them into blessings.

[363] **seat**
abode.

[361–3]
The triad of the highest Christian virtues, Faith, Hope and Love.

[364] **Counts** ,
considers, thinks.

[364]
'Nature' here is the object to 'faith' of the previous line. 'Nature' is on the retreat in this image of battle and warfare; note how the line reworks 'Till pitying nature signs the last release' of line 309.

[366] **to gain**
intransitive, 'to have advantage', 'to be advanced in interest or happiness', Johnson, *Dictionary*.

[367] **celestial wisdom**
a Christianised adaptation of *caelestis sapientia*, Horace, *Epistles*, 1, 3, 27. Happiness is seldom to be found or discovered as something that already exists; it must be 'made' or created by an attitude of mind. Cf. Johnson's contribution to the conclusion of Goldsmith's *The Traveller*: 'How small, of all that human hearts endure,/ That part which laws or kings can cause or cure!/ Still to ourselves in every place consign'd,/ Our own felicity we make or find', lines 429–32.

[343–68]
Johnson transforms Juvenal's Stoic conclusion into a Christian one. Later, in *Idler*, No. 41, he wrote:

The precepts of Epicurus, who teaches us to endure what the laws of the universe make necessary, may silence but not content us. The dictates of Zeno, who commands us to look with indifference on external things, may dispose us to conceal our sorrow, but cannot assuage it. Real alleviation of the loss of friends, and rational tranquillity in the prospect of our own dissolution, can be received only from the promises of him in whose hands are life and death, and from the assurance of another and better state, in which all tears will be wiped from the eyes, and the whole soul shall be filled with joy. Philosophy may infuse stubbornness, but religion only can give patience.

———◇———

28 / *On the Death of Dr Robert Levet*

Condemned to hope's delusive mine,
  As on we toil from day to day,
By sudden blasts, or slow decline,
  Our social comforts drop away.

Well tried through many a varying year,   5
  See Levet to the grave descend;
Officious, innocent, sincere,
  Of every friendless name the friend.

Yet still he fills affection's eye,
  Obscurely wise, and coarsely kind;   10
Nor, lettered arrogance, deny
  Thy praise to merit unrefined.

When fainting nature called for aid,
  And hovering death prepared the blow,
His vigorous remedy displayed   15
  The power of art without the show.

In misery's darkest caverns known,
  His useful care was ever nigh,
Where hopeless anguish poured his groan,
  And lonely want retired to die.   20

No summons mocked by chill delay,
  No petty gain disdained by pride,
The modest wants of every day
  The toil of every day supplied.

His virtues walked their narrow round,   25
  Nor made a pause, nor left a void;
And sure th'Eternal Master found
  The single talent well employed.

The busy day, the peaceful night,
  Unfelt, uncounted, glided by;   30
His frame was firm, his powers were bright,
  Though now his eightieth year was nigh.

Then with no throbbing fiery pain,
No cold gradations of decay,
Death broke at once the vital chain,
And freed his soul the nearest way.

35

This short poem was written towards the end of Johnson's life. It is an elegy on the loss of a friend. Though Johnson did have a separate criterion of sincerity of feeling for the poetry of love and personal loss, by which he judged Milton's *Lycidas* and the love-poems of Donne to be deficient, the grief expressed in *Levet* is also general and formal. Indeed, Johnson seems more concerned with broad reflections on life and death rather than personal feeling.

On the Death of Dr Robert Levet is written in the four-line stanza which conveyed a greater fervour and personal feeling than the heroic couplet. Above all it was free from the satiric edge that had come to be so closely associated with the couplet form. The language, though not entirely devoid of the characteristic Augustan abstractions and personifications, is relatively simple and more straightforward.

Title

Dr Levet, physician and close friend of Samuel Johnson's, lived in the same house with him for several years. *Thraliana* records that Levet

lived with Johnson as a sort of *necessary man*, or surgeon to the wretched household he held in Bolt Court; where blind Mrs. Williams, dropsical Mrs. Desmoulines, black Francis and his white wife's bastard, with a wretched Mrs. White and a thing that he called Poll, shared his bounty, and increased his dirt.

Boswell wrote of Levet as

an obscure practiser in physick among the lower people ... such was Johnson's predilection for him, and fanciful estimate of his moderate abilities, that I have heard him say he should not be satisfied, though attended by all the College of Physicians, unless he had Mr. Levet with him. (*Life of Johnson*)

Robert Levet died on 17 January 1782 in his seventy-seventh year. Johnson wrote this poem shortly after his death.

[1] **Condemned**
consigned; *delusive* apt to deceive;

hope's delusive mine cf. 'Since hope but soothes to double my distress', *London*, line 39. See also 'Delusive fortune hears th'incessant call', *The Vanity of Human Wishes*, line 75; it was a common punishment in Roman times to condemn culprits to lead mines, and the word became commonplace for relentless drudgery (see Fleeman, 1971).

[3]
The image of the 'mine' in line 1 is sustained.

[4] **social comforts**
Johnson here refers to the quiet friendships and pleasures on which he placed much store as opposed to 'luxury' and the false appetites that it generated.

[5]
Levet was an old friend of Johnson's.

[7] **Officious**
'kind, doing good offices', Johnson, *Dictionary*; *innocent* 'pure from mischief; unhurtful', Johnson, *Dictionary*; *sincere* 'honest; undissembling; uncorrupt', Johnson, *Dictionary*.

[10] **Obscurely**
'out of sight; privately; without notice', Johnson, *Dictionary*.

[10]
Johnson characterises Levet like one

of the dwellers of Goldsmith's *Deserted Village*, or the countryside depicted in Gray's *Elegy*.

[11–12]

In these lines Johnson continues on the same note, addressing the 'learned proud' not to overlook the merit of those less urbane than themselves. He is reported by Boswell to have said, 'Levet, madam, is a brutal fellow, but . . . his brutality is in his manners, not in his mind', *Life of Johnson*.

[13–14] **fainting nature . . . hovering death**

the construction of present participle and abstract noun, with a gentle touch of personification, so often used by Johnson. Cf. 'groaning nation's', *London*, line 65; 'hissing infamy', *The Vanity of Human Wishes*, line 342.

[16]

Cf. *Essay on Criticism*, lines 74–5: 'Art from that fund each just supply provides,/ Works without show, and without pomp presides'.

[17] **misery's darkest caverns**

to some extent the image of the mine is sustained.

[18] **useful care**

Johnson is concerned to distinguish, in Augustan fashion, between the 'useful' and the unnecessary or superfluous.

[21] **summons**

'a call of authority', Johnson, *Dictionary*.

[22] **petty**

small; *disdained* scorned.

[23–4]

The moral tone here again is in keeping with the idea of few wants as opposed to artificially created desires.

[25–6]

The Renaissance image of the circle as symbolic of perfection, as something complete and invulnerable. Cf. 'Though all these rare endowments of the mind/ Were in a narrow space of life confined,/ The figure was with full perfection crowned;/ Though not so large an orb, as truly round', Dryden, *Eleonara*, lines 270–3; 'And after all his wand'ring ways are done,/ His circle fills, and ends where he begun', Dryden, *To my Honour'd Kinsman, John Driden*, lines 63–4; see also the concluding lines of Donne's *A Valediction Forbidding Mourning*: 'Thy firmness makes my circle just,/ And makes me end where I begun'.

[26–7]

A reference to the Parable of the Talents, Matthew 25: 24–9. Johnson was deeply unhappy because he believed that in his life he had not lived up to the expectations that his 'Master' had of him.

[30] **glided**

passed smoothly.

[31] **bright**

'acute', Johnson, *Dictionary*.

[35–6]

Cf. 'Dear Sovereign break at once these vital strings,/ That bind me to my clay', Isaac Watts.

CHARLES WESLEY

(1707–88)

The younger brother of John Wesley, the founder of the
Methodist movement, Charles experienced a spiritual awakening in 1728–9 and took holy orders in the Church of England in
1735. Like his brother, he was a powerful itinerant preacher,
and they worked closely together in the movement in the 1740s
and 1750s. Later, they grew apart, disagreeing in particular over
John's ordination of priests (1784 onwards), a move which
ensured the separation of the Methodists from the Church of
England. Charles began writing hymns after a spiritual crisis in
1738, and it is for his hymns that he is chiefly remembered
today.

Further Reading

A modern selection of Wesley's poetry is available in F. Baker
(ed.), *Charles Wesley: Representative Verse* (New York: Abingdon
Press, 1963). His hymns are also readily available either in
collections of eighteenth-century poetry, or more especially in
hymn books.

A worthwhile biography is E. Meyers, *Singer of a Thousand
Songs: A Life of Charles Wesley* (New York: T. Nelson, 1965). A
general introduction to the brothers' poetry is provided by
Samuel J. Rogal in *John and Charles Wesley* (Boston, Mass.:
Twayne, 1983). There is also useful material in Madeleine Forell
Marshall and Janet Todd, *English Congregational Hymns in the
Eighteenth Century* (Lexington: University Press of Kentucky,
1982).

29 / *'Christ, whose glory'*

Christ, whose glory fills the skies,
   Christ, the true, the only light,
Sun of righteousness, arise,
   Triumph o'er the shades of night:
Day-spring from on high, be near: 5
Day-star in my heart appear.

Dark and cheerless is the morn
   Unaccompanied by thee,
Joyless is the day's return,
   Till thy mercy's beams I see;   10
Till they inward light impart,
Glad my eyes, and warm my heart.

Visit then this soul of mine,
   Pierce the gloom of sin and grief,
Fill me, radiancy divine,   15
   Scatter all my unbelief,
More and more thyself display,
Shining to the perfect day.

'Christ, whose glory' (1740) is a hymn to morning written towards the beginning of Charles's career as a hymn-writer. Any such poem in English must recall the devotions of Adam and Eve in *Paradise Lost* (v, 153–208). Like Milton, Wesley also looks back to those psalms which express joy at the creation.

Wesley wrote these hymns for the growing Methodist movement, publishing them in joint volumes with his brother, John. In their simplicity, they reflect the aim of the Methodists to reach out to people of all classes (particularly the poor). In their use of many biblical words, phrases and allusions, they reflect a kind of 'fundamentalist' Bible Protestantism.

The metre is basically trochaic (stress/unstress – dumde), with each line having four trochaic feet and the unstressed syllable of the last foot omitted (dumdedumdedumdedum). The poem is organised in verses of six lines, rhymed ABABCC.

[1] **glory**
splendour, magnificence; also, ring of light. The word, thus, refers both to Christ as God and to His role in the poem as dawn.
[2] **light**
Again there is a double reference to Christ as 'the true light, which

lighteth every man that cometh into the world' (John 1: 9), and Christ metaphorically as the dawn.
[3] **Sun**
punning on 'sun' and 'son'. The pun is an old one, used for instance by John Donne in *Good Friday, 1613: Riding Westward*, in which the poet

meditates upon the crucifixion: 'There should I see a sun by rising set' (line 11); *arise* a verb appropriate both to Christ entering the battle between good and evil, and to the sun in the morning.

[4] **Triumph ... night**
The victory of the sun over darkness is paralleled with the victory of Christ over evil. This, the central idea of the hymn, is suggested in Milton's morning hymn: 'if the night/ Have gathered aught of evil or concealed,/ Disperse it, as now light dispels the dark' (*Paradise Lost*, v, 206–8); *o'er* over.

[5] **Day-spring**
daybreak, but also a biblical title for Jesus: 'the dayspring from on high hath visited us' (Luke 1: 78).

[6] **Day-star**
echoing a sentiment from the second epistle of St Peter: 'ye do well that ye take heed, as unto a light that shineth in a dark place, until the day dawn and the day star arise in your hearts' (2 Peter 1: 19). The reference to 'my heart' also introduces a new personal element into the hymn; the battle between good and evil is not only a cosmic fight but also one that takes place in the individual heart.

[7–8] **Dark ... thee**
The sense of waiting here may echo

Psalm 130: 'my soul waits for the Lord more than they that watch for morning' (Psalms 130: 6).

[10] **mercy's beams**
The reference to mercy reflects Wesley's version of Christianity, with its emphasis on the sinfulness of all. If all are bad, all need mercy.

[11] **inward light**
There may be an echo here of St Paul: 'though our outward man may perish, yet the inward man is renewed day by day' (2 Corinthians 4: 16).

[12] **Glad**
gladden.

[16] **unbelief**
The word is used frequently in the Bible, perhaps most relevantly by the father of the child with the 'dumb spirit'. Jesus asks if the man can believe the child can be healed, to which the man replies 'Lord, I believe. Help thou my unbelief' (Mark 9: 23–4).

[17] **Thyself**
yourself; the familiar form of you, by Wesley's time used chiefly as a form of address to God.

[18] **Shining ... day**
'The path of the just is as a shining light, that shines more and more unto the perfect day' (Proverbs 4: 18).

◇

---

30 / *'Jesu, lover of my soul'*

Jesu, lover of my soul,
   Let me to thy bosom fly,
While the nearer waters roll,
   While the tempest still is high.
Hide me, O my Saviour, hide,   5
   Till the storm of life is past.
Safe into the haven guide;
   O receive my soul at last.

Other refuge have I none,
　Hangs my helpless soul on thee.　　　　10
Leave, ah leave me not alone,
　Still support and comfort me.
All my trust on thee is stayed,
　All my help from thee I bring;
Cover my defenceless head　　　　　　　15
　With the shadow of thy wing.

Wilt thou not regard my call?
　Wilt thou not accept my prayer?
Lo, I sink, I faint, I fall!
　Lo, on thee I cast my care.　　　　　　20
Reach me out thy gracious hand!
　While I of thy strength receive,
Hoping against hope I stand
　Dying, and behold I live!

Thou, O Christ, art all I want;　　　　　25
　More than all in thee I find.
Raise the fallen, cheer the faint,
　Heal the sick, and lead the blind.
Just and holy is thy name,
　I am all unrighteousness.　　　　　　　30
False and full of sin I am,
　Thou art full of truth and grace.

Plenteous grace with thee is found,
　Grace to cover all my sin:
Let the healing streams abound,　　　　　35
　Make and keep me pure within.
Thou of life the fountain art,
　Freely let me take of thee,
Spring thou up within my heart,
　Rise to all eternity!　　　　　　　　　40

Like that of the previous hymn, the metre of 'Jesu, lover of my soul' (1740) is basically trochaic. There are four feet in each line, with the final syllable of the last foot omitted (dumdedumdedumdedum). The poem is organised into verses of eight lines, with a rhyming pattern of *ABABCDCD*.

CHARLES WESLEY

[1] **Jesu**
Jesus; *lover* The distinguishing feature
of Christianity among other religions
is the emphasis it lays upon God's
love. Wesley here uses that element of
Christianity in order to write a religious song which is also a love song,
an idea which goes back to Christian
interpretations of the Old Testament
'Song of Solomon'. Wesley exploits
the possibilities of the amorous
metaphor less daringly than, say,
John Donne in 'Batter my heart': 'Yet
dearly I love you, and would be loved
fain,/ But am bethrothed unto your
enemy./ Divorce me, untie, or break
that knot again;/ Take me to you,
imprison me, for I/ Except you
enthrall me never shall be free,/ Nor
ever chaste unless you ravish me.'
[2] **bosom**
The image has connotations of closeness both to a lover and to God. To
'rest in Abraham's bosom' is to die
(Luke 16: 22) – cf. Rochester's 'Absent
from thee', line 10 and note.
[3] **waters**
The idea of threatening waters used in
tandem with that of a safe bosom is
something of a mixed metaphor (ships
not bosoms are useful against waves).
However, the incongruity is not very
apparent since both metaphors are
justified by their biblical source.
Waves and waters are stock
metaphors of threat in the psalms,
often recalling the destruction of the
Egyptian pursuers of Moses: 'If it had
not been the lord who was on our side
when men rose up against us ... then
the waters would have overwhelmed
us, the stream would have gone over
our soul; then the proud waters
would have gone over our soul'
(Psalms 124: 2–5).
[5] **Hide**
In the Old Testament, the word is
used to mean the provision of safety:
'hide me under the shadow of thy
wings, from the wicked that oppress
me' (Psalms 17: 8–9). In the New, it
suggests also a desirable closeness to
God: 'your life is hid with Christ in

God' (Colossians 3: 3); *Saviour* Jesus.
His purpose in coming to earth was to
save mankind which had separated
itself from God.
[6] **storm of life**
The idea of life as a choppy sea journey is traditional and particularly
common in medieval literature – see,
for example, the anonymous *The
Pilgrimage of the Life of Manhood*.
[7] **haven**
'Thou hast been a strength to the
poor, a strength to the needy in his
distress, a refuge from the storm, a
shadow from the heat' (Isaiah 25: 4).
[9] **refuge**
Wesley abandons the storm/haven
imagery and writes more generally in
terms of a threat and refuge. A result
is that the hymn begins to resemble
those psalms which pray for help in
trouble, protection from enemies.
[13] **stayed**
placed.
[14–16] **All my ... wing**
Cf. 'Because thou hast been my help,
therefore in the shadow of thy wings
will I rejoice' (Psalms 63: 7).
[19] **Lo**
look!; *I sink ... fall* It is interesting to
speculate that P.B. Shelley may have
this line in mind when composing his
rather feverish poem *The Indian
Serenade* (1819): 'Oh lift me from the
grass!/ I die! I faint! I fail!/ Let thy love
in kisses rain/ On my lips and eyelids
pale' (lines 17–20).
[21] **gracious**
used in its religious sense: inclined to
show mercy. The word is biblical.
[24] **Dying ... live**
echoing St Paul's description of Christian workers: 'As unknown and yet
well known; as dying, and behold, we
live; as chastened and not killed' (2
Corinthians 6: 9).
[25] **art**
are (the correct form of the verb with
'thou').
[26] **More than all**
echoing the sentiment of Revelation:
'I am alpha and omega, the beginning
and the ending, says the Lord, which

is, and which was, and which is to come, the Almighty' (Revelation 1: 8).

[27] **Raise the fallen**
Both literally in that Jesus healed the lame, and figuratively in that He raised all fallen (sinful) people.

[28] **Heal the sick**
'And Jesus went about... healing every sickness and every disease among people' (Matthew 9: 35); *lead the blind* Although Jesus healed the blind, Wesley refers not to that but to guiding them. Jesus accused the Pharisees of being 'blind guides' (Matthew 23: 16), an idea which Wesley turns round.

[32] **grace**
the favour of God, freely given by Him and undeserved by the recipient. The Methodists emphasised that salvation could be attained only through God's grace and not through good works or a good life.

[34] **Cover... sin**
The phrase is used in Psalm 32: 'Blessed is he whose transgression is forgiven, whose sin is covered' (Psalms 32: 1). It is repeated by St Paul in a passage where he is discussing justification by faith, i.e. grace as opposed to works (Romans 4: 7).

[35] **healing streams**
Elisha cured Naaman the Syrian of leprosy by having him bathe himself in the Jordan (2 Kings 5: 1–14). There is also a reference to baptism. In the Church of England baptismal service, the priest prays that God will 'sanctify this water to the mystical washing away of sin'; *abound* be many.

[37] **life... fountain**
'For with thee is the fountain of life' (Psalms 36: 9).

THOMAS GRAY

(1716–71)

◇

Though of middle-class origins, Gray was educated at Eton where he first made the acquaintance of Horace Walpole, Richard West and Thomas Ashton. This 'Quadruple Alliance' was to continue at Cambridge University, where Gray was admitted at Peterhouse. After Cambridge Gray joined the Inner Temple with a view to a legal career. He did a 'grand tour' of Europe with his friend Horace Walpole. The death of his father in 1741, however, left him and his family financially insecure. Gray, it seems, hoped to solve the problem by advancing in the legal profession, and indeed, graduated as Bachelor of Laws in 1743. But in October 1742 he had already returned to Cambridge, where he spent almost all the rest of his life in a quiet scholarly existence.

When Gray returned to England in 1741–2 after his tour he entered into one of the most creative years of his life. During this period he wrote his *Ode on the Spring*, *Ode to Adversity* and his *Eton Ode*. He also wrote his *Sonnet on the Death of Mr Richard West* around this time after the death of his friend on 1 June 1742. The *Sonnet* was not published until 1775. It is believed by many that he started his *Elegy* in this year too, though 1746 is favoured by others as the more likely time. The famous *Odes* were the product of the early 1750s, *Progress of Poesy* having been begun around 1752 and *The Bard* and *Ode on Vicissitude* around 1754. The *Odes* were published in 1757. A collected edition of Gray's *Poems* was published in 1768 by Robert Dodsley.

In 1762 Gray had been disappointed in his hope of the Regius Professorship of Modern History at Cambridge. The year 1768 proved fortunate in that regard. Gray died in 1771 at Cambridge, and is buried at Stoke Poges.

Further Reading

The standard edition of Gray's work is Roger Lonsdale (ed.), *Thomas Gray and William Collins: Poetical Works* (Oxford: Oxford University Press, 1977).

The present editors are deeply indebted to Roger Lonsdale (ed.), *The Poems of Thomas Gray, William Collins, Oliver Goldsmith* (London: Longman, 1969), which has detailed annotations. Roger Lonsdale's book has proved invaluable for our Collins and Goldsmith poems as well. Another edition of Gray that has been useful is J. Crofts (ed.), *Gray: Poetry and Prose* (Oxford: Clarendon Press, 1926, reprinted 1971).

Two good biographies are R.W. Ketton-Cremer's *Thomas Gray: A Biography* (Cambridge: Cambridge University Press, 1955), and A.L. Lytton Sells (assisted by Iris Lytton Sells), *Thomas Gray: His Life and Works* (London: Allen and Unwin, 1980). A valuable full-length study is Norris Golden, *Thomas Gray* (Boston, Mass.: Twayne, 1988), and a useful collection of essays is James Downey and Ben Jones (eds), *Fearful Joy: Papers from the Thomas Gray Bicentenary Conference at Carleton University* (Montreal and London: McGill–Queen's University Press, 1974). Two further books of essays are devoted to the *Elegy* alone: Herbert W. Starr (ed.), *Twentieth-Century Interpretations of Gray's 'Elegy': A Collection of Critical Essays* (Englewood Cliffs, NJ: Prentice Hall, 1968) and Harold Bloom (ed.), *Thomas Gray's 'Elegy Written in a Country Churchyard'* (New York: Chelsea, 1987).

The editors also wish to acknowledge James Michie's translation, *The Odes of Horace* (Harmondsworth: Penguin, 1964).

————◇————

31 /   Sonnet On the Death of Mr Richard West

In vain to me the smiling mornings shine,
And reddening Phoebus lifts his golden fire:
The birds in vain their amorous descant join,
Or cheerful fields resume their green attire:
These ears, alas! for other notes repine,   5
A different object do these eyes require.
My lonely anguish melts no heart but mine;
And in my breast the imperfect joys expire.
Yet morning smiles the busy race to cheer,
And new-born pleasure brings to happier men   10
The fields to all their wonted tribute bear;
To warm their little loves the birds complain:
I fruitless mourn to him that cannot hear,
And weep the more because I weep in vain.

This poem has become the *locus classicus* for critical debate about Augustan poetic diction. Wordsworth in his *Preface* to the *Lyrical Ballads* quoted the whole poem to illustrate Gray's 'curiously elaborate...poetic diction', which worked against the expression of grief at which the poem aimed. Coleridge challenged Wordsworth's arguments in his *Biographia Literaria*. Hopkins followed up with praise for the poem's 'rythmical beauty', and pointed to the structural organisation of the whole poem, as opposed to Wordsworth's fragmentation of it. The poem, situating the poet at a configuration of formal poetical language and personal experience, is interesting for the modern reader.

[1]
Cf. 'Awake, the morning shines, and the fresh field/ Calls us', *Paradise Lost*, v, 20–1; several other lines from *Paradise Lost* come to mind: 'Then when fair morning first smiles on the world', v, 124; 'the morn,/ All unconcerned with our unrest, begins/ Her rosie progress smiling', xi, 173–5.

[2] **reddening Phoebus**
Cf. 'reddening dawn', Pope, *Odyssey*, xvii, 517. The combination of the adjectival present participle and noun is a popular feature of the descriptive poetry of this period. The pattern is often used to suggest personification.

[3] **amorous descant**
Cf. 'amorous descant', *Paradise Lost*, iv, 602.

[4] **green attire**
Cf. 'Earth in her rich attire', *Paradise Lost*, vii, 501.

[1–4]
The description of nature in these lines is in anthropomorphic terms.

[5] **repine**
fret for.

[6] **require**
need; also in the sense of 'seek for' (see Lonsdale, 1969).

[8] **imperfect**
frail; *the imperfect joys expire* Cf. 'And on her tongue imperfect accents die', Pope, *Odyssey*, iv, 937.

[9] **busy race**
a periphrasis for human beings.

[10] **new-born pleasure**
fresh happiness.

[11] **wonted tribute**
usual offerings.
[13] **fruitless**
fruitlessly; *to him that cannot hear*
Gray refers here to his friend, Richard
West, who is dead, and therefore
cannot hear him.

[14]
I cry, not only for the loss of my
friend, but also because I cannot
convey my grief to him. The poet
emphasises the isolation of personal
grief and loss.

————◇————

32 /   Elegy Written in a Country Church-yard

The curfew tolls the knell of parting day,
The lowing herd wind slowly o'er the lea,
The ploughman homeward plods his weary way,
And leaves the world to darkness, and to me.

Now fades the glimmering landscape on the sight,   5
And all the air a solemn stillness holds,
Save where the beetle wheels his droning flight,
And drowsy tinklings lull the distant folds;

Save that from yonder ivy-mantled tower
The moping owl does to the moon complain   10
Of such as wandering near her secret bower,
Molest her ancient solitary reign.

Beneath those rugged elms, that yew-tree's shade,
Where heaves the turf in many a mouldering heap,
Each in his narrow cell for ever laid,   15
The rude forefathers of the hamlet sleep.

The breezy call of incense-breathing morn,
The swallow twittering from the straw-built shed,
The cock's shrill clarion, or the echoing horn,
No more shall rouse them from their lowly bed.   20

For them no more the blazing hearth shall burn,
Or busy housewife ply her evening care,
No children run to lisp their sire's return,
Or climb his knees the envied kiss to share.

Oft did the harvest to their sickle yield,   25
Their furrow oft the stubborn glebe has broke:
How jocund did they drive their team afield!
How bowed the woods beneath their sturdy stroke!

Let not ambition mock their useful toil,
Their homely joys and destiny obscure;   30
Nor grandeur hear with a disdainful smile,
The short and simple annals of the poor.

The boast of heraldry, the pomp of power,
And all that beauty, all that wealth e'er gave,
Awaits alike th'inevitable hour: 35
The paths of glory lead but to the grave.

Nor you, ye proud, impute to these the fault,
If memory o'er their tomb no trophies raise,
Where through the long-drawn isle and fretted vault
The pealing anthem swells the note of praise.   40

Can storied urn or animated bust
Back to its mansion call the fleeting breath?
Can honour's voice provoke the silent dust,
Or flattery soothe the dull cold ear of death?

Perhaps in this neglected spot is laid   45
Some heart once pregnant with celestial fire,
Hands that the rod of empire might have swayed,
Or waked to ecstasy the living lyre.

But knowledge to their eyes her ample page
Rich with the spoils of time did ne'er unroll: 50
Chill penury repressed their noble rage,
And froze the genial current of the soul.

Full many a gem of purest ray serene,
The dark unfathomed caves of ocean bear:
Full many a flower is born to blush unseen,   55
And waste its sweetness on the desert air.

403

Some village-Hampden that with dauntless breast
The little tyrant of his fields withstood;
Some mute inglorious Milton here may rest,
Some Cromwell guiltless of his country's blood.   60

Th'applause of listening senates to command,
The threats of pain and ruin to despise,
To scatter plenty o'er a smiling land,
And read their history in a nation's eyes,

Their lot forbad: nor circumscribed alone   65
Their growing virtues, but their crimes confined;
Forbade to wade through slaughter to a throne,
And shut the gates of mercy on mankind,

The struggling pangs of conscious truth to hide,
To quench the blushes of ingenuous shame,   70
Or heap the shrine of luxury and pride
With incense kindled at the muse's flame.

Far from the madding crowd's ignoble strife,
Their sober wishes never learned to stray:
Along the cool sequestered vale of life   75
They kept the noiseless tenor of their way.

Yet ev'n these bones from insult to protect
Some frail memorial still erected nigh,
With uncouth rhymes and shapeless sculpture decked,
Implores the passing tribute of a sigh.   80

Their name, their years, spelt by th'unlettered muse,
The place of fame and elegy supply;
And many a holy text around she strews,
That teach the rustic moralist to die.

For who to dumb forgetfulness a prey,   85
This pleasing anxious being e'er resigned,
Left the warm precincts of the cheerful day,
Nor cast one longing lingering look behind?

On some fond breast the parting soul relies,
Some pious drops the closing eye requires: 90
Ev'n from the tomb the voice of nature cries,
Ev'n in our ashes live their wonted fires.

For thee who mindful of th'unhonoured dead
Dost in these lines their artless tale relate: 95
If chance, by lonely contemplation led,
Some kindred spirit shall inquire thy fate,

Haply some hoary-headed swain may say:
'Oft have we seen him at the peep of dawn
Brushing with hasty steps the dews away
To meet the sun upon the upland lawn.   100

'There at the foot of yonder nodding beech
That wreathes its old fantastic roots so high,
His listless length at noontide would he stretch,
And pore upon the brook that babbles by.

'Hard by yon wood, now smiling as in scorn,   105
Muttering his wayward fancies he would rove,
Now drooping, woeful wan, like one forlorn
Or crazed with care, or crossed in hopeless love.

'One morn I missed him on the customed hill,
Along the heath and near his favourite tree: 110
Another came; nor yet beside the rill,
Nor up the lawn, nor at the wood was he.

'The next with dirges due in sad array
Slow through the church-way path we saw him borne.
Approach and read (for thou can'st read) the lay,   115
Graved on the stone beneath yon aged thorn.'

The Epitaph

Here rests his head upon the lap of earth
A youth to fortune and to fame unknown;
Fair science frowned not on his humble birth,
And melancholy marked him for her own.   120

405

Large was his bounty, and his soul sincere,
Heaven did a recompense as largely send;
He gave to misery all he had, a tear,
He gained from heaven ('twas all he wished) a friend.

No farther seek his merits to disclose,   125
Or draw his frailties from their dread abode,
(There they alike in trembling hope repose)
The bosom of his Father and his God.

Religious note ✳

The history of the publication of the *Elegy* is interesting; it also elucidates the
social context in which the poem was written, and Gray's particular dilemma in
being both a coterie and public poet. Gray's continuing interest in his poems,
and his tendency to revise them, mark him out as a writer in the classical tradition. The poem was widely circulated in manuscript by Horace Walpole among
friends and acquaintances, and was much acclaimed. Robert Dodsley published
it in 1751 at Gray's urgent request in order to prevent its publication by the none
too reputable *Magazine of Magazines*, which hoped to cash in on its popularity.
Gray instructed Dodsley to publish the poem without his name, and 'without
any interval between the stanza's, because the sense is some places continued
beyond them'. He also gave the title as 'Elegy, wrote in a Country Church-yard',
and suggested two improvements to the text. Later Gray separated the stanzas,
and the 1768 edition of his *Poems* keeps them separate. In this matter, and also
with regard to the two substantially different versions that we have of the poem
(see note to line 72), the *Elegy* is interesting material for both conventional
textual criticism, and contemporary questions about what constitutes a text.
    The poem was instantly popular. It was translated into Latin and Greek,
quoted, imitated and parodied. Samuel Johnson praised it for its 'sentiments to
which every bosom returns an echo'; and readers the world over have shared
the response of Johnson's 'common reader'.
    Gray's *Elegy* is the best known of the 'graveyard' poems that appeared in the
1740s: Blair's *The Grave* (1743), Young's *Night Thoughts* (1742–5). Indeed, its title
page was illustrated with skulls and crossbones, picks and shovels, and hour-
glasses. The *Elegy* also has affinities with other poems of the period such as
Akenside's *Pleasures of the Imagination* (1744) and *Odes* (1745), the odes of Collins
and Joseph Warton (1746) and Thomas Warton's *The Pleasures of Melancholy*
(1747).
    The poem, as it originally ended with the four stanzas that follow line 72 in
the Eton manuscript, was clearly in the 'rural retirement' tradition. This classical
tradition had been freshly brought to the fore of the English literary consciousness in Dryden's translation of Virgil's second *Georgic*. Horace's second *Epode*
also lies at the back of the English 'rural' imagination. In both Virgil and Gray,
however, the praise of country life is not entirely unqualified. Dryden's rendering: 'O happy, if he knew his happy state,/ The swain, who, free from business
and debate' (*Georgics*, ii, 639–40) points to a certain limitation of consciousness
that is at the heart of rural bliss; this is different from the 'poet's first petition'
to know 'the ways of wandering stars' (*Georgics*, ii, 676–7). Johnson, in his
London, had already stressed the importance of the poet's utterance that not

only bestowed self-consciousness on the rural imagination, but marked the poet's ultimate fulfilment in the public voice of his poetry. The direction of Gray's *Elegy* is somewhat different. The first version rests on a quietude and stoical resignation, which is fraught with the tragic awareness that an escape from human suffering is accompanied by the denial of human potential. The second version affirms the need for reputation and fame as a shared human need among rich and poor, country folk and city dwellers alike. The expanded *Elegy*, far from exhibiting a confidence in the public voice of the poet, reveals a trembling uncertainty about the poet's role. This is balanced by the restrained religious note on which the poem ends.

We may consider the poem as written in four-line stanzas. The form was much less widespread at the time than the heroic couplet or Miltonic blank verse; nevertheless Dryden had used it in *Annus Mirabilis* and Davenant in *Gondibert*. Thomas Hobbes used it for his translation of Homer. Closer to Gray's time, the elegiac potential of the form had been explored by Hammond in his *Elegies*.

The most significant aspect of Gray's style is its allusiveness. He was aware that his poems echoed and reechoed with phrases from other poets, and in the 1768 text acknowledged some of his borrowings. He is recorded to have told Nicholls that 'he never sat down to compose poetry without reading Spenser for a considerable time previously'. Allusions to Shakespeare and Milton abound in his verse; more contemporary poets like Pope and Dryden formed part of the poetic imagination of his times. His poetry is also deeply influenced by the classical poets of ancient Rome. Gray's verse is rich in texture and meaning. Even the *Elegy*, perhaps one of the most popular poems in English literature, is finally available only to the learned reader. Gray himself described his *Odes*, for instance, as being *'vocal to the Intelligent alone'*. An Augustan restraint and patterning balance the rich allusiveness of texture and indeterminacy of syntax in the *Elegy*. The subtle interweaving of different kinds of style corresponds to the equally fine intermixture between the public voice and individual experience in the poem.

[1] **curfew**
an evening peal marking the end of the day; by extension suggesting departure, or even death; cf. 'A sullen bell/ Remembered tolling a departed friend', *I Henry IV*, I, i, 102–3; see also 'That tolls the knell for their departed sense', Dryden, *Prologue to Troilus and Cressida*, 22; *knell* a sound announcing the passing away of something, in this case the day.

[2] **lowing**
'to bellow as a cow', Johnson, *Dictionary*; *lowing herd* cf. 'As from fresh pastures and the dewy fields . . ./ The lowing herds return', Pope, *Odyssey*, x, 485–7. Note the preponderance of the adjectival present participle plus noun combination; *wind* go on one's way; 'herd' as a collective noun may be allowed the plural form of the verb. *lea* meadow.

[3]
Several parallels may be listed for this line, in particular from Virgil and Horace; pastoral poets of the eighteenth century also offer comparisons, largely because they drew heavily on the classical pastoral. Spenser's line in *Faerie Queene*, 'And now she was upon the weary way' (6.7. 39, 1) is interesting. Of course it is the 'ploughman' who is 'weary' and not the 'way'; this is one of several cases of the transferred epithet in Gray.

[6] **all . . . holds**
'stillness' is the subject, 'air' the object, and 'holds' the verb, so that the line works out as 'a solemn stillness holds all the air'. Such inversions are very common in the poetry of this period. The determining influence here, as elsewhere, is Milton, and the learned reader is expected to respond

to the fluidity of the syntax. Cf. 'A solemn stillness reigns o'er land and seas', William Broome, *Paraphrase of Job*, line 40 (see Lonsdale, 1969).

[7] **wheels**
moves in a spiral or curve; *droning* emitting a low buzz or hum; cf. 'ere to black Hecate's summons/ The shard-borne beetle with his drowsy hums/ Hath rung night's yawning peal', *Macbeth*, III ii, 41–3, and 'Which drowsily like humming beetles rise', Dryden, *Indian Emperor*, 1, i, 119.

[8] **folds**
flocks of sheep; *drowsy tinklings lull the distant folds* the meaning is suspended between the 'tinklings' that are 'drowsy', and that make 'drowsy' or 'lull' the 'distant folds'.

[5–8]
The 'silence . . . save where' formula was often used in descriptions of evening by the 1740s, cf. 'No wakeful sound the moonlight valley knows,/ Save where the brook its liquid murmur pours,/ And lulls the waving scene to more profound repose', Collins, *Ode to Evening*, lines 9–12.

[9] **ivy-mantled**
twined with ivy; cf. 'the mantling vine', *Paradise Lost*, iv, 258.

[10] **moping**
drowsy, dull; cf. 'moping Melancholy/ And moon-struck madness', *Paradise Lost*, xi, 485–6.

[11] **wandering**
straying; *secret bower* cf. 'For the Screech-owl to build her balefull bower', Spenser, *Ruines of Time*, line 130. Spenser also has 'secret bowre', *Faerie Queene*, 4.5. 5, 4.

[12] **Molest**
'to disturb; to trouble; to vex', Johnson, *Dictionary*.

[13] **rugged elms . . . yew tree's shade**
elms and yew trees were planted in churchyards as signs of solemnity.

[14] **heaves**
swells or bulges. The other sense of moaning or sobbing could accompany the primary meaning in this context;

turf earth covered with grass; *mouldering* crumbling.

[16] **rude**
rustic, uneducated, unlearned; *hamlet* village.

[17] **breezy**
attended by breezes or low winds; *incense-breathing morn* emitting fragrance in the morning; cf. 'the humid Flowers that breathed/ Their morning incense', *Paradise Lost*, ix, 193–4.

[18] **twittering**
'to make a sharp, tremulous, intermitted noise', Johnson, *Dictionary*; an epithet often used for the swallow; cf. 'Or swallows twitter on the chimney tops', Dryden, *Georgics*, iv, 434; *straw-built* Milton has the compound 'straw-built citadel', *Paradise Lost*, i, 773.

[19] **clarion**
'a trumpet', Johnson, *Dictionary*; in this instance the crowing of the cock; cf. 'While the cock with lively din,/ Scatters the rear of darkness thin,/ And to the stack, or the barn door,/ Oft listening how the hounds and horn/ Chearly rouse the slumbering morn,/ From the side of some hoar hill, / Through the high wood echoing shrill', Milton, *L'Allegro*, lines 49–56; *echoing horn* the hunting horn. The sense of 'clarion' as related to 'a trumpet' suits with 'the horn'.

[22] **ply**
attend diligently to; work on anything closely; *care* responsibilities, domestic duties.

[23]
Cf. 'And stammering babes are taught to lisp thy name', Dryden, *Absalom and Achitophel*, line 243.

[21–4]
The sentiment in these lines can be traced back to Lucretius, and Dryden's translation of it: 'But to be snatched from all thy household joys,/ From thy chaste wife, and thy dear prattling boys,/ Whose little arms about thy legs are cast,/ And climbing for a kiss prevent their mother's haste', *Latter Part of the 3rd Book of*

Lucretius, lines 76–9 (see Lonsdale, 1969); see also: 'In vain for him the officious wife prepares/ The fire fair-blazing and the vestment warm;/ In vain his little children, peeping out,/ Into the mingling storm demand their sire/ With tears of artless innocence. Alas!/ Nor wife nor children more shall he behold', Thomson, *Winter*, lines 311–16.

[26] **furrow**
narrow trench made in the earth with a plough for the sowing of seed; *glebe* a piece of cultivated land, a field; *stubborn glebe has broke* the idea was expressed by Dryden: 'Commands/ Th'unwilling soil, and tames the stubborn lands', *Georgics*, i, 143–4; Pope: 'Or tames the genius of the stubborn plain', *Imitations of Horace, Satire*, II, i, 131.

[27] **jocund**
cheerful, blithe; *their team* a set of draught animals harnessed to draw together; *afield* in the field. Cf. 'Under the opening eye-lids of the morn,/ We drove a field', Milton, *Lycidas*, lines 26–7.

[28] **How bowed the woods**
Cf. 'Low the woods/ Bow their hoar head', Thomson, *Winter*, lines 235–6; *sturdy stroke* strong blows; cf. 'And labour him with many a sturdy stroke', Dryden, *Georgics*, iii, 639.

[30] **homely**
rustic; *destiny obscure* one of many Miltonic inversions.

[35] **Awaits**
if the text reads 'awaits' then the subject is 'hour'; *th'inevitable hour* cf. 'Th'inevitable hour of Naples' fate', Gay, *Trivia*, iii, 388.

[36]
Cf. 'With equal steps the paths of glory trace', Pope, *Odyssey*, i, 392.

[33–6]
The sentiment had become a favourite, oft-repeated one. It can be traced back to Horace, *Odes* I, iv, 13–14: 'Pale death at the poor man's shack and the pasha's palace kicking/ Impartially'; and 'One night of darkness waits for every creature;/ One

road we tread once only – to the tomb'; I, xxviii, 15–16 (trans. Mitchie). Cf. 'Ah me! what boots us all our boasted power,/ Our golden treasure, and our purpled state,/ They cannot ward th'inevitable hour,/ Nor stay the fearful violence of fate', Richard West, *Monody on the Death of Queen Caroline* (see Crofts, 1971).

[39] **fretted vault**
decorated. Cf. 'This majestical roof fretted with golden fire', *Hamlet*, II, ii, 293; 'The roof was fretted gold', *Paradise Lost*, i, 717; 'Wide vaults appear, and roofs of fretted gold', Pope, *Temple of Fame*, line 137; *vault* arched roof.

[40] **pealing**
resounding; *anthem* music or song of praise or gladness; *swells* in music to become gradually louder or fuller; *pealing anthem swells the note of praise* cf. 'There let the pealing organ blow/ To the full-voiced choir below,/ In service high, and anthems clear', Milton, *Il Penseroso*, lines 161–3; also 'And swelling organs lift the rising soul', Pope, *Eloisa to Abelard*, line 272. It seems that the line refers to organ music.

[37–40]
There is a shift of scene between the first two and the last two lines of this stanza. In the earlier lines the poet advises the 'proud' that it is not the fault of the humble dead that they have not been commemorated; the next lines refer to a scene inside a much grander church than the one in the 'country churchyard'; it is the kind of church which the 'proud' might attend.

[41] **storied**
having legends and myths figured or engraved on it, or bearing an inscription. Cf. 'And storied windows richly dight', Milton, *Il Penseroso*, line 159; 'The trophy'd arches, story'd halls', Pope, *Essay on Man*, iv, 303. Another meaning, 'celebrated or recorded in story or history' as describing the 'urn', could co-exist with the more common sense of 'decorated with

stories'; *animated* as if alive, life-like. Gray's is an ironical use of the word.

[42] **mansion**
a place of abode (used here figuratively). Cf. 'The immortal mind that hath forsook/ Her mansion in this fleshly nook', *Il Penseroso*, lines 91–2.

[43] **provoke**
to urge or stimulate to action.

[44] **flattery**
referring to the eulogic epitaphs on the tombs of the great; *dull* unresponsive. Cf.'When I am forgotten, as I shall be,/ And sleep in dull cold marble', *Henry VIII*, III, ii, 434–4.

[46] **pregnant**
teeming; *celestial fire* heavenly courage, passion. Cf. 'pregnant with infernal flame', *Paradise Lost*, vi, 483; see also: 'a soul,/ Which boasts her lineage from celestial fire', Young, *Night Thoughts*, vi, 378–9.

[48] **ecstasy**
rapturous emotion; *living lyre* cf. 'where Cowley strung/ His living harp', Pope, *Windsor-Forest*, lines 279–80.

[47–8]
The image of 'hands' in these lines works both literally and figuratively. 'Hands' would literally play the lyre; on the other hand they would 'sway the rod of empire' only metaphorically. The image of the lyre, however, is itself a figure for poetry.

[49] **ample page**
extended records.

[50] **Rich with the spoils of time**
Cf. 'Rich with spoils of many a conquer'd land', Dryden, *Palamon and Arcite*, ii, 452; *unroll* as in unrolling a scroll.

[51] **penury**
poverty, indigence; *repressed* crushed; *noble rage* rapture, ardour, inspiration; cf. 'Here noble Surrey felt the sacred rage', Pope, *Windsor-Forest*, line 291.

[52] **genial**
as opposed to 'froze', which refers back to the 'chill' of the previous line, it would mean ' warm'; in relation to

'current' the meaning would be 'moving, alive, creative'.

[51–2]
Thomson, in *Winter*, has a passage expressing sentiments similar to those of Gray here: 'if doomed/ In powerless humble fortune to repress/ These ardent risings of the kindling soul,/ Then even superior to ambition, we/ Would learn the private virtues', lines 597–601.

[53] **Full**
has an intensive sense with words of indefinite quantity like 'many'; *purest ray serene* a typical Miltonic placement of adjectives, one before and the other after the noun.

[55–6]
'There kept my charms concealed from mortal eye,/ Like roses that in deserts bloom and die', Pope, *Rape of the Lock*, iv, 157–8.

[57] **Hampden**
John Hampden (1594–1643). English statesman and patriot known for his resistance to Charles I; *dauntless breast* intrepid courage; cf. 'Stems a wild deluge with a dauntless breast', Dryden, *Eleonara*, line 362.

[60] **Cromwell**
Oliver Cromwell, Lord Protector, 1653–8; leader of the Puritan revolt that resulted in the execution of Charles I in 1649. It is interesting to note that Gray had had Cato, Tully and Caesar in the Eton manuscript instead of Hampden, Milton and Cromwell. He substituted English for Roman characters in the interests of intelligibility and relevance to his readers, and in deference to the very 'English' landscape of the poem.

[57–60]
These lines on unrealised greatness among the village-dwellers have been compared to: 'As when some dire usurper heav'n provides,/ To scourge his country with a lawless sway:/ His birth, perhaps some petty village hides,/ And sets his cradle out of fortune's sway:// Till fully ripe his swelling fate breaks out,/ And hurries him to mighty mischief on', Dryden,

Annus Mirabilis, lines 849–54 (see Lonsdale, 1969). Gray has chosen examples of great people who worked in some way to destabilise their country. His three references are to the activists and supporters of the Civil War of the previous century. Gray is concerned with the question of unrealised potential; it could be a serious loss to civilisation as in the case of 'mute inglorious Milton'; or it could be the absence of treachery and murder as in the case of Cromwell. The irony here is that Milton should have been of Cromwell's party; the poet's suggestion is of the weaving together, in a web of power, of the good and bad; he does not idealise the rural unremembered as being necessarily good.

[61] **listening senates**
'the listening senate', Thomson, *Winter*, line 680; *senate* the governing or legislative assembly of a nation; often applied to the British Parliament; *command* have the power to elicit.

[64] **read**
discern; cf. 'Let not my sister read it in your eye', *Comedy of Errors*, III, ii, 9, but also 'interpret' in the modern sense. The combination with 'history' also points to the common meaning of 'read'.

[65] **lot**
fate.

[65–6]
Not just the virtuous and good aspects of their personalities, but almost more importantly, if we look at the next lines, the greater potential for evil is circumscribed or contained by a rural existence.

[67] **wade through slaughter**
Cf. 'I am in blood/ Stepp'd in so far, that, should I wade no more', *Macbeth*, III, iv, 135–6. The image was used many times by Shakespeare, and later by eighteenth-century poets.

[70] **quench the blushes**
Cf. 'Quench your blushes', *The Winter's Tale*, IV, iv, 67; *ingenuous*

natural, or noble; *shame* cf. 'The passion felt when reputation is supposed to be lost; the passion expressed sometimes by blushes', Johnson, *Dictionary*.

[71] **Luxury**
Something that conduces to enjoyment over and above the necessaries of life. Gray has in mind a sense of excess, especially in the writing of poetry, as the next line suggests.

[72]
After this line the original manuscript has the following four stanzas, which were probably originally intended to conclude the poem:

The thoughtless world to majesty
             may bow
Exalt the brave and idolise success
But more to innocence their safety
             owe
Than power and genius e'er
          conspired to bless

And thou, who mindful of the
         unhonoured dead
Dost in these notes their artless tale
            relate
By night and lonely contemplation
            led
To linger in the gloomy walks of fate

Hark how the sacred calm, that
         broods around
Bids every fierce tumultuous passion
           cease
In still small accents whispering
         from the ground
A grateful earnest of eternal peace.

No more with reason and thyself at
           strife;
Give anxious cares and endless
         wishes room
But through the cool sequestered
         vale of life
Pursue the silent tenour of thy
          doom.

[73] **madding crowd's ignoble strife**
Cf. 'Horrible discord, and the madding wheels/ Of brazen chariots

raged', Milton, *Paradise Lost*, vi, 210–11; *ignoble* dishonourable.

[74] **sober wishes**
temperate desires; *never learned to stray* cf. 'His soul proud science never taught to stray', Pope, *Essay on Man*, i, 102. Living, as they did, far from the deranged conduct of mobs, they remained always temperate and serious in their attitudes.

[75] **the cool sequestered vale of life**
Cf. 'let woods and rivers be/ My quiet, though inglorious destiny:/ In life's cool vale let my low scene be laid', Cowley, *Imitation of Virgil, Georgics*, ii, 45–7 (see Lonsdale, 1969).

[76] **noiseless**
quiet, unobtrusive; *tenor* 'constant mode', Johnson, *Dictionary*; cf. 'Correctly cold, and regularly low,/ That shunning faults, one quiet tenor keep', Pope, *Essay on Criticism*, lines 240–1. Pope's context, of course, is satirical.

[77] **insult**
'act of insolence or contempt', Johnson, *Dictionary*.

[78] **still erected**
always erected.

[79] **uncouth rhymes**
unpolished verses; cf. 'uncouth speech', Spenser, *Faerie Queene*, 5.5. 37, I; and 'uncouth words', 6.8. 18, 4.

[80] **the passing tribute of a sigh**
a fleeting recognition by those who pass by; cf. 'The tribute of a tear is all I crave', Pope, *Odyssey*, xi, 89.

[86] **anxious**
capable of thought, of anticipation and recollection.

[85–6]
Cf. 'And them immortal make, which else would die/ In foul forgetfulness', Spenser, *Ruins of Time*, lines 377–8; see also 'for who would loose,/ Though full of pain, this intellectual being,/ Those thoughts that wander through eternity,/ To perish rather, swallowed up and lost/ In the wide womb of uncreated night,/ Devoid of sense and motion', Milton, *Paradise Lost*, ii, 146–51. Lonsdale (1969) offers

three possible interpretations of Gray's line: 'For who, about to become a prey to dumb forgetfulness (=oblivion)'; 'For who ever resigned this being to dumb forgetfulness (=oblivion)'; and 'For who was already so much the prey of forgetfulness (=insensibility) as to resign'.

[87] **warm precincts**
comfortable regions; cf. 'the precincts of light', *Paradise Lost*, iii, 88; *day* same as 'life'; Spenser has 'cheerfull day', *Faerie Queene*, 1.3. 27, 7.

[88]
'Nor casts one pitying look behind', Rowe, *The Fair Penitent*, II, i, Song.

[90] **pious**
'Careful of the duties of a near relation', Johnson, *Dictionary*.

[89–90]
Note the syntactical inversion. Cf. 'ev'n he whose soul now melts in mournful lays,/ Shall shortly want the gen'rous tear he pays;/ Then from his closing eyes thy form shall part', Pope, *Elegy to an Unfortunate Lady*, lines 77–9.

[91] **voice of nature**
wishes natural to the living. Cf. 'the faithful voice of nature', Akenside, *Pleasures of the Imagination*, ii, 357–8.

[92] **wonted**
usual, common.

[93] **For thee**
The poet addresses himself.

[95] **If chance**
by chance, if it should chance; *by lonely contemplation led* cf. 'Where lonely contemplation keeps her cave', Rowe, *Jane Grey*, II, i, 96.

[96] **kindred**
allied in nature, having similar qualities.

[95–6]
The syntax, again, needs to be unravelled: If, by chance, some kindred spirit, guided by lonely contemplation, should ask about you.

[97] **Haply**
perhaps; *hoary-headed* grey-haired. A common compound in Spenser and Dryden.

[98] **peep**
'peep' as a verb for dawn was common. Cf. 'The nice morn on th'Indian steep/ From her cabined loophole peep', Milton, *Comus*, lines 139–40. Spenser also uses the verb 'peep' for dawn.

[99]
Cf. 'though from off the boughs each morn/ We brush mellifluous dews', Milton, *Paradise Lost*, v, 428–9.

[100] **upland lawn**
stretch of grass on a hillside. Cf. 'upland fallows grey', Collins, *Ode to Evening*, line 31.

[102] **wreathes**
coils; *fantastic* wild, arbitrarily devised, grotesque in design.

[104] **brook that babbles by**
Cf. 'divided by a babbling brook', Thomson, *Spring*, line 646.

[105] **Hard by**
close by.

[106] **wayward**
capricious, intractable; *fancies* whimsical ideas.

[107] **wan**
'pale, as with a sickness', Johnson, *Dictionary*.

[107–8]
Cf. 'For pale and wan he was (alas the while,)/ May seem he loved, or else some care he took', Spenser, *Shepherd's Calendar*, 'Jan', lines 8–9.

[109] **customed**
accustomed. Cf. 'th'accustom'd oak', Milton, *Il Penseroso*, line 60.

[111] **Another came**
another day came.

[114] **through the church-way path**
Cf. 'church-way paths', *A Midsummer Nights's Dream*, V, ii, 391.

[115] **lay**
short lyric or poem.

[117] **lap of earth**
Cf. 'mother earth's dear lap', Spenser, *Faerie Queene*, 5.7. 9, 2.

[119] **Fair science**
'Science' used in the non-specialised sense of 'knowledge' or 'learning'; 'Fair' because it is personified as a muse.

[120] **melancholy**
Lonsdale makes the point that the meaning of the word 'melancholy' is crucial to the 'Epitaph':

Gray does not mean simply that the poet has been made melancholy (= gloomy) because his education made him aware of abilities which he has been unable to fulfil; if that had been the case the 'And' of this line would have logically been a 'But'. The favourable sense of 'melancholy', implying a valuable kind of sensibility, though not found in Johnson's *Dictionary*, was becoming fashionable at this time. The heightened sensibility of the melancholy man ideally expresses itself in benevolence and other social virtues, rather than merely in solitary wandering, although that usually precedes it.

Thomson, *Autumn*, lines 1004–10 speaks of the 'sacred influence' of 'the power/ Of philosophic melancholy'; see also 'that elegance of soul refined/ Whose soft sensation feels a quicker joy/ From melancholy's scenes, than the dull pride/ Of tasteless splendour and magnificence/ Can e'er afford', T. Warton, *Pleasures of Melancholy*, lines 92–5 (see Lonsdale, 1969). Gray's image of 'Melancholy' in *Ode to Adversity* offers a gloss: 'Wisdom in sable garb arrayed,/ Immersed in rapturous thought profound,/ And Melancholy, silent maid/ With leaden eye that loves the ground,/ Still on thy solemn steps attend:/ Warm charity, the general friend,/ With justice to herself severe,/ And pity, dropping soft the sadly-pleasing tear', lines 25–32. Melancholy here is associated with wisdom, charity, justice and pity. Such an interpretation leads on to the social virtues that are described in the next stanza.

[121] **Large**
abundant, generous; *soul* in the sense of 'heart'.

[122]
Cf. 'Heav'n, that had largely giv'n,

was largely pay'd', Dryden, *Eleonara*, line 25.

[126] **dread abode**
revered, awe inspiring dwelling, i.e. the grave or death.

[127] **trembling hope**
filled with a sense of apprehension. 'Trembling, hoping, ling'ring, flying', Pope, *Dying Christian to his Soul*, line 3.

WILLIAM COLLINS

(1721–59)

◇

William Collins was born at Chichester in 1721. Though his father was only a hatter he was mayor of the town in 1714 and 1721. In 1734 Collins was admitted to Winchester College where Joseph Warton and James Hampton were his fellow students. He matriculated at Queen's College in Oxford in 1740 and took his degree in 1743.

Collins started to write verse early in his life; his *Persian Eclogues* were published in 1742; and his *Verses Humbly Addres'd to Sir Thomas Hanmer* in 1743. Like many poets of the century he headed for London in 1744 where he soon became part of the literati, counting among his friends Johnson and Garrick, Quin and Foote. In London he planned to write both tragedies and a translation of Aristotle's *Poetics*. In 1746 he projected a joint publication of his Odes with Joseph Warton, but abandoned the idea; his *Odes on Several Descriptive and Allegoric Subjects* was published in that same year by Andrew Millar. Warton went on to publish separately with Robert Dodsley.

In 1747 Collins moved to Richmond where James Thomson was among his friends. Some of his poems including *Ode to Evening* were reprinted in Dodsley's *Collection* of 1748. Thomas Warton reports that he often saw Collins in London around 1750. He fell ill in 1751, and over the next few years travelled to France and Bath in the hope of a cure. His health continued to decline, though he did visit Oxford in 1754. Even so his interest in *The History of the Revival of Learning*, which he had planned as early as 1744, continued. William Collins died at Chichester in 1759 and is buried in St Andrew's Church.

Further Reading

Two editions of Collins may be considered standard: Roger Lonsdale (ed.), *Thomas Gray and William Collins: Poetical Works* (Oxford: Oxford University Press, 1977), and Richard Wendorf and Charles Ryskamp, *The Works of William Collins* (Oxford: Clarendon Press, 1979).

A life is provided by P.L. Carver, *The Life of a Poet: A Biographical Sketch of William Collins* (London: Sidgwick and Jackson, 1967), and a general critical account by Oliver F. Sigworth, *William Collins* (New York: Twayne, 1965). Two further books place the poet in different kinds of context. They are: Richard Wendorf, *William Collins and Eighteenth-Century English Poetry* (Minneapolis: University of Minnesota Press, 1981) and Paul S. Sherwin, *Precious Bane: Collins and the Miltonic Legacy* (Austin and London: University of Texas Press, 1977).

———◇———

33 / *Ode on the Poetical Character*

As once, if not with light regard,
I read aright that gifted bard,
(Him whose school above the rest
His loveliest elfin queen has blessed.)
One, only one, unrivalled fair,   5
Might hope the magic girdle wear,
At solemn tourney hung on high,
The wish of each love-darting eye.
Lo! to each other nymph in turn applied,
    As if, in air unseen, some hovering hand,   10
Some chaste and angel-friend to virgin-fame,
    With whispered spell had burst the starting band,
It left unblest her loathed, dishonoured side:
    Happier hopeless fair, if never
    Her baffled hand with vain endeavour   15
Had touched that fatal zone to her denied!

Young Fancy thus, to me divinest name,
  To whom, prepared and bathed in heaven,
  The cest of amplest power is given,
  To few the god-like gift assigns,   20
  To gird their blest prophetic loins,
And gaze her visions wild, and feel unmixed her flame!

2

The band, as fairy legends say,
Was wove on that creating day,
When He, who called with thought to birth   25
Yon tented sky, this laughing earth,
And dressed with springs, and forests tall,
And poured the main engirting all,
Long by the loved enthusiast woo'd,
Himself in some diviner mood,   30
Retiring, sate with her alone,
And placed her on his sapphire throne,
The whiles, the vaulted shrine around,
Seraphic wires were heard to sound,
Now sublimest triumph swelling,   35
Now on love and mercy dwelling;
And she, from out the veiling cloud,
Breathed her magic notes aloud;
And thou, thou rich-haired youth of morn,
And all thy subject life was born!   40
Thy dangerous passions kept aloof,
Far from the sainted growing woof:
But near it sat ecstatic wonder,
Listening the deep applauding thunder:
And truth, in sunny vest arrayed,   45
By whose the tarsel's eyes were made;
All the shadowy tribes of mind
In braided dance their murmurs joined,
And all the bright uncounted powers,
Who feed on heaven's ambrosial flowers.   50
Where is the bard, whose soul can now
Its high presuming hopes avow?
Where he who thinks, with rapture blind,
This hallowed work for him designed?

3

High on some cliff, to heaven up-piled,   55
Of rude access, of prospect wild,
Where, tangled round the jealous steep,
Strange shades o'erbrow the valleys deep,
And holy genii guard the rock,
Its glooms embrown, its springs unlock,   60
While on its rich ambitious head,
An Eden, like his own, lies spread.
I view that oak, the fancied glades among,
By which as Milton lay, his evening ear,
From many a cloud that dropped ethereal dew,   65
Nigh sphered in heaven its native strains could hear,
On which that ancient trump he reached was hung:
    Thither oft his glory greeting,
    From Waller's myrtle shades retreating,
With many a vow from hope's aspiring tongue,   70
My trembling feet his guiding steps pursue:
    In vain – such bliss to one alone,
    Of all the sons of soul was known,
    And heaven, and fancy, kindred powers,
    Have now o'erturned the inspiring bowers,   75
Or curtained close such scene from every future view.

The two Odes presented here are selected from Collins' *Odes on Several Descriptive and Allegoric Subjects*, first published in 1746 (dated 1747). As Collins had originally intended to publish with Warton, it is worth looking at the 'Advertisement' to *Odes on Various Subjects* (1746):

> The public has been so much accustomed of late to didactic poetry alone, and essays on moral subjects, that any work where the imagination is much indulged, will perhaps not be relished or regarded. The author therefore of these pieces is in some pain lest certain austere critics should think them too fanciful and descriptive. But as he is convinced that the fashion of moralising in verse has been carried too far, and as he looks upon invention and imagination to be the chief faculties of a poet, so he will be happy if the following Odes may be looked upon as an attempt to bring back poetry into its right channel.

These are ideas with which Collins was probably in agreement.

Collins' poems, far removed from Augustan moralising, aim at imaginative creativity; they are also concerned about the nature of poetic creativity. The poems write themselves and write about themselves. This dual consciousness requires a kind of critical attention that many were unable to give to them during Collins' lifetime, and his works were often dismissed as obscure. Collins, however, revised his manuscripts extensively before publishing; many that he did not consider fit, he destroyed. His comparative unpopularity during his lifetime indicates that he was writing against the grain of Augustan clarity, and especially against the precise syntax of the heroic couplet.

Both *Ode to the Poetical Character* and *Ode to Evening* are, as their titles suggest, serious and celebratory poems, elevated in style and elaborate in stanza structure. *Ode on the Poetical Character* is in the form established by and called after the Greek poet Pindar. Ever since Cowley, however misguidedly, popularised the Pindaric form, it offered an alternative to the better known forms of the elegy and the sonnet. Later Congreve established the rigour of the Pindaric form when he pointed out that the ode usually consisted of three stanzas, the strophe, the antistrophe, and the epode. The poet chose the stanza form of the strophe, but was committed to duplicate it in the antistrophe; the epode permitted another, often a contrasting stanza form. Gray, Gilbert West and Collins were among the English writers of the Pindaric Ode who observed fairly closely the formality of its poetic structure.

Collins offered a slight variation on it when he moved the epode to occupy the middle position between the strophe and the antistrophe. By this placement in the *Ode on the Poetical Character* Collins achieves a central position for the passage on the Creation, bordered by the opening strophe about Spenser's Florimel legend, and followed by the invocation of Milton's Eden; these are conceived as the two high-water marks of English poetry beyond which the modern poet cannot look.

Ode to Evening on the other hand is a Horatian poem which repeats a single stanza form and is calm and meditative in tone rather than ecstatic. The blank verse reduces the sharp outlines that the stanzaic method usually creates. The poem was originally printed in continuous form. *Ode to Evening* is more reminiscent of Joseph Warton's *Ode to Fancy*, and of Milton's poetry, than of the Pindaric Odes of the mid-eighteenth century.

The style of Collins' poems is deeply literary, evoking earlier writers continuously, most especially Milton. Clearly the reader is expected to be familiar with the works of Milton, Spenser, and other Renaissance and eighteenth-century poets. The wealth of recognisable allusions in Collins' Odes direct the reader to what may be called a 'poetical experience', rather than the reading of an isolated poem. Poems like these Odes suggest a different reading habit and different expectations from poetry. Collins' allusions are more sustained than those of Gray, for instance, and he is more identifiably Miltonic in his syntax. Again, as different from Gray, his sentence structure is often difficult to unravel, and the poems are read through a series of impressions, some of then highly visual.

Because of the acknowledged influence of Milton and Spenser, Collins also expects the reader to respond to his archaisms and unusual use of words. Once again, it seems that he is concerned with a different kind of reading capability than that engendered by the heroic couplet.

The poem illustrates poetic creativity and the power of the poetic imagination through a retelling of Spenser's story of Florimel's girdle and Milton's description of Eden. The first couplet echoes two lines from Spenser, the poet who is also the subject of praise in this Ode: cf. 'But she thereto would lend but light regard', *Faerie Queene*, 3.8. 14, 6; and 'Full hard it is (quoth he) to read aright', 1.9. 6, 6. Collins establishes from the start the literary nature of his work.

[1] **regard**
attention.

[3] **school**
of followers. Spenser had many imitators.

[4] **elfin queen**
Cf. 'To serve again his sovereign Elfin Queene', *Faerie Queene*, 2.1. 1, 6.
[7] **tourney**
tournament. Cf. 'A solemn feast, with public tourneying', *Faerie Queene*, 4.2. 26, 8, at which the competition for the girdle was held; see also 'great bards beside,/ In sage and solemn tunes have sung,/ Of tourneys and of trophies hung', Milton, *Il Penseroso*, lines 116–18.
[8] **love-darting eye**
Cf. 'Love-darting eyes', Milton, *Comus*, line 753; see also 'And those love-darting eyes must roll no more', Pope, *Elegy to the Memory of an Unfortunate Lady*, line 34.
[9] **nymph**
(in poetry) a young and beautiful woman; *applied* brought into contact.
[10–11]
The lines recall 'Thou hovering angel girt with golden wings,/ And thou unblemished form of chastity', *Comus*, lines 214–15. Milton has 'Angel guest' in *Paradise Lost*, v, 328. Pope's sylphs come to mind by way of both theme and allusion: 'Straight hover round the fair her airy band', *Rape of the Lock*, iii, 113.
[12] **whispered spell**
Cf. 'breathed spell', Milton, *Nativity Ode*, line 179; *burst* to break, snap, shatter suddenly; *starting* moving suddenly, involuntarily as a result of surprise, terror.
[13] **unblest**
unprotected; *loathed* that which excites aversion; *dishonoured* treated with indignity.
[15] **baffled**
confused.
[16] **fatal**
gravely mischievous; *zone* belt or girdle, common poetic usage; see: 'Scarce could the goddess from her nymph be known,/ But by the crescent and the golden zone', Pope, *Windsor-Forest*, lines 175–6.
[5–16]
In a note Collins himself referred back to the story of Florimel's girdle in

Spenser: '*Florimel*. See *Spenser* Leg. 4th.' Spenser describes the competition amongst the various ladies of the court when the girdle was offered as a prize. The girdle, of course, had magical moral qualities: 'That girdle gave the virtue of chaste love,/ And wifehood true, to all that did it bear;/ But whosoever contrary doth prove,/ Might not the same about her middle wear,/ But it would loose, or else a sunder tear', *Faerie Queene*, 4.5. 3, 1–5. The competition was not attended by Florimel, the true owner of the girle; the false Florimel won the girdle but could not fasten it: 'For ever as they fastened it, it loosed/ And fell away, as feeling secret blame./ Full oft about her waist she it enclosed,/ And it as oft was from her waist disclosed', *Faerie Queene*, 4.5. 16, 6–9; Finally, of course, the girdle was restored to its true owner.
[17–22]
The magical-moral power of Florimel's girdle is an illustration of the power of the poetic imagination; yet it is worth noting that the poet's language describing the creative imagination goes further to mutate the language of myth into the language of religion. The poet's use of words like 'divinest', 'heaven', 'godlike', 'blest', 'prophetic' and 'visions' is significant of a change in perspective. The poetic persona enters the poem here in the first person, against the background of the Florimel legend which focuses on Florimel (the individual) as at once morally privileged and unique. Moving beyond the legend the poet looks into the future with strong feeling. This is suggested by 'prophetic loins', 'visions wild' and 'feel unmixed her flame'.
[19] **cest**
belt or girdle for the waist; cf. 'That goodly belt was Cestus hight by name', *Faerie Queene*, 4.5. 6, 1. The word was often used for Aphrodite's girdle. Johnson defines *cestus* as: 'the girdle of Venus', *Dictionary*;

amplest 'unlimited; without restriction', Johnson, *Dictionary*.

[20] **assigns**
transfers, allots.

[22] **gaze**
to look at with regard; *visions wild* creations of the imagination; *feel unmixed her flame* to experience fancy's creative power in its pure form.

[24] **that creating day**
here, the fourth day of the creation.

[23–5]
This passage has been variously interpreted. Collins goes back to the image of the girdle in 'the band', but views it now in terms of the original creation by God which parallels poetic creativity. Though Collins' idea is not new, his presentation is strikingly dramatic. Cf. 'As first a various unformed hint we find/ Rise in some god-like poet's fertile mind,/ Till all the parts and words their places take,/ And with just marches verse and music make;/ Such was God's poem, this world's new essay;/ So wild and rude in its first draught it lay;/Th'ungoverned parts no correspondence knew,/ An artless war from thwarting motions grew;/ Till they to number and fixt rules were brought/ By the eternal Mind's Poetic Thought', Cowley, *Davideis*, i, 446–56. The idea had been explored by Akenside in *Pleasures of Imagination*. Collins, like Akenside, suggests an interpenetrating relationship in which God is a poet and the poet is God-like.

[26] **tented**
tent-like; *laughing* 'In poetry. To appear gay, favourable, pleasant, or fertile' , Johnson, *Dictionary*.

[27] **dressed**
adorned.

[28] **the main engirting all**
The all-surrounding sea.

[29] **enthusiast**
refers back to 'Fancy' from line 17, here introduced as a female consort. The word 'enthusiast', also used by Dryden – for instance, 'The sweet enthusiast', *Alexander's Feast*, line 163

– meant one who is in touch with the divine. Collins is in keeping with a tradition of personifying divine attributes as female companions. Cf. Milton's invocation to Urania, the Muse of sacred song: 'Before the hills appeared, or fountain flowed,/ Thou with eternal wisdom didst converse,/ Wisdom thy sister, and with her didst play/ In presence of th'Almighty Father, pleased/ With thy celestial song', *Paradise Lost*, vii, 8–12.

[31] **Retiring**
in privacy; away from the public eye. Akenside presents God, 'deep-retired/ In his unfathomed essence, viewed at large/ The uncreated images of things;/ . . . till in time complete,/ What he admired and loved, his vital smile/ Unfolded into being', *Pleasures of Imagination*, i, 59–78.

[33] **The whiles**
an archaism, common in Spenser.

[34] **wires**
metal strings for musical instruments.

[32–4]
Cf.

And above the firmament that was over their heads was the likeness of a throne, as the appearance of a sapphire stone. . . . As the appearance of the bow that is in the cloud in the day of rain, so was the appearance of the brightness round about. This was the appearance of the likeness of the glory of the Lord. (Ezekiel 1: 26, 28)

Also 'Then I looked, and behold, in the firmament that was above the head of the cherubims there appeared over them as it were a sapphire stone, as the appearance of the likeness of a throne', Ezekiel 10: 1. Milton, in a passage that draws on the Ezekiel text, has 'Sapphire throne', *Paradise Lost*, vi, 758, as he does in *At a Solemn Music*, 6–13: 'That undisturbed song of pure content,/ Ay sung before the sapphire-coloured throne/ . . . Where the bright Seraphim in burning row/ Their loud uplifted angel trumpets blow,/ And the cherubic host in thousand choirs/ Touch their immortal harps of golden wires'. Collins may have been thinking of this last passage.

[33–4]
Whilst the music of the seraphs was heard around the cave-like shrine.

[35] **sublimest triumph**
glorious victory. Cf. 'Exulting in triumph now swell the bold notes', Pope, *Ode for St Cecilia's Day*, line 16.

[36] **dwelling**
'to fix the mind upon', Johnson, *Dictionary*.

[37] **veiling**
concealing.

[38] **Breathed**
uttered.

[39] **rich-haired youth of morn**
Cf. Collins' own phrase 'bright-haired sun' in *Ode to Evening*, line 5. The phrase does appear to refer to the sun, the creation of which marked the high point of God's creation, of which the poetic act is a divine re-creation. The other interpretation that the phrase refers to the birth of 'the Poet', through a union of God with Fancy, cannot be ruled out but seems lacking in the fluidity that characterises this poem.

[40] **subject life**
again the phrase reverberates between life on earth that is sustained by the sun, and life as a subject of the poet's renderings. The whole passage is strongly reminiscent of visual depictions of goddesses emanating radiantly from clouds, carrying with them connotations of Truth.

[41] **dangerous**
haughty, arrogant. It seems that Collins has in mind this older sense of the word; *kept aloof* a Spenserian phrase.

[42] **sainted**
sacred; cf. 'Amongst the enthroned gods on sainted seats', Milton, *Comus*, line 11; *growing woof* growing fabric.

[43] **ecstatic wonder**
Addison in his *Spectator*, No. 412 had talked of the novel, or that which inspires wonder, as the source of imaginative pleasure. Akenside

adopts the idea of 'novelty or wonderfulness' in *Pleasures of Imagination*, i, 222–70.

[44] **deep applauding thunder**
Cf. 'I answered thee in thunder deep', Milton, *Psalm*, lxxxi, 29.

[45] **vest**
garment.

[46] **tarsel**
tercel, a male hawk.

[46]
The eyes of the hawk are as sharp and discerning as truth itself.

[48] **braided**
woven; *murmurs* low, indistinct sounds.

[50] **ambrosial**
divinely fragrant; capable of bestowing immortality. 'Ambrosial odours and ambrosial flowers', *Paradise Lost*, ii, 245.

[47–50]
An attempt to describe the creative process reminiscent of: 'Anon ten thousand shapes,/ Like spectres.../ Fleet swift before him. From the womb of earth,/ From ocean's bed they come: th'eternal heavens/ Disclose their splendors, and the dark abyss/ Pours out her births unknown. With fixed gaze/ He marks the rising phantoms. Now compares/ Their different forms; now blends them, now divides;/ Inlarges and extenuates by turns;/ Opposes, ranges in fantastic bands,/ And infinitely varies', Akenside, *Pleasures of Imagination*, iii, 385–95. Sir William Temple in *Of Poetry* had written:

There must be a spritely imagination or fancy, fertile in a thousand productions, ranging over infinite ground, piercing into every corner, and by the light of that true poetical fire discovering a thousand little bodies or images in the world, and similitudes among them, unseen to common eyes, and which could not be discovered without the rays of that sun. (see Lonsdale, 1969)

We see here, and in the passages from Akenside and Collins, attempts to define the poetic imagination, as different from the scientific tradition generated by Hobbes. The poem moves from the physical creation of the world (lines 25–9) and the life-giving power of the sun (lines 37–40) to the creation of the world of the mind, the 'shadowy tribes' that await the poet's powers of articulation. These are ideas that lead up to Coleridge's definition of the imagination.

[51–4]
Where is the poet who can now realise his highest role and aspirations? Where is he who, blinded by rapture, believes God's creation was designed for his (the poet's) work of recreation? The 'rapture blind' harks back to Homer, and more especially to Milton's blindness. See also 'But, O Melpomene, for whom/ Awakes thy golden shell again?/ What mortal breath shall e'er presume/ To echo that unbounded strain?', Akenside, *On Lyric Poetry*, in *Odes*, 1745 (see Lonsdale, 1969).

[56] **rude**
rough; *prospect* view or scene.

[57] **jealous**
suspiciously vigilant and protective.

[58] **shades**
shadows, darkness.

[60] **embrown**
darken or make brown. See 'and where the unpierced shade,/ Embrowned the noontide bowers', Milton, *Paradise Lost*, iv, 245–6; *its springs unlock* cf. 'Unlock your springs, and open all your shades', Pope, *Windsor-Forest*, line 4; this is a formula also found in Dryden: 'Once more unlock for thee the sacred spring', *Georgics*, ii, 245.

[61] **ambitious head**
swelling, towering, even in the sense of 'aspiring'. Cf. 'Or helps th'ambitious hill the heav'n to scale', Pope, *Epistles to Several Persons*, iv, 59.

[55–61]
Cf. 'Of Eden, where delicious Paradise,/ Now nearer, crowns with her enclosure green,/ As with a rural

mound the champaign head/ Of a steep wilderness, whose hairy sides/ With thicket overgrown, grotesque and wild,/ Access denied; and over head up grew/ Insuperable highth of loftiest shade', *Paradise Lost*, iv, 132–8; and 'Now to the ascent of that steep savage hill/ Satan had journeyed on, pensive and slow;/ But further way found none, so thick entwined,/ As one continued brake, the undergrowth/ Of shrubs and tangling bushes had perplexed/ All path of man or beast that past that way', *Paradise Lost*, iv, 172–7. Collins consciously evokes Milton's description of the difficult and arduous ascent to 'Eden' or the journey of the creative imagination; Milton, in turn, imitated God's creative powers in his imaginative reconstruction of Eden. His description of the eastern gate of Paradise is also relevant: 'it was a rock/ Of alabaster, piled up to the clouds,/ Conspicuous far, winding with one ascent/ Accessible from earth, one entrance high;/ The rest was craggy cliff, that overhung/ Still as it rose, impossible to climb', iv, 543–8.

[62] **An ... spread**
referring to Milton's poetic imagination.

[63–4]
Milton describes himself as listening to Philomel's 'even-song': 'While Cynthia checks her dragon yoke,/ Gently o'er th'accustomed oak', *Il Penseroso*, lines 59–60. The oak was sacred to the Druids. Once again the poetic persona asserts his presence in the first person in relation to the poets of earlier times.

[65]
Cf. 'Come gentle Spring, ethereal mildness, come;/ And from the bosom of yon dropping cloud', Thomson, *Spring*, lines 1–2.

[66] **Nigh sphered in heaven**
the allusion may be to the music of the spheres that Adam and Eve could hear in Paradise, *Paradise Lost*, iv, 680–8; Milton also has 'Spheared in a radiant cloud', *Paradise Lost*, vii, 247;

native strains through rather convoluted syntax Collins highlights Milton's unique achievement in 'listening' to the heavenly music of the spheres in his native English.

[67] **ancient trump**
Cf. 'The wakeful trump', Milton, *Nativity Ode*, line 156; the ancient instrument of prophecy.

[69] **myrtle**
sacred to Venus and an emblem of love. Collins associates it with the amorous verse of Waller.

[68–71]
Collins declares his allegiance to Milton and Spenser, as opposed to the more 'correct' school of Waller, who wrote mainly shorter love poems. Akenside had preceded Collins in making a similar, but less strong contrast between Shakespeare and Waller, *Pleasures of Imagination*, iii, 550–67.

[74] **kindred**
related. 'Heaven' and 'Fancy' both conspire to keep inspiration away from the younger poet.

[75]
Collins may have had in mind Guyon's destruction of the Bower of Bliss in 'But all those pleasant bowers and palace brave,/ Guyon broke down, with rigour pitiless', *Faerie Queene*, 2.12. 83, 1–2. His own reference is to the fall.

[76] **curtained close**
concealed. Cf.'close-curtained sleep', *Comus*, line 554; *future view* here meaning any viewers after Milton. Compare 'future views', Pope, *Essay on Man*, iv, 72.

---

34 / *Ode to Evening*

If aught of oaten stop or pastoral song,
May hope, chaste Eve, to soothe thy modest ear,
    Like thy own solemn springs,
    Thy springs, and dying gales,
O nymph reserved, while now the bright-haired sun   5
Sits in yon western tent, whose cloudy skirts,
    With brede ethereal wove,
    O'erhang his wavy bed;
Now air is hushed, save where the weak-eyed bat,
With short shrill shriek flits by on leathern wing,   10
    Or where the beetle winds
    His small but sullen horn,
As oft he rises midst the twilight path,
Against the pilgrim borne in heedless hum;
    Now teach me, maid composed,   15
    To breathe some softened strain,
Whose numbers stealing through thy darkening vale,

May not unseemly with its stillness suit,
   As musing slow, I hail
   Thy genial loved return!   20
For when thy folding star arising shows
His paly circlet, at his warning lamp
   The fragrant hours, and elves
   Who slept in flowers the day,
And many a nymph who wreathes her brows with sedge,   25
And sheds the freshening dew, and lovelier still,
   The pensive pleasures sweet
   Prepare thy shadowy car.
Then lead, calm vot'ress, where some sheety lake
Cheers the lone heath, or some time-hallowed pile,   30
   Or up-land fallows grey,
   Reflect its last cool gleam.
But when chill blustering winds, or driving rain,
Forbid my willing feet, be mine the hut,
   That from the mountain's side,   35
   Views wilds, and swelling floods,
And hamlets brown, and dim-discovered spires,
And hears their simple bell, and marks o'er all
   Thy dewy fingers draw
   The gradual dusky veil.   40
While spring shall pour his showers, as oft he wont,
And bathe thy breathing tresses, meekest Eve!
   While summer loves to sport,
   Beneath thy lingering light:
While sallow autumn fills thy lap with leaves,   45
Or winter yelling through the troublous air,
   Affrights thy shrinking train,
   And rudely rends thy robes.
So long, sure-found beneath the sylvan shed,
Shall fancy, friendship, science, rose-lipped health,   50
   Thy gentlest influence own,
   And hymn thy favourite name!

---

[1] **aught**
anything; *If aught* a phrase frequently used by Spenser. The first line goes on to imitate *Comus*, line 345: 'Or sound of pastoral reed with oaten stops'. As in *Ode on the Poetical Character* Collins here conveys his allegiance to Spenser and Milton; *oaten stop* shepherd's reed flute.

[3] **springs**
brooks.

[4] **dying gales**
Cf. 'The dying gales that pant upon the trees', Pope, *Eloisa to Abelard*, line 159.

[5] **reserved**
'modest; not loosely free', Johnson, *Dictionary*; **bright-haired sun** cf. 'rich-haired youth of morn', *Ode on the Poetical Character*, line 39; see also 'bright-hair'd Vesta', *Il Penseroso*, line 23.

[6] **skirts**
used often to describe the border of a cloud. Cf. 'a cloud... / ... / Whose skirts were bordered with bright sunny beams', *Faerie Queene*, 5.9. 28, 4, 6; 'Till the sun paint your fleecy skirts with gold', *Paradise Lost*, v, 187; and 'fluid skirts of that same watry cloud', xi, 878. The expression is used by both Akenside and Thomson, while Pope parodies it.

[6]
Cf. 'Arraying with reflected purple and gold/ The clouds that on his western throne attend:/ Now came still evening on', *Paradise Lost*, iv, 596–8; and 'yon western cloud', xi, 205.

[7] **brede**
embroidery; a poetical usage describing the interweaving of colours, especially the colours of the rainbow. In *Pleasures of Imagination*, ii, 118–19 Akenside describes the 'brede of colours' in the rainbow; **ethereal** formed of ether.

[8] **wavy bed**
Cf. 'So when the sun in bed,/ Curtained with cloudy red,/ Pillows his chin upon an Orient wave', *Nativity Ode*, lines 229–31.

[9]
This corresponds to what had almost become a formula: 'silence... save where' which is found most notably in Gray: 'And all the air a solemn stillness holds,/ Save where the beetle wheels his droning flight', *Elegy Written in a Country Church-yard*, lines 6–7. It was used by Thomas Warton: 'Here what a solemn silence reigns,/ Save the tinklings of a rill' *Poems* (1748),

and 'No wakeful sound the moonlight valley knows,/ Save where the brook its liquid murmur pours,/ And lulls the waving scene to more profound repose', Akenside, *Ode to Sleep*, lines 18–20 (see Lonsdale, 1969).

[10] **leathern wing**
In *A Midsummer Night's Dream* there is a reference to the bat's 'leathern wings', II, ii, 4.

[11] **winds**
to blow, as in a wind-instrument.

[12] **sullen**
solemn, serious.

[11–12]
Cf. 'What time the gray-fly winds her sultry horn', *Lycidas*, line 28.

[13] **As oft he rises**
referring to the beetle; **twilight path** cf. 'twilight meadows', *Comus*, line 844, and 'twilight groves', *Il Penseroso*, line 133.

[14] **Against**
in opposite movement, as in 'brushing against'; **pilgrim** traveller; **borne in heedless hum** in a state of unawareness or oblivion to the sound the beetle makes.

[9–14]
'Ere the bat hath flown/ His cloistered flight; ere... / The shard-borne beetle with his drowsy hums/ Hath rung night's yawning peal', *Macbeth*, III, iii, 40–3.

[15] **composed**
calm and tranquil.

[16]
frequently used thus for musical utterance. Cf. 'Can any mortal mixture of earth's mould,/ Breathe such divine enchanting ravishment?', *Comus*, line 245; 'And as I wake, sweet music breathe', *Il Penseroso*, line 151.

[17] **numbers**
versification, rhythm; **stealing** moving almost imperceptibly.

[16–17]
Cf. 'While melting music steals upon the sky,/ And soften'd sounds along the waters die', Pope, *Rape of the Lock*, ii, 49–50.

[18] **suit**
be in agreement or harmony with.

[19] **musing**
pondering, contemplative thinking; *slow* slowly.

[20] **genial**
cheering, enlivening. Seems to be first used in this sense by Collins.

[21] **thy folding star**
Hesperus, the evening star; when it appears in the early evening it is a signal to the shepherd to drive his sheep into the fold. Cf. 'The star that bids the shepherd fold', *Comus*, line 93; 'the unfolding star', *Measure for Measure*, IV, ii, 218.

[22] **paly circlet**
pale circle of light. Cf. 'Sure pledge of day, that crownest the smiling morn/ With thy bright circlet', *Paradise Lost*, v, 169. Milton, of course, is referring to the morning star.

[23] **hours**
female divinities presiding over changes in season and time.

[25] **wreathes**
adorns; *sedge* grassy plants growing in the wet by a river. The image here is that of a river-nymph in connection with dew.

[27] **pensive**
'sorrowfully thoughtful', Johnson, *Dictionary*.

[28] **shadowy**
nature of a shadow, unsubstantial and fleeting. The adjective captures the visual image of fading light; *car* chariot. Cf. 'the gilded car of day', *Comus*, line 95, and 'car of night', *Paradise Lost*, ix, 65.

[29] **vot'ress**
nun, one who is bound by religious vows. Cf. 'the gray-hooded Ev'n/ Like a sad votarist in palmer's weed', *Comus*, lines 188–9; *sheety* like a broad expanse of glistening water surface.

[30] **Cheers**
animates, brightens; *time-hallowed pile* heap of stones that has been present for such a long time that it has the aura of a sacred ruin.

[31] **up-land fallows**
uncultivated fields at higher altitudes. The distribution of the adjectives in

up-land fallows grey, one before and the other after the noun, is very Miltonic. Cf. also 'Fallows grey', and 'upland hamlets', *L'Allegro*, lines 71, 92.

[32] **its**
syntactically it is difficult to decide what this pronoun refers back to. It could be either 'Evening's car' or the 'sheety lake' ; both choices would relate to the 'last cool gleam'; the 'lake' would suit the visual interpretation of 'reflect' better. On the other hand the metaphorical sense might be predominant, emphasising 'reflectiveness' in relation to 'calm vot'ress'.

[33] **blustering winds**
Cf. 'The sound of blustering winds, which all night long/ Had roused the sea', *Paradise Lost*, ii, 286–7 (also found in Spenser).

[34] **Forbid**
prevent; *my willing feet* cf. 'with wearied wings, and willing feet', *Paradise Lost*, iii, 73.

[36] **swelling floods**
Often used in poetry for seas and rivers; partially periphrastic.

[37] **hamlets brown**
dusky dwellings; *dim-discovered spires* hardly visible; cf. 'dim-discovered', Thomson, *Summer*, line 946.

[39] **dewy fingers**
Cf. 'morning's dewy fingers', Akenside, *Pleasures of Imagination*, iii, 247.

[40] **gradual**
'advancing step by step', Johnson, *Dictionary*.

[40]
'The cloudy curtain of refreshing eve', Akenside, *Pleasures of Imagination*, ii, 504.

[42] **breathing**
fragrant.

[45] **sallow**
brownish yellow.

[46] **yelling**
uttering strident cries; *troublous* stormy.

[48] **rudely**
violently, roughly; *rends* tears. Cf.

'Her looser golden locks he rudely rent', *Faerie Queene*, 2.1. 11, 5.

[49] **sure-found**
an interesting and unusual compound; *sylvan shed* green shade.

[46–9]
There are many characteristically Spenserian words in these lines: troublous, yelling, affrights, regardful.

[51] **influence**
power.

[52] **hymn**
'to praise in song; to worship with hymns', Johnson, *Dictionary*.

[41–52]
Collins follows the sequence of the seasons from: 'When young-eyed Spring profusely throws/ From her green lap the pink and rose,/ When the soft turtle of the dale/ To summer tells her tender tale,/ When autumn cooling caverns seeks,/ And stains with wine his jolly cheeks,/ When Winter, like poor pilgrim old,/ Shakes his silver beard with cold,/ At every season let my ear/ Thy solemn whispers, Fancy, hear', Joseph Warton's *Ode to Fancy*, lines 107–16. Collins, however, personifies Evening as Eve in terms of 'breathing tresses', 'lap', and 'robes'; he also sees it visually in terms of its 'lingering light'.

MARY LEAPOR

(1722–46)

Mary Leapor is exceptional among the poets of this volume in three ways: she was a woman, she died when she was only 24, and she came from a relatively modest social class. Her father was a gardener, and she spent some of her adult life as a cook's maid, some as her father's housekeeper. Although her verse was circulated during her lifetime and she was 'discovered' by a local gentlewoman, publication only came posthumously.

The poetry is often witty and probing. Given her youth and her very limited opportunities, it is astonishingly accomplished.

Further Reading

There is no modern edition of Leapor's poems. Readers wanting to find more of her work are best advised to turn to Roger Lonsdale (ed.), *Eighteenth-Century Women Poets: An Oxford Anthology* (Oxford: Oxford University Press, 1990). That anthology reproduces sixteen poems.

Critics and biographers have not so far turned their attention to Leapor.

35 /   *Man the Monarch*

Amazed we read of nature's early throes,
How the fair heavens and the ponderous earth arose,
How blooming trees unplanted first began,
And beasts submissive to their tyrant, man;
To man, invested with despotic sway,   5
While his mute brethren tremble and obey;
Till heaven beheld him insolently vain,
And checked the limits of his haughty reign.
Then from their lord the rude deserters fly,
And grinning back his fruitless rage defy.   10
Pards, tigers, wolves to gloomy shades retire,
And mountain goats in purer gales respire.
To humble valleys, where soft flowers blow,
And fattening streams in crystal mazes flow,
Full of new life, the untamed coursers run,   15
And roll and wanton in the cheerful sun,
Round their gay hearts in dancing spirits rise,
And rouse the lightnings in their rolling eyes.
To craggy rocks destructive serpents glide,
Where mossy crannies hide their speckled pride,   20
And monstrous whales on foamy billows ride.
Then joyful birds ascend their native sky –
But where, ah, where shall helpless woman fly?

Here smiling Nature brought her choicest stores,
And roseate beauty on her favourite pours.   25
Pleased with her labour, the officious dame
Withheld no grace would deck the rising frame.
Then viewed her work, and viewed and smiled again,
And kindly whispered, 'Daughter, live and reign.'
But now the matron mourns her latest care,   30
And sees the sorrows of her darling fair,
Beholds a wretch whom she designed a queen,
And weeps that e'er she formed the weak machine.
In vain she boasts her lips of scarlet dyes,
Cheeks like the morning, and far-beaming eyes,   35
Her neck refulgent, fair and feeble arms –
A set of useless and neglected charms.
She suffers hardship with afflictive moans,

Small tasks of labour suit her slender bones.
Beneath a load her weary shoulders yield,   40
Nor can her fingers grasp the sounding shield.
She sees and trembles at approaching harms,
And fear and grief destroy her fading charms.
Then her pale lips no pearly teeth disclose,
And time's rude sickle cuts the yielding rose.   45
Thus, wretched woman's shortlived merit dies.
In vain to Wisdom's sacred help she flies,
Or sparkling Wit but lends a feeble aid.
'Tis all delirium from a wrinkled maid.

    A tattling dame, no matter where or who –   50
Me it concerns and it need not you –
Once told this story to the listening muse,
Which we, as now it serves our turn, shall use.

    When our grandsire named the feathered kind,
Pondering their natures in his careful mind,   55
'Twas then, if on our author we rely,
He viewed his consort with an envious eye.
Greedy of power he hugged the tottering throne,
Pleased with the homage, and would reign alone.
And better to secure his doubtful rule   60
Rolled his wise eyeballs, and pronounced her 'fool'.
The regal blood to distant ages runs.
Sires, brothers, husbands and commanding sons,
The sceptre claim. And every cottage brings
A long succession of domestic kings.   65

The poem is a deft and rather heterodox retelling of the Fall from a woman's point of view, and as such it looks back both to Genesis and to *Paradise Lost*. In her *Essay on Woman* Leapor describes woman as 'but a slave at large'. Here, she examines the other side of the equation. If woman is a slave, man is a master – or a monarch. The poem is not, though, 'feminist' in the modern meaning of the word. Leapor's sense of her own sex which is set out in detail in the second verse paragraph is very much that of a beautiful, weak and frightened creature.

The poem is written in heroic couplets. It betrays some of the adjectival padding, which was the characteristic vice both of the couplet and of the poetry of the middle eighteenth century generally. But much of the poem, perhaps especially the closing lines, is handled with considerable skill.

[1] **read**
There is something of a contradiction in the poem in that here the story of creation is read, and later it is heard (line 52); *throes* spasms of pain, specifically of childbirth. The phrase 'nature's throes' refers to the creation in a way that is both unbiblical and unmiltonic. There is here none of the sense of a creator's majestic work.

[2] **arose**
The choice of verb again avoids any sense of willed creation.

[4] **tyrant man**
The phrase 'tyrant man' occurs in Finch's *Nocturnal Reverie*. But whereas Finch uses 'man' to mean 'humanity at large', Leapor is thinking only of the male portion of it.

[5] **despotic sway**
absolute power. In Genesis God says to man and woman: 'Be fruitful and multiply, and fill the earth and subdue it; and have dominion over the fish of the sea and over the birds of the air and over every living thing that moves upon the earth' (Genesis 1: 28). Leapor's line recalls the passage, but both alters the nature of dominion by adding the word 'despotic', and limits the despotism to male human beings.

[6] **mute brethren**
i.e. the animals.

[7–8] **Till heaven...reign**
This couplet accounts for the Fall, i.e. humanity's 'first disobedience' to God, and the punishment consequent upon that. In the biblical account, God places Adam and Eve in a garden with the command not to eat the fruit of the tree of knowledge of good and evil. Eve eats and gives the fruit to Adam, upon which both are banished from the garden and death is introduced into the world (Genesis 3). Leapor makes no mention of Eve's part in this. Instead, it is the man's unspecified insolence and vanity which anger heaven, and which are curtailed by punishment.

[9] **rude**
rough, uncultivated (i.e. of animals); *deserters* Milton describes how the

awe of animals for Adam ends with the Fall (*Paradise Lost*, x, 712–14).

[10] **grinning...defy**
Compare 'or with countenance grim/ Glared on him passing' (*Paradise Lost*, x, 713–14).

[11] **Pards**
panthers, leopards.

[15] **coursers**
stallions.

[23] **woman**
the first mention of woman in the poem. The previous twelve lines have represented animals fleeing from male tyranny to a freedom away from man. This line implies that woman wishes, perhaps needs, to fly in such a way. This is consistent with the whole argument of the poem. Rather than as the authoress of the Fall, woman is represented as man's helpless victim.

[24] **smiling Nature**
The following lines imagine the creation of woman, by personifying Nature as a kind of matronly waiting maid; *choicest stores* Milton portrays Eve as 'adorned/ With all that earth or heaven could bestow/ To make her amiable' (*Paradise Lost*, viii, 482–4).

[25] **roseate**
A pinkish complexion was regarded as beautiful.

[26] **officious dame**
Nature in the role of waiting maid again. 'Officious' meant obliging, generous or dutiful. It had none of the pejorative modern sense of interfering.

[27] **grace**
ornament, charm; *rising frame* the first woman's body. It is 'rising' because Leapor is imagining the body at the moment of creation. As with the earlier descriptions (lines 1–3), there is little hint of a creator's forming hand. Even Nature does not create woman but only 'decks' her out with a number of pleasing qualities.

[29] **whispered...reign**
Dominion is given by female Nature to woman – compare note to line 5.

[30] **But now**
Leapor shifts from considering the

position of woman at the creation to her current position. The 'matron' here is Nature.

[31] **fair**
used as a noun for a beautiful woman.

[33] **machine**
The word could at that time be used to mean the human body as a combination of various parts. Leapor's emphasis in the second verse paragraph is very much upon the physical nature of women.

[35] **far-beaming eyes**
The description relies upon the conventional poetic comparison of beautiful eyes to the sun, an idea which Shakespeare had turned on its head 150 years earlier in the first line of Sonnet 130: 'My mistress' eyes are nothing like the sun.'

[36] **refulgent**
shining, radiant – rather an odd adjective for a neck.

[37] **neglected**
The following lines make clear that these charms are neglected because woman is forced to do the hard labour for which she is not fitted. Leapor's interest here is in a different kind of women from those portrayed elsewhere in this anthology – she is thinking of working women.

[38] **afflictive**
painful, tending to afflict. It is hard to see how the moans themselves can be 'afflictive'.

[40] **load ... shoulders**
A number of carrying tasks might fall to the lot of women, including carrying buckets of milk or water on a yoke across the shoulders.

[41] **sounding shield**
The warriors of the ancient world beat their shields before going into battle – the phrase is an image of martial ardour.

[42] **She ... harms**
Perhaps the line in the poem which most exposes Leapor's sense of the fragility of women.

[44] **pearly teeth**
The description of teeth as pearls is a poetic convention.

[46] **merit**
The 'merit' of woman has been imagined solely in terms of physical beauty.

[47–8] **In vain ... aid**
The futility of a woman expecting help from wit or wisdom suggests that it is the world's opinion which places her merit solely in beauty.

[49] **delirium ... maid**
i.e. the world regards wit and wisdom as madness in woman if they are not supported by youth and beauty.

[50] **tattling dame**
As line 52 makes clear, the 'tattling dame' is supposed to be the source of the heterodox account of the Fall. This contradicts the opening line's assertion that 'we read' of creation.

[51] **Me it ... you**
i.e. the identity of the source of the tale does not matter. The line seems to be a filler.

[52] **muse**
goddess of poetry – here, presumably, the poetess (Leapor) herself.

[54] **grandsire**
grandfather, male ancestor, Adam. 'Sire' must be pronounced as two syllables – 'sigh er', The idea of naming glances back to Genesis:

So out of the ground the Lord God formed every beast of the field and every bird of the air, and brought them to the man to see what he would call them; and whatever the man called every living creature, that was its name. (Genesis 2: 19)

feathered kind It is not clear why Leapor specifies the moment of naming birds as the time of Adam's first envy, but *Paradise Lost* may be her source. There the birds are represented as particularly servile (each 'stooped on his wing') at the naming (viii, 351), and Leapor will in a moment note Adam's pleasure in homage (line 59). However, Milton's naming takes place before the creation of woman, which makes a nonsense of Leapor's account. The chronology of events in the biblical account is less certain.

[55] **Pondering . . . natures**
An echo of Milton's Adam who says of the animals: 'I named them as they passed, and understood/ Their nature, with such knowledge God endued/ My sudden apprehension' (*Paradise Lost*, viii, 352–4). In view of line 61 and the tenor of the whole poem, the line must be regarded as ironic.

[56] **author**
the source of the tale, the 'tattling dame' of line 50.

[57] **consort**
wife, i.e. Eve.

[58] **tottering**
Presumably, the throne has begun to totter because of the heavenly wrath referred to in lines 7–8.

[59] **homage**
i.e. of the animals. Milton is the source again, for his Adam describes how the animals approached to receive their names, 'these cowering low/ With blandishment' (viii, 350–1).

[60] **doubtful**
threatened, uncertain.

[61] **pronounced her 'fool'**
The common insult of bullying men is traced back to Adam's first act of naming.

[64] **sceptre**
a symbol of kingship; *cottage* The word in the eighteenth century signified a much more humble dwelling than it does today – something closer to a hovel than to the 'cottages' we know. The implied poverty heightens the irony of the phrase 'domestic kings' with which the poem ends.

CHRISTOPHER SMART

(1722–71)

◇

Smart's early career was that of a successful student, prize-winning poet, hack writer and convivial drinking companion. In 1755, however, he was confined for madness, a confinement which lasted until 1763. His madness was associated with intense religious feelings, involving fervent and unceasing prayer. In 1769, Smart was imprisoned for debt, and his life ended in a debtor's prison.

Further Reading

The authoritative edition of Smart's poetry is the four-volume Marcus Walsh and Karina Williamson (eds), *The Poetical Works of Christopher Smart* (Oxford: Clarendon Press, 1980–7). The same editors have also brought out with Penguin a good single volume selection, *Christopher Smart: Selected Poems*.

The standard biography is Arthur Sherbo, *Christopher Smart: Scholar of the University* (Ann Arbor: Michigan State University Press, 1967). Two useful critical books are Moira Dearnley, *The Poetry of Christopher Smart* (London: Routledge and Kegan Paul, 1968), and Sophia B. Blaydes, *Christopher Smart as a Poet of his Time: A Reappraisal* (The Hague and Paris: Mouton, 1966).

————◇————

36 / Hymn. The Nativity of Our Lord and Saviour Jesus Christ

Where is this stupendous stranger,
  Swains of Solyma, advise.
Lead me to my master's manger,
  Show me where my saviour lies.

O most mighty! O most holy!   5
  Far beyond the seraph's thought,
Art thou then so mean and lowly
  As unheeded prophets taught?

O the magnitude of meekness!
  Worth from worth immortal sprung;   10
O the strength of infant weakness,
  If eternal is so young!

If so young and thus eternal,
  Michael tune the shepherd's reed,
Where the scenes are ever vernal,   15
  And the loves be love indeed!

See the God blasphemed and doubted
  In the schools of Greece and Rome,
See the powers of darkness routed,
  Taken at their utmost gloom.   20

Nature's decorations glisten
  Far above their usual trim.
Birds on box and laurels listen,
  As so near the cherubs hymn.

Boreas now no longer winters   25
  On the desolated coast.
Oaks no more are riv'n in splinters
  By the whirlwind and his host.

Spinks and ouzels sing sublimely,
  'We too have a Saviour born';   30
Whiter blossoms burst untimely
  On the blessed Mosaic thorn.

God all-bounteous, all-creative,
Whom no ills from good dissuade,
Is incarnate, and a native   35
Of the very world he made.

There are two contexts in which the *Hymn* (1765) should be placed. The first is that of the intense religious feelings which Smart experienced and which were interpreted as madness. The second is that of eighteenth-century hymn-writing. Smart joined other poets in this anthology (Watts, Cowper and Wesley) by participating in the remarkable flowering of the English hymn in that period. As with other flowerings in other periods, one can only suppose that writers took mutual support and encouragement from others working in a similar way.

The metre of the *Hymn* is trochaic (stress, unstress), and the verse form is a simple four-line stanza with alternate rhymes. The even lines are shorter than the odd lines by a single syllable; each even line ends with a single stressed syllable. Odd rhymes are feminine, even rhymes masculine. (The stanza pattern is the same as that of *Gratitude*.)

[2] **Swains**
peasants, especially shepherds; *Solyma* Jerusalem, from the Latin name Hierosolyma – compare *Absalom*, line 513. The 'swains of Solyma' are the shepherds who visited the infant Jesus (Luke 2: 8–17).
[3] **manger**
feeding trough for animals, in which the infant Jesus was laid instead of a cradle.
[4] **saviour**
In Christian theology, the word 'saviour' refers to the way in which Jesus, by coming to earth, saved all humanity from death.
[5] **most mighty**
Smart plays upon the paradox that the helpless baby is also the all-powerful God.
[6] **seraph**
seraphim, the highest of the nine orders of angels.
[7] **thou**
the familiar form of 'you', used with family, children, close acquaintance and as an address to God – thus forming a contrast with the exalted description of the preceding lines; **mean** of low degree.
[8] **unheeded**
ignored, unnoticed. The prophecies of

the Old Testament which Christian belief regards as foretelling the coming of Christ were misunderstand by the Jews; **prophets taught** Micah foretold the birth in Bethlehem: 'But thou, Bethlehem Ephratah, though thou be little among the thousands of Judah, yet out of thee shall come forth he that is to be the ruler of Israel' (Micah 5: 2). More central to Smart's meaning is the famous passage in Isaiah in which Jesus is described as a suffering servant: 'He is despised and rejected of men; a man of sorrows and acquainted with grief: and we hid as it were our faces from him; he was despised, and we esteemed him not' (Isaiah 53: 3).
[9] **magnitude of meekness**
The paradox emphasises the Christian mystery of God becoming man.
[10] **Worth ... sprung**
echoing the Anglican creed, which reads: 'I believe in one Lord Jesus Christ, the only-begotten Son of God, begotten of his Father before all worlds, God of God, light of light, very God of very God.'
[11–12] **strength ... young**
again emphasising the paradox of the infant God.

437

[14] **Michael**
an archangel and traditionally the chief of the heavenly armies, described by Milton as 'of celestial armies prince' (*Paradise Lost*, vi, 44); *tune* play, make music with; *reed* a musical pipe made from a reed. The stock instrument of rustic simplicity in pastoral poetry. It is another paradox that Michael, the warrior angel, should be told to play upon a shepherd's pipe.

[15] **Where...**
The description which follows is of heaven; *vernal* spring-like.

[16] **loves**
representations of Cupid, the Roman god of love. Smart is thinking of the chubby, winged infant boys who adorned clouds and heavens in the decorative painting of the period. In the real heaven, he suggests, there will be, instead of such figures, a more holy love ('love indeed').

[17] **God...doubted**
refers to the scepticism which existed in Jesus' time.

[18] **schools**
academies.

[19] **powers...routed**
The coming of Jesus spelt the defeat of Satan.

[20] **utmost gloom**
greatest darkness. The idea is that the powers of darkness were at their height (hence the scepticism referred to in line 17) when Jesus arrived.

[21] **Nature's...glisten**
The idea that nature celebrated the birth is traditional.

[22] **trim**
condition, adornment.

[23] **box**
a type of small evergreen tree.

[24] **cherubs**
cherubim, an order of angels; *hymn* sing praises. In the Bible, the angel who announces the news of Christ's birth to the shepherds is suddenly joined by a host of angels 'praising God, and saying, glory to God in the highest, and on earth peace, good will towards men' (Luke 2: 13–14). Later

accounts of the nativity emphasise the angelic music. Compare Milton's lines: 'The helmed Cherubim/ And sworded Seraphim/ Are seen in glittering ranks with wings displayed,/ Harping in loud and solemn choir/ With unexpressive notes to Heaven's new-born heir' (*On the Morning of Christ's Nativity*, lines 112–16).

[25] **Boreas**
the north wind personified, the god of the north wind; *winters* spends winter.

[27] **riv'n**
torn.

[28] **his**
i.e. the whirlwind's. That wind, like the northern one (line 25), is personified.

[29] **Spinks**
finches, especially chaffinches; *ouzels* blackbirds; *sublimely* in a lofty, elevated manner. The word carried associations of lofty, heroic poetry, and particularly of the poetry of Milton.

[31] **Whiter blossoms**
thorn blossom. The connotation of purity is, of course, intended; *untimely* out of season, in that they are blooming in the middle of winter. The Glastonbury thorn (see below) blooms at Christmas, or rather bloomed close to Christmas. The adoption of the Gregorian Calendar in 1752 means they now bloom in January.

[32] **Mosaic thorn**
A number of references are at work here. One is to the rod of Aaron (brother of Moses) which produced blossom and almonds as a sign of his authority (Numbers 17: 8). Smart means his blossom to represent both nature's celebrations and Jesus himself, by drawing upon the common Old Testament metaphor of successors as the branches of their ancestors. The most famous example is the passage in Isaiah which is taken by Christians to be a prophecy of Jesus: 'And there shall come forth a rod out of the stem of Jesse, and a branch shall grow

out of his roots' (Isaiah 11: 1). The blossoming rod is also a part of medieval Christian legend. When St Christopher has carried his heavenly burden across the river, he pushes his staff into the earth and falls asleep. When he awakes, the staff has flowered. The origin of the Glastonbury thorn (see previous note) is explained by a similar legend. Joseph of Arimathea, the Jew who took Jesus' body from the cross (Luke 23: 50–3), is supposed to have come to England with relics of the crucifixion (the cup, the grail). Upon arriving at Glastonbury, he put his staff in the earth, thus producing the Glastonbury thorn. Whether Joseph's staff was ever associated with Moses' I have not been able to discover.

[34] **Whom . . . dissuade**
Despite our evil, God will not be diverted from good.
[35] **incarnate**
made flesh.

37 /　　　　　*Gratitude*

I upon the first creation
　Clapped my wings with loud applause,
Cherub of the highest station,
　Praising, blessing, without pause.

I in Eden's bloomy bowers　　　　　　　　5
　Was the heavenly gardener's pride,
Sweet of sweets, and flower of flowers
　With the scented tinctures dyed.

Hear, ye little children, hear me,
　I am God's delightful voice.　　　　　　10
They who sweetly still revere me,
　Still shall make the wisest choice.

Hear me not like Adam trembling,
　When I walked in Eden's grove,
And the host of heaven assembling　　　　15
　From the spot the traitor drove.

Hear me rather as the lover
　Of mankind, restored and free.
By the word ye shall recover
　More than that ye lost by me.　　　　　20

I'm the Phoenix of the singers
That in Upper Eden dwell.
Hearing me Euphrates lingers
As my wondrous tale I tell.

'Tis the story of the Graces,   25
Mercies without end or sum,
And the sketches and the traces
Of a thousand more to come.

List, my children, list within you,
Dread ye not the tempter's rod.   30
Christ our gratitude shall win you,
Weaned from earth, and led to God.

The poem is a religious lyric intended for children, and included in Smart's
volume *Hymns for the Amusement of Children* (1770). It seeks to characterise a quality by personifying it. Among its forebears are those psalms which sing of the
greatness of God: 'Praise ye the Lord. Praise God in his sanctuary. Praise him
in the firmament of his power. Praise him for his mighty acts. Praise him for his
excellent greatness. Praise him with the sound of the trumpet. Praise him with
the psaltery and the harp' (Psalms 150: 1–3). However, it also differs from such
psalms in that it seeks not only to express but also to analyse gratitude.

The *Hymns for the Amusement of Children* were Smart's last poems. They were
composed in the debtor's prison where he spent the last one and a half years
of his life and where he died. Publication was posthumous.

The stanza pattern is the same as that of the previous poem.

Title
A number of Smart's hymns for children are given abstract virtues as their
titles.
[1–2] I upon ... applause
The main source for these lines is the
book of Job, in which after thirty-
seven chapters of Job's complaints,
God answers 'out of the whirlwind':
'Where wast thou when I laid the
foundations of the earth? ... When
the morning stars sang together and
all the sons of God shouted for joy'
(Job 38: 4–7). The poem moves across
the span of history (beginning here
with the creation) as it is seen by
Christians.
[2] Clapped
flapped, applauded. The word is used

as a metaphor of applause for God's
creation in the psalms: 'Make a joyful
noise unto the Lord, all the earth ...
Let the sea roar and the fulness
thereof ... Let the floods clap their
hands, let the hills be joyful together'
(Psalms 98: 4–8).
[3] Cherub
angel; one of the second order of
angels (not the highest as Smart
goes on to say); beautiful (winged
child).
[4] blessing
adoring, worshipping.
[5] Eden
the garden paradise in which Adam
and Eve lived. This second stanza
deals with the period of time after the
creation and before the fall; *bloomy*

flowery; *bowers* dwellings, shady hollows formed by trees.

[6] **heavenly gardener**
God, the creator of the garden of Eden; *pride* This is in keeping with the general sense of the poem that gratitude is a preeminent spiritual virtue (hence 'highest station' in line 3).

[7] **Sweet**
pleasure, delight; the sense of sweetness of taste or scent prepares for the subsequent idea of scented flowers.

[8] **tincture**
dye, colour, shade; also, the quintessence of something.

[9] **little children**
The address to children is in keeping with a poem written for them. It also echoes the first epistle of St John: 'My little children, these things I write unto you that ye sin not' (1 John 2: 1).

[10] **God's ... voice**
Although angels can act as God's messengers (His voice), the following verse makes clear that the phrases should be taken literally. Thus, the speaker (gratitude) has shifted from being an angel in the first stanza, a flower in the second, to an attribute of God here, the voice which speaks to Adam and Eve in the garden (Genesis 1: 28). It is a little hard to see how God, the creator of all things, can feel gratitude, but in Genesis He is represented as taking delight in His own creation: 'And God saw everything that he had made, and behold it was very good' (Genesis 1: 31); *delightful* implying a contrast with the other possible voices of God, the authoritative, the angry and so on.

[12] **Still**
The word adds little meaning to the line but creates a balance by echoing the 'still' of the previous line. Also, it provides Smart with the first syllable stress which he needs for his trochaic metre.

[13-14] **Hear ... grove**
The poem moves now to the Fall of Adam. After the eating the fruit of the tree of knowledge of good and evil,

Adam and Eve hide:

And they heard the voice of the Lord God walking in the garden in the cool of the day; and Adam and his wife hid themselves from the presence of the Lord God ... And the Lord God called unto Adam and said to him, Where art thou? And he said, I heard thy voice in the garden, and I was afraid because I was naked' (Genesis 3: 8–10)

The speaker is still associated with God, and Smart recommends a joyful rather than a fearful reception of Him.

[15-16] **And the host ... drove**
Adam and Eve were sent from Eden in punishment for their disobedience (referred to here with the word 'traitor'). The 'host' (army) of heaven is present in the biblical account in the cherubims which are placed to guard the gate of the garden of Eden (Genesis 3: 24). 'Host of heaven' is a biblical phrase; the angel who greeted the shepherds on the night of Christ's birth, for example, is suddenly surrounded by a 'multitude of the heavenly host' (Luke 2: 13).

[17-18] **lover/ Of mankind**
Jesus; thus, the poem leaps forward from the Fall to the Redemption. Also, the speaker again changes personality – here, from God the Father to God the Son.

[18] **restored**
referring to the idea that the death of Jesus restored humanity to God's favour; *free* The freedom to be gained by submission to the will of God is a theme of St Paul's: 'The liberty wherewith Christ has made us free' (Galatians 5: 1).

[19] **word**
word of God, Jesus. The 'word' is used as a title for Jesus in the gospel of St John: 'In the beginning was the word' (John 1: 1).

[20] **More ... by me**
Since the 'I' is here speaking as Jesus, the sense seems to be that the gain of salvation (through the word) is greater than the loss of Jesus through his death.

[21] **Phoenix**
a legendary bird, of which only one exists, supposed to burn to death every five hundred years or so, then rise again from its ashes. Sometimes used as a metaphor for a paragon, sometimes for Jesus. But the speaker is becoming again the personified quality of the opening.

[22] **Upper Eden**
by transference, heaven.

[23] **Euphrates**
one of the rivers of the earthly Eden (Genesis 2: 14).

[25] **Graces**
In classical myth, the three sister goddesses who bestow beauty. Here used more in the sense of divine favours, mercies.

[30] **tempter's rod**
In keeping with his theme of a loving God, Smart gives the rod, the instrument of punishment, to Satan rather than God.

[31] **Christ...win you**
i.e. our gratitude shall win you Christ.

OLIVER GOLDSMITH

(1730–74)

Oliver Goldsmith was born, probably, in 1730, second son of Rev. Charles Goldsmith. He attended village schools in Lissoy where his family moved in his early childhood. In 1745 he was admitted as a sizar to Trinity College in Dublin. His family, already fairly poverty-stricken, lost its only source of income on the death of his father in 1747, and economic hardship was to plague Goldsmith for the rest of his life. He graduated in 1750, after which he made some futile attempts to enter the church. In 1752 Goldsmith went to Edinburgh to study medicine; he continued his medical studies at Leyden, where he remained till early 1755.

In 1755 Goldsmith did a sort of 'grand tour' of Europe, travelling through Germany and Switzerland to Italy, and returning to England through France. In the summer of the same year he began writing *The Traveller*. He supported himself by some amount of journalistic writing and translations. In fact Goldsmith's early life followed, in financial terms, the same pattern as that of Samuel Johnson's, and may have been the reason for Johnson's consistent sympathy for him. In 1759 Goldsmith published *An Enquiry into the Present State of Learning in Europe*, in which he surveyed national characteristics and the different systems of patronage. Now began a period of widening literary acquaintance that was to include Thomas Percy, Tobias Smollett, Arthur Murphy, Edmund Burke and Samuel Johnson. Around this time Goldsmith wrote *The Bee*, and was soon to start his 'Chinese Letters' that were later published in book form and called *The Citizen of the World* (1762). In 1762 he also wrote his essay *The Revolution in Low Life*, expressing concerns and ideas that were to dominate his major poems.

Goldsmith was a founder member of The Club, with Johnson,

Reynolds, Burke, Garrick and others. The 1760s was a decade of activity and relative affluence for him. *The Traveller, or A Prospect of Society* was published in 1764 and in 1766 *The Vicar of Wakefield*. In 1769 Goldsmith was appointed Professor of Ancient History at the Royal Academy. Though his comedy, *A Good Natured Man*, was a failure at its first performance in 1768, Goldsmith managed to get a good run out of it later. His greatest triumph was *The Deserted Village* (1770), the poem by which he continues to be known, and placed alongside Samuel Johnson. *She Stoops to Conquer* (1773) was a success at Covent Garden.

Goldsmith was afflicted by illness in his last years, and died in March 1774, deeply in debt. His *History of the Earth, and Animated Nature* was published posthumously in July 1774.

A monument to him, with an epitaph in Latin by Samuel Johnson, was erected in Westminster Abbey in 1776.

Further Reading

The standard edition of Goldsmith's works is the five-volume A. Friedman (ed.), *Collected Works of Oliver Goldsmith* (Oxford: Clarendon Press, 1966) to which the present editors are indebted. There is also a useful single volume edition available: Tom Davis (ed.), *Goldsmith: Poems and Plays* (London: J.M. Dent, 1990).

R.M. Wardle's *Oliver Goldsmith* (Lawrence: University of Kansas Press, 1957) is an excellent biography, and John Ginger's, *The Notable Man: The Life and Times of Oliver Goldsmith* (London: Hamish Hamilton, 1977), is also readable. Two critical books are Clara M. Kirk, *Oliver Goldsmith* (New York: Twayne, 1967) and Robert M. Hopkins, *The True Genius of Oliver Goldsmith* (Baltimore: Johns Hopkins University Press, 1969). A more recent full-length study is Andrew Swarbrick's *The Art of Oliver Goldsmith* (London & Totowa: Vision, 1984). There are useful essays in Harold Bloom (ed.), *Oliver Goldsmith* (New York: Chelsea, 1987), and contemporary and nineteenth-century reactions are reprinted in G.S. Rousseau (ed.), *Goldsmith: The Critical Heritage* (London: Methuen, 1964).

The editors also wish to acknowledge Roger Lonsdale (ed.), *The Poems of Thomas Gray, William Collins, Oliver Goldsmith* (London: Longman, 1969).

38 /   *The Deserted Village*

Sweet Auburn, loveliest village of the plain,
Where health and plenty cheered the labouring swain,
Where smiling spring its earliest visit paid,
And parting summer's lingering blooms delayed;
Dear lovely bowers of innocence and ease,   5
Seats of my youth, when every sport could please,
How often have I loitered o'er thy green,
Where humble happiness endeared each scene:
How often have I paused on every charm,
The sheltered cot, the cultivated farm,   10
The never-failing brook, the busy mill,
The decent church that topped the neighbouring hill,
The hawthorn bush with seats beneath the shade,
For talking age and whispering lovers made.
How often have I blessed the coming day,   15
When toil remitting lent its turn to play,
And all the village train from labour free,
Led up their sports beneath the spreading tree,
While many a pastime circled in the shade,
The young contending as the old surveyed;   20
And many a gambol frolicked o'er the ground,
And sleights of art and feats of strength went round.
And still as each repeated pleasure tired,
Succeeding sports the mirthful band inspired:
The dancing pair that simply sought renown   25
By holding out to tire each other down;
The swain mistrustless of his smutted face,
While secret laughter tittered round the place,
The bashful virgin's side-long looks of love,
The matron's glance that would those looks reprove.   30
These were thy charms, sweet village; sports like these,
With sweet succession, taught even toil to please:
These round thy bowers their cheerful influence shed,
These were thy charms – but all these charms are fled.

    Sweet smiling village, loveliest of the lawn,   35
Thy sports are fled, and all thy charms withdrawn:
Amidst thy bowers the tyrant's hand is seen,
And desolation saddens all thy green;
One only master grasps the whole domain,

And half a tillage stints thy smiling plain: 40
No more thy glassy brook reflects the day,
But choked with sedges, works its weedy way.
Along thy glades, a solitary guest,
The hollow-sounding bittern guards its nest;
Amidst thy desert walks the lapwing flies, 45
And tires their echoes with unvaried cries.
Sunk are thy bowers in shapeless ruin all,
And the long grass o'ertops the mouldering wall,
And trembling, shrinking from the spoiler's hand,
Far, far away thy children leave the land. 50

Ill fares the land, to hastening ills a prey,
Where wealth accumulates, and men decay:
Princes and lords may flourish, or may fade,
A breath can make them, as a breath has made.
But a bold peasantry, their country's pride, 55
When once destroyed, can never be supplied.

A time there was, ere England's griefs began,
When every rood of ground maintained its man:
For him light labour spread her wholesome store,
Just gave what life required, but gave no more: 60
His best companions, innocence and health;
And his best riches, ignorance of wealth.

But times are altered; trade's unfeeling train
Usurp the land and dispossess the swain:
Along the lawn, where scattered hamlets rose, 65
Unwieldy wealth, and cumbrous pomp repose;
And every want to opulence allied,
And every pang that folly pays to pride.
Those gentle hours that plenty bade to bloom,
Those calm desires that asked but little room, 70
Those healthful sports that graced the peaceful scene,
Lived in each look, and brightened all the green;
These far departing seek a kinder shore,
And rural mirth and manners are no more.

Sweet Auburn! parent of the blissful hour, 75
Thy glades forlorn confess the tyrant's power:

Here as I take my solitary rounds,
Amidst thy tangling walks, and ruined grounds,
And many a year elapsed, return to view
Where once the cottage stood, the hawthorn grew,   80
Remembrance wakes with all her busy train,
Swells at my breast, and turns the past to pain.

In all my wanderings round this world of care,
In all my griefs, and God has given my share:
I still had hopes my latest hours to crown,   85
Amidst these humble bowers to lay me down;
To husband out life's taper at the close,
And keep the flame from wasting by repose.
I still had hopes, for pride attends us still,
Amidst the swains to show my book-learned skill,   90
Around my fire an evening group to draw,
And tell of all I felt, and all I saw;
And, as a hare whom hounds and horns pursue,
Pants to the place from whence at first she flew,
I still had hopes, my long vexations past,   95
Here to return – and die at home at last.

O blest retirement, friend to life's decline,
Retreats from care that never must be mine;
How happy he who crowns in shades likes these,
A youth of labour with an age of ease;   100
Who quits a world where strong temptations try,
And, since 'tis hard to combat, learns to fly.
For him no wretches, born to work and weep,
Explore the mine, or tempt the dangerous deep;
No surly porter stands in guilty state   105
To spurn imploring famine from the gate;
But on he moves to meet his latter end,
Angels around befriending virtue's friend;
Bends to the grave with unperceived decay,
While resignation gently slopes the way;   110
And all his prospects brightening to the last,
His heaven commences ere the world be past!

Sweet was the sound when oft at evening's close,
Up yonder hill the village murmur rose:

There as I passed with careless steps and slow,   115
The mingling notes came softened from below;
The swain responsive as the milk-maid sung,
The sober herd that lowed to meet their young;
The noisy geese that gabbled o'er the pool,
The playful children just let loose from school;   120
The watch-dog's voice that bayed the whispering wind,
And the loud laugh that spoke the vacant mind,
These all in sweet confusion sought the shade,
And filled each pause the nightingale had made.
But now the sounds of population fail,   125
No cheerful murmurs fluctuate in the gale,
No busy steps the grass-grown foot-way tread,
For all the bloomy flush of life is fled.
All but yon widowed, solitary thing
That feebly bends beside the plashy spring;   130
She, wretched matron, forced, in age, for bread,
To strip the brook with mantling cresses spread,
To pick her wintry faggot from the thorn,
To seek her nightly shed, and weep till morn;
She only left of all the harmless train,   135
The sad historian of the pensive plain.

    Near yonder copse, where once the garden smiled,
And still where many a garden flower grows wild:
There, where a few torn shrubs the place disclose,
The village preacher's modest mansion rose.   140
A man he was, to all the country dear,
And passing rich with forty pounds a year;
Remote from towns he ran his godly race,
Nor e'er had changed, nor wished to change his place;
Unpracticed he to fawn, or seek for power,   145
By doctrines fashioned to the varying hour;
Far other aims his heart had learned to prize,
More skilled to raise the wretched than to rise.
His house was known to all the vagrant train,
He chid their wanderings, but relieved their pain;   150
The long-remembered beggar was his guest,
Whose beard descending swept his aged breast;
The ruined spendthrift, now no longer proud,
Claimed kindred there, and had his claims allowed;

The broken soldier, kindly bade to stay,   155
Sat by his fire, and talked the night away;
Wept o'er his wounds, or tales of sorrow done,
Shouldered his crutch, and showed how fields were won.
Pleased with his guests, the good man learned to glow,
And quite forgot their vices in their woe;   160
Careless their merits, or their faults to scan,
His pity gave ere charity began.

Thus to relieve the wretched was his pride,
And even his failings leaned to virtue's side:
But in his duty prompt at every call,   165
He watched and wept, he prayed and felt, for all.
And, as a bird each fond endearment tries,
To tempt its new-fledged offspring to the skies;
He tried each art, reproved each dull delay,
Allured to brighter worlds, and led the way.   170

Beside the bed where parting life was laid,
And sorrow, guilt, and pain, by turns dismayed,
The reverend champion stood. At his control
Despair and anguish fled the struggling soul;
Comfort came down the trembling wretch to raise,   175
And his last faltering accents whispered praise.

At church, with meek and unaffected grace,
His looks adorned the venerable place:
Truth from his lips prevailed with double sway,
And fools, who came to scoff, remained to pray.   180
The service past, around the pious man,
With steady zeal each honest rustic ran;
Even children followed with endearing wile,
And plucked his gown, to share the good man's smile.
His ready smile a parent's warmth expressed,   185
Their welfare pleased him, and their cares distressed;
To them his heart, his love, his griefs were given,
But all his serious thoughts had rest in heaven.
As some tall cliff that lifts its aweful form,
Swells from the vale, and midway leaves the storm,   190
Though round its breast the rolling clouds are spread,
Eternal sunshine settles on its head.

449

Beside yon straggling fence that skirts the way,
With blossomed furze unprofitably gay,
There, in his noisy mansion, skilled to rule,   195
The village master taught his little school:
A man severe he was, and stern to view,
I knew him well, and every truant knew;
Well had the boding tremblers learned to trace
The day's disasters in his morning face;   200
Full well they laughed with counterfeited glee,
At all his jokes, for many a joke had he;
Full well the busy whisper circling round,
Conveyed the dismal tidings when he frowned;
Yet he was kind, or if severe in aught,   205
The love he bore to learning was in fault;
The village all declared how much he knew;
'Twas certain he could write, and cipher too;
Lands he could measure, terms and tides presage,
And even the story ran that he could gauge.   210
In arguing too, the parson owned his skill,
For e'en though vanquished, he could argue still;
While words of learned length and thundering sound,
Amazed the gazing rustics ranged around,
And still they gazed, and still the wonder grew,   215
That one small head could carry all he knew.

But past is all his fame. The very spot
Where many a time he triumphed, is forgot:
Near yonder thorn, that lifts its head on high,
Where once the sign-post caught the passing eye,   220
Low lies that house where nut-brown draughts inspired,
Where grey-beard mirth and smiling toil retired,
Where village statesmen talked with looks profound,
And news much older than their ale went round.
Imagination fondly stoops to trace   225
The parlour splendours of that festive place;
The white-washed wall, the nicely sanded floor,
The varnished clock that clicked behind the door;
The chest contrived a double debt to pay,
A bed by night, a chest of drawers by day;   230
The pictures placed for ornament and use,
The twelve good rules, the royal game of goose;

The hearth, except when winter chilled the day,
With aspen boughs, and flowers, and fennel gay,
While broken tea-cups, wisely kept for show,   235
Ranged o'er the chimney, glistened in a row.

Vain transitory splendours! Could not all
Reprieve the tottering mansion from its fall!
Obscure it sinks, nor shall it more impart
An hour's importance to the poor man's heart: 240
Thither no more the peasant shall repair
To sweet oblivion of his daily care;
No more the farmer's news, the barber's tale,
No more the woodman's ballad shall prevail;
No more the smith his dusky brow shall clear,   245
Relax his ponderous strength and lean to hear;
The host himself no longer shall be found
Careful to see the mantling bliss go round;
Nor the coy maid, half willing to be pressed,
Shall kiss the cup to pass it to the rest.   250

Yes! let the rich deride, the proud disdain,
These simple blessings of the lowly train,
To me more dear, congenial to my heart,
One native charm, than all the gloss of art;
Spontaneous joys, where nature has its play,   255
The soul adopts, and owns their first-born sway,
Lightly they frolic o'er the vacant mind,
Unenvied, unmolested, unconfined.
But the long pomp, the midnight masquerade,
With all the freaks of wanton wealth arrayed,   260
In these, ere triflers half their wish obtain,
The toiling pleasure sickens into pain;
And, even while fashion's brightest arts decoy,
The heart distrusting asks, if this be joy.

Ye friends to truth, ye statesmen who survey   265
The rich man's joys increase, the poor's decay,
'Tis yours to judge how wide the limits stand
Between a splendid and an happy land.
Proud swells the tide with loads of freighted ore,
And shouting folly hails them from her shore: 270

Hoards, even beyond the miser's wish abound,
And rich men flock from all the world around.
Yet count our gains. This wealth is but a name
That leaves our useful products still the same.
Not so the loss. The man of wealth and pride, 275
Takes up a space that many poor supplied:
Space for his lake, his park's extended bounds,
Space for his horses, equipage, and hounds;
The robe that wraps his limbs in silken sloth,
Has robbed the neighbouring fields of half their growth; 280
His seat, where solitary sports are seen,
Indignant spurns the cottage from the green;
Around the world each needful product flies,
For all the luxuries the world supplies;
While thus the land adorned for pleasure all, 285
In barren splendour feebly waits the fall.

As some fair female unadorned and plain,
Secure to please while youth confirms her reign,
Slights every borrowed charm that dress supplies,
Nor shares with art the triumph of her eyes; 290
But when those charms are passed, for charms are frail,
When time advances, and when lovers fail,
She then shines forth solicitous to bless,
In all the glaring impotence of dress.
Thus fares the land, by luxury betrayed, 295
In nature's simplest charms at first arrayed,
But verging to decline, its splendours rise,
Its vistas strike, its palaces surprise;
While scourged by famine from the smiling land,
The mournful peasant leads his humble band; 300
And while he sinks without one arm to save,
The country blooms – a garden, and a grave.

Where then, ah where, shall poverty reside,
To scape the pressure of contiguous pride?
If to some common's fenceless limits strayed, 305
He drives his flock to pick the scanty blade,
Those fenceless fields the sons of wealth divide,
And even the bare-worn common is denied.

If to the city sped – what waits him there?
To see profusion that he must not share; 310
To see ten thousand baneful arts combined
To pamper luxury, and thin mankind;
To see those joys the sons of pleasure know,
Extorted from his fellow-creature's woe.
Here, while the courtier glitters in brocade, 315
There the pale artist plies the sickly trade;
Here, while the proud their long-drawn pomps display,
There the black gibbet glooms beside the way.
The dome where pleasure holds her midnight reign,
Here, richly decked, admits the gorgeous train, 320
Tumultuous grandeur crowds the blazing square,
The rattling chariots clash, the torches glare;
Sure scenes like these no troubles e're annoy!
Sure these denote one universal joy!
Are these thy serious thoughts? – Ah, turn thine eyes 325
Where the poor, houseless, shivering female lies.
She once, perhaps, in village plenty blest,
Has wept at tales of innocence distressed;
Her modest looks the cottage might adorn,
Sweet as the primrose peeps beneath the thorn, 330
Now lost to all; her friends, her virtue fled,
Near her betrayer's door she lays her head,
And pinched with cold, and shrinking from the shower,
With heavy heart deplores that luckless hour,
When idly first, ambitious of the town, 335
She left her wheel and robes of country brown.

Do thine, sweet Auburn, thine, the loveliest train,
Do thy fair tribes participate her pain?
Even now, perhaps, by cold and hunger led,
At proud men's doors they ask a little bread! 340

Ah, no. To distant climes, a dreary scene,
Where half the convex world intrudes between,
Through torrid tracts with fainting steps they go,
Where wild Altama murmurs to their woe.
Far different there from all that charmed before, 345
The various terrors of that horrid shore:
Those blazing suns that dart a downward ray,

453

And fiercely shed intolerable day;
Those matted woods where birds forget to sing,
But silent bats in drowsy clusters cling,   350
Those poisonous fields with rank luxuriance crowned,
Where the dark scorpion gathers death around;
Where at each step the stranger fears to wake
The rattling terrors of the vengeful snake;
Where crouching tigers wait their hapless prey,   355
And savage men more murderous still than they;
While oft in whirls the mad tornado flies,
Mingling the ravaged landscape with the skies;
Far different these from every former scene,
The cooling brook, the grassy-vested green,   360
The breezy covert of the warbling grove,
That only sheltered thefts of harmless love.

    Good Heaven! what sorrows gloomed that parting day,
That called them from their native walks away:
When the poor exiles, every pleasure past,   365
Hung round their bowers, and fondly looked their last,
And took a long farewell, and wished in vain
For seats like these beyond the western main;
And shuddering still to face the distant deep,
Returned and wept, and still returned to weep.   370
The good old sire the first prepared to go
To new-found worlds, and wept for others' woe.
But for himself, in conscious virtue brave,
He only wished for worlds beyond the grave.
His lovely daughter, lovelier in her tears,   375
The fond companion of his helpless years,
Silent went next, neglectful of her charms,
And left a lover's for a father's arms.
With louder plaints the mother spoke her woes,
And blessed the cot where every pleasure rose;   380
And kissed her thoughtless babes with many a tear,
And clasped them close in sorrow doubly dear;
Whilst her fond husband strove to lend relief
In all the silent manliness of grief.

    O luxury! Thou cursed by heaven's decree,   385
How ill exchanged are things like these for thee!

How do thy potions with insidious joy,
Diffuse their pleasures only to destroy!
Kingdoms, by thee to sickly greatness grown,
Boast of a florid vigour not their own.   390
At every draught more large and large they grow,
A bloated mass of rank unwieldy woe;
Till sapped their strength, and every part unsound,
Down, down they sink, and spread a ruin round.

Even now the devastation is begun,   395
And half the business of destruction done;
Even now, methinks, as pondering here I stand,
I see the rural virtues leave the land.
Down where yon anchoring vessel spreads the sail,
That idly waiting flaps with every gale,   400
Downward they move, a melancholy band,
Pass from the shore, and darken all the strand.
Contented toil, and hospitable care,
And kind connubial tenderness are there;
And piety with wishes placed above,   405
And steady loyalty, and faithful love.
And thou, sweet Poetry, thou loveliest maid,
Still first to fly where sensual joys invade;
Unfit in these degenerate times of shame,
To catch the heart, or strike for honest fame;   410
Dear charming nymph, neglected and decried,
My shame in crowds, my solitary pride;
Thou source of all my bliss, and all my woe,
That found'st me poor at first, and keep'st me so;
Thou guide by which the nobler arts excel,   415
Thou nurse of every virtue, fare thee well.
Farewell, and O where'er thy voice be tried,
On Torno's cliffs, or Pambamarca's side,
Whether where equinoctial fervours glow,
Or winter wraps the polar world in snow,   420
Still let thy voice prevailing over time,
Redress the rigours of the inclement clime;
Aid slighted truth, with thy persuasive strain
Teach erring man to spurn the rage of gain;
Teach him that states of native strength possessed,   425
Though very poor, may still be very blessed;

455

That trade's proud empire hastes to swift decay,
As ocean sweeps the laboured mole away;
While self-dependent power can time defy,
As rocks resist the billows and the sky.   430

Goldsmith had been concerned with the problem of rural depopulation and urban luxury long before he expressed it in *The Deserted Village*. He had focused on the subject in his early essay *The Revolution in Low Life*. The same ideas had been handled in *The Traveller*, so that there is some truth to the charge that Goldsmith worked and reworked his material too often. But it is also true that Goldsmith was still writing in the Augustan tradition that did not prize novelty; and that he tuned to contemporary problems the heritage of Virgil's *Georgics*, especially the passage on rural retirement in the second book, and the accents of Milton, particularly those of *Il Penseroso*, *L'Allegro*, *Lycidas* and *Paradise Lost*.

The Deserted Village may be regarded as a pastoral with considerable admixture of the descriptive and didactic elements of eighteenth-century verse. But it is also in the long tradition of topographical poems like *Cooper's Hill* and *Windsor-Forest*. Goldsmith offers a generalised version of the topographical poem, deliberately eschewing definitive localisation; Denham and Pope, on the other hand, provide topographical and historical detail, and thus invite identification of the location.

The generalised attitude of the poet in *The Deserted Village* is balanced by a personal tone which often emerges very clearly in the poet's use of the first person voice. Even as the poem debates issues of national importance it is clear that the poet feels the effect of them in his own life. The public loss and disappointment is also a personal one. Indeed, it is the configuration of the poet's critical overview of the political and social situation, and his personal imprisonment in it, that enriches the texture of the poem and creates tautness. For too long Goldsmith's poem has been considered simply emotional and diffuse. It is important to recognise that the emotional, chiefly melancholic and elegiac, stance of the poem is informed by the poet's capacity to rise above it; and that Augustan generalisation is animated by personal detail.

Goldsmith expressed unqualified commitment to the heroic couplet by his consistent use of it in his verse; he expressed grave doubts as to the suitability of other metrical forms in his prose writings. In his Dedication to *The Traveller* he talked of the absurdity of defending 'blank verse and Pindaric odes, choruses, anapaests and iambics, alliterative care and happy negligence'. Earlier, in his *Present State of Learning*, he had referred to the 'affected obscurity of our odes, the tuneless flow of our blank verse, the pompous epithet, laboured diction, and every other deviation from common sense'.

Goldsmith's use of the ten-syllable couplet is versatile. He can extend it into verse paragraphs that describe landscape in the manner of Thomson's blank verse, or sharpen a satiric edge to it in the style of Pope. Lines like: 'Sunk are thy bowers in shapeless ruin all,/ And the long grass o'ertops the mouldering wall', offer visual description; a couplet like: 'The chest contrived a double debt to pay,/ A bed by night, a chest of drawers by day', has all the wit, based on antithesis, of a couplet by Pope. The second couplet of the poem: 'Where smiling spring its earliest visit paid,/ And parting summer's lingering blooms delayed', rests on stock poetic diction to evoke a generalised picture of the village. The threefold repetition of 'I still had hopes' in the sixth verse paragraph of the poem insists on the personal voice, on the individual's subjection to those very forces that he chisels his verse against. It is possible that the blending of these many different modes blurs the focus of the poem; looked at another way it re-creates the sense of dispersal that is also the poet's subject, and in so doing affirms the poet's final triumph.

Dedication

To Sir Joshua Reynolds

Dear Sir,

I can have no expectations in an address of this kind, either to add to your reputation, or to establish my own. You can gain nothing from my admiration, as I am ignorant of that art in which you are said to excel; and I may lose much by the severity of your judgement, as few have a juster taste in poetry than you. Setting interest therefore aside, to which I never paid much attention, I must be indulged at present in following my affections. The only dedication I ever made was to my brother, because I loved him better than most other men. He is since dead. Permit me to inscribe this poem to you.

How far you may be pleased with the versification and mere mechanical parts of this attempt, I don't pretend to enquire; but I know you will object (and indeed several of our best and wisest friends concur in the opinion) that the depopulation it deplores is no where to be seen, and the disorders it laments are only to be found in the poet's own imagination. To this I can scarce make any other answer than that I sincerely believe what I have written; that I have taken all possible pains, in my country excursions, for these four or five years past, to be certain of what I allege, and that all my views and enquiries have led me to believe those miseries real, which I here attempt to display. But this is not the place to enter into an enquiry, whether the country be depopulating, or not; the discussion would take up much room, and I should prove myself, at best, an indifferent politician, to tire the reader with a long preface, when I want his unfatigued attention to a long poem.

In regretting the depopulation of the country, I inveigh against the increase of our luxuries; and here also I expect the shout of modern politicians against me. For twenty or thirty years past, it has been the fashion to consider luxury as one of the greatest national advantages; and all the wisdom of antiquity in that particular, as erroneous. Still however, I must remain a professed ancient on that head, and continue to think those luxuries prejudicial to states, by which so many vices are introduced, and so many kingdoms have been undone. Indeed so much has been poured out of late on the other side of the question, that, merely for the sake of novelty and variety, one would sometimes wish to be in the right.

I am,
Dear Sir,
Your sincere friend,
and ardent admirer,
Oliver Goldsmith

[1] **Auburn**
Several sources have been traced for the name of Goldsmith's village; Auburn or Aldbourne in Wiltshire is referred to often. Whatever the origin of the name, there is now general agreement that Goldsmith was not writing about any particular village either in England or Ireland, but was describing the general plight of the countryside as he saw it. This marks a change from attempts to identify Auburn with Lissoy, the Irish village where Goldsmith was brought up. In critical terms this marks the shift away from biographical criticism. But Goldsmith did claim that he had depicted the social conditions in the English countryside with care and authenticity; further he was aware that he was writing against the current political opinion.

[2] **swain**
peasant.

[3] **smiling spring**
Cf. 'smiling mornings', Gray, *Sonnet on West*, line 1.

[4] **parting summer's lingering blooms**
Goldsmith's verse abounds in the adjectival present participle and noun combination. See note on *Sonnet on West*, line 2.

[6] **Seats**
abodes, dwellings.

[7] **green**
grassy plain.

[9] **paused**
'to deliberate', Johnson, *Dictionary*.

[10] **cot**
cottage, small house; *cultivated* improved through manual industry.

[12] **decent**
becoming.

[12–13] **The decent church . . . / The hawthorn bush**
Though both these have been identified as landmarks in Lissoy it is evident that they suggest a generalised and typical eighteenth-century village.

[16] **remitting**
abating, relaxing.

[17] **village train**
the people of the village.

[18] **Led up**
began.

[20] **contending**
contesting; *surveyed* looked on, viewed without participating.

[24] **Succeeding sports**
new games following the old ones.

[25] **simply**
in a simple, naive way (rather than merely).

[27] **mistrustless**
unsuspecting; *smutted* a game in which the victim is told to imitate someone else; both players are given plates, to be held face upwards, but the bottom of the victim's plate is smeared with black. The action to be imitated is drawing lines on your face after rubbing your fingers on the plate. The victim unsuspectingly covers his face with black.

[28] **secret**
hidden; *tittered* 'a restrained laugh', Johnson, *Dictionary*.

[29] **side-long looks of love**
Cf. 'The kiss, snatched hasty from the sidelong maid', Thomson, *Winter*, line 625, and 'In sidelong glances from her downcast eye', *Summer*, line 1280.

[30] **reprove**
check, censure.

[32] **sweet succession**
following one after the other in a pleasing way.

[35] **lawn**
open space of grass-covered land, not necessarily cultivated or trimmed.

[36] **withdrawn**
taken away.

[37] **tyrant**
large landowners, who further increased their holdings by implementing Enclosure Acts, which allowed them, on certain conditions, to enclose the common land. This measure greatly impoverished the small farmers.

[38] **desolation**
'to deprive of inhabitants', Johnson, *Dictionary*; *saddens* makes gloomy.

[40] **tillage**
tilled or ploughed land; *stints* confines or limits; *half a tillage* only half of the land being under cultivation resulting in reduced prosperity.
[39–40]
Cf. Goldsmith's comment on the fate of villagers in his essay *The Revolution in Low Life*: 'I was informed that a merchant of immense fortune in London, who had lately purchased the estate on which they lived, intended to lay the whole out in a seat of pleasure for himself.' Cf. also 'Seen opulence, her grandeur to maintain,/ Lead stern depopulation in her train,/ And over fields where scattered hamlets rose,/ In barren solitary pomp repose?', *The Traveller*, lines 401–4.
[42] **choked with sedges**
overgrown with weeds, untended.
[44] **The hollow-sounding bittern**
Goldsmith recalled his boyhood memories of the sound of the bittern:

there is none [sound] so dismally hollow as the booming of the bittern. It is impossible for words to give those who have not heard this evening-call an adequate idea of its solemnity. It is like the interrupted bellowing of a bull, but hollower and louder, and is heard at a mile's distance, as if issuing from some formidable being that resided at the bottom of the waters . . . I remember in the place where I was a boy with what terror this bird's note affected the whole village; they considered it as the presage of some sad event; and generally found or made one to succeed it. (*An History of the Earth, and Animated Nature*)

See Friedman; see also: 'so that scarce/ The bittern knows his time with bill engulfed/ To shake the sounding marsh', Thomson, *Spring*, lines 21–3.
[45] **desert**
solitary; *lapwing* Goldsmith had said of the lapwing that it chiefly chose to breed in unhabited islands. In the case of both the bittern and the lapwing he pointed out that they preferred soli-

tude. In the context of the poem 'solitary guest' invokes the solitude sought by these birds; but it also emphasises the surrounding desolation, and is a poignant reminder of vanished good-fellowship and hospitality.
[49] **spoiler's**
plunderer's.
[52] **decay**
decline.
[54] **A breath . . . has made**
Cf. 'Who pants for glory finds but short repose,/ A breath revives him, or a breath o'erthrows', Pope, *Imitations of Horace, Epistles*, II, i, 300–1.
[55] **bold**
brave, stout.
[56] **supplied**
replaced.
[55–6]
Goldsmith had expressed a similar sentiment in *The Revolution in Low Life*: 'I was grieved to see a generous, virtuous race of men, who should be considered as the strength and ornament of their country, torn from their little habitations.' See also: ' Have we not seen, round Britain's peopled shore,/ Her useful sons exchanged for useless ore?', *The Traveller*, lines 397–8.
[57] **England's griefs**
it would appear that Goldsmith is here talking about an English village.
[58] **rood**
about one-fourth of an acre.
[59] **light labour spread her wholesome store**
the daily wants of life were provided by none too strenuous work.
[61] **His**
referring back to 'man' of line 58.
[62]
Cf. 'Increase his riches, and his peace destroy', Johnson, *The Vanity of Human Wishes*, line 40.
[63] **trade's unfeeling train**
the insensitive followers of commerce.
[65] **hamlets**
small villages.
[66] **Unwieldy wealth**
stolid constructions of the rich; *cumbrous* cumbersome, oppressive; *repose* lodge, dwell.

[67] **opulence**
wealth, affluence.
[67]
All needs are related to affluence and show.
[68]
All pain is caused by a foolish deference to pride.
[69]
Those quiet times which flourished with a sense of plenty. Cf. 'With homebred plenty the rich owner bless', Dryden, *Georgics*, ii, 657.
[72] **Lived in each look**
that all could share.
[74] **manners**
customs, codes of behaviour and morality, i.e. the whole rural way of life.
[75] **parent**
origin, source.
[76] **confess**
attest to.
[78] **tangling**
here substituted for 'tangled'; the replacement of the passive by the active form was a part of the poetic idiom.
[84]
Cf. 'Ye mute companions of my toils, that bear,/ In all my griefs, a more than equal share!', Collins, *Persian Eclogues*, ii, 21–2.
[87] **husband**
manage carefully and economically; to put to good use; *taper* declining light; the metaphor of light as signifying life is continued in the 'flame' of the next line.
[83–7]
Cf.:

After a long life of the most dissipated variety, after having strayed through so many countries without being regarded, or known, with what enthusiasm do I again revisit the happy island where I drew my first breath, and received the early pleasures and instructions of life? . . . here let me spend the small remainder of my days in tranquillity and content . . .
(Goldsmith, 'A Comparative View of

Races and Nations' in *Royal Magazine*, 11 (1760); see Friedman, 1966)

[88]
To prevent destruction of life's vitality through proper rest.
[89] **still**
even then; *still* always.
[93–6]
Cf. 'The hare, in pastures or in plains is found,/ Emblem of human life, who runs the round;/ And, after all his wand'ring ways are done,/ His circle fills, and ends where he begun', Dryden, *To my Honour'd Kinsman, John Driden*, 11, 62–5. Dryden's lines point to the emblematic tradition of the Renaissance which both poets explore, though Goldsmith does it in a muted way. Within this tradition Donne's lines are relevant: 'Thy firmness makes my circle just,/ And makes me end where I begun', *A Valediction Forbidding Mourning*, lines 35–6. The emblem of the circle marked not only perfection in human achievement, but also a 'homecoming', or the final return. Cf. Goldsmith's sentiments in *Citizen of the World*, Letter CIII:

There is something so seducing in that spot in which we first had existence, that nothing but it can please; whatever vicissitudes we experience in life, however we toil, or wheresoever we wander, our fatigued wishes still recur to home for tranquillity, we long to die in that spot which gave us birth, and in the pleasing expectation opiate every calamity.
(see Friedman, 1966)

[95] **vexations**
troubles.
[97–100]
Cf. 'Happy next him who to these shades retires,/ Whom nature charms, and whom the Muse inspires,/ Whom humbler joys of home-felt quiet please,/ Successive study, exercise and ease', Pope, *Windsor-Forest*, lines 237–40. The *locus classicus* of this and

other passages on rural retirement is in the second book of Virgil's *Georgics*; Dryden, in his rather free translation of *Georgics*, had made Virgil's ideas available in the poetic idiom of the Augustans. Thomson had reiterated these ideas in *Winter*, lines 600ff.: 'Then, even superior to ambition, we/ Would learn the private virtues – how to glide/ Through shades and plains along the smoothest stream/ Of rural life'.

[99]
Cf. 'And rural pleasures crown his happiness', Dryden, *Georgics*, ii, 658.

[101–2]
Cf. 'by struggling with misfortunes, we are sure to receive some wounds in the conflict. The only method to come off victorious, is by running away', Goldsmith, *The Bee*, No. ii (see Friedman, 1966).

[104] **tempt**
attempt, venture on; *dangerous deep* periphrastic reference for the ocean; very much part of the current poetic idiom; see: 'finny deep', Goldsmith, *The Traveller*, line 187.

[105–6]
Cf. 'The houses of the great are as inaccessible as a frontier garrison at mid-night. I never see a noble-man's door half opened that some surly porter or footman does not stand full in the breach', Goldsmith, *Citizen of the World*, Letter XXX (see Friedman, 1966).

[108] **befriending virtue's friend**
'To virtue only, and her friends, a friend', Pope, *Imitations of Horace, Satire*, II, i, 121.

[109] **bends**
sinks; *unperceived decay* cf. 'An age that melts with unperceived decay', Johnson, *The Vanity of Human Wishes*, line 293, and: 'And varied life steal unperceived away', Johnson, *Irene*, II, vii, 91.

[110] **resignation**
Sir Joshua Reynolds gave the name *Resignation* to the engraving Thomas Warton made in 1772 of his picture of

'An Old Man', done in 1771. It was inscribed: 'This attempt to express a character in *The Deserted Village*, is dedicated to Dr. Goldsmith, by his sincere friend, and admirer Joshua Reynolds' (see Lonsdale, 1969).

[111–12]
His future becomes ever brighter, so that he is virtually in heaven before his death.

[115] **careless**
free from care, carefree; *careless steps and slow* Cf. 'with solemn pace and slow', Milton, *Paradise Lost*, xii, 648; 'with pensive steps and slow', Pope, *Odyssey*, xi, 397; see also: 'By timid steps, and slow', Pope, *Dunciad*, iv, 465.

[117] **responsive**
singing in response; *The swain responsive* Cf. 'responsive each to other's note', Milton, *Paradise Lost*, iv, 683; 'responsive to the cuckoo's note', Gray, *Ode on the Spring*, line 6.

[118] **sober herd**
solemn herd of cows; *lowed* bellowed. Cf. 'The lowing herd wind slowly o'er the lea', Gray, *Elegy*, line 2.

[121] **bayed**
followed with barking.

[122] **spoke**
proclaimed; *vacant* free from preoccupation, not 'vacuous' as we would interpret it.

[123] **sweet**
pleasing; *confusion* blending, or mingling together.

[124] **each pause the nightingale had made**
Goldsmith had characterised the nightingale's sound : 'Her note is soft, various, and interrupted; she seldom holds it without a pause above the time that one can count twenty. The nightingale's pausing song would be the proper epithet for this bird's music with us', *Animated Nature* (see Friedman, 1966).

[125] **the sounds of population fail**
In *The Revolution in Low Life* Goldsmith lamented the displacement of the village populations by wealthy

merchants from the big cities:

I spent part of last summer in a little village, distant about fifty miles from town, consisting of near one hundred houses . . . Upon my first arrival I felt a secret pleasure in observing this happy community . . . But this satisfaction was soon repressed, when I understood that they were shortly to leave this abode of felicity, of which they and their ancestors had been in possession for time immemorial, and that they had received orders to seek for a new habitation. I was informed that a merchant of immense fortune in London, who had lately purchased the estate on which they lived, intended to lay the whole out in a seat of pleasure for himself.

[126] **fluctuate**
i.e. waves of sound are heard, now loud, now soft; *gale* simply 'wind' or a gentle wind; without the sense of force we would now give it.

[130] **plashy**
marshy, with many pools.

[132] **mantling cresses**
watercress covering the surface of the brook; see 'ivy-mantled', Gray, *Elegy*, line 9.

[133] **faggot**
bundle of firewood.

[134] **nightly shed**
temporary shelter for the night; see 'monarch of a shed', Goldsmith, *The Traveller*, line 192.

[135] **harmless**
innocent; *train* retinue, group of followers.

[136] **sad historian**
sorrowful, grieving narrator, or representative.

[140] **The village preacher**
identified by Goldsmith's sister as his father; *mansion* dwelling, without any sense of grandeur. The word is used in the same sense in lines 195 and 238.

[142] **passing rich**
very rich, exceedingly wealthy; *forty pounds a year* in his Dedication to *The Traveller* Goldsmith had described his brother Henry as 'a man, who

despising fame and fortune, has retired early to happiness and obscurity, with an income of forty pounds a year'. Cf. 'Or, some remote, inferior post,/ With forty pounds a year at most', Swift, *A Libel on Dr Delany*, lines 133–4; Parson Adams, in Fielding's *Joseph Andrews*, also had an income of forty pounds a year.

[143] **ran his godly race**
led his virtuous life.

[144] **place**
living.

[145] **Unpracticed**
unskilful.

[149] **vagrant train**
beggars and tramps.

[151] **The long-remembered beggar**
beggars who had marked out rounds which they traversed year after year, and were therefore remembered by the people.

[155] **The broken soldier**
The Seven Years War had resulted in many disabled soldiers.

[159]
Cf. 'So perish all, whose breast ne'er learned to glow/ For others' good, or melt at others' woe', Pope, *Elegy to an Unfortunate Lady*, lines 45–6.

[161] **Careless**
not concerning himself with.

[162]
His 'pity' or feeling of sympathy for his fellow beings is contrasted with 'charity' or the mere duty of almsgiving.

[164] **failings**
indiscriminate and unquestioning benevolence, as appears from the earlier lines.

[169] **dull**
sluggish, slow of motion; *delay* procrastination.

[170]
Cf. 'And saints who taught, and led, the way to Heav'n', Tickell, *On the Death of Mr Addison*, line 42 (see Lonsdale, 1969).

[172] **dismayed**
frightened, terrified; 'Fall of courage; terror felt; desertion of mind', Johnson, *Dictionary*; see 'Which then not minded in dismay, yet now/ Assures

me that the bitterness of death/ Is past and we shall live', Milton, *Paradise Lost*, xi, 156–8.

[173] **reverend**
both as an appellation for the clergy and in the sense of venerable; *champion* hero; *control* authority, governance.

[176] **his**
the dying man's; *accents* voice.

[179] **prevailed**
gained influence; *double sway* because he not only preached but practised.

[180]
Cf. 'And sent us back to praise, who came to pray', Dryden, *Britannia Rediviva*, 4.

[182] **steady zeal**
unchanging ardour.

[189] **aweful**
inspiring awe.

[192] **Eternal sunshine**
Cf. 'Eternal sunshine of thy spotless mind', Pope, *Eloisa to Abelard*, line 209.

[189–93]
Cf.: 'As some tall tow'r, or lofty mountains's brow,/ Detains the sun, illustrious from its height,/ While rising vapours, and descending shades,/ With damps and darkness down the spacious vale:/ Undampt by doubt, undarken'd by despair,/ Philander, thus augustly rears his head', Young, *The Complaint: or Night-Thoughts* (near end of 'Night the Second'). Goldsmith's lines also recall: 'In short, that reas'ning, high, immortal thing,/ Just less than Jove, and much above a king,/ Nay half in Heav'n – except (what's mighty odd)/ A fit of vapours clouds this demi-god', Pope, *Imitations of Horace, Epistles*, II, i, 185–9.

[194] **furze**
gorse; *unprofitably* without pecuniary advantage; *gay* ornamented. The gorse was decorative though it had no commercial value.

[195] **skilled to rule**
suggests that he was adept in keeping discipline; but the idea that he was practised in using the ruler, both in

mathematics and also to maintain discipline, is present. The latter idea is related to the expression of his 'sternness'.

[199] **boding**
anticipating trouble.

[199–204]
Steele's passage from *Spectator*, No. 49 is usually cited as expressing a similar situation:

Eubulus has so great an authority in his little diurnal audience, that when he shakes his head at any piece of public news, they all of them appear dejected; and on the contrary, go home to their dinners with a good stomach and cheerful aspect, when Eubulus seems to intimate that things go well.

But see also: 'Practised their master's notions to embrace,/ Repeat his maxims, and reflect his face;/ . . . To shake with laughter ere the jest they hear,/ To pour at will the counterfeited tear', Johnson, *London*, lines 136–7, 140–1.

[208] **cipher**
do calculations.

[209] **terms**
days fixed for the payment of rent and other dues; *tides* church festivals.

[210] **gauge**
measure, to measure the contents of a barrel.

[214] **Amazed**
put into confusion with wonder.

[222] **grey-beard mirth and smiling toil**
muted personifications in the tradition of Johnson and Pope.

[223]
Could mean simply 'where village statesmen, with profound looks, talked'; but the possibility of 'where village statesmen talked through profound looks' cannot be overlooked.

[224] **news much older**
their concerns were those of long-time dwellers.

[225–6]
Only the imagination can outline the splendour and gaiety of that place

now. Goldsmith deliberately uses elevated phrases like 'parlour splendours' and 'festive place' to highlight the simplicity of the description that follows.

[227] **sanded**
covered with sand.

[228] **clicked**
'to make a sharp successive noise', Johnson, *Dictionary*.

[229] **contrived**
planned; *double debt to pay* to perform a double function.

[231] **ornament and use**
expressing concern here with 'usefulness', a moral preoccupation with the Augustans. Goldsmith's description emphasises the economy of village life as opposed to the luxury and ostentation of city life.

[232]
'The twelve good rules' were attributed to Charles I, as they appeared beneath a woodcut of his execution. The rules were: 1. Urge no healths. 2. Profane no divine ordinances. 3. Touch no state matters. 4. Reveal no secrets. 5. Pick no quarrels. 6. Make no comparisons. 7. Maintain no ill opinions. 8. Keep no bad company. 9. Encourage no vice. 10. Make no long meals. 11. Repeat no grievances. 12. Lay no wagers; 'the royal game of goose' was a game of different compartments with different titles through which the player progresses according to the number he throws with his dice. At every fourth or fifth compartment is depicted a goose, and if the player's cast falls upon one of these, he moves forward double the number of his throw (see Lonsdale, 1969). It is curious that the two pictures chosen to decorate the walls of the village preacher's house should carry the contrary messages of good conduct on the one hand, and the dominance of chance in human affairs, on the other. There is also some ambivalence in the 'good rules' being appended to a drawing of Charles I's execution.

[234] **fennel**
a fragrant plant.

[226–36]
This passage is a reworking of Goldsmith, *Description of an Author's Bedchamber*, lines 9–20: 'The sanded floor that grits beneath the tread,/ The humid wall with paltry pictures spread:/ The royal game of goose was there in view,/ And the twelve rules the royal martyr drew;/ The seasons framed with listing found a place,/ The brave Prince William showed his lamp-black face:/ The morn was cold, he views with keen desire/ The rusty grate unconscious of a fire:/ With beer and milk arrears the frieze was scored,/ And five cracked teacups dressed the chimney board./ A nightcap decked his brows instead of bay,/ A cap by night – a stocking all the day!'

[226, 237] **parlour splendours, Vain transitory splendours**
Goldsmith, like other poets of the period, describes lavish interiors in the course of presenting the fall of great men or houses – see Johnson, *The Vanity*, lines 84–90, 113–20. Hence his rather incongruous use of 'splendours' in the context of the village preacher's house; read straight the passage could be construed as presenting 'true splendours'; on the other hand Goldsmith's repeated 'no more' in lines 241–5 is both elegiac and satiric.

[238] **Reprieve**
give a respite to; *tottering mansion* the falling building.

[239] **Obscure it sinks**
It sinks into obscurity.

[241] **repair**
to betake oneself to.

[244] **prevail**
be listened to.

[246] **ponderous**
heavy.

[248] **Careful**
taking care; *mantling bliss* frothing beer. Another interesting periphrasis; cf. 'Mantling in the goblet see', Gray, *The Descent of Odin, An Ode*, line 43.

[249–50]
The usual comparison is with 'the earthen mug went round. Miss touched the cup, the stranger pledged the parson', Goldsmith, *The History of Miss Stanton* in the *British Magazine*, 1760 (see Friedman, 1966). But the maid's 'coyness' and 'half-willingness' and the image of her 'kissing the cup' interacts with the 'broken tea-cups' of line 235. The idea of broken chinaware carrying sexual suggestions, especially of loss of virginity, is raised by this interrelationship; cf. 'Whether the nymph shall break Diana's law,/ Or some frail China jar receive a flaw', Pope, *The Rape of the Lock*, ii, 105–6.

[251–2]
Cf. 'Let not ambition mock their useful toil,/ Their homely joys and destiny obscure;/ Nor grandeur hear with a disdainful smile,/ The short and simple annals of the poor', Gray, *Elegy*, lines 29–32.

[253] **congenial to my heart**
close to my heart.

[254] **native**
produced by nature; *gloss* superficial lustre.

[255] **play**
expression.

[256] **adopts**
accepts; *owns their first-born sway* recognises the importance of original, as opposed to secondary, pleasures.

[257] **vacant**
see line 122 and note.

[258]
Goldsmith uses the triple negative like Milton did; cf. 'Unrespited, unpitied, unreprieved', *Paradise Lost*, ii, 185, and 'Unshaken, unseduced, unterrified', v, 899.

[259] **midnight masquerade**
Cf. 'In courtly balls, and midnight masquerades', Pope, *The Rape of the Lock*, i, 72.

[260] **freaks**
capricious; out of the order of nature; *wanton* self-indulgent, capricious, lascivious.

[261] **triflers**
'One who acts with levity; one who talks with folly', Johnson, *Dictionary*.

[262]
Cf. 'Abstract what others feel, what others think,/ All pleasures sicken', Pope, *Essay on Man*, iv, 45–6.

[263] **fashion's**
prevailing mode, as opposed to 'nature' which is unchanging; *decoy* allure.

[251–64]
Cf.

Artificial pleasure may amuse us for a moment, but the nearer Nature the longer every thing pleases, and as we recede from it we only make approaches to anxiety and discontent ... The midnight masquerade, the prolonged brag party, the five hours labour of the toilet are only the pleasures of fashion and caprice ... Happy they who pursue pleasure as far as Nature directs and no farther; pleasure, rightly understood, and prudently followed, is but another name for virtue! (Goldsmith, *A Lady of Fashion in the Time of Anna Bullen compared with one of Modern Times* from the *Lady's Magazine*, October 1760; see Friedman, 1966)

[261–4]
Cf. 'those fantastic joys/ That still amuse the wanton, still deceive;/ A face of pleasure, but a heart of pain;/ Their hollow moments undelighted all', Thomson, *Autumn*, lines 1253–6.

[266]
Cf. 'Wherever the traveller turns, while he sees one part of the inhabitants of the country becoming immensely rich, he sees the other growing miserably poor, and the happy equality of condition now entirely removed', *The Revolution in Low Life*.

[267–8]
Cf. 'there is a wide difference between a conquering and a flourishing empire', Goldsmith, *Citizen*, Letter XXV.

[270] **shouting folly**
triumphant depravity of mind.
[279] **silken sloth**
luxuriousness tending to sinfulness.
[284] **luxuries**
Cf. 'while luxury/ In palaces lay straining her low thought/ To form unreal wants', Thomson, *Winter*, lines 1057–9.
[273–86]
'Let others felicitate their country upon the encrease of foreign commerce and the extension of our foreign conquests; but for my part, this new introduction of wealth gives me but very little satisfaction', Goldsmith, *The Revolution in Low Life*. Further in the same essay: 'A country ... where the inhabitants are thus divided into the very rich and the very poor, is, indeed, of all others the most helpless; without courage and without strength; neither enjoying peace within itself, and, after a time, unable to resist foreign invasion.'
[285] **adorned for pleasure all**
all of it laid out for pleasure.
[286] **barren splendour**
useless show.
[288] **confirms her reign**
establishes her power.
[290]
Her beauty is natural, not created by art.
[293] **solicitous to bless**
anxious to brandish her beauty.
[294] **glaring impotence**
obvious powerlessness.
[297] **verging**
tending towards; *splendours* yet another derogatory use of the word; *decline ... rise* the poet establishes an inverse relationship between 'nature's simplest charms' and the 'splendours' of luxury, or artificial want.
[299] **scourged**
forced, driven out; carrying also, in relation to 'famine', the sense of 'to exhaust the fertility of land'.
[302] **blooms**
used satirically; *The ... grave* pointing to the two extremes of the rich and the poor; for the rich the whole

country is a garden, for the poor it is like a grave.
[304] **scape**
escape; *contiguous pride* pride that presses close, without any intervening space. Cf. 'Or ruminate in the contiguous shade', Thomson, *Winter*, line 86.
[305] **common's**
the village parcel of common grazing land.
[305–8]
Goldsmith refers here to the enclosure of the common lands for private use by wealthy landlords.
[310]
'He ... only guards those luxuries he is not fated to share', *Animated Nature*.
[316] **artist**
artisan.
[318]
Public executions were still practised; *glooms* frowns.
[319] **dome**
simply a building.
[321–2]
Cf. 'th'affrighted crowd's tumultuous cries/ Roll through the streets, and thunder to the skies', Johnson, *London*, lines 182–3.
[325] **Ah, turn thine eyes**
Cf. 'Deign on the passing world to turn thine eyes', Johnson, *London*, line 157.
[326]
Cf.

These poor shivering females, have once seen happier days, and been flattered into beauty. They have been prostituted to the gay luxurious villain, and are now turned out to meet the severity of the winter in the streets. Perhaps now lying at the door of their betrayers they sue to wretches whose hearts are insensible to calamity. (Goldsmith, *A City Night-Piece* in *The Bee*, No. iv; see Friedman, 1966)

The innocent country girl debauched by the corrupt city had become a stock-piece in the writings and the paintings of the eighteenth century, for example Hogarth's *The Harlot's Progress*.

[335] **idly**
unthinkingly.

[336] **wheel**
spinning-wheel.

[338] **fair tribes**
periphrasis for 'women'; *participate* share.

[342] **half the convex world**
half the globe; *intrudes* is placed.

[343] **torrid tracts**
parched regions.

[343]
Cf. 'They hand in hand with wandering steps and slow', *Paradise Lost*, xii, 648.

[344] **Altama**
a river in Georgia, in North America; it is likely that Goldsmith had some detailed knowledge of the American state of Georgia; on the other hand here he does not give a specific description; *murmurs to their woe* the sounds of the river are responsive to the sorrow of the travellers.

[346] **horrid**
rough, rugged, and by extension unpleasing, offensive.

[349] **matted**
twisted together, like in a mat; hence without light, so that the birds do not know when it is day.

[356]
Cf. 'But savage beasts, or men as wild as they', Waller, *Upon the Death of My Lady Rich*, line 4 (see Lonsdale, 1969).

[358] **ravaged**
laid waste; ruined.

[360] **grassy vested**
dressed in or covered with grass; *green* grassy plain.

[361] **covert**
shelter or hiding place.

[363] **gloomed**
made gloomy. Cf. 'A night that glooms us in the noontide ray', Young, *Night-Thoughts*, ii, 358.

[366] **fondly looked their last**
had their last look at.

[379] **plaints**
complaints; *spoke* expressed.

[381] **thoughtless**
free from thought, preoccupation or care.

[375–84]
Cf.

The modest matron followed her husband in tears, and often looked back at the little mansion where she had passed her life in innocence, and to which she was nevermore to return; while the beautiful daughter parted for ever from her lover, who was now become too poor to maintain her as his wife. (*The Revolution in Low Life*)

See also: 'Have we not seen at pleasure's lordly call,/ The smiling long-frequented village fall?/ Behold the duteous son, the sire decayed,/ The modest matron and the blushing maid,/ Forced from their homes, a melancholy train,/ To traverse climes beyond the western main', *The Traveller*, lines 405–10.

[386]
Cf. 'England, therefore, must make an exchange of her best and bravest subjects for raw silk, hemp, and tobacco; her hardy veterans and honest tradesmen, must be truck'd for a box of snuff or a silk petticoat', *Citizen*, Letter XVII. Also 'Have we not seen, round Britain's peopled shore,/ Her useful sons exchanged for useless ore?', *The Traveller*, lines 397–8. Goldsmith did not always condemn luxury. But he did indict it when it was accompanied with a sense of degeneracy and waste, when it marked indulgence by the rich at the cost of the poor.

[387] **potions**
draughts; *insidious* treacherous.

[388] **Diffuse**
distribute, spread widely.

[389–94]
London was described by Smollett in similar terms in the context of luxury:

the capital is become an overgrown monster; which, like a dropsical head, will in time leave the body and extremities without nourishment and support . . . What wonder that our villages are depopulated, and our farms in want of day-labourers?... The tide of luxury has swept all the inhabitants from the open country. (*Humphrey Clinker*)

[402] **darken all the strand**
Cf. 'Cov'ring the beach, and black'ning all the strand', Dryden, *Absalom and Achitophel*, line 272.

[407–8]
Goldsmith identifies 'Poetry' with his 'rural virtues'; he slightly modifies the tradition of Thomson's *Liberty*, Collins' *Ode to Liberty*, and Gray's *Progress of Poesy*. In the last verse paragraph of *The Deserted Village* Goldsmith also strikes a personal note affirming the power of his poetic vocation in the face of inevitable change and decline. This alignment of poetry with virtue, and the poet's faith in it, against the odds that he describes,

bring the conclusion close to that of Johnson's *London*.

[411–16] **charming nymph...nurse of every virtue**
It is interesting to note these personifications of Poetry and the personal and intimate relationship expressed by the repeated use of first person pronouns. The power accorded to Poetry is in contrast to the helpless presentation of other female figures in the poem.

[418] **Torno**
name of a river and lake in Sweden; *Pambamarca* a mountain in the province of Quito, then in Peru.

[419] **equinoctial fervours**
intense heat.

[428] **laboured mole**
artificial breakwater; a dyke.

[427–30]
In 1783 Johnson marked the last four lines of the poem as the ones that he had written for Goldsmith.

GEORGE CRABBE

(1754–1832)

◇

George Crabbe was born in Aldeburgh, Suffolk, son of the collector of salt-duties. He grew up amidst poverty and dissolution. His father, who was inclined to drink, gave him only a modest education; for the rest Crabbe did a series of jobs, some manual, and had much time to spare.

He was rescued from his depressed existence by Edmund Burke to whom he sent a portion of *The Village*. Burke's attention drew him into the circle of Samuel Johnson and Joshua Reynolds. In fact Johnson helped him revise his *The Village*, and its publication in 1783 established his reputation as a poet. Meanwhile he had taken holy orders and performed his clerical duties with Methodist inclinations. His poetic career was erratic, and after *The Village* there was a gap of many years before his *Poems* (a reprint of earlier works with additions) was published in 1807. *The Borough* appeared in 1810. Crabbe continued to write verse, and in 1819 brought out *Tales of the Hall*. But for our purposes *The Village* remains his most interesting poem.

Further Reading

The standard edition of Crabbe's poetry is Norma Dalrymple-Champneys and Arthur Pollard (eds), *George Crabbe: The Complete Poetical Works* (Oxford: Clarendon Press, 1988). Good selections can also be found in Gavin Edwards' Penguin edition, *George Crabbe: Selected Poems,* and in Jem Poster (ed.), *George Crabbe: Selected Poetry* (Manchester: Carcanet, 1986).

A modern biography is available in Neville Blackburn, *The Restless Ocean: The Story of George Crabbe, the Aldeburgh Poet* (Lavenham: Dalton, 1972). Lillian Haddakin's *The Poetry of*

Crabbe (London: Chatto and Windus, 1955) and Robert L. Chamberlain's *George Crabbe* (New York: Twayne, 1965) are both useful critical books. Three more recent books deserve mention: Terence Bareham, *George Crabbe* (New York: Barnes and Noble, 1977), Peter New, *George Crabbe's Poetry* (New York: St. Martin's, 1976), and Beth George Nelson, *George Crabbe and the Progress of Eighteenth-Century Narrative Verse* (Cranbury, NJ: Bucknell University Press, 1976). A collection of eighteenth- and nineteenth-century reactions is provided by Arthur Pollard (ed.), *Crabbe: The Critical Heritage* (London: Routledge and Kegan Paul, 1972).

———◇———

39 / From *The Village*

Book I

The village life, and every care that reigns
O'er youthful peasants and declining swains:
What labour yields, and what, that labour past,
Age, in its hour of languor, finds at last:
What form the real picture of the poor,   5
Demand a song – The muse can give no more.

Fled are those times, when, in harmonious strains,
The rustic poet praised his native plains;
No shepherds now in smooth alternate verse,
Their country's beauty or their nymph's rehearse: 10
Yet still for these we frame the tender strain,
Still in our lays fond Corydons complain,
And shepherds' boys their amorous pains reveal,
The only pains, alas! they never feel.

On Mincio's bank, in Caesar's bounteous reign,   15
If Tityrus found the golden age again,
Must sleepy bards the flattering dream prolong,
Mechanic echoes of the Mantuan song?
From truth and nature shall we widely stray?
Where Virgil, not where fancy leads the way?   20

470

Yes, thus the muses sing of happy swains,
Because the muses never knew their pains;
They boast their peasants' pipes, but peasants now
Resign their pipes and plod behind the plough;
And few amid the rural-tribe have time   25
To number syllables and play with rhyme:
Save honest Duck, what son of verse could share
The poet's rapture and the peasant's care?
Or the great labours of the field degrade
With the new peril of a poorer trade?   30

From this chief cause these idle praises spring,
That, themes so easy, few forbear to sing;
For no deep thought the trifling subjects ask;
To sing of shepherds is an easy task:
The happy youth assumes the common strain,   35
A nymph his mistress and himself a swain;
With no sad scenes he clouds his tuneful prayer,
But all, to look like her, is painted fair.

I grant indeed that fields and flocks have charms,
For him that grazes or for him that farms: 40
But when amid such pleasing scenes I trace
The poor laborious natives of the place,
And see the mid-day sun, with fervid ray,
On their bare heads and dewy temples play;
While some, with feebler heads and fainter hearts,   45
Deplore their fortune, yet sustain their parts,
Then shall I dare these real ills to hide,
In tinsel trappings of poetic pride?

No, cast by fortune on a frowning coast,
Which neither groves nor happy valleys boast: 50
Where other cares than those the muse relates,
And other shepherds dwell with other mates:
By such examples taught, I paint the cot,
As truth will paint it, and as bards will not:
Nor you, ye poor, of lettered scorn complain,   55
To you the smoothest song is smooth in vain;
O'ercome by labour and bowed down by time,

471

Feel you the barren flattery of a rhyme?
Can poets soothe you, when you pine for bread,
By winding myrtles round your ruined shed?   60
Can their light tales your weighty griefs o'erpower,
Or glad with airy mirth the toilsome hour?

Lo! where the heath with withering brake grown o'er,
Lends the light turf that warms the neighbouring poor:
From thence a length of burning sand appears,   65
Where the thin harvest waves its withered ears;
Rank weeds, that every art and care defy,
Reign o'er the land and rob the blighted rye:
There thistles stretch their prickly arms afar,
And to the ragged infant threaten war: 70
There poppies nodding, mock the hope of toil,
There the blue bugloss paints the sterile soil;
Hardy and high, above the slender sheaf,
The slimy mallow waves her silky leaf;
O'er the young shoot the charlock throws a shade,   75
And clasping tares cling round the sickly blade:
With mingled tints the rocky coasts abound,
And a sad splendour vainly shines around.

So looks the nymph whom wretched arts adorn,
Betrayed by man, then left for man to scorn: 80
Whose cheek in vain assumes the mimic rose,
While her sad eyes the troubled breast disclose;
Whose outward splendour is but folly's dress,
Exposing most, when most it gilds distress.

Here joyless roam a wild amphibious race,   85
With sullen woe displayed in every face;
Who far from civil arts and social fly,
And scowl at strangers with suspicious eye.

Here too the lawless merchant of the main
Draws from his plough th'intoxicated swain: 90
Want only claimed the labour of the day,
But vice now steals his nightly rest away.

Where are the swains, who, daily labour done,
With rural games played down the setting sun:
Who struck with matchless force the bounding ball,   95
Or made the ponderous quoit obliquely fall;
While some huge Ajax, terrible and strong,
Engaged some artful stripling of the throng,
And fell beneath him, foiled, while far around
Hoarse triumph rose, and rocks returned the sound?   100
Where now are these? Beneath yon cliff they stand,
To show the freighted pinnace where to land,
To load the ready steed with guilty haste,
To fly in terror o'er the pathless waste,
Or when detected in their straggling course,   105
To foil their foes by cunning or by force;
Or, yielding part (which equal knaves demand),
To gain a lawless passport through the land.

Here wandering long among these frowning fields,
I sought the simple life that nature yields: 110
Rapine and wrong and fear usurped her place,
And a bold, artful, surly, savage race;
Who, only skilled to take the finny tribe,
The yearly dinner, or septennial bribe,
Wait on the shore, and as the waves run high,   115
On the tossed vessel bend their eager eye;
Which to their coast directs its vent'rous way,
Theirs, or the ocean's miserable prey.

As on their neighbouring beach yon swallows stand,
And wait for favouring winds to leave the land;   120
While still for flight the ready wing is spread;
So waited I the favouring hour, and fled;
Fled from these shores where guilt and famine reign,
And cried, Ah! hapless they who still remain;
Who still remain to hear the ocean roar,   125
Whose greedy waves devour the lessening shore;
Till some fierce tide, with more imperious sway,
Sweeps the low hut, and all it holds away;
When the sad tenant weeps from door to door,
And begs a poor protection from the poor.   130

But these are scenes where nature's niggard hand
Gave a spare portion to the famished land:
Hers is the fault if here mankind complain
Of fruitless toil and labour spent in vain;
But yet in other scenes more fair in view,   135
Where plenty smiles: alas! she smiles for few,
And those who taste not, yet behold her store,
Are as the slaves that dig the golden ore,
The wealth around them makes them doubly poor;
Or will you deem them amply paid in health,   140
Labour's fair child, that languishes with wealth?
Go then! and see them rising with the sun,
Through a long course of daily toil to run;
See them beneath the dog-star's raging heat,
When the knees tremble and the temples beat;   145
Behold them leaning on their scythes, look o'er
The labour past, and toils to come explore;
See them alternate suns and showers engage,
And hoard up aches and anguish for their age;
Through fens and marshy moors their steps pursue,   150
When their warm pores imbibe the evening dew;
Then own that labour may as fatal be
To these thy slaves, as thine excess to thee.

Amid this tribe too oft a manly pride
Strives in strong toil the fainting heart to hide;   155
There may you see the youth of slender frame
Contend with weakness, weariness, and shame;
Yet urged along, and proudly loth to yield,
He strives to join his fellows of the field;
Till long contending nature droops at last,   160
Declining health rejects his poor repast,
His cheerless spouse the coming danger sees,
And mutual murmurs urge the slow disease.
Yet grant them health, 'tis not for us to tell,
Though the head droops not, that the heart is well;   165
Or will you praise that homely, healthy fare,
Plenteous and plain, that happy peasants share!
Oh! trifle not with wants you cannot feel,
Nor mock the misery of a stinted meal;
Homely not wholesome, plain not plenteous, such   170
As you who praise would never deign to touch.

Ye gentle souls who dream of rural ease,
Whom the smooth stream and smoother sonnet please;
Go! if the peaceful cot your praises share,
Go look within, and ask if peace be there: 175
If peace be his – that drooping weary sire,
Or theirs, that offspring round their feeble fire,
Or hers, that matron pale, whose trembling hand
Turns on the wretched hearth th'expiring brand.
Nor yet can time itself obtain for these 180
Life's latest comforts, due respect and ease:
For yonder see that hoary swain, whose age
Can with no cares except his own engage;
Who, propped on that rude staff, looks up to see
The bare arms broken from the withering tree; 185
On which, a boy, he climbed the loftiest bough,
Then his first joy, but his sad emblem now.
He once was chief in all the rustic trade,
His steady hand the straightest furrow made;
Full many a prize he won, and still is proud 190
To find the triumphs of his youth allowed;
A transient pleasure sparkles in his eyes,
He hears and smiles, then thinks again and sighs:
For now he journeys to his grave in pain;
The rich disdain him; nay, the poor disdain; 195
Alternate masters now their slave command,
Urge the weak efforts of his feeble hand;
And, when his age attempts its task in vain,
With ruthless taunts of lazy poor complain.

Oft may you see him when he tends the sheep, 200
His winter charge beneath the hillock weep:
Oft hear him murmur to the winds that blow
O'er his white locks, and bury them in snow;
When roused by rage and muttering in the morn,
He mends the broken hedge with icy thorn. 205

'Why do I live, when I desire to be
At once from life and life's long labour free?
Like leaves in spring, the young are blown away,
Without the sorrows of a slow decay;
I, like yon withered leaf, remain behind, 210

475

Nipped by the frost and shivering in the wind;
There it abides till younger buds come on,
As I, now all my fellow swains are gone;
Then from the rising generation thrust,
It falls, like me, unnoticed to the dust. 215

'These fruitful fields, these numerous flocks I see,
Are others' gain, but killing cares to me;
To me the children of my youth are lords,
Cool in their looks, but hasty in their words;
Wants of their own demand their care, and who 220
Feels his own want and succours others too?
A lonely, wretched man, in pain I go,
None need my help, and none relieve my woe:
Then let my bones beneath the turf be laid,
And men forget the wretch they would not aid.' 225

Thus groan the old, till by disease oppressed,
They taste a final woe, and then they rest.
Theirs is yon house that holds the parish poor,
Whose walls of mud scarce bear the broken door;
There, where the putrid vapours flagging, play, 230
And the dull wheel hums doleful through the day,
There children dwell who know no parents' care,
Parents, who know no children's love, dwell there;
Heart-broken matrons on their joyless bed,
Forsaken wives and mothers never wed; 235
Dejected widows with unheeded tears,
And crippled age with more than childhood-fears;
The lame, the blind, and far, the happiest they!
The moping idiot and the madman gay.

Here too the sick their final doom receive, 240
Here brought amid the scenes of grief, to grieve;
Where the loud groans from some sad chamber flow,
Mixed with the clamours of the crowd below:
Here sorrowing, they each kindred sorrow scan,
And the cold charities of man to man. 245
Whose laws indeed for ruined age provide,
And strong compulsion plucks the scrap from pride;
But still that scrap is bought with many a sigh,
And pride embitters what it can't deny.

Say ye, oppressed by some fantastic woes,   250
Some jarring nerve that baffles your repose;
Who press the downy couch, while slaves advance,
With timid eye, to read the distant glance;
Who with sad prayers the weary doctor tease
To name the nameless ever-new disease;   255
Who with mock patience dire complaints endure,
Which real pain, and that alone can cure;
How would you bear in real pain to lie,
Despised, neglected, left alone to die?
How would you bear to draw your latest breath,   260
Where all that's wretched paves the way for death?

Such is that room which one rude beam divides,
And naked rafters form the sloping sides:
Where the vile bands that bind the thatch are seen,
And lath and mud are all that lie between;   265
Save one dull pane, that, coarsely patched, gives way
To the rude tempest, yet excludes the day:
Here, on a matted flock, with dust o'erspread,
The drooping wretch reclines his languid head;
For him no hand the cordial cup applies,   270
Or wipes the tear that stagnates in his eyes;
No friends with soft discourse his pain beguile,
Or promise hope till sickness wears a smile.

But soon a loud and hasty summons calls,
Shakes the thin roof, and echoes round the walls;   275
Anon, a figure enters, quaintly neat,
All pride and business, bustle and conceit:
With looks unaltered by these scenes of woe,
With speed that entering, speaks his haste to go;
He bids the gazing throng around him fly,   280
And carries fate and physic in his eye:
A potent quack, long versed in human ills,
Who first insults the victim whom he kills;
Whose murderous hand a drowsy bench protect,
And whose most tender mercy is neglect.   285

Paid by the parish for attendance here,
He wears contempt upon his sapient sneer:

In haste he seeks the bed where misery lies,
Impatience marked in his averted eyes;
And, some habitual queries hurried o'er,   290
Without reply, he rushes on the door;
His drooping patient, long inured to pain,
And long unheeded, knows remonstrance vain;
He ceases now the feeble help to crave
Of man: and silent sinks into the grave.   295

But ere his death some pious doubts arise,
Some simple fears which 'bold bad' men despise:
Fain would he ask the parish priest to prove
His title certain to the joys above;
For this he sends the murmuring nurse, who calls   300
The holy stranger, to these dismal walls;
And doth not he, the pious man, appear,
He 'passing rich with forty pounds a year?'
Ah! no, a shepherd of a different stock,
And far unlike him, feeds this little flock;   305
A jovial youth, who thinks his Sunday's task
As much as God or man can fairly ask;
The rest he gives to loves and labours light,
To fields the morning, and to feasts the night;
None better skilled, the noisy pack to guide,   310
To urge their chase, to cheer them or to chide;
A sportsman keen, he shoots through half the day,
And, skilled at whist, devotes the night to play:
Then, while such honours bloom around his head,
Shall he sit sadly by the sick man's bed   315
To raise the hope he feels not, or with zeal
To combat fears that e'en the pious feel?

Now once again the gloomy scene explore,
Less gloomy now; the bitter hour is o'er,
The man of many sorrows sighs no more.   320
Up yonder hill, behold how sadly slow
The bier moves winding from the vale below;
There lie the happy dead, from trouble free,
And the glad parish pays the frugal fee;
No more, O Death! thy victim starts to hear   325
Churchwarden stern, or kingly overseer;

No more the farmer claims his humble bow,
Thou art his lord, the best of tyrants thou.

Now to the church behold the mourners come,
Sedately torpid and devoutly dumb: 330
The village children now their games suspend,
To see the bier that bears their ancient friend:
For he was one in all their idle sport,
And like a monarch ruled their little court;
The pliant bow he formed, the flying ball,   335
The bat, the wicket, were his labours all;
Him now they follow to his grave, and stand
Silent and sad, and gazing, hand in hand;
While bending low, their eager eyes explore
The mingled relics of the parish poor: 340
The bell tolls late, the moping owl flies round,
Fear marks the flight and magnifies the sound;
The busy priest, detained by weightier care,
Defers his duty till the day of prayer;
And waiting long, the crowd retire distressed,   345
To think a poor man's bones could lie unblessed.

Crabbe was writing at a time when the neo-classical vision and conventions were on the decline. Both volumes of Joesph Warton's *An Essay on the Writings and Genius of Pope*, which adjudged Pope to be lacking in the 'true poetical spirit', had already appeared. Crabbe's *The Village*, too, marks the end of established poetic perspectives in favour of genuine sympathy with the lot of the rural poor. Boswell believed that Johnson's satisfaction with *The Village* rested on 'its sentiments as to false notions of rustic happiness and rustic virtue'. Clearly, Crabbe's poem also echoed Johnson's view of the pastoral form as 'easy, vulgar, and therefore disgusting', on the one hand, and as offering 'no nature . . . no truth', on the other.

The Village is an anti-pastoral in which the traditional image of rural bliss is challenged by a realistic depiction of the sufferings of the poor. The poet seems to have borne in mind Johnson's *London* and Goldsmith's *The Deserted Village*, when he wrote the poem. He offers a denial of the young Johnson's desire for the 'rural retreat', and of Goldsmith's nostalgia for the unspoiled countryside. Instead he chalks out a new path for the poet, to tell the truth about the peasants' lives, to paint, as he says, 'the real picture of the poor'. He invokes the ideas of 'truth and nature' in the context of not an idealist, but a realist vision.

Crabbe wrote in the rhymed couplet of ten syllables, a verse form that was popular in the eighteenth century. His style is simple and straightforward; but it is at the same time 'literary', in the sense that the presence of other poems of the period is discernible. In many ways Crabbe is writing 'against' a backdrop of poetry that extolled the virtues of the countryside.

[2] **declining**
a combination of 'old in years' and 'waning in strength and vigour'; *swains* rustic or peasant; 'A country servant employed in husbandry', Johnson, *Dictionary*.

[4] **languor**
fatigue, inactivity.

[9] **smooth**
flowing in an even pace; without starts or obstruction; the word was a favourite with the critics of the first half of the century in connection with versification; *alternate verse* lines in poetry following one after the other in a pattern of rhyme and metre.

[10] **nymph**
a lady; *rehearse* recount.

[11] **these**
the non-existent shepherds; *we* contemporary poets; *frame* compose; *tender strain* a periphrasis for poetry.

[12] **fond**
foolishly tender; *Corydons* the traditional rustic lover in pastoral poetry; *complain* the traditional posture of the lover, expressing anguish in love.

[15–18]
These lines are by Samuel Johnson.

[15] **Mincio**
a river running through the Italian city of Mantua. Mantua was traditionally believed to be the birthplace of the famous Roman poet Virgil (70–19 BC); Virgil's early poems were pastorals.

[16] **Tityrus**
a character in Virgil's first eclogue, through whom he speaks.

[18] **Mechanic**
mean, servile; *Mantuan* Virgilian.

[20]
This line is also by Samuel Johnson.

[20] **fancy**
'Imagination; the power by which the mind forms to itself images and representations'; 'image; conception; thought', Johnson, *Dictionary*.

[25] **rural-tribe**
Cf. 'fair tribes', Goldsmith, *The Deserted Village*, line 338.

[27] **Duck**
Stephen Duck (1705–56), a minor poet

who was patronised by Queen Caroline, George II's consort.

[28] **poet's rapture ... peasant's care**
pointing, by satiric contrast, to the impossibility of combining the two.

[29] **degrade**
diminish, lessen.

[32] **forbear**
omit.

[35] **assumes the common strain**
adopts the traditional posture.

[36] **mistress**
a woman beloved and courted; *swain* pastoral lover, especially in poetry.

[38] **painted fair**
applies satirically to the mistress as well; cf. 'A painted mistress, or a purling stream', Pope, *An Epistle to Dr Arbuthnot*, line 150.

[42] **laborious**
hard-worked.

[43] **fervid**
hot, burning.

[44] **dewy**
with perspiration.

[45] **with feebler heads and fainter hearts**
with less stamina and courage; cf. 'Others with softer smiles, and subtler art', Johnson, *London*, line 75.

[46]
Lament their poverty, yet perpetuate their roles in false presentations of rural bliss.

[49] **frowning coast**
inhospitable shore.

[53] **cot**
cottage, small abode; cf. 'The sheltered cot, the cultivated farm', Goldsmith, *The Deserted Village*, line 10; *I paint the cot* a parody of the epic 'I sing' formula.

[55] **lettered scorn**
neglect or mockery of the learned; cf. 'spelt by the unlettered muse', Gray, *Elegy*, line 81.

[56]
Cf. 'And the smooth stream in smoother numbers flows', Pope, *An Essay on Criticism*, line 367.

[60] **shed**
shelter.

[62] **glad**
gladden, make happier.

[63] **brake**
brambles.

[64] **Lends**
provides.

[70]
Are dangerous for the wandering children of the poor.

[72] **bugloss**
'The herb ox-tongue', Johnson, *Dictionary*.

[73] **Hardy**
bold, strong.

[74] **mallow**
'a common wild plant having hairy stems and leaves, and deeply cleft reddish purple flowers. It is very mucilaginous', *OED*; *slimy mallow* because of the viscous fluid it oozes.

[75] **charlock**
'A weed growing among the corn with a yellow flower', Johnson, *Dictionary*; *throws a shade* prevents from growing.

[76] **tares**
an injurious weed growing among corn.

[77] **mingled tints**
the blended hues of the weeds and wild plants.

[78] **sad splendour**
'splendour' because of the different colours; 'sad' because the splendour derives from the useless and destructive plants.

[79–84]
Crabbe may have had in mind the following presentations: 'As some fair female, unadorned and plain,/ [. . .] She then shines forth, solicitous to bless,/ In all the glaring impotence of dress./ [. . .] Where the poor houseless shivering female lies./ [. . .] Now lost to all; her friends, her virtue fled,/ Near her betrayer's door she lays her head,/ And pinched with cold, and shrinking from the shower,/ With heavy heart deplores that luckless hour,/ When idly first, ambitious of the town,/ She left her wheel, and robes of country brown', Goldsmith,

The Deserted Village, lines 287, 293–4, 326, 331–6.

[84] **gilds**
covers with brighter matter.

[85] **wild amphibious race**
a periphrastic phrase usually applied to animals; in this instance reductively used for the people who inhabit the shore.

[86] **sullen**
'Gloomy; angry; sluggishly discontented', Johnson, *Dictionary*.

[87] **civil arts and social**
organised modes of community life and conduct.

[87]
Note the syntactical inversion in the line.

[89] **lawless merchant of the main**
coastal smugglers; also pirates.

[94] **played down the setting sun**
continued their games until the sun set; metaphorically, as if their playing overcame the sun.

[97]
Cf. 'When Ajax strives, some rock's vast weight to throw', Pope, *Essay on Criticism*, line 370.

[98] **artful stripling**
skilled, though weak and puny.

[99] **foiled**
defeated.

[102] **freighted**
loaded; cf. 'loads of freighted ore', Goldsmith, *The Deserted Village*, line 269; *pinnace* a small boat, often in attendance on a larger vessel.

[104] **pathless waste**
Cf. 'No pathless waste, or undiscovered shore', Johnson, *London*, line 170.

[105] **straggling**
without clear direction.

[108] **lawless passport**
illegal thoroughfare.

[111]
Cf. 'Here malice, rapine, accident conspire', Johnson, *London*, line 13.

[113] **finny tribe**
periphrasis for fish.

[114] **yearly dinner**
given at Christmas by landlords to their tenants; *septennial* parliamentary elections were held every seven

years. Cf. 'With weekly libels and septennial ale', Johnson, *The Vanity of
Human Wishes*, line 97.

[117] **vent'rous**
hazardous.

[130] **poor**
inadequate; *protection* shelter.

[132] **spare**
scanty.

[137]
Cf. 'To see profusion that he must
not share', Goldsmith, *The Deserted
Village*, line 310.

[144]
The hot weather of July and August.
Sirius, the 'dog-star', it was believed,
caused this hot season; cf. 'The dog-
star rages', Pope, *An Epistle to Dr
Arbuthnot*, line 3; 'Nor dog-day's
parching heat that splits the rocks',
Dryden, *Georgics*, ii, 520.

[154] **tribe**
a distinct body of people.

[157] **Contend**
struggle with, combat; see also line
160; the literal sense occurs in 'The
young contending as the old surveyed', Goldsmith, *The Deserted
Village*, line 20.

[169] **stinted**
limited to an assigned portion.

[173]
See line 56.

[181] **Life's latest comforts**
the main supports of old age.

[184] **rude**
crudely made.

[190] **Full many a prize**
Cf. 'Full many a gem', Gray, *Elegy*,
line 53.

[191] **allowed**
praised, approved.

[196] **Alternate masters**
others who have become masters
now.

[197] **Urge**
press on.

[200]
Cf. 'Oft have we seen him at the peep
of dawn', Gray, *Elegy*, line 98.

[230] **putrid vapours**
foul or noxious exhalations; *flagging*
without energy to ascend.

[247] **plucks**
forces; *scrap* a little piece, a frag-
ment.

[250] **fantastic**
imaginary.

[251] **jarring nerve**
an unpleasing, obtrusive sensation;
baffles disturbs, destroys.

[254] **sad**
'vexatious', Johnson, *Dictionary*.

[264] **vile bands**
unsightly materials used for binding.

[265] **lath**
'A small long piece of wood used to
support the tiles of houses', Johnson,
Dictionary.

[268] **matted flock**
bed made of ragged cloth.

[270] **cordial cup**
reviving drink.

[276] **Anon**
quickly; *quaintly* exactly, scru-
pulously.

[277] **conceit**
self-centred, fond of himself.

[279] **speaks**
declares; cf. 'And the loud laugh that
spoke the vacant mind', Goldsmith,
The Deserted Village, line 122.

[280] **gazing throng**
the people of the poor-house. The
phrase is in the manner of contemporary periphrases.

[281]
His eyes declare his power over their
health and their lives.

[282] **potent**
powerful.

[284] **drowsy bench**
inattentive, sleeping judges.

[287] **sapient sneer**
wise and contemptuous look.

[292] **inured**
used to, habituated to.

[293] **remonstrance**
protest.

[294]
syntactical inversion.

[298] **Fain**
gladly.

[299] **title**
entitlement, claim.

[301] **holy stranger**
the parish priest who does not care to visit the poor house unless called.

[303] **'passing rich with forty pounds a year'**
Cf. 'And passing rich with forty pounds a year', Goldsmith, *The Deserted Village*, line 142. Goldsmith draws an idealised portrait of the village preacher.

[321] **Up yonder hill**
Cf. 'Up yonder hill the village murmur rose', Goldsmith, *The Deserted Village*, line 114; *sadly* heavy with grief.

[330] **Sedately torpid**
sluggish with indifference; *devoutly dumb* silent, apparently out of religious duty.

[340] **mingled relics**
the poor are buried in a common grave.

[341] **The bell tolls late**
Cf. 'The curfew tolls the knell of parting day', Gray, *Elegy*, line 1; *the moping owl flies round* Cf. 'The moping owl does to the moon complain', Gray, *Elegy*, line 10.

[343] **weightier care**
more important concerns.

WILLIAM COWPER

(1731–1800)

William Cowper was born in 1731. His childhood was on the whole a happy one. Six good years at Westminster School gave him a conservative education, devoted to the classics. He was admitted to the Middle Temple in 1754 and in 1757 joined the more fashionable Inner Temple.

By 1760 he belonged to a group of London literati who formed the Nonsense Club and were known as 'the Geniuses'. These were still happy years in Cowper's life. In 1763, however, he suffered a complete mental and physical breakdown that was marked by several attempts at suicide. One of the causes for his disturbed state of mind may have been his unfulfilled love for his cousin Theadora, whom he had addressed in his poems as 'Delia'. He experienced a 'conversion' in 1764, by his own account, on reading Romans 3: 25: 'In a moment I believed, and received the gospel'. At this time he espoused Evangelical Christianity.

Cowper seriously began writing poetry only after the age of 50. His *Olney Hymns* (1779) are Evangelical poems written in response to the faith he had espoused for a brief period. A relapse into insanity in 1773 was followed by a slow recovery from 1779 onwards when Cowper experienced a revival of his creativity. *Poems by William Cowper of the Inner Temple, Esq.*, was published in 1782. Written under the influence of Pope, the work's moral tone and gentle satire appealed to Samuel Johnson. *The Task* was published in 1785. *The Castaway*, written in March 1799, marks the end of a fairly short literary career. William Cowper died in 1800. In his last years, despite his fame, Cowper continued to suffer from troubled and unhappy states of mind.

Further Reading

The standard edition of Cowper's poems is H.S. Milford (ed.), corrected by Norma Russell, *Cowper: Poetical Works* (1934; London: Oxford University Press, 1967). A selections is also available in Norman Nicholson (ed.), *A Choice of Cowper's Verse* (London: Faber and Faber, 1975).

Cowper has been well served by biographers. David Cecil's *The Stricken Deer* (London: Constable, 1929) remains very readable, while Charles Ryskamp's *William Cowper of the Inner Temple, Esq.* is well researched (Cambridge: Cambridge University Press, 1959), as is James King's *William Cowper: A Biography* (Durham, NC: Duke University Press, 1986). A good general account is provided by William N. Free: *William Cowper* (New York: Twayne, 1970). Three more recent critical books deserve mention: Bill Hutchings, *The Poetry of William Cowper* (London: Croom Helm, 1983); Martin Priestman, *Cowper's Task: Structure and Influence* (Cambridge: Cambridge University Press, 1983); and Vincent Newey, *Cowper's Poetry: A Critical Reassessment* (Totowa, NJ: Barnes and Noble, 1982).

40 / *The Poplar-Field*

The poplars are felled, farewell to the shade
And the whispering sound of the cool colonnade,
The winds play no longer, and sing in the leaves,
Nor Ouse on his bosom their image receives.

Twelve years have elapsed since I first took a view   5
Of my favourite field and the bank where they grew,
And now in the grass behold they are laid,
And the tree is my seat that once lent me a shade.

The blackbird has fled to another retreat
Where the hazels afford him a screen from the heat,   10
And the scene where his melody charmed me before,
Resounds with his sweet-flowing ditty no more.

My fugitive years are all hasting away,
And I must ere long lie as lowly as they,
With a turf on my breast, and a stone at my head,   15
Ere another such grove shall arise in its stead.

'Tis a sight to engage me, if any thing can,
To muse on the perishing pleasures of man;
Though his life be a dream, his enjoyments, I see,
Have a being less durable even than he.   20

Cowper's poems seem to have originated in personal experience. Of *The Poplar-Field* he wrote to Lady Hesketh (Harriot Cowper, sister of Theadora):

There was indeed, some time since, in a neighbouring parish called Lavendon, a field one side of which formed a terrace, and the other was planted with poplars, at whose foot ran the Ouse, that I used to account a little paradise: but the poplars have been felled, and the scene has suffered so much by the loss, that though still in point of prospect beautiful, it has not charm sufficient to attract me now.

[2] **colonnade**
a series of trees.
[12] **Resounds**
echoes; *ditty* song.

[13] **fugitive**
apt to fly away, quickly passing.
[18] **muse**
to ponder, to reflect on; *perishing* of short duration, apt to decay.

————◇————

41 /   From *The Task, Book III*

The Garden

As one who long in thickets and in brakes
Entangled, winds now this way and now that
His devious course uncertain, seeking home;
Or having long in miry ways been foiled
And sore discomfited, from slough to slough   5
Plunging, and half despairing of escape,
If chance at length he find a green-sward smooth
And faithful to the foot, his spirits rise,
He chirrups brisk his ear-erecting steed,
And winds his way with pleasure and with ease: 10
So I, designing other themes, and called

T'adorn the sofa with eulogium due,
To tell its slumbers and to paint its dreams,
Have rambled wide. In country, city, seat
Of academic fame (howe'er deserved),   15
Long held, and scarcely disengaged at last.
But now with pleasant pace, a cleanlier road
I mean to tread: I feel myself at large,
Courageous, and refreshed for future toil,
If toil await me, or if dangers new.   20

.   .   .   .

Domestic happiness, thou only bliss
Of Paradise that has survived the fall!
Though few now taste thee unimpaired and pure,
Or tasting, long enjoy thee, too infirm
Or too incautious to preserve thy sweets   25
Unmixed with drops of bitter, which neglect
Or temper sheds into thy crystal cup.
Thou art the nurse of virtue. In thine arms
She smiles, appearing, as in truth she is,
Heaven born, and destined to the skies again.   30
Thou art not known where pleasure is adored,
That reeling goddess with the zoneless waist
And wandering eyes, still leaning on the arm
Of novelty, her fickle frail support:
For thou art meek and constant, hating change,   35
And finding in the calm of truth-tried love
Joys that her stormy raptures never yield.
Forsaking thee, what shipwreck have we made
Of honour, dignity, and fair renown,
'Till prostitution elbows us aside   40
In all our crowded streets, and senates seem
Convened for purposes of empire less,
Than to release th'adultress from her bond.

.   .   .   .

I was a stricken deer that left the herd
Long since; with many an arrow deep infixt   45
My panting side was charged when I withdrew
To seek a tranquil death in distant shades.

There was I found by one who had himself
Been hurt by th'archers. In his side he bore
And in his hands and feet the cruel scars.　50
With gentle force soliciting the darts
He drew them forth, and healed and bade me live.
Since then, with few associates, in remote
And silent woods I wander, far from those
My former partners of the peopled scene;　55
With few associates, and not wishing more.
Here much I ruminate, as much I may,
With other views of men and manners now
Than once, and others of a life to come.
I see that all are wanderers, gone astray,　60
Each in his own delusions; they are lost
In chase of fancied happiness, still wooed
And never won. Dream after dream ensues,
And still they dream that they shall still succeed,
And still are disappointed; rings the world　65
With the vain stir. I sum up half mankind,
And add two-thirds of the remaining half,
And find the total of their hopes and fears
Dreams, empty dreams.

.　.　.　.　.　.　.

God never meant that man should scale the heavens　70
By strides of human wisdom. In his works
Though wondrous, he commands us in his word
To seek him rather, where his mercy shines.
The mind indeed enlightened from above
Views him in all. Ascribes to the grand cause　75
The grand effect. Acknowledges with joy
His manner, and with rapture tastes his style:
But never yet did philosophic tube
That brings the planets home into the eye
Of observation, and discovers, else　80
Not visible, his family of worlds,
Discover him that rules them; such a veil
Hangs over mortal eyes, blind from the birth
And dark in things divine. Full often too
Our wayward intellect, the more we learn　85

Of nature, overlooks her author more,
From instrumental causes proud to draw
Conclusions retrograde and mad mistake.
But if his word once teach us, shoot a ray
Through all the heart's dark chambers, and reveal   90
Truths undiscerned but by that holy light,
Then all is plain. Philosophy baptised
In the pure fountain of eternal love
Has eyes indeed; and viewing all she sees
As meant to indicate a God to man,   95
Gives him his praise, and forfeits not her own.
Learning has borne such fruit in other days
On all her branches. Piety has found
Friends in the friends of science, and true prayer
Has flowed from lips wet with Castalian dews,   100
Such was thy wisdom, Newton, childlike sage;
Sagacious reader of the works of God,
And in his word sagacious. Such too thine,
Milton, whose genius had angelic wings,
And fed on manna. And such thine, in whom   105
Our British Themis gloried with just cause,
Immortal Hale! for deep discernment praised
And sound integrity not more, than famed
For sanctity of manners undefiled.

All flesh is grass, and all its glory fades   110
Like the fair flower dishevelled in the wind;
Riches have wings, and grandeur is a dream;
The man we celebrate must find a tomb,
And we that worship him, ignoble graves.
Nothing is proof against the general curse   115
Of vanity, that seizes all below.
The only amaranthine flower on earth
Is virtue, th'only lasting treasure, truth.
But what is truth? 'twas Pilate's question put
To Truth itself, that deigned him no reply.   120
And wherefore? will not God impart his light
To them that ask it? – Freely – 'tis his joy,
His glory, and his nature to impart.
But to the proud, uncandid, insincere
Or negligent enquirer, not a spark.   125

What's that which brings contempt upon a book
And him who writes it, though the style be neat,
The method clear, and argument exact?
That makes a minister in holy things
The joy of many and the dread of more,   130
His name a theme for praise and for reproach?
That while it gives us worth in God's account,
Depreciates and undoes us in our own?
What pearl is it that rich men cannot buy,
That learning is too proud to gather up: 135
But which the poor and despised of all
Seek and obtain, and often find unsought?
Tell me, and I will tell thee, what is truth.

. . . .

Who loves a garden, loves a green-house too.
Unconscious of a less propitious clime   140
There blooms exotic beauty, warm and snug,
While the winds whistle, and the snows descend.
The spiry myrtle with unwithering leaf
Shines there and flourishes. The golden boast
Of Portugal and western India there,   145
The ruddier orange and the paler lime
Peep through their polished foliage at the storm,
And seem to smile at what they need not fear.
Th'amomum there with intermingling flowers
And cherries hangs her twigs. Geranium boasts   150
Her crimson honours, and the spangled beau
Ficoides, glitters bright the winter long.
All plants of every leaf that can endure
The winter's frown if screened from his shrewd bite,
Live there and prosper. Those Ausonia claims,   155
Levantine regions these; the Azores send
Their jessamine, her jessamine remote
Caffraia; foreigners from many lands
They form one social shade, as if convened
By magic summons of th'Orphean lyre.   160
Yet just arrangement, rarely brought to pass
But by a master's hand, disposing well
The gay diversities of leaf and flower,

Must lend its aid to illustrate all their charms,
And dress the regular yet various scene.   165
Plant behind plant aspiring, in the van
The dwarfish, in the rear retired, but still
Sublime above the rest, the statelier stand.
So once were ranged the sons of ancient Rome,
A noble show! while Roscius trod the stage;   170
And so, while Garrick as renowned as he,
The sons of Albion; fearing each to lose
Some note of nature's music from his lips,
And covetous of Shakespeare's beauty seen
In every flash of his far-beaming eye.   175

.   .   .   .

My charmer is not mine alone; my sweets
And she that sweetens all my bitters too,
Nature, enchanting nature, in whose form
And lineaments divine I trace a hand
That errs not, and find raptures still renewed,   180
Is free to all men, universal prize.
Strange that so fair a creature should yet want
Admirers, and be destined to divide
With meaner objects, ev'n the few she finds.
Stripped of her ornaments, her leaves and flowers,   185
She loses all her influence. Cities then
Attract us, and neglected nature pines
Abandoned, as unworthy of our love.
But are not wholesome airs, though unperfumed
By roses, and clear suns though scarcely felt,   190
And groves if unharmonious, yet secure
From clamour, and whose very silence charms,
To be preferred to smoke, to the eclipse
That metropolitan volcanoes make,
Whose Stygian throats breathe darkness all day long,   195
And to the stir of commerce, driving slow,
And thundering loud, with his ten thousand wheels?
They would be, were not madness in the head
And folly in the heart; were England now
What England was, plain, hospitable, kind,   200
And undebauched. But we have bid farewell

491

To all the virtues of those better days,
And all their honest pleasures. Mansions once
Knew their own masters, and laborious hinds
Who had survived the father, served the son.   205
Now the legitimate and rightful Lord
Is but a transient guest, newly arrived
And soon to be supplanted. He that saw
His patrimonial timber cast its leaf,
Sells the last scantling, and transfers the price   210
To some shrewd sharper, ere it buds again.
Estates are landscapes, gazed upon a while,
Then advertised, and auctioneered away.   ·
The country starves, and they that feed th'o'ercharged
And surfeited lewd town with her fair dues,   215
By a just judgement strip and starve themselves.
The wings that waft our riches out of sight
Grow on the gamester's elbows, and th'alert
And nimble motion of those restless joints
That never tire, soon fans them all away.   220
Improvement too, the idol of the age,
Is fed with many a victim. Lo, he comes –
The omnipotent magician, Brown, appears.
Down falls the venerable pile, th'abode
Of our forefathers, a grave whiskered race,   225
But tasteless. Springs a palace in its stead,
But in a distant spot, where more exposed
It may enjoy th'advantage of the north,
And aguish east, till time shall have transformed
Those naked acres to a sheltering grove.   230
He speaks. The lake in front becomes a lawn,
Woods vanish, hills subside, and valleys rise,
And streams, as if created for his use,
Pursue the track of his directing wand
Sinuous or straight, now rapid and now slow,   235
Now murmuring soft, now roaring in cascades,
E'en as he bids. The enraptured owner smiles.
'Tis finished. And yet finished as it seems,
Still wants a grace, the loveliest it could show,
A mine to satisfy the enormous cost.   240
Drained to the last poor item of his wealth,
He sighs, departs, and leaves the accomplished plan

That he has touched, retouched, many a long day
Laboured, and many a night pursued in dreams,
Just when it meets his hopes, and proves the heaven   245
He wanted, for a wealthier to enjoy.

.   .   .   .

   Ambition, avarice, penury incurred
By endless riot; vanity, the lust
Of pleasure and variety, dispatch,
As duly as the swallows disappear,   250
The world of wandering knights and squires to town.
London engulfs them all. The shark is there
And the shark's prey. The spendthrift and the leech
That sucks him. There the sycophant and he
Who with bare-headed and obsequious bows   255
Begs a warm office, doomed to a cold jail
And groat per diem if his patron frown.
The levee swarms, as if in golden pomp
Were charactered on every statesman's door,
'Battered and bankrupt fortunes mended here.'   260
These are the charms that sully and eclipse
The charms of nature. 'Tis the cruel gripe
That lean hard-handed poverty inflicts,
The hope of better things, the chance to win,
The wish to shine, the thirst to be amused,   265
That at the sound of winter's hoary wing,
Unpeople all our counties, of such herds
Of fluttering, loitering, cringing, begging, loose
And wanton vagrants, as make London, vast
And boundless as it is, a crowded coop.   270

   Oh thou resort and mart of all the earth,
Checkered with all complexions of mankind,
And spotted with all crimes; in whom I see
Much that I love, and more that I admire,
And all that I abhor; thou freckled fair   275
That pleasest and yet shockest me, I can laugh
And I can weep, can hope, and can despond,
Feel wrath and pity when I think on thee!
Ten righteous would have saved a city once,

And thou hast many righteous. – Well for thee –   280
That salt preserves thee; more corrupted else,
And therefore more obnoxious at this hour,
Than Sodom in her day had power to be,
For whom God heard his Abraham plead in vain.

The Task (1785) was the product of Cowper's response to Lady Austen's suggestion to write about 'the sofa'. Cowper referred to her as 'the muse who had
inspired the subject'.
Cowper began his poem with the mock-epic opening: 'I sing the sofa', and
proceeded to write a little over five thousand lines of poetry covering six books.
He did not stick to a regular design, but worked on the then fashionable principle of association. By his own claim the poem falls into the country-versus-city
category. As he wrote to William Unwin on 10 October 1784:

> If the work cannot boast a regular plan . . . it may yet boast that the reflections
> are naturally suggested always by the preceding passage, and that . . . the
> whole has one tendency: to discountenance the modern enthusiasm after a
> London life, and to recommend rural ease and leisure as friendly to the cause
> of piety and virtue.

In the same letter Cowper went on to disavow imitation and to assert authenticity for experiences in the poem: 'My descriptions are all from nature. Not one
of them second-handed. My delineations of the heart are from my own
experience.' Clearly, even within the conventional country–city formula
Cowper's poetics extends to ideas of self-expression and the validity of the
individual's interpretation.
Cowper experimented with a number of forms in his writings. *John Gilpin* is
probably one of the best known comic ballads. Today vastly popular with church
congregations, Cowper's hymns, in his own day, were sung at private religious
meetings. *The Task* is a fluid combination of genres: the English Georgic like
Gay's *Trivia*, the descriptive nature poem like Thomson's *The Seasons*, mock-
Miltonic verse like John Philips's *The Splendid Shilling*, all go into its making.
In his expression Cowper aimed to be 'as clear as possible'. He felt that per-
spicuity was all the more necessary in blank verse in order to offset its syntactical
obscurity.

[1] **thickets**
a close wood; *brakes* brambles.
[3] **devious**
wandering, rambling, erring; *devious
course uncertain* note the adjectives
placed on either side of the noun; a
characteristic of Milton's style. Cf.
'dun air sublime', Milton, *Paradise
Lost*, iii, 72; 'circumfluous waters
calm', *Paradise Lost*, vii, 270.
[4] **miry ways**
muddy, slushy paths; *foiled* defeated.
[5] **sore**
sorely, painfully; *discomfited* discon-

certed; *slough* a deep miry place, a
bog; signifying spiritual despair as in
Bunyan.
[7] **chance**
by chance; *at length* after a long time;
green-sward the turf on which grass
grows, a grassy bank.
[8] **faithful to the foot**
firm, without any concealed declivities.
[9] **chirrups**
makes a sound that urges a horse;
brisk briskly; *ear-erecting* as the
master chirrups the steed erects its
ears.

[1–10]
A long simile in the epic mode.

[11] **designing other themes**
planning or following other subjects.

[12] **eulogium**
praise, encomium.

[16] **disengaged**
set free from.

[17] **cleanlier road**
a purer pursuit.

[18] **at large**
without restraint.

[23] **taste**
experience, have perception of; **unimpaired** undiminished; **pure** not sullied.

[24] **enjoy**
take or keep possession of; cf. 'and he who to enjoy/ Plato's Elysium, leaped into the sea', Milton, *Paradise Lost*, iii, 471–2.

[25] **sweets**
pleasures.

[26] **bitter**
pain or hurt. Cowper extends the idea of 'taste' in its sense of 'relish by the palate'.

[27] **temper**
in the sense of 'ill-temper'; **sheds** spills.

[28] **nurse of virtue**
protectress and nourisher of moral goodness.

[31] **pleasure**
loose gratification; **adored** worshipped, paid homage to.

[32] **reeling**
staggering; **zoneless** unbelted, without a girdle.

[33] **wandering**
roving, errant.

[34] **fickle**
inconstant, subject to change; **frail** weak, liable to error; **support** prop; **fickle frail support** a gentle echo of 'Herself, though fairest unsupported flower', *Paradise Lost*, ix, 432.

[37–8]
Cowper sustains the metaphor of storm and shipwreck.

[39] **fair renown**
honest reputation.

[44] **stricken**
wounded in a chase.

[45] **deep infixt**
driven in deep.

[46] **charged**
overloaded with arrows.

[45–6]
Note the syntactical inversion.

[48–50]
Referring to the wounds of Christ.

[51] **soliciting**
removing carefully, gently.

[57] **ruminate**
meditate, think over again and again.

[64–5] **still**
always, ever.

[65–6] **rings the world/ With the vain stir**
syntactical inversion in the style of Milton.

[70] **scale**
ascend to, measure.

[71] **strides**
long steps.

[71–2] **works ... wondrous**
See 'O God, thou hast taught me from my youth; and hitherto have I declared thy wondrous works', Psalms 71: 17; 'Hearken unto this, O Job: stand still and consider the wondrous works of God'; Job 37: 14.

[72] **wondrous**
admirable, creating a sense of wonder.

[71–3]
Cowper directs the reader to God's 'word', as opposed to a deistic celebration of his 'works' or the created world.

[75–6] **Ascribes to the grand cause/ The grand effect**
attributes to the original efficient or prime mover the consequence. The repetition of the word 'grand' introduces the idea of succession.

[77] **manner**
form or method; **style** mode of expression, custom.

[78] **philosophic tube**
referring here to the telescope. Milton, too, referred to the telescope, and Galileo's particular use of it, in *Paradise Lost*, i, 286–91: ' ... the broad circumference/ Hung on his shoulders like the moon, whose orb/ Through

optic glass the Tuscan artist views/ At evening from the top of Fesole,/ Or in Valdarno, to descry new lands,/ Rivers or mountains in her spotty globe.'

[79] **home**
to the point designed.

[80] **discovers**
brings to light; makes known.

[81] **his**
referring to God; *family* class or species; *family of worlds* group of heavenly bodies.

[70–84]
Cf. 'heaven is for thee too high/ To know what passes there; be lowly wise:/ Think only on what concerns thee and thy being;/ Dream not of other worlds', *Paradise Lost*, viii, 172–8; also: 'That not to know at large of things remote/ From use, obscure and subtle, but to know/ That which before us lies in daily life,/ Is the prime wisdom, what is more, is fume,/ Or emptiness, or fond impertinence,/ And renders us in things that most concern/ Unpractised, unprepared, and still to seek./ Therefore from this high pitch let us descend/ A lower flight, and speak of things at hand/Useful', *Paradise Lost*, viii, 191–200. Cowper is writing in the Renaissance tradition of the distrust of astronomical investigation. Swift, in the third book of *Gulliver's Travels*, and Johnson in his chapter on the mad astronomer in *Rasselas* expressed similar views.

[84] **dark**
lacking in knowledge of; ignorant; *Full often* very often.

[85] **wayward**
perverse; wrongheaded.

[86] **nature**
'the creative and regulative physical power which is conceived of as operating in the material world and as the immediate cause of all its phenomena', *OED*; 'the state or operation of the material world', Johnson, *Dictionary*; *author* God.

[87] **instrumental**
subordinate, merely means to an end;

causes that which produces an end or result.

[88] **Conclusions**
'Collections from propositions premised; consequence', Johnson, *Dictionary*; *retrograde* moving backward.

[87–8] **proud to draw/ Conclusions retrograde**
scientific studies, divorced from the revealed world of God, led to false knowledge, pride and mental derangement.

[89] **shoot**
discharge, send forth with speed and force; *ray* a beam of light, corporeal or intellectual.

[90] **dark**
without light, unenlightened, ignorant; see line 84.

[91] **undiscerned**
not distinguished; *holy light* divine illumination; cf. 'Hail, holy light, offspring of heaven first-born,/ Or of the eternal co-eternal beam', *Paradise Lost*, iii, 1–2. Cowper affirms that divine illumination is to found through God's 'word'.

[92] **Philosophy**
science; *baptised* administered the sacrament with holy water; the image is extended to the 'fountain' of the next line.

[95] **indicate**
to show.

[96] **him**
God; *forfeits not* does not lose.

[97–8]
referring by satiric inversion to the biblical fruit of the tree of the knowledge of good and evil, that led to the Fall.

[100] **Castalian dews**
poetic inspiration associated with the Castalian spring at the foot of Mount Parnassus.

[106] **Themis**
the Greek goddess who was a personification of justice. Mother of Prometheus and, by Zeus, mother of the Seasons.

[107] **Hale**
Sir Matthew Hale (1609–76), author

of religious and legal works; *discernment* having the power to distinguish, to understand.

[111] **dishevelled**
disordered.

[110–16]
Everything is subject to decay; see 'The boast of heraldry, the pomp of power,/ And all that beauty, all that wealth e'er gave,/ Awaits alike th'inevitable hour,/ The paths of glory lead but to the grave', Gray, *Elegy*, 33–6.

[117] **amaranthine flower**
the imaginary flower that was immortal.

[119] **Pilate's question**
See 'Pilate saith unto him, What is truth? And when he had said this, he went out again unto the Jews, and saith unto them, I find in him no fault at all', John 18: 38.

[119–20] **put/ To Truth itself**
addressed to Jesus Christ.

[120] **deigned him no reply**
did not think him worthy of an answer.

[121] **And wherefore?**
And why?; *impart* to give, to bestow.

[124] **uncandid**
disingenuous, deceitful.

[125] **negligent enquirer**
heedless, habitually inattentive.

[127] **neat**
elegant, but not elevated.

[128] **method**
order, organisation; *exact* accurate.

[126–31]
Pose a series of rhetorical questions, broadly expressing the view that the learned, those with a religious education, and the wealthy cannot necessarily identify what is good. The 'poor and the despised' often find unsought what those imbued with a sense of their own importance never do.

[132] **account**
estimation.

[133] **depreciates**
brings down the value of.

[134] **pearl**
something invaluable; metaphor-ically, something of spiritual worth that cannot be bought with material wealth.

[134]
Cf. 'Again, the kingdom of heaven is like unto a merchant man, seeking goodly pearls: Who when he had found one pearl of great price, went and sold all that he had, and bought it', Matthew 13: 45–6.

[140] **Unconscious**
unaware; *less propitious clime* a less favourable climate.

[141] **exotic**
belonging to foreign lands.

[142] **descend**
fall.

[143] **spiry**
curled.

[144] **Shines**
is gay or resplendent; *golden boast* a typical transferred epithet, the 'golden' in fact applicable to the 'orange' of line 146.

[149] **amomum**
an aromatic plant, though Johnson glosses it as 'a sort of fruit', *Dictionary*.

[151] **crimson honours**
periphrasis for flowers.

[152] **Ficoides**
a botanical name applied to the ice-plant.

[154] **screened from his shrewd bite**
protected from winter's dangerous effect. The poet works on an idea similar to 'frost-bite'.

[155] **Ausonia**
Italy.

[158] **Caffraia**
South Africa.

[159] **convened**
assembled.

[160] **Orphean lyre**
the playing of the lyre by Orpheus, the legendary Greek musician, charmed all the animals and plants.

[161] **just**
orderly, well-proportioned.

[162] **disposing**
arranging, managing.

[163] **diversities**
different varieties.

[164] **illustrate**
to elucidate.

[165] **regular yet various**
made up of many different kinds, but well-ordered, or well-arranged.

[166] **aspiring**
rising; *van* the first line, or front.

[167] **dwarfish**
small ones; *retired* withdrawn.

[168] **Sublime above the rest**
exalted by nature, higher than the others; *statelier* the loftier ones, taller and more majestic.

[139–68]
The garden passage has all the connotations of the world as God's garden with God as the chief gardener; the passage harks back to the biblical Garden of Eden and the many English renderings of it, the most important being Milton's in *Paradise Lost*. Cowper emphasises the orderly and well-arranged nature of the garden, as well as its multiplicity and diversity. Cowper may be accused of what is today called 'Orientalism', politically reductive presentations of distant parts of the empire, which are metonymically signified by a single plant or tree. Pope, in his description of Belinda's dressing table in *The Rape of the Lock*, i, 133–8, also used this method with self-conscious reductiveness: 'This casket India's glowing gems unlocks,/ And all Arabia breathes from yonder box./ The tortoise here and elephant unite,/ Transformed to combs, the speckled and the white./ Here files of pins extend their shining rows,/ Puffs, powders, patches, Bibles, billet-doux.' The last two lines make clear Pope's general satiric context. Cowper may again be seen as 'subjecting' distant parts of the world to the Graeco-Roman civilisation when he invokes the image of Orpheus as calling together plants and trees from different regions. This is in spite of his well-known pronouncements against racial discrimination, slavery and colonialism in the second book of *The Task*, and elsewhere.

[170] **Roscius**
Quintus Roscius Gallus (died 62 BC), a famous Roman comic actor. The name of Roscius came to be used in English literature for an actor generally, not just in comedy.

[171] **Garrick**
David Garrick, famous London actor and manager of Drury Lane theatre. A friend of Samuel Johnson's, he was sometimes referred to as the English Roscius.

[172] **Albion**
Britain.

[173] **Some note of nature's music**
Shakespeare was widely considered 'the poet of nature' in the eighteenth century; Johnson lent authority to the phrase by his use of it in his *Preface to Shakespeare*. Cowper's phrase could also refer to Garrick's more natural and less stilted style on the stage.

[174–5]
Garrick staged several of Shakespeare's plays and in his time was considered the 'restorer' of Shakespeare from the ravages of the seventeenth-century adapters. In retrospect, however, we feel that Garrick himself offered a considerably mangled Shakespeare interlaced with operatic scenes and music.

[177] **sweetens**
makes less painful, makes pleasing; *bitters* unpleasant experiences.

[178] **form**
'Form is the essential, special modification of the matter, so as to give it such a peculiar manner of existence', Johnson, *Dictionary*.

[177–8]
a conventional personification of Nature as a woman.

[179] **lineaments**
'Feature; discriminating mark in the form', Johnson, *Dictionary*.

[179–80]
Cowper may be indebted to Pope's 'Unerring nature, still divinely bright,/ One clear, unchanged, and universal light' (*Essay on Criticism*, lines 70–1) for his phraseology, but he emphasises the unerring hand of God

as different from Pope's 'unerring nature'.

[183] **divide**
share.

[182–4]
It is odd that Nature, though so beautiful, should have so few admirers, and even those that she does have she is compelled to share with others much beneath her.

[185]
Cowper shifts to a very restricted conception of Nature in his contrast of the country with the city.

[193–4] **the eclipse/ That metropolitan volcanoes make**
the fog caused by the smoke of the city factories.

[195] **Stygian**
hellish and dark, like the river Styx, the principal river of the underworld.

[196] **commerce**
trade; see 'trade's unfeeling train,/ Usurp the land and dispossess the swain', Goldsmith, *The Deserted Village*, lines 63–4.

[197] **ten thousand wheels**
Cf. 'To see ten thousand baneful arts combined', Goldsmith, *The Deserted Village*, line 311.

[199–201]
The passage is in the tradition of nostalgia for England's past. In Johnson's *London* there are many references to a golden age of the past in contrast to present decadence; see 'In pleasing dreams the blissful age renew,/ And call Britannia's glories back to view', *London*, lines 25–6; and 'A single jail in Alfred's golden reign,/ Could half the nation's criminals contain', lines 248–9; see also 'A time there was, ere England's griefs began,/ When every rood of ground maintained its man', Goldsmith, *The Deserted Village*, lines 57–8.

[204] **laborious**
diligent, hardworking; **hinds** peasants.

[206–8]
Cf. 'Some hireling senator's deserted seat', Johnson, *London*, line 213.

Cowper is concerned about the sale of country estates.

[209] **patrimonial timber**
trees planted by his forefathers; *cast its leaf* shed their leaves.

[210] **scantling**
a small bit.

[211] **shrewd sharper**
cunning rascal.

[214–15]
Goldsmith in *The Deserted Village*, lines 309–36, expresses similar resentment against the imbalance between the city and the country in terms of wealth, and the exploitation of the one by the other. See 'Kingdoms by thee, to sickly greatness grown,/ Boast of a florid vigour not their own./ At every draught more large and large they grow,/ A bloated mass of rank unwieldy woe', *The Deserted Village*, lines 389–92.

[217] **waft**
carry through the air.

[218] **gamester**
gambler, one viciously addicted to play. Generally used in a morally deprecatory sense.

[220] **them**
referring to 'riches' in line 217.

[221] **Improvement**
'to advance a thing nearer to perfection', Johnson, *Dictionary*. Here used in connection with landscaping and the laying out of gardens through which estates were redesigned for better prospects and beauty. Such 'improvements' were conceived as collaborations between the artist and nature. They also aimed to be morally instructive; *idol of the age* in the eighteenth century landscaping had become a passion. Cowper's stance is satiric.

[222] **Is fed with many a victim**
landscaping is personified as a monster devouring old-fashioned estates.

[223] **omnipotent**
generally used for God; see 'God omnipotent', *Paradise Lost*, ix, 927; here in satirical juxtaposition with 'magician'; *Brown* Lancelot 'Capability' Brown (1715–83), the

famous landscape gardener of the time.

[224] **venerable pile**
the edifice or building which ought to be treated with reverence.

[225] **grave whiskered race**
the older generation of people; this is a periphrasis in keeping with the genus plus differentiae formula of the period, for example, 'household feathery people' for 'birds' in *Winter*, line 87. Cowper's use here is tinged with the mockery with which the older generation is viewed, for the phrase conjures up the image of mice.

[226] **tasteless**
lacking in intellectual distinction.

[224–6] **Down falls . . . Springs**
sharp contrast satirising the activity of the landscape gardeners.

[227] **exposed**
laid open or bare.

[228] **th'advantage of the north**
superiority over the northern side, where, in fact, the 'palace' is more vulnerable to the cold wintry winds.

[229] **aguish**
alternately hot and cold. Again lines 228–9 are critical of the advantages of the new prospect; *till time shall have transformed* finally there is no getting away from the gradual benefits of natural growth.

[231] **He speaks**
'Capability' Brown gives the command.

[231–7]
A parody of the act of creation. Brown proceeds to work against the grain of nature, hence hills 'subside' and valleys 'rise'.

[234] **directing wand**
extending the metaphor of the 'omnipotent magician'.

[235] **sinuous**
bending.

[240–6]
The enormous cost of landscaping which also diminishes the productive capacity of the land causes the landlord to desert his newly designed estate, even as it is completed.

[247–52]
In the context of this list of vices Johnson's *London* comes to mind. Cowper paints the picture of a moral 'winter' in which the residents of the country, like birds of passage, disappear.

[251] **The world of wandering knights and squires**
a deliberately archaic picture emphasising the passing away of the old order.

[252] **London engulfs them all**
Cf. 'London! the needy villains' gen'ral home./ The common sewer of Paris and of Rome' ('sewer' is the reading in the 1787 version), Johnson, *London*, lines 93–4.

[252–3] **The shark is there/ And the shark's prey**
The city is depicted in terms of sharks that devour man, and human beings as being fatally attracted to them.

[254–5]
Cf. the picture of the sycophant in *London*, line 111: 'Obsequious, artful, voluble and gay'.

[256–7] **doomed to a cold jail/ And groat per diem if his patron frown**
Cf. 'There mark what ills the scholar's life assail,/ Toil, envy, want, the patron and the jail', Johnson, *The Vanity of Human Wishes*, lines 159–60; *groat* a four-penny coin.

[258] **levee**
those who crowd round a man of power in the morning; *swarms* crowded, like a swarm of bees.

[259] **charactered**
inscribed, written.

[262] **gripe**
hard seizure of the hand, clasp, crushing power.

[263] **lean**
poor, thin; *hard-handed* continuing the idea in 'gripe'.

[265]
The staccato rhythm of this line creates a satiric effect. Cf. 'Athirst for wealth, and burning to be great;/ . . ./They mount, they shine, evaporate, and fall', Johnson, *The Vanity of Human Wishes*, lines 74, 76.

[266] **hoary**
whitish.
[268] **fluttering**
moving in a disorderly way.
[268-9] **loose/ And wanton**
unrestrained.
[270] **coop**
a cage for animals like hens and sheep.
[271]
Addressing the city of London; *resort* confluence; *mart* market, place for public traffic.
[275] **freckled fair**
blemished but beautiful, generally referring to a woman. Here the phrase personifies London as a desirable but dangerous woman.

[279]
See 'And he said, Oh let not the Lord be angry, and I will speak yet but this once: Peradventure ten shall be found there. And he said, I will not destroy it for ten's sake', Genesis 18: 32.
[281] **salt**
worked as a preservative. Cowper's use here, in the context of the biblical story about Lot's wife turning into a pillar of salt, is satirical.
[282] **obnoxious**
liable to punishment.
[283-4]
See Genesis 18-19 for the story of the destruction of Sodom and Gomorrah.

---

42 / *The Castaway*

Obscurest night involved the sky,
   Th'Atlantic billows roared;
When such a destined wretch as I,
   Washed headlong from on board,
Of friends, of hope, of all bereft,   5
His floating home for ever left.

No braver chief could Albion boast
   Than he, with whom he went,
Nor ever ship left Albion's coast
   With warmer wishes sent.   10
He loved them both, but both in vain,
Nor him beheld nor her again.

Not long beneath the 'whelming brine,
   Expert to swim, he lay;
Nor soon he felt his strength decline,   15
   Or courage die away;
But waged with death a lasting strife,
Supported by despair of life.

He shouted: nor his friends had failed
    To check the vessel's course,   20
But so the furious blast prevailed,
    That, pitiless perforce,
They left their out-cast mate behind,
And scudded still before the wind.

Some succour yet they could afford;   25
    And, such as storms allow,
The cask, the coop, the floated cord,
    Delayed not to bestow.
But he (they knew) nor ship, nor shore,
Whate'er they gave, should visit more.   30

Nor, cruel as it seemed, could he
    Their haste himself condemn,
Aware that flight, in such a sea,
    Alone could rescue them;
Yet bitter felt it still to die   35
Deserted, and his friends so nigh.

He long survives, who lives an hour
    In ocean, self-upheld:
And so long he, with unspent power,
    His destiny repelled: 40
And ever, as the minutes flew,
Intreated help, or cried – 'Adieu!'

At length his transient respite past,
    His comrades, who before
Had heard his voice in every blast,   45
    Could catch the sound no more.
For then, by toil subdued, he drank
The stifling wave, and then he sank.

No poet wept him: but the page
    Of narrative sincere,   50
That tells his name, his worth, his age,
    Is wet with Anson's tear.
And tears by bards or heroes shed
Alike immortalise the dead.

I therefore purpose not, or dream,   55
  Descanting on his fate,
To give the melancholy theme
  A more enduring date.
But misery still delights to trace
  Its 'semblance in another's case.   60

No voice divine the storm allayed,
  No light propitious shone;
When, snatched from all effectual aid,
  We perished, each alone;
But I beneath a rougher sea,   65
  And whelmed in deeper gulfs than he.

In Richard Walter's *A Voyage Round the World, by (Lord) George Anson* (1748) Cowper found the following account of a sailor's being swept away. This provided him with the central figure of his poem:

> [In a severe storm] one of our ablest seamen was canted over-board; we per-ceived that, notwithstanding the prodigious agitation of the waves, he swam very strong, and it was with the utmost concern that we found ourselves incapable of assisting him; indeed we were the more grieved at his unhappy fate, as we lost sight of him struggling with the waves, and conceived from the manner in which he swam, that he might continue sensible, for a con-siderable time longer, of the horror attending his irretrievable situation.

The poem is interesting for its different narrative voices, especially when they merge into one another creating for the reader a complex experience. In the opening stanza a first person voice talks of being hurled from on board a ship, but the second stanza moves on to a third person narrative of a shipwreck. This is sustained till the fourth stanza. Next the poem offers different reactions to the central event, from the point of view of the sailors left behind on the ship, and also from the perspective of the drowning man. The poet's voice follows with reflective generalisations, and the narrative is taken up again soon after. From line 48 onwards the poem strikes an elegiac note denying any poetic ampli-fication of the story, which is recorded instead in Anson's simple but moving narrative. Here the poet apparently directs us to the sincere quality of his poem; but when he equates the power of bards with the immortalising power of heroes in the final couplet of the stanza we catch a suggestion of the redemptive quality of poetry. In the last but one stanza the poet both presents himself in the first person, and resumes his stance of humility. Finally, from line 60 onwards the first person plural 'we' makes explicit the identification between the drowning sailor and the poet's own drowning soul, and asserts his greater doom.

The poem may undoubtedly be read on a simple level; its diction especially appears accessible to all, and the neat stanzas of short line length make it very readable. But as in other elegies of this period – Johnson's poem on *Levet* comes to mind – Cowper's language works on different planes. While it is not directly allusive, one senses the Bible as ever present in his images. There are many intertwined texts in operation that thicken and enrich the texture of the poem.

[1] **Obscurest**
Dark, gloomy, hindering sight; *involved* enwrapped.
[3] **destined**
doomed to punishment or misery; *wretch* miserable creature.
[4] **headlong**
with head foremost; metaphorically it would mean suddenly or precipitately. Cf. 'And rose up, and thrust him out of the city, and led him unto the brow of the hill whereon their city was built, that they might cast him down headlong', Luke 4: 29; see also 'Hurled headlong flaming from the ethereal sky', Milton, *Paradise Lost*, i, 45.
[5] **bereft**
deprived of.
[6] **floating home**
continuing the metaphor of the shipwreck introduced earlier in 'Atlantic billows' and 'Washed headlong from on board'. The sense of flux suggested by 'floating' nudges against the certainty usually implied in the idea of 'home'.
[1–6]
The lines work through several inversions in syntax reminiscent of Milton's verse.
[7] **Albion**
England.
[11] **them both**
The captain of the ship and his country, England.
[12]
Did not see either his captain, or England again.
[16] **courage die away**
in the sense of 'to sink, or faint' coupled with the more usual sense. Cf. 'that his heart died within him, and he became as stone', 1 Samuel 25: 37. The idea of sinking courage suits well with the central image of the poem.
[17] **lasting strife**
long battle or struggle.
[18] **supported**
sustained; *despair* hopelessness.
[20] **check**
stop; *course* movement along a chalked out path.

[21] **furious blast**
raging storm; *prevailed* continued in force.
[22] **pitiless perforce**
forced to be so by the violence of the storm.
[23] **out-cast**
deliberately ambivalent, hovering between the literal sense of 'one who has been physically thrown out', and the slightly metaphoric sense of 'one expelled or banished from a group or community'. Cf. 'For I will restore health unto thee and I will heal thee of thy wounds, saith the Lord; because they called thee an outcast', Jeremiah 30: 17. It is possible that Cowper is reworking key terms from the Bible in his poem.
[24] **scudded**
hastened away; *still* ever; *before the wind* in the power of the storm.
[25] **succour**
help or assistance.
[27] **cask**
floating barrel; *coop* another word for barrel; *floated cord* the rope thrown out to save people from drowning.
[28] **bestow**
give.
[36] **deserted**
abandoned. The literal sense is tinged with the ideas of 'left solitary' and 'with the feeling that divine grace has been withdrawn'; the word is informed by a sense of spiritual despondency.
[38] **self-upheld**
'self-sustained', but with a bias towards the literal meaning of 'being held up from sinking by one's own efforts'. Contrasts with 'Upheld by me, yet once more he shall stand/ On even ground against his mortal foe,/ By me upheld, that he may know how frail/ His fallen condition is', Milton, *Paradise Lost*, iii, 178–81.
[39] **unspent power**
unexhausted strength.
[40] **repelled**
drove back, held out forcefully against.
[41] **ever**
all the time.

[43] **transient respite**
short reprive from capital punishment or death.
[45] **blast**
gust of wind.
[47] **subdued**
overcome, conquered.
[48] **stifling**
suffocating.
[49–51]
Cf. 'Their name, their years, spelt by the unlettered muse/ The place of fame and elegy supply', Gray, *Elegy*, lines 81–2.
[52] **Anson**
Lord George Anson, whose *A Voyage Round the World* provided Cowper with the prevailing figure of his poem. See introductory note.
[56] **descanting**
discoursing.
[60] **'semblance**
resemblance.
[61] **voice divine**
a typically Miltonic inversion; *allayed* abated.
[62] **propitious**
favourable, kind.
[63] **effectual**
efficacious.
[66] **whelmed**
sunk deep into, buried.

INDEX OF TITLES AND FIRST LINES

◇

A-Level
CHEMISTRY
FOURTH EDITION

E.N. Ramsden

B.Sc., Ph.D., D.Phil.
Formerly of Wolfreton School, Hull

Stanley Thornes (Publishers) Ltd.

© E.N. Ramsden 1985, 1990, 1994, 2000

The right of Eileen Ramsden to be identified as author of this work has been asserted by her in accordance with the Copyright, Designs and Patents Act 1988.

First published in 1985 by

Stanley Thornes (Publishers) Ltd
Delta Place
27 Bath Road
Cheltenham
GL53 7TH
United Kingdom

Second Edition 1990
Third Edition 1994
Fourth Edition 2000

00 01 02 03 04 / 10 9 8 7 6 5 4 3 2

Front cover: Photomicrograph of a smectic liquid crystal.
              Courtesy Standard Telecommunications Laboratories, Harlow, England

A catalogue record of this book is available from the British Library.

ISBN 0 7487 5299 4

Typeset by Mathematical Composition Setters Ltd, Salisbury, Wiltshire.
Printed and bound in Italy by G. Canale & C.S.p.A., Borgaro T.se, Turin